NBA REGISTER

1985-86 EDITION

W9-COE-107

Editors/NBA Register
MIKE DOUCHANT
ALEX SACHARE

Contributing Editors/NBA Register
JOHN DUXBURY
TERRY LYONS
BRIAN McINTYRE
DAVE SLOAN

President-Chief Executive Officer
RICHARD WATERS

Editor
TOM BARNIDGE

Director of Books and Periodicals
RON SMITH

NBA Statistics by Elias Sports Bureau

Published by

The Sporting News

1212 North Lindbergh Boulevard
P.O. Box 56 — St. Louis, MO 63166

Copyright © 1985
The Sporting News Publishing Company
a Times Mirror company

ISBN 0-89204-193-5   ISSN 0739-3067

Table
of
Contents

★ ★ ★

★ ★ ★

On the cover: Los Angeles Laker center Kareem Abdul-Jabbar rebounded from a poor performance in Game 1 to lead the Lakers to a six-game World Championship Series triumph over Boston last season. Abdul-Jabbar was unanimously voted as the series' most valuable player.
Photo by Andrew D. Bernstein

Career Records of NBA Players

The following records are of players who appeared in at least one game during the 1984-85 NBA season. Also included are records of players with previous NBA experience who were invited to training camp this year or were on the injured list for the entire 1984-85 season.

†Indicates college freshman or junior varsity participant.

KAREEM ABDUL-JABBAR

(Formerly known as Lew Alcindor.)

Born April 16, 1947 at New York, N. Y. Height 7:02. Weight 232.

High School—New York, N. Y., Power Memorial.

College—University of California at Los Angeles, Los Angeles, Calif.

Drafted by Milwaukee on first round, 1969 (1st pick).

Traded by Milwaukee with Walt Wesley to Los Angeles for Elmore Smith, Brian Winters, Dave Meyers and Junior Bridgeman, June 16, 1975.

—COLLEGIATE RECORD—

Year	G.	Min.	FGA	FGM	Pct.	FTA	FTM	Pct.	Reb.	Pts.	Avg.
65-66†	21	....	432	295	.683	179	106	.592	452	696	33.1
66-67	30	....	519	346	.667	274	178	.650	466	870	29.0
67-68	28	....	480	294	.613	237	146	.616	461	734	26.2
68-69	30	....	477	303	.635	188	115	.612	440	721	24.0
Varsity Totals	88	....	1476	943	.639	699	439	.628	1367	2325	26.4

NBA REGULAR SEASON RECORD

Sea.—Team	G.	Min.	FGA	FGM	Pct.	FTA	FTM	Pct.	Reb.	Ast.	PF	Disq.	Pts.	Avg.
69-70—Milwaukee	82	3534	1810	938	.518	743	485	.653	1190	337	283	8	2361	28.8
70-71—Milwaukee	82	3288	1843	1063	.577	681	470	.690	1311	272	264	4	2596	31.7
71-72—Milwaukee	81	3583	2019	1159	.574	732	504	.689	1346	370	235	1	2822	34.8
72-73—Milwaukee	76	3254	1772	982	.554	460	328	.713	1224	379	208	0	2292	30.2

Sea.—Team	G.	Min.	FGA	FGM	Pct.	FTA	FTM	Pct.	Off.	Def.	Tot.	Ast.	PF	Dq.	Stl.	Blk.	Pts.	Avg.
73-74—Milwaukee	81	3548	1759	948	.539	420	295	.702	287	891	1178	386	238	2	112	283	2191	27.0
74-75—Milwaukee	65	2747	1584	812	.513	426	325	.763	194	718	912	264	205	2	65	212	1949	30.0
75-76—Los Angeles	82	3379	1728	914	.529	636	447	.703	272	1111	1383	413	292	6	119	338	2275	27.7
76-77—Los Angeles	82	3016	1533	888	.579	536	376	.701	266	824	1090	319	262	4	101	261	2152	26.2
77-78—Los Angeles	62	2265	1205	663	.550	350	274	.783	186	615	801	269	182	1	103	185	1600	25.8
78-79—Los Angeles	80	3157	1347	777	.577	474	349	.736	207	818	1025	431	230	3	76	316	1903	23.8
79-80—Los Angeles	82	3143	1383	835	.604	476	364	.765	190	696	886	371	216	2	81	280	2034	24.8
80-81—Los Angeles	80	2976	1457	836	.574	552	423	.766	197	624	821	272	244	4	59	228	2095	26.2
81-82—Los Angeles	76	2677	1301	753	.579	442	312	.706	172	487	659	225	224	0	63	207	1818	23.9
82-83—Los Angeles	79	2554	1228	722	.588	371	278	.749	167	425	592	200	220	1	61	170	1722	21.8
83-84—Los Angeles	80	2622	1238	716	.578	394	285	.723	169	418	587	211	211	1	55	143	1717	21.5
84-85—L.A. Lakers	79	2630	1207	723	.599	395	289	.732	162	460	622	249	238	3	63	162	1735	22.0
Totals	1249	48373	24414	13729	.562	8088	5804	.718			15627	4968	3752	42	958	2785	33262	26.6

Three-Point Field Goals: 1979-80, 0-for-1. 1980-81, 0-for-1. 1981-82, 0-for-3. 1982-83, 0-for-2. 1983-84, 0-for-1. 1984-85, 0-for-1. Totals, 0-for-9.

NBA PLAYOFF RECORD

Sea.—Team	G.	Min.	FGA	FGM	Pct.	FTA	FTM	Pct.	Reb.	Ast.	PF	Disq.	Pts.	Avg.
69-70—Milwaukee	10	435	245	139	.567	101	74	.733	168	41	25	1	352	35.2
70-71—Milwaukee	14	577	295	152	.515	101	68	.673	238	35	45	0	372	26.6
71-72—Milwaukee	11	510	318	139	.437	54	38	.704	200	56	35	0	316	28.7
72-73—Milwaukee	6	276	138	59	.428	35	19	.543	97	17	26	0	137	22.8

Sea.—Team	G.	Min.	FGA	FGM	Pct.	FTA	FTM	Pct.	Off.	Def.	Tot.	Ast.	PF	Dq.	Stl.	Blk.	Pts.	Avg.
73-74—Milwaukee	16	758	402	224	.557	91	67	.736	67	186	253	78	41	0	20	39	515	32.2
76-77—Los Angeles	11	467	242	147	.607	120	87	.725	51	144	195	45	42	0	19	38	381	34.6
77-78—Los Angeles	3	134	73	38	.521	9	5	.556	14	27	41	11	14	1	2	12	81	27.0
78-79—Los Angeles	8	367	152	88	.579	62	52	.839	18	83	101	38	26	0	8	33	228	28.5
79-80—Los Angeles	15	618	346	198	.572	105	83	.790	51	130	181	46	51	0	17	58	479	31.9
80-81—Los Angeles	3	134	65	30	.462	28	20	.714	13	37	50	12	14	0	3	8	80	26.7
81-82—Los Angeles	14	493	221	115	.520	87	55	.632	33	86	119	51	45	0	14	45	285	20.4
82-83—Los Angeles	15	588	287	163	.568	106	80	.755	25	90	115	42	61	1	17	45	406	27.1
83-84—Los Angeles	21	767	371	206	.555	120	90	.750	56	117	173	79	71	2	23	45	502	23.9
84-85—L.A. Lakers	19	610	300	168	.560	103	80	.777	50	104	154	76	67	1	23	36	416	21.9
Totals	166	6734	3455	1866	.540	1122	818	.729			2085	627	563	6	146	369	4550	27.4

Three-Point Field Goals: 1982-83, 0-for-1.

Season—Team	Min.	FGA	FGM	Pct.	FTA	FTM	Pct.	Reb.	Ast.	PF	Disq.	Pts.
1970—Milwaukee	18	8	4	.500	2	2	1.000	11	4	6	1	10
1971—Milwaukee	30	16	8	.500	4	3	.750	14	1	2	0	19
1972—Milwaukee	19	10	5	.500	2	2	1.000	7	2	0	0	12
1973—Milwaukee							Selected, Did Not Play.					

								—Rebounds—								
Season—Team	Min	FGA	FGM	Pct.	FTA	FTM	Pct.	Off.	Def.	Tot.	Ast.	PF	Dq.	Stl.	Blk.	Pts.
1974—Milwaukee	23	11	7	.636	0	0	.000	1	7	8	6	2	0	1	1	14
1975—Milwaukee	19	10	3	.300	2	1	.500	5	5	10	3	2	0	0	1	7
1976—Los Angeles	36	16	9	.563	4	4	1.000	2	13	15	3	3	0	0	3	22
1977—Los Angeles	23	14	8	.571	6	5	.833	3	1	4	2	1	0	0	1	21
1979—Los Angeles	28	12	5	.417	2	1	.500	1	7	8	3	4	0	1	1	11
1980—Los Angeles	30	17	6	.353	6	5	.833	5	11	16	9	5	0	0	6	17
1981—Los Angeles	23	9	6	.667	3	3	1.000	2	4	6	4	3	0	0	4	15
1982—Los Angeles	22	10	1	.100	0	0	.000	1	2	3	1	3	0	0	2	2
1983—Los Angeles	32	12	9	.750	3	2	.667	2	4	6	5	1	0	1	4	20
1984—Los Angeles	37	19	11	.579	4	3	.750	5	8	13	2	5	0	0	1	25
1985—L.A. Lakers	23	10	5	.500	2	1	.500	0	6	6	1	5	0	1	1	11
Totals	363	174	87	.500	39	32	.821			127	46	42	1	4	25	206

Named to NBA 35th Anniversary All-Time Team, 1980. . . . NBA Most Valuable Player, 1971, 1972, 1974, 1976, 1977, 1980. . . . All-NBA First Team, 1971, 1972, 1973, 1974, 1976, 1977, 1980, 1981, 1984. . . . All-NBA Second Team, 1970, 1978, 1979, 1983, 1985. . . . NBA All-Defensive First Team, 1974, 1975, 1979, 1980, 1981. . . . NBA All-Defensive Second Team, 1970, 1971, 1976, 1977, 1978, 1984. . . . NBA Rookie of the Year, 1970. . . . NBA All-Rookie Team, 1970. . . . NBA Playoff MVP, 1971 and 1985. . . . Member of NBA championship teams, 1971, 1980, 1982, 1985. . . . Led NBA in scoring, 1971 and 1972. . . . Led NBA in rebounding, 1976. . . . Led NBA in field-goal percentage, 1977. . . . Led NBA in blocked shots, 1975, 1976, 1979, 1980. . . . Shares NBA record for most seasons played, 16. . . . Holds all-time NBA records for points, field goals made, field goals attempted and blocked shots. . . . Holds records for most points scored and most field goals made in NBA playoffs. . . . Holds NBA All-Star Game records for most games played, 14, and most personal fouls. . . . THE SPORTING NEWS College Player of the Year, 1967 and 1969. . . . THE SPORTING NEWS All-America First Team, 1967, 1968, 1969. . . . NCAA Tournament Most Outstanding Player, 1967, 1968, 1969. . . . Member of NCAA championship teams, 1967, 1968, 1969. . . . Led NCAA in field-goal percentage, 1967 and 1969.

ALVAN LEIGH ADAMS

Born July 19, 1954 at Lawrence, Kan.   Height 6:09.   Weight 220.

High School—Putnam City, Okla.

College—University of Oklahoma, Norman, Okla.

Drafted by Phoenix on first round as hardship case, 1975 (4th pick).

—COLLEGIATE RECORD—

Year	G.	Min.	FGA	FGM	Pct.	FTA	FTM	Pct.	Reb.	Pts.	Avg.
72-73	21	....	356	195	.548	110	74	.673	277	464	22.1
73-74	26	....	437	236	.540	116	80	.690	315	552	21.2
74-75	26	....	524	279	.532	183	133	.727	346	691	26.6
Totals	73	....	1317	710	.539	409	287	.702	938	1707	23.4

NBA REGULAR SEASON RECORD

								—Rebounds—									
Sea.—Team	G.	Min.	FGA	FGM	Pct.	FTA	FTM	Pct.	Off.	Def.	Tot.	Ast.	PF	Dq.	Stl.	Blk.	Pts.	Avg.
75-76—Phoenix	80	2656	1341	629	.469	355	261	.735	215	512	727	450	274	6	121	116	1519	19.0
76-77—Phoenix	72	2278	1102	522	.474	334	252	.754	180	472	652	322	260	4	95	87	1296	18.0
77-78—Phoenix	70	1914	895	434	.485	293	214	.730	158	407	565	225	242	8	86	63	1082	15.5
78-79—Phoenix	77	2364	1073	569	.530	289	231	.799	220	485	705	360	246	4	110	63	1369	17.8
79-80—Phoenix	75	2168	875	465	.531	236	188	.797	158	451	609	322	237	4	108	55	1118	14.9
80-81—Phoenix	75	2054	870	458	.526	259	199	.768	157	389	546	344	226	2	106	69	1115	14.9
81-82—Phoenix	79	2393	1027	507	.494	233	182	.781	138	448	586	356	269	2	114	78	1196	15.1
82-83—Phoenix	80	2447	981	477	.486	217	180	.829	161	387	548	376	287	7	114	74	1135	14.2
83-84—Phoenix	70	1452	582	269	.462	160	132	.825	118	201	319	219	195	1	73	31	670	9.6
84-85—Phoenix	82	2136	915	476	.520	283	250	.883	153	347	500	308	254	2	115	48	1202	14.7
Totals	760	21862	9661	4806	.497	2659	2089	.786	1658	4099	5757	3282	2490	45	1042	684	11702	15.4

Three-Point Field Goals: 1979-80, 0-for-2. 1981-82, 0-for-1. 1982-83, 1-for-3 (.333). 1983-84, 0-for-4. Totals, 1-for-10 (.100).

NBA PLAYOFF RECORD

								—Rebounds—									
Sea.—Team	G.	Min.	FGA	FGM	Pct.	FTA	FTM	Pct.	Off.	Def.	Tot.	Ast.	PF	Dq.	Stl.	Blk.	Pts.	Avg.
75-76—Phoenix	19	668	303	137	.452	82	67	.817	54	137	191	98	60	1	24	20	341	17.9
77-78—Phoenix	2	71	33	15	.455	2	2	1.000	8	8	16	4	8	0	2	1	32	16.0
78-79—Phoenix	12	372	139	66	.475	31	22	.710	25	65	90	53	41	1	11	12	154	12.8
79-80—Phoenix	8	251	99	56	.566	19	17	.895	18	59	77	46	24	1	7	10	129	16.1
80-81—Phoenix	7	218	60	27	.450	28	20	.714	11	30	41	26	20	0	4	1	74	10.6
81-82—Phoenix	7	233	92	48	.522	28	22	.786	19	32	51	26	22	0	14	10	118	16.9
82-83—Phoenix	3	84	32	15	.469	7	5	.714	3	15	18	14	15	0	2	5	35	11.7
83-84—Phoenix	17	312	126	53	.421	53	36	.679	27	60	87	42	53	0	17	11	142	8.4
84-85—Phoenix	3	79	46	23	.500	6	5	.833	4	13	17	11	8	0	7	1	51	17.0
Totals	78	2288	930	440	.473	256	196	.766	169	419	588	320	251	3	88	71	1076	13.8

NBA ALL-STAR GAME RECORD

Season—Team	Min.	FGA	FGM	Pct.	FTA	FTM	Pct.	Rebounds Off.	Def.	Tot.	Ast.	PF	Dq.	Stl.	Blk.	Pts.
1976—Phoenix	11	4	2	.500	0	0	.000	2	1	3	0	1	0	0	0	4

Named NBA Rookie of the Year, 1976. . . . NBA All-Rookie Team, 1976.

MARK ANTHONY AGUIRRE

Born December 10, 1959 at Chicago, Ill. Height 6:06. Weight 235.

High Schools—Chicago, Ill., Austin (Sophomore)
and Chicago, Ill., Westinghouse (Junior and Senior).

College—DePaul University, Chicago, Ill.

Drafted by Dallas on first round as an undergraduate, 1981 (1st pick).

—COLLEGIATE RECORD—

Year	G.	Min.	FGA	FGM	Pct.	FTA	FTM	Pct.	Reb.	Pts.	Avg.
78-79	32	....	581	302	.520	213	163	.765	244	767	24.0
79-80	28	....	520	281	.540	244	187	.766	213	749	26.8
80-81	29	1069	481	280	.582	137	106	.774	249	666	23.0
Totals	89	....	1582	863	.546	594	456	.768	706	2182	24.5

NBA REGULAR SEASON RECORD

Sea.—Team	G.	Min.	FGA	FGM	Pct.	FTA	FTM	Pct.	Rebounds Off.	Def.	Tot.	Ast.	PF	Dq.	Stl.	Blk.	Pts.	Avg.
81-82—Dallas	51	1468	820	381	.465	247	168	.680	89	160	249	164	152	0	37	22	955	18.7
82-83—Dallas	81	2784	1589	767	.483	589	429	.728	191	317	508	332	247	5	80	26	1979	24.4
83-84—Dallas	79	2900	1765	925	.524	621	465	.749	161	308	469	358	246	5	80	22	2330	29.5
84-85—Dallas	80	2699	1569	794	.506	580	440	.759	188	289	477	249	250	3	60	24	2055	25.7
Totals	291	9851	5743	2867	.499	2037	1502	.737	629	1074	1703	1103	895	13	257	94	7319	25.2

Three-Point Field Goals: 1981-82, 25-for-71 (.352). 1982-83, 16-for-76 (.211). 1983-84, 15-for-56 (.268). 1984-85, 27-for-85 (.318). Totals, 83-for-288 (.288).

NBA PLAYOFF RECORD

Sea.—Team	G.	Min.	FGA	FGM	Pct.	FTA	FTM	Pct.	Rebounds Off.	Def.	Tot.	Ast.	PF	Dq.	Stl.	Blk.	Pts.	Avg.
83-84—Dallas	10	350	184	88	.478	57	44	.772	21	55	76	32	34	2	5	5	220	22.0
84-85—Dallas	4	164	89	44	.494	32	27	.844	16	14	30	16	16	1	3	0	116	29.0
Totals	14	514	273	132	.484	89	71	.798	37	69	106	48	50	3	8	5	336	24.0

Three-Point Field Goals: 1983-84, 0-for-5. 1984-85, 1-for-2 (.500). Totals, 1-for-7 (.143).

NBA ALL-STAR GAME RECORD

Season—Team	Min.	FGA	FGM	Pct.	FTA	FTM	Pct.	Rebounds Off.	Def.	Tot.	Ast.	PF	Dq.	Stl.	Blk.	Pts.
1984—Dallas	13	8	5	.625	4	3	.750	1	0	1	2	1	0	1	1	13

Named THE SPORTING NEWS College Player of the Year, 1981. . . . THE SPORTING NEWS All-America First Team, 1980 and 1981. . . . Member of U.S. Olympic Team, 1980.

DANIEL RAE AINGE
(Danny)

Born March 17, 1959 at Eugene, Ore. Height 6:04. Weight 175.

High School—Eugene, Ore., North.

College—Brigham Young University, Provo, Utah.

Drafted by Boston on second round, 1981 (31st pick).

—COLLEGIATE RECORD—

Year	G.	Min.	FGA	FGM	Pct.	FTA	FTM	Pct.	Reb.	Pts.	Avg.
77-78	30	....	473	243	.514	169	146	.864	173	632	21.1
78-79	27	922	376	206	.548	112	86	.768	102	498	18.4
79-80	29	984	430	229	.533	124	97	.782	114	555	19.1
80-81	32	1212	596	309	.518	199	164	.824	152	782	24.4
Totals	118	....	1875	987	.526	604	493	.816	541	2467	20.9

NBA REGULAR SEASON RECORD

Sea.—Team	G.	Min.	FGA	FGM	Pct.	FTA	FTM	Pct.	Rebounds Off.	Def.	Tot.	Ast.	PF	Dq.	Stl.	Blk.	Pts.	Avg.
81-82—Boston	53	564	221	79	.357	65	56	.862	25	31	56	87	86	1	37	3	219	4.1
82-83—Boston	80	2048	720	357	.496	97	72	.742	83	131	214	251	259	2	109	6	791	9.9
83-84—Boston	71	1154	361	166	.460	56	46	.821	29	87	116	162	143	2	41	4	384	5.4
84-85—Boston	75	2564	792	419	.529	136	118	.868	76	192	268	399	228	4	122	6	971	12.9
Totals	279	6330	2094	1021	.488	354	292	.825	213	441	654	899	716	9	309	19	2365	8.5

DANNY AINGE

Three-Point Field Goals: 1981-82, 5-for-17 (.294). 1982-83, 5-for-29 (.172). 1983-84, 6-for-22 (.273). 1984-85, 15-for-56 (.268). Totals, 31-for-124 (.250).

NBA PLAYOFF RECORD

Sea.—Team	G.	Min.	FGA	FGM	Pct.	FTA	FTM	Pct.	—Rebounds— Off.	Def.	Tot.	Ast.	PF	Dq.	Stl.	Blk.	Pts.	Avg.
81-82—Boston	10	129	45	19	.422	13	10	.769	6	7	13	11	21	0	2	1	50	5.0
82-83—Boston	7	201	72	28	.389	11	8	.727	2	12	14	25	24	0	5	1	66	9.4
83-84—Boston	19	253	90	41	.456	10	7	.700	4	12	16	38	36	0	9	2	91	4.8
84-85—Boston	21	687	208	97	.466	39	30	.769	20	38	58	121	76	1	32	1	231	11.0
Totals	57	1270	415	185	.446	73	55	.753	32	69	101	195	157	1	48	5	438	7.7

Three-Point Field Goals: 1981-82, 2-for-4 (.500). 1982-83, 2-for-5 (.400). 1983-84, 2-for-9 (.222). 1984-85, 7-for-16 (.438). Totals, 13-for-34 (.382).

RECORD AS BASEBALL PLAYER

Year	Club	League	Pos.	G.	AB.	R.	H.	2B.	3B.	HR.	RBI.	B.A.	PO.	A.	E.	F.A.
1978—Syracuse	....	Int.	SS-2B	119	389	33	89	10	1	4	30	.229	206	328	29	.948
1979—Syracuse	....	Int.	2B	27	101	10	25	4	2	0	8	.248	56	77	4	.971
1979—Toronto	....	Amer.	2B	87	308	26	73	7	1	2	19	.237	198	261	11	.977
1980—Syracuse	....	Int.	3-O-SS	80	295	37	72	9	1	2	17	.244	111	140	3	.988
1980—Toronto	....	Amer.	OF-3-2	38	111	11	27	6	1	0	4	.243	69	12	1	.988
1981—Toronto	....	Amer.	3-SS-O-2	86	246	20	46	6	2	0	14	.187	88	146	12	.951
Major League Totals		....		211	665	57	146	19	4	2	37	.220	355	419	24	.970

Member of NBA championship team, 1984. . . . Named to THE SPORTING NEWS All-America First Team, 1981. . . . Drafted by Toronto Blue Jays in 15th round of free-agent draft, June 7, 1977.

CHARLES ALEKSINAS
(Chuck)

Born February 26, 1959 at Litchfield, Conn. Height 6:11. Weight 260.

High School—Litchfield, Conn., Wamogo.

Colleges—University of Kentucky, Lexington, Ky., and University of Connecticut, Storrs, Conn.

Drafted by Chicago on fourth round, 1982 (76th pick).

Draft rights relinquished by Chicago, October 22, 1982; signed by Golden State as a free agent, September 7, 1984. Played in Spain during 1983-84 season.

—COLLEGIATE RECORD—
Kentucky

Year	G.	Min.	FGA	FGM	Pct.	FTA	FTM	Pct.	Reb.	Pts.	Avg.
77-78	27	216	65	37	.569	36	25	.694	60	99	3.7
78-79	13	366	125	58	.464	45	33	.733	79	149	11.5
Ky. Totals...............	40	582	190	95	.500	81	58	.716	139	248	6.2

Connecticut

Year	G.	Min.	FGA	FGM	Pct.	FTA	FTM	Pct.	Reb.	Pts.	Avg.
79-80					Transfer—Did Not Play						
80-81	29	889	244	154	.631	120	93	.775	202	401	13.8
81-82	27	760	217	116	.535	132	89	.674	139	321	11.9
Conn. Totals...........	56	1649	461	270	.586	252	182	.722	341	722	12.9
College Totals	96	2231	651	365	.561	333	240	.721	480	970	10.1

NBA REGULAR SEASON RECORD

Sea.—Team	G.	Min.	FGA	FGM	Pct.	FTA	FTM	Pct.	—Rebounds— Off.	Def.	Tot.	Ast.	PF	Dq.	Stl.	Blk.	Pts.	Avg.
84-85—Golden State	74	1114	337	161	.478	75	55	.733	87	183	270	36	171	1	15	15	377	5.1

Three-Point Field Goals: 1984-85, 0-for-1.

Member of NCAA championship team, 1978.

MITCHELL KEITH ANDERSON
(J.J.)

Born September 23, 1960 at Chicago, Ill. Height 6:08. Weight 195.

High School—Chicago, Ill., Metro.

College—Bradley University, Peoria, Ill.

Drafted by Philadelphia on second round, 1982 (36th pick).

Waived by Philadelphia, December 20, 1982; signed by Utah as a free agent, December 23, 1982.

—COLLEGIATE RECORD—

Year	G.	Min.	FGA	FGM	Pct.	FTA	FTM	Pct.	Reb.	Pts.	Avg.
78-79	26	994	503	232	.461	113	81	.717	144	545	21.0
79-80	33	1264	644	295	.458	126	90	.714	291	680	20.6
80-81	27	....	475	229	.482	99	67	.677	237	525	19.4
81-82	36	....	467	220	.471	206	151	.733	275	591	16.4
Totals	122	....	2089	976	.467	544	389	.715	947	2341	19.2

NBA REGULAR SEASON RECORD

Sea.—Team	G.	Min.	FGA	FGM	Pct.	FTA	FTM	Pct.	Off.	Def.	Tot.	Ast.	PF	Dq.	Stl.	Blk.	Pts.	Avg.
82-83—Phil.-Utah	65	1202	379	190	.501	175	100	.571	119	175	294	67	153	1	63	21	480	7.4
83-84—Utah	48	311	130	55	.423	29	12	.414	38	25	63	22	28	0	15	9	122	2.5
84-85—Utah	44	457	149	61	.409	45	27	.600	29	53	82	21	70	0	29	9	149	3.4
Totals	157	1970	658	306	.465	249	139	.558	186	253	439	110	251	1	107	39	751	4.8

Three-Point Field Goals: 1982-83, 0-for-4. 1983-84, 0-for-3. 1984-85, 0-for-2. Totals, 0-for-9.

NBA PLAYOFF RECORD

Sea.—Team	G.	Min.	FGA	FGM	Pct.	FTA	FTM	Pct.	Off.	Def.	Tot.	Ast.	PF	Dq.	Stl.	Blk.	Pts.	Avg.
1983-84—Utah	5	13	8	5	.625	0	0	.000	3	1	4	0	2	0	0	1	11	2.2

Three-Point Field Goals: 1983-84, 1-for-1 (1.000).

RONALD GENE ANDERSON
(Ron)

Born October 15, 1958 at Chicago, Ill.   Height 6:07.   Weight 215.

High School—Chicago, Ill., Bowen (Did not play basketball)

Colleges—Santa Barbara City College, Santa Barbara, Calif.,
and Fresno State University, Fresno, Calif.

Drafted by Cleveland on second round, 1984 (27th pick).

—COLLEGIATE RECORD—
Santa Barbara

Year	G.	Min.	FGA	FGM	Pct.	FTA	FTM	Pct.	Reb.	Pts.	Avg.
80-81	33	....	333	167	.502	75	56	.747	328	390	11.8
81-82	32	....	448	292	.652	84	66	.786	340	650	20.3
JC Totals	65	....	781	459	.588	159	122	.767	668	1040	16.0

Fresno State

Year	G.	Min.	FGA	FGM	Pct.	FTA	FTM	Pct.	Reb.	Pts.	Avg.
82-83	35	1303	426	234	.549	128	104	.813	204	572	16.3
83-84	33	1197	437	249	.570	104	82	.788	200	580	17.6
Totals	68	2500	863	483	.560	232	186	.802	404	1152	16.9

NBA REGULAR SEASON RECORD

Sea.—Team	G.	Min.	FGA	FGM	Pct.	FTA	FTM	Pct.	Off.	Def.	Tot.	Ast.	PF	Dq.	Stl.	Blk.	Pts.	Avg.
84-85—Cleveland	36	520	195	84	.431	50	41	.820	39	49	88	34	40	0	9	7	210	5.8

Three-Point Field Goals: 1984-85, 1-for-2 (.500).

NBA PLAYOFF RECORD

Sea.—Team	G.	Min.	FGA	FGM	Pct.	FTA	FTM	Pct.	Off.	Def.	Tot.	Ast.	PF	Dq.	Stl.	Blk.	Pts.	Avg.
84-85—Cleveland	2	9	3	0	.000	0	0	.000	1	2	3	0	0	0	0	0	0	0.0

JOHN EDWARD BAGLEY

Born April 23, 1960 at Bridgeport, Conn.   Height 6:00.   Weight 190.

High School—Bridgeport, Conn., Warren Harding.

College—Boston College, Chestnut Hill, Mass.

Drafted by Cleveland on first round as an undergraduate, 1982 (12th pick).

—COLLEGIATE RECORD—

Year	G.	Min.	FGA	FGM	Pct.	FTA	FTM	Pct.	Reb.	Pts.	Avg.
79-80	29	....	270	130	.481	115	83	.722	91	343	11.8
80-81	30	965	418	209	.500	245	193	.788	115	611	20.4
81-82	32	1065	513	257	.501	202	161	.797	122	675	21.1
Totals	91	....	1201	596	.496	562	437	.778	328	1629	17.9

Sea.—Team	G.	Min.	FGA	FGM	Pct.	FTA	FTM	Pct.	—Rebounds— Off.	Def.	Tot.	Ast.	PF	Dq.	Stl.	Blk.	Pts.	Avg.
82-83—Cleveland	68	990	373	161	.432	84	64	.762	17	79	96	167	74	0	54	5	386	5.7
83-84—Cleveland	76	1712	607	257	.423	198	157	.793	49	107	156	333	113	1	78	4	673	8.9
84-85—Cleveland	81	2401	693	338	.488	167	125	.749	54	237	291	697	132	0	129	5	804	9.9
Totals	225	5103	1673	756	.452	449	346	.771	120	423	543	1197	319	1	261	14	1863	8.3

Three-Point Field Goals: 1982-83, 0-for-14. 1983-84, 2-for-17 (.118). 1984-85, 3-for-26 (.115). Totals, 5-for-57 (.088).

NBA PLAYOFF RECORD

Sea.—Team	G.	Min.	FGA	FGM	Pct.	FTA	FTM	Pct.	—Rebounds— Off.	Def.	Tot.	Ast.	PF	Dq.	Stl.	Blk.	Pts.	Avg.
84-85—Cleveland	4	168	56	22	.393	10	7	.700	1	15	16	40	7	0	10	0	51	12.8

Three-Point Field Goals: 1984-85, 0-for-3.

JAMES L. BAILEY

Born May 21, 1957 at Dublin, Ga. Height 6:09. Weight 220.

High School—Westwood, Mass., Xaverian.

College—Rutgers University, New Brunswick, N. J.

Drafted by Seattle on first round, 1979 (6th pick).

Traded by Seattle to New Jersey for Ray Tolbert and a 1984 2nd round draft choice, November 25, 1981.
Traded by New Jersey to Houston for two 2nd round draft choices (1983 and 1985), November 10, 1982.
Traded by Houston with a 1985 2nd round draft choice and cash to San Antonio for John Lucas and a 1985 3rd round draft choice, October 4, 1984.
Traded by San Antonio to New York for a 1986 3rd round draft choice and cash, October 24, 1984.

—COLLEGIATE RECORD—

Year	G.	Min.	FGA	FGM	Pct.	FTA	FTM	Pct.	Reb.	Pts.	Avg.
75-76	33	790	240	121	.504	68	40	.588	233	282	8.5
76-77	28	927	342	185	.541	141	98	.695	304	468	16.7
77-78	31	1061	533	312	.585	164	106	.646	290	730	23.5
78-79	30	1028	443	231	.521	140	92	.657	247	554	18.5
Totals	122	3806	1558	849	.545	513	336	.655	1074	2034	16.7

NBA REGULAR SEASON RECORD

Sea.—Team	G.	Min.	FGA	FGM	Pct.	FTA	FTM	Pct.	—Rebounds— Off.	Def.	Tot.	Ast.	PF	Dq.	Stl.	Blk.	Pts.	Avg.
79-80—Seattle	67	726	271	122	.450	101	68	.673	71	126	197	28	116	1	21	54	312	4.7
80-81—Seattle	82	2539	889	444	.499	361	256	.709	192	415	607	98	332	11	74	143	1145	14.0
81-82—Sea-N.J.	77	1468	505	261	.517	224	137	.612	127	264	391	65	270	5	42	83	659	8.6
82-83—N.J.-Hou.	75	1765	774	385	.497	322	226	.702	171	303	474	67	271	7	43	60	996	13.3
83-84—Houston	73	1174	517	254	.491	192	138	.719	104	190	294	79	197	8	33	40	646	8.8
84-85—New York	74	1297	349	156	.447	108	73	.676	122	222	344	39	286	10	30	50	385	5.2
Totals	448	8969	3305	1622	.491	1308	898	.687	787	1520	2307	376	1472	42	243	430	4143	9.2

Three-Point Field Goals: 1980-81, 1-for-2 (.500). 1982-83, 0-for-1. 1983-84, 0-for-1. 1984-85, 0-for-1. Totals, 1-for-5 (.200).

NBA PLAYOFF RECORD

Sea.—Team	G.	Min.	FGA	FGM	Pct.	FTA	FTM	Pct.	—Rebounds— Off.	Def.	Tot.	Ast.	PF	Dq.	Stl.	Blk.	Pts.	Avg.
79-80—Seattle	12	138	44	21	.477	20	13	.650	8	17	25	5	22	0	9	9	55	4.6
81-82—New Jersey	2	26	3	1	.333	2	2	1.000	2	4	6	1	5	0	2	1	4	2.0
Totals	14	164	47	22	.468	22	15	.682	10	21	31	6	27	0	11	10	59	4.2

Named to THE SPORTING NEWS All-America First Team, 1979. . . . THE SPORTING NEWS All-America Second Team, 1978.

THURL LEE BAILEY

Born April 7, 1961 at Washington, D. C. Height 6:11. Weight 215.

High School—Bladensburg, Md.

College—North Carolina State University, Raleigh, N. C.

Drafted by Utah on first round, 1983 (7th pick).

—COLLEGIATE RECORD—

Year	G.	Min.	FGA	FGM	Pct.	FTA	FTM	Pct.	Reb.	Pts.	Avg.
79-80	28	....	101	44	.436	55	37	.673	102	125	4.5
80-81	27	....	278	146	.525	53	39	.736	165	331	12.3
81-82	32	....	312	171	.548	118	96	.814	216	438	13.7
82-83	36	....	499	250	.501	127	91	.717	276	601	16.7
Totals	123	....	1190	611	.513	353	263	.745	759	1495	12.2

NBA REGULAR SEASON RECORD

Sea.—Team	G.	Min.	FGA	FGM	Pct.	FTA	FTM	Pct.	Off.	Def.	Tot.	Ast.	PF	Dq.	Stl.	Blk.	Pts.	Avg.
83-84—Utah	81	2009	590	302	.512	117	88	.752	113	349	464	129	193	1	38	122	692	8.5
84-85—Utah	80	2481	1034	507	.490	234	197	.842	153	372	525	138	215	2	51	105	1212	15.2
Totals	161	4490	1624	809	.498	351	285	.812	268	721	989	267	408	3	89	227	1904	11.8

Three-Point Field Goals: 1984-85, 1-for-1 (1.000).

NBA PLAYOFF RECORD

Sea.—Team	G.	Min.	FGA	FGM	Pct.	FTA	FTM	Pct.	Off.	Def.	Tot.	Ast.	PF	Dq.	Stl.	Blk.	Pts.	Avg.
83-84—Utah	11	340	97	50	.515	21	17	.810	15	46	61	10	33	0	2	11	117	10.6
84-85—Utah	10	375	152	62	.408	55	45	.818	21	71	92	27	30	0	5	18	169	16.9
Totals	21	715	249	112	.450	76	62	.816	36	117	153	37	63	0	7	29	286	13.6

Three-Point Field Goals: 1983-84, 0-for-2.

Named to NBA All-Rookie Team, 1984. . . . Member of NCAA championship team, 1983.

GREGORY BALLARD
(Greg)

Born January 29, 1955 at Los Angeles, Calif.   Height 6:07.   Weight 215.

High School—Pomona, Calif., Garey.

College—University of Oregon, Eugene, Ore.

Drafted by Washington on first round, 1977 (4th pick).

Traded by Washington to Golden State for 1985 and 1987 2nd round draft choices, June 17, 1985.

—COLLEGIATE RECORD—

Year	G.	Min.	FGA	FGM	Pct.	FTA	FTM	Pct.	Reb.	Pts.	Avg.
73-74	26	761	152	71	.467	138	102	.739	230	244	9.4
74-75	30	874	322	157	.488	144	106	.736	288	420	14.0
75-76	30	965	398	209	.525	155	118	.761	313	536	17.9
76-77	29	1017	452	238	.527	179	153	.855	283	629	21.7
Totals	115	3617	1324	675	.510	616	479	.778	1114	1829	15.9

NBA REGULAR SEASON RECORD

Sea.—Team	G.	Min.	FGA	FGM	Pct.	FTA	FTM	Pct.	Off.	Def.	Tot.	Ast.	PF	Dq.	Stl.	Blk.	Pts.	Avg.
77-78—Washington	76	936	334	142	.425	114	88	.772	102	164	266	62	90	1	30	13	372	4.9
78-79—Washington	82	1552	559	260	.465	172	119	.692	143	307	450	116	167	3	58	30	639	7.8
79-80—Washington	82	2438	1101	545	.495	227	171	.753	240	398	638	159	197	2	90	36	1277	15.6
80-81—Washington	82	2610	1186	549	.463	196	166	.847	167	413	580	195	194	1	118	39	1271	15.5
81-82—Washington	79	2946	1307	621	.475	283	235	.830	136	497	633	250	204	0	137	22	1486	18.8
82-83—Washington	78	2840	1274	603	.473	233	182	.781	123	385	508	262	176	2	135	25	1401	18.0
83-84—Washington	82	2701	1061	510	.481	208	166	.798	140	348	488	290	214	1	94	35	1188	14.5
84-85—Washington	82	2664	978	469	.480	151	120	.795	150	381	531	208	221	0	100	33	1072	13.1
Totals	643	18687	7800	3699	.474	1584	1247	.787	1201	2893	4094	1542	1463	10	762	233	8706	13.5

Three-Point Field Goals: 1979-80, 16-for-47 (.340). 1980-81, 7-for-32 (.219). 1981-82, 9-for-22 (.409). 1982-83, 13-for-37 (.351). 1983-84, 2-for-15 (.133). 1984-85, 14-for-46 (.304). Totals, 61-for-199 (.307).

NBA PLAYOFF RECORD

Sea.—Team	G.	Min.	FGA	FGM	Pct.	FTA	FTM	Pct.	Off.	Def.	Tot.	Ast.	PF	Dq.	Stl.	Blk.	Pts.	Avg.
77-78—Washington	19	243	63	21	.333	41	32	.780	27	52	79	18	29	0	9	3	74	3.9
78-79—Washington	19	312	101	53	.525	41	31	.756	34	58	92	17	28	0	9	6	137	7.2
79-80—Washington	2	73	28	9	.321	7	4	.571	2	12	14	7	8	0	1	1	22	11.0
81-82—Washington	7	268	100	36	.360	25	21	.840	22	41	63	22	20	1	14	3	93	13.3
83-84—Washington	4	168	59	27	.458	13	12	.923	7	17	24	14	12	0	7	4	66	16.5
84-85—Washington	4	65	24	11	.458	9	8	.889	4	10	14	6	7	0	3	0	30	7.5
Totals	55	1129	375	157	.419	136	108	.794	96	190	286	84	104	1	43	16	422	7.7

Three-Point Field Goals: 1983-84, 0-for-1. 1984-85, 0-for-2. Totals, 0-for-3.

Member of NBA championship team, 1978. . . . Drafted by Montreal Expos in 15th round of free-agent draft, June 5, 1973.

EUGENE LAVON BANKS
(Gene)

Born May 15, 1959 at Philadelphia, Pa.   Height 6:07.   Weight 215.

High School—Philadelphia, Pa., West.

College—Duke University, Durham, N. C.

Drafted by San Antonio on second round, 1981 (28th pick).

Traded by San Antonio to Chicago for Steve Johnson and a 1985 2nd round draft choice, June 18, 1985.

Year	G.	Min.	FGA	FGM	Pct.	FTA	FTM	Pct.	Reb.	Pts.	Avg.
77-78	34	....	451	238	.528	146	105	.719	292	581	17.1
78-79	30	....	353	175	.496	126	79	.627	255	429	14.3
79-80	33	1165	404	212	.525	183	146	.798	254	570	17.3
80-81	27	933	350	202	.577	134	95	.709	184	499	18.5
Totals	124	....	1558	827	.531	589	425	.722	985	2079	16.8

NBA REGULAR SEASON RECORD

Sea.—Team	G.	Min.	FGA	FGM	Pct.	FTA	FTM	Pct.	Off.	Def.	Tot.	Ast.	PF	Dq.	Stl.	Blk.	Pts.	Avg.
81-82—San Antonio	80	1700	652	311	.477	212	145	.684	157	254	411	147	199	2	55	17	767	9.6
82-83—San Antonio	81	2722	919	505	.550	278	196	.705	222	390	612	279	229	3	78	21	1206	14.9
83-84—San Antonio	80	2600	747	424	.568	270	200	.741	204	378	582	254	256	5	105	23	1049	13.1
84-85—San Antonio	82	2091	493	289	.586	257	199	.774	133	312	445	234	220	3	65	13	778	9.5
Totals	323	9113	2811	1529	.544	1017	740	.728	716	1334	2050	914	904	13	303	74	3800	11.8

Three-Point Field Goals: 1981-82, 0-for-8. 1982-83, 0-for-5. 1983-84, 1-for-6 (.167). 1984-85, 1-for-3 (.333). Totals, 2-for-22 (.091).

NBA PLAYOFF RECORD

Sea.—Team	G.	Min.	FGA	FGM	Pct.	FTA	FTM	Pct.	Off.	Def.	Tot.	Ast.	PF	Dq.	Stl.	Blk.	Pts.	Avg.
81-82—San Antonio	9	146	65	30	.462	10	4	.400	21	22	43	9	12	0	4	3	64	7.1
82-83—San Antonio	11	398	150	76	.507	35	23	.657	27	49	76	50	25	1	11	1	175	15.9
84-85—San Antonio	1	10	1	0	.000	0	0	.000	0	0	0	1	3	0	0	0	0	0.0
Totals	21	554	216	106	.491	45	27	.600	48	71	119	60	40	1	15	4	239	11.4

Three-Point Field Goals: 1981-82, 0-for-1.

KENNETH BANNISTER
(Ken)

Born April 1, 1960 at Baltimore, Md.   Height 6:09.   Weight 235.

High School—Baltimore, Md., Southwestern.

Colleges—Trinidad State Junior College, Trinidad, Colo.; Indiana State University, Terre Haute, Ind., and St. Augustine's College, Raleigh, N. C.

Drafted by New York on seventh round, 1984 (156th pick).

—COLLEGIATE RECORD—
Trinidad State J.C.

Year	G.	Min.	FGA	FGM	Pct.	FTA	FTM	Pct.	Reb.	Pts.	Avg.
79-80					Statistics Unavailable						
80-81					Statistics Unavailable						

Indiana State

Year	G.	Min.	FGA	FGM	Pct.	FTA	FTM	Pct.	Reb.	Pts.	Avg.
81-82	27	786	304	153	.503	117	69	.590	177	375	13.9

St. Augustine's
82-83 .... Did Not Play—Transfer Student

Year	G.	Min.	FGA	FGM	Pct.	FTA	FTM	Pct.	Reb.	Pts.	Avg.
83-84	21	....	256	142	.555	117	64	.547	276	348	16.6
Totals	48	....	560	295	.527	234	133	.568	453	723	15.1

NBA REGULAR SEASON RECORD

Sea.—Team	G.	Min.	FGA	FGM	Pct.	FTA	FTM	Pct.	Off.	Def.	Tot.	Ast.	PF	Dq.	Stl.	Blk.	Pts.	Avg.
84-85—New York	75	1404	445	209	.470	192	91	.474	108	222	330	39	279	16	38	40	509	6.8

CHARLES WADE BARKLEY

Born February 20, 1963 at Leeds, Ala.   Height 6:06.   Weight 260.

High School—Leeds, Ala.

College—Auburn University, Auburn, Ala.

Drafted by Philadelphia on first round as an undergraduate, 1984 (5th pick).

—COLLEGIATE RECORD—

Year	G.	Min.	FGA	FGM	Pct.	FTA	FTM	Pct.	Reb.	Pts.	Avg.
81-82	28	746	242	144	.595	107	68	.636	275	356	12.7
82-83	28	782	250	161	.644	130	82	.631	266	404	14.4
83-84	28	794	254	162	.638	145	99	.683	265	423	15.1
Totals	84	2322	746	467	.636	382	249	.652	806	1183	14.1

CHARLES BARKLEY

NBA REGULAR SEASON RECORD

Sea.—Team	G.	Min.	FGA	FGM	Pct.	FTA	FTM	Pct.	—Rebounds— Off.	Def.	Tot.	Ast.	PF	Dq.	Stl.	Blk.	Pts.	Avg.
84-85—Philadelphia	82	2347	783	427	.545	400	293	.733	266	437	703	155	301	5	95	80	1148	14.0

Three-Point Field Goals: 1984-85, 1-for-6 (.167).

NBA PLAYOFF RECORD

Sea.—Team	G.	Min.	FGA	FGM	Pct.	FTA	FTM	Pct.	—Rebounds— Off.	Def.	Tot.	Ast.	PF	Dq.	Stl.	Blk.	Pts.	Avg.
84-85—Philadelphia	13	408	139	75	.540	63	40	.635	52	92	144	26	49	0	23	15	194	14.9

Three-Point Field Goals: 1984-85, 4-for-6 (.667).

Named to NBA All-Rookie Team, 1985.

MICHAEL KENT BENSON

(Known by middle name.)

Born December 27, 1954 at New Castle, Ind.   Height 6:10.   Weight 245.

High School—New Castle, Ind., Chrysler.

College—Indiana University, Bloomington, Ind.

Drafted by Milwaukee on first round, 1977 (1st pick).

Traded by Milwaukee with a 1980 1st round draft choice to Detroit for Bob Lanier, February 4, 1980.

—COLLEGIATE RECORD—

Year	G.	Min.	FGA	FGM	Pct.	FTA	FTM	Pct.	Reb.	Pts.	Avg.
73-74	27	....	224	113	.504	40	24	.600	222	250	9.3
74-75	32	....	366	198	.541	113	84	.743	286	480	15.0
75-76	32	....	410	237	.578	117	80	.684	282	554	17.3
76-77	23	....	346	174	.503	144	108	.750	241	456	19.8
Totals	114	....	1346	722	.536	414	296	.715	1031	1740	15.3

NBA REGULAR SEASON RECORD

Sea.—Team	G.	Min.	FGA	FGM	Pct.	FTA	FTM	Pct.	—Rebounds— Off.	Def.	Tot.	Ast.	PF	Dq.	Stl.	Blk.	Pts.	Avg.
77-78—Milwaukee	69	1288	473	220	.465	141	92	.652	89	206	295	99	177	1	69	54	532	7.7
78-79—Milwaukee	82	2132	798	413	.518	245	180	.735	187	397	584	204	280	4	89	81	1006	12.3
79-80—Mil.-Det.	73	1891	618	299	.484	141	99	.702	126	327	453	178	246	4	73	92	698	9.6
80-81—Detroit	59	1956	770	364	.473	254	196	.772	124	276	400	172	184	1	72	67	924	15.7
81-82—Detroit	75	2467	802	405	.505	158	127	.804	219	434	653	159	214	2	66	98	940	12.5
82-83—Detroit	21	599	182	85	.467	50	38	.760	53	102	155	49	61	0	14	17	208	9.9
83-84—Detroit	82	1734	451	248	.550	101	83	.822	117	292	409	130	230	4	71	53	579	7.1
84-85—Detroit	72	1401	397	201	.506	94	76	.809	103	221	324	93	207	4	53	44	478	6.6
Totals	533	13468	4491	2235	.498	1184	891	.753	1018	2255	3273	1084	1599	20	507	506	5365	10.1

Three-Point Field Goals: 1979-80, 1-for-5 (.200). 1980-81, 0-for-4. 1981-82, 3-for-11 (.273). 1982-83, 0-for-1. 1983-84, 0-for-1. 1984-85, 0-for-3. Totals, 4-for-25 (.160).

NBA PLAYOFF RECORD

Sea.—Team	G.	Min.	FGA	FGM	Pct.	FTA	FTM	Pct.	—Rebounds— Off.	Def.	Tot.	Ast.	PF	Dq.	Stl.	Blk.	Pts.	Avg.
77-78—Milwaukee	9	103	23	11	.478	11	6	.545	5	10	15	3	20	0	5	3	28	3.1
83-84—Detroit	5	129	37	16	.432	10	6	.600	9	21	30	7	14	0	5	7	38	7.6
84-85—Detroit	9	142	46	25	.543	15	13	.867	9	27	36	4	27	0	8	2	63	7.0
Totals	23	374	106	52	.491	36	25	.694	23	58	81	14	61	0	18	12	129	5.6

Named to THE SPORTING NEWS All-America First Team, 1977. . . . NCAA Division I Tournament Most Outstanding Player, 1976. . . . Member of NCAA championship team, 1976.

LARRY JOE BIRD

Born December 7, 1956 at French Lick, Ind.   Height 6:09.   Weight 220.

High School—French Lick, Ind., Springs Valley.

Colleges—Indiana University, Bloomington, Ind.; Northwood Institute, West Baden, Ind., and Indiana State University, Terre Haute, Ind.

Drafted by Boston on first round as junior eligible, 1978 (6th pick).

—COLLEGIATE RECORD—

Indiana

Year	G.	Min.	FGA	FGM	Pct.	FTA	FTM	Pct.	Reb.	Pts.	Avg.
74-75					Did Not Play						

Indiana State

Year	G.	Min.	FGA	FGM	Pct.	FTA	FTM	Pct.	Reb.	Pts.	Avg.
75-76				Did Not Play—Transfer Student							
76-77	28	1033	689	375	.544	200	168	.840	373	918	32.8
77-78	32	....	769	403	.524	193	153	.793	369	959	30.0
78-79	34	....	707	376	.532	266	221	.831	505	973	28.6
Totals	94	....	2165	1154	.533	659	542	.822	1247	2850	30.3

NBA REGULAR SEASON RECORD

Sea.—Team	G.	Min.	FGA	FGM	Pct.	FTA	FTM	Pct.	—Rebounds— Off.	Def.	Tot.	Ast.	PF	Dq.	Stl.	Blk.	Pts.	Avg.
79-80—Boston	82	2955	1463	693	.474	360	301	.836	216	636	852	370	279	4	143	53	1745	21.3
80-81—Boston	82	3239	1503	719	.478	328	283	.863	191	704	895	451	239	2	161	63	1741	21.2
81-82—Boston	77	2923	1414	711	.503	380	328	.863	200	637	837	447	244	0	143	66	1761	22.9
82-83—Boston	79	2982	1481	747	.504	418	351	.840	193	677	870	458	197	0	148	71	1867	23.6
83-84—Boston	79	3028	1542	758	.492	421	374	.888	181	615	796	520	197	0	144	69	1908	24.2
84-85—Boston	80	3161	1760	918	.522	457	403	.882	164	678	842	531	208	0	129	98	2295	28.7
Totals	479	18288	9163	4546	.496	2364	2040	.863	1145	3947	5092	2777	1364	6	868	420	11317	23.6

Three-Point Field Goals: 1979-80, 58-for-143 (.406). 1980-81, 20-for-74 (.270). 1981-82, 11-for-52 (.212). 1982-83, 22-for-77 (.286). 1983-84, 18-for-73 (.247). 1984-85, 56-for-131 (.427). Totals, 185-for-550 (.336).

NBA PLAYOFF RECORD

Sea.—Team	G.	Min.	FGA	FGM	Pct.	FTA	FTM	Pct.	—Rebounds— Off.	Def.	Tot.	Ast.	PF	Dq.	Stl.	Blk.	Pts.	Avg.
79-80—Boston	9	372	177	83	.469	25	22	.880	22	79	101	42	30	0	14	8	192	21.3
80-81—Boston	17	750	313	147	.470	85	76	.894	49	189	238	103	53	0	39	17	373	21.9
81-82—Boston	12	490	206	88	.427	45	37	.822	33	117	150	67	43	0	23	17	214	17.8
82-83—Boston	6	240	116	49	.422	29	24	.828	20	55	75	41	15	0	13	3	123	20.5
83-84—Boston	23	961	437	229	.524	190	167	.879	62	190	252	136	71	0	54	27	632	27.5
84-85—Boston	20	815	425	196	.461	136	121	.890	53	129	182	115	54	0	34	19	520	26.0
Totals	87	3628	1674	792	.473	510	447	.876	239	759	998	504	266	0	177	91	2054	23.6

Three-Point Field Goals: 1979-80, 4-for-15 (.267). 1980-81, 3-for-8 (.375). 1981-82, 1-for-6 (.167). 1982-83, 1-for-4 (.250). 1983-84, 7-for-17 (.412). 1984-85, 7-for-25 (.280). Totals, 23-for-75 (.307).

NBA ALL-STAR GAME RECORD

Season—Team	Min.	FGA	FGM	Pct.	FTA	FTM	Pct.	—Rebounds— Off.	Def.	Tot.	Ast.	PF	Dq.	Stl.	Blk.	Pts.
1980—Boston	23	6	3	.500	0	0	.000	3	3	6	7	1	0	1	0	7
1981—Boston	18	5	1	.200	0	0	.000	1	3	4	3	1	0	1	0	2
1982—Boston	28	12	7	.583	8	5	.625	0	12	12	5	3	0	1	1	19
1983—Boston	29	14	7	.500	0	0	.000	3	10	13	7	4	0	2	0	14
1984—Boston	33	18	6	.333	4	4	1.000	1	6	7	3	1	0	2	0	16
1985—Boston	31	16	8	.500	6	5	.833	5	3	8	2	3	0	0	1	21
Totals	162	71	32	.451	18	14	.778	13	37	50	27	13	0	7	2	79

Three-Point Field Goals: 1980, 1-for-2 (.500). 1983, 0-for-1. 1985, 0-for-1. Totals, 1-for-4 (.250).

NBA Most Valuable Player, 1984 and 1985.... Named to All-NBA First Team, 1980, 1981, 1982, 1983, 1984, 1985.... NBA All-Defensive Second Team, 1982, 1983, 1984.... NBA Rookie of the Year, 1980.... NBA All-Rookie Team, 1980.. .. Member of NBA championship teams, 1981 and 1984.... NBA Playoff MVP, 1984.... Holds NBA playoff record for most points in one year, 1984.... Led NBA in free-throw percentage, 1984.... NBA All-Star Game MVP, 1982.... THE SPORTING NEWS College Player of the Year, 1979. ... Named to THE SPORTING NEWS All-America First Team, 1978 and 1979.

OTIS LEE BIRDSONG

Born December 9, 1955 at Winter Haven, Fla.   Height 6:04.   Weight 195.

High School—Winter Haven, Fla.

College—University of Houston, Houston, Tex.

Drafted by Kansas City on first round, 1977 (2nd pick).

Traded by Kansas City with a 1981 2nd round draft choice to New Jersey for Cliff Robinson, June 8, 1981.

—COLLEGIATE RECORD—

Year	G.	Min.	FGA	FGM	Pct.	FTA	FTM	Pct.	Reb.	Pts.	Avg.
73-74	26	673	312	154	.494	92	64	.696	110	372	14.3
74-75	26	965	460	268	.583	143	104	.727	122	640	24.6
75-76	28	1082	582	302	.519	191	126	.660	176	730	26.1
76-77	36	1342	794	452	.569	249	186	.747	159	1090	30.3
Totals	116	4062	2148	1176	.547	675	480	.711	567	2832	24.4

NBA REGULAR SEASON RECORD

Sea.—Team	G.	Min.	FGA	FGM	Pct.	FTA	FTM	Pct.	—Rebounds— Off.	Def.	Tot.	Ast.	PF	Dq.	Stl.	Blk.	Pts.	Avg.
77-78—Kansas City	73	1878	955	470	.492	310	216	.697	70	105	175	174	179	1	74	12	1156	15.8
78-79—Kansas City	82	2839	1456	741	.509	408	296	.725	176	178	354	281	255	2	125	17	1778	21.7
79-80—Kansas City	82	2885	1546	781	.505	412	286	.694	170	161	331	202	226	2	136	22	1858	22.7
80-81—Kansas City	71	2593	1306	710	.544	455	317	.697	119	139	258	233	172	2	93	18	1747	24.6

Sea.—Team	G.	Min.	FGA	FGM	Pct.	FTA	FTM	Pct.	Off.	Def.	Tot.	Ast.	PF	Dq.	Stl.	Blk.	Pts.	Avg.
										—Rebounds—								
81-82—New Jersey	37	1025	480	225	.469	127	74	.583	30	67	97	124	74	0	30	5	524	14.2
82-83—New Jersey	62	1885	834	426	.511	145	82	.566	53	97	150	239	155	0	85	16	936	15.1
83-84—New Jersey	69	2168	1147	583	.508	319	194	.608	74	96	170	266	180	2	86	17	1365	19.8
84-85—New Jersey	56	1842	968	495	.511	259	161	.622	60	88	148	232	145	1	84	7	1155	20.6
Totals	532	17115	8692	4431	.510	2435	1626	.668	752	931	1683	1751	1386	10	713	114	10519	19.8

Three-Point Field Goals: 1979-80, 10-for-36 (.278). 1980-81, 10-for-35 (.286). 1981-82, 0-for-10. 1982-83, 2-for-6 (.333). 1983-84, 5-for-20 (.250). 1984-85, 4-for-21 (.190). Totals, 31-for-128 (.242).

NBA PLAYOFF RECORD

Sea.—Team	G.	Min.	FGA	FGM	Pct.	FTA	FTM	Pct.	Off.	Def.	Tot.	Ast.	PF	Dq.	Stl.	Blk.	Pts.	Avg.
										—Rebounds—								
78-79—Kansas City	5	168	76	39	.513	38	27	.711	8	10	18	9	13	0	10	0	105	21.0
79-80—Kansas City	3	112	62	30	.484	14	6	.429	11	12	23	7	5	0	4	0	66	22.0
80-81—Kansas City	8	234	98	56	.571	18	11	.611	8	13	21	27	13	1	12	0	124	15.5
82-83—New Jersey	2	37	16	6	.375	2	1	.500	1	1	2	9	3	0	3	0	13	6.5
83-84—New Jersey	11	387	171	71	.415	48	25	.521	7	19	26	41	38	0	20	1	167	15.2
Totals	29	938	423	202	.478	120	70	.583	35	55	90	93	72	1	49	1	475	16.4

Three-Point Field Goals: 1979-80, 0-for-3. 1980-81, 1-for-1. 1982-83, 0-for-1. 1983-84, 0-for-1. Totals, 1-for-6 (.167).

NBA ALL-STAR GAME RECORD

Season—Team	Min.	FGA	FGM	Pct.	FTA	FTM	Pct.	Off.	Def.	Tot.	Ast.	PF	Dq.	Stl.	Blk.	Pts.
									—Rebounds—							
1979—Kansas City..	14	6	4	.667	2	1	.500	1	1	2	0	1	0	2	0	9
1980—Kansas City..	14	2	1	.500	0	0	.000	0	0	0	0	1	0	1	0	2
1981—Kansas City..	12	3	0	.000	2	1	.500	1	0	1	1	0	0	0	0	1
1984—New Jersey..	12	5	1	.200	0	0	.000	2	1	3	1	1	0	0	0	2
Totals	52	16	6	.375	4	2	.500	4	2	6	2	3	0	3	0	14

Named to All-NBA Second Team, 1981. . . . THE SPORTING NEWS All-America First Team, 1977.

ROLANDO ANTONIO BLACKMAN

Born February 26, 1959 at Panama City, Panama.   Height 6:06.   Weight 190.

High School—Brooklyn, N. Y., William Grady.

College—Kansas State University, Manhattan, Kan.

Drafted by Dallas on first round, 1981 (9th pick).

—COLLEGIATE RECORD—

Year	G.	Min.	FGA	FGM	Pct.	FTA	FTM	Pct.	Reb.	Pts.	Avg.
77-78	29	....	269	127	.472	93	61	.656	187	315	10.9
78-79	28	....	392	200	.510	113	83	.735	110	483	17.3
79-80	31	....	419	226	.539	145	100	.690	145	552	17.8
80-81	33	....	380	202	.532	115	90	.783	165	494	15.0
Totals	121	....	1460	755	.517	466	334	.717	607	1844	15.2

NBA REGULAR SEASON RECORD

Sea.—Team	G.	Min.	FGA	FGM	Pct.	FTA	FTM	Pct.	Off.	Def.	Tot.	Ast.	PF	Dq.	Stl.	Blk.	Pts.	Avg.
										—Rebounds—								
81-82—Dallas	82	1979	855	439	.513	276	212	.768	97	157	254	105	122	0	46	30	1091	13.3
82-83—Dallas	75	2349	1042	513	.492	381	297	.780	108	185	293	185	116	0	37	29	1326	17.7
83-84—Dallas	81	3025	1320	721	.546	458	372	.812	124	249	373	288	127	0	56	37	1815	22.4
84-85—Dallas	81	2834	1230	625	.508	413	342	.828	107	193	300	289	96	0	61	16	1598	19.7
Totals	319	10187	4447	2298	.517	1528	1223	.800	436	784	1220	867	461	0	200	112	5830	18.3

Three-Point Field Goals: 1981-82, 1-for-4 (.250). 1982-83, 3-for-15 (.200). 1983-84, 1-for-11 (.091). 1984-85, 6-for-20 (.300). Totals, 11-for-50 (.220).

NBA PLAYOFF RECORD

Sea.—Team	G.	Min.	FGA	FGM	Pct.	FTA	FTM	Pct.	Off.	Def.	Tot.	Ast.	PF	Dq.	Stl.	Blk.	Pts.	Avg.
										—Rebounds—								
83-84—Dallas	10	397	175	93	.531	63	53	.841	15	26	41	40	15	0	6	4	239	23.9
84-85—Dallas	4	169	92	47	.511	38	36	.947	11	15	26	19	8	0	2	2	131	32.8
Totals	14	566	267	140	.524	101	89	.881	26	41	67	59	23	0	8	6	370	26.4

Three-Point Field Goals: 1984-85, 1-for-2 (.500).

NBA ALL-STAR GAME RECORD

Season—Team	Min.	FGA	FGM	Pct.	FTA	FTM	Pct.	Off.	Def.	Tot.	Ast.	PF	Dq.	Stl.	Blk.	Pts.
									—Rebounds—							
1985—Dallas	23	14	7	.500	2	1	.500	1	2	3	2	1	0	1	1	15

Named to THE SPORTING NEWS All-America First Team, 1981. . . . Member of U.S. Olympic team, 1980.

ROLANDO BLACKMAN

CORY BLACKWELL

Born March 27, 1963 at Chicago, Ill. Height 6:06. Weight 210.

High School—Chicago, Ill., Crane Tech.

College—University of Wisconsin, Madison, Wis.

Drafted by Seattle on second round as an undergraduate, 1984 (28th pick).

—COLLEGIATE RECORD—

Year	G.	Min.	FGA	FGM	Pct.	FTA	FTM	Pct.	Reb.	Pts.	Avg.
81-82	27	869	330	147	.445	103	71	.689	137	365	13.5
82-83	28	995	465	215	.462	113	80	.708	206	511	18.3
83-84	28	1045	439	201	.458	181	127	.702	243	529	18.9
Totals	83	2909	1234	563	.456	397	278	.700	586	1405	16.9

Three-Point Field Goals: 1982-83, 1-for-4 (.250).

NBA REGULAR SEASON RECORD

									—Rebounds—								
Sea.—Team	G.	Min.	FGA	FGM	Pct.	FTA	FTM	Pct.	Off.	Def.	Tot.	Ast.	PF	Dq.	Stl.	Blk.	Pts.	Avg.
84-85—Seattle	60	551	237	87	.367	55	28	.509	42	54	96	26	55	0	25	3	202	3.4

Three-Point Field Goals: 1984-85, 0-for-2.

SAMUEL PAUL BOWIE
(Sam)

Born March 17, 1961 at Lebanon, Pa. Height 7:01. Weight 235.

High School—Lebanon, Pa.

College—University of Kentucky, Lexington, Ky.

Drafted by Portland on first round, 1984 (2nd pick).

—COLLEGIATE RECORD—

Year	G.	Min.	FGA	FGM	Pct.	FTA	FTM	Pct.	Reb.	Pts.	Avg.
79-80	34	886	311	165	.531	144	110	.764	276	440	12.9
80-81	28	895	356	185	.520	164	118	.720	254	488	17.4
81-82					Did Not Play—Injured						
82-83					Did Not Play—Injured						
83-84	34	980	258	133	.516	126	91	.722	313	357	10.5
Totals	96	2761	925	483	.522	434	319	.735	843	1285	13.4

NBA REGULAR SEASON RECORD

									—Rebounds—								
Sea.—Team	G.	Min.	FGA	FGM	Pct.	FTA	FTM	Pct.	Off.	Def.	Tot.	Ast.	PF	Dq.	Stl.	Blk.	Pts.	Avg.
84-85—Portland	76	2216	557	299	.537	225	160	.711	207	449	656	215	278	9	55	203	758	10.0

NBA PLAYOFF RECORD

									—Rebounds—								
Sea.—Team	G.	Min.	FGA	FGM	Pct.	FTA	FTM	Pct.	Off.	Def.	Tot.	Ast.	PF	Dq.	Stl.	Blk.	Pts.	Avg.
84-85—Portland	9	259	59	26	.441	25	14	.560	16	60	76	21	36	2	4	21	66	7.3

Named to NBA All-Rookie Team, 1985. . . . Member of 1980 U.S. Olympic team. . . . Named to THE SPORTING NEWS All-America Second Team, 1984.

DUDLEY LEROY BRADLEY

Born March 19, 1957 at Baltimore, Md. Height 6:06. Weight 195.

High School—Edgewood, Md.

College—University of North Carolina, Chapel Hill, N. C.

Drafted by Indiana on first round, 1979 (13th pick).

Traded by Indiana to Phoenix for two 2nd round draft choices (1981 and 1982), June 8, 1981.
Signed by Chicago as Veteran Free Agent, October 1, 1982. Phoenix agreed not to exercise its right of first refusal in exchange for a 1983 3rd round draft choice, October 2, 1983.
Waived by Chicago, October 25, 1983; signed by Detroit as a free agent, July 6, 1984.
Waived by Detroit, September 4, 1984; signed by Washington as a free agent, September 27, 1984.
Played in Continental Basketball Association with Toronto Tornados and Detroit Spirits, 1983-84.

—COLLEGIATE RECORD—

Year	G.	Min.	FGA	FGM	Pct.	FTA	FTM	Pct.	Reb.	Pts.	Avg.
75-76	27	....	65	19	.292	16	8	.500	33	46	1.7
76-77	33	....	48	17	.354	9	2	.222	39	36	1.1
77-78	31	....	159	76	.478	41	22	.537	108	174	5.6
78-79	29	....	213	109	.512	79	48	.608	105	266	9.2
Totals	120	....	485	221	.456	145	80	.552	285	522	4.4

SAM BOWIE

MINOR LEAGUE REGULAR-SEASON RECORD

				—2-Point—			—3-Point—								
Sea.—Team	G.	Min.	FGM	FGA	Pct.	FGM	FGA	Pct.	FTM	FTA	Pct.	Reb.	Ast.	Pts.	Avg.
83-84—Tor.-Det. CBA	38	1282	211	451	.467	8	28	.286	125	179	.698	172	154	571	15.0

NBA REGULAR SEASON RECORD

									—Rebounds—								
Sea.—Team	G.	Min.	FGA	FGM	Pct.	FTA	FTM	Pct.	Off.	Def.	Tot.	Ast.	PF	Dq.	Stl.	Blk.	Pts.	Avg.
79-80—Indiana	82	2027	609	275	.452	174	136	.782	69	154	223	252	194	1	211	48	688	8.4
80-81—Indiana	82	1867	559	265	.474	178	125	.702	70	123	193	188	236	2	186	37	657	8.0
81-82—Phoenix	64	937	281	125	.445	100	74	.740	30	57	87	80	115	0	78	10	325	5.1
82-83—Chicago	58	683	159	82	.516	45	36	.800	27	78	105	106	91	0	49	10	201	3.5
84-85—Washington	73	1232	299	142	.475	79	54	.684	34	100	134	173	152	0	96	21	358	4.9
Totals	359	6746	1907	889	.466	576	425	.738	230	512	742	799	788	3	620	126	2229	6.2

Three-Point Field Goals: 1979-80, 2-for-5 (.400). 1980-81, 2-for-16 (.125). 1981-82, 1-for-4 (.250). 1982-83, 1-for-5 (.200). 1984-85, 20-for-65 (.308). Totals, 26-for-95 (.274).

NBA PLAYOFF RECORD

									—Rebounds—								
Sea.—Team	G.	Min.	FGA	FGM	Pct.	FTA	FTM	Pct.	Off.	Def.	Tot.	Ast.	PF	Dq.	Stl.	Blk.	Pts.	Avg.
80-81—Indiana	2	19	9	3	.333	2	2	1.000	1	1	2	2	4	0	2	0	9	4.5
81-82—Phoenix	7	24	8	2	.250	1	1	1.000	0	1	1	5	3	0	1	1	5	0.7
84-85—Washington	4	41	9	5	.556	4	3	.750	2	4	6	6	5	0	2	0	14	3.5
Totals	13	84	26	10	.385	7	6	.857	3	6	9	13	12	0	5	1	28	2.2

Three-Point Field Goals: 1980-81, 1-for-1. 1984-85, 1-for-5 (.200). Totals, 2-for-6 (.333).

Named to NBA All-Defensive Second Team, 1981. . . . Named to CBA All-Defensive First Team, 1984.

MICHAEL LOUIS BRATZ
(Mike)

Born October 17, 1955 at Lompoc, Calif.   Height 6:02.   Weight 185.

High School—Lompoc, Calif.

Colleges—Allan Hancock College, Santa Maria, Calif., and
Stanford University, Stanford, Calif.

Drafted by Phoenix on third round, 1977 (66th pick).

Selected from Phoenix by Dallas in expansion draft, May 28, 1980.
Traded by Dallas to Cleveland for a 1984 1st round draft choice, September 16, 1980.
Traded by Cleveland to San Antonio for a 1983 3rd round draft choice, October 28, 1981.
Traded by San Antonio to Chicago for a 1983 4th round draft choice, March 8, 1983.
Signed by Golden State as Veteran Free Agent, September 30, 1983; Chicago agreed not to exercise its right of first refusal in exchange for a 1984 4th round draft choice.

—COLLEGIATE RECORD—
Allan Hancock

Year	G.	Min.	FGA	FGM	Pct.	FTA	FTM	Pct.	Reb.	Pts.	Avg.
73-74	35	....	392	183	.467	85	73	.859	152	439	12.5

Stanford

Year	G.	Min.	FGA	FGM	Pct.	FTA	FTM	Pct.	Reb.	Pts.	Avg.
74-75	26	....	122	58	.475	22	12	.545	31	128	4.9
75-76	27	....	295	129	.437	88	69	.784	82	327	12.1
76-77	27	943	423	205	.485	145	118	.814	95	528	19.6
Totals	80	....	840	392	.467	255	199	.780	208	983	12.3

NBA REGULAR SEASON RECORD

									—Rebounds—								
Sea.—Team	G.	Min.	FGA	FGM	Pct.	FTA	FTM	Pct.	Off.	Def.	Tot.	Ast.	PF	Dq.	Stl.	Blk.	Pts.	Avg.
77-78—Phoenix	80	933	395	159	.403	68	56	.824	42	73	115	123	104	1	39	5	374	4.7
78-79—Phoenix	77	1297	533	242	.454	170	139	.818	55	86	141	179	151	0	64	7	623	8.1
79-80—Phoenix	82	1589	687	269	.392	162	141	.870	50	117	167	223	165	0	93	9	700	8.5
80-81—Cleveland	80	2595	817	319	.390	132	107	.811	66	132	198	452	194	1	136	17	802	10.0
81-82—San Antonio	81	1616	565	230	.407	152	119	.783	40	126	166	438	183	0	65	11	625	7.7
82-83—Chicago	15	140	42	14	.333	13	10	.769	3	16	19	23	20	0	7	0	39	2.6
83-84—Golden State	82	1428	521	213	.409	137	120	.876	41	102	143	252	155	0	84	6	561	6.8
84-85—Golden State	56	746	250	106	.424	82	69	.841	11	47	58	122	76	1	47	4	287	5.1
Totals	553	10344	3810	1552	.407	916	761	.831	308	699	1007	1812	1048	3	535	59	4011	7.3

Three-Point Field Goals: 1979-80, 21-for-86 (.244). 1980-81, 57-for-169 (.337). 1981-82, 46-for-138 (.333). 1982-83, 1-for-8 (.125). 1983-84, 15-for-51 (.294). 1984-85, 6-for-26 (.231). Totals, 146-for-478 (.305).

NBA PLAYOFF RECORD

									—Rebounds—								
Sea.—Team	G.	Min.	FGA	FGM	Pct.	FTA	FTM	Pct.	Off.	Def.	Tot.	Ast.	PF	Dq.	Stl.	Blk.	Pts.	Avg.
77-78—Phoenix	2	9	5	1	.200	0	0	.000	0	0	0	1	0	0	0	0	2	1.0
78-79—Phoenix	15	293	115	57	.496	59	45	.763	10	11	21	30	42	0	15	3	159	10.6

Sea.—Team	G.	Min.	FGA	FGM	Pct.	FTA	FTM	Pct.	Off.	Def.	Tot.	Ast.	PF	Dq.	Stl.	Blk.	Pts.	Avg.
										—Rebounds—								
79-80—Phoenix	8	169	84	43	.512	10	9	.900	6	14	20	16	20	0	9	0	104	13.0
81-82—San Antonio	9	180	52	15	.288	10	8	.800	2	12	14	48	20	0	9	0	43	4.8
Totals	34	651	256	116	.453	79	62	.785	18	37	55	95	82	0	33	3	308	9.1

Three-Point Field Goals: 1979-80, 9-for-23 (.391). 1981-82, 5-for-18 (.278). Totals, 14-for-41. (.341).

Holds NBA playoff game records for most three-point field goals made, 5, and attempted, 10, vs. Los Angeles, April 8, 1980.

RANDALL W. BREUER
(Randy)

Born October 11, 1960 at Lake City, Minn.   Height 7:03.   Weight 230.

High School—Lake City, Minn.

College—University of Minnesota, Minneapolis, Minn.

Drafted by Milwaukee on first round, 1983 (18th pick).

—COLLEGIATE RECORD—

Year	G.	Min.	FGA	FGM	Pct.	FTA	FTM	Pct.	Reb.	Pts.	Avg.
79-80	31	....	172	96	.558	74	48	.648	98	240	7.7
80-81	30	....	313	180	.575	141	97	.688	166	457	15.2
81-82	29	....	325	180	.554	168	127	.756	209	487	16.8
82-83	29	....	384	225	.586	186	143	.769	257	593	20.4
Totals	119	....	1194	681	.570	569	415	.729	730	1777	14.9

NBA REGULAR SEASON RECORD

Sea.—Team	G.	Min.	FGA	FGM	Pct.	FTA	FTM	Pct.	Off.	Def.	Tot.	Ast.	PF	Dq.	Stl.	Blk.	Pts.	Avg.
										—Rebounds—								
83-84—Milwaukee	57	472	177	68	.384	46	32	.696	48	61	109	17	98	1	11	38	168	2.9
84-85—Milwaukee	78	1083	317	162	.511	127	89	.701	92	164	256	40	179	4	21	82	413	5.3
Totals	135	1555	494	230	.466	173	121	.699	140	225	365	57	277	5	32	120	581	4.3

NBA PLAYOFF RECORD

Sea.—Team	G.	Min.	FGA	FGM	Pct.	FTA	FTM	Pct.	Off.	Def.	Tot.	Ast.	PF	Dq.	Stl.	Blk.	Pts.	Avg.
										—Rebounds—								
83-84—Milwaukee	12	66	26	11	.423	5	3	.600	6	11	17	4	18	0	0	6	25	2.1
84-85—Milwaukee	8	104	26	15	.577	21	14	.667	9	15	24	0	15	0	2	2	44	5.5
Totals	20	170	52	26	.500	26	17	.654	15	26	41	4	33	0	2	8	69	3.5

RONALD CHARLES BREWER
(Ron)

Born September 16, 1955 at Fort Smith, Ark.   Height 6:04.   Weight 185.

High School—Fort Smith, Ark., Northside.

Colleges—Westark Community College, Fort Smith, Ark., and University of Arkansas, Fayetteville, Ark.

Drafted by Portland on first round, 1978 (7th pick).

Traded by Portland to San Antonio for Mike Gale and a 1982 1st round draft choice, December 19, 1980.

Traded by San Antonio with Reggie Johnson and cash to Cleveland for Mike Mitchell and Roger Phegley, December 23, 1981.

Traded by Cleveland to Golden State for World B. Free, December 15, 1982.

Traded by Golden State to San Antonio for a 1985 2nd round draft choice and cash, January 20, 1984.

Waived by San Antonio, December 5, 1984; signed by New Jersey as a free agent, March 21, 1985.

—COLLEGIATE RECORD—

Westark CC

Year	G.	Min.	FGA	FGM	Pct.	FTA	FTM	Pct.	Reb.	Pts.	Avg.
74-75	35	....	534	267	.500	112	85	.759	245	619	17.7

Arkansas

Year	G.	Min.	FGA	FGM	Pct.	FTA	FTM	Pct.	Reb.	Pts.	Avg.
75-76	28	....	226	130	.575	99	74	.748	105	334	11.9
76-77	27	930	326	199	.610	97	61	.629	85	459	17.0
77-78	36	1291	486	258	.531	157	131	.834	112	647	18.0
Totals	91	....	1038	587	.566	353	266	.754	302	1440	15.8

NBA REGULAR SEASON RECORD

Sea.—Team	G.	Min.	FGA	FGM	Pct.	FTA	FTM	Pct.	Off.	Def.	Tot.	Ast.	PF	Dq.	Stl.	Blk.	Pts.	Avg.
										—Rebounds—								
78-79—Portland	81	2454	878	434	.494	256	210	.820	88	141	229	165	181	3	102	79	1078	13.3
79-80—Portland	82	2815	1182	548	.464	219	184	.840	54	160	214	216	154	0	98	48	1286	15.7

Sea.—Team	G.	Min.	FGA	FGM	Pct.	FTA	FTM	Pct.	—Rebounds— Off.	Def.	Tot.	Ast.	PF	Dq.	Stl.	Blk.	Pts.	Avg.
80-81—Port.-S.A.	75	1452	631	275	.436	114	91	.798	34	52	86	148	95	0	61	34	642	8.6
81-82—S.A.-Clev.	72	2319	1194	569	.477	260	211	.812	55	106	161	188	151	0	82	30	1357	18.8
82-83—Clev.-G.S.	74	1964	807	344	.426	170	142	.835	59	85	144	96	123	0	90	25	837	11.3
83-84—G.S.-S.A.	53	992	403	179	.444	67	52	.776	22	41	63	50	64	0	24	21	413	7.8
84-85—S.A.-N.J.	20	326	118	62	.525	25	23	.920	9	12	21	17	23	0	6	6	147	7.4
Totals	457	12322	5213	2411	.462	1111	913	.822	321	597	918	880	791	3	463	243	5760	12.6

Three-Point Field Goals: 1979-80, 6-for-32 (.188). 1980-81, 1-for-7 (.143). 1981-82, 8-for-31 (.258). 1982-83, 7-for-18 (.389). 1983-84, 3-for-14 (.214). 1984-85, 0-for-2. Totals, 25-for-104 (.240).

NBA PLAYOFF RECORD

Sea.—Team	G.	Min.	FGA	FGM	Pct.	FTA	FTM	Pct.	—Rebounds— Off.	Def.	Tot.	Ast.	PF	Dq.	Stl.	Blk.	Pts.	Avg.
78-79—Portland	3	94	39	22	.564	13	9	.692	4	7	11	8	7	0	1	9	53	17.7
79-80—Portland	3	106	61	26	.426	9	5	.556	1	2	3	6	10	0	3	1	57	19.0
80-81—San Antonio	7	118	61	29	.475	29	21	.724	0	5	5	13	6	0	1	6	80	11.4
84-85—New Jersey	3	93	30	15	.500	8	6	.750	1	4	5	5	7	0	3	0	36	12.0
Totals	16	411	191	92	.482	59	41	.695	6	18	24	32	30	0	8	16	226	14.1

Three-Point Field Goals: 1979-80, 0-for-3. 1980-81, 1-for-3 (.333). 1984-85, 0-for-1. Totals, 1-for-7 (.143).
Named to NBA All-Rookie Team, 1979.

FRANK BRICKOWSKI

Born August 14, 1959 at Bayville, N. Y.   Height 6:10.   Weight 240.

High School—Locust Valley, N. Y.

College—Penn State University, University Park, Pa.

Drafted by New York on third round, 1981 (57th pick).

Draft rights relinquished by New York, June 30, 1983; signed by Seattle as a free agent, September 23, 1984.
Played in Italy during 1981-82 season.
Played in France during 1982-83 season.
Played in Israel during 1983-84 season.

COLLEGIATE RECORD

Year	G.	Min.	FGA	FGM	Pct.	FTA	FTM	Pct.	Reb.	Pts.	Avg.
77-78	25	266	81	37	.457	25	21	.840	64	95	3.8
78-79	24	349	99	49	.495	48	38	.792	109	136	5.7
79-80	27	692	213	111	.521	105	82	.781	202	304	11.3
80-81	24	615	218	131	.601	63	49	.778	150	311	13.0
Totals	100	1922	611	328	.537	241	190	.788	525	846	8.5

NBA REGULAR SEASON RECORD

Sea.—Team	G.	Min.	FGA	FGM	Pct.	FTA	FTM	Pct.	—Rebounds— Off.	Def.	Tot.	Ast.	PF	Dq.	Stl.	Blk.	Pts.	Avg.
1984-85—Seattle	78	1115	305	150	.492	127	85	.669	76	184	260	100	171	1	34	15	385	4.9

Three-Point Field Goals: 1984-85, 0-for-4.

ULYSSES LEE BRIDGEMAN
(Junior)

Born September 17, 1953 at East Chicago, Ind.   Height 6:05.   Weight 210.

High School—East Chicago, Ind., Washington.

College—University of Louisville, Louisville, Ky.

Drafted by Los Angeles on first round, 1975 (8th pick).

Traded by Los Angeles with Elmore Smith, Brian Winters and David Meyers to Milwaukee for Kareem Abdul-Jabbar and Walt Wesley, June 16, 1975.
Traded by Milwaukee with Marques Johnson, Harvey Catchings and cash to Los Angeles Clippers for Terry Cummings, Craig Hodges and Ricky Pierce, September 29, 1984.

—COLLEGIATE RECORD—

Year	G.	Min.	FGA	FGM	Pct.	FTA	FTM	Pct.	Reb.	Pts.	Avg.
71-72†	16	....	260	144	.554	97	61	.629	202	349	21.8
72-73	28	....	338	164	.485	84	58	.690	190	386	13.8
73-74	28	878	332	179	.539	134	103	.769	237	461	16.5
74-75	31	1034	356	187	.525	156	127	.814	230	501	16.2
Varsity Totals	87	....	1026	530	.517	374	288	.770	657	1348	15.5

NBA REGULAR SEASON RECORD

Sea.—Team	G.	Min.	FGA	FGM	Pct.	FTA	FTM	Pct.	—Rebounds— Off.	Def.	Tot.	Ast.	PF	Dq.	Stl.	Blk.	Pts.	Avg.
75-76—Milwaukee	81	1646	651	286	.439	161	128	.795	113	181	294	157	235	3	52	21	700	8.6
76-77—Milwaukee	82	2410	1094	491	.449	228	197	.864	129	287	416	205	221	3	82	26	1179	14.4
77-78—Milwaukee	82	1876	947	476	.503	205	166	.810	114	176	290	175	202	1	72	30	1118	13.6

Sea.—Team	G.	Min.	FGA	FGM	Pct.	FTA	FTM	Pct.	Off.	Def.	Tot.	Ast.	PF	Dq.	Stl.	Blk.	Pts.	Avg.
78-79—Milwaukee	82	1963	1067	540	.506	228	189	.829	113	184	297	163	184	2	88	41	1269	15.5
79-80—Milwaukee	81	2316	1243	594	.478	266	230	.865	104	197	301	237	216	3	94	20	1423	17.6
80-81—Milwaukee	77	2215	1102	537	.487	241	213	.884	78	211	289	234	182	2	88	28	1290	16.8
81-82—Milwaukee	41	924	433	209	.483	103	89	.864	37	88	125	109	91	0	28	3	511	12.5
82-83—Milwaukee	70	1855	856	421	.492	196	164	.837	44	202	246	207	155	0	40	9	1007	14.4
83-84—Milwaukee	81	2431	1094	509	.465	243	196	.807	80	252	332	265	224	2	53	14	1220	15.1
84-85—L.A. Clippers	80	2042	990	460	.465	206	181	.879	55	175	230	171	128	0	47	18	1115	13.9
Totals	757	19678	9477	4523	.477	2077	1753	.844	867	1953	2820	1923	1838	16	644	210	10832	14.3

Three-Point Field Goals: 1979-80, 5-for-27 (.185). 1980-81, 3-for-21 (.143). 1981-82, 4-for-9 (.444). 1982-83, 1-for-13 (.077). 1983-84, 6-for-31 (.194). 1984-85, 14-for-39 (.359). Totals, 33-for-140 (.236).

NBA PLAYOFF RECORD

Sea.—Team	G.	Min.	FGA	FGM	Pct.	FTA	FTM	Pct.	Off.	Def.	Tot.	Ast.	PF	Dq.	Stl.	Blk.	Pts.	Avg.
75-76—Milwaukee	3	67	20	9	.450	11	7	.636	4	7	11	5	10	0	1	0	25	8.3
77-78—Milwaukee	9	178	91	44	.484	8	6	.750	6	12	18	11	31	0	9	2	94	10.4
79-80—Milwaukee	5	124	56	20	.357	15	11	.733	4	15	19	17	17	0	5	2	51	10.2
80-81—Milwaukee	7	183	91	42	.462	16	13	.813	6	9	15	23	27	0	6	0	98	14.0
82-83—Milwaukee	9	308	130	61	.469	30	28	.933	21	24	45	28	26	1	10	2	152	16.9
83-84—Milwaukee	16	499	193	88	.456	65	53	.815	12	52	64	44	37	1	6	5	230	14.4
Totals	49	1359	581	264	.454	145	118	.814	53	119	172	128	148	2	37	11	650	13.3

Three-Point Field Goals: 1979-80, 0-for-1. 1980-81, 1-for-1. 1982-83, 2-for-5 (.400). 1983-84, 1-for-9 (.111). Totals, 4-for-16 (.250).

MICHAEL ANTHONY BROOKS

Born August 17, 1958 at Philadelphia, Pa.   Height 6:07.   Weight 220.

High School—Philadelphia, Pa., West Catholic.

College—La Salle College, Philadelphia, Pa.

Drafted by San Diego on first round, 1980 (9th pick).

Missed entire 1984-85 season due to injury.

—COLLEGIATE RECORD—

Year	G.	Min.	FGA	FGM	Pct.	FTA	FTM	Pct.	Reb.	Pts.	Avg.
76-77	29	....	490	241	.492	152	97	.638	311	579	20.0
77-78	28	967	490	288	.588	164	120	.732	358	696	24.9
78-79	26	....	443	245	.553	161	116	.720	347	606	23.3
79-80	31	....	553	290	.524	237	167	.705	356	747	24.1
Totals	114	....	1976	1064	.538	714	500	.700	1372	2628	23.1

NBA REGULAR SEASON RECORD

Sea.—Team	G.	Min.	FGA	FGM	Pct.	FTA	FTM	Pct.	Off.	Def.	Tot.	Ast.	PF	Dq.	Stl.	Blk.	Pts.	Avg.
80-81—San Diego	82	2479	1018	488	.479	320	226	.706	210	232	442	208	234	2	99	31	1202	14.7
81-82—San Diego	82	2750	1066	537	.504	267	202	.757	207	417	624	236	285	7	113	39	1276	15.6
82-83—San Diego	82	2457	830	402	.484	277	193	.697	239	282	521	262	297	6	112	39	1002	12.2
83-84—San Diego	47	1405	445	213	.479	151	104	.689	142	200	342	88	125	1	50	14	530	11.3
Totals	293	9091	3359	1640	.488	1015	725	.714	798	1131	1929	794	941	16	374	123	4010	13.7

Three-Point Field Goals: 1980-81, 0-for-6. 1981-82, 0-for-7. 1982-83, 5-for-15 (.333). 1983-84, 0-for-5. Totals, 5-for-33 (.152).

Named to THE SPORTING NEWS All-America Second Team, 1980.... Member of U.S. Olympic Team, 1980.

RICKEY DARNELL BROWN

Born August 20, 1958 at Madison County, Miss.   Height 6:10.   Weight 235.

High School—Atlanta, Ga., West Fulton.

College—Mississippi State University, Mississippi State, Miss.

Drafted by Golden State on first round, 1980 (13th pick).

Traded by Golden State to Atlanta for a 1984 2nd round draft choice and cash, February 15, 1983.

—COLLEGIATE RECORD—

Year	G.	Min.	FGA	FGM	Pct.	FTA	FTM	Pct.	Reb.	Pts.	Avg.
76-77	27	824	443	225	.508	97	70	.722	292	520	19.3
77-78	26	756	304	140	.461	100	69	.690	179	349	13.4
78-79	27	842	370	178	.481	88	60	.682	232	416	15.4
79-80	27	964	471	231	.490	136	91	.669	389	553	20.5
Totals	107	3386	1588	774	.487	421	290	.689	1092	1838	17.2

Sea.—Team	G.	Min.	FGA	FGM	Pct.	FTA	FTM	Pct.	Off.	Def.	Tot.	Ast.	PF	Dq.	Stl.	Blk.	Pts.	Avg.
80-81—Golden State	45	580	162	83	.512	21	16	.762	52	114	166	21	103	4	9	14	182	4.0
81-82—Golden State	82	1260	418	192	.459	122	86	.705	136	228	364	19	243	4	36	29	470	5.7
82-83—G.S.-Atl.	76	1048	349	167	.479	105	65	.619	91	175	266	25	172	1	13	26	399	5.3
83-84—Atlanta	68	785	201	94	.468	65	48	.738	67	114	181	29	161	4	18	23	236	3.5
84-85—Atlanta	69	814	192	78	.406	68	39	.574	76	147	223	25	117	0	19	22	195	2.8
Totals	340	4487	1322	614	.464	381	254	.667	422	778	1200	119	796	13	95	114	1482	4.4

Three-Point Field Goals: 1982-83, 0-for-3.

NBA PLAYOFF RECORD

Sea.—Team	G.	Min.	FGA	FGM	Pct.	FTA	FTM	Pct.	Off.	Def.	Tot.	Ast.	PF	Dq.	Stl.	Blk.	Pts.	Avg.
82-83—Atlanta	2	15	3	1	.333	2	1	.500	0	3	3	0	3	0	0	0	3	1.5
83-84—Atlanta	5	83	21	10	.476	12	10	.833	5	14	19	2	19	0	0	1	30	6.0
Totals	7	98	24	11	.458	14	11	.786	5	17	22	2	22	0	0	1	33	4.7

ANTHONY WILLIAM BROWN
(Tony)

Born July 29, 1960 at Chicago, Ill. Height 6:06. Weight 185.

High School—Chicago, Ill., Farragut.

College—University of Arkansas, Fayetteville, Ark.

Drafted by New Jersey on fourth round, 1982 (82nd pick).

Waived by New Jersey, October 25, 1982; signed by Detroit as a free agent, May 1983.
Waived by Detroit, August 19, 1983; signed by Indiana as a free agent, September 28, 1984.
Played in Continental Basketball Association with Ohio Mixers, 1982-83.

—COLLEGIATE RECORD—

Year	G.	Min.	FGA	FGM	Pct.	FTA	FTM	Pct.	Reb.	Pts.	Avg.
78-79	23	354	66	38	.576	14	11	.786	29	87	3.8
79-80	28	299	68	37	.544	23	13	.565	39	87	3.1
80-81	32	654	113	63	.558	46	29	.630	88	155	4.8
81-82	27	826	185	109	.589	68	52	.765	87	270	10.0
Totals	110	2133	432	247	.572	151	105	.695	243	599	5.4

MINOR LEAGUE REGULAR SEASON RECORD

Sea.—Team	G.	Min.	2-Point FGM	2-Point FGA	2-Point Pct.	3-Point FGM	3-Point FGA	3-Point Pct.	FTM	FTA	Pct.	Reb.	Ast.	Pts.	Avg.
82-83—Ohio. CBA	44	1584	371	745	.497	0	5	.000	223	321	.694	304	115	965	21.9

NBA REGULAR SEASON RECORD

Sea.—Team	G.	Min.	FGA	FGM	Pct.	FTA	FTM	Pct.	Off.	Def.	Tot.	Ast.	PF	Dq.	Stl.	Blk.	Pts.	Avg.
84-85—Indiana	82	1586	465	214	.460	171	116	.678	146	142	288	159	212	3	59	12	544	6.6

Three-Point Field Goals: 1984-85, 0-for-6.

WALLACE GORDON BRYANT JR.

Born July 14, 1959 at Madrid, Spain. Height 7:00. Weight 245.

High School—Gary, Ind., Emerson.

College—University of San Francisco, San Francisco, Calif.

Drafted by Chicago on second round, 1982 (30th pick).

Traded by Chicago to Dallas for a 1986 2nd round draft choice, September 14, 1984.
Played in Italy during 1982-83 season.

—COLLEGIATE RECORD—

Year	G.	Min.	FGA	FGM	Pct.	FTA	FTM	Pct.	Reb.	Pts.	Avg.
78-79	29	502	192	83	.432	40	23	.575	157	189	6.5
79-80	29	....	330	159	.482	105	68	.648	301	386	13.3
80-81	29	991	390	202	.518	125	78	.624	267	482	16.6
81-82	31	1050	397	193	.486	133	86	.647	337	472	15.2
Totals	118	....	1309	637	.487	403	255	.633	1062	1529	13.0

ITALIAN LEAGUE RECORD

Year	G.	Min.	FGA	FGM	Pct.	FTA	FTM	Pct.	Reb.	Pts.	Avg.
82-83—Pall. Canter.....	36	1306	554	270	.487	167	100	.599	319	640	17.8

NBA REGULAR SEASON RECORD

Sea.—Team	G.	Min.	FGA	FGM	Pct.	FTA	FTM	Pct.	Off.	Def.	Tot.	Ast.	PF	Dq.	Stl.	Blk.	Pts.	Avg.
83-84—Chicago	29	317	133	52	.391	33	14	.424	37	43	80	13	48	0	9	11	118	4.1
84-85—Dallas	56	860	148	67	.453	44	30	.682	74	167	241	84	110	1	21	24	164	2.9
Totals	85	1177	281	119	.423	77	44	.571	111	210	321	97	158	1	30	35	282	3.3

NBA PLAYOFF RECORD

Sea.—Team	G.	Min.	FGA	FGM	Pct.	FTA	FTM	Pct.	Off.	Def.	Tot.	Ast.	PF	Dq.	Stl.	Blk.	Pts.	Avg.
84-85—Dallas	2	36	1	0	.000	2	2	1.000	1	6	7	1	5	0	1	1	2	1.0

WILLIAM QUINN BUCKNER
(Known by middle name.)

Born August 20, 1954 at Phoenix, Ill.   Height 6:03.   Weight 205.
High School—Dolton, Ill., Thornridge.
College—Indiana University, Bloomington, Ind.
Drafted by Milwaukee on first round, 1976 (7th pick).

Traded by Milwaukee to Boston for Dave Cowens, September 9, 1982.

—COLLEGIATE RECORD—

Year	G.	Min.	FGA	FGM	Pct.	FTA	FTM	Pct.	Reb.	Pts.	Avg.
72-73	28	....	318	130	.409	69	41	.594	134	301	10.8
73-74	28	....	273	103	.377	41	23	.561	106	229	8.2
74-75	32	....	335	165	.493	84	49	.583	123	379	11.8
75-76	32	....	279	123	.441	82	40	.488	91	286	8.9
Totals	120	....	1205	521	.432	276	153	.554	454	1195	10.0

NBA REGULAR SEASON RECORD

Sea.—Team	G.	Min.	FGA	FGM	Pct.	FTA	FTM	Pct.	Off.	Def.	Tot.	Ast.	PF	Dq.	Stl.	Blk.	Pts.	Avg.
76-77—Milwaukee	79	2095	689	299	.434	154	83	.539	91	173	264	372	291	5	192	21	681	8.6
77-78—Milwaukee	82	2072	671	314	.468	203	131	.645	78	169	247	456	287	6	188	19	759	9.3
78-79—Milwaukee	81	1757	553	251	.454	125	79	.632	57	153	210	468	224	1	156	17	581	7.2
79-80—Milwaukee	67	1690	655	306	.467	143	105	.734	69	169	238	383	202	1	135	4	719	10.7
80-81—Milwaukee	82	2384	956	471	.493	203	149	.734	88	210	298	384	271	3	197	3	1092	13.3
81-82—Milwaukee	70	2156	822	396	.482	168	110	.655	77	173	250	328	218	2	174	3	906	12.9
82-83—Boston	72	1565	561	248	.442	117	74	.632	62	125	187	275	195	2	108	5	570	7.9
83-84—Boston	79	1249	323	138	.427	74	48	.649	41	96	137	214	187	0	84	3	324	4.1
84-85—Boston	75	858	193	74	.383	50	32	.640	26	61	87	148	142	0	63	2	180	2.4
Totals	687	15826	5423	2497	.460	1237	811	.656	589	1329	1918	3028	2017	20	1297	77	5812	8.5

Three-Point Field Goals: 1979-80, 2-for-5 (.400). 1980-81, 1-for-6 (.167). 1981-82, 4-for-15 (.267). 1982-83, 0-for-4 (.000). 1983-84, 0-for-6. 1984-85, 0-for-1. Totals, 7-for-37 (.189).

NBA PLAYOFF RECORD

Sea.—Team	G.	Min.	FGA	FGM	Pct.	FTA	FTM	Pct.	Off.	Def.	Tot.	Ast.	PF	Dq.	Stl.	Blk.	Pts.	Avg.
77-78—Milwaukee	9	257	86	43	.500	23	15	.652	3	24	27	62	30	0	18	1	101	11.2
79-80—Milwaukee	7	165	53	18	.340	11	7	.636	6	10	16	31	20	0	15	0	43	6.1
80-81—Milwaukee	7	183	60	26	.433	16	11	.688	5	15	20	35	26	1	11	0	63	9.0
82-83—Boston	7	98	37	16	.432	2	0	.000	1	9	10	2	18	1	1	0	32	4.6
83-84—Boston	23	268	79	32	.405	22	12	.545	12	23	35	28	52	0	13	0	76	3.3
84-85—Boston	15	86	22	13	.591	8	5	.625	2	5	7	12	24	0	6	0	31	2.1
Totals	68	1057	337	148	.439	82	50	.610	29	86	115	170	170	2	64	1	346	5.1

Three-Point Field Goals: 1979-80, 0-for-1. 1982-83, 0-for-2. 1983-84, 0-for-1. Totals, 0-for-4.

Member of NBA championship team, 1984. . . . Named to NBA All-Defensive Second Team, 1978, 1980, 1981, 1982. . . . Member of NCAA championship team, 1976. . . . Member of U.S. Olympic team, 1976. . . . Selected by Washington Redskins in 14th round of 1976 National Football League draft.

STEVEN DWAYNE BURTT
(Steve)

Born November 5, 1962 at New York, N. Y.   Height 6:02.   Weight 185.
High School—New York, N. Y., Charles Evans Hughes.
College—Iona College, New Rochelle, N. Y.
Drafted by Golden State on second round, 1984 (30th pick).

—COLLEGIATE RECORD—

Year	G.	Min.	FGA	FGM	Pct.	FTA	FTM	Pct.	Reb.	Pts.	Avg.
80-81	28	800	309	149	.482	126	83	.659	73	381	13.6
81-82	31	1148	496	251	.506	251	182	.725	108	684	22.1
82-83	31	1139	544	294	.540	171	132	.772	129	720	23.2
83-84	31	1065	574	309	.538	179	131	.732	109	749	24.2
Totals	121	4152	1923	1003	.522	727	528	.726	419	2534	20.9

NBA REGULAR SEASON RECORD

Sea.—Team	G.	Min.	FGA	FGM	Pct.	FTA	FTM	Pct.	Off.	Def.	Tot.	Ast.	PF	Dq.	Stl.	Blk.	Pts.	Avg.
84-85—Golden State	47	418	188	72	.383	77	53	.688	10	18	28	20	76	0	21	4	197	4.2

Three-Point Field Goals: 1984-85, 0-for-1.

DONALD R. BUSE
(Don)

Born August 10, 1950 at Huntingburg, Ind.   Height 6:04.   Weight 195.

High School—Holland, Ind.

College—University of Evansville, Evansville, Ind.

Drafted by Phoenix on third round, 1972 (34th pick).

Selected by Virginia on fifth round of ABA draft, 1972.
Draft rights sold by Virginia to Indiana, 1972.
Entered NBA with Indiana, 1976.
Traded by Indiana to Phoenix for Ricky Sobers, September 6, 1977.
Traded by Phoenix to Indiana for two 2nd round draft choices (1981 and 1982), November 25, 1980.
Rights traded by Indiana to Portland for cash and other considerations, January 7, 1983.
Waived by Portland, August 22, 1983; signed by Kansas City as a free agent, September 28, 1983.

—COLLEGIATE RECORD—

Year	G.	Min.	FGA	FGM	Pct.	FTA	FTM	Pct.	Reb.	Pts.	Avg.
68-69†	..	....	...	...	....	...	...	....	....	...	16.8
69-70	26	....	334	169	.506	112	81	.723	171	419	16.1
70-71	30	....	383	203	.530	171	139	.813	185	545	18.2
71-72	28	....	352	159	.452	181	144	.796	172	462	16.5
Varsity Totals	84	....	1069	531	.497	464	364	.784	528	1426	17.0

ABA REGULAR SEASON RECORD

Sea.—Team	G.	Min.	2-Point FGM	FGA	Pct.	3-Point FGM	FGA	Pct.	FTM	FTA	Pct.	Reb.	Ast.	Pts.	Avg.
72-73—Indiana	77	1484	158	336	.470	5	24	.208	82	109	.752	210	223	413	5.4
73-74—Indiana	77	1877	134	320	.419	36	107	.336	48	70	.686	254	258	424	5.5
74-75—Indiana	80	2369	178	377	.472	38	123	.309	47	59	.797	272	335	517	6.5
75-76—Indiana	84	3380	328	679	.483	72	208	.346	179	220	.814	322	689	1051	12.5
Totals	318	9107	798	1712	.466	151	462	.327	356	458	.777	1058	1505	2405	7.6

ABA PLAYOFF RECORD

Sea.—Team	G.	Min.	2-Point FGM	FGA	Pct.	3-Point FGM	FGA	Pct.	FTM	FTA	Pct.	Reb.	Ast.	Pts.	Avg.
72-73—Indiana	14	163	16	38	.421	0	7	.000	13	21	.619	25	17	45	3.2
73-74—Indiana	14	331	23	46	.500	7	22	.320	6	9	.667	37	36	73	5.7
74-75—Indiana	18	576	33	77	.429	6	26	.230	16	30	.533	58	80	100	5.6
75-76—Indiana	3	138	12	24	.500	3	9	.333	4	4	1.000	14	26	37	12.3
Totals	49	1208	84	185	.454	16	64	.250	39	64	.609	134	159	255	5.2

ABA ALL-STAR GAME RECORD

Sea.—Team	Min.	2-Point FGM	FGA	Pct.	3-Point FGM	FGA	Pct.	FTM	FTA	Pct.	Reb.	Ast.	Pts.	Avg.
1976—Indiana	14	2	4	.500	0	0	.000	1	2	.500	1	3	5	5.0

NBA REGULAR SEASON RECORD

Sea.—Team	G.	Min.	FGA	FGM	Pct.	FTA	FTM	Pct.	Off.	Def.	Tot.	Ast.	PF	Dq.	Stl.	Blk.	Pts.	Avg.
76-77—Indiana	81	2947	639	266	.416	145	114	.786	66	204	270	685	129	0	281	16	646	8.0
77-78—Phoenix	82	2547	626	287	.458	136	112	.824	59	190	249	391	144	0	185	14	686	8.4
78-79—Phoenix	82	2544	576	285	.495	91	70	.769	44	173	217	356	149	0	156	18	640	7.8
79-80—Phoenix	81	2499	589	261	.443	128	85	.664	70	163	233	320	111	0	132	10	626	7.7
80-81—Indiana	58	1095	287	114	.397	65	50	.769	19	65	84	140	61	0	74	8	297	5.1
81-82—Indiana	82	2529	685	312	.455	123	100	.813	46	177	223	407	176	0	164	27	797	9.7
82-83—Portland	41	643	182	72	.396	46	41	.891	19	35	54	115	60	0	44	2	194	4.7
83-84—Kansas City	76	1327	352	150	.426	80	63	.788	29	87	116	303	62	0	86	1	381	5.0
84-85—Kansas City	65	939	203	82	.404	30	23	.767	21	40	61	203	75	0	38	1	218	3.4
Totals	648	17070	4139	1829	.442	844	658	.780	373	1134	1507	2920	967	0	1160	97	4485	6.9

Three-Point Field Goals: 1979-80, 19-for-79 (.241). 1980-81, 19-for-58 (.328). 1981-82, 73-for-189 (.386). 1982-83, 9-for-35 (.257). 1983-84, 18-for-59 (.305). 1984-85, 31-for-87 (.356). Totals, 169-for-507 (.333).

Sea.—Team	G.	Min.	FGA	FGM	Pct.	FTA	FTM	Pct.	Off.	Def.	Tot.	Ast.	PF	Dq.	Stl.	Blk.	Pts.	Avg.
77-78—Phoenix	2	76	11	4	.364	0	0	.000	0	5	5	4	3	0	4	0	8	4.0
78-79—Phoenix	15	512	116	47	.405	33	24	.727	17	38	55	52	31	0	23	5	118	7.9
79-80—Phoenix	8	236	64	28	.438	11	7	.636	8	13	21	44	15	0	6	0	68	8.5
80-81—Indiana	2	35	8	1	.125	2	2	1.000	0	5	5	7	4	0	3	0	5	2.5
82-83—Portland	5	31	8	2	.250	4	3	.750	0	2	2	7	2	0	0	0	7	1.4
83-84—Kansas City	3	50	16	7	.438	6	4	.667	0	3	3	11	5	0	1	1	21	7.0
Totals	35	940	223	89	.399	56	40	.714	25	66	91	125	60	0	37	6	227	6.5

Three-Point Field Goals: 1979-80, 5-for-13 (.385). 1980-81, 1-for-4 (.250). 1982-83, 0-for-0 (.000). 1983-84, 3-for-6 (.500). Totals, 9-for-23 (.391).

Season—Team	Min.	FGA	FGM	Pct.	FTA	FTM	Pct.	Off.	Def.	Tot.	Ast.	PF	Dq.	Stl.	Blk.	Pts.
1977—Indiana..........	19	4	2	.500	0	0	.000	0	2	2	5	0	0	4	0	4

Named to NBA All-Defensive First Team, 1977, 1978, 1979, 1980. . . . Led NBA in assists and steals, 1977. . . . Holds NBA record for most steals in one season, 1977. . . . ABA All-Star Second Team, 1976. . . . ABA All-Defensive Team, 1975 and 1976. . . . Member of ABA championship team, 1973. . . . NCAA Division II Tournament Most Outstanding Player, 1971. . . . Member of NCAA Division II championship team, 1971.

MICHAEL JEROME CAGE

Born January 28, 1962 at West Memphis, Ark. Height 6:09. Weight 225.

High School—West Memphis, Ark.

College—San Diego State University, San Diego, Calif.

Drafted by Los Angeles Clippers on first round, 1984 (14th pick).

—COLLEGIATE RECORD—

Year	G.	Min.	FGA	FGM	Pct.	FTA	FTM	Pct.	Reb.	Pts.	Avg.
80-81	27	1031	206	115	.558	86	65	.756	355	295	10.9
81-82	29	1076	252	123	.488	109	72	.661	256	318	11.0
82-83	28	1070	335	191	.570	221	165	.747	354	547	19.5
83-84	28	1085	445	250	.562	251	186	.741	352	686	24.5
Totals	112	4262	1238	679	.548	667	488	.732	1317	1846	16.5

NBA REGULAR SEASON RECORD

Sea.—Team	G.	Min.	FGA	FGM	Pct.	FTA	FTM	Pct.	Off.	Def.	Tot.	Ast.	PF	Dq.	Stl.	Blk.	Pts.	Avg.
84-85—L.A. Clippers	75	1610	398	216	.543	137	101	.737	126	266	392	51	164	1	41	32	533	7.1

ANTHONY CAMPBELL
(Tony)

Born May 7, 1962 at Teaneck, N. J. Height 6:07. Weight 215.

High School—Teaneck, N. J.

College—Ohio State University, Columbus, Ohio.

Drafted by Detroit on first round, 1984 (20th pick).

—COLLEGIATE RECORD—

Year	G.	Min.	FGA	FGM	Pct.	FTA	FTM	Pct.	Reb.	Pts.	Avg.
80-81	14	55	24	10	.417	6	3	.500	9	23	1.6
81-82	31	986	356	151	.424	119	95	.798	154	397	12.8
82-83	30	1122	451	227	.503	144	115	.799	250	569	19.0
83-84	29	1095	392	201	.513	171	138	.807	215	540	18.6
Totals	104	3258	1223	589	.482	440	351	.798	628	1529	14.7

NBA REGULAR SEASON RECORD

Sea.—Team	G.	Min.	FGA	FGM	Pct.	FTA	FTM	Pct.	Off.	Def.	Tot.	Ast.	PF	Dq.	Stl.	Blk.	Pts.	Avg.
84-85—Detroit	56	625	262	130	.496	70	56	.800	41	48	89	24	107	1	28	3	316	5.6

Three-Point Field Goals: 1984-85, 0-for-1.

NBA PLAYOFF RECORD

Sea.—Team	G.	Min.	FGA	FGM	Pct.	FTA	FTM	Pct.	Off.	Def.	Tot.	Ast.	PF	Dq.	Stl.	Blk.	Pts.	Avg.
84-85—Detroit	2	9	3	1	.333	0	0	.000	0	2	2	1	1	0	0	0	2	1.0

RICHARD PRESTON CARLISLE
(Rick)

Born October 27, 1959 at Ogdensburg, N. Y. Height 6:05. Weight 210.

High School—Lisbon, N. Y., Central.

Prep School—Worcester Academy, Worcester, Mass.

Colleges—University of Maine, Orono, Me., and University of Virginia, Charlottesville, Va.

Drafted by Boston on third round, 1984 (69th pick).

—COLLEGIATE RECORD—
Maine

Year	G.	Min.	FGA	FGM	Pct.	FTA	FTM	Pct.	Reb.	Pts.	Avg.
79-80	28	....	236	131	.555	97	83	.856	96	345	12.3
80-81	28	....	322	176	.547	126	102	.810	118	454	16.2
Maine Totals	56	....	558	307	.550	223	185	.830	214	799	14.3

Virginia

Year	G.	Min.	FGA	FGM	Pct.	FTA	FTM	Pct.	Reb.	Pts.	Avg.
81-82				Did Not Play—Transfer Student							
82-83	34	965	277	142	.513	104	87	.837	100	379	11.1
83-84	33	959	289	149	.516	96	67	.698	93	365	11.1
Va. Totals	67	1924	566	291	.514	200	154	.770	193	744	11.1
College Totals	123	....	1124	598	.532	443	339	.765	407	1543	12.5

Three-Point Field Goals: 1982-83, 8-for-12 (.750).

NBA REGULAR SEASON RECORD

Sea.—Team	G.	Min.	FGA	FGM	Pct.	FTA	FTM	Pct.	Off.	Def.	Tot.	Ast.	PF	Dq.	Stl.	Blk.	Pts.	Avg.
										—Rebounds—								
84-85—Boston	38	179	67	26	.388	17	15	.882	8	13	21	25	21	0	3	0	67	1.8

Three-Point Field Goals: 1984-85, 0-for-2.

ANTOINE LABOTTE CARR

Born July 23, 1961 at Oklahoma City, Okla. Height 6:09. Weight 225.

High School—Wichita, Kan., Wichita Heights.

College—Wichita State University, Wichita, Kan.

Drafted by Detroit on first round, 1983 (8th pick).

Draft rights traded by Detroit with Cliff Levington and 1986 and 1987 2nd round draft choices to Atlanta for Dan Roundfield, June 18, 1984.

Played in Italy during 1983-84 season.

—COLLEGIATE RECORD—

Year	G.	Min.	FGA	FGM	Pct.	FTA	FTM	Pct.	Reb.	Pts.	Avg.
79-80	29	818	355	178	.501	129	86	.667	171	442	15.2
80-81	33	1030	360	211	.586	132	101	.765	241	523	15.8
81-82	28	785	316	179	.566	115	91	.791	196	449	16.0
82-83	22	727	339	195	.575	136	104	.765	168	497	22.6
Totals	112	3360	1370	763	.557	512	382	.746	776	1911	17.1

Three-Point Field Goals: 1982-83, 3-for-5 (.600).

ITALIAN LEAGUE RECORD

Year	G.	Min.	FGA	FGM	Pct.	FTA	FTM	Pct.	Reb.	Pts.	Avg.
83-84—Milan Olym.	20	701	329	183	.556	101	61	.604	174	427	21.4

NBA REGULAR SEASON RECORD

Sea.—Team	G.	Min.	FGA	FGM	Pct.	FTA	FTM	Pct.	Off.	Def.	Tot.	Ast.	PF	Dq.	Stl.	Blk.	Pts.	Avg.
										—Rebounds—								
84-85—Atlanta	62	1195	375	198	.528	128	101	.789	79	153	232	80	219	4	29	78	499	8.0

Three-Point Field Goals: 1984-85, 2-for-6 (.333).

Named to THE SPORTING NEWS All-America First Team, 1983.

KENNETH ALAN CARR
(Kenny)

Born August 15, 1955 at Washington, D. C. Height 6:07. Weight 230.

High School—Hyattsville, Md., DeMatha.

College—North Carolina State University, Raleigh, N. C.

Drafted by Los Angeles on first round as an undergraduate, 1977 (6th pick).

Traded by Los Angeles to Cleveland for two 2nd round draft choices (1980 and 1981), October 24, 1979.
Traded by Cleveland with Bill Laimbeer to Detroit for Paul Mokeski, Phil Hubbard and two 1982 draft choices (1st and 2nd round), February 16, 1982.
Traded by Detroit to Portland for a 1982 1st round draft choice, June 23, 1982.

—COLLEGIATE RECORD—

Year	G.	Min.	FGA	FGM	Pct.	FTA	FTM	Pct.	Reb.	Pts.	Avg.
74-75	28	....	301	158	.525	101	70	.693	201	386	13.8
75-76	30	....	607	322	.530	218	154	.706	310	798	26.6
76-77	28	....	467	230	.493	198	128	.646	278	588	21.0
Totals	86		1375	710	.516	517	352	.681	789	1772	20.6

NBA REGULAR SEASON RECORD

Sea.—Team	G.	Min.	FGA	FGM	Pct.	FTA	FTM	Pct.	Off.	Def.	Tot.	Ast.	PF	Dq.	Stl.	Blk.	Pts.	Avg.
77-78—Los Ang.	52	733	302	134	.444	85	55	.647	53	155	208	26	127	0	18	14	323	6.2
78-79—Los Ang.	72	1149	450	225	.500	137	83	.606	70	222	292	60	152	0	38	31	533	7.4
79-80—L. A.-Clev.	79	1838	768	378	.492	263	173	.658	199	389	588	77	246	3	66	52	929	11.8
80-81—Cleveland	81	2615	918	469	.511	409	292	.714	260	575	835	192	296	3	76	42	1230	15.2
81-82—Clev.-Det.	74	1926	692	348	.503	302	198	.656	167	364	531	86	249	0	64	22	895	12.1
82-83—Portland	82	2331	717	362	.505	366	255	.697	182	407	589	116	306	10	62	42	981	12.0
83-84—Portland	82	2455	923	518	.561	367	247	.673	208	434	642	157	274	3	68	33	1283	15.6
84-85—Portland	48	1120	363	190	.523	164	118	.720	90	233	323	56	141	0	25	17	498	10.4
Totals	570	14167	5133	2624	.511	2093	1421	.679	1229	2779	4008	770	1791	19	417	253	6672	11.7

Three-Point Field Goals: 1979-80, 0-for-4. 1980-81, 0-for-4. 1981-82, 1-for-10 (.100). 1982-83, 2-for-6 (.333). 1983-84, 0-for-5. 1984-85, 0-for-3. Totals, 3-for-32 (.094).

NBA PLAYOFF RECORD

Sea.—Team	G.	Min.	FGA	FGM	Pct.	FTA	FTM	Pct.	Off.	Def.	Tot.	Ast.	PF	Dq.	Stl.	Blk.	Pts.	Avg.
77-78—Los Ang.	2	17	8	3	.375	0	0	.000	0	4	4	0	2	0	1	0	6	3.0
78-79—Los Ang.	8	117	35	19	.543	8	5	.625	4	13	17	4	18	0	4	2	43	5.4
82-83—Portland	7	171	60	26	.433	23	18	.783	15	36	51	10	26	0	3	5	70	10.0
83-84—Portland	5	180	59	31	.525	19	12	.632	11	24	35	6	22	1	2	2	74	14.8
84-85—Portland	9	265	95	50	.526	20	16	.800	30	40	70	10	40	2	3	2	116	12.9
Totals	31	750	257	129	.502	70	51	.729	60	117	177	30	108	3	13	11	309	10.0

Three-Point Field Goals: 1984-85, 0-for-1.

Member of U. S. Olympic team, 1976.

MICHAEL LEON CARR
(M. L.)

Born January 9, 1951 at Wallace, N. C.   Height 6:06.   Weight 205.
High School—Teachey, N. C., Wallace Rose Hill.
College—Guilford College, Greensboro, N. C.
Drafted by Kansas City-Omaha on fifth round, 1973 (76th pick).

Selected by Kentucky on third round of ABA draft, 1973.
Released by Kentucky, September 15, 1973; signed as a free agent by St. Louis ABA, July 31, 1975.
Waived by Kansas City-Omaha, September 30, 1974; signed by Boston as a free agent, October 10, 1974.
Waived by Boston, October 15, 1974; signed by Detroit as a free agent, June 12, 1976.
Signed by Boston as Veteran Free Agent, July 24, 1979. Detroit received Bob McAdoo and Boston received two 1980 1st round draft choices to complete compensation, September 6, 1979.
Played in Eastern Basketball Association with Hamilton and Scranton, 1973-74 and 1974-75.
Played in Israel during 1974-75 season.

—COLLEGIATE RECORD—

Year	G.	Min.	FGA	FGM	Pct.	FTA	FTM	Pct.	Reb.	Pts.	Avg.
69-70	36	....	411	249	.606	144	84	.583	383	582	16.2
70-71	28	....	347	203	.585	151	102	.675	292	508	18.1
71-72	13	....	204	122	.598	67	33	.493	164	277	21.3
72-73	34	....	526	278	.529	106	70	.660	426	626	18.4
Totals	111	....	1488	852	.573	468	289	.618	1265	1993	18.0

MINOR LEAGUE REGULAR SEASON RECORD

Sea.—Team			—2-Point—			—3-Point—							
	G.	Min.	FGM	FGA	Pct.	FGM	FGA	Pct.	FTM	FTA	Pct.	Reb.	Ast.	Pts.	Avg.
73-74—Hamilton EBA	27	....	162	...	....	0	...	....	81	119	.681	194	52	405	15.0
74-75—Scranton EBA	2	....	3	...	....	0	0	....	5	9	.556	7	2	11	5.5

ABA REGULAR SEASON RECORD

Sea.—Team			—2-Point—			—3-Point—							
	G.	Min.	FGM	FGA	Pct.	FGM	FGA	Pct.	FTM	FTA	Pct.	Reb.	Ast.	Pts.	Avg.
75-76—St. Louis	74	2174	371	762	.487	9	24	.375	137	206	.665	459	224	906	12.2

NBA REGULAR SEASON RECORD

Sea.—Team	G.	Min.	FGA	FGM	Pct.	FTA	FTM	Pct.	Off.	Def.	Tot.	Ast.	PF	Dq.	Stl.	Blk.	Pts.	Avg.
76-77—Detroit	82	2643	931	443	.476	279	205	.735	211	420	631	181	287	8	165	58	1091	13.3
77-78—Detroit	79	2556	857	390	.455	271	200	.738	202	355	557	185	243	4	147	27	980	12.4
78-79—Detroit	80	3207	1143	587	.514	435	323	.743	219	370	589	262	279	2	197	46	1497	18.7
79-80—Boston	82	1994	763	362	.474	241	178	.739	106	224	330	156	214	1	120	36	914	11.1
80-81—Boston	41	655	216	97	.449	67	53	.791	26	57	83	56	74	0	30	18	248	6.0
81-82—Boston	56	1296	409	184	.450	116	82	.707	56	94	150	128	136	2	67	21	455	8.1
82-83—Boston	77	883	315	135	.429	81	60	.741	51	86	137	71	140	0	48	10	333	4.3
83-84—Boston	60	585	171	70	.409	48	42	.875	26	49	75	49	67	0	17	4	185	3.1
84-85—Boston	47	397	149	62	.416	17	17	1.000	21	22	43	24	44	0	21	6	150	3.2
Totals	604	14216	4954	2330	.470	1555	1160	.746	918	1677	2595	1112	1484	17	812	226	5853	9.7

Three-Point Field Goals: 1979-80, 12-for-41 (.293). 1980-81, 1-for-14 (.071). 1981-82, 5-for-17 (.294). 1982-83, 3-for-19 (.158). 1983-84, 3-for-15 (.200). 1984-85, 9-for-23 (.391). Totals, 33-for-129 (.256).

NBA PLAYOFF RECORD

Sea.—Team	G.	Min.	FGA	FGM	Pct.	FTA	FTM	Pct.	Off.	Def.	Tot.	Ast.	PF	Dq.	Stl.	Blk.	Pts.	Avg.
76-77—Detroit	3	112	31	12	.387	7	4	.571	9	8	17	6	9	0	1	3	28	9.3
79-80—Boston	9	172	80	32	.400	24	16	.667	14	19	33	11	20	0	6	1	82	9.1
80-81—Boston	17	288	101	42	.416	24	18	.750	8	17	25	14	32	0	10	6	102	6.0
81-82—Boston	12	305	105	37	.352	23	15	.652	21	22	43	28	30	0	11	0	89	7.4
82-83—Boston	3	22	8	2	.250	2	2	1.000	1	0	1	0	3	0	2	0	6	2.0
83-84—Boston	16	82	32	13	.406	11	10	.909	5	3	8	4	13	0	7	0	38	2.4
84-85—Boston	7	24	15	4	.267	0	0	.000	1	1	2	1	4	0	1	0	9	1.3
Totals	67	1005	372	142	.382	91	65	.714	59	70	129	64	111	0	38	10	354	5.3

Three-Point Field Goals: 1979-80, 2-for-5 (.400). 1980-81, 0-for-4. 1981-82, 0-for-4. 1982-83, 0-for-1 (.000). 1983-84, 2-for-6 (.333). 1984-85, 1-for-2 (.500). Totals, 5-for-22 (.227).

Named to NBA All-Defensive Second Team, 1979. . . . Led NBA in steals, 1979. . . . Member of NBA championship teams, 1981 and 1984. . . . ABA All-Rookie Team, 1976. . . . Member of NAIA championship team, 1973.

JOSEPH BARRY CARROLL
(Joe Barry)

Born July 24, 1958 at Pine Bluff, Ark.   Height 7:00.   Weight 250.

High School—Denver, Colo., East.

College—Purdue University, West Lafayette, Ind.

Drafted by Golden State on first round, 1980 (1st pick).

Signed by Milwaukee as Veteran Free Agent, June 14, 1985; Golden State matched offer, June 28, 1985. Played in Italy during 1984-85 season, averaging 24.9 points in 25 games.

—COLLEGIATE RECORD—

Year	G.	Min.	FGA	FGM	Pct.	FTA	FTM	Pct.	Reb.	Pts.	Avg.
76-77	28	573	187	93	.497	54	34	.630	206	220	7.9
77-78	27	855	312	163	.522	143	95	.664	288	421	15.6
78-79	35	1235	545	318	.583	253	162	.640	352	798	22.8
79-80	33	1168	558	301	.539	203	134	.660	302	736	22.3
Totals	123	3831	1602	875	.546	653	425	.651	1148	2175	17.7

NBA REGULAR SEASON RECORD

Sea.—Team	G.	Min.	FGA	FGM	Pct.	FTA	FTM	Pct.	Off.	Def.	Tot.	Ast.	PF	Dq.	Stl.	Blk.	Pts.	Avg.
80-81—Golden State	82	2919	1254	616	.491	440	315	.716	274	485	759	117	313	10	50	121	1547	18.9
81-82—Golden State	76	2627	1016	527	.519	323	235	.728	220	423	633	64	265	8	64	127	1289	17.0
82-83—Golden State	79	2988	1529	785	.513	469	337	.719	220	468	688	169	260	7	108	155	1907	24.1
83-84—Golden State	80	2962	1390	663	.477	433	313	.723	235	401	636	193	244	9	103	142	1639	20.5
Totals	317	11496	5189	2591	.499	1665	1200	.721	939	1777	2716	548	1082	34	325	545	6382	20.1

Three-Point Field Goals: 1980-81, 0-for-2. 1981-82, 0-for-1. 1982-83, 0-for-3. 1983-84, 0-for-1. Totals, 0-for-7.

Named to NBA All-Rookie Team, 1981. . . . THE SPORTING NEWS All-America First Team, 1980.

CLARENCE EUGENE CARTER
(Butch)

Born June 11, 1958 at Springfield, O.   Height 6:05.   Weight 195.

High School—Middletown, O.

College—Indiana University, Bloomington, Ind.

Drafted by Los Angeles on second round, 1980 (37th pick).

Traded by Los Angeles to Indiana for a 1982 3rd round draft choice, October 15, 1981.
Traded by Indiana to New York for a 1985 2nd round draft choice, October 19, 1984.

Year	G.	Min.	FGA	FGM	Pct.	FTA	FTM	Pct.	Reb.	Pts.	Avg.
76-77	23	....	69	27	.391	23	14	.609	50	68	3.0
77-78	29	....	61	31	.508	31	21	.677	39	83	2.9
78-79	33	....	226	116	.513	66	49	.742	100	281	8.5
79-80	29	....	223	122	.547	104	79	.760	101	323	11.1
Totals	114	....	579	296	.511	224	163	.728	290	755	6.6

NBA REGULAR SEASON RECORD

Sea.—Team	G.	Min.	FGA	FGM	Pct.	FTA	FTM	Pct.	Off.	Def.	Tot.	Ast.	PF	Dq.	Stl.	Blk.	Pts.	Avg.
80-81—Los Angeles	54	672	247	114	.462	95	70	.737	34	31	65	52	99	0	23	1	301	5.6
81-82—Indiana	75	1035	402	188	.468	70	58	.829	30	49	79	60	110	0	34	11	442	5.9
82-83—Indiana	81	1716	706	354	.501	154	124	.805	62	88	150	194	207	5	78	13	849	10.5
83-84—Indiana	73	2045	862	413	.479	178	136	.764	70	83	153	206	211	1	128	13	977	13.4
84-85—New York	69	1279	476	214	.450	134	109	.813	36	59	95	167	151	1	57	5	548	7.9
Totals	352	6747	2693	1283	.476	631	497	.788	232	310	542	679	778	7	320	43	3117	8.9

Three-Point Field Goals: 1980-81, 3-for-10 (.300). 1981-82, 8-for-25 (.320). 1982-83, 17-for-51 (.333). 1983-84, 15-for-46 (.326). 1984-85, 11-for-43 (.256). Totals, 54-for-175 (.309).

Holds NBA record for most points in an overtime period, 14, vs. Boston, March 20, 1984.

HOWARD O'NEAL CARTER

Born October 26, 1961 at Baton Rouge, La.   Height 6:05.   Weight 215.

High School—Baton Rouge, La., Redemptorist.

College—Louisiana State University, Baton Rouge, La.

Drafted by Denver on first round, 1983 (15th pick).

Traded by Denver to Dallas for Dallas' agreement not to match Denver's offer sheet for Elston Turner, August 23, 1984.

—COLLEGIATE RECORD—

Year	G.	Min.	FGA	FGM	Pct.	FTA	FTM	Pct.	Reb.	Pts.	Avg.
79-80	32	907	287	140	.488	72	55	.764	113	335	10.5
80-81	36	1209	450	233	.518	137	110	.803	148	576	16.0
81-82	28	1144	420	199	.474	95	69	.726	156	467	16.7
82-83	32	1104	472	234	.496	114	96	.842	151	564	17.6
Totals	128	4364	1629	806	.495	418	330	.789	568	1942	15.2

NBA REGULAR SEASON RECORD

Sea.—Team	G.	Min.	FGA	FGM	Pct.	FTA	FTM	Pct.	Off.	Def.	Tot.	Ast.	PF	Dq.	Stl.	Blk.	Pts.	Avg.
83-84—Denver	55	688	316	145	.459	61	47	.770	38	48	86	71	81	0	19	4	342	6.2
84-85—Dallas	11	66	23	4	.174	1	1	1.000	1	2	3	4	4	0	1	0	9	0.8
Totals	66	754	339	149	.440	62	48	.774	39	50	89	75	85	0	20	4	351	5.3

Three-Point Field Goals: 1983-84, 5-for-19 (.263). 1984-85, 0-for-3. Totals, 5-for-22 (.227).

NBA PLAYOFF RECORD

Sea.—Team	G.	Min.	FGA	FGM	Pct.	FTA	FTM	Pct.	Off.	Def.	Tot.	Ast.	PF	Dq.	Stl.	Blk.	Pts.	Avg.
83-84—Denver	5	60	22	7	.318	0	0	.000	1	4	5	5	3	0	4	1	15	3.0

Three-Point Field Goals: 1983-84, 1-for-5 (.200).

JAMES WILLIAM CARTWRIGHT
(Bill)

Born July 30, 1957 at Lodi, Calif.   Height 7:01.   Weight 245.

High School—Elk Grove, Calif.

College—University of San Francisco, San Francisco, Calif.

Drafted by New York on first round, 1979 (3rd pick).

Missed entire 1984-85 season due to injury.

—COLLEGIATE RECORD—

Year	G.	Min.	FGA	FGM	Pct.	FTA	FTM	Pct.	Reb.	Pts.	Avg.
75-76	30	845	285	151	.530	98	72	.735	207	374	12.5
76-77	31	969	426	241	.566	161	118	.733	262	600	19.4
77-78	21	712	252	168	.667	131	96	.733	213	432	20.6
78-79	29	1020	443	268	.605	237	174	.734	455	710	24.5
Totals	111	3546	1406	828	.589	627	460	.734	1137	2116	19.1

NBA REGULAR SEASON RECORD

Sea.—Team	G.	Min.	FGA	FGM	Pct.	FTA	FTM	Pct.	Off.	Def.	Tot.	Ast.	PF	Dq.	Stl.	Blk.	Pts.	Avg.
79-80—New York	82	3150	1215	665	.547	566	451	.797	194	532	726	165	279	2	48	101	1781	21.7
80-81—New York	82	2925	1118	619	.554	518	408	.788	161	452	613	111	259	2	48	83	1646	20.1
81-82—New York	72	2060	694	390	.562	337	257	.763	116	305	421	87	208	2	48	65	1037	14.4
82-83—New York	82	2468	804	455	.566	511	380	.744	185	405	590	136	315	7	41	127	1290	15.7
83-84—New York	77	2487	808	453	.561	502	404	.805	195	454	649	107	262	4	44	97	1310	17.0
Totals	395	13090	4639	2582	.557	2434	1900	.781	851	2148	2999	606	1323	17	229	473	7064	17.9

Three-Point Field Goals: 1980-81, 0-for-1. 1983-84, 0-for-1. Totals, 0-for-2.

NBA PLAYOFF RECORD

Sea.—Team	G.	Min.	FGA	FGM	Pct.	FTA	FTM	Pct.	Off.	Def.	Tot.	Ast.	PF	Dq.	Stl.	Blk.	Pts.	Avg.
80-81—New York	2	49	17	6	.353	12	8	.667	4	9	13	1	7	0	1	1	20	10.0
82-83—New York	6	172	43	25	.581	22	17	.773	9	25	34	4	25	0	3	7	67	11.2
83-84—New York	12	398	126	70	.556	80	69	.863	27	72	99	5	44	0	2	14	209	17.4
Totals	20	619	186	101	.543	114	94	.825	40	106	146	10	76	0	6	22	296	14.8

NBA ALL-STAR GAME RECORD

Season—Team	Min.	FGA	FGM	Pct.	FTA	FTM	Pct.	Off.	Def.	Tot.	Ast.	PF	Dq.	Stl.	Blk.	Pts.
1980—New York.....	14	8	4	.500	0	0	.000	1	2	3	1	1	0	0	0	8

Named to NBA All-Rookie Team, 1980. . . . THE SPORTING NEWS All-America First Team, 1979.

HARVEY LEE CATCHINGS

Born September 2, 1951 at Jackson, Miss.   Height 6:09.   Weight 218.

High School—Jackson, Miss., Jim Hill.

Colleges—Weatherford College, Weatherford, Tex., and
Hardin-Simmons University, Abilene, Tex.

Drafted by Philadelphia on third round, 1974 (42nd pick).

Traded by Philadelphia with Ralph Simpson and cash to New Jersey for Eric Money and Al Skinner, February 7, 1979.

Traded by New Jersey to Milwaukee for John Gianelli and a 1979 1st round draft choice, May 31, 1979.

Traded by Milwaukee with Marques Johnson, Junior Bridgeman and cash to Los Angeles Clippers for Terry Cummings, Craig Hodges and Ricky Pierce, September 29, 1984.

—COLLEGIATE RECORD—

Weatherford

Year	G.	Min.	FGA	FGM	Pct.	FTA	FTM	Pct.	Reb.	Pts.	Avg.
69-70	..	....	...	...	....	...	...	....	....	....	....

Hardin-Simmons

Year	G.	Min.	FGA	FGM	Pct.	FTA	FTM	Pct.	Reb.	Pts.	Avg.
70-71				Did Not Play—Red Shirt							
71-72	26	....	305	158	.518	138	88	.638	285	404	15.5
72-73	25	....	348	184	.529	101	62	.614	282	430	17.2
73-74	25	....	354	187	.528	97	63	.649	278	437	17.5
Totals	76	....	1007	529	.525	336	213	.634	845	1271	16.7

NBA REGULAR SEASON RECORD

Sea.—Team	G.	Min.	FGA	FGM	Pct.	FTA	FTM	Pct.	Off.	Def.	Tot.	Ast.	PF	Dq.	Stl.	Blk.	Pts.	Avg.
74-75—Philadelphia	37	528	74	41	.554	25	16	.640	49	104	153	21	82	1	10	60	98	2.6
75-76—Philadelphia	75	1731	242	103	.426	96	58	.604	191	329	520	63	262	6	21	164	264	3.5
76-77—Philadelphia	53	864	123	62	.504	47	33	.702	64	170	234	30	130	1	23	78	157	3.0
77-78—Philadelphia	61	748	178	70	.393	55	34	.618	105	145	250	34	124	1	20	67	174	2.9
78-79—Phila.-NJ	56	948	243	102	.420	78	60	.769	101	201	302	48	132	3	23	91	264	4.7
79-80—Milwaukee	72	1366	244	97	.398	62	39	.629	164	246	410	82	191	1	23	162	233	3.2
80-81—Milwaukee	77	1635	300	134	.447	92	59	.641	154	319	473	99	284	7	33	184	327	4.2
81-82—Milwaukee	80	1603	224	94	.420	69	41	.594	129	227	356	97	237	3	42	135	229	2.9
82-83—Milwaukee	74	1554	197	90	.457	92	62	.674	132	276	408	77	224	4	26	148	242	3.3
83-84—Milwaukee	69	1156	153	61	.399	42	22	.524	89	182	271	43	172	3	25	81	144	2.1
84-85—L.A. Clippers	70	1049	149	72	.483	89	59	.663	89	173	262	14	162	0	15	57	203	2.9
Totals	724	13182	2127	926	.435	747	483	.647	1267	2372	3639	608	2000	30	261	1227	2335	3.2

Three-Point Field Goals: 1979-80, 0-for-1. 1983-84, 0-for-1. 1984-85, 0-or-1. Totals, 0-for-3.

NBA PLAYOFF RECORD

Sea.—Team	G.	Min.	FGA	FGM	Pct.	FTA	FTM	Pct.	Off.	Def.	Tot.	Ast.	PF	Dq.	Stl.	Blk.	Pts.	Avg.
75-76—Philadelphia	3	87	13	8	.615	3	1	.333	12	16	28	6	11	0	0	9	17	5.7
76-77—Philadelphia	8	54	5	2	.400	3	0	.000	5	7	12	1	9	0	0	4	4	0.5
77-78—Philadelphia	7	26	8	3	.375	4	3	.750	3	6	9	0	4	0	1	3	9	1.3
78-79—New Jersey	2	26	6	1	.167	3	0	.000	5	3	8	1	4	0	0	1	2	1.0

Sea.—Team	G.	Min.	FGA	FGM	Pct.	FTA	FTM	Pct.	—Rebounds— Off.	Def.	Tot.	Ast.	PF	Dq.	Stl.	Blk.	Pts.	Avg.
79-80—Milwaukee	6	64	6	2	.333	4	2	.500	5	16	21	2	13	0	0	8	6	1.0
80-81—Milwaukee	7	109	16	3	.188	2	2	1.000	10	16	26	8	24	0	0	11	8	1.1
81-82—Milwaukee	6	26	3	2	.667	0	0	.000	3	4	7	0	9	0	0	3	4	0.7
82-83—Milwaukee	6	139	19	9	.474	3	3	1.000	15	23	38	4	18	0	2	10	21	2.3
83-84—Milwaukee	5	25	2	1	.500	2	1	.500	2	3	5	1	7	0	0	0	3	0.6
Totals	50	556	78	31	.397	24	12	.500	60	94	154	23	99	0	3	49	74	1.5

RONNIE GOODALL CAVENALL
(Ron)

Born April 30, 1959 at Beaumont, Tex.   Height 7:01. Weight 230.

High School—Beaumont, Tex., Charlton-Pollard.

College—Texas Southern University, Houston, Tex.

Never drafted by an NBA franchise.

Signed by New York as a free agent, August, 1984.
Waived by New York, October 25, 1984; re-signed by New York, November 9, 1984.
Played with Harlem Wizards, 1983-84.

—COLLEGIATE RECORD—

Year	G.	Min.	FGA	FGM	Pct.	FTA	FTM	Pct.	Reb.	Pts.	Avg.
77-78	18	....	39	19	.487	9	3	.333	46	41	2.3
78-79	27	....	158	78	.494	33	17	.515	170	173	6.4
79-80	24	....	90	43	.478	50	32	.640	103	118	4.9
80-81	26	....	174	84	.483	39	21	.538	181	189	7.3
Totals	95	....	461	224	.486	131	73	.557	500	521	5.5

NBA REGULAR SEASON RECORD

Sea.—Team	G.	Min.	FGA	FGM	Pct.	FTA	FTM	Pct.	—Rebounds— Off.	Def.	Tot.	Ast.	PF	Dq.	Stl.	Blk.	Pts.	Avg.
84-85—New York	53	653	86	28	.326	39	22	.564	53	113	166	19	123	2	12	42	78	1.5

THOMAS DOANE CHAMBERS
(Tom)

Born June 21, 1959 at Ogden, Utah.   Height 6:10.   Weight 225.

High School—Boulder, Colo., Fairview.

College—University of Utah, Salt Lake City, Utah.

Drafted by San Diego on first round, 1981 (8th pick).

Traded by San Diego with Al Wood, a 1987 2nd round draft choice and a future 3rd round draft choice to Seattle for James Donaldson, Greg Kelser, Mark Radford, a 1984 1st round draft choice and a 1985 2nd round draft choice, August 18, 1983.

—COLLEGIATE RECORD—

Year	G.	Min.	FGA	FGM	Pct.	FTA	FTM	Pct.	Reb.	Pts.	Avg.
77-78	28	355	139	69	.496	64	40	.625	104	178	6.4
78-79	30	853	379	206	.544	127	69	.543	266	481	16.0
79-80	28	792	359	195	.543	129	92	.713	244	482	17.2
80-81	30	959	372	221	.594	155	115	.742	262	557	18.6
Totals	116	2959	1249	691	.553	475	316	.665	876	1698	14.6

NBA REGULAR SEASON RECORD

Sea.—Team	G.	Min.	FGA	FGM	Pct.	FTA	FTM	Pct.	—Rebounds— Off.	Def.	Tot.	Ast.	PF	Dq.	Stl.	Blk.	Pts.	Avg.
81-82—San Diego	81	2682	1056	554	.525	458	284	.620	211	350	561	146	341	17	58	46	1392	17.2
82-83—San Diego	79	2665	1099	519	.472	488	353	.723	218	301	519	192	333	15	79	57	1391	17.6
83-84—Seattle	82	2570	1110	554	.499	469	375	.800	219	313	532	133	309	8	47	51	1483	18.1
84-85—Seattle	81	2923	1302	629	.483	571	475	.832	164	415	579	209	312	4	70	57	1739	21.5
Totals	323	10840	4567	2256	.494	1986	1487	.749	812	1379	2191	680	1295	44	254	211	6005	18.6

Three-Point Field Goals: 1981-82, 0-for-2. 1982-83, 0-for-8. 1983-84, 0-for-12. 1984-85, 6-for-22 (.273). Totals, 6-for-44 (.136).

NBA PLAYOFF RECORD

Sea.—Team	G.	Min.	FGA	FGM	Pct.	FTA	FTM	Pct.	—Rebounds— Off.	Def.	Tot.	Ast.	PF	Dq.	Stl.	Blk.	Pts.	Avg.
83-84—Seattle	5	191	59	28	.475	18	12	.667	4	29	33	8	23	0	5	3	68	13.6

TOM CHAMBERS

MAURICE EDWARD CHEEKS

Born September 8, 1956 at Chicago, Ill.   Height 6:01.   Weight 180.

High School—Chicago, Ill., DuSable.

College—West Texas State University, Canyon, Tex.

Drafted by Philadelphia on second round, 1978 (36th pick).

—COLLEGIATE RECORD—

Year	G.	Min.	FGA	FGM	Pct.	FTA	FTM	Pct.	Reb.	Pts.	Avg.
74-75	26	....	75	35	.467	53	31	.585	56	101	3.9
75-76	23	767	170	102	.600	84	52	.619	91	256	11.1
76-77	30	1095	246	149	.606	169	119	.704	119	417	13.9
77-78	27	941	319	174	.545	147	105	.714	152	453	16.8
Totals	106	....	810	460	.568	453	307	.678	418	1227	11.6

NBA REGULAR SEASON RECORD

Sea.—Team	G.	Min.	FGA	FGM	Pct.	FTA	FTM	Pct.	Off.	Def.	Tot.	Ast.	PF	Dq.	Stl.	Blk.	Pts.	Avg.
78-79—Philadelphia	82	2409	572	292	.510	140	101	.721	63	191	254	431	198	2	174	12	685	8.4
79-80—Philadelphia	79	2623	661	357	.540	231	180	.779	75	199	274	556	197	1	183	32	898	11.4
80-81—Philadelphia	81	2415	581	310	.534	178	140	.787	67	178	245	560	231	1	193	39	763	9.4
81-82—Philadelphia	79	2498	676	352	.521	220	171	.777	51	197	248	667	247	0	209	33	881	11.2
82-83—Philadelphia	79	2465	745	404	.542	240	181	.754	53	156	209	543	182	0	184	31	990	12.5
83-84—Philadelphia	75	2494	702	386	.550	232	170	.733	44	161	205	478	196	1	171	20	950	12.7
84-85—Philadelphia	78	2616	741	422	.570	199	175	.879	54	163	217	497	184	0	169	24	1025	13.1
Totals	553	17520	4678	2523	.539	1440	1118	.776	407	1245	1652	3732	1435	5	1283	191	6192	11.2

Three-Point Field Goals: 1979-80, 4-for-9 (.444). 1980-81, 3-for-8 (.375). 1981-82, 6-for-22 (.273). 1982-83, 1-for-6 (.167). 1983-84, 8-for-20 (.400). 1984-85, 6-for-26 (.231). Totals, 28-for-91 (.308).

NBA PLAYOFF RECORD

Sea.—Team	G.	Min.	FGA	FGM	Pct.	FTA	FTM	Pct.	Off.	Def.	Tot.	Ast.	PF	Dq.	Stl.	Blk.	Pts.	Avg.
78-79—Philadelphia	9	330	121	66	.545	56	37	.661	13	22	35	63	29	0	37	4	169	18.8
79-80—Philadelphia	18	675	174	89	.511	41	29	.707	22	52	74	111	43	0	45	4	208	11.6
80-81—Philadelphia	16	513	125	68	.544	42	32	.762	4	47	51	116	55	1	40	12	168	10.5
81-82—Philadelphia	21	765	265	125	.472	65	50	.769	15	47	62	172	58	0	48	6	301	14.3
82-83—Philadelphia	13	483	165	83	.503	64	45	.703	11	28	39	91	23	0	26	2	212	16.3
83-84—Philadelphia	5	171	67	35	.522	15	13	.867	2	10	12	19	18	0	13	0	83	16.6
84-85—Philadelphia	13	483	153	81	.529	42	36	.857	12	34	46	67	29	0	31	5	198	15.2
Totals	95	3420	1070	547	.511	325	242	.745	79	240	319	639	255	1	240	33	1339	14.1

Three-Point Field Goals: 1979-80, 1-for-5 (.200). 1980-81, 0-for-3. 1981-82, 1-for-9 (.111). 1982-83, 1-for-2 (.500). 1983-84, 0-for-1. 1984-85, 0-for-5. Totals, 3-for-25 (.120).

NBA ALL-STAR GAME RECORD

Season—Team	Min.	FGA	FGM	Pct.	FTA	FTM	Pct.	Off.	Def.	Tot.	Ast.	PF	Dq.	Stl.	Blk.	Pts.
1983—Phila.	18	8	3	.375	0	0	.000	0	1	1	1	0	0	0	0	6

Named to NBA All-Defensive First Team, 1983, 1984, 1985. . . . Member of NBA championship team, 1983.

CARLOS CLARK

Born August 10, 1960 at Somerville, Tenn.   Height 6:04.   Weight 210.

High School—Somerville, Tenn., Fayette-Ware.

College—University of Mississippi, University, Miss.

Drafted by Boston on fourth round, 1983 (91st pick).

—COLLEGIATE RECORD—

Year	G.	Min.	FGA	FGM	Pct.	FTA	FTM	Pct.	Reb.	Pts.	Avg.
79-80	29	662	128	70	.547	30	24	.800	73	164	5.7
80-81	28	967	289	154	.533	111	84	.757	110	392	14.0
81-82	30	1192	403	251	.623	162	132	.815	129	634	21.1
82-83	31	1027	477	235	.493	205	162	.790	154	632	20.4
Totals	118	3848	1297	710	.547	508	402	.791	466	1822	15.4

NBA REGULAR SEASON RECORD

Sea.—Team	G.	Min.	FGA	FGM	Pct.	FTA	FTM	Pct.	Off.	Def.	Tot.	Ast.	PF	Dq.	Stl.	Blk.	Pts.	Avg.
83-84—Boston	31	127	52	19	.365	18	16	.889	7	10	17	17	13	0	8	1	54	1.7
84-85—Boston	62	562	152	64	.421	53	41	.774	29	40	69	48	66	0	35	2	169	2.7
Totals	93	689	204	83	.407	71	57	.803	36	50	86	65	79	0	43	3	223	2.4

Three-Point Field Goals: 1983-84, 0-for-2. 1984-85, 0-for-5. Totals, 0-for-7.

NBA PLAYOFF RECORD

Sea.—Team	G.	Min.	FGA	FGM	Pct.	FTA	FTM	Pct.	Off.	Def.	Tot.	Ast.	PF	Dq.	Stl.	Blk.	Pts.	Avg.
									—Rebounds—									
83-84—Boston	8	20	10	4	.400	2	1	.500	1	0	1	1	3	0	1	2	9	1.1
84-85—Boston	3	11	5	3	.600	2	2	1.000	2	0	2	3	2	0	1	0	8	2.7
Totals	11	31	15	7	.467	4	3	.750	3	0	3	4	5	0	2	2	17	1.5

Member of NBA championship team, 1984.

DONALD COLLINS
(Don)

Born November 28, 1958 at Toledo, O. Height 6:06. Weight 190.

High School—Toledo, O., Scott.

College—Washington State University, Pullman, Wash.

Drafted by Atlanta on first round, 1980 (18th pick).

Traded by Atlanta to Washington for Wes Matthews, January 17, 1981.
Waived by Washington, October 27, 1983; signed by Golden State as a free agent, December 1, 1983.
Waived by Golden State, October 23, 1984; signed by Washington as a free agent, March 13, 1985.
Waived by Washington, May 1, 1985.
Played in Continental Basketball Association with Lancaster Lightning, 1984-85.

—COLLEGIATE RECORD—

Year	G.	Min.	FGA	FGM	Pct.	FTA	FTM	Pct.	Reb.	Pts.	Avg.
76-77	27	437	138	71	.514	35	21	.600	77	163	6.0
77-78	24	686	203	108	.532	99	80	.808	119	296	12.3
78-79	27	946	332	182	.548	117	93	.795	170	457	16.9
79-80	28	948	424	253	.597	183	141	.770	169	647	23.1
Totals	106	3017	1097	614	.560	434	335	.772	535	1563	14.7

NBA REGULAR SEASON RECORD

Sea.—Team	G.	Min.	FGA	FGM	Pct.	FTA	FTM	Pct.	Off.	Def.	Tot.	Ast.	PF	Dq.	Stl.	Blk.	Pts.	Avg.
									—Rebounds—									
80-81—Atl.-Wash.	81	1845	811	360	.444	272	211	.776	129	139	268	190	259	6	104	25	931	11.5
81-82—Washington	79	1609	653	334	.511	169	121	.716	101	95	196	148	195	3	89	24	790	10.0
82-83—Washington	65	1575	635	332	.523	136	101	.743	116	94	210	132	166	1	87	30	765	11.8
83-84—Golden State	61	957	387	187	.483	89	65	.730	62	67	129	67	119	1	43	14	440	7.2
84-85—Washington	11	91	34	12	.353	9	8	.889	10	9	19	7	5	0	7	4	32	2.9
Totals	297	6077	2520	1225	.486	675	506	.750	418	404	822	544	744	11	330	97	2958	10.0

Three-Point Field Goals: 1980-81, 0-for-6. 1981-82, 1-for-12 (.083). 1982-83, 0-for-6. 1983-84, 1-for-5 (.200). Totals, 2-for-29 (.069).

NBA PLAYOFF RECORD

Sea.—Team	G.	Min.	FGA	FGM	Pct.	FTA	FTM	Pct.	Off.	Def.	Tot.	Ast.	PF	Dq.	Stl.	Blk.	Pts.	Avg.
									—Rebounds—									
81-82—Washington	7	149	40	19	.432	7	5	.714	9	13	22	6	25	1	4	1	43	6.1
84-85—Washington	1	2	0	0	.000	0	0	.000	0	0	0	0	0	0	0	0	0	0.0
Totals	8	151	44	19	.432	7	5	.714	9	13	22	6	25	1	4	1	43	5.4

MINOR LEAGUE REGULAR SEASON RECORD

Sea.—Team	G.	Min.	FGM	FGA	Pct.	FGM	FGA	Pct.	FTM	FTA	Pct.	Reb.	Ast.	Pts.	Avg.
			—2-Point—			—3-Point—									
84-85—Lancaster CBA...........	48	1897	478	902	.529	1	22	.045	191	234	.816	261	124	1150	24.0

Named to CBA All-Star First Team, 1985. . . . . CBA Newcomer of the Year, 1985.

STEVE COLTER

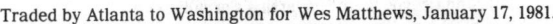

Born July 24, 1962 at Phoenix, Ariz. Height 6:03. Weight 165.

High School—Phoenix, Ariz., Union.

College—New Mexico State University, Las Cruces, N. M.

Drafted by Portland on second round, 1984 (33rd pick).

—COLLEGIATE RECORD—

Year	G.	Min.	FGA	FGM	Pct.	FTA	FTM	Pct.	Reb.	Pts.	Avg.
80-81	22	233	47	18	.383	41	28	.683	37	64	2.9
81-82	28	822	194	94	.485	87	66	.759	100	254	9.1
82-83	29	1079	329	166	.505	179	135	.754	137	469	16.2
83-84	28	1120	438	219	.500	138	108	.783	137	546	19.5
Totals	107	3254	1008	497	.493	445	337	.757	411	1333	12.5

Three-Point Field Goals: 1982-83, 2-for-6 (.333).

NBA REGULAR SEASON RECORD

Sea.—Team	G.	Min.	FGA	FGM	Pct.	FTA	FTM	Pct.	Off.	Def.	Tot.	Ast.	PF	Dq.	Stl.	Blk.	Pts.	Avg.
									—Rebounds—									
84-85—Portland	78	1462	477	216	.453	130	98	.754	40	110	150	243	142	0	75	9	556	7.1

Three-Point Field Goals: 1984-85, 26-for-74 (.351).

NBA PLAYOFF RECORD

Sea.—Team	G.	Min.	FGA	FGM	Pct.	FTA	FTM	Pct.	Off.	Def.	Tot.	Ast.	PF	Dq.	Stl.	Blk.	Pts.	Avg.
									—Rebounds—									
84-85—Portland	9	166	75	36	.480	8	5	.625	4	12	16	37	24	1	5	0	80	8.9

Three-Point Field Goals: 1984-85, 3-for-11 (.273).

LESTER ALLEN CONNER

Born September 17, 1959 at Memphis, Tenn. Height 6:04. Weight 185.

High School—Oakland, Calif., Fremont.

Colleges—Los Medanos College, Antioch, Calif.; Chabot College, Hayward, Calif., and Oregon State University, Corvallis, Ore.

Drafted by Golden State on first round, 1982 (14th pick).

—COLLEGIATE RECORD—
Los Medanos

Year	G.	Min.	FGA	FGM	Pct.	FTA	FTM	Pct.	Reb.	Pts.	Avg.
78-79	31	....	...	...	....	...	...	....	....	781	25.2

Chabot

Year	G.	Min.	FGA	FGM	Pct.	FTA	FTM	Pct.	Reb.	Pts.	Avg.
79-80	35	1179	549	319	.581	217	158	.728	215	796	22.7
JC Totals	66	...	...	...	...	...	...	...	....	1577	23.9

Oregon State

Year	G.	Min.	FGA	FGM	Pct.	FTA	FTM	Pct.	Reb.	Pts.	Avg.
80-81	28	790	141	68	.482	91	61	.670	119	197	7.0
81-82	30	1106	292	151	.517	196	146	.745	163	448	14.9
Totals	58	1896	433	219	.506	287	207	.721	282	645	11.1

NBA REGULAR SEASON RECORD

Sea.—Team	G.	Min.	FGA	FGM	Pct.	FTA	FTM	Pct.	Off.	Def.	Tot.	Ast.	PF	Dq.	Stl.	Blk.	Pts.	Avg.
									—Rebounds—									
82-83—Golden State	75	1416	303	145	.479	113	79	.699	69	152	221	253	141	1	116	7	369	4.9
83-84—Golden State	82	2573	730	360	.493	259	186	.718	132	173	305	401	176	1	162	12	907	11.1
84-85—Golden State	79	2258	546	246	.451	192	144	.750	87	159	246	369	136	1	161	13	640	8.1
Totals	236	6247	1579	751	.476	564	409	.725	288	484	772	1023	453	3	439	32	1916	8.1

Three-Point Field Goals: 1982-83, 0-for-4. 1983-84, 1-for-6 (.167). 1984-85, 4-for-20 (.200). Totals, 5-for-30 (.167).

DARWIN LOUIS COOK

Born August 6, 1958 at Los Angeles, Calif. Height 6:03. Weight 190.

High School—Los Angeles, Calif., Crenshaw.

College—University of Portland, Portland, Ore.

Drafted by Detroit on fourth round, 1980 (70th pick).

Waived by Detroit, July 3, 1980; signed by New Jersey as a free agent, July 17, 1980.

—COLLEGIATE RECORD—

Year	G.	Min.	FGA	FGM	Pct.	FTA	FTM	Pct.	Reb.	Pts.	Avg.
76-77	26	790	303	146	.482	78	50	.641	71	342	13.2
77-78	27	....	300	146	.487	85	66	.776	81	358	13.3
78-79	28	985	429	201	.469	127	91	.717	121	493	17.6
79-80	28	1001	394	204	.518	99	77	.778	113	485	17.3
Totals	109	....	1426	697	.489	389	284	.730	386	1678	15.4

NBA REGULAR SEASON RECORD

Sea.—Team	G.	Min.	FGA	FGM	Pct.	FTA	FTM	Pct.	Off.	Def.	Tot.	Ast.	PF	Dq.	Stl.	Blk.	Pts.	Avg.
									—Rebounds—									
80-81—New Jersey	81	1980	819	383	.468	180	132	.733	96	140	236	297	197	4	141	36	904	11.2
81-82—New Jersey	82	2090	803	387	.482	162	118	.728	52	103	155	319	196	2	146	24	899	11.0
82-83—New Jersey	82	2625	986	446	.449	242	186	.769	73	167	240	448	213	2	194	48	1080	13.2
83-84—New Jersey	82	1870	687	304	.443	126	95	.754	51	105	156	356	184	3	164	36	714	8.7
84-85—New Jersey	58	1063	453	212	.468	54	47	.870	21	71	92	160	96	0	74	10	473	8.2
Totals	385	9628	3748	1732	.462	764	578	.757	293	586	879	1580	886	11	719	154	4070	10.6

Three-Point Field Goals: 1980-81, 6-for-25 (.240). 1981-82, 7-for-31 (.226). 1982-83, 8-for-38 (.211). 1983-84, 11-for-46 (.239). 1984-85, 2-for-23 (.087). Totals, 34-for-163 (.209).

NBA PLAYOFF RECORD

Sea.—Team	G.	Min.	FGA	FGM	Pct.	FTA	FTM	Pct.	Off.	Def.	Tot.	Ast.	PF	Dq.	Stl.	Blk.	Pts.	Avg.
									\-Rebounds\-									
81-82—New Jersey	2	86	33	13	.394	6	2	.333	0	3	3	9	7	0	2	2	28	14.0
82-83—New Jersey	2	63	27	9	.333	2	2	1.000	3	3	6	10	8	0	1	0	20	10.0
83-84—New Jersey	11	185	82	30	.366	24	17	.708	8	10	18	31	26	0	15	0	81	7.4
84-85—New Jersey	1	7	4	3	.750	0	0	.000	0	0	0	1	2	0	0	0	6	6.0
Totals	16	341	146	55	.377	32	21	.656	11	16	27	51	43	0	18	2	135	8.4

Three-Point Field Goals: 1981-82, 0-for-3. 1982-83, 0-for-1. 1983-84, 4-for-13 (.308). Totals, 4-for-17 (.235).

JEFF JAMES COOK

Born October 21, 1956 at West Covina, Calif.   Height 6:10.   Weight 215.

High School—West Covina, Calif., Edgewood.

College—Idaho State University, Pocatello, Idaho.

Drafted by Kansas City on third round, 1978 (49th pick).

Waived by Kansas City, October 2, 1978; signed by Phoenix as a free agent, May 22, 1979.
Traded by Phoenix with a 1983 3rd round draft choice and cash to Cleveland for James Edwards, February 7, 1983.
Traded by Cleveland to San Antonio for Edgar Jones and cash, December 14, 1984.
Played in Western Basketball Association with Washington Lumberjacks, 1978-79.

—COLLEGIATE RECORD—

Year	G.	Min.	FGA	FGM	Pct.	FTA	FTM	Pct.	Reb.	Pts.	Avg.
74-75	20	....	45	19	.422	12	6	.500	51	44	2.2
75-76	24	....	95	42	.442	44	26	.591	108	110	4.6
76-77	30	....	267	143	.536	60	37	.617	259	323	10.8
77-78	26	....	274	134	.489	139	104	.748	302	372	14.3
Totals	100	....	681	338	.496	255	173	.678	720	849	8.5

MINOR LEAGUE REGULAR SEASON RECORD

Sea.—Team	G.	Min.	FGM	FGA	Pct.	FGM	FGA	Pct.	FTM	FTA	Pct.	Reb.	Ast.	Pts.	Avg.
78-79—Washington WBA.....	48	1822	301	634	.475	0	1	.000	163	226	.721	612	195	765	15.9

NBA REGULAR SEASON RECORD

Sea.—Team	G.	Min.	FGA	FGM	Pct.	FTA	FTM	Pct.	Off.	Def.	Tot.	Ast.	PF	Dq.	Stl.	Blk.	Pts.	Avg.
									\-Rebounds\-									
79-80—Phoenix	66	904	275	129	.469	129	104	.806	90	151	241	84	102	0	28	18	362	5.5
80-81—Phoenix	79	2192	616	286	.464	155	100	.645	170	297	467	201	236	3	82	54	672	8.5
81-82—Phoenix	76	1298	358	151	.422	134	89	.664	112	189	301	100	174	1	37	23	391	5.1
82-83—Phoe.-Clev.	75	1333	304	148	.487	104	79	.760	119	216	335	102	181	3	39	31	375	5.0
83-84—Cleveland	81	1950	387	188	.486	130	94	.723	174	310	484	123	282	7	68	47	471	5.8
84-85—Cle.-S.A.	72	1288	279	138	.495	64	47	.734	122	192	314	62	203	2	30	23	323	4.5
Totals	449	8965	2219	1040	.469	716	513	.716	787	1355	2142	672	1178	16	284	196	2594	5.8

Three-Point Field Goals: 1979-80, 0-for-3. 1980-81, 0-for-5. 1981-82, 0-for-2. 1982-83, 0-for-3. 1983-84, 1-for-2 (.500). 1984-85, 0-for-1. Totals, 1-for-16 (.063).

NBA PLAYOFF RECORD

Sea.—Team	G.	Min.	FGA	FGM	Pct.	FTA	FTM	Pct.	Off.	Def.	Tot.	Ast.	PF	Dq.	Stl.	Blk.	Pts.	Avg.
									\-Rebounds\-									
79-80—Phoenix	7	98	24	16	.667	26	22	.846	5	16	21	7	10	0	4	2	54	7.7
80-81—Phoenix	7	206	54	25	.463	19	14	.737	17	30	47	11	29	1	1	0	65	9.3
81-82—Phoenix	7	45	8	4	.500	0	0	.000	6	3	9	7	5	0	2	2	8	1.1
84-85—San Antonio	5	98	18	9	.500	25	17	.680	6	23	29	4	23	0	5	6	35	7.0
Totals	26	447	104	54	.519	70	53	.757	34	72	106	29	67	1	12	10	162	6.2

Three-Point Field Goals: 1980-81, 1-for-1. 1984-85, 0-for-1. Totals, 1-for-2 (.500).

ARTIS WAYNE COOPER
(Known by middle name.)

Born November 16, 1956 at Milan, Ga.   Height 6:10.   Weight 220.

High School—McRae, Ga., Telfair County.

College—University of New Orleans, New Orleans, La.

Drafted by Golden State on second round, 1978 (40th pick).

Traded by Golden State with a 1981 2nd round draft choice to Utah for Bernard King, September 11, 1980.
Traded by Utah with Allan Bristow to Dallas for Bill Robinzine, August 20, 1981.
Traded by Dallas with a 1985 1st round draft choice to Portland for Kelvin Ransey, June 28, 1982.
Traded by Portland with Lafayette Lever, Calvin Natt, a 1984 2nd round draft choice and a 1985 1st round draft choice to Denver for Kiki Vandeweghe, June 7, 1984.

Year	G.	Min.	FGA	FGM	Pct.	FTA	FTM	Pct.	Reb.	Pts.	Avg.
74-75	17	....	33	16	.485	4	3	.750	52	35	2.1
75-76	26	....	278	140	.504	47	34	.723	244	314	12.1
76-77	28	....	368	166	.451	55	38	.691	284	370	13.2
77-78	27	....	377	202	.536	111	86	.775	343	490	18.1
Totals	98	....	1056	524	.496	217	161	.742	923	1209	12.3

NBA REGULAR SEASON RECORD

Sea.—Team	G.	Min.	FGA	FGM	Pct.	FTA	FTM	Pct.	Off.	Def.	Tot.	Ast.	PF	Dq.	Stl.	Blk.	Pts.	Avg.
78-79—Golden State	65	795	293	128	.437	61	41	.672	90	190	280	21	118	0	7	44	297	4.6
79-80—Golden State	79	1781	750	367	.489	181	136	.751	202	305	507	42	246	5	20	79	871	11.0
80-81—Utah	71	1420	471	213	.452	90	62	.689	166	274	440	52	219	8	18	51	489	6.9
81-82—Dallas	76	1818	669	281	.420	160	119	.744	200	350	550	115	285	10	37	106	682	9.0
82-83—Portland	80	2099	723	320	.443	197	135	.685	214	397	611	116	318	5	27	136	775	9.7
83-84—Portland	81	1662	663	304	.459	230	185	.804	176	300	476	76	247	2	26	106	793	9.8
84-85—Denver	80	2031	856	404	.472	235	161	.685	229	402	631	86	304	2	28	197	969	12.1
Totals	532	11606	4425	2017	.456	1154	839	.727	1277	2218	3495	508	1737	32	163	719	4876	9.2

Three-Point Field Goals: 1979-80, 1-for-4 (.250). 1980-81, 1-for-3 (.333). 1981-82, 1-for-8 (.125). 1982-83, 0-for-5. 1983-84, 0-for-7. 1984-85, 0-for-2. Totals, 3-for-29 (.103).

NBA PLAYOFF RECORD

Sea.—Team	G.	Min.	FGA	FGM	Pct.	FTA	FTM	Pct.	Off.	Def.	Tot.	Ast.	PF	Dq.	Stl.	Blk.	Pts.	Avg.
82-83—Portland	7	228	74	36	.486	17	15	.882	24	32	56	9	33	3	2	8	87	12.4
83-84—Portland	5	104	27	10	.370	8	4	.500	11	9	20	4	14	0	1	4	24	4.8
84-85—Denver	15	321	143	67	.469	40	30	.750	34	59	93	20	52	0	8	36	164	10.9
Totals	27	653	244	113	.463	65	49	.754	69	100	169	33	99	3	11	48	275	10.2

JOSEPH EDWARD COOPER
(Joe)

Born September 1, 1957 at Houston, Tex.   Height 6:10.   Weight 230.

High School—Houston, Tex., Kashmere.

Colleges—Howard College, Big Spring, Tex.; University of Tulsa, Tulsa, Okla., and University of Colorado, Boulder, Colo.

Drafted by New Jersey on fifth round, 1981 (95th pick).

Waived by New Jersey, November 3, 1981; signed by Los Angeles as a free agent, September 20, 1982.
Waived by Los Angeles, November 8, 1982; signed by Washington as a free agent, November 18, 1982.
Waived by Washington, December 2, 1982; signed by San Diego as a free agent, March 21, 1983.
Waived by San Diego, August 9, 1983; signed by Milwaukee as a free agent, September 14, 1984.
Waived by Milwaukee, October 18, 1984; signed by Seattle as a free agent, April 11, 1985.
Played in Continental Basketball Association with Lancaster Lightning, 1981-82 through 1984-85 seasons.

—COLLEGIATE RECORD—
Howard College

Year	G.	Min.	FGA	FGM	Pct.	FTA	FTM	Pct.	Reb.	Pts.	Avg.
76-77	32	771	220	110	.500	61	33	.541	202	253	7.9
77-78	33	788	516	250	.484	138	90	.652	457	590	17.8
JC Totals	65	1559	736	360	.489	199	123	.618	659	843	13.0

Tulsa

Year	G.	Min.	FGA	FGM	Pct.	FTA	FTM	Pct.	Reb.	Pts.	Avg.
78-79	18	322	131	62	.473	50	38	.760	125	152	8.4

Colorado

Year	G.	Min.	FGA	FGM	Pct.	FTA	FTM	Pct.	Reb.	Pts.	Avg.
79-80				Did Not Play—Transfer Student							
80-81	28	660	219	126	.575	66	43	.652	199	295	10.5
College Totals	46	982	340	188	.553	116	71	.612	324	447	9.7

MINOR LEAGUE REGULAR SEASON RECORD

Sea.—Team	G.	Min.	2-Point			3-Point			FTM	FTA	Pct.	Reb.	Ast.	Pts.	Avg.
			FGM	FGA	Pct.	FGM	FGA	Pct.							
81-82—Lancaster CBA	44	1395	230	428	.537	0	0	.000	101	126	.801	374	45	561	12.8
82-83—Lancaster CBA	39	1458	192	373	.514	0	3	.000	112	163	.687	448	98	496	12.7
83-84—Lancaster CBA	38	1080	158	336	.470	0	1	.000	113	173	.653	305	56	429	11.3
84-85—Lancaster CBA	48	1573	309	601	.514	0	1	.000	237	325	.729	441	78	855	17.8

NBA REGULAR SEASON RECORD

Sea.—Team	G.	Min.	FGA	FGM	Pct.	FTA	FTM	Pct.	Off.	Def.	Tot.	Ast.	PF	Dq.	Stl.	Blk.	Pts.	Avg.
81-82—New Jersey	1	11	2	1	.500	0	0	.000	1	1	2	0	2	0	0	0	2	2.0
82-83—LA-Wa.-SD	20	333	72	37	.514	29	16	.552	42	44	86	17	49	0	9	20	90	4.5
84-85—Seattle	3	45	15	7	.467	6	3	.500	3	6	9	2	7	1	2	1	17	5.7
Totals	24	389	89	45	.506	35	19	.543	46	51	97	19	58	1	11	21	109	4.5

Named to CBA All-Star Second Team, 1985.

MICHAEL JEROME COOPER

Born April 15, 1956 at Los Angeles, Calif. Height 6:05. Weight 170.

High School—Pasadena, Calif.

Colleges—Pasadena City College, Pasadena, Calif., and
University of New Mexico, Albuquerque, N. M.

Drafted by Los Angeles on third round, 1978 (60th pick).

—COLLEGIATE RECORD—

Pasadena City

Year	G.	Min.	FGA	FGM	Pct.	FTA	FTM	Pct.	Reb.	Pts.	Avg.
74-75	23	....	336	177	.527	65	38	.585	91	392	17.0
75-76	28	....	473	261	.552	129	102	.791	230	624	22.3
JC Totals	51		809	438	.541	194	140	.722	321	1016	19.9

New Mexico

Year	G.	Min.	FGA	FGM	Pct.	FTA	FTM	Pct.	Reb.	Pts.	Avg.
76-77	30	957	333	171	.514	140	112	.800	150	454	15.1
77-78	28	830	387	189	.488	111	73	.658	158	451	16.1
Totals	58	1787	720	360	.500	251	185	.737	308	905	15.6

NBA REGULAR SEASON RECORD

Sea.—Team	G.	Min.	FGA	FGM	Pct.	FTA	FTM	Pct.	—Rebounds— Off.	Def.	Tot.	Ast.	PF	Dq.	Stl.	Blk.	Pts.	Avg.
78-79—Los Angeles	3	7	6	3	.500	0	0	.000	0	0	0	1	0	1	0	6	2.0
79-80—Los Angeles	82	1973	578	303	.524	143	111	.776	101	128	229	221	215	3	86	38	722	8.8
80-81—Los Angeles	81	2625	654	321	.491	149	117	.785	121	215	336	332	249	4	133	78	763	9.4
81-82—Los Angeles	76	2197	741	383	.517	171	139	.813	84	185	269	230	216	1	120	61	907	11.9
82-83—Los Angeles	82	2148	497	266	.535	130	102	.785	82	192	274	315	208	0	115	50	639	7.8
83-84—Los Angeles	82	2387	549	273	.497	185	155	.838	53	209	262	482	267	3	113	67	739	9.0
84-85—L.A. Lakers	82	2189	593	276	.465	133	115	.865	56	199	255	429	208	0	93	49	702	8.6
Totals	488	13526	3618	1825	.504	911	739	.811	497	1128	1625	2009	1364	11	661	343	4478	9.2

Three-Point Field Goals: 1979-80, 5-for-20 (.250). 1980-81, 4-for-19 (.211). 1981-82, 2-for-17 (.118). 1982-83, 5-for-21 (.238). 1983-84, 38-for-121 (.314). 1984-85, 35-for-123 (.285). Totals, 89-for-321 (.277).

NBA PLAYOFF RECORD

Sea.—Team	G.	Min.	FGA	FGM	Pct.	FTA	FTM	Pct.	—Rebounds— Off.	Def.	Tot.	Ast.	PF	Dq.	Stl.	Blk.	Pts.	Avg.
79-80—Los Angeles	16	464	140	57	.407	36	31	.861	28	31	59	58	54	0	24	11	145	9.1
80-81—Los Angeles	3	102	20	11	.550	14	10	.714	2	8	10	7	7	0	6	0	32	10.7
81-82—Los Angeles	14	383	124	70	.565	34	25	.735	19	42	61	62	47	0	24	11	166	11.9
82-83—Los Angeles	15	453	114	53	.465	41	34	.829	12	47	59	44	54	1	26	6	141	9.4
83-84—Los Angeles	21	723	191	88	.461	62	50	.806	20	62	82	119	80	1	24	20	238	11.3
84-85—L.A. Lakers	19	501	126	71	.563	52	48	.923	12	64	76	93	46	0	21	9	198	10.4
Totals	88	2626	715	350	.490	239	198	.828	93	254	347	383	288	2	125	57	920	10.5

Three-Point Field Goals: 1979-80, 0-for-2. 1980-81, 0-for-3. 1981-82, 1-for-2 (.500). 1982-83, 1-for-7 (.143). 1983-84, 12-for-36 (.333). 1984-85, 8-for-26 (.308). Totals, 22-for-76 (.289).

Named to NBA All-Defensive First Team, 1982, 1984, 1985. . . . NBA All-Defensive Second Team, 1981 and 1983. . . Member of NBA championship teams, 1980, 1982, 1985.

DAVID JOHN CORZINE
(Dave)

Born April 25, 1956 at Arlington Heights, Ill. Height 6:11. Weight 260.

High School—Arlington Heights, Ill., Hersey.

College—DePaul University, Chicago, Ill.

Drafted by Washington on first round, 1978 (18th pick).

Traded by Washington to San Antonio for two 2nd round draft choices (1981 and 1982), September 26, 1980.
Traded by San Antonio with Mark Olberding and cash to Chicago for Artis Gilmore, July 22, 1982.

—COLLEGIATE RECORD—

Year	G.	Min.	FGA	FGM	Pct.	FTA	FTM	Pct.	Reb.	Pts.	Avg.
74-75	25	....	309	134	.434	56	36	.643	216	304	12.2
75-76	29	....	386	181	.469	124	88	.710	256	450	15.5
76-77	27	....	448	219	.489	97	74	.763	339	512	19.0
77-78	30	....	462	255	.552	152	120	.789	340	630	21.0
Totals	111	....	1605	789	.492	429	318	.741	1151	1896	17.1

NBA REGULAR SEASON RECORD

Sea.—Team	G.	Min.	FGA	FGM	Pct.	FTA	FTM	Pct.	—Rebounds— Off.	Def.	Tot.	Ast.	PF	Dq.	Stl.	Blk.	Pts.	Avg.
78-79—Washington	59	532	118	63	.534	63	49	.778	52	95	147	49	67	0	10	14	175	3.0
79-80—Washington	78	826	216	90	.417	68	45	.662	104	166	270	63	120	1	9	31	225	2.9

									—Rebounds—									
Sea.—Team	G.	Min.	FGA	FGM	Pct.	FTA	FTM	Pct.	Off.	Def.	Tot.	Ast.	PF	Dq.	Stl.	Blk.	Pts.	Avg.
80-81—San Antonio	82	1960	747	366	.490	175	125	.714	228	408	636	117	212	0	42	99	857	10.5
81-82—San Antonio	82	2189	648	336	.519	213	159	.746	211	418	629	130	235	3	33	126	832	10.1
82-83—Chicago	82	2496	920	457	.497	322	232	.720	243	474	717	154	242	4	47	109	1146	14.0
83-84—Chicago	82	2674	824	385	.467	275	231	.840	169	406	575	202	227	3	58	120	1004	12.2
84-85—Chicago	82	2062	568	276	.486	200	149	.745	130	292	422	140	189	2	32	64	701	8.5
Totals	547	12739	4041	1973	.488	1316	990	.752	1137	2259	3396	855	1292	13	231	563	4940	9.0

Three-Point Field Goals: 1980-81, 0-for-3. 1981-82, 1-for-4 (.250). 1982-83, 0-for-2. 1983-84, 3-for-9 (.333). 1984-85, 0-for-1. Totals, 4-for-19 (.211).

NBA PLAYOFF RECORD

									—Rebounds—									
Sea.—Team	G.	Min.	FGA	FGM	Pct.	FTA	FTM	Pct.	Off.	Def.	Tot.	Ast.	PF	Dq.	Stl.	Blk.	Pts.	Avg.
78-79—Washington	12	63	15	4	.267	0	0	.000	12	13	25	5	9	0	2	0	8	0.7
79-80—Washington	2	9	5	4	.800	2	2	1.000	2	1	3	0	2	0	0	0	10	5.0
80-81—San Antonio	7	161	55	27	.491	13	9	.692	12	36	48	16	15	0	4	8	63	9.0
81-82—San Antonio	9	258	106	49	.462	34	24	.706	38	47	85	17	30	0	6	9	122	13.6
84-85—Chicago	4	77	21	14	.667	6	5	.833	9	13	22	3	14	0	2	1	33	8.3
Totals	34	568	202	98	.485	55	40	.727	73	110	183	41	70	0	14	18	236	6.9

CHARLES WASHINGTON CRISS JR.
(Charlie)

Born November 6, 1949 at Valhalla, N. Y. Height 5:08. Weight 165.
High School—Yonkers, N. Y.
Colleges—New Mexico Junior College, Hobbs, N. M., and
New Mexico State University, Las Cruces, N. M.

Signed by New York Knicks as a free agent, September 23, 1976.
Waived by New York, October 1, 1976; signed by Atlanta as a free agent, July 25, 1977.
Traded by Atlanta with Al Wood to San Diego for Freeman Williams, January 20, 1982.
Signed by Milwaukee as Veteran Free Agent, September 27, 1982.
Waived by Milwaukee, November 23, 1983; signed by Atlanta, February 4, 1984, to the first of consecutive 10-day contracts that expired, February 24, 1984.
Signed by Atlanta to a 10-day contract that expired, February 15, 1985.
Played in Eastern Basketball Association with Hartford, Cherry Hill and Scranton, 1972-73 through 1976-77.
Played in Continental Basketball Association with Albuquerque Silvers and Lancaster Lightning, 1983-84.

—COLLEGIATE RECORD—

New Mexico JC

Year	G.	Min.	FGA	FGM	Pct.	FTA	FTM	Pct.	Reb.	Pts.	Avg.
66-67	27	....	....	290	....	....	216	....	....	796	29.5

New Mexico State

Year	G.	Min.	FGA	FGM	Pct.	FTA	FTM	Pct.	Reb.	Pts.	Avg.
67-68	11	....	78	32	.411	27	20	.741	13	84	7.6
68-69	26	....	359	165	.460	131	104	.794	77	434	16.7
69-70	24	....	274	109	.398	112	82	.732	54	300	12.5
Totals	61	....	711	306	.430	270	206	.763	144	818	13.4

MINOR LEAGUE REGULAR SEASON RECORD

			——2-Point——			——3-Point——									
Sea.—Team	G.	Min.	FGM	FGA	Pct.	FGM	FGA	Pct.	FTM	FTA	Pct.	Reb.	Ast.	Pts.	Avg.
72-73—Hartford EBA	4	....	4	....	....	0	....	....	2	2	1.000	2	5	10	2.5
73-74—Hartford EBA	26	....	202	....	....	1	....	....	127	146	.870	59	70	534	20.5
74-75—Cherry Hill EBA	26	....	303	....	....	13	....	....	151	175	.863	84	59	796	30.6
75-76—Scranton EBA	24	....	324	762	.425	5	8	.625	261	295	.885	71	100	924	38.5
76-77—Scranton EBA	25	....	315	602	.523	3	11	.273	222	258	.861	82	109	861	34.4
83-84—Albu-Lan. CBA	4	62	10	20	.500	1	2	.500	13	14	.928	4	15	36	9.0

NBA REGULAR SEASON RECORD

									—Rebounds—									
Sea.—Team	G.	Min.	FGA	FGM	Pct.	FTA	FTM	Pct.	Off.	Def.	Tot.	Ast.	PF	Dq.	Stl.	Blk.	Pts.	Avg.
77-78—Atlanta	77	1935	751	319	.425	296	236	.797	24	97	121	294	143	0	108	5	874	11.4
78-79—Atlanta	54	879	289	109	.377	86	67	.779	19	41	60	138	70	0	41	3	285	5.3
79-80—Atlanta	81	1794	578	249	.431	212	172	.811	27	89	116	246	133	0	74	4	671	8.3
80-81—Atlanta	66	1708	485	220	.454	214	185	.864	26	74	100	283	87	0	61	3	626	9.5
81-82—Atl.-S.D.	55	1392	498	222	.446	159	141	.887	13	69	82	187	96	0	44	6	595	10.8
82-83—Milwaukee	66	922	375	169	.451	76	68	.895	14	65	79	127	44	0	27	0	412	6.2
83-84—Mil.-Atl.	15	215	52	20	.385	16	12	.750	5	15	20	38	11	0	8	0	53	3.5
84-85—Atlanta	4	115	17	7	.412	6	4	.667	2	12	14	22	5	0	3	0	18	4.5
Totals	418	8960	3045	1315	.432	1065	885	.831	130	462	592	1335	589	0	366	21	3534	8.5

Three-Point Field Goals: 1979-80, 1-for-17 (.059). 1980-81, 1-for-21 (.048). 1981-82, 10-for-29 (.345). 1982-83, 6-for-31 (.194). 1983-84, 1-for-6 (.167). 1984-85, 0-for-2. Totals, 19-for-106 (.179).

NBA PLAYOFF RECORD

Sea.—Team	G.	Min.	FGA	FGM	Pct.	FTA	FTM	Pct.	—Rebounds— Off.	Def.	Tot.	Ast.	PF	Dq.	Stl.	Blk.	Pts.	Avg.
77-78—Atlanta	2	65	24	10	.417	9	7	.778	0	4	4	3	5	0	4	1	27	13.5
78-79—Atlanta	9	99	29	12	.414	10	9	.900	2	3	5	16	5	0	3	0	33	3.7
79-80—Atlanta	5	152	59	29	.492	12	11	.917	0	5	5	22	12	0	6	0	70	14.0
82-83—Milwaukee	9	116	34	15	.441	18	17	.944	1	13	14	12	12	0	9	0	47	5.2
Totals	25	432	146	66	.452	49	44	.898	3	25	28	53	34	0	22	1	177	7.1

Three-Point Field Goals: 1979-80, 1-for-3 (.333). 1982-83, 0-for-1. Totals, 1-for-4 (.250).

Named Eastern Basketball Association Most Valuable Player, 1976 and 1977.... Led EBA in scoring, 1975, 1976, 1977.... Led EBA in free-throw percentage, 1976.... Member of EBA championship team, 1974.... Set EBA single-game record for points, 72, against Hazleton, January 25, 1976.

PATRICK MICHAEL CUMMINGS
(Pat)

Born July 11, 1956 at Johnstown, Pa. Height 6:09. Weight 235.

High School—Johnstown, Pa.

College—University of Cincinnati, Cincinnati, O.

Drafted by Milwaukee on third round as junior eligible, 1978 (59th pick).

Traded by Milwaukee to Dallas for a 1982 2nd round draft choice, June 28, 1982.

Signed by New York as Veteran Free Agent, June 27, 1984; Dallas agreed not to exercise its right of first refusal in exchange for a 1985 3rd round draft choice and a 1986 2nd round draft choice.

—COLLEGIATE RECORD—

Year	G.	Min.	FGA	FGM	Pct.	FTA	FTM	Pct.	Reb.	Pts.	Avg.
74-75	18	458	190	111	.584	39	29	.744	131	251	13.9
75-76	31	810	291	163	.560	57	37	.649	210	363	11.7
76-77					Did Not Play—Broken Foot						
77-78	27	854	330	212	.642	87	63	.724	206	487	18.0
78-79	27	1013	490	270	.551	147	121	.823	304	661	24.5
Totals	103	3135	1301	756	.581	330	250	.758	851	1762	17.1

NBA REGULAR SEASON RECORD

Sea.—Team	G.	Min.	FGA	FGM	Pct.	FTA	FTM	Pct.	—Rebounds— Off.	Def.	Tot.	Ast.	PF	Dq.	Stl.	Blk.	Pts.	Avg.
79-80—Milwaukee	71	900	370	187	.505	123	94	.764	81	157	238	53	141	0	22	17	468	6.6
80-81—Milwaukee	74	1084	460	248	.539	140	99	.707	97	195	292	62	192	4	31	19	595	8.0
81-82—Milwaukee	78	1132	430	219	.509	91	67	.736	61	184	245	99	227	6	22	8	505	6.5
82-83—Dallas	81	2317	878	433	.493	196	148	.755	225	443	668	144	296	9	57	35	1014	12.5
83-84—Dallas	80	2492	915	452	.494	190	141	.742	151	507	658	158	282	2	64	23	1045	13.1
84-85—New York	63	2069	797	410	.514	227	177	.780	139	379	518	109	247	6	50	17	997	15.8
Totals	447	9994	3850	1949	.506	967	726	.751	754	1865	2619	625	1385	27	246	119	4624	10.3

Three-Point Field Goals: 1980-81, 0-for-2. 1981-82, 0-for-2. 1982-83, 0-for-1. 1983-84, 0-for-2. 1984-85, 0-for-4. Totals, 0-for-11.

NBA PLAYOFF RECORD

Sea.—Team	G.	Min.	FGA	FGM	Pct.	FTA	FTM	Pct.	—Rebounds— Off.	Def.	Tot.	Ast.	PF	Dq.	Stl.	Blk.	Pts.	Avg.
79-80—Milwaukee	6	57	17	11	.647	6	5	.833	4	12	16	2	9	0	1	0	27	4.5
80-81—Milwaukee	5	25	11	3	.273	4	3	.750	3	3	6	0	2	0	1	0	9	1.8
81-82—Milwaukee	6	44	11	4	.364	2	1	.500	3	8	11	2	7	0	0	2	9	1.5
83-84—Dallas	10	300	115	47	.409	15	14	.933	26	46	72	15	30	0	4	2	108	10.8
Totals	27	426	154	65	.422	27	23	.852	36	69	105	19	48	0	6	4	153	5.7

ROBERT TERRELL CUMMINGS
(Terry)

Born March 15, 1961 at Chicago, Ill. Height 6:10. Weight 220.

High School—Chicago, Ill., Carver.

College—DePaul University, Chicago, Ill.

Drafted by San Diego on first round as an undergraduate, 1982 (2nd pick).

Traded by Los Angeles Clippers with Craig Hodges and Ricky Pierce to Milwaukee for Marques Johnson, Harvey Catchings, Junior Bridgeman and cash, September 29, 1984.

—COLLEGIATE RECORD—

Year	G.	Min.	FGA	FGM	Pct.	FTA	FTM	Pct.	Reb.	Pts.	Avg.
79-80	28	....	303	154	.508	107	89	.832	263	397	14.2
80-81	29	994	303	151	.498	100	75	.750	260	377	13.0
81-82	28	1031	430	244	.567	180	136	.756	334	624	22.3
Totals	85	2025	1036	549	.530	387	300	.775	857	1398	16.4

TERRY CUMMINGS

NBA REGULAR SEASON RECORD

Sea.—Team	G.	Min.	FGA	FGM	Pct.	FTA	FTM	Pct.	Off.	Def.	Tot.	Ast.	PF	Dq.	Stl.	Blk.	Pts.	Avg.
										—Rebounds—								
82-83—San Diego	70	2531	1309	684	.523	412	292	.709	303	441	744	177	294	10	129	62	1660	23.7
83-84—San Diego	81	2907	1491	737	.494	528	380	.720	323	454	777	139	298	6	92	57	1854	22.9
84-85—Milwaukee	79	2722	1532	759	.495	463	343	.741	244	472	716	228	264	4	117	67	1861	23.6
Totals	230	8160	4332	2180	.503	1403	1015	.723	870	1367	2237	544	856	20	338	186	5375	23.4

Three-Point Field Goals: 1982-83, 0-for-1. 1983-84, 0-for-3. 1984-85, 0-for-1. Totals, 0-for-5.

NBA PLAYOFF RECORD

Sea.—Team	G.	Min.	FGA	FGM	Pct.	FTA	FTM	Pct.	Off.	Def.	Tot.	Ast.	PF	Dq.	Stl.	Blk.	Pts.	Avg.
										—Rebounds—								
84-85—Milwaukee	8	311	149	86	.577	58	48	.828	21	49	70	20	33	1	12	7	220	27.5

Three-Point Field Goals: 1984-85, 0-for-1.

NBA ALL-STAR GAME RECORD

Season—Team	Min.	FGA	FGM	Pct.	FTA	FTM	Pct.	Off.	Def.	Tot.	Ast.	PF	Dq.	Stl.	Blk.	Pts.
										—Rebounds—						
1985—Milwaukee	16	17	7	.412	4	3	.750	4	3	7	0	1	0	0	1	17

Named to All-NBA Second Team, 1985. . . . Named NBA Rookie of the Year, 1983. . . . Named to NBA All-Rookie Team, 1983. . . . Named to THE SPORTING NEWS All-America First Team, 1982.

EARL CURETON

Born September 3, 1957 at Detroit, Mich. Height 6:09. Weight 215.

High School—Detroit, Mich., Finney.

Colleges—Robert Morris College, Coraopolis, Pa., and
University of Detroit, Detroit, Mich.
(Robert Morris, a junior college, became a four-year college between
the 1975-76 and 1976-77 school years.)

Drafted by Philadelphia on third round as junior eligible, 1979 (58th pick).

Signed by Detroit as Veteran Free Agent, November 12, 1983; Philadelphia agreed not to exercise its right of first refusal in exchange for 1989 and 1990 2nd round draft choices.

COLLEGIATE RECORD
Robert Morris JC

Year	G.	Min.	FGA	FGM	Pct.	FTA	FTM	Pct.	Reb.	Pts.	Avg.
75-76	28	....	...	...	....	...	...	....	227	405	14.5

Robert Morris (Four-year college)

Year	G.	Min.	FGA	FGM	Pct.	FTA	FTM	Pct.	Reb.	Pts.	Avg.
76-77	26	....	418	196	.469	101	54	.535	274	446	17.2

Detroit

Year	G.	Min.	FGA	FGM	Pct.	FTA	FTM	Pct.	Reb.	Pts.	Avg.
77-78					Did Not Play—Transfer Student						
78-79	28	744	270	138	.511	75	51	.680	251	327	11.7
79-80	27	893	448	236	.527	109	66	.606	246	538	19.9
Totals	55	1637	718	374	.521	184	117	.636	497	865	15.7
College Totals	81	....	1136	570	.502	285	171	.600	771	1311	16.2

NBA REGULAR SEASON RECORD

Sea.—Team	G.	Min.	FGA	FGM	Pct.	FTA	FTM	Pct.	Off.	Def.	Tot.	Ast.	PF	Dq.	Stl.	Blk.	Pts.	Avg.
										—Rebounds—								
80-81—Philadelphia	52	528	205	93	.454	64	33	.516	51	104	155	25	68	0	20	23	219	4.2
81-82—Philadelphia	66	956	306	149	.487	94	51	.543	90	180	270	32	142	0	31	27	349	5.3
82-83—Philadelphia	73	987	258	108	.419	67	33	.493	84	185	269	43	144	1	37	24	249	3.4
83-84—Detroit	73	907	177	81	.458	59	31	.525	86	201	287	36	143	3	24	31	193	2.6
84-85—Detroit	81	1642	428	207	.484	144	82	.569	169	250	419	83	216	1	56	42	496	6.1
Totals	345	5020	1374	638	.464	428	230	.537	480	920	1400	219	713	5	168	147	1506	4.4

Three-Point Field Goals: 1980-81, 0-for-1. 1981-82, 0-for-2. 1983-84, 0-for-1. 1984-85, 0-for-3. Totals, 0-for-7.

NBA PLAYOFF RECORD

Sea.—Team	G.	Min.	FGA	FGM	Pct.	FTA	FTM	Pct.	Off.	Def.	Tot.	Ast.	PF	Dq.	Stl.	Blk.	Pts.	Avg.
										—Rebounds—								
80-81—Philadelphia	9	36	18	6	.333	2	0	.000	1	8	9	2	3	0	1	2	12	1.3
81-82—Philadelphia	12	75	41	13	.317	9	6	.667	12	14	26	2	12	0	1	1	32	2.7
82-83—Philadelphia	5	25	4	1	.250	0	0	.000	0	5	5	1	5	0	2	0	2	0.4
83-84—Detroit	5	93	31	15	.484	6	2	.333	14	19	33	2	9	0	2	1	32	6.4
84-85—Detroit	9	133	34	16	.471	9	5	.556	10	31	41	4	20	0	9	2	37	4.1
Totals	40	362	128	51	.398	26	13	.500	37	77	114	11	49	0	15	6	115	2.9

Three-Point Field Goals: 1981-82, 0-for-1. 1984-85, 0-for-1. Totals, 0-for-2.

Member of NBA championship team, 1983.

QUINTIN DAILEY

Born January 22, 1961 at Baltimore, Md.   Height 6:03. Weight 180.

High School—Baltimore, Md., Cardinal Gibbons.

College—University of San Francisco, San Francisco, Calif.

Drafted by Chicago on first round as an undergraduate, 1982 (7th pick).

—COLLEGIATE RECORD—

Year	G.	Min.	FGA	FGM	Pct.	FTA	FTM	Pct.	Reb.	Pts.	Avg.
79-80	29	....	292	154	.527	134	85	.634	107	393	13.6
80-81	31	....	467	267	.572	206	159	.772	170	693	22.4
81-82	30	1138	524	286	.546	232	183	.789	156	755	25.2
Totals	90	....	1283	707	.551	572	427	.747	433	1841	20.5

NBA REGULAR SEASON RECORD

Sea.—Team	G.	Min.	FGA	FGM	Pct.	FTA	FTM	Pct.	Off.	Def.	Tot.	Ast.	PF	Dq.	Stl.	Blk.	Pts.	Avg.
82-83—Chicago	76	2081	1008	470	.466	282	206	.730	87	173	260	280	248	7	72	10	1151	15.1
83-84—Chicago	82	2449	1229	583	.474	396	321	.811	61	174	235	254	218	4	109	11	1491	18.2
84-85—Chicago	79	2101	1111	525	.473	251	205	.817	57	151	208	191	192	0	71	5	1262	16.0
Totals	237	6631	3348	1578	.471	929	732	.788	205	498	703	725	658	11	252	26	3904	16.5

Three-Point Field Goals: 1982-83, 5-for-25 (.200). 1983-84, 4-for-32 (.125). 1984-85, 7-for-30 (.233). Totals, 16-for-87 (.184).

NBA PLAYOFF RECORD

Sea.—Team	G.	Min.	FGA	FGM	Pct.	FTA	FTM	Pct.	Off.	Def.	Tot.	Ast.	PF	Dq.	Stl.	Blk.	Pts.	Avg.
84-85—Chicago	4	129	62	26	.419	11	8	.727	5	8	13	11	9	0	4	0	61	15.3

Three-Point Field Goals: 1984-85, 1-for-7 (.143).

Named to NBA All-Rookie Team, 1983. . . . THE SPORTING NEWS All-America First Team, 1982.

ADRIAN DELANO DANTLEY

Born February 28, 1956 at Washington, D. C.   Height 6:05.   Weight 210.

High School—Hyattsville, Md., DeMatha.

College—University of Notre Dame, Ind.

Drafted by Buffalo on first round as hardship case, 1976 (6th pick).

Traded by Buffalo with Mike Bantom to Indiana for Billy Knight, September 1, 1977.

Traded by Indiana with Dave Robisch to Los Angeles for James Edwards, Earl Tatum and cash, December 13, 1977.

Traded by Los Angeles to Utah for Spencer Haywood, September 13, 1979.

—COLLEGIATE RECORD—

Year	G.	Min.	FGA	FGM	Pct.	FTA	FTM	Pct.	Reb.	Pts.	Avg.
73-74	28	795	339	189	.558	161	133	.826	255	511	18.3
74-75	29	1091	581	315	.542	314	253	.806	296	883	30.4
75-76	29	1056	510	300	.588	294	229	.779	292	829	28.6
Totals	86	2942	1430	804	.562	769	615	.800	843	2223	25.8

NBA REGULAR SEASON RECORD

Sea.—Team	G.	Min.	FGA	FGM	Pct.	FTA	FTM	Pct.	Off.	Def.	Tot.	Ast.	PF	Dq.	Stl.	Blk.	Pts.	Avg.
76-77—Buffalo	77	2816	1046	544	.520	582	476	.818	251	336	587	144	215	2	91	15	1564	20.3
77-78—Ind.-L. A.	79	2933	1128	578	.512	680	541	.796	265	355	620	253	233	2	118	24	1697	21.5
78-79—Los Angeles	60	1775	733	374	.510	342	292	.854	131	211	342	138	162	0	63	12	1040	17.3
79-80—Utah	68	2674	1267	730	.576	526	443	.842	183	333	516	191	211	2	96	14	1903	28.0
80-81—Utah	80	3417	1627	909	.559	784	632	.806	192	317	509	322	245	1	109	18	2452	30.7
81-82—Utah	81	3222	1586	904	.570	818	648	.792	231	283	514	324	252	1	95	14	2457	30.3
82-83—Utah	22	887	402	233	.580	248	210	.847	58	82	140	105	62	2	20	0	676	30.7
83-84—Utah	79	2984	1438	802	.558	946	813	.859	179	269	448	310	201	0	61	4	2418	30.6
84-85—Utah	55	1971	964	512	.531	545	438	.804	148	175	323	186	133	0	57	8	1462	26.6
Totals	601	22679	10191	5586	.548	5471	4493	.821	1638	2361	3999	1973	1714	10	710	109	15669	26.1

Three-Point Field Goals: 1979-80, 0-for-2. 1980-81, 2-for-7 (.286). 1981-82, 1-for-3 (.333). 1983-84, 1-for-4 (.250). Totals, 4-for-16 (.250).

NBA PLAYOFF RECORD

Sea.—Team	G.	Min.	FGA	FGM	Pct.	FTA	FTM	Pct.	Off.	Def.	Tot.	Ast.	PF	Dq.	Stl.	Blk.	Pts.	Avg.
77-78—Los Angeles	3	104	35	20	.571	17	11	.647	9	16	25	11	9	0	5	3	51	17.0
78-79—Los Angeles	8	236	89	50	.562	52	41	.788	10	23	33	11	24	0	6	1	141	17.5
83-84—Utah	11	454	232	117	.504	139	120	.863	37	46	83	46	30	0	10	1	354	32.2
84-85—Utah	10	398	151	79	.523	122	95	.779	25	50	75	20	39	1	16	0	253	25.3
Totals	32	1192	507	266	.525	330	267	.809	81	135	216	88	102	1	37	5	799	25.0

Three-Point Field Goals: 1984-85, 0-for-1.

ADRIAN DANTLEY

NBA ALL-STAR GAME RECORD

Season—Team	Min.	FGA	FGM	Pct.	FTA	FTM	Pct.	Off.	Def.	Tot.	Ast.	PF	Dq.	Stl.	Blk.	Pts.
								—Rebounds—								
1980—Utah	30	15	8	.533	8	7	.875	4	1	5	2	1	0	2	0	23
1981—Utah	21	9	3	.333	2	2	1.000	2	3	5	0	1	0	1	0	8
1982—Utah	21	8	6	.750	1	0	.000	1	1	2	0	2	0	0	0	12
1984—Utah	18	8	1	.125	0	0	.000	0	2	2	1	4	0	1	0	2
1985—Utah	23	6	2	.333	6	6	1.000	0	2	2	1	4	0	1	0	10
Totals	113	46	20	.435	17	15	.882	7	9	16	4	12	0	5	0	55

Named to All-NBA Second Team, 1981 and 1984. . . . NBA Rookie of the Year, 1977. . . . NBA All-Rookie Team, 1977. . . . Led NBA in scoring, 1981 and 1984. . . . NBA Comeback Player of the Year, 1984. . . . Shares NBA record for most free throws made in one game, 28, vs. Houston, January 4, 1984. . . . THE SPORTING NEWS All-America First Team, 1975 and 1976. . . . Member of U.S. Olympic team, 1976.

BRADLEY ERNEST DAVIS
(Brad)

Born December 17, 1955 at Monaca, Pa.   Height 6:03.   Weight 180.

High School—Monaca, Pa.

College—University of Maryland, College Park, Md.

Drafted by Los Angeles on first round as an undergraduate, 1977 (15th pick).

Waived by Los Angeles, October 27, 1978; signed by Indiana as a free agent, February 14, 1979.
Waived by Indiana, October 22, 1979; signed by Utah to two 10-day contracts, that expired March 20, 1979.
Signed by Detroit as a free agent, July 9, 1980.
Waived by Detroit, October 8, 1980; signed by Dallas as a free agent, December 2, 1980.
Played in Western Basketball Association with Montana Sky, 1978-79.
Played in Continental Basketball Association with Anchorage Northern Knights, 1979-80 and 1980-81.

—COLLEGIATE RECORD—

Year	G.	Min.	FGA	FGM	Pct.	FTA	FTM	Pct.	Reb.	Pts.	Avg.
74-75	29	....	243	141	.580	100	82	.820	95	364	12.6
75-76	28	....	228	117	.513	116	92	.793	73	326	11.6
76-77	27	....	250	128	.512	102	80	.784	94	336	12.4
Totals	84	....	721	386	.535	318	254	.799	262	1026	12.2

MINOR LEAGUE REGULAR SEASON RECORD

Sea.—Team	G.	Min.	FGM	FGA	Pct.	FGM	FGA	Pct.	FTM	FTA	Pct.	Reb.	Ast.	Pts.	Avg.
				—2-Point—			—3-Point—								
78-79—Montana WBA	34	1395	194	362	.536	3	16	.188	105	133	.789	119	224	502	14.8
79-80—Anchorage CBA	40	955	206	361	.571	0	8	.000	120	139	.863	158	291	532	13.3
80-81—Anchorage CBA	5	165	18	43	.418	0	5	.000	12	16	.750	18	41	48	9.6

NBA REGULAR SEASON RECORD

Sea.—Team	G.	Min.	FGA	FGM	Pct.	FTA	FTM	Pct.	Off.	Def.	Tot.	Ast.	PF	Dq.	Stl.	Blk.	Pts.	Avg.
									—Rebounds—									
77-78—Los Angeles	33	334	72	30	.417	29	22	.759	4	31	35	83	39	1	15	2	82	2.5
78-79—L.A.-Ind.	27	298	55	31	.564	23	16	.696	1	16	17	52	32	0	16	2	78	2.9
79-80—Ind.-Utah	18	268	63	35	.556	16	13	.813	4	13	17	50	28	0	13	1	83	4.6
80-81—Dallas	56	1686	410	230	.561	204	163	.799	29	122	151	385	156	2	52	11	626	11.2
81-82—Dallas	82	2614	771	397	.515	230	185	.804	35	191	226	509	218	5	73	6	993	12.1
82-83—Dallas	79	2323	628	359	.572	220	186	.845	34	164	198	565	176	2	80	11	915	11.6
83-84—Dallas	81	2665	651	345	.530	238	199	.836	41	146	187	561	218	4	94	13	896	11.1
84-85—Dallas	82	2539	614	310	.505	178	158	.888	39	154	193	581	219	1	91	10	825	10.1
Totals	458	12727	3264	1737	.532	1138	942	.828	187	837	1024	1786	1086	15	434	56	4498	9.8

Three-Point Field Goals: 1979-80, 0-for-1. 1980-81, 3-for-17 (.176). 1981-82, 14-for-49 (.286). 1982-83, 11-for-43 (.256). 1983-84, 7-for-38 (.184). 1984-85, 47-for-115 (.409). Totals, 82-for-263 (.312).

NBA PLAYOFF RECORD

Sea.—Team	G.	Min.	FGA	FGM	Pct.	FTA	FTM	Pct.	Off.	Def.	Tot.	Ast.	PF	Dq.	Stl.	Blk.	Pts.	Avg.
									—Rebounds—									
83-84—Dallas	10	304	73	33	.452	19	15	.789	6	13	19	50	18	0	6	0	81	8.1
84-85—Dallas	4	113	26	13	.500	13	12	.923	1	7	8	22	11	0	4	1	41	10.3
Totals	14	417	99	46	.465	32	27	.844	7	20	27	72	29	0	10	1	122	8.7

Three-Point Field Goals: 1983-84, 0-for-2. 1984-85, 3-for-8 (.375). Totals, 3-for-10 (.300).

Member of CBA championship team, 1980.

—DID YOU KNOW—

That when Cleveland Coach George Karl was a guard at North Carolina, his team defeated Massachusetts by 40 points in a National Invitation Tournament game that turned out to be Julius Erving's last collegiate contest?

CHARLES EDWARD DAVIS
(Charlie)

Born October 5, 1958 at Nashville, Tenn.   Height 6:07.   Weight 215.

High School—Nashville, Tenn., McGavock.

College—Vanderbilt University, Nashville, Tenn.

Drafted by Washington on second round, 1981 (35th pick).

Waived by Washington, November 6, 1984; signed by Milwaukee as a free agent, November 11, 1984.

—COLLEGIATE RECORD—

Year	G.	Min.	FGA	FGM	Pct.	FTA	FTM	Pct.	Reb.	Pts.	Avg.
76-77	26	825	368	164	.446	94	71	.755	181	399	15.3
77-78	25	889	353	178	.504	87	63	.724	178	419	16.8
78-79	27	964	352	203	.577	130	96	.738	234	502	18.6
79-80	1	15	6	3	.500	0	0	.000	3	6	6.0
80-81	26	676	249	135	.542	99	79	.798	150	349	13.4
Totals	105	3369	1328	683	.514	410	309	.754	746	1675	16.0

(Granted extra year of eligibility because he was able to play only one game in 1979-80 because of tendinitis in left ankle.)

NBA REGULAR SEASON RECORD

Sea.—Team	G.	Min.	FGA	FGM	Pct.	FTA	FTM	Pct.	—Rebounds— Off.	Def.	Tot.	Ast.	PF	Dq.	Stl.	Blk.	Pts.	Avg.
81-82—Washington	54	575	184	88	.478	37	30	.811	54	79	133	31	89	0	10	13	206	3.8
82-83—Washington	74	1161	534	251	.470	89	56	.629	83	130	213	73	122	0	32	22	560	7.6
83-84—Washington	46	467	218	103	.472	39	24	.615	34	69	103	30	58	1	14	10	231	5.0
84-85—Wash.-Mil.	61	774	356	153	.430	62	51	.823	59	94	153	51	113	1	22	5	358	5.9
Totals	235	2977	1292	595	.461	229	161	.703	230	372	602	185	382	2	78	50	1355	5.8

Three-Point Field Goals: 1981-82, 0-for-2. 1982-83, 2-for-10 (.200). 1983-84, 1-for-9 (.111). 1984-85, 1-for-10 (.100). Totals, 4-for-31 (.129).

NBA PLAYOFF RECORD

Sea.—Team	G.	Min.	FGA	FGM	Pct.	FTA	FTM	Pct.	—Rebounds— Off.	Def.	Tot.	Ast.	PF	Dq.	Stl.	Blk.	Pts.	Avg.
81-82—Washington	6	52	17	7	.412	2	2	1.000	1	4	5	3	6	0	1	1	16	2.7
83-84—Washington	3	17	12	7	.583	0	0	.000	1	2	3	0	0	0	0	0	14	4.7
84-85—Milwaukee	5	51	20	8	.400	4	3	.750	6	4	10	4	2	0	0	0	19	3.8
Totals	14	120	49	22	.449	6	5	.883	8	10	18	7	8	0	1	1	49	3.5

Three-Point Field Goals: 1981-82, 0-for-1. 1984-85, 0-for-2. Totals, 0-for-3.

JOHNNY REGINALD DAVIS

Born October 21, 1955 at Detroit, Mich.   Height 6:02.   Weight 180.

High School—Detroit, Mich., Murray-Wright.

College—University of Dayton, Dayton, O.

Drafted by Portland on second round as hardship case, 1976 (22nd pick).

Traded by Portland with a 1978 1st round draft choice to Indiana for a 1978 1st round draft choice, June 8, 1978.
Traded by Indiana to Atlanta for a 1983 2nd round draft choice and cash, December 31, 1982.
Traded by Atlanta to Cleveland for Stewart Granger and John Garris, August 8, 1984.

—COLLEGIATE RECORD—

Year	G.	Min.	FGA	FGM	Pct.	FTA	FTM	Pct.	Reb.	Pts.	Avg.
73-74	29	....	407	173	.425	105	69	.657	106	415	14.3
74-75	26	1002	477	228	.478	158	125	.791	93	581	22.3
75-76	26	1007	453	206	.455	193	154	.798	85	566	21.8
Totals	81	....	1337	607	.454	456	348	.763	284	1562	19.3

NBA REGULAR SEASON RECORD

Sea.—Team	G.	Min.	FGA	FGM	Pct.	FTA	FTM	Pct.	—Rebounds— Off.	Def.	Tot.	Ast.	PF	Dq.	Stl.	Blk.	Pts.	Avg.
76-77—Portland	79	1451	531	234	.441	209	166	.794	62	64	126	148	128	1	41	11	634	8.0
77-78—Portland	82	2188	756	343	.454	227	188	.828	65	108	173	217	173	0	81	14	874	10.7
78-79—Indiana	79	2971	1240	565	.456	396	314	.793	70	121	191	453	177	1	95	22	1444	18.3
79-80—Indiana	82	2912	1159	496	.428	352	304	.864	102	124	226	440	178	0	110	23	1300	15.9
80-81—Indiana	76	2536	917	426	.465	299	238	.796	56	114	170	480	179	2	95	14	1094	14.4
81-82—Indiana	82	2664	1153	538	.467	394	315	.799	72	106	178	346	176	1	76	11	1396	17.0
82-83—Atlanta	53	1465	567	258	.455	206	164	.796	37	91	128	315	100	0	43	7	685	12.9
83-84—Atlanta	75	2079	800	354	.443	256	217	.848	53	86	139	326	146	0	62	6	925	12.3
84-85—Cleveland	76	1920	791	337	.426	300	255	.850	35	84	119	426	136	1	43	4	941	12.4
Totals	684	20186	7914	3551	.449	2639	2161	.819	552	898	1450	3151	1393	6	646	112	9293	13.6

Three-Point Field Goals: 1979-80, 4-for-42 (.095). 1980-81, 4-for-33 (.121). 1981-82, 5-for-27 (.185). 1982-83, 5-for-18 (.278). 1983-84, 0-for-8. 1984-85, 12-for-46 (.261). Totals, 30-for-174 (.172).

NBA PLAYOFF RECORD

Sea.—Team	G.	Min.	FGA	FGM	Pct.	FTA	FTM	Pct.	Off.	Def.	Tot.	Ast.	PF	Dq.	Stl.	Blk.	Pts.	Avg.
											—Rebounds—							
76-77—Portland	16	436	133	65	.489	53	38	.717	10	23	33	52	32	0	28	3	168	10.5
77-78—Portland	6	201	76	35	.461	23	16	.696	3	7	10	13	15	0	1	2	86	14.3
80-81—Indiana	2	74	35	14	.400	13	12	.923	2	6	8	11	6	0	2	0	40	20.0
82-83—Atlanta	3	113	52	21	.404	10	9	.900	1	4	5	27	6	0	0	0	51	17.0
83-84—Atlanta	5	131	55	22	.400	6	6	1.000	2	8	10	24	10	0	1	0	50	10.0
84-85—Cleveland	3	50	16	12	.750	5	4	.800	1	5	6	15	5	0	5	0	28	9.3
Totals	35	1005	367	169	.460	110	85	.773	19	53	72	142	74	0	37	5	423	12.1

Three-Point Field Goals: 1980-81, 0-for-1. 1982-83, 0-for-1. 1984-85, 0-for-1. Totals, 0-for-3.

Member of NBA championship team, 1977.

WALTER PAUL DAVIS

Born September 9, 1954 at Pineville, N. C.   Height 6:06.   Weight 200.

High School—Pineville, N. C., South Mecklenberg.

Prep School—Hockessin, Del., Sanford.

College—University of North Carolina, Chapel Hill, N. C.

Drafted by Phoenix on first round, 1977 (5th pick).

—COLLEGIATE RECORD—

Year	G.	Min.	FGA	FGM	Pct.	FTA	FTM	Pct.	Reb.	Pts.	Avg.
73-74	27	....	322	161	.500	82	65	.793	126	387	14.3
74-75	31	....	396	200	.505	130	98	.754	195	498	16.1
75-76	29	....	351	190	.541	130	101	.777	166	481	16.6
76-77	32	....	351	203	.578	117	91	.778	183	497	15.5
Totals	119	....	1420	754	.531	459	355	.773	670	1863	15.7

NBA REGULAR SEASON RECORD

Sea.—Team	G.	Min.	FGA	FGM	Pct.	FTA	FTM	Pct.	Off.	Def.	Tot.	Ast.	PF	Dq.	Stl.	Blk.	Pts.	Avg.
											—Rebounds—							
77-78—Phoenix	81	2590	1494	786	.526	466	387	.830	158	326	484	273	242	2	113	20	1959	24.2
78-79—Phoenix	79	2437	1362	764	.561	409	340	.831	111	262	373	339	250	5	147	26	1868	23.6
79-80—Phoenix	75	2309	1166	657	.563	365	299	.819	75	197	272	337	202	2	114	19	1613	21.5
80-81—Phoenix	78	2182	1101	593	.539	250	209	.836	63	137	200	302	192	3	97	12	1402	18.0
81-82—Phoenix	55	1182	669	350	.523	111	91	.820	21	82	103	162	104	1	46	3	794	14.4
82-83—Phoenix	80	2491	1289	665	.516	225	184	.818	63	134	197	397	186	2	117	12	1521	19.0
83-84—Phoenix	78	2546	1274	652	.512	270	233	.863	38	164	202	429	202	0	107	12	1557	20.0
84-85—Phoenix	23	570	309	139	.450	73	64	.877	6	29	35	98	42	0	18	0	345	15.0
Totals	549	16307	8664	4606	.532	2169	1807	.833	535	1331	1866	2337	1420	15	759	104	11059	20.1

Three-Point Field Goals: 1979-80, 0-for-4. 1980-81, 7-for-17 (.412). 1981-82, 3-for-16 (.188). 1982-83, 7-for-23 (.304). 1983-84, 20-for-87 (.230). 1984-85, 3-for-10 (.300). Totals, 40-for-157 (.255).

NBA PLAYOFF RECORD

Sea.—Team	G.	Min.	FGA	FGM	Pct.	FTA	FTM	Pct.	Off.	Def.	Tot.	Ast.	PF	Dq.	Stl.	Blk.	Pts.	Avg.
											—Rebounds—							
77-78—Phoenix	2	66	40	19	.475	16	12	.750	4	13	17	8	8	0	3	0	50	25.0
78-79—Phoenix	15	490	244	127	.520	96	78	.813	24	45	69	79	41	0	26	5	332	22.1
79-80—Phoenix	8	245	137	69	.504	38	28	.737	9	14	23	35	20	0	4	1	166	20.8
80-81—Phoenix	7	199	106	51	.481	17	10	.588	7	12	19	22	17	0	7	1	112	16.0
81-82—Phoenix	7	173	116	52	.448	24	22	.917	5	17	22	30	19	0	5	1	127	18.1
82-83—Phoenix	3	113	69	30	.435	21	17	.810	5	10	15	13	6	0	6	5	78	26.0
83-84—Phoenix	17	623	327	175	.535	78	70	.897	15	31	46	109	55	0	29	3	423	24.9
Totals	59	1909	1039	523	.503	290	237	.817	69	142	211	296	166	0	80	16	1288	21.8

Three-Point Field Goals: 1979-80, 0-for-3. 1980-81, 0-for-1. 1981-82, 1-for-3 (.333). 1982-83, 1-for-2 (.500). 1983-84, 3-for-11 (.273). Totals, 5-for-20 (.250).

NBA ALL-STAR GAME RECORD

Season—Team	Min.	FGA	FGM	Pct.	FTA	FTM	Pct.	Off.	Def.	Tot.	Ast.	PF	Dq.	Stl.	Blk.	Pts.
										—Rebounds—						
1978—Phoenix.........	15	6	3	.500	4	4	1.000	0	1	1	6	1	0	1	0	10
1979—Phoenix.........	19	9	4	.444	0	0	.000	1	3	4	4	0	0	1	0	8
1980—Phoenix.........	23	10	5	.500	2	2	1.000	2	2	4	2	2	0	4	0	12
1981—Phoenix.........	22	9	5	.556	2	2	1.000	1	6	7	1	2	0	0	0	12
1984—Phoenix.........	15	9	5	.556	0	0	.000	0	2	2	1	0	0	1	0	10
Totals	94	43	22	.512	8	8	1.000	4	14	18	14	5	0	7	0	52

Named to All-NBA Second Team, 1978 and 1979. . . . NBA Rookie of the Year, 1978. . . . NBA All-Rookie Team, 1978. . . . Member of U. S. Olympic Team, 1976.

DARRYL DAWKINS

Born January 11, 1957 at Orlando, Fla. Height 6:11. Weight 251.

High School—Orlando, Fla., Maynard Evans.

Did not attend college.

Drafted by Philadelphia on first round as hardship case, 1975 (5th pick).

Traded by Philadelphia to New Jersey for a 1983 1st round draft choice and cash, August 27, 1982.

NBA REGULAR SEASON RECORD

Sea.—Team	G.	Min.	FGA	FGM	Pct.	FTA	FTM	Pct.	Off.	Def.	Tot.	Ast.	PF	Dq.	Stl.	Blk.	Pts.	Avg.
75-76—Philadelphia	37	165	82	41	.500	24	8	.333	15	34	49	3	40	1	2	9	90	2.4
76-77—Philadelphia	59	684	215	135	.628	79	40	.506	59	171	230	24	129	1	12	49	310	5.3
77-78—Philadelphia	70	1722	577	332	.575	220	156	.709	117	438	555	85	268	5	34	125	820	11.7
78-79—Philadelphia	78	2035	831	430	.517	235	158	.672	123	508	631	128	295	5	32	143	1018	13.1
79-80—Philadelphia	80	2541	946	494	.522	291	190	.653	197	496	693	149	328	8	49	142	1178	14.7
80-81—Philadelphia	76	2088	697	423	.607	304	219	.720	106	439	545	109	316	9	38	112	1065	14.0
81-82—Philadelphia	48	1124	367	207	.564	164	114	.695	68	237	305	55	193	5	19	55	528	11.0
82-83—New Jersey	81	2093	669	401	.599	257	166	.646	127	293	420	114	379	23	67	152	968	12.0
83-84—New Jersey	81	2417	855	507	.593	464	341	.735	159	382	541	123	386	22	60	136	1357	16.8
84-85—New Jersey	39	972	339	192	.566	201	143	.711	55	126	181	45	171	11	14	35	527	13.5
Totals	649	15841	5578	3162	.567	2239	1535	.686	1026	3124	4150	835	2505	90	327	958	7861	12.1

Three-Point Field Goals: 1979-80, 0-for-6. 1981-82, 0-for-2. 1983-84, 2-for-5 (.400). 1984-85, 0-for-1. Totals, 2-for-14 (.143).

NBA PLAYOFF RECORD

Sea.—Team	G.	Min.	FGA	FGM	Pct.	FTA	FTM	Pct.	Off.	Def.	Tot.	Ast.	PF	Dq.	Stl.	Blk.	Pts.	Avg.
76-77—Philadelphia	18	331	95	50	.526	47	31	.660	9	89	98	17	46	1	8	18	131	7.3
77-78—Philadelphia	10	180	53	27	.509	17	9	.529	6	51	57	10	34	1	3	15	63	6.3
78-79—Philadelphia	9	255	106	56	.528	47	32	.681	21	61	82	12	42	1	2	16	144	16.0
79-80—Philadelphia	18	607	238	126	.529	93	60	.645	44	93	137	33	75	2	13	42	312	17.3
80-81—Philadelphia	16	421	153	86	.562	68	49	.721	28	70	98	14	71	2	3	16	221	13.8
81-82—Philadelphia	21	460	178	99	.556	50	33	.660	23	75	98	11	94	4	7	35	231	11.0
82-83—New Jersey	2	59	22	17	.773	2	2	1.000	2	8	10	2	7	0	4	5	36	18.0
83-84—New Jersey	11	340	118	66	.559	83	70	.843	22	46	68	13	52	4	5	10	202	18.4
84-85—New Jersey	3	64	23	11	.478	4	3	.750	4	10	14	4	13	1	2	6	25	8.3
Totals	108	2717	986	538	.546	411	289	.703	159	503	662	116	434	16	47	163	1365	12.6

Three-Point Field Goals: 1979-80, 0-for-3. 1982-83, 0-for-1. 1983-84, 0-for-3. Totals, 0-for-7.

Holds NBA record for most personal fouls in a season, 1984.

DARREN KEEFE DAYE

Born November 30, 1960 at Des Moines, Iowa. Height 6:08. Weight 220.

High School—Granada Hills, Calif., Kennedy.

College—University of California at Los Angeles, Los Angeles, Calif.

Drafted by Washington on third round, 1983 (57th pick).

—COLLEGIATE RECORD—

Year	G.	Min.	FGA	FGM	Pct.	FTA	FTM	Pct.	Reb.	Pts.	Avg.
79-80	32	497	103	59	.573	76	43	.566	60	161	5.0
80-81	27	717	225	131	.582	93	63	.677	117	325	12.0
81-82	26	606	140	76	.543	85	55	.647	101	207	8.0
82-83	29	979	347	186	.536	124	84	.677	174	456	15.7
Totals	114	2799	815	452	.555	378	245	.648	452	1149	10.1

NBA REGULAR SEASON RECORD

Sea.—Team	G.	Min.	FGA	FGM	Pct.	FTA	FTM	Pct.	Off.	Def.	Tot.	Ast.	PF	Dq.	Stl.	Blk.	Pts.	Avg.
83-84—Washington	75	1174	408	180	.441	133	95	.714	90	98	188	176	154	0	38	12	455	6.1
84-85—Washington	80	1573	504	258	.512	249	178	.715	93	179	272	240	164	1	53	19	695	8.7
Totals	155	2747	912	438	.480	382	273	.715	183	277	460	416	318	1	91	31	1150	7.4

Three-Point Field Goals 1983-84, 0-for-6. 1984-85, 1-for-7 (.143). Totals, 1-for-13 (.077).

NBA PLAYOFF RECORD

Sea.—Team	G.	Min.	FGA	FGM	Pct.	FTA	FTM	Pct.	Off.	Def.	Tot.	Ast.	PF	Dq.	Stl.	Blk.	Pts.	Avg.
83-84—Washington	3	15	5	1	.200	2	2	1.000	0	0	0	1	2	0	0	1	4	1.3
84-85—Washington	4	85	30	17	.567	16	7	.438	6	6	12	14	8	0	3	0	41	10.3
Totals	7	100	35	18	.514	18	9	.500	6	6	12	15	10	0	3	1	45	6.4

JAMES DONALDSON

JAMES LEE DONALDSON III

Born August 16, 1957 at Meachern, England. Height 7:02. Weight 278.
High School—Sacramento, Calif., Burbank.
College—Washington State University, Pullman, Wash.
Drafted by Seattle on fourth round, 1979 (73rd pick).

Traded by Seattle with Greg Kelser, Mark Radford, a 1984 1st round draft choice and a 1985 2nd round draft choice to San Diego for Tom Chambers, Al Wood, a 1987 2nd round draft choice and a 1984 3rd round draft choice, August 18, 1983.

Played in Europe during 1979-80 season.

—COLLEGIATE RECORD—

Year	G.	Min.	FGA	FGM	Pct.	FTA	FTM	Pct.	Reb.	Pts.	Avg.
75-76	9	36	7	4	.571	3	2	.667	17	10	1.1
76-77	22	297	59	34	.576	19	6	.316	74	74	3.4
77-78	27	999	251	131	.522	121	79	.653	305	341	12.6
78-79	26	946	216	120	.556	98	53	.541	281	293	11.3
Totals	84	2278	533	289	.542	241	140	.581	677	718	8.5

NBA REGULAR SEASON RECORD

									—Rebounds—									
Sea.—Team	G.	Min.	FGA	FGM	Pct.	FTA	FTM	Pct.	Off.	Def.	Tot.	Ast.	PF	Dq.	Stl.	Blk.	Pts.	Avg.
80-81—Seattle	68	980	238	129	.542	170	101	.594	107	202	309	42	79	0	8	74	359	5.3
81-82—Seattle	82	1710	419	255	.609	240	151	.629	138	352	490	51	186	2	27	139	661	8.1
82-83—Seattle	82	1789	496	289	.583	218	150	.688	131	370	501	97	171	1	19	101	728	8.9
83-84—San Diego	82	2525	604	360	.596	327	249	.761	165	484	649	90	214	1	40	139	969	11.8
84-85—L.A. Clippers	82	2392	551	351	.637	303	227	.749	168	500	668	48	217	1	28	130	929	11.3
Totals	396	9396	2308	1384	.600	1258	878	.698	709	1908	2617	328	867	5	122	583	3646	9.2

NBA PLAYOFF RECORD

									—Rebounds—									
Sea.—Team	G.	Min.	FGA	FGM	Pct.	FTA	FTM	Pct.	Off.	Def.	Tot.	Ast.	PF	Dq.	Stl.	Blk.	Pts.	Avg.
81-82—Seattle	8	189	43	18	.419	24	18	.750	25	49	74	7	16	0	2	5	54	6.8
82-83—Seattle	2	47	22	11	.500	3	2	.667	5	12	17	2	4	0	0	3	24	12.0
Totals	10	236	65	29	.446	27	20	.741	30	61	91	9	20	0	2	8	78	7.8

Led NBA in field-goal percentage, 1985.

JOHN EDWARD DREW

Born September 30, 1954 at Vredenburgh, Ala. Height 6:06. Weight 205.
High School—Beatrice, Ala., Shields.
College—Gardner-Webb College, Boiling Springs, N. C.
Drafted by Atlanta on second round as hardship case, 1974 (25th pick).

Traded by Atlanta with Freeman Williams and cash to Utah for draft rights to Dominique Wilkins, September 2, 1982.

Waived by Utah, December 10, 1984.

—COLLEGIATE RECORD—

Year	G.	Min.	FGA	FGM	Pct.	FTA	FTM	Pct.	Reb.	Pts.	Avg.
72-73	23	....	469	239	.510	123	84	.683	195	562	24.4
73-74	28	....	588	308	.524	156	109	.699	365	725	25.9
Totals	51	....	1057	547	.518	279	193	.692	560	1287	25.2

NBA REGULAR SEASON RECORD

									—Rebounds—									
Sea.—Team	G.	Min.	FGA	FGM	Pct.	FTA	FTM	Pct.	Off.	Def.	Tot.	Ast.	PF	Dq.	Stl.	Blk.	Pts.	Avg.
74-75—Atlanta	78	2289	1230	527	.428	544	388	.713	357	479	836	138	274	4	119	39	1442	18.5
75-76—Atlanta	77	2351	1168	586	.502	656	488	.744	286	374	660	150	261	11	138	30	1660	21.6
76-77—Atlanta	74	2688	1416	689	.487	577	412	.714	280	395	675	133	275	9	102	29	1790	24.2
77-78—Atlanta	70	2203	1236	593	.480	575	437	.760	213	298	511	141	247	8	119	27	1623	23.2
78-79—Atlanta	79	2410	1375	650	.473	677	495	.731	225	297	522	119	332	19	128	16	1795	22.7
79-80—Atlanta	80	2306	1182	535	.453	646	489	.757	203	268	471	101	313	10	91	23	1559	19.5
80-81—Atlanta	67	2075	1096	500	.456	577	454	.787	145	238	383	79	264	9	98	15	1454	21.7
81-82—Atlanta	70	2040	957	465	.486	491	364	.741	169	206	375	96	250	6	64	3	1298	18.5
82-83—Utah	44	1206	671	318	.474	392	296	.755	98	137	235	97	152	8	35	7	932	21.2
83-84—Utah	81	1797	1067	511	.479	517	402	.778	146	192	338	135	208	1	88	2	1430	17.7
84-85—Utah	19	463	260	107	.412	122	94	.770	36	46	82	35	65	0	22	2	308	16.2
Totals	739	21828	11658	5481	.470	5774	4319	.748	2158	2930	5088	1224	2641	85	1004	193	15291	20.7

Three-Point Field Goals: 1979-80, 0-for-7. 1980-81, 0-for-7. 1981-82, 4-for-12 (.333). 1982-83, 0-for-5. 1983-84, 6-for-22 (.273). 1984-85, 0-for-4. Totals, 10-for-57 (.175).

CLYDE DREXLER

NBA PLAYOFF RECORD

Sea.—Team	G.	Min.	FGA	FGM	Pct.	FTA	FTM	Pct.	Off.	—Rebounds— Def.	Tot.	Ast.	PF	Dq.	Stl.	Blk.	Pts.	Avg.
77-78—Atlanta	2	79	49	21	.429	16	10	.625	9	6	15	3	9	0	1	1	52	26.0
78-79—Atlanta	9	275	131	55	.420	46	35	.761	20	40	60	7	36	1	9	4	145	16.1
79-80—Atlanta	5	150	63	24	.381	35	25	.714	10	20	30	4	21	1	7	0	73	14.6
81-82—Atlanta	2	59	22	8	.364	12	7	.583	6	4	10	1	11	1	0	0	23	11.5
83-84—Utah	11	172	85	43	.506	33	26	.788	10	15	25	9	26	0	4	0	112	10.2
Totals	29	735	350	151	.431	142	103	.725	55	85	140	24	103	3	21	5	405	14.0

NBA ALL-STAR GAME RECORD

Season—Team	Min.	FGA	FGM	Pct.	FTA	FTM	Pct.	Off.	—Rebounds— Def.	Tot.	Ast.	PF	Dq.	Stl.	Blk.	Pts.
1976—Atlanta	9	3	1	.333	0	0	.000	1	2	3	0	2	0	0	0	2
1980—Atlanta	15	4	0	.000	5	4	.800	1	2	3	0	5	0	2	0	4
Totals	24	7	1	.143	5	4	.800	2	4	6	0	7	0	2	0	6

Named to NBA All-Rookie Team, 1975.

LARRY DONNELL DREW

Born April 2, 1958 at Kansas City, Kan. Height 6:01. Weight 180.

High School—Kansas City, Kan., Wyandotte.

College—University of Missouri, Columbia, Mo.

Drafted by Detroit on first round, 1980 (17th pick).

Traded by Detroit to Kansas City for two 2nd round draft choices (1982 and 1984), August 26, 1981.

—COLLEGIATE RECORD—

Year	G.	Min.	FGA	FGM	Pct.	FTA	FTM	Pct.	Reb.	Pts.	Avg.
76-77	28	....	175	75	.429	59	44	.746	77	194	6.9
77-78	30	1029	344	150	.436	105	80	.762	90	380	12.7
78-79	28	1037	366	181	.495	100	64	.640	73	426	15.2
79-80	31	1092	279	151	.541	121	99	.818	89	401	12.9
Totals	117	....	1164	557	.479	385	287	.745	329	1401	12.0

NBA REGULAR SEASON RECORD

Sea.—Team	G.	Min.	FGA	FGM	Pct.	FTA	FTM	Pct.	Off.	—Rebounds— Def.	Tot.	Ast.	PF	Dq.	Stl.	Blk.	Pts.	Avg.
80-81—Detroit	76	1581	484	197	.407	133	106	.797	24	96	120	249	125	0	88	7	504	6.6
81-82—Kansas City	81	1973	757	358	.473	189	150	.794	30	119	149	419	150	0	110	1	874	10.8
82-83—Kansas City	75	2690	1218	599	.492	378	310	.820	44	163	207	610	207	1	126	10	1510	20.1
83-84—Kansas City	73	2363	1026	474	.462	313	243	.776	33	113	146	558	170	0	121	10	1194	16.4
84-85—Kansas City	72	2373	913	457	.501	194	154	.794	39	125	164	484	147	0	93	8	1075	14.9
Totals	377	10980	4398	2085	.474	1207	963	.798	170	616	786	2320	799	1	538	36	5157	13.7

Three-Point Field Goals: 1980-81, 4-for-17. 1981-82, 8-for-27 (.296). 1982-83, 2-for-16 (.125). 1983-84, 3-for-10 (.300). 1984-85, 7-for-28 (.250). Totals, 24-for-98 (.245).

NBA PLAYOFF RECORD

Sea.—Team	G.	Min.	FGA	FGM	Pct.	FTA	FTM	Pct.	Off.	—Rebounds— Def.	Tot.	Ast.	PF	Dq.	Stl.	Blk.	Pts.	Avg.
83-84—Kansas City	3	70	19	7	.368	3	3	1.000	0	4	4	11	5	0	3	0	17	5.7

CLYDE DREXLER

Born June 22, 1962 at New Orleans, La. Height 6:07. Weight 210.

High School—Houston, Tex., Sterling.

College—University of Houston, Houston, Tex.

Drafted by Portland on first round as an undergraduate, 1983 (14th pick).

—COLLEGIATE RECORD—

Year	G.	Min.	FGA	FGM	Pct.	FTA	FTM	Pct.	Reb.	Pts.	Avg.
80-81	30	992	303	153	.505	85	50	.588	314	356	11.9
81-82	32	1077	362	206	.569	120	73	.608	336	485	15.2
82-83	34	1186	440	236	.536	95	70	.737	298	542	15.9
Totals	96	3255	1105	595	.538	300	193	.643	948	1383	14.4

NBA REGULAR SEASON RECORD

Sea.—Team	G.	Min.	FGA	FGM	Pct.	FTA	FTM	Pct.	Off.	—Rebounds— Def.	Tot.	Ast.	PF	Dq.	Stl.	Blk.	Pts.	Avg.
83-84—Portland	82	1408	559	252	.451	169	123	.728	112	123	235	153	209	2	107	29	628	7.7
84-85—Portland	80	2555	1161	573	.494	294	223	.759	217	259	476	441	265	3	177	68	1377	17.2
Totals	162	3963	1720	825	.480	463	346	.747	329	382	711	594	474	5	284	97	2005	12.4

Three-Point Field Goals: 1983-84, 1-for-4 (.250). 1984-85, 8-for-37 (.216). Totals, 9-for-41 (.220).

NBA PLAYOFF RECORD

Sea.—Team	G.	Min.	FGA	FGM	Pct.	FTA	FTM	Pct.	—Rebounds— Off.	Def.	Tot.	Ast.	PF	Dq.	Stl.	Blk.	Pts.	Avg.
83-84—Portland	5	85	35	15	.429	7	6	.857	7	10	17	8	11	0	5	1	36	7.2
84-85—Portland	9	339	134	55	.410	45	38	.844	27	28	55	83	37	0	23	9	150	16.7
Totals	14	424	169	70	.414	52	44	.846	34	38	72	91	48	0	28	10	186	13.3

Three-Point Field Goals: 1983-84, 0-for-1. 1984-85, 2-for-7 (.286). Totals, 2-for-8 (.250).

MICHAEL JOSEPH DUNLEAVY
(Mike)

Born March 21, 1954 at Brooklyn, N. Y.   Height 6:03.   Weight 180.
High School—Brooklyn, N. Y., Nazareth.
College—University of South Carolina, Columbia, S. C.
Drafted by Philadelphia on sixth round, 1976 (99th pick).

Waived by Philadelphia, November 14, 1977; signed by Houston as a free agent, March 10, 1978.
Signed by San Antonio as Veteran Free Agent, October 16, 1982; Houston agreed not to exercise its right of first refusal in exchange for a 1983 3rd round draft choice.
Signed by Milwaukee as Veteran Free Agent, March 8, 1984; San Antonio agreed not to exercise its right of first refusal in exchange for a 1984 4th round draft choice and cash.
Player-coach in All-America Basketball Alliance with Carolina Lightning, 1977-78.

—COLLEGIATE RECORD—

Year	G.	Min.	FGA	FGM	Pct.	FTA	FTM	Pct.	Reb.	Pts.	Avg.
72-73	29	803	236	122	.517	72	59	.819	60	303	10.4
73-74	27	983	369	167	.453	116	97	.836	85	431	16.0
74-75	28	1016	368	182	.495	119	91	.765	110	455	16.3
75-76	27	962	297	144	.485	139	109	.784	87	397	14.7
Totals	111	3764	1270	615	.484	446	356	.798	342	1586	14.3

MINOR LEAGUE REGULAR SEASON RECORD

Sea.—Team	G.	Min.	—2-Point— FGM	FGA	Pct.	—3-Point— FGM	FGA	Pct.	FTM	FTA	Pct.	Reb.	Ast.	Pts.	Avg.
77-78—Carolina AABA	10	332	66	123	.537	2	5	.400	53	60	.883	52	50	191	19.1

NBA REGULAR SEASON RECORD

Sea.—Team	G.	Min.	FGA	FGM	Pct.	FTA	FTM	Pct.	—Rebounds— Off.	Def.	Tot.	Ast.	PF	Dq.	Stl.	Blk.	Pts.	Avg.
76-77—Philadelphia	32	359	145	60	.414	45	34	.756	10	24	34	56	64	1	13	2	154	4.8
77-78—Phi-Houston	15	119	50	20	.400	18	13	.722	1	9	10	28	12	0	9	1	53	3.5
78-79—Houston	74	1486	425	215	.506	184	159	.864	28	100	128	324	168	2	56	5	589	8.0
79-80—Houston	51	1036	319	148	.464	134	111	.828	26	74	100	210	120	2	40	4	410	8.0
80-81—Houston	74	1609	632	310	.491	186	156	.839	28	90	118	268	165	1	64	2	777	10.5
81-82—Houston	70	1315	450	206	.458	106	75	.708	24	80	104	227	161	0	45	3	520	7.4
82-83—San Antonio	79	1619	510	213	.418	154	120	.779	18	116	134	437	210	1	74	4	613	7.8
83-84—Milwaukee	17	404	127	70	.551	40	32	.800	6	22	28	78	51	0	12	1	191	11.2
84-85—Milwaukee	19	433	135	64	.474	29	25	.862	6	25	31	85	55	1	15	3	169	8.9
Totals	431	8380	2793	1306	.468	896	725	.809	147	540	687	1713	1006	8	328	25	3476	8.1

Three-Point Field Goals: 1979-80, 3-for-20 (.150). 1980-81, 1-for-16 (.063). 1981-82, 33-for-86 (.384). 1982-83, 67-for-194 (.345). 1983-84, 19-for-45 (.422). 1984-85, 16-for-47 (.340). Totals, 139-for-408 (.341).

NBA PLAYOFF RECORD

Sea.—Team	G.	Min.	FGA	FGM	Pct.	FTA	FTM	Pct.	—Rebounds— Off.	Def.	Tot.	Ast.	PF	Dq.	Stl.	Blk.	Pts.	Avg.
76-77—Philadelphia	11	68	25	9	.360	5	4	.800	1	3	4	9	14	0	3	0	22	2.0
78-79—Houston	1	10	2	0	.000	0	0	.000	0	1	1	0	1	0	0	0	0	0.0
79-80—Houston	6	45	12	6	.500	6	5	.833	2	3	5	13	11	0	5	0	17	2.8
80-81—Houston	20	472	152	69	.454	38	33	.868	9	33	42	68	59	1	15	1	177	8.9
81-82—Houston	3	66	22	9	.409	6	5	.833	0	3	3	9	7	0	2	0	23	7.7
82-83—San Antonio	11	174	65	22	.338	13	9	.692	3	10	13	49	22	0	9	1	61	5.5
83-84—Milwaukee	15	393	129	59	.457	36	33	.917	10	25	35	46	59	2	17	0	169	11.3
Totals	67	1228	407	174	.428	104	89	.856	25	78	103	194	173	3	51	2	469	7.0

Three-Point Field Goals: 1979-80, 0-for-2. 1980-81, 6-for-15 (.400). 1981-82, 0-for-4. 1982-83, 8-for-30 (.267). 1983-84, 18-for-50 (.360). Totals, 32-for-101 (.317).

Led NBA in three-point field-goal percentage, 1983.

—DID YOU KNOW—

That the oldest NBA All-Star Game MVP was Len Wilkens? Wilkens, now the Seattle SuperSonics' general manager, was 33 in 1971 when he won the award.

THEODORE ROOSEVELT DUNN
(T. R.)

Born February 1, 1955 at Birmingham, Ala. Height 6:04. Weight 192.

High School—Birmingham, Ala., West End.

College—University of Alabama, University, Ala.

Drafted by Portland on second round, 1977 (41st pick).

Traded by Portland to Denver for a 1984 2nd round draft choice and other considerations, August 15, 1980.

—COLLEGIATE RECORD—

Year	G.	Min.	FGA	FGM	Pct.	FTA	FTM	Pct.	Reb.	Pts.	Avg.
73-74	25	839	232	99	.427	58	38	.655	199	236	9.4
74-75	27	948	297	140	.471	70	51	.729	176	331	12.3
75-76	28	961	303	118	.389	59	37	.627	145	273	9.8
76-77	31	1094	353	173	.490	86	61	.709	220	407	13.1
Totals	111	3842	1185	530	.447	273	187	.685	740	1247	11.2

NBA REGULAR SEASON RECORD

Sea.—Team	G.	Min.	FGA	FGM	Pct.	FTA	FTM	Pct.	Off.	Def.	Tot.	Ast.	PF	Dq.	Stl.	Blk.	Pts.	Avg.
77-78—Portland	63	768	240	100	.417	56	37	.661	63	84	147	45	74	0	46	8	237	3.8
78-79—Portland	80	1828	549	246	.448	158	122	.772	145	199	344	103	166	1	86	23	614	7.7
79-80—Portland	82	1841	551	240	.436	111	84	.757	132	192	324	147	145	1	102	31	564	6.9
80-81—Denver	82	1427	354	146	.412	121	79	.653	133	168	301	81	141	0	66	29	371	4.5
81-82—Denver	82	2519	504	258	.512	215	153	.712	211	348	559	188	210	1	135	36	669	8.2
82-83—Denver	82	2640	527	254	.482	163	119	.730	231	384	615	189	218	2	147	25	627	7.6
83-84—Denver	80	2705	370	174	.470	145	106	.731	195	379	574	228	233	5	173	32	454	5.7
84-85—Denver	81	2290	358	175	.489	116	84	.724	169	216	385	153	213	3	140	14	434	5.4
Totals	632	16018	3453	1593	.461	1085	784	.723	1279	1970	3249	1134	1400	13	895	198	3970	6.3

Three-Point Field Goals: 1979-80, 0-for-3. 1980-81, 0-for-2. 1981-82, 0-for-1. 1982-83, 0-for-1. 1983-84, 0-for-1. 1984-85, 0-for-2. Totals, 0-for-10.

NBA PLAYOFF RECORD

Sea.—Team	G.	Min.	FGA	FGM	Pct.	FTA	FTM	Pct.	Off.	Def.	Tot.	Ast.	PF	Dq.	Stl.	Blk.	Pts.	Avg.
77-78—Portland	4	35	4	2	.500	0	0	.000	1	4	5	3	3	0	1	0	4	1.0
78-79—Portland	3	52	11	5	.455	0	0	.000	2	4	6	4	7	0	5	0	10	3.3
79-80—Portland	3	24	8	2	.250	2	2	1.000	1	3	4	4	3	0	1	0	6	2.0
81-82—Denver	3	81	13	6	.462	8	7	.875	10	8	18	10	11	0	8	1	19	6.3
82-83—Denver	8	300	41	18	.439	8	5	.625	27	51	78	20	21	0	12	3	41	5.1
83-84—Denver	5	178	25	14	.560	7	5	.714	20	19	39	8	19	0	10	4	33	6.6
84-85—Denver	15	371	65	27	.415	19	14	.737	27	33	60	34	45	0	24	3	68	4.5
Totals	41	1041	167	74	.443	44	33	.750	88	122	210	83	109	0	61	11	181	4.4

Named to NBA All-Defensive Second Team, 1983, 1984, 1985.

DEVIN GEORGE DURRANT

Born October 20, 1960 at Provo, Utah. Height 6:07. Weight 200.

High School—Provo, Utah.

College—Brigham Young University, Provo, Utah.

Drafted by Indiana on second round, 1984 (25th pick).

—COLLEGIATE RECORD—

Year	G.	Min.	FGA	FGM	Pct.	FTA	FTM	Pct.	Reb.	Pts.	Avg.
78-79	28	795	263	142	.540	122	86	.705	146	370	13.2
79-80	29	836	265	147	.555	130	93	.715	170	387	13.3
82-83	29	1094	456	231	.507	261	200	.766	167	662	22.8
83-84	31	....	543	312	.575	307	242	.788	160	866	27.9
Totals	117	....	1527	832	.545	820	621	.757	643	2285	19.5

NBA REGULAR SEASON RECORD

Sea.—Team	G.	Min.	FGA	FGM	Pct.	FTA	FTM	Pct.	Off.	Def.	Tot.	Ast.	PF	Dq.	Stl.	Blk.	Pts.	Avg.
84-85—Indiana	59	756	274	114	.416	102	72	.706	49	75	124	80	106	0	19	10	300	5.1

Three-Point Field Goals: 1984-85, 0-for-3.

(Mormon missionary in Spain during the 1980-81 and 1981-82 seasons.)

Named to THE SPORTING NEWS All-America Second Team, 1984.

MARK EATON

MARK E. EATON

Born January 24, 1957 at Westminister, Calif.   Height 7:03.   Weight 280.

High School—Westminster, Calif.

Colleges—Cypress College, Cypress, Calif., and University
of California at Los Angeles, Los Angeles, Calif.

Drafted by Phoenix on fifth round, 1979 (107th pick). (Eligible
for NBA draft because he was out of school three seasons between
high school and college and his college class graduated in 1979.)

Drafted by Utah on fourth round, 1982 (72nd pick).

—COLLEGIATE RECORD—
Cypress

Year	G.	Min.	FGA	FGM	Pct.	FTA	FTM	Pct.	Reb.	Pts.	Avg.
78-79	35	....	319	202	.633	117	78	.667	381	482	13.8
79-80	25	....	289	167	.578	83	40	.482	218	374	15.0
JC Totals	60	....	608	369	.607	200	118	.590	599	856	14.3

UCLA

Year	G.	Min.	FGA	FGM	Pct.	FTA	FTM	Pct.	Reb.	Pts.	Avg.
80-81	19	155	37	17	.459	17	5	.294	49	39	2.1
81-82	11	41	12	5	.417	5	4	.800	22	14	1.3
Totals	30	196	49	22	.449	22	9	.409	71	53	1.8

NBA REGULAR SEASON RECORD

Sea.—Team	G.	Min.	FGA	FGM	Pct.	FTA	FTM	Pct.	Off.	Def.	Tot.	Ast.	PF	Dq.	Stl.	Blk.	Pts.	Avg.
										—Rebounds—								
82-83—Utah	81	1528	353	146	.414	90	59	.656	86	376	462	112	257	6	24	275	351	4.3
83-84—Utah	82	2139	416	194	.466	123	73	.593	148	447	595	113	303	4	25	351	461	5.6
84-85—Utah	82	2813	673	302	.449	267	190	.712	207	720	927	124	312	5	36	456	794	9.7
Totals	245	6480	1442	642	.445	480	322	.671	441	1543	1984	349	872	15	85	1082	1606	6.6

Three-Point Field Goals: 1982-83, 0-for-1. 1983-84, 0-for-1. Totals, 0-for-2.

NBA PLAYOFF RECORD

Sea.—Team	G.	Min.	FGA	FGM	Pct.	FTA	FTM	Pct.	Off.	Def.	Tot.	Ast.	PF	Dq.	Stl.	Blk.	Pts.	Avg.
										—Rebounds—								
83-84—Utah	11	254	41	21	.512	17	8	.471	19	57	76	9	33	1	5	34	50	4.5
84-85—Utah	5	158	34	12	.353	7	5	.714	11	34	45	5	19	0	4	29	29	5.8
Totals	16	412	75	33	.440	24	13	.542	30	91	121	14	52	1	9	63	79	4.9

**Named NBA Defensive Player of the Year, 1985. . . . NBA All-Defensive First Team, 1985. . . . Holds NBA record
for most blocked shots in a season, 1985. . . . Holds NBA playoff game record for most blocked shots, 10, vs. Denver,
April 26, 1985. . . . Led NBA in blocked shots, 1984 and 1985.**

JERRY LEE EAVES

Born February 8, 1959 at Louisville, Ky.   Height 6:04.   Weight 185.

High School—Louisville, Ky., Ballard.

College—University of Louisville, Louisville, Ky.

Drafted by Utah on third round, 1982 (55th pick).

Waived by Utah, October 11, 1984; signed by Atlanta as a free agent, October 15, 1984.
Waived by Atlanta, October 31, 1984.

—COLLEGIATE RECORD—

Year	G.	Min.	FGA	FGM	Pct.	FTA	FTM	Pct.	Reb.	Pts.	Avg.
78-79	32	472	96	47	.490	87	61	.701	33	155	4.8
79-80	34	878	179	92	.514	117	78	.667	61	262	7.7
80-81	30	915	310	155	.500	145	107	.738	69	417	13.9
81-82	33	1018	322	164	.509	119	88	.739	74	416	12.6
Totals	129	3283	907	458	.505	468	334	.714	237	1250	9.7

NBA REGULAR SEASON RECORD

Sea.—Team	G.	Min.	FGA	FGM	Pct.	FTA	FTM	Pct.	Off.	Def.	Tot.	Ast.	PF	Dq.	Stl.	Blk.	Pts.	Avg.
										—Rebounds—								
82-83—Utah	82	1588	575	280	.487	247	200	.810	34	88	122	210	116	0	51	3	761	9.3
83-84—Utah	80	1034	293	132	.451	132	92	.697	29	56	85	200	90	0	33	5	356	4.5
84-85—Atlanta	3	37	6	3	.500	6	5	.833	0	0	0	4	6	0	0	0	11	3.7
Totals	165	2659	874	415	.475	385	297	.771	63	144	207	414	212	0	84	8	1128	6.8

Three-Point Field Goals: 1982-83, 1-for-8 (.125). 1983-84, 0-for-6. Totals, 1-for-14 (.071).

NBA PLAYOFF RECORD

Sea.—Team	G.	Min.	FGA	FGM	Pct.	FTA	FTM	Pct.	—Rebounds— Off.	Def.	Tot.	Ast.	PF	Dq.	Stl.	Blk.	Pts.	Avg.
83-84—Utah	11	132	46	22	.478	13	10	.769	3	7	10	13	10	0	5	2	55	5.0

Three-Point Field Goals: 1983-84, 1-for-3 (.333).
Member of NCAA championship team, 1980.

KENTON SCOTT EDELIN

Born May 24, 1962 at Heidelburg, West Germany.   Height 6:08.   Weight 205.
High School—Alexandria, Va., Hayfield.
College—University of Virginia, Charlottesville, Va.
Drafted by Indiana on seventh round, 1984 (140th pick).

Waived by Indiana, October 24, 1984; re-signed by Indiana to a 10-day contract that expired, January 19, 1985. Signed by Indiana as a free agent, March 29, 1985.

—COLLEGIATE RECORD—

Year	G.	Min.	FGA	FGM	Pct.	FTA	FTM	Pct.	Reb.	Pts.	Avg.
80-81				Statistics Unavailable							
81-82	34	446	66	45	.682	54	31	.574	94	121	3.6
82-83	34	503	57	28	.491	46	14	.304	165	70	2.1
83-84	29	761	78	53	.679	40	21	.525	185	127	4.4
Varsity Totals	97	1710	201	126	.627	140	66	.471	444	318	3.3

NBA REGULAR SEASON RECORD

Sea.—Team	G.	Min.	FGA	FGM	Pct.	FTA	FTM	Pct.	—Rebounds— Off.	Def.	Tot.	Ast.	PF	Dq.	Stl.	Blk.	Pts.	Avg.
84-85—Indiana	10	143	13	4	.308	8	3	.375	8	18	26	10	39	1	5	4	11	1.1

FRANKLIN DELANO EDWARDS

Born February 2, 1959 at New York, N. Y.   Height 6:01.   Weight 170.
High School—New York, N. Y., Julia Richman.
College—Cleveland State University, Cleveland, O.
Drafted by Philadelphia on first round, 1981 (22nd pick).

Signed by Los Angeles Clippers as Veteran Free Agent to a 10-day contract that expired, March 20, 1985. Re-signed by Los Angeles Clippers to a second 10-day contract that expired, April 3, 1985. Philadelphia waived right of first refusal.
Played in Continental Basketball Association with Lancaster Lightning, 1984-85.

—COLLEGIATE RECORD—

Year	G.	Min.	FGA	FGM	Pct.	FTA	FTM	Pct.	Reb.	Pts.	Avg.
77-78	25	....	416	190	.457	122	87	.713	68	467	18.7
78-79	25	....	402	198	.493	93	71	.763	90	467	18.7
79-80	25	....	486	253	.521	153	131	.856	65	637	25.5
80-81	27	....	503	265	.527	152	134	.882	86	664	24.6
Totals	102	....	1807	906	.501	520	423	.813	309	2235	21.9

NBA REGULAR SEASON RECORD

Sea.—Team	G.	Min.	FGA	FGM	Pct.	FTA	FTM	Pct.	—Rebounds— Off.	Def.	Tot.	Ast.	PF	Dq.	Stl.	Blk.	Pts.	Avg.
81-82—Philadelphia	42	291	150	65	.433	27	20	.741	10	17	27	45	37	0	16	5	150	3.6
82-83—Philadelphia	81	1266	483	228	.472	113	86	.761	23	62	85	221	119	0	81	6	542	6.7
83-84—Philadelphia	60	654	221	84	.380	48	34	.708	12	47	59	90	78	1	31	5	202	3.4
84-85—L.A. Clippers	16	198	66	36	.545	24	19	.792	3	11	14	38	10	0	17	0	91	5.7
Totals	199	2429	920	413	.449	212	159	.750	48	137	185	394	244	1	145	16	985	4.9

Three-Point Field Goals: 1981-82, 0-for-9. 1982-83, 0-for-8. 1983-84, 0-for-1. Totals, 0-for-18.

NBA PLAYOFF RECORD

Sea.—Team	G.	Min.	FGA	FGM	Pct.	FTA	FTM	Pct.	—Rebounds— Off.	Def.	Tot.	Ast.	PF	Dq.	Stl.	Blk.	Pts.	Avg.
81-82—Philadelphia	9	32	20	12	.600	9	8	.889	2	3	5	5	0	0	3	0	33	3.7
82-83—Philadelphia	12	101	32	13	.406	17	14	.824	2	7	9	17	7	0	5	0	40	3.3
Totals	21	133	52	25	.481	26	22	.846	4	10	14	22	7	0	8	0	73	3.5

Three-Point Field Goals: 1981-82, 1-for-1 (1.000).

MINOR LEAGUE REGULAR SEASON RECORD

Sea.—Team	G.	Min.	2-Point			3-Point			FTM	FTA	Pct.	Reb.	Ast.	Pts.	Avg.
			FGM	FGA	Pct.	FGM	FGA	Pct.							
84-85—Lancaster CBA.........	18	660	134	258	.519	1	2	.500	74	80	.925	42	173	345	19.2

Member of NBA championship team, 1983.

JAMES FRANKLIN EDWARDS

Born November 22, 1955 at Seattle, Wash. Height 7:00. Weight 225.

High School—Seattle, Wash., Roosevelt.

College—University of Washington, Seattle, Wash.

Drafted by Los Angeles on third round, 1977 (46th pick).

Traded by Los Angeles with Earl Tatum and cash to Indiana for Adrian Dantley and Dave Robisch, December 13, 1977.

Signed by Cleveland as Veteran Free Agent, May 25, 1981; Indiana agreed not to exercise its right of first refusal in exchange for two 2nd round draft choices (1981 and 1982), June 8, 1981.

Traded by Cleveland to Phoenix for Jeff Cook, a 1983 3rd round draft choice and cash, February 7, 1983.

—COLLEGIATE RECORD—

Year	G.	Min.	FGA	FGM	Pct.	FTA	FTM	Pct.	Reb.	Pts.	Avg.
73-74	25	....	160	68	.425	62	34	.548	115	170	6.8
74-75	26	575	264	125	.473	129	70	.543	198	320	12.3
75-76	28	811	392	205	.523	137	83	.606	200	493	17.6
76-77	27	940	404	223	.552	184	119	.647	282	565	20.9
Totals	106	....	1220	621	.509	512	306	.598	795	1548	14.6

NBA REGULAR SEASON RECORD

Sea.—Team	G.	Min.	FGA	FGM	Pct.	FTA	FTM	Pct.	Off.	Def.	Tot.	Ast.	PF	Dq.	Stl.	Blk.	Pts.	Avg.
77-78—LA-Ind.	83	2405	1093	495	.453	421	272	.646	197	418	615	85	322	12	53	78	1262	15.2
78-79—Indiana	82	2546	1065	534	.501	441	298	.676	179	514	693	92	363	16	60	109	1366	16.7
79-80—Indiana	82	2314	1032	528	.512	339	231	.681	179	399	578	127	324	12	55	104	1287	15.7
80-81—Indiana	81	2375	1004	511	.509	347	244	.703	191	380	571	212	304	7	32	128	1266	15.6
81-82—Cleveland	77	2539	1033	528	.511	339	232	.684	189	392	581	123	347	17	24	117	1288	16.7
82-83—Clev.-Phoe.	31	667	263	128	.487	108	69	.639	56	99	155	40	110	5	12	19	325	10.5
83-84—Phoenix	72	1897	817	438	.536	254	183	.720	108	240	348	184	254	3	23	30	1059	14.7
84-85—Phoenix	70	1787	766	384	.501	370	276	.746	95	292	387	153	237	5	26	52	1044	14.9
Totals	578	16530	7073	3546	.501	2619	1805	.689	1194	2734	3928	1016	2261	77	285	637	8897	15.4

Three-Point Field Goals: 1979-80, 0-for-1. 1980-81, 0-for-3. 1981-82, 0-for-4. 1983-84, 0-for-1. 1984-85, 0-for-3. Totals, 0-for-12.

NBA PLAYOFF RECORD

Sea.—Team	G.	Min.	FGA	FGM	Pct.	FTA	FTM	Pct.	Off.	Def.	Tot.	Ast.	PF	Dq.	Stl.	Blk.	Pts.	Avg.
80-81—Indiana	2	56	24	7	.292	0	0	.000	4	10	14	5	8	0	1	1	14	7.0
82-83—Phoenix	3	54	26	11	.423	6	6	1.000	6	12	18	4	7	0	1	1	28	9.3
83-84—Phoenix	17	463	189	93	.492	68	48	.706	22	69	91	27	62	3	4	11	234	13.8
Totals	22	573	239	111	.464	74	54	.730	32	91	123	36	77	3	6	13	276	12.5

JOEL CRAIG EHLO

(Known by middle name.)

Born August 11, 1961 at Lubbock, Tex. Height 6:06. Weight 180.

High School—Lubbock, Tex., Monterey.

Colleges—Odessa College, Odessa, Tex., and Washington State University, Pullman, Wash.

Drafted by Houston on third round, 1983 (48th pick).

—COLLEGIATE RECORD—

Odessa

Year	G.	Min.	FGA	FGM	Pct.	FTA	FTM	Pct.	Reb.	Pts.	Avg.
79-80	28	...	300	146	.487	84	60	.714	142	352	12.6
80-81	30	...	482	241	.500	180	139	.772	204	621	20.7
JC Totals................	58		782	387	.495	264	199	.754	346	973	16.8

Washington State

Year	G.	Min.	FGA	FGM	Pct.	FTA	FTM	Pct.	Reb.	Pts.	Avg.
81-82	30	592	119	57	.479	65	39	.600	65	153	5.1
82-83	30	911	265	145	.547	109	69	.633	97	359	12.0
Totals	60	1503	384	202	.526	174	108	.621	162	512	8.5

Sea.—Team	G.	Min.	FGA	FGM	Pct.	FTA	FTM	Pct.	Off.	Def.	Tot.	Ast.	PF	Dq.	Stl.	Blk.	Pts.	Avg.
										—Rebounds—								
83-84—Houston	7	63	27	11	.407	1	1	1.000	4	5	9	6	13	0	3	0	23	3.3
84-85—Houston	45	189	69	34	.493	30	19	.633	8	17	25	26	26	0	11	3	87	1.9
Totals	52	252	96	45	.469	31	20	.645	12	22	34	32	39	0	14	3	110	2.1

Three-Point Field Goals: 1984-85, 0-for-3.

NBA PLAYOFF RECORD

Sea.—Team	G.	Min.	FGA	FGM	Pct.	FTA	FTM	Pct.	Off.	Def.	Tot.	Ast.	PF	Dq.	Stl.	Blk.	Pts.	Avg.
										—Rebounds—								
84-85—Houston	3	6	1	1	1.000	2	2	1.000	0	0	0	0	3	0	4	0	4	1.3

DALE ELLIS

Born August 6, 1960 at Marietta, Ga.   Height 6:07.   Weight 205.

High School—Marietta, Ga.

College—University of Tennessee, Knoxville, Tenn.

Drafted by Dallas on first round, 1983 (9th pick).

—COLLEGIATE RECORD—

Year	G.	Min.	FGA	FGM	Pct.	FTA	FTM	Pct.	Reb.	Pts.	Avg.
79-80	27	573	182	81	.445	40	31	.775	96	193	7.1
80-81	29	1057	360	215	.597	111	83	.748	185	513	17.7
81-82	30	1134	393	257	.654	152	121	.796	189	635	21.2
82-83	32	1179	464	279	.601	221	166	.751	209	724	22.6
Totals	118	4943	1399	832	.595	523	401	.767	679	2065	17.5

NBA REGULAR SEASON RECORD

Sea.—Team	G.	Min.	FGA	FGM	Pct.	FTA	FTM	Pct.	Off.	Def.	Tot.	Ast.	PF	Dq.	Stl.	Blk.	Pts.	Avg.
										—Rebounds—								
83-84—Dallas	67	1059	493	225	.456	121	87	.719	106	144	250	56	118	0	41	9	549	8.2
84-85—Dallas	72	1314	603	274	.454	104	77	.740	100	138	238	56	131	1	46	7	667	9.3
Totals	139	2373	1096	499	.455	225	164	.729	206	282	488	112	249	1	87	16	1216	8.7

Three-Point Field Goals: 1983-84, 12-for-29 (.414). 1984-85, 42-for-109 (.385). Totals, 54-for-138 (.391).

NBA PLAYOFF RECORD

Sea.—Team	G.	Min.	FGA	FGM	Pct.	FTA	FTM	Pct.	Off.	Def.	Tot.	Ast.	PF	Dq.	Stl.	Blk.	Pts.	Avg.
										—Rebounds—								
83-84—Dallas	8	178	80	26	.325	8	6	.750	19	23	42	4	17	0	10	2	59	7.4
84-85—Dallas	4	68	23	10	.435	2	1	.500	4	3	7	3	3	0	4	0	23	5.8
Totals	12	246	103	36	.350	10	7	.700	23	26	49	7	20	0	14	2	82	6.8

Three-Point Field Goals: 1983-84, 1-for-12 (.083). 1984-85, 2-for-5 (.400). Totals, 3-for-17 (.176).

Named to THE SPORTING NEWS All-America First Team, 1983.

CHRISTOPHER AARON ENGLER
(Chris)

Born March 1, 1959 at Stillwater, Minn.   Height 7:00.   Weight 248.

High School—Stillwater, Minn.

Colleges—University of Minnesota, Minneapolis, Minn., and
University of Wyoming, Laramie, Wyo.

Drafted by Golden State on third round, 1982 (60th pick).

Waived by Golden State, October 23, 1984; signed by New Jersey, December 22, 1984, to first of consecutive 10-day contracts that expired, January 12, 1985.
Signed by Chicago, January 14, 1985, to first of consecutive 10-day contracts that expired, February 4, 1985.
Signed by Los Angeles Clippers to a 10-day contract that expired, February 28, 1985.
Signed by Milwaukee as a free agent, April 2, 1985.
Played in Continental Basketball Association with Wyoming Wildcatters, 1984-85.

—COLLEGIATE RECORD—
Minnesota

Year	G.	Min.	FGA	FGM	Pct.	FTA	FTM	Pct.	Reb.	Pts.	Avg.
77-78	8	....	10	4	.400	1	0	.000	10	8	1.0
78-79	8	....	4	1	.250	0	0	.000	8	2	0.3
Minn. Totals	16	....	14	5	.357	1	0	.000	18	10	0.6

Wyoming

Year	G.	Min.	FGA	FGM	Pct.	FTA	FTM	Pct.	Reb.	Pts.	Avg.
79-80											
					Did Not Play—Transfer Student						

Year	G.	Min.	FGA	FGM	Pct.	FTA	FTM	Pct.	Reb.	Pts.	Avg.
80-81	30	649	190	97	.511	50	35	.700	158	229	7.6
81-82	30	877	251	144	.574	77	58	.753	192	346	11.5
Wyo. Totals............	60	1526	441	241	.546	127	93	.732	350	575	9.6
College Totals	76	....	455	246	.541	128	93	.727	368	585	7.7

MINOR LEAGUE REGULAR SEASON RECORD

Sea.—Team	G.	Min.	2-Point			3-Point			FTM	FTA	Pct.	Reb.	Ast.	Pts.	Avg.
			FGM	FGA	Pct.	FGM	FGA	Pct.							
84-85—Wyoming CBA...........	25	842	135	278	.485	0	1	.000	80	104	.769	221	34	350	14.0

NBA REGULAR SEASON RECORD

Sea.—Team	G.	Min.	FGA	FGM	Pct.	FTA	FTM	Pct.	Off.	Def.	Tot.	Ast.	PF	Dq.	Stl.	Blk.	Pts.	Avg.
82-83—Golden State	54	369	94	38	.404	16	5	.313	43	61	104	11	95	1	7	17	81	1.5
83-84—Golden State	46	360	83	33	.398	23	14	.609	27	70	97	11	68	0	9	3	80	1.7
84-85—N.J.-Chi.-Mil.	11	82	20	8	.400	9	5	.556	12	18	30	0	5	0	2	5	21	1.9
Totals	111	811	197	79	.401	48	24	.500	82	149	231	22	168	1	18	25	182	1.6

NBA PLAYOFF RECORD

Sea.—Team	G.	Min.	FGA	FGM	Pct.	FTA	FTM	Pct.	Off.	Def.	Tot.	Ast.	PF	Dq.	Stl.	Blk.	Pts.	Avg.
84-85—Milwaukee	1	6	1	1	1.000	0	0	.000	0	2	2	0	2	0	0	0	2	2.0

ALEXANDER ENGLISH
(Alex)

Born January 5, 1954 at Columbia, S. C.   Height 6:08.   Weight 190.

High School—Columbia, S. C., Dreher.

College—University of South Carolina, Columbia, S. C.

Drafted by Milwaukee on second round, 1976 (23rd pick).

Signed by Indiana as Veteran Free Agent, June 8, 1978; Milwaukee received a 1979 1st round draft choice as compensation, October 3, 1978.

Traded by Indiana with a 1980 1st round draft choice to Denver for George McGinnis, February 1, 1980.

—COLLEGIATE RECORD—

Year	G.	Min.	FGA	FGM	Pct.	FTA	FTM	Pct.	Reb.	Pts.	Avg.
72-73	29	1037	368	189	.514	70	44	.629	306	422	14.6
73-74	27	1007	395	209	.529	112	75	.670	237	493	18.3
74-75	28	1024	359	199	.554	77	49	.636	244	447	16.0
75-76	27	1045	468	258	.551	134	94	.701	277	610	22.6
Totals	111	4113	1590	855	.538	393	262	.667	1064	1972	17.8

NBA REGULAR SEASON RECORD

Sea.—Team	G.	Min.	FGA	FGM	Pct.	FTA	FTM	Pct.	Off.	Def.	Tot.	Ast.	PF	Dq.	Stl.	Blk.	Pts.	Avg.
76-77—Milwaukee	60	648	277	132	.477	60	46	.767	68	100	168	25	78	0	17	18	310	5.2
77-78—Milwaukee	82	1552	633	343	.542	143	104	.727	144	251	395	129	178	1	41	55	790	9.6
78-79—Indiana	81	2696	1102	563	.511	230	173	.752	253	402	655	271	214	3	70	78	1299	16.0
79-80—Ind.-Den.	78	2401	1113	553	.501	266	210	.789	269	336	605	224	206	0	73	62	1318	16.9
80-81—Denver	81	3093	1555	768	.494	459	390	.850	273	373	646	290	255	2	106	100	1929	23.8
81-82—Denver	82	3015	1553	855	.551	443	372	.840	210	348	558	433	261	2	87	120	2082	25.4
82-83—Denver	82	2988	1857	959	.516	490	406	.829	263	338	601	397	235	1	116	126	2326	28.4
83-84—Denver	82	2870	1714	907	.529	427	352	.824	216	248	464	406	252	3	83	95	2167	26.4
84-85—Denver	81	2924	1812	939	.518	462	383	.829	203	255	458	344	259	1	101	46	2262	27.9
Totals	709	22187	11616	6019	.518	2980	2436	.817	1899	2651	4550	2519	1938	13	694	700	14483	20.4

Three-Point Field Goals: 1979-80, 2-for-6 (.333). 1980-81, 3-for-5 (.600). 1981-82, 0-for-8. 1982-83, 2-for-12 (.167). 1983-84, 1-for-7 (.143). 1984-85, 1-for-5 (.200). Totals, 9-for-43 (.209).

NBA PLAYOFF RECORD

Sea.—Team	G.	Min.	FGA	FGM	Pct.	FTA	FTM	Pct.	Off.	Def.	Tot.	Ast.	PF	Dq.	Stl.	Blk.	Pts.	Avg.
77-78—Milwaukee	9	208	78	48	.615	32	25	.781	16	26	42	13	20	0	6	7	121	13.4
81-82—Denver	3	118	55	26	.473	7	6	.857	8	15	23	17	6	0	3	3	58	19.3
82-83—Denver	7	270	150	67	.447	53	47	.887	20	24	44	42	21	0	4	7	181	25.9
83-84—Denver	5	203	102	60	.588	28	25	.893	16	24	40	28	17	0	3	2	145	29.0
84-85—Denver	14	536	304	163	.536	109	97	.890	36	56	92	63	40	1	17	5	423	30.2
Totals	38	1335	689	364	.528	229	200	.873	96	145	241	163	104	1	33	24	928	24.4

Three-Point Field Goals: 1982-83, 0-for-2. 1983-84, 0-for-1. 1984-85, 0-for-1. Totals, 0-for-4.

ALEX ENGLISH

NBA ALL-STAR GAME RECORD

Season—Team	Min.	FGA	FGM	Pct.	FTA	FTM	Pct.	Off.	Def.	Tot.	Ast.	PF	Dq.	Stl.	Blk.	Pts.
								—Rebounds—								
1982—Denver	12	6	2	.333	0	0	.000	2	3	5	1	2	0	1	0	4
1983—Denver	23	14	7	.500	1	0	.000	2	2	4	0	2	0	1	2	14
1984—Denver	19	8	6	.750	1	1	1.000	0	0	0	2	2	0	1	1	13
1985—Denver	14	3	0	.000	0	0	.000	1	1	2	1	1	0	0	0	0
Totals	68	31	15	.484	2	1	.500	5	6	11	4	7	0	3	3	31

Named to All-NBA Second Team, 1982 and 1983. . . . Led NBA in scoring, 1983.

JULIUS WINFIELD ERVING II
(Dr. J)

Born February 22, 1950 at Roosevelt, N. Y.   Height 6:07.   Weight 205.

High School—Roosevelt, N. Y.

College—University of Massachusetts, Amherst, Mass.

Drafted by Milwaukee on first round, 1972 (12th pick).

Signed as an undergraduate free agent by Virginia ABA, April 6, 1971.

Traded by Virginia with Willie Sojourner to New York for George Carter, draft rights to Kermit Washington and cash, August 1, 1973.

Entered NBA with New York Nets, 1976.

Sold by Nets to Philadelphia, October 20, 1976.

—COLLEGIATE RECORD—

Year	G.	Min.	FGA	FGM	Pct.	FTA	FTM	Pct.	Reb.	Pts.	Avg.
68-69†	15	....	216	112	.519	81	49	.605	214	273	18.2
69-70	25	969	468	238	.509	230	167	.726	522	643	25.7
70-71	27	1029	609	286	.470	206	155	.752	527	727	26.9
Varsity Totals	52	1998	1077	524	.487	436	322	.739	1049	1370	26.3

ABA REGULAR SEASON RECORD

Sea.—Team	G.	Min.	FGM	FGA	Pct.	FGM	FGA	Pct.	FTM	FTA	Pct.	Reb.	Ast.	Pts.	Avg.
			—2-Point—			—3-Point—									
1971-72—Virginia	84	3513	907	1810	.501	3	16	.188	467	627	.745	1319	335	2290	27.3
1972-73—Virginia	71	2993	889	1780	.499	5	24	.208	475	612	.776	867	298	2268	31.9
1973-74—New York	84	3398	897	1742	.515	17	43	.395	454	593	.766	899	434	2299	27.4
1974-75—New York	84	3402	885	1719	.515	29	87	.333	486	608	.799	914	462	2343	27.9
1975-76—New York	84	3244	915	1770	.517	34	103	.330	530	662	.801	925	423	2462	29.3
Totals	407	16550	4493	8821	.509	88	273	.322	2412	3102	.778	4924	1952	11662	28.7

ABA PLAYOFF RECORD

Sea.—Team	G.	Min.	FGM	FGA	Pct.	FGM	FGA	Pct.	FTM	FTA	Pct.	Reb.	Ast.	Pts.	Avg.
			—2-Point—			—3-Point—									
71-72—Virginia	11	504	146	280	521	1	4	.250	71	85	.835	224	72	366	33.3
72-73—Virginia	5	219	59	109	.541	0	3	.000	30	40	.750	45	16	148	29.6
73-74—New York	14	579	156	294	.531	5	11	.455	63	85	.741	135	67	390	27.9
74-75—New York	5	211	55	113	.487	0	8	.000	27	32	.844	49	28	137	27.4
75-76—New York	13	551	156	286	.545	4	14	.286	127	158	.804	164	64	451	34.7
Totals	48	3577	572	1082	.529	10	40	.250	318	400	.795	617	247	1492	31.1

ABA ALL-STAR GAME RECORD

Sea.—Team	Min.	FGM	FGA	Pct.	FGM	FGA	Pct.	FTM	FTA	Pct.	Reb.	Ast.	Pts.	Avg.
		—2-Point—			—3-Point—									
1972—Virginia	25	9	15	.600	0	0	.000	2	2	1.000	6	3	20	20.0
1973—Virginia	30	8	16	.500	0	0	.000	6	8	.750	5	1	22	22.0
1974—New York	27	6	15	.400	0	0	.000	2	2	1.000	11	8	14	14.0
1975—New York	27	5	11	.455	1	1	1.000	8	10	.800	7	7	21	21.0
1976—New York	25	9	12	.750	0	1	.000	5	7	.714	7	5	23	23.0
Totals	134	37	69	.536	1	2	.500	23	29	.793	36	24	100	20.0

NBA REGULAR SEASON RECORD

Sea.—Team	G.	Min.	FGA	FGM	Pct.	FTA	FTM	Pct.	Off.	Def.	Tot.	Ast.	PF	Dq.	Stl.	Blk.	Pts.	Avg.
									—Rebounds—									
76-77—Philadelphia	82	2940	1373	685	.499	515	400	.777	192	503	695	306	251	1	159	113	1770	21.6
77-78—Philadelphia	74	2429	1217	611	.502	362	306	.845	179	302	481	279	207	0	135	97	1528	20.6
78-79—Philadelphia	78	2802	1455	715	.491	501	373	.745	198	366	564	357	207	0	133	100	1803	23.1
79-80—Philadelphia	78	2812	1614	838	.519	534	420	.787	215	361	576	355	208	0	170	140	2100	26.9
80-81—Philadelphia	82	2874	1524	794	.521	536	422	.787	244	413	657	364	233	0	173	147	2014	24.6
81-82—Philadelphia	81	2789	1428	780	.546	539	411	.763	220	337	557	319	229	1	161	141	1974	24.4
82-83—Philadelphia	72	2421	1170	605	.517	435	330	.759	173	318	491	263	202	1	112	131	1542	21.4
83-84—Philadelphia	77	2683	1324	678	.512	483	364	.754	190	342	532	309	217	3	141	139	1727	22.4
84-85—Philadelphia	78	2535	1236	610	.494	442	338	.765	172	242	414	233	199	0	135	109	1561	20.0
Totals	702	24285	12341	6316	.512	4347	3364	.774	1783	3184	4967	2785	1953	6	1319	1117	16019	22.8

Three-Point Field Goals: 1979-80, 4-for-20 (.200). 1980-81, 4-for-18 (.222). 1981-82, 3-for-11 (.273). 1982-83, 2-for-7 (.286). 1983-84, 7-for-21 (.333). 1984-85, 3-for-14 (.214). Totals, 23-for-91 (.253).

NBA PLAYOFF RECORD

Sea.—Team	G.	Min.	FGA	FGM	Pct.	FTA	FTM	Pct.	Off.	Def.	Tot.	Ast.	PF	Dq.	Stl.	Blk.	Pts.	Avg.
76-77—Philadelphia	19	758	390	204	.523	134	110	.821	41	81	122	85	45	0	41	23	518	27.3
77-78—Philadelphia	10	358	180	88	.489	56	42	.750	40	57	97	40	30	0	15	18	218	21.8
78-79—Philadelphia	9	372	172	89	.517	67	51	.761	29	41	70	53	22	0	18	17	229	25.4
79-80—Philadelphia	18	694	338	165	.488	136	108	.794	31	105	136	79	56	0	36	37	440	24.4
80-81—Philadelphia	16	592	301	143	.475	107	81	.757	52	62	114	54	54	0	22	41	367	22.9
81-82—Philadelphia	21	780	324	168	.519	165	124	.752	57	99	156	99	55	0	37	37	461	22.0
82-83—Philadelphia	13	493	211	95	.450	68	49	.721	32	67	99	44	42	1	15	27	239	18.4
83-84—Philadelphia	5	194	76	36	.474	22	19	.864	9	23	32	25	14	0	8	6	91	18.2
84-85—Philadelphia	13	434	187	84	.449	63	54	.857	29	44	73	48	34	0	25	11	222	17.1
Totals	124	4675	2179	1072	.492	818	638	.780	320	579	899	527	352	1	217	217	2785	22.5

Three-Point Field Goals: 1979-80, 2-for-9 (.222). 1980-81, 0-for-1. 1981-82, 1-for-6 (.167). 1982-83, 0-for-1. 1983-84, 0-for-1. 1984-85, 0-for-1. Totals, 3-for-19 (.158).

NBA ALL-STAR GAME RECORD

Season—Team	Min.	FGA	FGM	Pct.	FTA	FTM	Pct.	Off.	Def.	Tot.	Ast.	PF	Dq.	Stl.	Blk.	Pts.
1977—Philadelphia	30	20	12	.600	6	6	1.000	5	7	12	3	2	0	4	1	30
1978—Philadelphia	27	14	3	.214	12	10	.833	2	6	8	3	1	0	0	1	16
1979—Philadelphia	39	22	10	.455	12	9	.750	6	2	8	5	4	0	2	0	29
1980—Philadelphia	20	12	4	.333	4	3	.750	2	3	5	2	5	0	2	1	11
1981—Philadelphia	29	15	6	.400	7	6	.857	3	0	3	2	2	0	2	1	18
1982—Philadelphia	32	16	7	.438	4	2	.500	3	5	8	2	4	0	1	2	16
1983—Philadelphia	28	19	11	.579	3	3	1.000	3	3	6	3	1	0	1	2	25
1984—Philadelphia	36	22	14	.636	8	6	.750	4	4	8	5	4	0	2	2	34
1985—Philadelphia	23	15	5	.333	2	2	1.000	2	2	4	3	3	0	1	0	12
Totals	264	155	72	.465	58	47	.810	30	32	62	28	26	0	15	10	191

Named to NBA 35th Anniversary All-Time Team, 1980. . . . Named NBA Most Valuable Player, 1981. . . . Named to All-NBA First Team, 1978, 1980, 1981, 1982, 1983. . . . All-NBA Second Team, 1977 and 1984. . . . Member of NBA championship team, 1983. . . . NBA All-Star Game MVP, 1977 and 1983. . . . Holds NBA All-Star Game record for most free throws attempted in one quarter, 11, in 1978. . . . Shares NBA All-Star Game record for most free throws made in one quarter, 9, in 1978. . . . ABA Most Valuable Player, 1974 and 1976. . . . ABA co-MVP, 1975. . . . ABA All-Star First Team, 1973, 1974, 1975, 1976. . . . ABA All-Star Second Team, 1972. . . . ABA Playoff MVP, 1974 and 1976. . . . Member of ABA championship team, 1974 and 1976. . . . ABA All-Defensive Team, 1976. . . . ABA All-Rookie Team, 1972. . . . Led ABA in scoring, 1973, 1974, 1976. . . . One of only seven players to average over 20 points and 20 rebounds per game during NCAA career.

MIKE LEEROYALL EVANS

Born April 19, 1955 at Goldsboro, N. C.   Height 6:01.   Weight 170.

High School—Goldsboro, N. C.

Prep School—Laurinburg, N. C., Institute.

College—Kansas State University, Manhattan, Kan.

Drafted by Denver on first round, 1978 (21st pick).

Draft rights traded by Denver with Darnell Hillman to Kansas City for Ron Boone and a 1979 2nd round draft choice, June 26, 1978.
Waived by Kansas City, October 11, 1978; signed by San Antonio as a free agent, April 26, 1979.
Sold by San Antonio to Milwaukee, October 7, 1980.
Waived by Milwaukee, December 29, 1981; re-signed by Milwaukee, January 8, 1982.
Waived by Milwaukee, February 11, 1982; signed by Cleveland as a free agent, February 20, 1982.
Signed as Veteran Free Agent by San Diego, October 11, 1982.
Waived by San Diego, October 29, 1982; signed by Denver as a free agent, January 12, 1983.
Played in Western Basketball Association with Washington Lumberjacks, 1978-79.
Played in Continental Basketball Association with Montana Golden Nuggets, 1982-83.

—COLLEGIATE RECORD—

Year	G.	Min.	FGA	FGM	Pct.	FTA	FTM	Pct.	Reb.	Pts.	Avg.
74-75	29	....	446	213	.478	81	66	.815	103	492	17.0
75-76	28	....	425	216	.508	82	70	.854	94	502	17.9
76-77	31	....	468	227	.485	145	112	.772	110	566	18.3
77-78	29	....	471	234	.497	120	87	.725	86	555	19.1
Totals	117	....	1810	890	.492	428	335	.783	393	2115	18.1

MINOR LEAGUE REGULAR SEASON RECORD

			—2-Point—			—3-Point—									
Sea.—Team	G.	Min.	FGM	FGA	Pct.	FGM	FGA	Pct.	FTM	FTA	Pct.	Reb.	Ast.	Pts.	Avg.
78-79—Washington WBA.....	4	94	16	36	.444	0	0	....	0	0	....	6	4	32	8.0
82-83—Montana CBA............	16	504	109	201	.542	5	14	.357	42	50	.840	35	77	275	17.2

NBA REGULAR SEASON RECORD

									—Rebounds—									
Sea.—Team	G.	Min.	FGA	FGM	Pct.	FTA	FTM	Pct.	Off.	Def.	Tot.	Ast.	PF	Dq.	Stl.	Blk.	Pts.	Avg.
79-80—San Antonio	79	1246	464	208	.448	85	58	.682	29	78	107	230	194	2	60	9	486	6.2

Sea.—Team	G.	Min.	FGA	FGM	Pct.	FTA	FTM	Pct.	Off.	Def.	Tot.	Ast.	PF	Dq.	Stl.	Blk.	Pts.	Avg.
80-81—Milwaukee	71	911	291	134	.460	64	50	.781	22	65	87	167	114	0	34	4	320	4.5
81-82—Mil.-Clev.	22	270	86	35	.407	20	13	.650	5	17	22	42	36	1	13	0	83	3.8
82-83—Denver	42	695	243	115	.473	41	33	.805	4	54	58	113	94	3	23	3	263	6.3
83-84—Denver	78	1687	564	243	.431	131	111	.847	23	115	138	288	175	2	61	4	629	8.1
84-85—Denver	81	1437	661	323	.489	131	113	.863	26	93	119	231	174	2	65	12	816	10.1
Totals	373	6246	2309	1058	.458	472	378	.801	109	422	531	1071	787	10	256	32	2597	7.0

Three-Point Field Goals: 1979-80, 12-for-42 (.286). 1980-81, 2-for-14 (.143). 1981-82, 0-for-6. 1982-83, 0-for-9. 1983-84, 32-for-89 (.360). 1984-85, 57-for-157 (.363). Totals, 103-for-317 (.325).

NBA PLAYOFF RECORD

Sea.—Team	G.	Min.	FGA	FGM	Pct.	FTA	FTM	Pct.	Off.	Def.	Tot.	Ast.	PF	Dq.	Stl.	Blk.	Pts.	Avg.
79-80—San Antonio	2	12	8	3	.375	4	3	.750	0	2	2	2	2	0	0	0	11	5.5
80-81—Milwaukee	4	38	17	9	.529	8	7	.875	0	1	1	6	9	0	0	1	25	6.3
82-83—Denver	8	183	74	36	.486	17	11	.647	2	17	19	38	20	0	5	0	86	10.8
83-84—Denver	5	77	28	9	.321	4	4	1.000	1	2	3	12	13	0	0	0	23	4.6
84-85—Denver	15	281	143	62	.434	17	14	.824	3	29	32	46	39	0	13	3	155	10.3
Totals	34	591	270	119	.441	50	39	.780	6	51	57	104	83	0	18	4	300	8.8

Three-Point Field Goals: 1979-80, 2-for-4 (.500). 1980-81, 0-for-2. 1982-83, 3-for-10 (.300). 1983-84, 1-for-8 (.125). 1984-85, 17-for-51 (.333). Totals, 23-for-75 (.307).

KENNETH FIELDS
(Kenny)

Born February 9, 1962 at Iowa City, Iowa.   Height 6:07.   Weight 220.

High School—Los Angeles, Calif., Verbum Dei.

College—University of California at Los Angeles, Los Angeles, Calif.

Drafted by Milwaukee on first round, 1984 (21st pick).

—COLLEGIATE RECORD—

Year	G.	Min.	FGA	FGM	Pct.	FTA	FTM	Pct.	Reb.	Pts.	Avg.
80-81	25	588	185	110	.595	56	33	.589	122	253	10.1
81-82	27	867	286	158	.552	84	60	.714	160	376	13.9
82-83	29	998	405	224	.553	121	75	.620	192	523	18.0
83-84	28	943	384	194	.505	134	98	.731	193	486	17.4
Totals	109	3396	1260	686	.544	395	266	.673	667	1638	15.0

NBA REGULAR SEASON RECORD

Sea.—Team	G.	Min.	FGA	FGM	Pct.	FTA	FTM	Pct.	Off.	Def.	Tot.	Ast.	PF	Dq.	Stl.	Blk.	Pts.	Avg.
84-85—Milwaukee	51	535	191	84	.440	36	27	.750	41	43	84	38	84	2	9	10	195	3.8

VERN FLEMING

Born February 4, 1961 at New York, N.Y.   Height 6:05.   Weight 195.

High School—Long Island City, N. Y., Mater Christi.

College—University of Georgia, Athens, Ga.

Drafted by Indiana on first round, 1984 (18th pick).

—COLLEGIATE RECORD—

Year	G.	Min.	FGA	FGM	Pct.	FTA	FTM	Pct.	Reb.	Pts.	Avg.
80-81	30	1082	225	108	.480	122	85	.697	80	301	10.0
81-82	31	1079	236	117	.496	114	73	.640	120	307	9.9
82-83	34	1130	424	227	.535	169	121	.716	158	575	16.9
83-84	30	1030	493	248	.503	130	98	.754	120	594	19.8
Totals	125	4321	1378	700	.508	535	377	.705	478	1777	14.2

NBA REGULAR SEASON RECORD

Sea.—Team	G.	Min.	FGA	FGM	Pct.	FTA	FTM	Pct.	Off.	Def.	Tot.	Ast.	PF	Dq.	Stl.	Blk.	Pts.	Avg.
84-85—Indiana	80	2486	922	433	.470	339	260	.767	148	175	323	247	232	4	99	8	1126	14.1

Member of U.S. Olympic team, 1984.

—DID YOU KNOW—

That Sacramento's Otis Thorpe, not New York's Pat Ewing, is the all-time leading rebounder in the Big East Conference?

ERIC A. FLOYD
(Sleepy)

Born March 6, 1960 at Gastonia, N. C.   Height 6:03.   Weight 175.

High School—Gastonia, N. C., Hunter Huss.

College—Georgetown University, Washington, D. C.

Drafted by New Jersey on first round, 1982 (13th pick).

Traded by New Jersey with Mickey Johnson to Golden State for Micheal Ray Richardson, February 6, 1983.

—COLLEGIATE RECORD—

Year	G.	Min.	FGA	FGM	Pct.	FTA	FTM	Pct.	Reb.	Pts.	Avg.
78-79	29	975	388	177	.456	155	126	.813	119	480	16.6
79-80	32	1052	444	246	.554	140	106	.757	98	598	18.7
80-81	32	1115	508	237	.467	165	133	.806	133	607	19.0
81-82	37	1200	494	249	.504	168	121	.720	127	619	16.7
Totals	130	4342	1834	909	.496	628	486	.774	477	2304	17.7

NBA REGULAR SEASON RECORD

Sea.—Team	G.	Min.	FGA	FGM	Pct.	FTA	FTM	Pct.	Off.	Def.	Tot.	Ast.	PF	Dq.	Stl.	Blk.	Pts.	Avg.
82-83—N.J.-G.S.	76	1248	527	226	.429	180	150	.833	56	81	137	138	134	3	58	17	612	8.1
83-84—Golden State	77	2555	1045	484	.463	386	315	.816	87	184	271	269	216	0	103	31	1291	16.8
84-85—Golden State	82	2873	1372	610	.445	415	336	.810	62	140	202	406	226	1	134	41	1598	19.5
Totals	235	6676	2944	1320	.448	981	801	.817	205	405	610	813	576	4	295	89	3501	14.9

Three-Point Field Goals: 1982-83, 10-for-25 (.400). 1983-84, 8-for-45 (.178). 1984-85, 42-for-143 (.294). Totals, 60-for-213 (.282).

Named to THE SPORTING NEWS All-America Second Team, 1982.

PHIL JACKSON FORD

Born February 9, 1956 at Rocky Mount, N. C.   Height 6:02.   Weight 186.

High School—Rocky Mount, N. C.

College—University of North Carolina, Chapel Hill, N. C.

Drafted by Kansas City on first round, 1978 (2nd pick).

Traded by Kansas City to New Jersey for Ray Williams, June 29, 1982.

Traded by New Jersey with a 1983 2nd round draft choice to Milwaukee for Mickey Johnson and the rights to Fred Roberts, November 10, 1982.

Signed by Houston as Veteran Free Agent, October 5, 1983; Milwaukee waived its right of first refusal in exchange for a 1984 6th round draft choice and cash.

Waived by Houston, December 18, 1984.

—COLLEGIATE RECORD—

Year	G.	Min.	FGA	FGM	Pct.	FTA	FTM	Pct.	Reb.	Pts.	Avg.
74-75	31	....	370	191	.516	161	126	.783	85	508	16.4
75-76	29	....	387	206	.532	164	128	.780	51	540	18.6
76-77	33	....	431	230	.534	184	157	.853	63	617	18.7
77-78	30	....	452	238	.527	184	149	.810	62	625	20.8
Totals	123	....	1640	865	.527	693	560	.808	261	2290	18.6

NBA REGULAR SEASON RECORD

Sea.—Team	G.	Min.	FGA	FGM	Pct.	FTA	FTM	Pct.	Off.	Def.	Tot.	Ast.	PF	Dq.	Stl.	Blk.	Pts.	Avg.
78-79—Kansas City	79	2723	1004	467	.465	401	326	.813	33	149	182	681	245	3	174	6	1260	15.9
79-80—Kansas City	82	2621	1058	489	.462	423	346	.818	29	143	172	610	208	0	136	4	1328	16.2
80-81—Kansas City	66	2287	887	424	.478	354	294	.831	26	102	128	580	190	3	99	6	1153	17.5
81-82—Kansas City	72	1952	649	285	.439	166	136	.819	24	81	105	451	160	0	63	1	713	9.9
82-83—N.J.-Milw.	77	1610	445	213	.479	123	97	.789	18	85	103	290	190	2	52	3	524	6.8
83-84—Houston	81	2020	470	236	.502	117	98	.838	28	109	137	410	243	7	59	8	572	7.1
84-85—Houston	25	290	47	14	.298	18	16	.889	3	24	27	61	33	0	6	1	44	1.8
Totals	482	13503	4560	2128	.467	1602	1313	.820	161	693	854	3083	1269	15	589	29	5594	11.6

Three-Point Field Goals: 1979-80, 4-for-23 (.174). 1980-81, 11-for-36 (.306). 1981-82, 7-for-32 (.219). 1982-83, 1-for-9 (.111). 1983-84, 2-for-15 (.133). 1984-85, 0-for-4. Totals, 25-for-119 (.210).

NBA PLAYOFF RECORD

Sea.—Team	G.	Min.	FGA	FGM	Pct.	FTA	FTM	Pct.	Off.	Def.	Tot.	Ast.	PF	Dq.	Stl.	Blk.	Pts.	Avg.
78-79—Kansas City	5	143	57	15	.263	16	9	.563	2	10	12	29	14	0	12	0	39	7.8
79-80—Kansas City	3	110	43	20	.465	11	9	.818	0	6	6	26	6	0	5	0	52	17.3
80-81—Kansas City	5	158	35	15	.429	13	9	.692	1	7	8	29	9	0	5	0	39	7.8
82-83—Milwaukee	2	5	2	0	.000	6	6	1.000	0	0	0	1	1	0	0	0	6	3.0
Totals	15	416	137	50	.365	46	33	.717	3	23	26	85	30	0	22	0	136	9.1

Three-Point Field Goals: 1979-80, 3-for-4 (.750). 1980-81, 0-for-1. Totals, 3-for-5 (.600).

Named to All-NBA Second Team, 1979. . . . NBA Rookie of the Year, 1979. . . . NBA All-Rookie Team, 1979. . . . THE SPORTING NEWS College Player of the Year, 1978. . . . THE SPORTING NEWS All-America First Team, 1976 and 1978. . . . THE SPORTING NEWS All-America Second Team, 1977. . . . Member of U. S. Olympic team, 1976.

RODERICK ALLEN FOSTER
(Rod)

Born October 10, 1960 at Birmingham, Ala.   Height 6:01.   Weight 160.

High School—New Britain, Conn., Aquinas.

College—University of California at Los Angeles, Los Angeles, Calif.

Drafted by Phoenix on second round, 1983 (28th pick).

—COLLEGIATE RECORD—

Year	G.	Min.	FGA	FGM	Pct.	FTA	FTM	Pct.	Reb.	Pts.	Avg.
79-80	32	839	263	144	.548	95	80	.842	59	368	11.5
80-81	25	664	244	124	.508	66	60	.909	41	308	12.3
81-82	27	577	199	92	.462	100	95	.950	39	279	10.3
82-83	29	835	310	168	.542	90	74	.822	52	410	14.1
Totals	113	2915	1016	528	.520	351	309	.880	191	1365	12.1

NBA REGULAR SEASON RECORD

Sea.—Team	G.	Min.	FGA	FGM	Pct.	FTA	FTM	Pct.	Off.	Def.	Tot.	Ast.	PF	Dq.	Stl.	Blk.	Pts.	Avg.
83-84—Phoenix	80	1424	580	260	.448	155	122	.787	39	81	120	172	193	0	54	9	664	8.3
84-85—Phoenix	79	1318	636	286	.450	110	83	.755	27	53	80	186	171	1	61	0	696	8.8
Totals	159	2742	1216	546	.449	265	205	.774	66	134	200	358	364	1	115	9	1360	8.6

Three-Point Field Goals: 1983-84, 22-for-84 (.262). 1984-85, 41-for-126 (.325). Totals, 63-for-210 (.300).

NBA PLAYOFF RECORD

Sea.—Team	G.	Min.	FGA	FGM	Pct.	FTA	FTM	Pct.	Off.	Def.	Tot.	Ast.	PF	Dq.	Stl.	Blk.	Pts.	Avg.
83-84—Phoenix	16	128	39	10	.256	9	9	1.000	6	7	13	18	21	0	5	1	29	1.8
84-85—Phoenix	3	56	25	7	.280	8	6	.750	0	3	3	7	4	0	5	0	20	6.7
Totals	19	184	64	17	.266	17	15	.882	6	10	16	25	25	0	10	1	49	2.6

Three-Point Field Goals: 1983-84, 0-for-5. 1984-85, 0-for-4. Totals, 0-for-9.

Holds NCAA Division I record for free-throw percentage in a season, 1982.

WORLD B. FREE
(Formerly known as Lloyd Free.)

Born December 9, 1953 at Atlanta, Ga.   Height 6:02.   Weight 185.

High School—Brooklyn, N. Y., Canarsie.

College—Guilford College, Greensboro, N. C.

Drafted by Philadelphia on second round as hardship case, 1975 (23rd pick).

Traded by Philadelphia to San Diego for a 1984 1st round draft choice, October 12, 1978.
Traded by San Diego to Golden State for Phil Smith and a 1984 1st round draft choice, August 28, 1980.
Traded by Golden State to Cleveland for Ron Brewer, December 15, 1982.

—COLLEGIATE RECORD—

Year	G.	Min.	FGA	FGM	Pct.	FTA	FTM	Pct.	Reb.	Pts.	Avg.
72-73	33	....	572	272	.476	217	153	.705	191	697	21.1
73-74	24	....	456	216	.474	225	165	.733	200	597	24.9
74-75	28	....	486	247	.508	291	218	.749	163	712	25.4
Totals	85	....	1514	735	.485	733	536	.731	554	2006	23.6

NBA REGULAR SEASON RECORD

Sea.—Team	G.	Min.	FGA	FGM	Pct.	FTA	FTM	Pct.	Off.	Def.	Tot.	Ast.	PF	Dq.	Stl.	Blk.	Pts.	Avg.
75-76—Philadelphia	71	1121	533	239	.448	186	112	.602	64	61	125	104	107	0	37	6	590	8.3
76-77—Philadelphia	78	2253	1022	467	.457	464	334	.720	97	140	237	266	207	2	75	25	1268	16.3
77-78—Philadelphia	76	2050	857	390	.455	562	411	.731	92	120	212	306	199	0	68	41	1191	15.7
78-79—San Diego	78	2954	1653	795	.481	865	654	.756	127	174	301	340	253	8	111	35	2244	28.8
79-80—San Diego	68	2585	1556	737	.474	760	572	.753	129	109	238	283	195	0	81	32	2055	30.2
80-81—Golden State	65	2370	1157	516	.446	649	528	.814	48	111	159	361	183	1	85	11	1565	24.1
81-82—Golden State	78	2796	1452	650	.448	647	479	.740	118	130	248	419	222	1	71	8	1789	22.9
82-83—G.S.-Clev.	73	2638	1423	649	.456	583	430	.738	92	109	201	290	241	4	97	15	1743	23.4

WORLD B. FREE

Sea.—Team	G.	Min.	FGA	FGM	Pct.	FTA	FTM	Pct.	Off.	Def.	Tot.	Ast.	PF	Dq.	Stl.	Blk.	Pts.	Avg.
											—Rebounds—							
83-84—Cleveland	75	2375	1407	626	.445	504	395	.784	89	128	217	226	214	2	94	8	1669	22.3
84-85—Cleveland	71	2249	1328	609	.459	411	308	.749	61	150	211	320	163	0	75	16	1597	22.5
Totals	733	23391	12388	5678	.458	5631	4223	.750	917	1232	2149	2915	1984	18	794	197	15711	21.4

Three-Point Field Goals: 1979-80, 9-for-25 (.360). 1980-81, 5-for-31 (.161). 1981-82, 10-for-56 (.179). 1982-83, 15-for-45 (.333). 1983-84, 22-for-69 (.319). 1984-85, 71-for-193 (.368). Totals, 132-for-419 (.315).

NBA PLAYOFF RECORD

Sea.—Team	G.	Min.	FGA	FGM	Pct.	FTA	FTM	Pct.	Off.	Def.	Tot.	Ast.	PF	Dq.	Stl.	Blk.	Pts.	Avg.
											—Rebounds—							
75-76—Philadelphia	3	62	28	11	.393	13	10	.769	1	0	1	5	6	0	3	0	32	10.7
76-77—Philadelphia	15	281	170	63	.371	77	53	.688	10	22	32	29	33	0	12	8	179	11.9
77-78—Philadelphia	10	268	124	51	.411	81	59	.728	10	21	31	37	26	0	4	6	161	16.1
84-85—Cleveland	4	150	93	41	.441	25	23	.920	4	6	10	31	12	0	6	0	105	26.3
Totals..............	32	761	415	166	.400	196	145	.740	25	49	74	102	77	0	25	14	477	14.9

Three-Point Field Goals: 1984-85, 0-for-4.

NBA ALL-STAR GAME RECORD

Season—Team	Min.	FGA	FGM	Pct.	FTA	FTM	Pct.	Off.	Def.	Tot.	Ast.	PF	Dq.	Stl.	Blk.	Pts.
									—Rebounds—							
1980—San Diego	21	13	7	.538	1	0	.000	1	2	3	5	1	0	0	1	14

Named to All-NBA Second Team, 1979. . . . Most Valuable Player in NAIA tournament, 1973. . . . Member of NAIA championship team, 1973.

BILL PATRICK GARNETT

Born April 22, 1960 at Kansas City, Mo.   Height 6:09.   Weight 225.

High School—Denver, Colo., Regis.

College—University of Wyoming, Laramie, Wyo.

Drafted by Dallas on first round, 1982 (4th pick).

Traded by Dallas with Terence Stansbury to Indiana for a future 1st round draft choice, October 22, 1984.

—COLLEGIATE RECORD—

Year	G.	Min.	FGA	FGM	Pct.	FTA	FTM	Pct.	Reb.	Pts.	Avg.
78-79	27	818	162	86	.531	116	79	.681	183	251	9.3
79-80	28	992	268	144	.537	113	88	.779	212	376	13.4
80-81	30	1051	306	154	.503	142	115	.810	203	423	14.1
81-82	30	1093	312	190	.609	208	164	.788	242	544	18.1
Totals	115	3954	1048	574	.548	579	446	.770	840	1594	13.9

NBA REGULAR SEASON RECORD

Sea.—Team	G.	Min.	FGA	FGM	Pct.	FTA	FTM	Pct.	Off.	Def.	Tot.	Ast.	PF	Dq.	Stl.	Blk.	Pts.	Avg.
											—Rebounds—							
82-83—Dallas	75	1411	319	141	.533	174	129	.741	141	265	406	103	245	3	48	70	469	6.3
83-84—Dallas	80	1529	299	141	.472	176	129	.733	123	208	331	128	217	4	44	66	411	5.1
84-85—Indiana	65	1123	310	149	.481	174	120	.690	98	188	286	67	196	3	28	15	418	6.4
Totals	220	4063	928	460	.496	524	378	.721	362	661	1023	298	658	10	120	151	1298	5.9

Three-Point Field Goals: 1982-83, 0-for-3. 1983-84, 0-for-2. 1984-85, 0-for-2. Totals, 0-for-7.

NBA PLAYOFF RECORD

Sea.—Team	G.	Min.	FGA	FGM	Pct.	FTA	FTM	Pct.	Off.	Def.	Tot.	Ast.	PF	Dq.	Stl.	Blk.	Pts.	Avg.
											—Rebounds—							
83-84—Dallas	8	74	30	15	.500	8	7	.875	10	12	22	4	10	0	0	2	38	4.8

Three-Point Field Goals: 1983-84, 1-for-1 (1.000).

Named to THE SPORTING NEWS All-America Second Team, 1982.

GEORGE GERVIN

Born April 27, 1952 at Detroit, Mich.   Height 6:07.   Weight 185.

High School—Detroit, Mich., Martin Luther King.

Colleges—Long Beach State, Long Beach, Calif., and

Eastern Michigan University, Ypsilanti, Mich.

Drafted by Phoenix on third round, 1974 (40th pick).

Selected as an undergraduate by Virginia on first round of ABA special circumstance draft, 1973.

Sold by Virginia to San Antonio, January 30, 1974.

Entered NBA with San Antonio, 1976.

Played in Continental Basketball Association with the Pontiac Capparells during 1972-73 season (averaged 37.4 points per game).

—COLLEGIATE RECORD—
Long Beach State

Year	G.	Min.	FGA	FGM	Pct.	FTA	FTM	Pct.	Reb.	Pts.	Avg.
69-70					Dropped out of school prior to basketball season.						

Eastern Michigan

Year	G.	Min.	FGA	FGM	Pct.	FTA	FTM	Pct.	Reb.	Pts.	Avg.
70-71	9	300	123	65	.528	39	28	.718	104	158	17.6
71-72	30	1098	571	339	.594	265	208	.785	458	886	29.5
Totals	39	1398	694	404	.582	304	236	.776	562	1044	26.8

ABA REGULAR SEASON RECORD

Sea.—Team	G.	Min.	2-Point			3-Point			FTM	FTA	Pct.	Reb.	Ast.	Pts.	Avg.
			FGM	FGA	Pct.	FGM	FGA	Pct.							
72-73—Virginia	30	689	155	315	.492	6	26	.231	96	118	.814	128	34	424	14.1
73-74—Va.-S.A.	74	2511	664	1370	.485	8	56	.143	378	464	.815	624	142	1730	23.4
74-75—San Antonio	84	3113	767	1600	.479	17	55	.309	380	458	.830	697	207	1965	23.4
75-76—San Antonio	81	2748	692	1359	.509	14	55	.255	342	399	.857	546	201	1768	21.8
Totals	269	9061	2278	4644	.491	45	192	.234	1196	1439	.831	1977	584	5887	21.9

ABA PLAYOFF RECORD

Sea.—Team	G.	Min.	2-Point			3-Point			FTM	FTA	Pct.	Reb.	Ast.	Pts.	Avg.
			FGM	FGA	Pct.	FGM	FGA	Pct.							
72-73—Virginia	5	200	33	72	.458	1	5	.200	23	34	.676	38	8	93	18.6
73-74—San Antonio	7	226	56	114	.491	1	1	1.000	29	31	.935	52	19	144	20.6
74-75—San Antonio	6	276	76	159	.478	3	12	.250	43	52	.827	84	8	204	34.0
75-76—San Antonio	7	288	67	125	.536	0	3	.000	56	69	.812	64	19	190	27.1
Totals	25	990	232	470	.494	5	21	.238	151	186	.812	238	54	631	25.2

ABA ALL-STAR GAME RECORD

Sea.—Team	Min.	2-Point			3-Point			FTM	FTA	Pct.	Reb.	Ast.	Pts.	Avg.
		FGM	FGA	Pct.	FGM	FGA	Pct.							
1974—Virginia	21	3	8	.375	0	1	.000	3	4	.750	5	3	9	9.0
1975—San Antonio	30	8	14	.571	0	1	.000	7	8	.875	6	3	23	23.0
1976—San Antonio	16	3	13	.231	0	0	.000	1	2	.500	6	1	8	8.0
Totals	67	14	35	.400	0	2	.000	11	14	.786	17	7	40	13.3

NBA REGULAR SEASON RECORD

Sea.—Team	G.	Min.	FGA	FGM	Pct.	FTA	FTM	Pct.	Rebounds			Ast.	PF	Dq.	Stl.	Blk.	Pts.	Avg.
									Off.	Def.	Tot.							
76-77—San Antonio	82	2705	1335	726	.544	532	443	.833	134	320	454	238	286	12	105	104	1895	23.1
77-78—San Antonio	82	2857	1611	864	.536	607	504	.830	118	302	420	302	255	3	136	110	2232	27.2
78-79—San Antonio	80	2888	1749	947	.541	570	471	.826	142	258	400	219	275	5	137	91	2365	29.6
79-80—San Antonio	78	2934	1940	1024	.528	593	505	.852	154	249	403	202	208	0	110	79	2585	33.1
80-81—San Antonio	82	2765	1729	850	.492	620	512	.826	126	293	419	260	212	4	56	42	2221	27.1
81-82—San Antonio	79	2817	1987	993	.500	642	555	.864	138	254	392	187	215	2	77	45	2551	32.3
82-83—San Antonio	78	2830	1553	757	.487	606	517	.853	111	246	357	264	243	5	88	67	2043	26.2
83-84—San Antonio	76	2584	1561	765	.490	507	427	.842	106	207	313	220	219	3	79	47	1967	25.9
84-85—San Antonio	72	2091	1182	600	.508	384	324	.844	79	155	234	178	208	2	66	48	1524	21.2
Totals	709	24471	14647	7526	.514	5061	4258	.841	1108	2284	3392	2070	2121	36	892	647	19383	27.3

Three-Point Field Goals: 1979-80, 32-for-102 (.314). 1980-81, 9-for-35 (.257). 1981-82, 10-for-36 (.278). 1982-83, 12-for-33 (.364). 1983-84, 10-for-24 (.417). 1984-85, 0-for-10. Totals, 73-for-240 (.304).

NBA PLAYOFF RECORD

Sea.—Team	G.	Min.	FGA	FGM	Pct.	FTA	FTM	Pct.	Rebounds			Ast.	PF	Dq.	Stl.	Blk.	Pts.	Avg.
									Off.	Def.	Tot.							
76-77—San Antonio	2	62	44	19	.432	15	12	.800	5	6	11	3	9	1	1	2	50	25.0
77-78—San Antonio	6	227	142	78	.549	56	43	.768	11	23	34	19	23	0	6	16	199	33.2
78-79—San Antonio	14	513	295	158	.536	104	84	.808	33	49	82	35	51	1	27	14	400	28.6
79-80—San Antonio	3	122	74	37	.500	30	26	.867	9	11	20	12	8	0	5	3	100	33.3
80-81—San Antonio	7	274	154	77	.500	45	36	.800	9	26	35	24	19	1	5	5	190	27.1
81-82—San Antonio	9	373	228	103	.452	71	59	.831	19	47	66	41	36	1	10	4	265	29.4
82-83—San Antonio	11	437	208	108	.519	69	61	.884	21	53	74	37	39	1	12	4	277	25.2
84-85—San Antonio	5	183	79	42	.532	34	27	.794	3	15	18	14	19	0	3	3	111	22.2
Totals	57	2191	1224	622	.508	424	348	.821	110	230	340	185	204	5	69	51	1592	27.9

Three-Point Field Goals: 1979-80, 0-for-2. 1980-81, 0-for-3. 1981-82, 0-for-3. 1982-83, 0-for-2. 1984-85, 0-for-3. Totals, 0-for-13.

NBA ALL-STAR GAME RECORD

Season—Team	Min.	FGA	FGM	Pct.	FTA	FTM	Pct.	Rebounds			Ast.	PF	Dq.	Stl.	Blk.	Pts.
								Off.	Def.	Tot.						
1977—San Antonio	12	6	0	.000	0	0	.000	0	1	1	0	1	0	0	1	0
1978—San Antonio	18	11	4	.364	3	1	.333	1	1	2	1	2	0	2	1	9
1979—San Antonio	34	16	8	.500	11	10	.909	2	4	6	2	4	0	1	1	26
1980—San Antonio	40	26	14	.538	9	6	.667	4	6	10	3	2	0	3	0	34
1981—San Antonio	24	9	5	.556	2	1	.500	1	2	3	0	3	0	2	1	11
1982—San Antonio	27	14	5	.357	2	2	1.000	1	5	6	1	3	0	3	3	12
1983—San Antonio	14	8	3	.375	2	2	1.000	0	0	0	3	3	0	2	0	9
1984—San Antonio	21	6	5	.833	3	3	1.000	0	2	2	1	5	0	0	1	13

Season—Team	Min.	FGA	FGM	Pct.	FTA	FTM	Pct.	Off.	Def.	Tot.	Ast.	PF	Dq.	Stl.	Blk.	Pts.
1985—San Antonio..	25	12	10	.833	4	3	.750	0	3	3	1	2	0	3	1	23
Totals	215	108	54	.500	36	28	.778	9	24	33	12	25	0	16	9	137

Three-Point Field Goals: 1983, 0-for-1.

Named to All-NBA First Team, 1978, 1979, 1980, 1981, 1982 .... All-NBA Second Team, 1977 and 1983.... NBA All-Star Game MVP, 1980.... Holds NBA record for most points in one quarter, 33, against New Orleans, April 9, 1978.... Led NBA in scoring, 1978, 1979, 1980, 1982.... One of only two players in NBA history to win four scoring titles.... Named to ABA All-Star Second Team, 1975 and 1976.... Brother of Derrick Gervin, 4th-round draft choice of Philadelphia 76ers in 1985 NBA draft.

MICHAEL JEROME GIBSON
(Mike)

Born October 27, 1960 at Williamsburg County, S. C. Height 6:10. Weight 205.

High School—Hemingway, S. C.

College—University of South Carolina at Spartanburg,
Spartanburg, S. C.

Drafted by Washington on second round, 1982 (44th pick).

Traded by Washington with Rick Mahorn to Detroit for Dan Roundfield, June 17, 1985.
Played in Italy during 1984-85 season.
Played briefly in Philippines during 1982-83 season.
Played in Continental Basketball Association with Maine Lumberjacks and Rochester Zeniths, 1982-83.

—COLLEGIATE RECORD—

Year	G.	Min.	FGA	FGM	Pct.	FTA	FTM	Pct.	Reb.	Pts.	Avg.
78-79	25	....	141	71	.504	33	23	.697	80	165	6.6
79-80	29	....	395	207	.524	58	35	.603	256	449	15.5
80-81	34	....	472	260	.551	89	66	.742	299	586	17.2
81-82	32	....	382	220	.576	105	82	.781	295	522	16.3
Totals	120	....	1390	758	.545	285	206	.723	930	1722	14.4

MINOR LEAGUE REGULAR SEASON RECORD

Sea.—Team	G.	Min.	2-Point FGM	FGA	Pct.	3-Point FGM	FGA	Pct.	FTM	FTA	Pct.	Reb.	Ast.	Pts.	Avg.
82-83—Maine-Roch. CBA.....	43	1234	222	441	.503	0	1	.000	84	105	.800	382	52	528	12.3

NBA REGULAR SEASON RECORD

Sea.—Team	G.	Min.	FGA	FGM	Pct.	FTA	FTM	Pct.	Off.	Def.	Tot.	Ast.	PF	Dq.	Stl.	Blk.	Pts.	Avg.
83-84—Washington	32	229	55	21	.382	17	11	.647	29	37	66	9	30	1	5	7	53	1.7

Member of NAIA championship team, 1982.

ARTIS GILMORE

Born September 21, 1949 at Chipley, Fla. Height 7:02. Weight 255.

High Schools—Chipley, Fla., Roulhac and Dothan, Ala., Carver (Senior).

Colleges—Gardner-Webb Junior College, Boiling Springs, N.C., and
Jacksonville University, Jacksonville, Fla.

Drafted by Chicago on seventh round, 1971 (117th pick).

Selected by Kentucky on first round of ABA draft, 1971.
Selected by Chicago NBA from Kentucky for $1,100,000 in ABA dispersal draft, August 5, 1976.
Traded by Chicago to San Antonio for Dave Corzine, Mark Olberding and cash, July 22, 1982.

—COLLEGIATE RECORD—
Gardner Webb JC

Year	G.	Min.	FGA	FGM	Pct.	FTA	FTM	Pct.	Reb.	Pts.	Avg.
67-68	31	....	...	296	....	...	121	....	....	713	23.0
68-69	36	....	...	326	....	...	140	....	....	792	22.0
JC Totals.................	67	....	....	622	....	....	261	....	....	1505	22.5

Jacksonville

Year	G.	Min.	FGA	FGM	Pct.	FTA	FTM	Pct.	Reb.	Pts.	Avg.
69-70	28	....	529	307	.580	202	128	.634	621	742	26.5
70-71	26	....	405	229	.565	188	112	.596	603	570	21.9
Totals	54	....	934	536	.574	390	240	.615	1224	1312	24.3

ABA REGULAR SEASON RECORD

Sea.—Team	G.	Min.	2-Point FGM	FGA	Pct.	3-Point FGM	FGA	Pct.	FTM	FTA	Pct.	Reb.	Ast.	Pts.	Avg.
71-72—Kentucky	84	3666	806	1348	.598	0	0	.000	391	605	.646	1491	230	2003	23.8
72-73—Kentucky	84	3502	686	1226	.560	1	2	.500	368	572	.643	1476	295	1743	20.9
73-74—Kentucky	84	3502	621	1257	.494	0	3	.000	326	489	.667	1538	329	1568	18.7
74-75—Kentucky	84	3493	783	1349	.580	1	2	.500	412	592	.696	1361	208	1081	23.6
75-76—Kentucky	84	3286	773	1401	.552	0	0	.000	521	764	.682	1303	211	2067	24.6
Totals	420	17449	3669	6581	.558	2	7	.286	2018	3022	.668	7169	1273	9362	22.3

ABA PLAYOFF RECORD

Sea.—Team	G.	Min.	2-Point FGM	FGA	Pct.	3-Point FGM	FGA	Pct.	FTM	FTA	Pct.	Reb.	Ast.	Pts.	Avg.
71-72—Kentucky	6	285	52	90	.577	0	0	.000	27	38	.711	106	25	131	21.8
72-73—Kentucky	19	780	142	261	.544	0	0	.000	77	123	.626	260	75	361	19.0
73-74—Kentucky	8	344	71	127	.559	0	0	.000	38	66	.576	149	28	180	22.5
74-75—Kentucky	15	679	132	245	.539	0	0	.000	98	127	.772	264	38	362	24.1
75-76—Kentucky	10	390	93	153	.608	0	0	.000	56	75	.747	152	19	242	24.2
Totals	58	2478	500	876	.571	0	0	.000	296	429	.690	931	185	1280	22.1

ABA ALL-STAR GAME RECORD

Sea.—Team	Min.	2-Point FGM	FGA	Pct.	3-Point FGM	FGA	Pct.	FTM	FTA	Pct.	Reb.	Ast.	Pts.	Avg.
1972—Kentucky	27	4	5	.800	0	0	.000	6	10	.600	10	2	14	14.0
1973—Kentucky	31	3	8	.375	0	0	.000	4	8	.500	16	0	10	10.0
1974—Kentucky	27	8	12	.667	0	0	.000	2	3	.667	13	1	18	18.0
1975—Kentucky	28	4	8	.500	0	0	.000	3	7	.429	13	2	11	11.0
1976—Kentucky	27	5	7	.714	0	0	.000	6	7	.857	7	1	14	14.0
Totals	140	24	40	.600	0	0	.000	21	35	.600	59	6	67	13.4

NBA REGULAR SEASON RECORD

Sea.—Team	G.	Min.	FGA	FGM	Pct.	FTA	FTM	Pct.	Rebounds Off.	Def.	Tot.	Ast.	PF	Dq.	Stl.	Blk.	Pts.	Avg.
76-77—Chicago	82	2877	1091	570	.522	586	387	.660	313	757	1070	199	266	4	44	203	1527	18.6
77-78—Chicago	82	3067	1260	704	.559	669	471	.704	318	753	1071	263	261	4	42	181	1879	22.9
78-79—Chicago	82	3265	1310	753	.575	587	434	.739	293	750	1043	274	280	2	50	156	1940	23.7
79-80—Chicago	48	1568	513	305	.595	344	245	.712	108	324	432	133	167	5	29	59	855	17.8
80-81—Chicago	82	2832	816	547	.670	532	375	.705	220	608	828	172	295	2	47	198	1469	17.9
81-82—Chicago	82	2796	837	546	.652	552	424	.768	224	611	835	136	287	4	49	220	1517	18.5
82-83—San Antonio	82	2797	888	556	.626	496	367	.740	299	685	984	126	273	4	40	192	1479	18.0
83-84—San Antonio	64	2034	556	351	.631	390	280	.718	213	449	662	70	229	4	36	132	982	15.3
84-85—San Antonio	81	2756	854	532	.623	646	484	.749	231	615	846	131	306	4	40	173	1548	19.1
Totals	685	23992	8125	4864	.599	4802	3467	.722	2219	5552	7771	1504	2364	33	377	1514	13196	19.3

Three-Point Field Goals: 1981-82, 1-for-1. 1982-83, 0-for-6. 1983-84, 0-for-3. 1984-85, 0-for-2. Totals, 1-for-12 (.083).

NBA PLAYOFF RECORD

Sea.—Team	G.	Min.	FGA	FGM	Pct.	FTA	FTM	Pct.	Rebounds Off.	Def.	Tot.	Ast.	PF	Dq.	Stl.	Blk.	Pts.	Avg.
76-77—Chicago	3	126	40	19	.475	23	18	.783	15	24	39	6	9	0	3	8	56	18.7
80-81—Chicago	6	247	60	35	.583	55	38	.691	24	43	67	12	15	0	6	17	108	18.0
82-83—San Antonio	11	401	132	76	.576	46	32	.696	37	105	142	18	46	1	9	34	184	16.7
84-85—San Antonio	5	185	52	29	.558	45	31	.689	10	40	50	7	18	0	2	7	89	17.8
Totals	25	959	284	159	.560	169	119	.704	86	212	298	43	88	1	20	66	437	17.5

NBA ALL-STAR GAME RECORD

Season—Team	Min.	FGA	FGM	Pct.	FTA	FTM	Pct.	Rebounds Off.	Def.	Tot.	Ast.	PF	Dq.	Stl.	Blk.	Pts.
1978—Chicago	13	4	2	.500	8	6	.750	0	2	2	0	1	0	1	2	10
1979—Chicago	15	4	3	.750	2	2	1.000	1	0	1	2	1	0	0	0	8
1981—Chicago	22	7	5	.714	2	1	.500	1	5	6	2	4	0	0	1	11
1982—Chicago	16	6	3	.500	1	1	1.000	1	2	3	2	4	0	0	1	7
1983—San Antonio	16	4	2	.500	2	1	.500	1	4	5	1	4	0	1	0	5
Totals	82	25	15	.600	15	11	.733	4	13	17	7	14	0	2	4	41

Named to NBA All-Defensive Second Team, 1978.... NBA all-time field-goal percentage leader.... Led NBA in field-goal percentage, 1981, 1982, 1983, 1984.... ABA All-Star First Team, 1972, 1973, 1974, 1975, 1976.... ABA Most Valuable Player and Rookie of the Year, 1972.... ABA All-Rookie Team, 1972.... ABA All-Defensive Team, 1973, 1974, 1975, 1976.... ABA All-Star Game MVP, 1974.... ABA Playoff MVP, 1975.... Member of ABA championship team, 1975.... Led ABA in rebounding, 1972, 1973, 1974, 1976.... Led ABA in field-goal percentage, 1972 and 1973.... Led ABA in blocked shots, 1973.... Named to THE SPORTING NEWS All-America First Team, 1971.... THE SPORTING NEWS All-America Second Team, 1970.... NCAA career leading rebounding average, 22.7.... Led NCAA in rebounding, 1970 and 1971.... One of only seven players to average over 20 points and 20 rebounds per game during NCAA career.

—DID YOU KNOW—

That former NBA star Zelmo Beaty was the last coach of the ill-fated Virginia Squires in the defunct American Basketball Association?

MIKE THEODORE GLENN

Born September 10, 1955 at Rome, Ga.   Height 6:03.   Weight 185.

High School—Rome, Ga., Coosa.

College—Southern Illinois University, Carbondale, Ill.

Drafted by Chicago on second round, 1977 (23rd pick).

Waived by Chicago, December 8, 1977; signed by Buffalo as a free agent, December 14, 1977.
Signed by New York as Veteran Free Agent, June 12, 1978.
Signed by Atlanta as a Veteran Free Agent, October 12, 1981. New York agreed not to exercise its right of first refusal in exchange for a 1982 2nd round draft choice.

—COLLEGIATE RECORD—

Year	G.	Min.	FGA	FGM	Pct.	FTA	FTM	Pct.	Reb.	Pts.	Avg.
73-74	25	....	339	182	.537	25	18	.720	49	382	15.3
74-75	27	....	321	196	.611	56	48	.857	82	440	16.3
75-76	23	696	359	199	.554	54	49	.907	51	447	19.4
76-77	29	1009	478	278	.582	57	53	.930	82	609	21.0
Totals	104	....	1497	855	.571	192	168	.875	264	1878	18.1

NBA REGULAR SEASON RECORD

Sea.—Team	G.	Min.	FGA	FGM	Pct.	FTA	FTM	Pct.	Off.	Def.	Tot.	Ast.	PF	Dq.	Stl.	Blk.	Pts.	Avg.
77-78—Buffalo	56	947	370	195	.527	65	51	.785	14	65	79	78	98	0	35	5	441	7.9
78-79—New York	75	1171	486	263	.541	63	57	.905	28	54	82	136	113	0	37	6	583	7.8
79-80—New York	75	800	364	188	.516	73	63	.863	21	45	66	85	79	0	35	7	441	5.9
80-81—New York	82	1506	511	285	.558	110	98	.891	27	61	88	108	126	0	72	5	672	8.2
81-82—Atlanta	49	833	291	158	.543	67	59	.881	5	56	61	87	80	0	26	3	376	7.7
82-83—Atlanta	73	1124	444	230	.518	89	74	.831	16	74	90	125	132	0	30	9	534	7.3
83-84—Atlanta	81	1503	554	312	.563	70	56	.800	17	87	104	171	146	1	46	5	681	8.4
84-85—Atlanta	60	1126	388	228	.588	76	62	.816	20	61	81	122	74	0	27	0	518	8.6
Totals	551	9010	3408	1859	.545	613	520	.848	148	503	651	912	848	1	308	40	4246	7.7

Three-Point Field Goals: 1979-80, 2-for-10 (.200). 1980-81, 4-for-11 (.364). 1981-82, 1-for-2 (.500). 1982-83, 0-for-1. 1983-84, 1-for-2 (.500). 1984-85, 0-for-2. Totals, 8-for-28 (.286).

NBA PLAYOFF RECORD

Sea.—Team	G.	Min.	FGA	FGM	Pct.	FTA	FTM	Pct.	Off.	Def.	Tot.	Ast.	PF	Dq.	Stl.	Blk.	Pts.	Avg.
80-81—New York	2	26	7	4	.571	3	3	1.000	1	3	4	1	0	0	1	0	11	5.5
81-82—Atlanta	2	35	7	5	.714	2	2	1.000	0	1	1	2	3	0	3	0	12	6.0
82-83—Atlanta	3	67	22	12	.545	4	4	1.000	0	5	5	3	10	0	2	0	28	9.3
83-84—Atlanta	5	53	14	5	.357	0	0	.000	1	4	5	5	9	0	2	0	10	2.0
Totals	12	181	50	26	.520	9	9	1.000	2	13	15	11	22	0	8	0	61	5.1

Three-Point Field Goals: 1980-81, 0-for-1.

MICHAEL THOMAS GMINSKI
(Mike)

Born August 3, 1959 at Monroe, Conn.   Height 6:11.   Weight 250.

High School—Monroe, Conn., Masuk.

College—Duke University, Durham, N. C.

Drafted by New Jersey on first round, 1980 (7th pick).

—COLLEGIATE RECORD—

Year	G.	Min.	FGA	FGM	Pct.	FTA	FTM	Pct.	Reb.	Pts.	Avg.
76-77	27	....	340	175	.515	91	64	.703	289	414	15.3
77-78	32	....	450	246	.547	176	148	.841	319	640	20.0
78-79	30	....	420	218	.519	177	129	.729	275	565	18.8
79-80	33	1192	487	262	.538	214	180	.841	359	704	21.3
Totals	122	....	1697	901	.531	658	521	.792	1242	2323	19.0

NBA REGULAR SEASON RECORD

Sea.—Team	G.	Min.	FGA	FGM	Pct.	FTA	FTM	Pct.	Off.	Def.	Tot.	Ast.	PF	Dq.	Stl.	Blk.	Pts.	Avg.
80-81—New Jersey	56	1579	688	291	.423	202	155	.767	137	282	419	72	127	1	54	100	737	13.2
81-82—New Jersey	64	740	270	119	.441	118	97	.822	70	116	186	41	69	0	17	48	335	5.2
82-83—New Jersey	80	1255	426	213	.500	225	175	.778	154	228	382	61	118	0	35	116	601	7.5
83-84—New Jersey	82	1655	462	237	.513	184	147	.799	161	272	433	92	162	0	37	70	621	7.6
84-85—New Jersey	81	2418	818	380	.465	328	276	.841	229	404	633	158	135	0	38	92	1036	12.8
Totals	363	7647	2664	1240	.465	1057	850	.804	751	1302	2053	424	611	1	181	426	3330	9.2

Three-Point Field Goals: 1980-81, 0-for-1. 1982-83, 0-for-1. 1983-84, 0-for-3. 1984-85, 0-for-1. Totals, 0-for-6.

NBA PLAYOFF RECORD

Sea.—Team	G.	Min.	FGA	FGM	Pct.	FTA	FTM	Pct.	—Rebounds— Off.	Def.	Tot.	Ast.	PF	Dq.	Stl.	Blk.	Pts.	Avg.
81-82—New Jersey	1	10	3	2	.667	2	1	.500	0	2	2	0	2	0	0	0	5	5.0
82-83—New Jersey	2	29	9	6	.667	4	3	.750	4	5	9	1	2	0	0	4	15	7.5
83-84—New Jersey	11	223	50	29	.580	52	36	.692	22	33	55	6	17	0	7	15	94	8.5
84-85—New Jersey	3	81	33	18	.545	6	6	1.000	4	15	19	4	5	0	3	5	42	14.0
Totals	17	343	95	55	.579	64	46	.719	30	55	85	11	26	0	10	24	156	9.2

Named to THE SPORTING NEWS All-America Second Team, 1979 and 1980.

LANCASTER GORDON

Born June 24, 1962 at Jackson, Miss.   Height 6:03.   Weight 185.

High School—Jackson, Miss., Jim Hill.

College—University of Louisville, Louisville, Ky.

Drafted by Los Angeles Clippers on first round, 1984 (8th pick).

—COLLEGIATE RECORD—

Year	G.	Min.	FGA	FGM	Pct.	FTA	FTM	Pct.	Reb.	Pts.	Avg.
80-81	30	630	234	109	.466	56	39	.696	74	257	8.6
81-82	33	956	301	148	.492	71	53	.746	77	349	10.6
82-83	36	1164	400	208	.520	99	76	.768	120	492	13.7
83-84	35	1177	418	217	.519	107	82	.766	122	516	14.7
Totals	134	3927	1353	682	.504	333	250	.751	393	1614	12.0

NBA REGULAR SEASON RECORD

Sea.—Team	G.	Min.	FGA	FGM	Pct.	FTA	FTM	Pct.	—Rebounds— Off.	Def.	Tot.	Ast.	PF	Dq.	Stl.	Blk.	Pts.	Avg.
84-85—L.A. Clippers	63	682	287	110	.383	49	37	.755	26	35	61	88	61	0	33	6	259	4.1

Three-Point Field Goals: 1984-85, 2-for-9 (.222).

Named to THE SPORTING NEWS All-America Second Team, 1984.

STEWART FRANCIS GRANGER

Born October 27, 1961 at Montreal, Canada.   Height 6:03.   Weight 190.

High School—Brooklyn, N. Y., Nazareth.

College—Villanova University, Villanova, Pa.

Drafted by Cleveland on first round, 1983 (24th pick).

Traded by Cleveland with John Garris to Atlanta for Johnny Davis, August 8, 1984.

—COLLEGIATE RECORD—

Year	G.	Min.	FGA	FGM	Pct.	FTA	FTM	Pct.	Reb.	Pts.	Avg.
79-80	30	392	83	43	.518	49	35	.714	36	121	4.0
80-81	31	1122	288	150	.521	136	98	.721	60	398	12.8
81-82	32	1089	296	145	.490	105	80	.762	52	370	11.6
82-83	32	1055	310	160	.516	128	98	.766	59	418	13.1
Totals	125	3658	977	498	.510	418	311	.744	207	1307	10.5

NBA REGULAR SEASON RECORD

Sea.—Team	G.	Min.	FGA	FGM	Pct.	FTA	FTM	Pct.	—Rebounds— Off.	Def.	Tot.	Ast.	PF	Dq.	Stl.	Blk.	Pts.	Avg.
83-84—Cleveland	56	738	226	97	.429	70	53	.757	8	47	55	134	97	0	24	0	251	4.5
84-85—Atlanta	9	92	17	6	.353	8	4	.500	1	5	6	12	13	0	2	0	16	1.8
Totals	65	830	243	103	.424	78	57	.731	9	52	61	146	110	0	26	0	267	4.1

Three-Point Field Goals: 1983-84, 4-for-13 (.308). 1984-85, 0-for-1. Totals, 4-for-14 (.286).

EARL G. GRAVES JR.
(Butch)

Born January 5, 1962 at Scarsdale, N.Y.   Height 6:03.   Weight 200.

High School—Scarsdale, N. Y.

College—Yale University, New Haven, Conn.

Drafted by Philadelphia on third round, 1984 (68th pick).

Waived by Philadelphia, October 10, 1984; signed by Milwaukee as a free agent, October 12, 1984.
Waived by Milwaukee, October 22, 1984; signed by Cleveland, January 10, 1985, to the first of consecutive 10-day contracts that expired, January 30, 1985.

—COLLEGIATE RECORD—

Year	G.	Min.	FGA	FGM	Pct.	FTA	FTM	Pct.	Reb.	Pts.	Avg.
80-81	26	862	344	165	.479	137	81	.591	116	411	15.8
81-82	25	843	346	182	.526	137	101	.737	91	465	18.6
82-83	26	997	427	223	.522	227	160	.705	167	606	23.3
83-84	26	966	518	246	.475	178	117	.657	151	609	23.4
Totals	103	3668	1635	816	.499	679	459	.676	525	2091	20.3

NBA REGULAR SEASON RECORD

Sea.—Team	G.	Min.	FGA	FGM	Pct.	FTA	FTM	Pct.	Off.	Def.	Tot.	Ast.	PF	Dq.	Stl.	Blk.	Pts.	Avg.
84-85—Cleveland	4	11	6	2	.333	5	1	.200	0	2	2	1	4	0	1	0	5	1.3

Three-Point Field Goals: 1984-85, 0-for-1.

STUART ALLAN GRAY

Born May 27, 1963 in the Panama Canal Zone. Height 7:00. Weight 235.

High School—Granada Hills, Calif., Kennedy.

College—University of California at Los Angeles, Los Angeles, Calif.

Drafted by Indiana on second round as an undergraduate, 1984 (29th pick).

—COLLEGIATE RECORD—

Year	G.	Min.	FGA	FGM	Pct.	FTA	FTM	Pct.	Reb.	Pts.	Avg.
81-82	27	589	111	57	.514	44	19	.432	129	133	4.9
82-83	23	570	134	78	.582	45	20	.444	158	176	7.7
83-84	28	860	177	107	.605	90	62	.689	220	276	9.9
Totals	78	2019	422	242	.573	179	101	.564	507	585	7.5

NBA REGULAR SEASON RECORD

Sea.—Team	G.	Min.	FGA	FGM	Pct.	FTA	FTM	Pct.	Off.	Def.	Tot.	Ast.	PF	Dq.	Stl.	Blk.	Pts.	Avg.
84-85—Indiana	52	391	92	35	.380	47	32	.681	29	94	123	15	82	1	9	14	102	2.0

RICKEY GREEN

Born August 18, 1954 at Chicago, Ill. Height 6:01. Weight 170.

High School—Chicago, Ill., Hirsch.

Colleges—Vincennes University, Vincennes, Ind., and University of Michigan, Ann Arbor, Mich.

Drafted by Golden State on first round, 1977 (16th pick).

Traded by Golden State to Detroit for a 1980 2nd round draft choice, October 9, 1978.
Waived by Detroit, December 11, 1978; signed by Chicago as a free agent, August 12, 1980.
Waived by Chicago, October 8, 1980; signed by Utah as a free agent, December 2, 1980.
Played in Continental Basketball Association with Hawaii and Billings Volcanos, 1979-80 and 1980-81.

COLLEGIATE RECORD
Vincennes

Year	G.	Min.	FGA	FGM	Pct.	FTA	FTM	Pct.	Reb.	Pts.	Avg.
73-74	36	....	633	254	.401	163	114	.699	237	622	17.3
74-75	32	....	600	302	.503	105	69	.657	208	673	21.0
JC Totals	68	....	1233	556	.451	268	183	.683	445	1295	19.0

Michigan

Year	G.	Min.	FGA	FGM	Pct.	FTA	FTM	Pct.	Reb.	Pts.	Avg.
75-76	32	....	542	266	.491	135	106	.785	117	638	19.9
76-77	28	....	464	224	.483	128	98	.766	81	546	19.5
Totals	60	....	1006	490	.487	263	204	.776	198	1184	19.7

MINOR LEAGUE REGULAR SEASON RECORD

Sea.—Team	G.	Min.	2-Point			3-Point			FTM	FTA	Pct.	Reb.	Ast.	Pts.	Avg.
			FGM	FGA	Pct.	FGM	FGA	Pct.							
79-80—Hawaii CBA	44	1753	408	824	.495	3	17	.176	155	205	.756	188	345	980	22.3
80-81—Billings CBA	5	197	47	95	.494	0	1	.000	19	24	.791	22	32	113	22.6

NBA REGULAR SEASON RECORD

Sea.—Team	G.	Min.	FGA	FGM	Pct.	FTA	FTM	Pct.	Off.	Def.	Tot.	Ast.	PF	Dq.	Stl.	Blk.	Pts.	Avg.
77-78—Golden State	76	1098	375	143	.381	90	54	.600	49	67	116	149	95	0	58	1	340	4.5
78-79—Detroit	27	431	177	67	.379	67	45	.672	15	25	40	63	37	0	25	1	179	6.6
80-81—Utah	47	1307	366	176	.481	97	70	.722	30	86	116	235	123	2	75	1	422	9.0
81-82—Utah	81	2822	1015	500	.493	264	202	.765	85	158	243	630	183	0	185	9	1202	14.8

Sea.—Team	G.	Min.	FGA	FGM	Pct.	FTA	FTM	Pct.	Off.	Def.	Tot.	Ast.	PF	Dq.	Stl.	Blk.	Pts.	Avg.
82-83—Utah	78	2783	942	464	.493	232	185	.797	62	161	223	697	154	0	220	4	1115	14.3
83-84—Utah	81	2768	904	439	.486	234	192	.821	56	174	230	748	155	1	215	13	1072	13.2
84-85—Utah	77	2431	798	381	.477	267	232	.869	37	152	189	597	131	0	132	3	1000	13.0
Totals	467	13640	4577	2170	.474	1251	980	.783	334	823	1157	3119	878	3	910	32	5330	11.4

Three-Point Field Goals: 1980-81, 0-for-1. 1981-82, 0-for-8. 1982-83, 2-for-13 (.154). 1983-84, 2-for-17 (.118). 1984-85, 6-for-20 (.300). Totals, 10-for-59 (.169).

NBA PLAYOFF RECORD

								—Rebounds—										
Sea.—Team	G.	Min.	FGA	FGM	Pct.	FTA	FTM	Pct.	Off.	Def.	Tot.	Ast.	PF	Dq.	Stl.	Blk.	Pts.	Avg.
83-84—Utah	11	404	151	64	.424	43	32	.744	9	25	34	104	17	0	19	4	161	14.6
84-85—Utah	10	302	106	57	.538	38	35	.921	10	20	30	75	23	0	12	0	150	15.0
Totals	21	706	257	121	.471	81	67	.827	19	45	64	179	40	0	31	4	311	14.8

Three-Point Field Goals: 1983-84, 1-for-4 (.250). 1984-85, 1-for-7 (.143). Totals, 2-for-11 (.182).

NBA ALL-STAR GAME RECORD

							—Rebounds—								
Season—Team	Min.	FGA	FGM	Pct.	FTA	FTM	Pct.	Off.	Def.	Tot.	Ast.	PF	Dq.	Stl.	Blk.	Pts.
1984—Utah	19	8	3	.375	0	0	.000	0	0	0	11	1	0	1	0	6

Shares NBA playoff game record for most assists in one quarter, 9, vs. Phoenix, April 29, 1984. . . . Led NBA in steals, 1984. . . . Named to THE SPORTING NEWS All-America First Team, 1977.

SIDNEY GREEN

Born January 4, 1961 at Brooklyn, N. Y.   Height 6:09.   Weight 220.

High School—Brooklyn, N. Y., Jefferson.

College—University of Nevada at Las Vegas, Las Vegas, Nev.

Drafted by Chicago on first round, 1983 (5th pick).

—COLLEGIATE RECORD—

Year	G.	Min.	FGA	FGM	Pct.	FTA	FTM	Pct.	Reb.	Pts.	Avg.
79-80	32	1024	388	201	.518	132	96	.727	354	498	15.6
80-81	26	817	297	153	.515	120	85	.708	284	391	15.0
81-82	30	963	374	200	.535	130	100	.769	270	500	16.7
82-83	31	1120	491	269	.548	203	142	.700	368	684	22.1
Totals	119	3924	1550	823	.531	585	423	.723	1276	2073	17.4

Three-Point Field Goals: 1982-83, 4-for-12 (.333).

NBA REGULAR SEASON RECORD

								—Rebounds—										
Sea.—Team	G.	Min.	FGA	FGM	Pct.	FTA	FTM	Pct.	Off.	Def.	Tot.	Ast.	PF	Dq.	Stl.	Blk.	Pts.	Avg.
83-84—Chicago	49	667	228	100	.439	77	55	.714	58	116	174	25	128	1	18	17	255	5.2
84-85—Chicago	48	740	250	108	.432	98	79	.806	72	174	246	29	102	0	11	11	295	6.1
Totals	97	1407	478	208	.435	175	134	.766	130	290	420	54	230	1	29	28	550	5.7

Three-Point Field Goals: 1984-85, 0-for-4.

NBA PLAYOFF RECORD

								—Rebounds—										
Sea.—Team	G.	Min.	FGA	FGM	Pct.	FTA	FTM	Pct.	Off.	Def.	Tot.	Ast.	PF	Dq.	Stl.	Blk.	Pts.	Avg.
84-85—Chicago	3	54	24	12	.500	11	7	.636	10	5	15	2	8	0	0	1	31	10.3

Named to THE SPORTING NEWS All-America Second Team, 1983.

DAVID KASIM GREENWOOD
(Dave)

Born May 27, 1957 at Lynwood, Calif.   Height 6:09.   Weight 232.

High School—Los Angeles, Calif., Verbum Dei.

College—University of California at Los Angeles, Los Angeles, Calif.

Drafted by Chicago on first round, 1979 (2nd pick).

—COLLEGIATE RECORD—

Year	G.	Min.	FGA	FGM	Pct.	FTA	FTM	Pct.	Reb.	Pts.	Avg.
75-76	31	403	122	62	.508	35	28	.800	114	152	4.9
76-77	29	979	395	202	.511	112	80	.714	280	484	16.7
77-78	28	978	364	196	.538	133	97	.729	319	489	17.5
78-79	30	1069	421	247	.587	126	102	.810	309	596	19.9
Totals	118	3439	1302	707	.543	406	307	.756	1022	1721	14.6

NBA REGULAR SEASON RECORD

Sea.—Team	G.	Min.	FGA	FGM	Pct.	FTA	FTM	Pct.	Off.	Def.	Tot.	Ast.	PF	Dq.	Stl.	Blk.	Pts.	Avg.

Sea.—Team	G.	Min.	FGA	FGM	Pct.	FTA	FTM	Pct.	Off.	Def.	Tot.	Ast.	PF	Dq.	Stl.	Blk.	Pts.	Avg.
79-80—Chicago	82	2791	1051	498	.474	416	337	.810	223	550	773	182	313	8	60	129	1334	16.3
80-81—Chicago	82	2710	989	481	.486	290	217	.748	243	481	724	218	282	5	77	124	1179	14.4
81-82—Chicago	82	2914	1014	480	.473	291	240	.825	192	594	786	262	292	1	70	93	1200	14.6
82-83—Chicago	79	2355	686	312	.455	233	165	.708	217	548	765	151	261	5	54	90	789	10.0
83-84—Chicago	78	2718	753	369	.490	289	213	.737	214	572	786	139	265	9	67	72	951	12.2
84-85—Chicago	61	1523	332	152	.458	94	67	.713	108	280	388	78	190	1	34	21	371	6.1
Totals	464	15011	4825	2292	.475	1613	1239	.768	1197	3025	4222	1030	1603	29	362	529	5824	12.6

Three-Point Field Goals: 1979-80, 1-for-7 (.143). 1980-81, 0-for-2. 1981-82, 0-for-3. 1982-83, 0-for-4. 1983-84, 0-for-1. 1984-85, 0-for-1. Totals, 1-for-18 (.056).

NBA PLAYOFF RECORD

Sea.—Team	G.	Min.	FGA	FGM	Pct.	FTA	FTM	Pct.	Off.	Def.	Tot.	Ast.	PF	Dq.	Stl.	Blk.	Pts.	Avg.
80-81—Chicago	6	212	87	51	.586	12	5	.417	16	28	44	11	26	0	9	5	107	17.8
84-85—Chicago	4	139	28	15	.536	10	8	.800	10	21	31	5	14	0	6	4	38	9.5
Totals	10	351	115	66	.574	22	13	.591	26	49	75	16	40	0	15	9	145	14.5

Three-Point Field Goals: 1980-81, 0-for-2.

Named to NBA All-Rookie Team, 1980. . . . THE SPORTING NEWS All-America Second Team, 1979.

KEVIN MICHAEL GREVEY

Born May 12, 1953 at Hamilton, O.   Height 6:05.   Weight 210.

High School—Hamilton, O., Taft.

College—University of Kentucky, Lexington, Ky.

Drafted by Washington on first round, 1975 (18th pick).

Traded by Washington to Milwaukee for a 1984 2nd round draft choice, September 30, 1983.

—COLLEGIATE RECORD—

Year	G.	Min.	FGA	FGM	Pct.	FTA	FTM	Pct.	Reb.	Pts.	Avg.
71-72†	21	....	363	174	.479	149	118	.792	192	466	22.2
72-73	28	919	441	236	.535	76	52	.684	168	524	18.7
73-74	25	843	457	232	.508	100	83	.830	180	547	21.9
74-75	31	1023	592	303	.512	157	124	.790	199	730	23.5
Varsity Totals	84	2785	1490	771	.517	333	259	.778	547	1801	21.4

NBA REGULAR SEASON RECORD

Sea.—Team	G.	Min.	FGA	FGM	Pct.	FTA	FTM	Pct.	Off.	Def.	Tot.	Ast.	PF	Dq.	Stl.	Blk.	Pts.	Avg.
75-76—Washington	56	504	213	79	.371	58	52	.897	24	36	60	27	65	0	13	3	210	3.8
76-77—Washington	76	1306	530	224	.423	119	79	.664	73	105	178	68	148	1	29	9	527	6.9
77-78—Washington	81	2121	1128	505	.448	308	243	.789	124	166	290	155	203	4	61	17	1253	15.5
78-79—Washington	65	1856	922	418	.453	224	173	.772	90	142	232	153	159	1	46	14	1009	15.5
79-80—Washington	65	1818	804	331	.412	249	216	.867	80	107	187	177	158	0	56	16	912	14.0
80-81—Washington	75	2616	1103	500	.453	290	244	.841	67	152	219	300	161	1	68	17	1289	17.2
81-82—Washington	71	2164	857	376	.439	193	165	.855	57	138	195	149	151	1	44	23	945	13.3
82-83—Washington	41	756	294	114	.388	69	54	.783	18	31	49	49	61	0	18	7	297	7.2
83-84—Milwaukee	64	923	395	178	.451	84	75	.893	30	51	81	75	95	0	27	4	446	7.0
84-85—Milwaukee	78	1182	424	190	.448	107	88	.822	27	76	103	94	85	1	30	2	476	6.1
Totals	672	15246	6670	2915	.437	1701	1389	.817	590	1004	1594	1247	1286	9	392	112	7364	11.0

Three-Point Field Goals: 1979-80, 34-for-92 (.370). 1980-81, 45-for-136 (.331). 1981-82, 28-for-82 (.341). 1982-83, 15-for-38 (.395). 1983-84, 15-for-53 (.283). 1984-85, 8-for-33 (.242). Totals, 145-for-434 (.334).

NBA PLAYOFF RECORD

Sea.—Team	G.	Min.	FGA	FGM	Pct.	FTA	FTM	Pct.	Off.	Def.	Tot.	Ast.	PF	Dq.	Stl.	Blk.	Pts.	Avg.
75-76—Washington	2	3	2	1	.500	0	0	.000	0	0	0	0	1	0	0	0	2	1.0
76-77—Washington	9	225	88	36	.409	23	15	.652	10	6	16	8	20	0	2	5	87	9.7
77-78—Washington	21	584	284	126	.444	90	73	.811	25	36	61	42	71	2	11	3	325	15.5
78-79—Washington	19	527	256	102	.398	53	40	.755	26	22	48	30	62	1	15	7	244	12.8
79-80—Washington	2	72	30	16	.533	4	4	1.000	1	5	6	8	9	1	5	2	41	20.5
81-82—Washington	7	159	56	23	.411	19	16	.842	2	8	10	11	12	0	3	1	66	9.4
83-84—Milwaukee	5	27	9	2	.222	6	4	.667	0	2	2	1	1	0	0	0	8	1.6
84-85—Milwaukee	5	28	13	4	.308	4	4	1.000	1	1	2	2	5	0	2	0	12	2.4
Totals	70	1625	738	310	.420	199	156	.784	65	80	145	102	181	4	38	18	785	11.2

Three-Point Field Goals: 1979-80, 5-for-10 (.500). 1981-82, 4-for-8 (.500). Totals, 9-for-18 (.500).

Member of NBA championship team, 1978. . . . Named to THE SPORTING NEWS All-America Second Team, 1975.

DARRELL GRIFFITH

DARRELL STEVEN GRIFFITH

Born June 16, 1958 at Louisville, Ky.   Height 6:04. Weight 190.

High School—Louisville, Ky., Male.

College—University of Louisville, Louisville, Ky.

Drafted by Utah on first round, 1980 (2nd pick).

—COLLEGIATE RECORD—

Year	G.	Min.	FGA	FGM	Pct.	FTA	FTM	Pct.	Reb.	Pts.	Avg.
76-77	28	652	299	150	.502	93	59	.634	109	359	12.8
77-78	30	996	460	240	.522	110	78	.709	162	558	18.6
78-79	32	1001	487	242	.497	151	107	.709	140	591	18.5
79-80	36	1246	631	349	.553	178	127	.713	174	825	22.9
Totals	126	3895	1877	981	.523	532	371	.697	585	2333	18.5

NBA REGULAR SEASON RECORD

Sea.—Team	G.	Min.	FGA	FGM	Pct.	FTA	FTM	Pct.	Off.	Def.	Tot.	Ast.	PF	Dq.	Stl.	Blk.	Pts.	Avg.
80-81—Utah	81	2867	1544	716	.464	320	229	.716	79	209	288	194	219	0	106	40	1671	20.6
81-82—Utah	80	2597	1429	689	.482	271	189	.697	128	177	305	187	213	0	95	34	1582	19.8
82-83—Utah	77	2787	1554	752	.484	246	167	.679	100	204	304	270	184	0	138	33	1709	22.2
83-84—Utah	82	2650	1423	697	.490	217	151	.696	95	243	338	283	202	1	114	23	1636	20.0
84-85—Utah	78	2776	1593	728	.457	298	216	.725	124	220	344	243	178	1	133	30	1764	22.6
Totals	398	13677	7543	3582	.475	1352	952	.704	526	1053	1579	1177	996	2	586	160	8362	21.0

Three-Point Field Goals: 1980-81, 10-for-52 (.192). 1981-82, 15-for-52 (.288). 1982-83, 38-for-132 (.288). 1983-84, 91-for-252 (.361). 1984-85, 92-for-257 (.358). Totals, 246-for-745 (.330).

NBA PLAYOFF RECORD

Sea.—Team	G.	Min.	FGA	FGM	Pct.	FTA	FTM	Pct.	Off.	Def.	Tot.	Ast.	PF	Dq.	Stl.	Blk.	Pts.	Avg.
83-84—Utah	11	417	183	81	.443	48	33	.688	16	49	65	41	24	0	19	2	211	19.2
84-85—Utah	10	340	158	72	.456	25	18	.720	6	23	29	25	21	0	12	5	175	17.5
Totals	21	757	341	153	.449	73	51	.699	22	72	94	66	45	0	31	7	386	18.4

Three-Point Field Goals: 1983-84, 16-for-45 (.356). 1984-85, 13-for-36 (.361). Totals, 29-for-81 (.358).

Named NBA Rookie of the Year, 1981.... NBA All-Rookie Team, 1981.... NBA's all-time three-point field goal leader.... Holds NBA record for most three-point field goals in a season, 1985.... Led NBA in three-point field goal percentage, 1984 and 1985.... THE SPORTING NEWS College Player of the Year, 1980.... THE SPORTING NEWS All-America First Team, 1979 and 1980. ... THE SPORTING NEWS All-America Second Team, 1978. ... NCAA Tournament Most Outstanding Player, 1980.... Member of NCAA championship team, 1980.

ERNEST GRUNFELD
(Ernie)

Born April 24, 1955 at Satu-Mare, Romania.   Height 6:06.   Weight 215.

High School—Forest Hills, N. Y.

College—University of Tennessee, Knoxville, Tenn.

Drafted by Milwaukee on first round, 1977 (11th pick).

Traded by Milwaukee with a 1980 2nd round draft choice and cash to Kansas City for Richard Washington, October 9, 1979.

Signed by New York as Veteran Free Agent, September 10, 1982.

—COLLEGIATE RECORD—

Year	G.	Min.	FGA	FGM	Pct.	FTA	FTM	Pct.	Reb.	Pts.	Avg.
73-74	26	....	363	180	.496	128	93	.727	188	453	17.4
74-75	20	....	401	184	.459	132	107	.811	128	475	23.8
75-76	27	....	485	255	.526	214	173	.808	172	683	25.3
76-77	28	....	463	248	.536	179	142	.793	176	638	23.8
Totals	101	....	1712	867	.506	653	515	.789	664	2249	22.3

NBA REGULAR SEASON RECORD

Sea.—Team	G.	Min.	FGA	FGM	Pct.	FTA	FTM	Pct.	Off.	Def.	Tot.	Ast.	PF	Dq.	Stl.	Blk.	Pts.	Avg.
77-78—Milwaukee	73	1261	461	204	.443	143	94	.657	70	124	194	145	150	1	54	19	502	6.9
78-79—Milwaukee	82	1778	661	326	.493	251	191	.761	124	236	360	216	220	3	58	15	843	10.3
79-80—Kansas City	80	1397	420	186	.443	131	101	.771	87	145	232	109	151	1	56	9	474	5.9
80-81—Kansas City	79	1584	486	260	.535	101	75	.743	31	175	206	205	155	1	60	15	595	7.5
81-82—Kansas City	81	1892	822	420	.511	229	188	.821	55	127	182	276	191	0	72	39	1030	12.7
82-83—New York	77	1422	377	167	.443	98	81	.827	42	121	163	136	172	1	40	10	415	5.4
83-84—New York	76	1119	362	166	.459	83	64	.771	24	97	121	108	151	0	43	7	398	5.2
84-85—New York	69	1061	384	188	.490	104	77	.740	41	110	151	105	129	2	50	7	455	6.6
Totals	617	11514	3973	1917	.483	1140	871	.764	474	1135	1609	1300	1319	9	433	121	4712	7.6

Three-Point Field Goals: 1979-80, 1-for-2 (.500). 1981-82, 2-for-14 (143). 1982-83, 0-for-4. 1983-84, 2-for-9 (.222). 1984-85, 2-for-8 (.250). Totals, 7-for-37 (.189).

NBA PLAYOFF RECORD

Sea.—Team	G.	Min.	FGA	FGM	Pct.	FTA	FTM	Pct.	Off.	Def.	Tot.	Ast.	PF	Dq.	Stl.	Blk.	Pts.	Avg.
									—Rebounds—									
77-78—Milwaukee	7	77	32	17	.531	5	4	.800	4	7	11	17	6	0	3	1	38	5.4
79-80—Kansas City	3	32	9	5	.556	3	1	.333	1	0	1	0	3	0	1	0	11	3.7
80-81—Kansas City	15	633	201	98	.488	67	54	.806	11	52	63	88	51	1	30	9	252	16.8
82-83—New York	6	118	34	15	.441	19	18	.947	2	6	8	10	17	0	7	2	48	8.0
83-84—New York	11	84	23	11	.478	4	4	1.000	1	8	9	6	12	0	2	0	26	2.4
Totals	42	944	299	146	.488	98	81	.827	19	73	92	121	89	0	43	12	375	8.9

Three-Point Field Goals: 1980-81, 2-for-4 (.500).

Named to THE SPORTING NEWS All-America Second Team, 1977.

ROBERT LOUIS HANSEN II
(Bob)

Born January 18, 1961 at Des Moines, Iowa. Height 6:06. Weight 190.

High School—Des Moines, Iowa, Dowling.

College—University of Iowa, Iowa City, Iowa.

Drafted by Utah on third round, 1983 (54th pick).

—COLLEGIATE RECORD—

Year	G.	Min.	FGA	FGM	Pct.	FTA	FTM	Pct.	Reb.	Pts.	Avg.
79-80	33	....	167	71	.425	73	43	.589	67	185	5.6
80-81	22	....	156	70	.449	53	45	.849	75	185	8.4
81-82	25	....	237	117	.494	93	65	.699	102	299	12.0
82-83	31	....	378	184	.487	129	98	.760	166	476	15.4
Totals	111	....	938	442	.471	388	251	.647	410	1145	10.3

Three-Point Field Goals: 1982-83, 10-for-20 (.500).

NBA REGULAR SEASON RECORD

Sea.—Team	G.	Min.	FGA	FGM	Pct.	FTA	FTM	Pct.	Off.	Def.	Tot.	Ast.	PF	Dq.	Stl.	Blk.	Pts.	Avg.
									—Rebounds—									
83-84—Utah	55	419	145	65	.448	28	18	.643	13	35	48	44	62	0	15	4	148	2.7
84-85—Utah	54	646	225	110	.489	72	40	.556	20	50	70	75	88	0	25	1	261	4.8
Totals	109	1065	370	175	.473	100	58	.580	33	85	118	119	150	0	40	5	409	3.8

Three-Point Field Goals: 1983-84, 0-for-8. 1984-85, 1-for-7 (.143). Totals, 1-for-15 (.067).

NBA PLAYOFF RECORD

Sea.—Team	G.	Min.	FGA	FGM	Pct.	FTA	FTM	Pct.	Off.	Def.	Tot.	Ast.	PF	Dq.	Stl.	Blk.	Pts.	Avg.
									—Rebounds—									
83-84—Utah	4	18	7	2	.286	2	1	.500	2	5	7	2	4	0	0	0	7	1.8
84-85—Utah	8	34	8	2	.250	8	5	.625	1	3	4	6	6	0	3	0	9	1.1
Totals	12	52	15	4	.267	10	6	.600	3	8	11	8	10	0	3	0	16	1.3

Three-Point Field Goals: 1983-84, 2-for-3 (.667).

WILLIAM HENRY HANZLIK
(Bill)

Born December 6, 1957 at Middletown, O. Height 6:07. Weight 185.

High Schools—Lake Oswego, Ore. (Junior) and

Beloit, Wis., Memorial (Senior).

College—University of Notre Dame, Notre Dame, Ind.

Drafted by Seattle on first round, 1980 (20th pick).

Traded by Seattle to Denver to complete deal for David Thompson, July 20, 1982. Seattle's earlier trade of the rights to free agent Wally Walker and a 1982 1st round draft choice for Thompson was nullified when Walker's rights were ruled non-transferable by an arbitrator.

—COLLEGIATE RECORD—

Year	G.	Min.	FGA	FGM	Pct.	FTA	FTM	Pct.	Reb.	Pts.	Avg.
76-77	28	274	91	38	.418	55	39	.709	51	115	4.1
77-78	30	307	78	40	.513	38	30	.789	57	110	3.7
78-79	29	654	164	95	.579	77	63	.818	84	253	8.7
79-80	22	603	135	61	.452	60	44	.733	74	166	7.5
Totals	109	1838	468	234	.500	230	176	.765	266	644	5.9

NBA REGULAR SEASON RECORD

Sea.—Team	G.	Min.	FGA	FGM	Pct.	FTA	FTM	Pct.	Off.	Def.	Tot.	Ast.	PF	Dq.	Stl.	Blk.	Pts.	Avg.
									—	Rebounds	—							
80-81—Seattle	74	1259	289	138	.478	150	119	.793	67	86	153	111	168	1	58	20	396	5.4
81-82—Seattle	81	1974	357	167	.468	176	138	.784	99	167	266	183	250	3	81	30	472	5.8
82-83—Denver	82	1547	437	187	.428	160	125	.781	80	156	236	268	220	0	75	15	500	6.1
83-84—Denver	80	1469	306	132	.431	207	167	.807	66	139	205	252	255	6	68	19	434	5.4
84-85—Denver	80	1673	522	220	.421	238	180	.756	88	119	207	210	291	5	84	26	621	7.8
Totals	397	7922	1911	844	.442	931	729	.783	400	667	1067	1024	1184	15	366	110	2423	6.1

Three-Point Field Goals: 1980-81, 1-for-5 (.200). 1981-82, 0-for-4. 1982-83, 1-for-7 (.143). 1983-84, 3-for-12 (.250). 1984-85, 1-for-15 (.067). Totals, 6-for-43 (.139).

NBA PLAYOFF RECORD

Sea.—Team	G.	Min.	FGA	FGM	Pct.	FTA	FTM	Pct.	Off.	Def.	Tot.	Ast.	PF	Dq.	Stl.	Blk.	Pts.	Avg.
									—	Rebounds	—							
81-82—Seattle	8	203	34	16	.471	22	20	.909	10	22	32	20	26	1	6	5	52	6.5
82-83—Denver	8	157	50	20	.400	17	14	.824	3	22	25	21	26	0	6	5	54	6.8
83-84—Denver	5	82	19	11	.579	6	6	1.000	3	5	8	21	16	0	3	0	28	5.6
84-85—Denver	15	310	92	45	.489	41	30	.732	24	22	46	33	57	2	14	6	120	8.0
Totals	36	752	195	92	.472	86	70	.814	40	71	111	95	125	3	29	16	254	7.1

Three-Point Field Goals: 1981-82, 0-for-1. 1982-83, 0-for-2. 1983-84, 0-for-2. 1984-85, 0-for-1. Totals, 0-for-6.

Member of U. S. Olympic team, 1980.

DEREK RICARDO HARPER

Born October 13, 1961 at Elberton, Ga. Height 6:04. Weight 185.

High School—West Palm Beach, Fla., North Shore.

College—University of Illinois, Champaign, Ill.

Drafted by Dallas on first round as an undergraduate, 1983 (11th pick).

—COLLEGIATE RECORD—

Year	G.	Min.	FGA	FGM	Pct.	FTA	FTM	Pct.	Reb.	Pts.	Avg.
80-81	29	934	252	104	.413	46	33	.717	75	241	8.3
81-82	29	1059	230	105	.457	45	34	.756	133	244	8.4
82-83	32	1182	369	198	.537	123	83	.675	112	492	15.4
Totals	90	3175	851	407	.478	214	150	.701	320	977	10.9

Three-Point Field Goals: 1982-83, 13-for-24 (.542).

NBA REGULAR SEASON RECORD

Sea.—Team	G.	Min.	FGA	FGM	Pct.	FTA	FTM	Pct.	Off.	Def.	Tot.	Ast.	PF	Dq.	Stl.	Blk.	Pts.	Avg.
									—	Rebounds	—							
83-84—Dallas	82	1712	451	200	.443	98	66	.673	53	119	172	239	143	0	95	21	469	5.7
84-85—Dallas	82	2218	633	329	.520	154	111	.721	47	152	199	360	194	1	144	37	790	9.6
Totals	164	3930	1084	529	.488	252	177	.702	100	271	371	599	337	1	239	58	1259	7.7

Three-Point Field Goals: 1983-84, 3-for-26 (.115). 1984-85, 21-for-61 (.344). Totals, 24-for-87 (.276).

NBA PLAYOFF RECORD

Sea.—Team	G.	Min.	FGA	FGM	Pct.	FTA	FTM	Pct.	Off.	Def.	Tot.	Ast.	PF	Dq.	Stl.	Blk.	Pts.	Avg.
									—	Rebounds	—							
83-84—Dallas	10	226	54	21	.389	7	5	.714	8	12	20	28	16	0	11	2	50	5.0
84-85—Dallas	4	132	21	10	.476	7	5	.714	1	11	12	20	12	0	6	1	26	6.5
Totals	14	358	75	31	.413	14	10	.714	9	23	32	48	28	0	17	3	76	5.4

Three-Point Field Goals: 1983-84, 3-for-8 (.375). 1984-85, 1-for-3 (.333). Totals, 4-for-11 (.364).

SCOTT ALAN HASTINGS

Born June 3, 1960 at Independence, Kan. Height 6:10. Weight 235.

High School—Independence, Kan.

College—University of Arkansas, Fayetteville, Ark.

Drafted by New York on second round, 1982 (29th pick).

Traded by New York with cash to Atlanta for Rory Sparrow, February 12, 1983.

—COLLEGIATE RECORD—

Year	G.	Min.	FGA	FGM	Pct.	FTA	FTM	Pct.	Reb.	Pts.	Avg.
78-79	30	753	191	97	.508	74	54	.730	138	248	8.3
79-80	29	1033	322	172	.534	160	125	.781	194	469	16.2
80-81	32	1054	341	192	.563	189	139	.735	173	523	16.3
81-82	29	1040	369	204	.553	177	131	.740	175	539	18.6
Totals	120	3880	1223	665	.544	600	449	.748	680	1779	14.8

DEREK HARPER

NBA REGULAR SEASON RECORD

								—Rebounds—									
Sea.—Team	G.	Min.	FGA	FGM	Pct.	FTA	FTM	Pct.	Off.	Def.	Tot.	Ast.	PF	Dq.	Stl.	Blk.	Pts. Avg.
82-83—N.Y.-Atl.	31	140	38	13	.342	20	11	.550	15	26	41	3	34	0	6	1	37 1.2
83-84—Atlanta	68	1135	237	111	.468	104	82	.788	96	174	270	46	220	7	40	36	305 4.5
84-85—Atlanta	64	825	188	89	.473	81	63	.778	59	100	159	46	135	1	24	23	241 3.8
Totals	163	2100	463	213	.460	205	156	.761	170	300	470	95	389	8	70	60	583 3.6

Three-Point Field Goals: 1982-83, 0-for-3. 1983-84, 1-for-4 (.250). Totals, 1-for-7 (.143).

NBA PLAYOFF RECORD

								—Rebounds—									
Sea.—Team	G.	Min.	FGA	FGM	Pct.	FTA	FTM	Pct.	Off.	Def.	Tot.	Ast.	PF	Dq.	Stl.	Blk.	Pts. Avg.
83-84—Atlanta	5	32	9	2	.222	4	3	.750	2	6	8	1	4	0	1	0	7 1.4

STEVEN LEONARD HAYES
(Steve)

Born August 2, 1955 at American Falls, Idaho.   Height 7:00.   Weight 235.

High School—Aberdeen, Idaho.

College—Idaho State University, Pocatello, Idaho.

Drafted by New York Knicks on fourth round, 1977 (76th pick).

Waived by New York Knicks, 1977; signed by Portland as a free agent, August 28, 1979.
Waived by Portland, September 27, 1979; signed by Chicago as a free agent, July 28, 1981.
Waived by Chicago, November 9, 1981; signed to two 10-day contracts by San Antonio that expired January 18, 1982.
Signed by Detroit as a free agent, February 28, 1982.
Traded by Detroit to Cleveland for a 1986 2nd round draft choice, October 7, 1982.
Waived by Cleveland, October 19, 1983; signed by Seattle as a free agent, November 13, 1983.
Waived by Seattle, September 24, 1984; signed by New Jersey as a free agent, October 8, 1984.
Waived by New Jersey, October 23, 1984; signed by Philadelphia, March 19, 1985, to first of consecutive 10-day contracts that expired, April 7, 1985.
Signed by Utah as a free agent, May 23, 1985.
Played in Italy during 1977-78, 1978-79 and 1979-80 seasons.
Played in Continental Basketball Association with Anchorage Northern Knights, 1979-80 and 1981-82, and Tampa Bay Thrillers, 1984-85.

—COLLEGIATE RECORD—

Year	G.	Min.	FGA	FGM	Pct.	FTA	FTM	Pct.	Reb.	Pts.	Avg.
73-74	27	....	210	107	.510	76	50	.658	183	264	9.8
74-75	26	....	393	213	.542	137	105	.766	346	531	20.4
75-76	27	....	395	216	.547	142	101	.711	286	533	19.7
76-77	30	....	437	240	.549	181	125	.691	332	605	20.2
Totals	110	....	1435	776	.541	536	381	.711	1147	1933	17.6

ITALIAN LEAGUE RECORD

Year	G.	Min.	FGA	FGM	Pct.	FTA	FTM	Pct.	Reb.	Pts.	Avg.
77-78—Bologna............	34	....	552	312	.565	108	77	.713	302	701	20.6
78-79—Bologna............	25	....	307	192	.625	86	55	.640	207	439	17.6
80-81—T.G. Gorizia	24	....	365	200	.548	63	35	.556	257	435	18.1

MINOR LEAGUE REGULAR SEASON RECORD

			—2-Point—			—3-Point—									
Sea.—Team	G.	Min.	FGM	FGA	Pct.	FGM	FGA	Pct.	FTM	FTA	Pct.	Reb.	Ast.	Pts.	Avg.
79-80—Anchorage CBA........	45	762	215	430	.500	0	2	.000	93	146	.637	351	72	522	11.6
81-82—Anchorage CBA........	23	745	159	288	.552	0	0	.000	63	88	.715	226	42	381	16.6
84-85—Tampa Bay CBA	46	1688	367	653	.562	0	0	.000	208	264	.787	411	77	942	20.5

NBA REGULAR SEASON RECORD

								—Rebounds—									
Sea.—Team	G.	Min.	FGA	FGM	Pct.	FTA	FTM	Pct.	Off.	Def.	Tot.	Ast.	PF	Dq.	Stl.	Blk.	Pts. Avg.
81-82—S.A.-Det.	35	487	111	54	.486	53	32	.604	39	78	117	28	71	0	4	20	140 4.0
82-83—Cleveland	65	1058	217	104	.479	51	29	.569	102	134	236	36	215	9	17	41	237 3.6
83-84—Seattle	43	253	50	26	.520	14	5	.357	19	43	62	13	52	0	5	18	57 1.3
84-85—Philadelphia	11	101	18	10	.556	4	2	.500	11	23	34	1	19	0	1	4	22 2.0
Totals	154	1899	396	194	.490	122	68	.557	171	278	449	78	357	9	27	83	456 3.0

Three-Point Field Goals: 1982-83, 0-for-1.

Named CBA Most Valuable Player, 1985. . . . CBA Playoff MVP, 1980. . . . Member of CBA championship team, 1980. . . . Named to CBA All-Star First Team, 1985. . . . CBA All-Star Second Team, 1982. . . . CBA All-Defensive First Team, 1985.

JEROME McKINLEY HENDERSON
(Gerald)

Born January 16, 1956 at Richmond, Va.   Height 6:02.   Weight 175.

High School—Richmond, Va., Huguenot.

College—Virginia Commonwealth University, Richmond, Va.

Drafted by San Antonio on third round, 1978 (64th pick).

Waived by San Antonio, September 20, 1978; signed by Boston as a free agent, June 25, 1979.
Traded by Boston to Seattle for a 1986 1st round draft choice, October 16, 1984.
Played in Western Basketball Association with Tucson Gunners, 1978-79.

—COLLEGIATE RECORD—

Year	G.	Min.	FGA	FGM	Pct.	FTA	FTM	Pct.	Reb.	Pts.	Avg.
74-75	25	....	182	73	.401	39	21	.538	64	167	6.7
75-76	25	....	395	196	.496	43	27	.628	71	419	16.8
76-77	25	903	465	228	.490	81	50	.617	102	506	20.2
77-78	28	939	377	185	.491	121	80	.661	94	450	16.1
Totals	103	....	1419	682	.481	284	178	.627	331	1542	15.0

MINOR LEAGUE REGULAR SEASON RECORD

Sea.—Team	G.	Min.	2-Point FGM	2-Point FGA	2-Point Pct.	3-Point FGM	3-Point FGA	3-Point Pct.	FTM	FTA	Pct.	Reb.	Ast.	Pts.	Avg.
78-79—Tucson, WBA	48	1288	239	447	.535	1	7	.143	124	173	.717	138	140	605	12.6

NBA REGULAR SEASON RECORD

Sea.—Team	G.	Min.	FGA	FGM	Pct.	FTA	FTM	Pct.	Off.	Def.	Tot.	Ast.	PF	Dq.	Stl.	Blk.	Pts.	Avg.
79-80—Boston	76	1061	382	191	.500	129	89	.690	37	46	83	147	96	0	45	15	473	6.2
80-81—Boston	82	1608	579	261	.451	157	113	.720	43	89	132	213	177	0	79	12	636	7.8
81-82—Boston	82	1844	705	353	.501	172	125	.727	47	105	152	252	199	3	82	11	833	10.2
82-83—Boston	82	1551	618	286	.463	133	96	.722	57	67	124	195	190	6	95	3	671	8.2
83-84—Boston	78	2088	718	376	.524	177	136	.768	68	79	147	300	209	1	117	14	908	11.6
84-85—Seattle	79	2648	891	427	.479	255	199	.780	71	119	190	559	196	1	140	9	1062	13.4
Totals	479	10800	3893	1894	.487	1023	758	.741	323	505	828	1666	1067	11	558	64	4583	9.6

Three-Point Field Goals: 1979-80, 2-for-6 (.333). 1980-81, 1-for-16 (.063). 1981-82, 2-for-12 (.167). 1982-83, 3-for-16 (.188). 1983-84, 20-for-57 (.351). 1984-85, 9-for-38 (.237). Totals, 37-for-145 (.255).

NBA PLAYOFF RECORD

Sea.—Team	G.	Min.	FGA	FGM	Pct.	FTA	FTM	Pct.	Off.	Def.	Tot.	Ast.	PF	Dq.	Stl.	Blk.	Pts.	Avg.
79-80—Boston	9	101	37	15	.405	20	12	.600	4	6	10	12	8	0	4	0	42	4.7
80-81—Boston	16	228	86	41	.477	12	10	.833	10	15	25	26	24	0	10	3	92	5.8
81-82—Boston	12	310	93	38	.409	35	24	.686	12	13	25	48	30	0	14	2	100	8.3
82-83—Boston	7	187	85	35	.412	7	6	.857	8	6	14	31	25	1	11	1	76	10.9
83-84—Boston	23	616	237	115	.485	75	54	.720	23	29	52	97	78	0	34	1	287	12.5
Totals	67	1442	538	344	.639	149	106	.711	57	69	126	214	165	1	73	7	597	8.9

Three-Point Field Goals: 1979-80, 0-for-2. 1980-81, 0-for-1. 1981-82, 0-for-2. 1982-83, 0-for-3. 1983-84, 3-for-11 (.273). Totals, 3-for-19 (.158).

Member of NBA championship teams, 1981 and 1984.

RODERICK DWAYNE HIGGINS
(Rod)

Born January 31, 1960 at Monroe, La.   Height 6:07.   Weight 205.

High School—Harvey, Ill., Thornton.

College—Fresno State University, Fresno, Calif.

Drafted by Chicago on second round, 1982 (31st pick).

—COLLEGIATE RECORD—

Year	G.	Min.	FGA	FGM	Pct.	FTA	FTM	Pct.	Reb.	Pts.	Avg.
78-79	22	....	153	79	.516	66	49	.742	127	207	9.4
79-80	24	....	235	119	.506	86	72	.837	136	310	12.9
80-81	29	941	319	178	.558	108	92	.852	158	448	15.4
81-82	29	1025	335	178	.531	105	81	.771	182	437	15.1
Totals	104	....	1042	554	.532	365	294	.805	603	1402	13.5

NBA REGULAR SEASON RECORD

Sea.—Team	G.	Min.	FGA	FGM	Pct.	FTA	FTM	Pct.	Off.	Def.	Tot.	Ast.	PF	Dq.	Stl.	Blk.	Pts.	Avg.
82-83—Chicago	82	2196	698	313	.448	264	209	.792	159	207	366	175	248	3	66	65	848	10.3

Sea.—Team	G.	Min.	FGA	FGM	Pct.	FTA	FTM	Pct.	Off.	Def.	Tot.	Ast.	PF	Dq.	Stl.	Blk.	Pts.	Avg.
83-84—Chicago	78	1577	432	193	.447	156	113	.724	87	119	206	116	161	0	49	29	500	6.4
84-85—Chicago	68	942	270	119	.441	90	60	.667	55	92	147	73	91	0	21	13	308	4.5
Totals	228	4715	1400	625	.446	510	382	.749	301	418	719	364	500	3	136	107	1656	7.3

Three-Point Field Goals: 1982-83, 13-for-41 (.317). 1983-84, 1-for-22 (.045). 1984-85, 10-for-37 (.270). Totals, 24-for-100 (.240).

NBA PLAYOFF RECORD

Sea.—Team	G.	Min.	FGA	FGM	Pct.	FTA	FTM	Pct.	Off.	Def.	Tot.	Ast.	PF	Dq.	Stl.	Blk.	Pts.	Avg.
84-85—Chicago	1	1	0	0	.000	0	0	.000	0	0	0	0	0	0	0	0	0	0.0

ROY MANUS HINSON

Born May 2, 1961 at Trenton, N. J.   Height 6:09.   Weight 210.

High School—Somerset, N. J., Franklin Township.

College—Rutgers University, New Brunswick, N. J.

Drafted by Cleveland on first round, 1983 (20th pick).

—COLLEGIATE RECORD—

Year	G.	Min.	FGA	FGM	Pct.	FTA	FTM	Pct.	Reb.	Pts.	Avg.
79-80	28	796	228	115	.504	76	42	.553	157	272	9.7
80-81	30	952	309	150	.485	98	59	.602	218	359	12.0
81-82	30	1015	316	153	.484	119	70	.588	215	376	12.5
82-83	31	1048	377	199	.528	184	118	.641	268	516	16.6
Totals	119	3811	1230	617	.502	477	289	.606	858	1523	12.8

NBA REGULAR SEASON RECORD

Sea.—Team	G.	Min.	FGA	FGM	Pct.	FTA	FTM	Pct.	Off.	Def.	Tot.	Ast.	PF	Dq.	Stl.	Blk.	Pts.	Avg.
83-84—Cleveland	80	1858	371	184	.496	117	69	.590	175	324	499	69	306	11	31	145	437	5.5
84-85—Cleveland	76	2344	925	465	.503	376	271	.721	186	410	596	68	311	13	51	173	1201	15.8
Totals	156	4202	1296	649	.501	493	340	.690	361	734	1095	137	617	24	82	318	1638	10.5

Three-Point Field Goals: 1984-85, 0-for-3.

NBA PLAYOFF RECORD

Sea.—Team	G.	Min.	FGA	FGM	Pct.	FTA	FTM	Pct.	Off.	Def.	Tot.	Ast.	PF	Dq.	Stl.	Blk.	Pts.	Avg.
84-85—Cleveland	4	120	48	26	.542	23	15	652	10	20	30	3	18	1	3	9	67	16.8

CRAIG ANTHONY HODGES

Born June 27, 1960 at Park Forest, Ill.   Height 6:03.   Weight 190.

High School—Park Forest, Ill., Rich East.

College—California State University at Long Beach, Long Beach, Calif.

Drafted by San Diego on third round, 1982 (48th pick).

Traded by Los Angeles Clippers with Terry Cummings and Ricky Pierce to Milwaukee for Marques Johnson, Harvey Catchings, Junior Bridgeman and cash, September 29, 1984.

—COLLEGIATE RECORD—

Year	G.	Min.	FGA	FGM	Pct.	FTA	FTM	Pct.	Reb.	Pts.	Avg.
78-79	28	801	234	122	.521	49	38	.776	56	282	10.1
79-80	33	1148	361	180	.499	68	57	.838	70	417	12.6
80-81	26	755	275	127	.462	55	33	.600	67	287	11.0
81-82	28	1005	444	211	.475	92	68	.739	89	490	17.5
Totals	115	3709	1314	640	.487	264	196	.742	282	1476	12.8

NBA REGULAR SEASON RECORD

Sea.—Team	G.	Min.	FGA	FGM	Pct.	FTA	FTM	Pct.	Off.	Def.	Tot.	Ast.	PF	Dq.	Stl.	Blk.	Pts.	Avg.
82-83—San Diego	76	2022	704	318	.452	130	94	.723	53	69	122	275	192	3	82	4	750	9.9
83-84—San Diego	76	1571	573	258	.450	88	66	.750	22	64	86	116	166	2	58	1	592	7.8
84-85—Milwaukee	82	2496	733	359	.490	130	106	.815	74	112	186	349	262	8	96	1	871	10.6
Totals	234	6089	2010	935	.465	348	266	.764	149	245	394	740	620	13	236	6	2213	9.5

Three-Point Field Goals: 1982-83, 20-for-90 (.222). 1983-84, 10-for-46 (.217). 1984-85, 47-for-135 (.348). Totals, 77-for-271 (.284).

NBA PLAYOFF RECORD

Sea.—Team	G.	Min.	FGA	FGM	Pct.	FTA	FTM	Pct.	Off.	Def.	Tot.	Ast.	PF	Dq.	Stl.	Blk.	Pts.	Avg.
84-85—Milwaukee	8	216	77	28	.364	5	4	.800	2	11	13	26	29	2	12	1	64	8.0

Three-Point Field Goals: 1984-85, 4-for-23 (.174).

ROY HINSON

LIONEL EUGENE HOLLINS

Born October 19, 1953 at Arkansas City, Kan.   Height 6:03.   Weight 185.

High School—Las Vegas, Nev., Rancho.

Colleges—Dixie College, St. George, Utah, and
Arizona State University, Tempe, Ariz.

Drafted by Portland on first round, 1975 (6th pick).

Traded by Portland to Philadelphia for a 1981 1st round draft choice and cash, February 8, 1980.

Traded by Philadelphia to San Diego for a 1983 4th round draft choice and a 1984 2nd round draft choice, October 27, 1982.

Signed by Detroit as Veteran Free Agent, December 22, 1983; San Diego elected not to exercise its right of first refusal.

Signed by Houston as Veteran Free Agent, September 26, 1984; Detroit elected not to exercise its right of first refusal.

—COLLEGIATE RECORD—
Dixie

Year	G.	Min.	FGA	FGM	Pct.	FTA	FTM	Pct.	Reb.	Pts.	Avg.
71-72	..	....	...	...	....	...	...	....	....	....	....
72-73	..	....	...	...	....	...	...	....	....	....	....
JC Totals	53	....	....	503	....	301	225	.748	632	1231	23.2

Arizona State

Year	G.	Min.	FGA	FGM	Pct.	FTA	FTM	Pct.	Reb.	Pts.	Avg.
73-74	27	840	401	194	.484	120	79	.658	102	467	17.3
74-75	29	911	409	194	.474	132	96	.727	84	484	16.7
Totals	56	1751	810	388	.479	252	175	.694	186	951	17.0

NBA REGULAR SEASON RECORD

Sea.—Team	G.	Min.	FGA	FGM	Pct.	FTA	FTM	Pct.	Off.	Def.	Tot.	Ast.	PF	Dq.	Stl.	Blk.	Pts.	Avg.
75-76—Portland	74	1891	738	311	.421	247	178	.721	39	136	175	306	235	5	131	28	800	10.8
76-77—Portland	76	2224	1046	452	.432	287	215	.749	52	158	210	313	265	5	166	38	1119	14.7
77-78—Portland	81	2741	1202	531	.442	300	223	.743	81	196	277	380	268	4	157	29	1285	15.9
78-79—Portland	64	1967	886	402	.454	221	172	.778	32	117	149	325	199	3	114	24	976	15.3
79-80—Port.-Phil.	47	1209	526	212	.403	140	101	.721	29	60	89	162	103	0	76	10	528	11.2
80-81—Philadelphia	82	2154	696	327	.470	171	125	.731	47	144	191	352	205	2	104	18	781	9.5
81-82—Philadelphia	81	2257	797	380	.477	188	132	.702	35	152	187	316	198	1	103	20	894	11.0
82-83—San Diego	56	1844	717	313	.437	179	129	.721	30	98	128	373	155	2	111	14	758	13.5
83-84—Detroit	32	216	63	24	.381	13	11	.846	4	18	22	62	26	0	13	1	59	1.8
84-85—Houston	80	1950	540	249	.461	136	108	.794	33	140	173	417	187	1	78	10	609	7.6
Totals	673	18453	7211	3201	.444	1882	1394	.741	382	1219	1601	3006	1841	23	1053	192	7809	11.6

Three-Point Field Goals: 1979-80, 3-for-20 (.150). 1980-81, 2-for-15 (.133). 1981-82, 2-for-16 (.125). 1982-83, 3-for-21 (.143). 1983-84, 0-for-2. 1984-85, 3-for-13 (.231). Totals, 13-for-87 (.149).

NBA PLAYOFF RECORD

Sea.—Team	G.	Min.	FGA	FGM	Pct.	FTA	FTM	Pct.	Off.	Def.	Tot.	Ast.	PF	Dq.	Stl.	Blk.	Pts.	Avg.
76-77—Portland	19	682	321	134	.417	88	60	.682	13	39	52	85	74	2	47	5	328	17.3
77-78—Portland	6	223	89	40	.449	29	20	.690	5	24	29	33	21	1	7	0	100	16.7
78-79—Portland	3	66	26	8	.308	7	5	.714	1	2	3	5	8	0	3	0	21	7.0
79-80—Philadelphia	18	618	233	97	.416	68	54	.794	17	54	71	113	49	0	27	3	248	13.8
80-81—Philadelphia	16	490	152	67	.441	37	29	.784	8	26	34	65	42	0	17	1	163	10.2
81-82—Philadelphia	8	114	49	15	.306	6	4	.667	1	8	9	25	11	0	9	1	34	4.3
83-84—Detroit	2	6	1	0	.000	0	0	.000	0	0	0	0	0	0	1	0	0	0.0
84-85—Houston	5	94	26	8	.308	1	1	1.000	1	8	9	18	16	1	4	0	17	3.4
Totals	77	2293	897	369	.411	236	173	.733	46	161	207	344	221	4	114	11	911	11.8

Three-Point Field Goals: 1979-80, 0-for-10. 1980-81, 0-for-1. 1981-82, 0-for-1. Totals, 0-for-12.

NBA ALL-STAR GAME RECORD

Season—Team	Min.	FGA	FGM	Pct.	FTA	FTM	Pct.	Off.	Def.	Tot.	Ast.	PF	Dq.	Stl.	Blk.	Pts.
1978—Portland	23	8	3	.375	5	4	.800	0	0	0	8	2	0	2	0	10

Named to NBA All-Defensive First Team, 1978. . . . NBA All-Defensive Second Team, 1979. . . . NBA All-Rookie Team, 1976. . . . Member of NBA championship team, 1977. . . . Named to THE SPORTING NEWS All-America First Team, 1975.

MICHAEL DAVID HOLTON

Born August 4, 1961 at Seattle, Wash.   Height 6:04.   Weight 185.

High School—Pasadena, Calif., Pasadena.

College—University of California at Los Angeles, Los Angeles, Calif.

Drafted by Golden State on third round, 1982 (53rd pick).

Waived by Golden State, October 5, 1983; signed by Phoenix as a free agent, September 24, 1984.

Played in Continental Basketball Association with Puerto Rico Coquis, 1983-84.

—COLLEGIATE RECORD—

Year	G.	Min.	FGA	FGM	Pct.	FTA	FTM	Pct.	Reb.	Pts.	Avg.
79-80	32	802	105	55	.524	73	54	.740	78	164	5.1
80-81	27	734	161	79	.491	67	53	.791	75	211	7.8
81-82	27	677	154	75	.487	65	46	.708	64	196	7.3
82-83	29	721	161	88	.547	75	64	.853	78	240	8.3
Totals	115	2934	581	297	.511	280	217	.775	295	811	7.1

MINOR LEAGUE REGULAR SEASON RECORD

Sea.—Team	G.	Min.	2-Point FGM	FGA	Pct.	3-Point FGM	FGA	Pct.	FTM	FTA	Pct.	Reb.	Ast.	Pts.	Avg.
83-84—Puerto Rico CBA	44	1646	293	574	.510	6	23	.261	207	250	.828	149	198	811	18.4

NBA REGULAR SEASON RECORD

Sea.—Team	G.	Min.	FGA	FGM	Pct.	FTA	FTM	Pct.	Off.	Def.	Tot.	Ast.	PF	Dq.	Stl.	Blk.	Pts.	Avg.
84-85—Phoenix	74	1761	576	257	.446	118	96	.814	30	102	132	198	141	0	59	6	624	8.4

Three-Point Field Goals: 1984-85, 14-for-45 (.311).

NBA PLAYOFF RECORD

Sea.—Team	G.	Min.	FGA	FGM	Pct.	FTA	FTM	Pct.	Off.	Def.	Tot.	Ast.	PF	Dq.	Stl.	Blk.	Pts.	Avg.
84-85—Phoenix	3	55	19	9	.474	4	4	1.000	0	2	2	9	8	0	0	0	22	7.3

Three-Point Field Goals: 1984-85, 0-for-4.

PHILLIP GREGORY HUBBARD
(Phil)

Born December 13, 1956 at Canton, O.   Height 6:08.   Weight 215.

High School—Canton, O., McKinley.

College—University of Michigan, Ann Arbor, Mich.

Drafted by Detroit on first round as junior eligible, 1979 (15th pick).

Traded by Detroit with Paul Mokeski and two 1982 draft choices (1st and 2nd round) to Cleveland for Kenny Carr and Bill Laimbeer, February 16, 1982.

—COLLEGIATE RECORD—

Year	G.	Min.	FGA	FGM	Pct.	FTA	FTM	Pct.	Reb.	Pts.	Avg.
75-76	32	....	381	208	.546	113	66	.584	352	482	15.1
76-77	30	....	410	228	.556	195	132	.677	389	588	19.6
77-78					Did Not Play—Knee Injury						
78-79	26	....	311	154	.495	128	77	.602	238	385	14.8
Totals	88	....	1102	590	.535	436	275	.631	979	1455	16.5

NBA REGULAR SEASON RECORD

Sea.—Team	G.	Min.	FGA	FGM	Pct.	FTA	FTM	Pct.	Off.	Def.	Tot.	Ast.	PF	Dq.	Stl.	Blk.	Pts.	Avg.
79-80—Detroit	64	1189	451	210	.466	220	165	.750	114	206	320	70	202	9	48	10	585	9.1
80-81—Detroit	80	2289	880	433	.492	426	294	.690	236	350	586	150	317	14	80	20	1161	14.5
81-82—Det.-Clev.	83	1839	665	326	.490	280	191	.682	187	286	473	91	292	3	65	19	843	10.2
82-83—Cleveland	82	1953	597	288	.482	296	204	.689	222	249	471	89	271	11	87	8	780	9.5
83-84—Cleveland	80	1799	628	321	.511	299	221	.739	172	208	380	86	244	3	71	6	863	10.8
84-85—Cleveland	76	2249	822	415	.505	494	371	.751	214	265	479	114	258	8	81	9	1201	15.8
Totals	465	11318	4043	1993	.493	2015	1446	.718	1145	1564	2709	600	1584	48	432	72	5433	11.7

Three-Point Field Goals: 1979-80, 0-for-2. 1980-81, 1-for-3 (.333). 1981-82, 0-for-4. 1982-83, 0-for-2. 1983-84, 0-for-1. 1984-85, 0-for-4. Totals, 1-for-16 (.063).

NBA PLAYOFF RECORD

Sea.—Team	G.	Min.	FGA	FGM	Pct.	FTA	FTM	Pct.	Off.	Def.	Tot.	Ast.	PF	Dq.	Stl.	Blk.	Pts.	Avg.
84-85—Cleveland	4	101	45	24	.533	17	13	.765	11	9	20	3	16	0	3	0	62	15.5

Three-Point Field Goals: 1984-85, 1-for-1 (1.000).

Member of U. S. Olympic team, 1976.

JOHN JAY HUMPHRIES
(Known by middle name.)

Born October 17, 1962 at Los Angeles, Calif.   Height 6:03.   Weight 185.

High School—Inglewood, Calif.

College—University of Colorado, Boulder, Colo.

Drafted by Phoenix on first round, 1984 (13th pick).

—COLLEGIATE RECORD—

Year	G.	Min.	FGA	FGM	Pct.	FTA	FTM	Pct.	Reb.	Pts.	Avg.
80-81	28	762	143	74	.517	47	31	.660	59	179	6.4
81-82	27	948	242	113	.467	83	53	.639	71	279	10.3
82-83	28	1034	339	170	.501	95	60	.632	91	400	14.3
83-84	29	1120	334	170	.509	137	108	.788	94	448	15.4
Totals	112	3864	1058	527	.498	362	252	.696	315	1306	11.7

NBA REGULAR SEASON RECORD

Sea.—Team	G.	Min.	FGA	FGM	Pct.	FTA	FTM	Pct.	—Rebounds— Off.	Def.	Tot.	Ast.	PF	Dq.	Stl.	Blk.	Pts.	Avg.
84-85—Phoenix	80	2062	626	279	.446	170	141	.829	32	132	164	350	209	2	107	8	703	8.8

Three-Point Field Goals: 1984-85, 4-for-20 (.200).

NBA PLAYOFF RECORD

Sea.—Team	G.	Min.	FGA	FGM	Pct.	FTA	FTM	Pct.	—Rebounds— Off.	Def.	Tot.	Ast.	PF	Dq.	Stl.	Blk.	Pts.	Avg.
84-85—Phoenix	3	90	31	20	.645	12	9	.750	1	4	5	16	12	0	2	0	49	16.3

GEOFFREY ANGIER HUSTON
(Geoff)

Born November 8, 1957 at Brooklyn, N. Y.   Height 6:02.   Weight 175.

High School—Brooklyn, N. Y., Canarsie.

College—Texas Tech University, Lubbock, Tex.

Drafted by New York on third round, 1979 (50th pick).

Selected from New York by Dallas in expansion draft, May 28, 1980.
Traded by Dallas with a 1983 3rd round draft choice to Cleveland for Chad Kinch and a 1985 1st round draft choice, February 7, 1981.
Waived by Cleveland, December 7, 1984.

—COLLEGIATE RECORD—

Year	G.	Min.	FGA	FGM	Pct.	FTA	FTM	Pct.	Reb.	Pts.	Avg.
75-76	31	557	194	91	.469	54	36	.667	42	218	7.0
76-77	29	891	222	128	.577	59	34	.576	58	290	10.0
77-78	27	754	197	96	.487	53	39	.736	46	231	8.6
78-79	30	911	286	142	.497	53	41	.774	70	325	10.8
Totals	117	3113	899	457	.508	219	150	.685	216	1064	9.1

NBA REGULAR SEASON RECORD

Sea.—Team	G.	Min.	FGA	FGM	Pct.	FTA	FTM	Pct.	—Rebounds— Off.	Def.	Tot.	Ast.	PF	Dq.	Stl.	Blk.	Pts.	Avg.
79-80—New York	71	923	241	94	.390	38	28	.737	14	44	58	159	83	0	39	5	219	3.1
80-81—Dall.-Clev.	81	2434	942	461	.489	212	150	.708	45	93	138	394	148	1	58	7	1073	13.2
81-82—Cleveland	78	2409	672	325	.484	200	153	.765	53	97	150	590	169	1	70	11	806	10.3
82-83—Cleveland	80	2716	832	401	.482	245	168	.686	41	118	159	487	215	1	74	4	974	12.2
83-84—Cleveland	77	2041	699	348	.498	154	110	.714	32	64	96	413	126	0	38	1	808	10.5
84-85—Cleveland	8	93	25	12	.480	3	2	.667	0	1	1	23	8	0	0	0	26	3.3
Totals	395	10616	3411	1641	.481	852	611	.717	185	417	602	2066	749	3	279	28	3906	9.9

Three-Point Field Goals: 1979-80, 3-for-17 (.176). 1980-81, 1-for-5 (.200). 1981-82, 3-for-10 (.300). 1982-83, 4-for-12 (.333). 1983-84, 2-for-11 (.182). Totals, 13-for-55 (.236).

MARCUS JOHN IAVARONI
(Marc)

Born September 15, 1956 at Jamaica, N. Y.   Height 6:09.   Weight 225.

High School—Plainview, N. Y., Kennedy.

College—University of Virginia, Charlottesville, Va.

Drafted by New York on third round, 1978 (55th pick).

Waived by New York, October 9, 1980; signed by Philadelphia as free agent, August, 1982.
Traded by Philadelphia to San Antonio for a 1986 3rd round draft choice, December 15, 1984.
Played in Italy during 1978-79, 1979-80 and 1981-82 seasons.

—COLLEGIATE RECORD—

Year	G.	Min.	FGA	FGM	Pct.	FTA	FTM	Pct.	Reb.	Pts.	Avg.
74-75	25	846	213	105	.493	83	61	.735	198	271	10.8
75-76	30	830	261	138	.529	157	106	.675	168	382	12.7
76-77	28	791	272	118	.434	122	80	.656	178	316	11.3
77-78	27	800	188	97	.516	119	81	.681	174	275	10.2
Totals	110	3267	934	458	.490	481	328	.682	718	1244	11.3

ITALIAN LEAGUE RECORD

Year	G.	Min.	FGA	FGM	Pct.	FTA	FTM	Pct.	Reb.	Pts.	Avg.
78-79—P. I. Brescia	26	....	297	139	.468	87	65	.747	199	343	13.2
79-80—P. I. Brescia	27	....	291	148	.411	87	66	.758	212	362	13.4
81-82—Recoard	34	1329	592	340	.574	185	137	.741	364	817	24.0

NBA REGULAR SEASON RECORD

Sea.—Team	G.	Min.	FGA	FGM	Pct.	FTA	FTM	Pct.	—Rebounds— Off.	Def.	Tot.	Ast.	PF	Dq.	Stl.	Blk.	Pts.	Avg.
82-83—Philadelphia	80	1612	353	163	.462	113	78	.690	117	212	329	83	238	0	32	44	404	5.1
83-84—Philadelphia	78	1532	322	149	.463	131	97	.740	91	219	310	95	222	1	36	55	395	5.1
84-85—Phil.-S.A.	69	1334	354	162	.458	128	87	.680	95	209	304	119	217	5	35	35	411	6.0
Totals	227	4478	1029	474	.461	372	262	.704	303	640	943	297	677	6	103	134	1210	5.3

Three-Point Field Goals: 1982-83, 0-for-2. 1983-84, 0-for-2. 1984-85, 0-for-4. Totals, 0-for-8.

NBA PLAYOFF RECORD

Sea.—Team	G.	Min.	FGA	FGM	Pct.	FTA	FTM	Pct.	—Rebounds— Off.	Def.	Tot.	Ast.	PF	Dq.	Stl.	Blk.	Pts.	Avg.
82-83—Philadelphia	13	283	52	29	.558	18	9	.500	22	35	57	19	42	1	8	7	67	5.2
83-84—Philadelphia	4	64	15	7	.467	8	7	.875	3	5	8	3	18	1	1	1	22	4.5
84-85—San Antonio	5	116	28	15	.536	20	15	.750	8	18	26	13	23	1	5	2	45	9.0
Totals	22	463	95	51	.537	46	31	.674	33	58	91	35	83	3	14	10	134	6.1

Three-Point Field Goals: 1983-84, 1-for-2 (.500). 1984-85, 0-for-1. Totals, 1-for-3 (.333).

Member of NBA championship team, 1983.

DANIEL PAUL ISSEL
(Dan)

Born October 25, 1948 at Batavia, Ill. Height 6:09. Weight 240.

High School—Batavia, Ill.

College—University of Kentucky, Lexington, Ky.

Drafted by Detroit on eighth round, 1970 (122nd pick).

Selected by Kentucky on first round of ABA draft, 1970.
Traded by Kentucky to Baltimore for Tom Owens and cash, September 19, 1975.
Traded by Baltimore to Denver for Dave Robisch and cash, October 8, 1975.
Entered NBA with Denver, 1976.

—COLLEGIATE RECORD—

Year	G.	Min.	FGA	FGM	Pct.	FTA	FTM	Pct.	Reb.	Pts.	Avg.
66-67†	20	....	332	168	.506	111	80	.721	355	416	20.8
67-68	27	836	390	171	.438	154	102	.662	328	444	16.4
68-69	28	1063	534	285	.534	232	176	.759	381	746	26.6
69-70	28	1044	667	369	.553	275	210	.764	369	948	33.9
Varsity Totals	83	2943	1591	825	.519	661	488	.738	1078	2138	25.8

ABA REGULAR SEASON RECORD

Sea.—Team	G.	Min.	—2-Point— FGM	FGA	Pct.	—3-Point— FGM	FGA	Pct.	FTM	FTA	Pct.	Reb.	Ast.	Pts.	Avg.
70-71—Kentucky	83	3274	938	1989	.472	0	5	.000	604	748	.807	1093	162	2480	29.9
71-72—Kentucky	83	3570	969	1990	.487	3	11	.273	591	753	.785	931	195	2538	30.6
72-73—Kentucky	84	3531	899	1742	.516	3	15	.200	485	635	.764	922	220	2292	27.3
73-74—Kentucky	83	3347	826	1709	.483	3	17	.176	457	581	.787	847	137	2118	25.5
74-75—Kentucky	83	2864	614	1298	.473	0	5	.000	237	321	.738	710	188	1465	17.7
75-76—Denver	84	2858	751	1468	.512	1	4	.250	425	521	.816	923	201	1930	23.0
Totals	500	19444	4997	10196	.490	10	57	.175	2799	3559	.787	5426	1103	12823	25.6

ABA PLAYOFF RECORD

Sea.—Team	G.	Min.	—2-Point— FGM	FGA	Pct.	—3-Point— FGM	FGA	Pct.	FTM	FTA	Pct.	Reb.	Ast.	Pts.	Avg.
70-71—Kentucky	19	670	207	408	.507	0	0	.000	123	141	.872	221	28	536	27.9
71-72—Kentucky	6	269	47	113	.416	0	1	.000	38	50	.760	54	5	132	22.0
72-73—Kentucky	19	821	197	392	.503	1	6	.167	124	156	.795	225	28	521	27.4
73-74—Kentucky	8	311	60	135	.444	0	0	.000	28	33	.848	87	14	148	18.5
74-75—Kentucky	15	578	122	261	.467	0	0	.000	60	74	.811	119	29	304	20.3
75-76—Denver	13	470	111	226	.491	0	1	.000	44	56	.786	156	32	266	20.5
Totals	80	3119	744	1535	.485	1	8	.125	417	510	.818	949	136	1907	23.8

ABA ALL-STAR GAME RECORD

Sea.—Team	Min.	—2-Point— FGM	FGA	Pct.	—3-Point— FGM	FGA	Pct.	FTM	FTA	Pct.	Reb.	Ast.	Pts.	Avg.
1971—Kentucky...........	34	8	15	.533	0	0	.000	5	8	.625	11	0	21	21.0
1972—Kentucky...........	23	9	13	.692	0	0	.000	3	4	.750	9	5	21	21.0

DAN ISSEL

Sea.—Team	Min.	FGM	2-Point FGA	Pct.	FGM	3-Point FGA	Pct.	FTM	FTA	Pct.	Reb.	Ast.	Pts.	Avg.
1973—Kentucky	29	6	14	.429	0	0	.000	2	2	1.000	7	4	14	14.0
1974—Kentucky	26	10	15	.667	0	0	.000	1	1	1.000	4	1	21	21.0
1975—Kentucky	20	3	6	.500	0	0	.000	1	2	.500	7	1	7	7.0
1976—Denver	31	6	16	.375	0	0	.000	7	9	.778	9	5	19	19.0
Totals	163	42	79	.532	0	0	.000	19	26	.731	41	16	103	17.2

NBA REGULAR SEASON RECORD

Sea.—Team	G.	Min.	FGA	FGM	Pct.	FTA	FTM	Pct.	Off.	Rebounds— Def.	Tot.	Ast.	PF	Dq.	Stl.	Blk.	Pts.	Avg.
76-77—Denver	79	2507	1282	660	.515	558	445	.797	211	485	696	177	246	7	91	29	1765	22.3
77-78—Denver	82	2851	1287	659	.512	547	428	.782	253	577	830	304	279	5	100	41	1746	21.3
78-79—Denver	81	2742	1030	532	.517	419	316	.754	240	498	738	255	233	6	61	46	1380	17.0
79-80—Denver	82	2938	1416	715	.505	667	517	.775	236	483	719	198	190	1	88	54	1951	23.8
80-81—Denver	80	2641	1220	614	.503	684	519	.759	229	447	676	158	249	6	83	53	1749	21.9
81-82—Denver	81	2472	1236	651	.527	655	546	.834	174	434	608	179	245	4	67	55	1852	22.9
82-83—Denver	80	2431	1296	661	.510	479	400	.835	151	445	596	223	227	0	83	43	1726	21.6
83-84—Denver	76	2076	1153	569	.493	428	364	.850	112	401	513	173	182	2	60	44	1506	19.8
84-85—Denver	77	1684	791	363	.459	319	257	.806	80	251	331	137	171	1	65	31	984	12.8
Totals	718	22342	10711	5424	.506	4756	3792	.797	1686	4021	5707	1804	2022	32	698	396	14659	20.4

Three-Point Field Goals: 1979-80, 4-for-12 (.333). 1980-81, 2-for-12 (.167). 1981-82, 4-for-6 (.667). 1982-83, 4-for-19 (.211). 1983-84, 4-for-19 (.211). 1984-85, 1-for-7 (.143). Totals, 19-for-75 (.253).

NBA PLAYOFF RECORD

Sea.—Team	G.	Min.	FGA	FGM	Pct.	FTA	FTM	Pct.	Off.	Rebounds— Def.	Tot.	Ast.	PF	Dq.	Stl.	Blk.	Pts.	Avg.
76-77—Denver	6	222	96	49	.510	45	34	.756	18	40	58	17	20	0	5	4	132	22.0
77-78—Denver	13	460	212	103	.486	65	56	.862	41	93	134	53	43	1	7	3	262	20.2
78-79—Denver	3	109	45	24	.533	31	25	.806	7	21	28	10	15	0	0	0	73	24.3
81-82—Denver	3	103	60	32	.533	12	12	1.000	8	13	21	5	10	0	3	1	76	25.3
82-83—Denver	8	227	136	69	.507	29	25	.862	13	45	58	25	18	0	9	5	163	20.4
83-84—Denver	5	153	102	52	.510	39	32	.821	10	30	40	8	15	0	6	6	137	27.4
84-85—Denver	15	325	159	73	.459	48	39	.813	14	40	54	27	36	0	12	5	186	12.4
Totals	53	1599	810	402	.496	269	223	.829	111	282	393	145	157	1	42	24	1029	19.4

Three-Point Field Goals: 1982-83, 0-for-1. 1983-84, 1-for-2 (.500). 1984-85, 1-for-1 (1.000). Totals, 2-for-4 (.500).

NBA ALL-STAR GAME RECORD

Season—Team	Min.	FGA	FGM	Pct.	FTA	FTM	Pct.	Off.	Rebounds— Def.	Tot.	Ast.	PF	Dq.	Stl.	Blk.	Pts.
1977—Denver	10	3	0	.000	0	0	.000	1	0	1	0	0	0	0	0	0

Named to ABA All-Star First Team, 1972.... ABA All-Star Second Team, 1971, 1973, 1974, 1976.... ABA Rookie of the Year, 1971.... ABA All-Rookie Team, 1971.... ABA All-Star Game MVP, 1972.... Member of ABA championship team, 1975.... Led ABA in scoring, 1971.... Set ABA record for most points in one season, 1972.... Named to THE SPORTING NEWS All-America First Team, 1970.... THE SPORTING NEWS All-America Second Team, 1969.

RALPH A. JACKSON III

Born October 26, 1962 at Los Angeles, Calif. Height 6:02. Weight 190.

High School—Inglewood, Calif.

College—University of California at Los Angeles, Los Angeles, Calif.

Drafted by Indiana on fourth round, 1984 (71st pick).

Waived by Indiana, November 9, 1984.

—COLLEGIATE RECORD—

Year	G.	Min.	FGA	FGM	Pct.	FTA	FTM	Pct.	Reb.	Pts.	Avg.
80-81	27	753	133	57	.429	51	32	.627	56	146	5.4
81-82	27	875	171	79	.462	61	39	.639	73	197	7.3
82-83	29	844	199	94	.472	65	48	.738	81	236	8.1
83-84	28	1030	274	139	.507	102	71	.696	74	349	12.5
Totals	111	3502	777	369	.475	279	190	.681	284	928	8.4

NBA REGULAR SEASON RECORD

Sea.—Team	G.	Min.	FGA	FGM	Pct.	FTA	FTM	Pct.	Off.	Rebounds— Def.	Tot.	Ast.	PF	Dq.	Stl.	Blk.	Pts.	Avg.
84-85—Indiana	1	12	3	1	.333	0	0	.000	1	0	1	4	1	0	2	0	2	2.0

—DID YOU KNOW—

That former baseball star Del Rice, also a 6-2 pro basketball forward, played for the Rochester Royals in the National Basketball League during the 1945-46 season (11 games) and caught in three games for the St. Louis Cardinals in the 1946 World Series?

CLARENCE STEPHEN JOHNSON
(Steve)

Born November 3, 1957 at Akron, O.   Height 6:10½.   Weight 245.

High School—San Bernardino, Calif., San Gorgonio.

College—Oregon State University, Corvallis, Ore.

Drafted by Kansas City on first round, 1981 (7th pick).

Traded by Kansas City with a 1984 2nd round draft pick and two 1985 2nd round draft picks to Chicago for Reggie Theus, February 15, 1984.

Traded by Chicago with a 1985 2nd round draft choice to San Antonio for Gene Banks, June 18, 1985.

—COLLEGIATE RECORD—

Year	G.	Min.	FGA	FGM	Pct.	FTA	FTM	Pct.	Reb.	Pts.	Avg.
76-77	28	616	267	159	.596	91	61	.670	156	379	13.5
77-78	3	62	45	26	.578	13	8	.615	29	60	20.0
78-79	27	724	298	197	.661	169	104	.615	178	498	18.4
79-80	30	711	297	211	.710	145	87	.600	207	509	17.0
80-81	28	716	315	235	.746	174	119	.684	215	589	21.0
Totals	116	2829	1222	828	.678	592	379	.640	785	2035	17.5

(Suffered broken left foot in 1977-78 season; granted extra year of eligibility).

NBA REGULAR SEASON RECORD

Sea.—Team	G.	Min.	FGA	FGM	Pct.	FTA	FTM	Pct.	Off.	Def.	Tot.	Ast.	PF	Dq.	Stl.	Blk.	Pts.	Avg.
81-82—Kansas City	78	1741	644	395	.613	330	212	.642	152	307	459	91	372	25	39	89	1002	12.8
82-83—Kansas City	79	1544	595	371	.624	324	186	.574	140	258	398	95	323	9	40	83	928	11.7
83-84—K.C.-Chi.	81	1487	540	302	.559	287	165	.575	162	256	418	81	307	15	37	69	769	9.5
84-85—Chicago	74	1659	516	281	.545	252	181	.718	146	291	437	64	265	7	37	62	743	10.0
Totals	312	6431	2295	1349	.588	1193	744	.624	600	1112	1712	331	1567	56	153	303	3442	11.0

Three-Point Field Goals: 1984-85, 0-for-3.

NBA PLAYOFF RECORD

Sea.—Team	G.	Min.	FGA	FGM	Pct.	FTA	FTM	Pct.	Off.	Def.	Tot.	Ast.	PF	Dq.	Stl.	Blk.	Pts.	Avg.
84-85—Chicago	3	22	7	2	.286	2	2	1.000	3	2	5	2	4	0	0	0	6	2.0

Named to THE SPORTING NEWS All-America Second Team, 1981. . . . Holds NCAA record for career field-goal percentage. . . . Led NCAA in field-goal percentage, 1980 and 1981.

CLEMON JOHNSON

Born September 12, 1956 at Monticello, Fla.   Height 6:10.   Weight 240.

High School—Tallahassee, Fla., Florida A&M University High.

College—Florida A&M University, Tallahassee, Fla.

Drafted by Portland on second round, 1978 (44th pick).

Traded by Portland to Indiana for a 1981 2nd round draft choice, October 9, 1979.

Traded by Indiana with a 1984 3rd round draft choice to Philadelphia for Russ Schoene, a 1983 1st round draft choice and a 1984 2nd round draft choice, February 15, 1983.

—COLLEGIATE RECORD—

Year	G.	Min.	FGA	FGM	Pct.	FTA	FTM	Pct.	Reb.	Pts.	Avg.
74-75	25	....	233	113	.485	45	23	.511	302	249	9.9
75-76	27	....	242	118	.488	53	30	.566	378	266	9.9
76-77	30	....	310	170	.548	89	54	.607	402	394	13.1
77-78	27	....	354	200	.565	117	72	.643	412	472	17.5
Totals	109	....	1139	601	.528	304	179	.589	1494	1381	12.7

NBA REGULAR SEASON RECORD

Sea.—Team	G.	Min.	FGA	FGM	Pct.	FTA	FTM	Pct.	Off.	Def.	Tot.	Ast.	PF	Dq.	Stl.	Blk.	Pts.	Avg.
78-79—Portland	74	794	217	102	.470	74	36	.486	83	143	226	78	121	1	23	36	240	3.2
79-80—Indiana	79	1541	396	199	.503	117	74	.632	145	249	394	115	211	2	48	121	472	6.0
80-81—Indiana	81	1643	466	235	.504	189	112	.593	173	295	468	144	185	1	44	119	582	7.2
81-82—Indiana	79	1979	641	312	.487	189	123	.651	184	387	571	127	241	3	60	112	747	9.5
82-83—Ind.-Phil.	83	1914	581	299	.515	180	111	.617	190	334	524	139	221	3	67	92	709	8.5
83-84—Philadelphia	80	1721	412	193	.468	113	69	.611	131	267	398	55	205	1	35	65	455	5.7
84-85—Philadelphia	58	875	235	117	.498	49	36	.735	92	129	221	33	112	0	15	44	270	4.7
Totals	534	10467	2948	1457	.494	911	561	.616	998	1804	2802	691	1296	11	292	589	3475	6.5

Three-Point Field Goals: 1980-81, 0-for-1. 1982-83, 0-for-1. 1984-85, 0-for-1. Totals, 0-for-3.

NBA PLAYOFF RECORD

Sea.—Team	G.	Min.	FGA	FGM	Pct.	FTA	FTM	Pct.	Off.	Def.	Tot.	Ast.	PF	Dq.	Stl.	Blk.	Pts.	Avg.
78-79—Portland	3	47	11	4	.364	11	6	.545	5	12	17	2	5	0	2	4	14	4.7
80-81—Indiana	2	55	12	5	.417	10	5	.500	10	10	20	3	3	0	4	2	15	7.5
82-83—Philadelphia	12	202	49	25	.510	4	0	.000	21	22	43	7	28	0	4	5	50	4.2
83-84—Philadelphia	5	45	12	4	.333	0	0	.000	3	3	6	0	8	0	1	4	8	1.6
84-85—Philadelphia	13	165	33	13	.394	21	16	.762	17	19	36	2	32	0	3	6	42	3.2
Totals	35	514	117	51	.436	46	27	.587	56	66	122	14	76	0	14	21	129	3.7

Three Point-Field Goals: 1984-85, 0-for-1.

Member of NBA championship team, 1983.

DENNIS WAYNE JOHNSON

Born September 18, 1954 at San Pedro, Calif.   Height 6:04.   Weight 200.

High School—Compton, Calif., Dominguez.

Colleges—Los Angeles Harbor Junior College, Wilmington, Calif., and Pepperdine University, Malibu, Calif.

Drafted by Seattle on second round as hardship case, 1976 (29th pick).

Traded by Seattle to Phoenix for Paul Westphal, June 4, 1980.
Traded by Phoenix with 1983 1st and 3rd round draft choices to Boston for Rick Robey and two 1983 2nd round draft choices, June 27, 1983.

—COLLEGIATE RECORD—
Los Angeles Harbor JC

Year	G.	Min.	FGA	FGM	Pct.	FTA	FTM	Pct.	Reb.	Pts.	Avg.
73-74	...	699	191	103	.539	82	45	.549	230	251	.....
74-75	28	967	....	....	....	...	...	....	336	511	18.3
JC Totals	...	1666	....	....	....	...	...	....	566	762	....

Pepperdine

Year	G.	Min.	FGA	FGM	Pct.	FTA	FTM	Pct.	Reb.	Pts.	Avg.
75-76	27	930	378	181	.479	112	63	.563	156	425	15.7

NBA REGULAR SEASON RECORD

Sea.—Team	G.	Min.	FGA	FGM	Pct.	FTA	FTM	Pct.	Off.	Def.	Tot.	Ast.	PF	Dq.	Stl.	Blk.	Pts.	Avg.
76-77—Seattle	81	1667	566	285	.504	287	179	.624	161	141	302	123	221	3	123	57	749	9.2
77-78—Seattle	81	2209	881	367	.417	406	297	.732	152	142	294	230	213	2	118	51	1031	12.7
78-79—Seattle	80	2717	1110	482	.434	392	306	.781	146	228	374	280	209	2	100	97	1270	15.9
79-80—Seattle	81	2937	1361	574	.422	487	380	.780	173	241	414	332	267	6	144	82	1540	19.0
80-81—Phoenix	79	2615	1220	532	.436	501	411	.820	160	203	363	291	244	2	136	61	1486	18.8
81-82—Phoenix	80	2937	1228	577	.470	495	399	.806	142	268	410	369	253	6	105	55	1561	19.5
82-83—Phoenix	77	2551	861	398	.462	369	292	.791	92	243	335	388	204	1	97	39	1093	14.2
83-84—Boston	80	2665	878	384	.437	330	281	.852	87	193	280	338	251	6	93	57	1053	13.2
84-85—Boston	80	2976	1066	493	.462	306	261	.853	91	226	317	543	224	2	96	39	1254	15.7
Totals	719	23274	9171	4092	.446	3573	2806	.785	1204	1885	3089	2894	2086	30	1012	538	11037	15.4

Three-Point Field Goals: 1979-80, 12-for-58 (.207). 1980-81, 11-for-51 (.216). 1981-82, 8-for-42 (.190). 1982-83, 5-for-31 (.161). 1983-84, 4-for-32 (.125). 1984-85, 7-for-26 (.269). Totals, 47-for-240 (.196).

NBA PLAYOFF RECORD

Sea.—Team	G.	Min.	FGA	FGM	Pct.	FTA	FTM	Pct.	Off.	Def.	Tot.	Ast.	PF	Dq.	Stl.	Blk.	Pts.	Avg.
77-78—Seattle	22	827	294	121	.412	159	112	.704	47	54	101	72	63	0	23	23	354	16.1
78-79—Seattle	17	691	302	136	.450	109	84	.771	44	60	104	69	63	0	28	26	356	20.9
79-80—Seattle	15	582	244	100	.410	62	52	.839	25	39	64	57	48	2	27	10	257	17.1
80-81—Phoenix	7	267	110	52	.473	42	32	.762	7	26	33	20	18	0	9	4	137	19.6
81-82—Phoenix	7	271	132	63	.477	39	30	.769	13	18	31	32	28	2	15	4	156	22.3
82-83—Phoenix	3	108	48	22	.458	12	10	.833	6	17	23	17	9	0	5	2	54	18.0
83-84—Boston	22	808	319	129	.404	120	104	.867	30	49	79	97	75	1	25	7	365	16.6
84-85—Boston	21	848	319	142	.445	93	80	.860	24	60	84	154	66	0	31	9	364	17.3
Totals	114	4402	1768	765	.433	636	504	.792	196	323	519	518	370	5	163	90	2043	17.9

Three-Point Field Goals: 1979-80, 5-for-15 (.333). 1980-81, 1-for-5 (.200). 1981-82, 0-for-3. 1982-83, 0-for-1. 1983-84, 3-for-7 (.429). 1984-85, 0-for-14. Totals, 9-for-45 (.200).

NBA ALL-STAR GAME RECORD

Season—Team	Min.	FGA	FGM	Pct.	FTA	FTM	Pct.	Off.	Def.	Tot.	Ast.	PF	Dq.	Stl.	Blk.	Pts.
1979—Seattle...........	27	7	5	.714	2	2	1.000	1	0	1	3	3	0	0	1	12
1980—Seattle...........	20	13	7	.538	6	5	.833	2	2	4	1	3	0	2	1	19
1981—Phoenix........	24	8	5	.625	10	9	.900	1	1	2	1	1	0	3	0	19

Season—Team	Min.	FGA	FGM	Pct.	FTA	FTM	Pct.	Off.	Def.	Tot.	Ast.	PF	Dq.	Stl.	Blk.	Pts.
1982—Phoenix	15	2	0	.000	2	1	.500	2	3	5	1	1	0	0	2	1
1985—Boston	12	7	3	.429	2	2	1.000	1	5	6	3	2	0	0	0	8
Totals	98	37	20	.541	22	19	.864	7	11	18	9	10	0	5	4	59

Named to All-NBA First Team, 1981. . . . All-NBA Second Team, 1980. . . . NBA All-Defensive First Team, 1979, 1980, 1981, 1982, 1983. . . . NBA All-Defensive Second Team, 1984 and 1985. . . . NBA Playoff MVP, 1979. . . . Member of NBA championship teams, 1979 and 1984. . . . Shares NBA record for most free throws made in one half of championship series game, 12, vs. Los Angeles, June 12, 1984.

EARVIN JOHNSON JR.
(Magic)

Born August 14, 1959 at Lansing, Mich.   Height 6:08.   Weight 215.

High School—Lansing, Mich., Everett.

College—Michigan State University, East Lansing, Mich.

Drafted by Los Angeles on first round as an undergraduate, 1979 (1st pick).

—COLLEGIATE RECORD—

Year	G.	Min.	FGA	FGM	Pct.	FTA	FTM	Pct.	Reb.	Pts.	Avg.
77-78	30	....	382	175	.458	205	161	.785	237	511	17.0
78-79	32	1159	370	173	.468	240	202	.842	234	548	17.1
Totals	62	....	752	348	.463	445	363	.816	471	1059	17.1

NBA REGULAR SEASON RECORD

Sea.—Team	G.	Min.	FGA	FGM	Pct.	FTA	FTM	Pct.	Off.	Def.	Tot.	Ast.	PF	Dq.	Stl.	Blk.	Pts.	Avg.
79-80—Los Angeles	77	2795	949	503	.530	462	374	.810	166	430	596	563	218	1	187	41	1387	18.0
80-81—Los Angeles	37	1371	587	312	.532	225	171	.760	101	219	320	317	100	0	127	27	798	21.6
81-82—Los Angeles	78	2991	1036	556	.537	433	329	.760	252	499	751	743	223	1	208	34	1447	18.6
82-83—Los Angeles	79	2907	933	511	.548	380	304	.800	214	469	683	829	200	1	176	47	1326	16.8
83-84—Los Angeles	67	2567	780	441	.565	358	290	.810	99	392	491	875	169	1	150	49	1178	17.6
84-85—L.A. Lakers	77	2781	899	504	.561	464	391	.843	90	386	476	968	155	0	113	25	1406	18.3
Totals	415	15412	5184	2827	.545	2322	1859	.801	922	2395	3317	4295	1065	4	961	223	7542	18.2

Three-Point Field Goals: 1979-80, 7-for-31 (.226). 1980-81, 3-for-17 (.176). 1981-82, 6-for-29 (.207). 1982-83, 0-for-21. 1983-84, 6-for-29 (.207). 1984-85, 7-for-37 (.189). Totals, 29-for-164 (.177).

NBA PLAYOFF RECORD

Sea.—Team	G.	Min.	FGA	FGM	Pct.	FTA	FTM	Pct.	Off.	Def.	Tot.	Ast.	PF	Dq.	Stl.	Blk.	Pts.	Avg.
79-80—Los Angeles	16	658	199	103	.518	106	85	.802	52	116	168	151	47	1	49	6	293	18.3
80-81—Los Angeles	3	127	49	19	.388	20	13	.650	8	33	41	21	14	1	8	3	51	17.0
81-82—Los Angeles	14	562	157	83	.529	93	77	.828	54	104	158	130	50	0	40	3	243	17.4
82-83—Los Angeles	15	643	206	100	.485	81	68	.840	51	77	128	192	49	0	34	2	268	17.9
83-84—Los Angeles	21	837	274	151	.551	100	80	.800	26	113	139	284	71	0	42	20	382	18.2
84-85—L.A. Lakers	19	687	226	116	.513	118	100	.847	19	115	134	289	48	0	32	4	333	17.5
Totals	88	3514	1111	572	.515	518	423	.817	210	558	768	1067	279	2	205	48	1570	17.8

Three-Point Field Goals: 1979-80, 2-for-8 (.250). 1981-82, 0-for-4. 1982-83, 0-for-11. 1983-84, 0-for-7. 1984-85, 1-for-7 (.143). Totals, 3-for-37 (.081).

NBA ALL-STAR GAME RECORD

Season—Team	Min.	FGA	FGM	Pct.	FTA	FTM	Pct.	Off.	Def.	Tot.	Ast.	PF	Dq.	Stl.	Blk.	Pts.
1980—Los Angeles	24	8	5	.625	2	2	1.000	2	0	2	4	3	0	3	2	12
1982—Los Angeles	23	9	5	.556	7	6	.857	3	1	4	7	5	0	0	0	16
1983—Los Angeles	33	16	7	.438	4	3	.750	3	2	5	16	2	0	5	0	17
1984—Los Angeles	37	13	6	.462	2	2	1.000	4	5	9	22	3	0	3	2	15
1985—L.A. Lakers	31	14	7	.500	8	7	.875	2	3	5	15	2	0	1	0	21
Totals	148	60	30	.500	23	20	.870	14	11	25	64	15	0	12	4	81

Three-Point Field Goals: 1980, 0-for-1. 1983, 0-for-2. 1983-84, 1-for-3 (.333). Totals, 1-for-5 (.200).

Named to All-NBA First Team, 1983, 1984, 1985. . . . All-NBA Second Team, 1982. . . . NBA All-Rookie Team, 1980. . . . NBA Playoff MVP, 1980 and 1982. . . . Recipient of Schick Pivotal Player Award, 1984. . . . Member of NBA championship teams, 1980, 1982, 1985. . . . Holds all-time NBA playoff record for most assists. . . . Holds NBA playoff game record for most assists, 24, vs. Phoenix, May 15, 1984. . . . Holds NBA playoff game record for most assists in one half, 15, vs. Portland, May 3, 1985. . . . Holds NBA championship series game records for most assists, 21, most assists in one half, 11, and shares record for most assists in one quarter, 8, vs. Boston, June 3, 1984. . . . Holds NBA All-Star Game record for most assists, 22, 1984. . . . Led NBA in steals, 1981 and 1982. . . . Led NBA in assists, 1983 and 1984. . . . Named to THE SPORTING NEWS All-America First Team, 1979. . . . NCAA Division I Tournament Most Outstanding Player, 1979. . . . Member of NCAA championship team, 1979.

—DID YOU KNOW—

That the only NBA championship series in which home teams won every game was in 1955, when Syracuse defeated Fort Wayne?

EDWARD JOHNSON JR.
(Eddie)

Born February 24, 1955 at Ocala, Fla.   Height 6:02.   Weight 190.
High School—Summerfield, Fla., Lake Weir.
College—Auburn University, Auburn, Ala.
Drafted by Atlanta on third round, 1977 (49th pick).

—COLLEGIATE RECORD—

Year	G.	Min.	FGA	FGM	Pct.	FTA	FTM	Pct.	Reb.	Pts.	Avg.
73-74	26	....	538	231	.429	130	105	.808	105	567	21.8
74-75	24	....	449	200	.445	116	102	.879	90	502	20.9
75-76	26	....	428	204	.477	142	105	.739	101	513	19.7
76-77	26	....	362	154	.425	124	98	.790	67	406	15.6
Totals	102	....	1777	789	.444	512	410	.801	363	1988	19.5

NBA REGULAR SEASON RECORD

									—Rebounds—									
Sea.—Team	G.	Min.	FGA	FGM	Pct.	FTA	FTM	Pct.	Off.	Def.	Tot.	Ast.	PF	Dq.	Stl.	Blk.	Pts.	Avg.
77-78—Atlanta	79	1875	686	332	.484	201	164	.816	51	102	153	235	232	4	100	4	828	10.5
78-79—Atlanta	78	2413	982	501	.510	292	243	.832	65	105	170	360	241	6	121	11	1245	16.0
79-80—Atlanta	79	2622	1212	590	.487	338	280	.828	95	105	200	370	216	2	120	24	1465	18.5
80-81—Atlanta	75	2693	1136	573	.504	356	279	.784	60	119	179	407	188	2	126	11	1431	19.1
81-82—Atlanta	68	2314	1011	455	.450	385	294	.764	63	128	191	358	188	1	102	16	1211	17.8
82-83—Atlanta	61	1813	858	389	.453	237	186	.785	26	98	124	318	138	2	61	6	978	16.0
83-84—Atlanta	67	1893	798	353	.442	213	164	.770	31	115	146	374	155	2	58	7	886	13.2
84-85—Atlanta	73	2367	946	453	.479	332	265	.798	38	154	192	566	184	1	43	7	1193	16.3
Totals	580	17990	7629	3646	.478	2354	1875	.797	429	926	1355	2988	1542	20	731	86	9237	15.9

Three-Point Field Goals: 1979-80, 5-for-13 (.385). 1980-81, 6-for-20 (.300). 1981-82, 7-for-30 (.233). 1982-83, 14-for-41 (.341). 1983-84, 16-for-43 (.372). 1984-85, 22-for-72 (.306). Totals, 70-for-219 (.320).

NBA PLAYOFF RECORD

									—Rebounds—									
Sea.—Team	G.	Min.	FGA	FGM	Pct.	FTA	FTM	Pct.	Off.	Def.	Tot.	Ast.	PF	Dq.	Stl.	Blk.	Pts.	Avg.
77-78—Atlanta	2	64	19	12	.632	8	7	.875	2	4	6	6	10	1	8	1	31	15.5
78-79—Atlanta	9	262	128	65	.508	25	18	.720	8	15	23	45	22	0	4	2	148	16.4
79-80—Atlanta	5	188	74	38	.514	28	21	.750	3	15	18	21	12	0	8	2	97	19.4
81-82—Atlanta	2	67	26	9	.346	4	4	1.000	0	6	6	9	8	0	0	1	22	11.0
83-84—Atlanta	5	123	54	19	.352	22	15	.682	2	7	9	24	11	0	6	0	54	10.8
Totals	23	704	301	143	.475	87	65	.747	15	47	62	105	63	1	26	6	352	15.3

Three-Point Field Goals: 1983-84, 1-for-6 (.167).

NBA ALL-STAR GAME RECORD

								—Rebounds—								
Season—Team	Min.	FGA	FGM	Pct.	FTA	FTM	Pct.	Off.	Def.	Tot.	Ast.	PF	Dq.	Stl.	Blk.	Pts.
1980—Atlanta	32	16	11	.688	0	0	.000	1	0	1	7	2	0	6	0	22
1981—Atlanta	28	12	7	.583	3	2	.667	1	1	2	2	1	0	1	0	16
Totals	60	28	18	.643	3	2	.667	2	1	3	9	3	0	7	0	38

Named to NBA All-Defensive Second Team, 1979 and 1980. . . . Brother of Washington Bullets guard Frank Johnson.

EDWARD A. JOHNSON
(Eddie)

Born May 1, 1959 at Chicago, Ill.   Height 6:08.   Weight 215.
High School—Chicago, Ill., Westinghouse.
College—University of Illinois, Champaign, Ill.
Drafted by Kansas City on second round, 1981 (29th pick).

—COLLEGIATE RECORD—

Year	G.	Min.	FGA	FGM	Pct.	FTA	FTM	Pct.	Reb.	Pts.	Avg.
77-78	27	469	234	100	.427	27	20	.741	84	220	8.1
78-79	30	786	405	168	.415	49	26	.531	170	362	12.1
79-80	35	1215	576	266	.462	119	78	.655	310	610	17.4
80-81	29	1009	443	219	.494	82	62	.756	267	500	17.2
Totals	121	3479	1658	753	.454	277	186	.671	831	1692	14.0

NBA REGULAR SEASON RECORD

									—Rebounds—									
Sea.—Team	G.	Min.	FGA	FGM	Pct.	FTA	FTM	Pct.	Off.	Def.	Tot.	Ast.	PF	Dq.	Stl.	Blk.	Pts.	Avg.
81-82—Kansas City	74	1517	643	295	.459	149	99	.664	128	194	322	109	210	6	50	14	690	9.3

EDDIE JOHNSON

Sea.—Team	G.	Min.	FGA	FGM	Pct.	FTA	FTM	Pct.	Off.	Def.	Tot.	Ast.	PF	Dq.	Stl.	Blk.	Pts.	Avg.
										—Rebounds—								
82-83—Kansas City	82	2933	1370	677	.494	317	247	.779	191	310	501	216	259	3	70	20	1621	19.8
83-84—Kansas City	82	2920	1552	753	.485	331	268	.810	165	290	455	296	266	4	76	21	1794	21.9
84-85—Kansas City	82	3029	1565	769	.491	373	325	.871	151	256	407	273	237	2	83	22	1876	22.9
Totals	320	10399	5130	2494	.486	1170	939	.803	635	1050	1685	894	972	15	279	77	5981	18.7

Three-Point Field Goals: 1981-82, 1-for-11 (.091). 1982-83, 20-for-71 (.282). 1983-84, 20-for-64 (.313). 1984-85, 13-for-54 (.241). Totals, 54-for-200 (.270).

NBA PLAYOFF RECORD

Sea.—Team	G.	Min.	FGA	FGM	Pct.	FTA	FTM	Pct.	Off.	Def.	Tot.	Ast.	PF	Dq.	Stl.	Blk.	Pts.	Avg.
										—Rebounds—								
83-84—Kansas City	3	107	48	21	.438	7	7	1.000	4	6	10	12	8	0	3	1	51	17.0

FRANKLIN LENARD JOHNSON
(Frank)

Born November 23, 1958 at Weirsdale, Fla.   Height 6:02.   Weight 185.

High School—Summerfield, Fla., Lake Weir.

College—Wake Forest University, Winston-Salem, N. C.

Drafted by Washington on first round, 1981 (11th pick).

—COLLEGIATE RECORD—

Year	G.	Min.	FGA	FGM	Pct.	FTA	FTM	Pct.	Reb.	Pts.	Avg.
76-77	30	1044	328	150	.457	69	48	.696	84	348	11.6
77-78	29	999	392	193	.492	122	84	.689	91	470	16.2
78-79	27	957	354	169	.477	125	96	.768	62	434	16.1
79-80	5	109	32	9	.281	10	10	1.000	9	28	5.6
80-81	29	945	359	187	.521	116	95	.819	60	469	16.2
Totals	120	4054	1465	708	.483	442	333	.753	306	1749	14.6

(Suffered broken bone in left foot prior to 1979-80 season; granted extra year of eligibility.)

NBA REGULAR SEASON RECORD

Sea.—Team	G.	Min.	FGA	FGM	Pct.	FTA	FTM	Pct.	Off.	Def.	Tot.	Ast.	PF	Dq.	Stl.	Blk.	Pts.	Avg.
										—Rebounds—								
81-82—Washington	79	2027	812	336	.414	204	153	.750	34	113	147	380	196	1	76	7	842	10.7
82-83—Washington	68	2324	786	321	.408	261	196	.751	46	132	178	549	170	1	110	6	852	12.5
83-84—Washington	82	2686	840	392	.467	252	187	.742	58	126	184	567	174	1	96	6	982	12.0
84-85—Washington	46	925	358	175	.489	96	72	.750	23	40	63	143	72	0	43	3	428	9.3
Totals	275	7962	2796	1224	.438	813	608	.748	161	411	572	1639	612	3	325	22	3104	11.3

Three-Point Field Goals: 1981-82, 17-for-79 (.215). 1982-83, 14-for-61 (.230). 1983-84, 11-for-43 (.256). 1984-85, 6-for-17 (.353). Totals, 48-for-200 (.240).

NBA PLAYOFF RECORD

Sea.—Team	G.	Min.	FGA	FGM	Pct.	FTA	FTM	Pct.	Off.	Def.	Tot.	Ast.	PF	Dq.	Stl.	Blk.	Pts.	Avg.
										—Rebounds—								
81-82—Washington	7	280	104	40	.385	28	24	.857	7	15	22	59	24	0	10	0	109	15.6
83-84—Washington	4	156	42	24	.571	8	8	1.000	4	9	13	25	16	0	5	0	57	14.3
84-85—Washington	2	39	14	4	.286	6	6	1.000	1	3	4	7	5	0	2	0	15	7.5
Totals	13	475	160	68	.425	42	38	.905	12	27	39	91	45	0	17	0	181	13.9

Three-Point Field Goals: 1981-82, 5-for-12 (.417). 1983-84, 1-for-3 (.333). 1984-85, 1-for-6 (.167). Totals, 7-for-21 (.333).

Named to THE SPORTING NEWS All-America Second Team, 1981. . . . Brother of Atlanta Hawks guard Eddie Johnson.

GEORGE L. JOHNSON

Born December 8, 1956 at Brooklyn, N. Y.   Height 6:07.   Weight 218.

High School—Brooklyn, N. Y., New Utrecht.

College—St. John's University, Jamaica, N. Y.

Drafted by Milwaukee on first round, 1978 (12th pick).

Sold by Milwaukee to Denver, October 19, 1979.
Sold by Denver to Milwaukee, May 16, 1980.
Traded by Milwaukee with a 1982 2nd round draft choice to Indiana for Mickey Johnson, September 11, 1980.
Signed by Philadelphia as Veteran Free Agent, December 15, 1984; Indiana agreed not to exercise its right of first refusal in exchange for two future 2nd round draft choices.

—COLLEGIATE RECORD—

Year	G.	Min.	FGA	FGM	Pct.	FTA	FTM	Pct.	Reb.	Pts.	Avg.
74-75	30	....	263	139	.529	53	35	.660	290	313	10.4
75-76	28	....	348	164	.471	76	57	.750	301	385	13.8
76-77	31	....	451	228	.506	114	84	.737	335	540	17.4
77-78	27	....	425	213	.501	128	99	.773	324	525	19.4
Totals	116	....	1487	744	.500	371	275	.741	1250	1763	15.2

NBA REGULAR SEASON RECORD

Sea.—Team	G.	Min.	FGA	FGM	Pct.	FTA	FTM	Pct.	Off.	Def.	Tot.	Ast.	PF	Dq.	Stl.	Blk.	Pts.	Avg.
									—Rebounds—									
78-79—Milwaukee	67	1157	342	165	.482	117	84	.718	106	254	360	81	187	5	75	49	414	6.2
79-80—Denver	75	1938	649	309	.476	189	148	.783	190	394	584	157	260	4	84	67	768	10.2
80-81—Indiana	43	930	394	182	.462	122	93	.762	99	179	278	86	120	1	47	23	457	10.6
81-82—Indiana	59	720	291	120	.412	80	60	.750	72	145	217	40	147	2	36	25	300	5.1
82-83—Indiana	82	2297	858	409	.477	172	126	.733	176	369	545	220	279	6	77	53	951	11.6
83-84—Indiana	81	2073	884	411	.465	270	223	.826	139	321	460	195	256	3	82	49	1056	13.0
84-85—Philadelphia	55	756	263	107	.407	56	49	.875	48	116	164	38	99	0	31	16	264	4.8
Totals	462	9871	3681	1703	.463	1006	783	.778	830	1778	2608	817	1348	21	432	282	4210	9.1

Three-Point Field Goals: 1979-80, 2-for-9 (.222). 1980-81, 0-for-5. 1981-82, 0-for-2. 1982-83, 7-for-38 (.184). 1983-84, 11-for-47 (.234). 1984-85, 1-for-10 (.100). Totals, 21-for-111 (.189).

NBA PLAYOFF RECORD

Sea.—Team	G.	Min.	FGA	FGM	Pct.	FTA	FTM	Pct.	Off.	Def.	Tot.	Ast.	PF	Dq.	Stl.	Blk.	Pts.	Avg.
									—Rebounds—									
80-81—Indiana	2	23	8	5	.625	0	0	.000	1	3	4	1	1	0	0	0	10	5.0
84-85—Philadelphia	5	24	8	5	.625	0	0	.000	3	4	7	0	2	0	0	0	11	2.2
Totals	7	47	16	10	.625	0	0	.000	4	7	11	1	3	0	0	0	21	3.0

Three-Point Field Goals: 1984-85, 1-for-1 (1.000).

Named to THE SPORTING NEWS All-America Second Team, 1978.

GEORGE THOMAS JOHNSON

Born December 18, 1948 at Tylertown, Miss.   Height 6:11.   Weight 205.

High School—Tylertown, Miss., Gulledge.

College—Dillard University, New Orleans, La.

Drafted by Chicago on fifth round, 1970 (79th pick).

Waived by Chicago, April 15, 1971; signed by Golden State as a free agent, September 28, 1972.

Traded by Golden State to Buffalo for a 1977 1st round draft choice, January 18, 1977.

Traded by Buffalo with a 1979 1st round draft choice to New Jersey for Nate Archibald, September 1, 1977.

Signed by San Antonio as Veteran Free Agent, August 15, 1980; New Jersey was awarded a 1981 1st round draft choice as compensation.

Traded by San Antonio to Atlanta for Jim Johnstone and two 2nd round draft choices (1983 and 1985), September 27, 1982.

Signed by New Jersey as Veteran Free Agent, September 27, 1984; Atlanta elected not to exercise its right of first refusal.

Played in Western Basketball Association with Martinez (Calif.) Muirs during 1971-72 season (averaged 13.8 points and 15.7 rebounds per game).

—COLLEGIATE RECORD—

Year	G.	Min.	FGA	FGM	Pct.	FTA	FTM	Pct.	Reb.	Pts.	Avg.
66-67	15	....	101	35	.347	75	41	.547	210	111	7.4
67-68	23	....	227	115	.507	74	37	.500	300	267	11.6
68-69	25	....	286	130	.455	90	59	.656	376	319	12.8
69-70	27	....	349	175	.501	90	57	.633	460	407	15.1
Totals	90	....	963	455	.472	329	194	.590	1346	1104	12.3

NBA REGULAR SEASON RECORD

Sea.—Team	G.	Min.	FGA	FGM	Pct.	FTA	FTM	Pct.	Off.	Def.	Tot.	Ast.	PF	Dq.	Stl.	Blk.	Pts.	Avg.
									—Rebounds—									
72-73—Golden State	56	349	100	41	.410	17	7	.412			138	8	40	0			89	1.6
73-74—Golden State	66	1291	358	173	.483	107	59	.551	190	332	522	73	176	3	35	124	405	6.1
74-75—Golden State	82	1439	319	152	.476	91	60	.659	217	357	574	67	206	1	32	136	364	4.4
75-76—Golden State	82	1745	341	165	.484	104	70	.673	200	427	627	82	275	6	51	174	400	4.9
76-77—G.S.-Buff.	78	1652	429	198	.462	98	71	.724	204	407	611	104	246	8	37	177	467	6.0
77-78—New Jersey	81	2411	721	285	.395	185	133	.719	245	534	779	111	339	20	78	274	703	8.7
78-79—New Jersey	78	2058	483	206	.427	138	105	.761	201	415	616	88	315	8	68	253	517	6.6
79-80—New Jersey	81	2119	543	248	.457	126	89	.706	192	410	602	173	312	7	53	258	585	7.2
80-81—San Antonio	82	1935	347	164	.473	109	80	.734	215	387	602	92	273	3	47	278	408	5.0
81-82—San Antonio	75	1578	195	91	.467	64	43	.672	152	302	454	79	259	6	20	234	225	3.0
82-83—Atlanta	37	461	57	25	.439	19	14	.737	44	73	117	17	69	0	10	59	64	1.7
84-85—New Jersey	65	800	79	42	.532	27	22	.815	74	111	185	22	151	2	19	78	107	1.6
Totals...............	863	17838	3972	1790	.451	1085	753	.694			5827	916	2661	64	450	2045	4334	5.0

Three-Point Field Goals: 1979-80, 0-for-1. 1984-85, 1-for-1 (1.000). Totals, 1-for-2 (.500).

NBA PLAYOFF RECORD

Sea.—Team	G.	Min.	FGA	FGM	Pct.	FTA	FTM	Pct.	Off.	Def.	Tot.	Ast.	PF	Dq.	Stl.	Blk.	Pts.	Avg.
									—Rebounds—									
72-73—Golden State	9	45	15	6	.400	4	1	.250			14	3	7	0			13	1.4
74-75—Golden State	17	321	63	36	.571	27	16	.593	54	72	126	15	50	1	9	40	88	5.2
75-76—Golden State	13	261	54	31	.574	19	14	.737	38	49	87	17	46	0	14	23	76	5.8
78-79—New Jersey	2	70	21	14	.667	3	1	.333	8	17	25	2	8	1	2	7	29	14.5
80-81—San Antonio	7	165	26	12	.462	10	7	.700	24	39	63	6	20	0	3	16	31	4.4

Sea.—Team	G.	Min.	FGA	FGM	Pct.	FTA	FTM	Pct.	Off.	Def.	Tot.	Ast.	PF	Dq.	Stl.	Blk.	Pts.	Avg.
81-82—San Antonio	9	175	8	4	.500	5	3	.600	12	34	46	12	34	0	6	15	11	1.2
82-83—Atlanta	1	2	0	0	.000	0	0	.000	0	0	0	0	0	0	0	0	0	0.0
84-85—New Jersey	1	4	0	0	.000	0	0	.000	0	0	0	0	0	0	0	0	0	0.0
Totals	59	1043	187	103	.551	68	42	.618			361	55	165	2	34	101	248	4.2

Named to NBA All-Defensive Second Team, 1981.... Member of NBA championship team, 1975.... Led NBA in blocked shots, 1978, 1981, 1982.

MARQUES KEVIN JOHNSON

Born February 8, 1956 at Nachitoches, La.   Height 6:07.   Weight 218.

High School—Los Angeles, Calif., Crenshaw.

College—University of California at Los Angeles, Los Angeles, Calif.

Drafted by Milwaukee on first round, 1977 (3rd pick).

Traded by Milwaukee with Harvey Catchings, Junior Bridgeman and cash to Los Angeles Clippers for Terry Cummings, Craig Hodges and Ricky Pierce, September 29, 1984.

—COLLEGIATE RECORD—

Year	G.	Min.	FGA	FGM	Pct.	FTA	FTM	Pct.	Reb.	Pts.	Avg.
73-74	27	....	131	83	.634	38	28	.737	90	194	7.2
74-75	29	....	254	138	.543	86	59	.686	205	335	11.6
75-76	32	1165	413	223	.540	140	106	.757	301	552	17.3
76-77	27	1004	413	244	.591	145	90	.621	301	578	21.4
Totals	115	....	1211	688	.568	409	283	.692	897	1659	14.4

NBA REGULAR SEASON RECORD

Sea.—Team	G.	Min.	FGA	FGM	Pct.	FTA	FTM	Pct.	Off.	Def.	Tot.	Ast.	PF	Dq.	Stl.	Blk.	Pts.	Avg.
77-78—Milwaukee	80	2765	1204	628	.522	409	301	.736	292	555	847	190	221	3	92	103	1557	19.5
78-79—Milwaukee	77	2779	1491	820	.550	437	332	.760	212	374	586	234	186	1	116	89	1972	25.6
79-80—Milwaukee	77	2686	1267	689	.544	368	291	.791	217	349	566	273	173	0	100	70	1671	21.7
80-81—Milwaukee	76	2542	1153	636	.552	381	269	.706	225	293	518	346	196	1	115	41	1541	20.3
81-82—Milwaukee	60	1900	760	404	.532	260	182	.700	153	211	364	213	142	1	59	35	990	16.5
82-83—Milwaukee	80	2853	1420	723	.509	359	264	.735	196	366	562	363	211	0	100	56	1714	21.4
83-84—Milwaukee	74	2715	1288	646	.502	340	241	.709	173	307	480	315	194	1	115	44	1535	20.7
84-85—L.A. Clippers	72	2448	1094	494	.452	260	190	.731	184	244	428	248	193	2	72	30	1181	16.4
Totals	596	20688	9677	5040	.521	2814	2070	.736	1652	2699	4351	2182	1516	9	769	469	12161	20.4

Three-Point Field Goals: 1979-80, 2-for-9 (.222). 1980-81, 0-for-9. 1981-82, 0-for-4. 1982-83, 4-for-20 (.200). 1983-84, 2-for-13 (.154). 1984-85, 3-for-13 (.231). Totals, 11-for-68 (.162).

NBA PLAYOFF RECORD

Sea.—Team	G.	Min.	FGA	FGM	Pct.	FTA	FTM	Pct.	Off.	Def.	Tot.	Ast.	PF	Dq.	Stl.	Blk.	Pts.	Avg.
77-78—Milwaukee	9	321	153	84	.549	64	48	.750	35	77	112	31	25	0	10	17	216	24.0
79-80—Milwaukee	7	303	128	54	.422	40	30	.750	17	31	48	20	20	0	5	6	139	19.9
80-81—Milwaukee	7	266	135	75	.556	32	23	.719	41	25	66	34	14	0	10	7	173	24.7
81-82—Milwaukee	6	235	100	44	.440	42	24	.571	23	21	44	20	25	0	6	2	113	18.8
82-83—Milwaukee	9	382	175	85	.486	43	28	.651	28	44	72	38	22	0	8	7	198	22.0
83-84—Milwaukee	16	605	273	129	.473	90	65	.722	29	56	85	55	50	0	17	6	324	20.3
Totals	54	2112	964	471	.489	311	218	.701	173	254	427	198	156	0	56	45	1163	21.5

Three-Point Field Goals: 1979-80, 1-for-3 (.333). 1980-81, 0-for-1. 1981-82, 1-for-4 (.250). 1982-83, 0-for-1. 1983-84, 1-for-4 (.250). Totals, 3-for-13 (.231).

NBA ALL-STAR GAME RECORD

Season—Team	Min.	FGA	FGM	Pct.	FTA	FTM	Pct.	Off.	Def.	Tot.	Ast.	PF	Dq.	Stl.	Blk.	Pts.
1979—Milwaukee....	20	11	3	.273	6	4	.667	3	3	6	2	1	0	0	0	10
1980—Milwaukee....	34	6	1	.167	2	2	1.000	1	3	4	1	2	0	1	1	4
1981—Milwaukee....	19	2	1	.500	6	5	.833	1	3	4	2	2	0	0	0	7
1983—Milwaukee....	20	10	3	.300	2	1	.500	2	0	2	2	1	0	0	1	7
Totals	93	29	8	.276	16	12	.750	7	9	16	7	6	0	1	2	28

Named to All-NBA First Team, 1979.... All-NBA Second Team, 1980 and 1981.... NBA All-Rookie Team, 1978... . THE SPORTING NEWS College Player of the Year, 1977.... THE SPORTING NEWS All-America First Team, 1977.... Member of NCAA championship team, 1975.

—DID YOU KNOW—

That Dick Surhoff, father of B.J. Surhoff, the No. 1 choice in the baseball free-agent draft last summer, played briefly with the New York Knicks? B.J. was chosen by the Milwaukee Brewers.

VINNIE JOHNSON

VINCENT JOHNSON
(Vinnie)

Born September 1, 1956 at Brooklyn, N. Y. Height 6:02. Weight 200.

High School—Brooklyn, N. Y., Franklin Roosevelt.

Colleges—McLennan Community College, Waco, Tex., and Baylor University, Waco, Tex.

Drafted by Seattle on first round, 1979 (7th pick).

Traded by Seattle to Detroit for Greg Kelser, November 23, 1981.

—COLLEGIATE RECORD—

McLennan CC

Year	G.	Min.	FGA	FGM	Pct.	FTA	FTM	Pct.	Reb.	Pts.	Avg.
75-76	35	....	...	398	....	...	169	....	....	965	27.6
76-77	31	....	...	382	....	...	152	....	....	916	29.5
JC Totals	66	....	....	780	....	...	321	....	....	1881	28.5

Baylor

Year	G.	Min.	FGA	FGM	Pct.	FTA	FTM	Pct.	Reb.	Pts.	Avg.
77-78	25	....	481	241	.501	141	93	.660	140	575	23.0
78-79	26	....	502	262	.522	170	132	.776	128	656	25.2
Totals	51	....	983	503	.512	311	225	.723	268	1231	24.1

NBA REGULAR SEASON RECORD

Sea.—Team	G.	Min.	FGA	FGM	Pct.	FTA	FTM	Pct.	—Rebounds— Off.	Def.	Tot.	Ast.	PF	Dq.	Stl.	Blk.	Pts.	Avg.
79-80—Seattle	38	325	115	45	.391	39	31	.795	19	36	55	54	40	0	19	4	121	3.2
80-81—Seattle	81	2311	785	419	.534	270	214	.793	193	173	366	341	198	0	78	20	1053	13.0
81-82—Sea.-Det.	74	1295	444	217	.489	142	107	.754	82	77	159	171	101	0	56	25	544	7.4
82-83—Detroit	82	2511	1013	520	.513	315	245	.778	167	186	353	301	263	2	93	49	1296	15.8
83-84—Detroit	82	1909	901	426	.473	275	207	.753	130	107	237	271	196	1	44	19	1063	13.0
84-85—Detroit	82	2093	942	428	.454	247	190	.769	134	118	252	325	205	2	71	20	1051	12.8
Totals	439	10444	4200	2055	.489	1288	994	.772	725	697	1422	1463	1003	5	361	137	5128	11.7

Three-Pgint Field Goals: 1979-80, 0-for-1. 1980-81, 1-for-5 (.200). 1981-82, 3-for-12 (.250). 1982-83, 11-for-40 (.275). 1983-84, 4-for-19 (.211). 1984-85, 5-for-27 (.185). Totals, 24-for-104 (.231).

NBA PLAYOFF RECORD

Sea.—Team	G.	Min.	FGA	FGM	Pct.	FTA	FTM	Pct.	—Rebounds— Off.	Def.	Tot.	Ast.	PF	Dq.	Stl.	Blk.	Pts.	Avg.
79-80—Seattle	5	12	3	1	.333	0	0	.000	0	2	2	2	1	0	1	0	2	0.4
83-84—Detroit	5	132	46	17	.370	19	17	.895	5	9	14	12	9	0	1	1	51	10.2
84-85—Detroit	9	235	103	53	.515	28	22	.786	15	12	27	29	24	0	6	1	128	14.2
Totals	19	379	152	71	.467	47	39	.830	20	23	43	43	34	0	8	2	181	9.5

Three-Point Field Goals: 1983-84, 0-for-1. 1984-85, 0-for-3. Totals, 0-for-4.

WALLACE EDGAR JOHNSON
(Mickey)

Born August 31, 1952 at Chicago, Ill. Height 6:10. Weight 190.

High School—Chicago, Ill., Lindbloom.

College—Aurora College, Aurora, Ill.

Drafted by Portland on fourth round, 1974 (56th pick).

Traded by Portland to Chicago for a 1975 3rd round draft choice, September 17, 1974.

Signed by Indiana as Veteran Free Agent, July 17, 1979; Chicago received Ricky Sobers as compensation.

Traded by Indiana to Milwaukee for George Johnson and a 1982 2nd round draft choice, September 11, 1980.

Traded by Milwaukee with the rights to Fred Roberts to New Jersey for Phil Ford and a 1983 2nd round draft choice, November 10, 1982.

Traded by New Jersey with Eric Floyd to Golden State for Micheal Ray Richardson, February 6, 1983.

—COLLEGIATE RECORD—

Year	G.	Min.	FGA	FGM	Pct.	FTA	FTM	Pct.	Reb.	Pts.	Avg.
70-71	22	....	438	252	.575	148	91	.615	419	595	27.0
71-72	24	....	412	232	.563	174	109	.626	492	573	23.9
72-73	24	....	483	278	.576	107	66	.617	550	622	25.9
73-74	24	....	520	288	.554	106	87	.821	506	663	27.6
Totals	94	....	1873	1050	.561	535	353	.660	1967	2453	26.1

NBA REGULAR SEASON RECORD

Sea.—Team	G.	Min.	FGA	FGM	Pct.	FTA	FTM	Pct.	—Rebounds— Off.	Def.	Tot.	Ast.	PF	Dq.	Stl.	Blk.	Pts.	Avg.
74-75—Chicago	38	291	118	53	.449	58	37	.638	32	62	94	20	57	1	10	11	143	3.8
75-76—Chicago	81	2390	1033	478	.463	360	283	.786	279	479	758	130	292	8	93	66	1239	15.3

Sea.—Team	G.	Min.	FGA	FGM	Pct.	FTA	FTM	Pct.	Off.	Def.	Tot.	Ast.	PF	Dq.	Stl.	Blk.	Pts.	Avg.
										—Rebounds—								
76-77—Chicago	81	2847	1205	538	.446	407	324	.796	297	531	828	195	315	10	103	64	1400	17.3
77-78—Chicago	81	2870	1215	561	.462	446	362	.812	218	520	738	267	317	8	92	68	1484	18.3
78-79—Chicago	82	2594	1105	496	.449	329	273	.830	193	434	627	380	286	9	88	59	1265	15.4
79-80—Indiana	82	2647	1271	588	.463	482	385	.799	258	423	681	344	291	11	153	112	1566	19.1
80-81—Milwaukee	82	2118	846	379	.448	332	262	.789	183	362	545	286	256	4	94	71	1023	12.5
81-82—Milwaukee	76	1934	757	372	.491	291	233	.801	133	321	454	215	240	4	72	45	978	12.9
82-83—Mil-NJ-GS	78	2053	921	391	.425	380	312	.821	163	331	494	255	288	10	82	46	1097	14.1
83-84—Golden State	78	2122	852	359	.421	432	339	.785	198	320	518	219	290	3	101	30	1062	13.6
84-85—Golden State	66	1565	714	304	.426	316	260	.823	149	247	396	149	221	5	70	35	875	13.3
Totals	825	23431	10037	4519	.450	3833	3070	.801	2103	4030	6133	2460	2853	73	958	607	12132	14.7

Three-Point Field Goals: 1979-80, 5-for-32 (.156). 1980-81, 3-for-18 (.167). 1981-82, 1-for-7 (.143). 1982-83, 3-for-36 (.083). 1983-84, 5-for-29 (.172). 1984-85, 7-for-30 (.233). Totals, 24-for-152 (.158).

NBA PLAYOFF RECORD

Sea.—Team	G.	Min.	FGA	FGM	Pct.	FTA	FTM	Pct.	Off.	Def.	Tot.	Ast.	PF	Dq.	Stl.	Blk.	Pts.	Avg.
										—Rebounds—								
74-75—Chicago	3	5	3	1	.333	0	0	.000	0	0	0	0	2	0	0	1	2	0.7
76-77—Chicago	3	124	72	34	.472	16	14	.875	14	25	39	7	13	0	5	2	82	27.3
80-81—Milwaukee	7	170	65	26	.400	35	30	.857	24	23	47	13	25	0	9	6	82	11.7
81-82—Milwaukee	6	206	75	43	.573	39	33	.846	15	17	32	18	27	1	8	4	119	19.8
Totals	19	505	215	104	.484	90	77	.856	53	65	118	38	67	1	22	13	285	15.0

Three-Point Field Goals: 1980-81, 0-for-1. 1981-82, 0-for-1. Totals, 0-for-2.

CALDWELL JONES

Born August 4, 1950 at McGehee, Ark. Height 6:11. Weight 225.

High School—Rohwer, Ark., Desha Central.

College—Albany State College, Albany, Ga.

Drafted by Philadelphia on second round, 1973 (32nd pick).

Selected by Virginia on third round of ABA draft, 1973.
Signed by San Diego; Larry Miller sent by San Diego to Virginia as compensation, October 29, 1973.
Signed by Philadelphia (for future services), February 25, 1975.
Purchased by Kentucky from disbanded San Diego franchise, November 14, 1975.
Traded by Kentucky to St. Louis for Maurice Lucas, December 17, 1975.
Traded by Philadelphia with a 1983 1st round draft choice to Houston for Moses Malone, September 15, 1982.
Traded by Houston to Chicago for Mitchell Wiggins and 1985 2nd and 3rd round draft choices, August 10, 1984.

—COLLEGIATE RECORD—

Year	G.	Min.	FGA	FGM	Pct.	FTA	FTM	Pct.	Reb.	Pts.	Avg.
69-70†	25	....	367	185	.504	108	80	.741	440	450	18.0
70-71	27	....	437	206	.471	137	76	.555	576	488	18.1
71-72	28	....	539	288	.534	219	156	.712	567	732	26.1
72-73	29		470	238	.506	134	91	.679	633	567	19.6
Varsity Totals	109	....	1813	917	.506	598	403	.674	2216	2237	20.5

ABA REGULAR SEASON RECORD

Sea.—Team	G.	Min.	2-Point			3-Point			FTM	FTA	Pct.	Reb.	Ast.	Pts.	Avg.
			FGM	FGA	Pct.	FGM	FGA	Pct.							
73-74—San Diego	79	2929	505	1083	.466	2	8	.250	171	230	.743	1095	144	1187	15.0
74-75—San Diego	76	3004	603	1229	.491	3	11	.273	264	335	.788	1074	162	1479	19.5
75-76—SD-Ky-St.L.	76	2674	423	893	.474	0	7	.000	140	186	.753	853	147	986	13.0
Totals....................	231	8607	1531	3205	.478	5	26	.192	575	751	.766	3022	453	3652	15.8

ABA PLAYOFF RECORD

Sea.—Team	G.	Min.	2-Point			3-Point			FTM	FTA	Pct.	Reb.	Ast.	Pts.	Avg.
			FGM	FGA	Pct.	FGM	FGA	Pct.							
73-74—San Diego	6	277	36	88	.409	0	0	.000	11	16	.688	94	15	83	13.8

ABA ALL-STAR GAME RECORD

Sea.—Team	Min.	2-Point			3-Point			FTM	FTA	Pct.	Reb.	Ast.	Pts.	Avg.
		FGM	FGA	Pct.	FGM	FGA	Pct.							
1975—San Diego..........	15	2	4	.500	0	0	.000	1	1	1.000	4	0	5	5.0

NBA REGULAR SEASON RECORD

Sea.—Team	G.	Min.	FGA	FGM	Pct.	FTA	FTM	Pct.	Off.	Def.	Tot.	Ast.	PF	Dq.	Stl.	Blk.	Pts.	Avg.
										—Rebounds—								
76-77—Philadelphia	82	2023	424	215	.507	116	64	.552	190	476	666	92	301	3	43	200	494	6.0
77-78—Philadelphia	80	1636	359	169	.471	153	96	.627	165	405	570	92	281	4	26	127	434	5.4
78-79—Philadelphia	78	2171	637	302	.474	162	121	.747	177	570	747	151	303	10	39	157	725	9.3
79-80—Philadelphia	80	2771	532	232	.436	178	124	.697	219	731	950	164	298	5	43	162	588	7.4
80-81—Philadelphia	81	2639	485	218	.449	193	148	.767	200	613	813	122	271	2	53	134	584	7.2
81-82—Philadelphia	81	2446	465	231	.497	219	179	.817	164	544	708	100	301	3	38	146	641	7.9
82-83—Houston	82	2440	677	307	.453	206	162	.786	222	446	668	138	278	2	46	131	776	9.5

Sea.—Team	G.	Min.	FGA	FGM	Pct.	FTA	FTM	Pct.	Off.	Def.	Tot.	Ast.	PF	Dq.	Stl.	Blk.	Pts.	Avg.
83-84—Houston	81	2506	633	318	.502	196	164	.837	168	414	582	156	335	7	46	80	801	9.9
84-85—Chicago	42	885	115	53	.461	47	36	.766	49	162	211	34	125	3	12	31	142	3.4
Totals	687	19517	4327	2045	.473	1470	1094	.744	1554	4361	5915	1049	2493	39	346	1168	5185	7.5

Three-Point Field Goals: 1979-80, 0-for-2. 1981-82, 0-for-3. 1982-83, 0-for-2. 1983-84, 1-for-3 (.333). 1984-85, 0-for-2. Totals, 1-for-12 (.083).

NBA PLAYOFF RECORD

Sea.—Team	G.	Min.	FGA	FGM	Pct.	FTA	FTM	Pct.	Off.	Def.	Tot.	Ast.	PF	Dq.	Stl.	Blk.	Pts.	Avg.
76-77—Philadelphia	19	513	73	37	.507	30	18	.600	38	112	150	20	81	4	9	40	92	4.8
77-78—Philadelphia	10	301	56	28	.500	10	8	.800	22	84	106	14	36	2	5	30	64	6.4
78-79—Philadelphia	9	320	89	43	.483	36	28	.778	37	84	121	21	36	0	4	22	114	12.7
79-80—Philadelphia	18	639	129	58	.450	52	42	.808	50	135	185	34	75	1	13	37	158	8.8
80-81—Philadelphia	16	580	95	54	.568	42	31	.738	37	118	155	27	53	0	7	31	139	8.7
81-82—Philadelphia	21	679	160	74	.463	41	35	.854	52	137	189	19	77	1	11	40	183	8.7
84-85—Chicago	2	18	6	5	.833	0	0	.000	1	4	5	0	7	1	0	1	10	5.0
Totals	95	3050	608	299	.492	211	162	.768	237	674	911	135	365	9	49	201	760	8.0

Three-Point Field Goals: 1979-80, 0-for-3. 1984-85, 0-for-1. Totals, 0-for-4.

Named to NBA All-Defensive First Team, 1981 and 1982. . . . Shares ABA record for most blocked shots in one game, 12, vs. Carolina, January 6, 1974. . . . Led ABA in blocked shots, 1974 and 1975. . . . Brother of Detroit Pistons forward Major Jones, Washington Bullets forward-center Charles Jones and former ABA and NBA forward Wilbert Jones.

CHARLES JONES

Born April 3, 1957 at McGehee, Ark.   Height 6:09.   Weight 215.

High School—McGehee, Ark., Delta.

College—Albany State College, Albany, Ga.

Drafted by Phoenix on eighth round, 1979 (165th pick).

Waived by Phoenix, October 1, 1979; signed by Portland as a free agent, April 14, 1980.
Waived by Portland, July 21, 1980; signed by New York as a free agent, September 30, 1983.
Waived by New York, October 24, 1983; signed by Philadelphia to a 10-day contract that expired March 2, 1984.
Signed by San Antonio as a free agent, May 2, 1984.
Waived by San Antonio, September 11, 1984; signed by Chicago as a free agent, September 20, 1984.
Waived by Chicago, November 16, 1984; signed by Washington as a free agent, February 14, 1985.
Played in Continental Basketball Association with Maine Lumberjacks during 1979-80 and 1982-83 seasons, with Bay State Bombardiers during 1983-84 season and with Tampa Bay Thrillers during 1984-85 season.
Played in France during 1980-81 season.
Played in Italy during 1981-82 season.

—COLLEGIATE RECORD—

Year	G.	Min.	FGA	FGM	Pct.	FTA	FTM	Pct.	Reb.	Pts.	Avg.
75-76	24	....	206	106	.515	35	16	.457	198	228	9.5
76-77	27	....	284	136	.479	84	39	.464	374	311	11.5
77-78	27	....	276	148	.536	100	68	.680	368	364	13.5
78-79	29	....	352	182	.517	97	66	.680	438	430	14.8
Totals	107	....	1118	572	.512	316	189	.598	1378	1333	12.5

MINOR LEAGUE REGULAR SEASON RECORD

Sea.—Team	G.	Min.	——2-Point——			——3-Point——			FTM	FTA	Pct.	Reb.	Ast.	Pts.	Avg.
			FGM	FGA	Pct.	FGM	FGA	Pct.							
79-80—Maine CBA	39	1606	222	459	.484	0	2	.000	60	94	.619	506	70	504	12.9
82-83—Maine CBA	24	914	105	215	.488	0	1	.000	70	89	.786	223	35	280	11.7
83-84—Bay State CBA	37	1365	149	297	.501	0	1	.000	94	139	.676	293	73	392	10.6
84-85—Tampa Bay CBA	24	802	80	154	.519	0	1	.000	38	53	.716	227	38	198	8.3

NBA REGULAR SEASON RECORD

Sea.—Team	G.	Min.	FGA	FGM	Pct.	FTA	FTM	Pct.	Off.	Def.	Tot.	Ast.	PF	Dq.	Stl.	Blk.	Pts.	Avg.
83-84—Philadelphia	1	3	1	0	.000	4	1	.250	0	0	0	0	1	0	0	0	1	1.0
84-85—Chi.-Wash.	31	667	127	67	.528	58	40	.690	71	113	184	26	107	3	22	79	174	5.6
Totals	32	670	128	67	.523	62	41	.661	71	113	184	26	108	3	22	79	175	5.5

NBA PLAYOFF RECORD

Sea.—Team	G.	Min.	FGA	FGM	Pct.	FTA	FTM	Pct.	Off.	Def.	Tot.	Ast.	PF	Dq.	Stl.	Blk.	Pts.	Avg.
84-85—Washington	4	110	19	10	.526	16	9	.563	11	15	26	3	16	0	3	10	29	7.3

ITALIAN LEAGUE

Year	G.	Min.	FGA	FGM	Pct.	FTA	FTM	Pct.	Reb.	Pts.	Avg.
81-82—S. Benedetto....	38	1458	398	215	.540	114	73	.640	429	503	13.2

Led CBA in blocked shots, 1980, 1983 and 1984. . . . Named to CBA All-Star Second Team, 1984. . . . CBA All-Defensive First Team, 1983 and 1984. . . . CBA All-Defensive Second Team, 1985. . . . Brother of Caldwell Jones, forward-center with Chicago Bulls, Major Jones, forward with Detroit Pistons, and former ABA and NBA forward Wilbert Jones.

CHARLES ALEXANDER JONES

Born January 12, 1962 at Scooba, Miss. Height 6:08. Weight 215.

High School—Scooba, Miss., East Kemper.

College—University of Louisville, Louisville, Ky.

Drated by Phoenix on second round, 1984 (36th pick).

—COLLEGIATE RECORD—

Year	G.	Min.	FGA	FGM	Pct.	FTA	FTM	Pct.	Reb.	Pts.	Avg.
80-81	27	538	105	54	.514	68	38	.559	106	146	5.4
81-82	31	553	102	60	.588	92	65	.707	122	185	6.0
82-83	36	1088	243	134	.551	184	123	.668	247	391	10.9
83-84	35	1210	280	159	.568	169	84	.497	338	402	11.5
Totals	129	3389	730	407	.558	513	310	.604	813	1124	8.7

NBA REGULAR SEASON RECORD

Sea.—Team	G.	Min.	FGA	FGM	Pct.	FTA	FTM	Pct.	—Rebounds— Off.	Def.	Tot.	Ast.	PF	Dq.	Stl.	Blk.	Pts.	Avg.
84-85—Phoenix	78	1565	454	236	.520	281	182	.648	139	255	394	128	149	0	45	61	654	8.4

Three-Point Field Goals: 1984-85, 0-for-4.

NBA PLAYOFF RECORD

Sea.—Team	G.	Min.	FGA	FGM	Pct.	FTA	FTM	Pct.	—Rebounds— Off.	Def.	Tot.	Ast.	PF	Dq.	Stl.	Blk.	Pts.	Avg.
84-85—Phoenix	2	34	5	3	.600	6	6	1.000	1	2	3	3	4	0	0	3	12	6.0

EARL JONES

Born January 13, 1961 at Oak Hill, W. Va. Height 7:00. Weight 230.

High Schools—Mt. Hope, W. Va. (Sophomore and Junior)
and Washington D.C., Spingarn (Senior).

College—University of District of Columbia, Washington, D. C.

Drafted by Los Angeles Lakers on first round, 1984 (23rd pick).

—COLLEGIATE RECORD—

Year	G.	Min.	FGA	FGM	Pct.	FTA	FTM	Pct.	Reb.	Pts.	Avg.
80-81	25	....	392	197	.503	137	98	.715	333	492	19.7
81-82	30	....	516	267	.517	222	173	.779	315	707	23.6
82-83	30	....	487	272	.559	247	183	.741	307	727	22.7
83-84	22	....	363	215	.592	237	200	.844	213	630	28.6
Totals	109	....	1758	951	.541	843	654	.776	1168	2556	23.4

NBA REGULAR SEASON RECORD

Sea.—Team	G.	Min.	FGA	FGM	Pct.	FTA	FTM	Pct.	—Rebounds— Off.	Def.	Tot.	Ast.	PF	Dq.	Stl.	Blk.	Pts.	Avg.
84-85—L.A. Lakers	2	7	1	0	.000	0	0	.000	0	0	0	0	0	0	0	0	0	0.0

Led NCAA Division II in rebounding, 1981. . . . Led NCAA Division II in scoring, 1984. . . . Member of NCAA Division II championship team, 1982.

EDGAR JONES JR.

Born June 17, 1956 at Fort Rucker, Ala. Height 6:10. Weight 225.

High School—Newark, N. J., Barringer.

College—University of Nevada at Reno, Reno, Nev.

Drafted by Milwaukee on second round, 1979 (31st pick).

Waived by Milwaukee, October 10, 1979; signed by New Jersey as a free agent, June 4, 1980.
Sold by New Jersey to Detroit, June 11, 1981.
Traded by Detroit to San Antonio for a 1984 2nd round draft choice and a 1985 3rd round draft choice, February 10, 1983.
Traded by San Antonio with cash to Cleveland for Jeff Cook, December 14, 1984.
Played in Continental Basketball Association with Lehigh Valley Jets, 1979-80.

—COLLEGIATE RECORD—

Year	G.	Min.	FGA	FGM	Pct.	FTA	FTM	Pct.	Reb.	Pts.	Avg.
75-76	26	....	348	181	.520	135	95	.704	161	457	17.6
76-77	27	997	489	247	.505	216	147	.681	355	641	23.7

Year	G.	Min.	FGA	FGM	Pct.	FTA	FTM	Pct.	Reb.	Pts.	Avg.
77-78	27	846	366	173	.473	135	91	.674	275	437	16.2
78-79	21	625	274	135	.493	105	72	.686	225	342	16.3
Totals	101	....	1477	736	.498	591	405	.685	1016	1877	18.6

MINOR LEAGUE REGULAR SEASON RECORD

Sea.—Team	G.	Min.	2-Point FGM	FGA	Pct.	3-Point FGM	FGA	Pct.	FTM	FTA	Pct.	Reb.	Ast.	Pts.	Avg.
79-80—Lehigh Valley CBA..	31	966	265	498	.532	0	2	.000	169	225	.751	339	36	697	22.5

NBA REGULAR SEASON RECORD

Sea.—Team	G.	Min.	FGA	FGM	Pct.	FTA	FTM	Pct.	Rebounds Off.	Def.	Tot.	Ast.	PF	Dq.	Stl.	Blk.	Pts.	Avg.
80-81—New Jersey	60	950	357	189	.529	218	146	.670	92	171	263	43	185	4	36	81	524	8.7
81-82—Detroit	48	802	259	142	.548	129	90	.698	70	137	207	40	149	3	28	92	375	7.8
82-83—Det.-S.A.	77	1658	479	237	.495	286	201	.703	136	312	448	89	267	10	42	108	677	8.8
83-84—San Antonio	81	1770	644	322	.500	242	176	.727	143	306	449	85	298	7	64	107	826	10.2
84-85—S.A.-Cle.	44	769	275	130	.473	111	82	.739	50	121	171	29	123	2	20	29	342	7.8
Totals	310	5949	2014	1020	.506	986	695	.705	491	1047	1538	386	1022	26	190	417	2744	8.9

Three-Point Field Goals: 1980-81, 0-for-4. 1981-82, 1-for-2 (.500). 1982-83, 2-for-9 (.222). 1983-84, 6-for-19 (.316). 1984-85, 0-for-4. Totals, 9-for-38 (.237).

NBA PLAYOFF RECORD

Sea.—Team	G.	Min.	FGA	FGM	Pct.	FTA	FTM	Pct.	Rebounds Off.	Def.	Tot.	Ast.	PF	Dq.	Stl.	Blk.	Pts.	Avg.
82-83—San Antonio	11	193	62	28	.452	33	19	.576	23	30	53	17	44	1	6	14	75	6.8
84-85—Cleveland	4	45	18	9	.500	8	7	.875	2	6	8	3	6	0	2	0	25	6.3
Totals	15	238	80	37	.463	41	26	.634	25	36	61	20	50	1	8	14	100	6.7

Three-Point Field Goals: 1982-83, 0-for-2. 1984-85, 0-for-1. Totals, 0-for-3.

Named to CBA All-Star First Team, 1980.

MAJOR JAMES BROOKS JONES

Born July 9, 1953 at McGehee, Ark. Height 6:09. Weight 225.

High School—Rohwer, Ark., Desha Central.

College—Albany State College, Albany, Ga.

Drafted by Portland on second round, 1976 (20th pick).

Released by Portland, September, 1976; signed by Buffalo as a free agent, September 23, 1976.
Waived by Buffalo, September 28, 1976; signed by Atlanta as a free agent, September 20, 1977.
Waived by Atlanta, October 12, 1977; signed by Houston as a free agent, September 10, 1979.
Waived by Houston, October 23, 1984; signed by Detroit as a free agent, November 7, 1984.
Played in Eastern Basketball Association with Allentown Jets, 1976-77 and 1977-78.
Played in All-America Basketball Alliance with the New York Guard, 1977-78.
Played in Western Basketball Association with Fresno Stars, 1978-79.

—COLLEGIATE RECORD—

Year	G.	Min.	FGA	FGM	Pct.	FTA	FTM	Pct.	Reb.	Pts.	Avg.
72-73	29	....	488	252	.516	100	61	.610	456	565	19.5
73-74	25	....	466	258	.554	144	74	.514	513	590	23.6
74-75	27	....	507	255	.503	155	92	.594	608	602	22.3
75-76	24	....	470	247	.526	127	73	.575	475	567	23.6
Totals	105	....	1931	1012	.524	526	300	.570	2052	2324	22.1

MINOR LEAGUE REGULAR SEASON RECORD

Sea.—Team	G.	Min.	2-Point FGM	FGA	Pct.	3-Point FGM	FGA	Pct.	FTM	FTA	Pct.	Reb.	Ast.	Pts.	Avg.
76-77—Allentown EBA	26	....	207	403	.514	0	1	.000	53	88	.602	342	26	467	18.0
77-78—Allentown EBA	15	527	157	284	.553	0	3	.000	48	69	.696	215	17	362	24.1
77-78—New York AABA	9	357	83	157	.546	0	1	.000	41	69	.594	135	21	207	23.0
78-79—Fresno WBA	31	1221	263	525	.501	0	1	.000	137	214	.640	430	76	650	21.0

NBA REGULAR SEASON RECORD

Sea.—Team	G.	Min.	FGA	FGM	Pct.	FTA	FTM	Pct.	Rebounds Off.	Def.	Tot.	Ast.	PF	Dq.	Stl.	Blk.	Pts.	Avg.
79-80—Houston	82	1545	392	188	.480	108	61	.565	147	234	381	67	186	0	50	67	438	5.3
80-81—Houston	68	1003	252	117	.464	101	64	.634	96	138	234	41	112	0	18	23	298	4.4
81-82—Houston	60	746	213	113	.531	77	42	.545	80	122	202	25	100	0	20	29	268	4.5
82-83—Houston	60	878	311	142	.457	102	56	.549	114	149	263	39	104	0	22	22	340	5.7
83-84—Houston	57	473	130	70	.538	49	30	.612	33	82	115	28	63	0	14	14	170	3.0
84-85—Detroit	47	418	87	48	.552	51	33	.647	48	80	128	15	58	0	9	14	129	2.7
Totals	374	5063	1385	678	.490	488	286	.586	518	805	1323	215	623	0	133	169	1643	4.4

Three-Point Field Goals: 1979-80, 1-for-3 (.333). 1980-81, 0-for-1. 1981-82, 0-for-3. 1982-83, 0-for-2. Totals, 1-for-9 (.111).

NBA PLAYOFF RECORD

Sea.—Team	G.	Min.	FGA	FGM	Pct.	FTA	FTM	Pct.	Off.	Def.	Tot.	Ast.	PF	Dq.	Stl.	Blk.	Pts.	Avg.
										—Rebounds—								
79-80—Houston	6	70	18	11	.611	9	6	.667	8	14	22	4	8	0	0	2	28	4.7
80-81—Houston	12	88	21	10	.476	5	2	.400	7	11	18	5	15	0	3	2	22	1.8
84-85—Detroit	1	4	1	1	1.000	0	0	.000	0	0	0	0	0	0	0	0	2	2.0
Totals	19	162	40	22	.550	14	8	.571	15	25	40	9	23	0	3	4	52	2.7

Led NCAA Division II in rebounding, 1975 and 1976. . . . Brother of Chicago Bulls forward-center Caldwell Jones, Washington Bullets center-forward Charles Jones and former ABA and NBA forward Wilbert Jones.

OZELL JONES

Born November 20, 1960 at Long Beach, Calif.   Height 6:11.   Weight 235.

High School—Long Beach, Calif., Poly.

Colleges—Wichita State University, Wichita, Kan., and
California State University, Fullerton, Calif.

Drafted by San Antonio on fourth round, 1984 (90th pick).

—COLLEGIATE RECORD—
Wichita State

Year	G.	Min.	FGA	FGM	Pct.	FTA	FTM	Pct.	Reb.	Pts.	Avg.
79-80	29	604	209	92	.440	42	18	.429	146	202	7.0
80-81	28	576	202	93	.460	52	32	.615	199	218	7.8
Wich. St. Totals.....	57	1180	411	185	.450	94	50	.532	345	420	7.4

California State-Fullerton

Year	G.	Min.	FGA	FGM	Pct.	FTA	FTM	Pct.	Reb.	Pts.	Avg.
81-82				Did Not Play—Transfer Student							
82-83	29	758	253	134	.530	85	50	.588	207	318	11.0
83-84	29	929	234	129	.551	103	46	.447	272	304	10.5
Cal. St. Totals	58	1687	487	263	.540	188	96	.511	479	622	10.7
College Totals	115	2867	898	448	.499	282	146	.578	824	1042	9.1

NBA REGULAR SEASON RECORD

Sea.—Team	G.	Min.	FGA	FGM	Pct.	FTA	FTM	Pct.	Off.	Def.	Tot.	Ast.	PF	Dq.	Stl.	Blk.	Pts.	Avg.
										—Rebounds—								
84-85—San Antonio	67	888	180	106	.589	83	33	.398	65	173	238	56	139	1	30	57	245	3.7

Three-Point Field Goals: 1984-85, 0-for-1.

NBA PLAYOFF RECORD

Sea.—Team	G.	Min.	FGA	FGM	Pct.	FTA	FTM	Pct.	Off.	Def.	Tot.	Ast.	PF	Dq.	Stl.	Blk.	Pts.	Avg.
										—Rebounds—								
84-85—San Antonio	5	73	11	8	.727	6	1	.167	5	12	17	4	18	1	1	4	17	3.4

ROBERT CLYDE JONES
(Bobby)

Born December 18, 1951 at Charlotte, N. C.   Height 6:09.   Weight 212.

High School—Charlotte, N. C., South Mecklenburg.

College—University of North Carolina, Chapel Hill, N. C.

Drafted by Houston on first round, 1974 (5th pick).

Selected by Carolina on second round of ABA special circumstance draft, 1973.
Carolina franchise transferred to St. Louis, which exchanged Jones' draft rights with Denver for draft rights to Marvin Barnes, 1974.
Entered NBA with Denver, 1976.
Traded by Denver with Ralph Simpson to Philadelphia for George McGinnis, August 16, 1978.

—COLLEGIATE RECORD—

Year	G.	Min.	FGA	FGM	Pct.	FTA	FTM	Pct.	Reb.	Pts.	Avg.
70-71	16	....	237	136	.574	113	86	.761	236	358	22.4
71-72	31	....	190	127	.668	95	62	.653	195	316	10.2
72-73	33	....	343	206	.601	128	84	.656	348	496	15.0
73-74	28	....	326	189	.580	120	74	.617	274	452	16.1
Varsity Totals	92	....	859	522	.608	343	220	.641	817	1264	13.7

ABA REGULAR SEASON RECORD

Sea.—Team	G.	Min.	2-Point			3-Point			FTM	FTA	Pct.	Reb.	Ast.	Pts.	Avg.
			FGM	FGA	Pct.	FGM	FGA	Pct.							
74-75—Denver	84	2706	529	875	.605	0	1	.000	187	269	.695	692	303	1245	14.8
75-76—Denver	83	2845	510	878	.581	0	0	.000	215	308	.698	791	331	1235	14.9
Totals.............................	167	5551	1039	1753	.593	0	1	.000	402	577	.697	1483	634	2480	14.9

ABA PLAYOFF RECORD

Sea.—Team	G.	Min.	2-Point FGM	FGA	Pct.	3-Point FGM	FGA	Pct.	FTM	FTA	Pct.	Reb.	Ast.	Pts.	Avg.
74-75—Denver	13	428	69	128	.539	0	1	.000	31	40	.775	111	38	169	13.0
75-76—Denver	13	433	74	127	.583	0	0	.000	30	41	.732	112	59	178	13.7
Totals	26	861	143	255	.561	0	1	.000	61	81	.753	223	97	347	13.3

ABA ALL-STAR GAME RECORD

Sea.—Team	Min.	2-Point FGM	FGA	Pct.	3-Point FGM	FGA	Pct.	FTM	FTA	Pct.	Reb.	Ast.	Pts.	Avg.
1976—Denver	29	8	12	.667	0	0	.000	8	11	.727	10	3	24	24.0

NBA REGULAR SEASON RECORD

Sea.—Team	G.	Min.	FGA	FGM	Pct.	FTA	FTM	Pct.	Rebounds Off.	Def.	Tot.	Ast.	PF	Dq.	Stl.	Blk.	Pts.	Avg.
76-77—Denver	82	2419	879	501	.570	329	236	.717	174	504	678	264	238	3	186	162	1238	15.1
77-78—Denver	75	2440	761	440	.578	277	208	.751	164	472	636	252	221	2	137	126	1088	14.5
78-79—Philadelphia	80	2304	704	378	.537	277	209	.755	199	332	531	201	245	2	107	96	965	12.1
79-80—Philadelphia	81	2125	748	398	.532	329	257	.781	152	298	450	146	223	3	102	118	1053	13.0
80-81—Philadelphia	81	2046	755	407	.539	347	282	.813	142	293	435	226	226	2	95	74	1096	13.5
81-82—Philadelphia	76	2181	737	416	.564	333	263	.790	109	284	393	189	211	3	99	112	1095	14.4
82-83—Philadelphia	74	1749	460	250	.543	208	165	.793	102	242	344	142	199	4	85	91	665	9.0
83-84—Philadelphia	75	1761	432	226	.523	213	167	.784	92	231	323	187	199	1	107	103	619	8.3
84-85—Philadelphia	80	1633	385	207	.538	216	186	.861	105	192	297	155	183	2	84	50	600	7.5
Totals	704	18658	5861	3223	.550	2529	1973	.780	1239	2848	4087	1762	1945	22	1002	932	8419	12.0

Three-Point Field Goals: 1979-80, 0-for-3. 1980-81, 0-for-3. 1981-82, 0-for-3. 1982-83, 0-for-1. 1983-84, 0-for-1. 1984-85, 0-for-4. Totals, 0-for-15.

NBA PLAYOFF RECORD

Sea.—Team	G.	Min.	FGA	FGM	Pct.	FTA	FTM	Pct.	Rebounds Off.	Def.	Tot.	Ast.	PF	Dq.	Stl.	Blk.	Pts.	Avg.
76-77—Denver	6	187	64	31	.484	17	10	.588	11	24	35	21	25	1	17	14	72	12.0
77-78—Denver	13	390	116	66	.569	46	34	.739	36	66	102	35	42	1	16	9	166	12.8
78-79—Philadelphia	9	260	87	48	.552	26	22	.846	12	31	43	19	30	0	5	4	118	13.1
79-80—Philadelphia	18	470	172	90	.523	62	53	.855	29	57	86	31	56	1	21	32	233	12.9
80-81—Philadelphia	16	443	160	81	.506	88	73	.830	35	53	88	33	60	1	18	21	235	14.7
81-82—Philadelphia	21	589	174	94	.540	81	68	.840	37	62	99	52	69	0	15	22	256	12.2
82-83—Philadelphia	12	324	78	43	.551	20	17	.850	19	39	58	34	29	0	15	18	103	8.6
83-84—Philadelphia	5	130	31	15	.484	19	18	.947	9	14	23	9	12	0	3	7	48	9.6
84-85—Philadelphia	13	309	78	46	.590	20	14	.700	22	26	48	16	38	0	12	15	106	8.2
Totals	113	3102	960	514	.535	379	309	.815	210	372	582	250	361	4	122	142	1337	11.8

Three-Point Field Goals: 1979-80, 0-for-1. 1982-83, 0-for-1. Totals, 0-for-2.

NBA ALL-STAR GAME RECORD

Season—Team	Min.	FGA	FGM	Pct.	FTA	FTM	Pct.	Rebounds Off.	Def.	Tot.	Ast.	PF	Dq.	Stl.	Blk.	Pts.
1977—Denver	14	4	1	.250	0	0	.000	0	0	0	3	0	0	0	1	2
1978—Denver	18	3	1	.333	0	0	.000	1	5	6	2	4	0	0	1	2
1981—Philadelphia	16	11	5	.455	1	1	1.000	1	3	4	0	2	0	1	1	11
1982—Philadelphia	14	5	2	.400	2	1	.500	1	3	4	1	2	0	1	0	5
Totals	62	23	9	.391	3	2	.667	3	11	14	6	8	0	2	3	20

Named to NBA All-Defensive First Team, 1977, 1978, 1979, 1980, 1981, 1982, 1983, 1984. . . . NBA All-Defensive Second Team, 1985. . . . Recipient of NBA Sixth Man Award, 1983. . . . Member of NBA championship team, 1983. . . . Led NBA in field-goal percentage, 1978. . . . ABA All-Star Second Team, 1976. . . . ABA All-Defensive Team, 1975 and 1976. . . . ABA All-Rookie Team, 1975. . . . Holds ABA record for highest field-goal percentage in one season, 1975. . . . Led ABA in field-goal percentage, 1975 and 1976. . . . Member of U. S. Olympic team, 1972.

MICHAEL JEFFERY JORDAN

Born February 17, 1963 at Brooklyn, N. Y. Height 6:06. Weight 195.

High School—Wilmington, N. C., Laney.

College—University of North Carolina, Chapel Hill, N. C.

Drafted by Chicago on first round as an undergraduate, 1984 (3rd pick).

—COLLEGIATE RECORD—

Year	G.	Min.	FGA	FGM	Pct.	FTA	FTM	Pct.	Reb.	Pts.	Avg.
81-82	34	....	358	191	.534	108	78	.722	149	460	13.5
82-83	36	....	527	182	.535	167	123	.737	197	721	20.0
83-84	31	....	448	247	.551	145	113	.779	163	607	19.6
Totals	101	....	1333	720	.540	420	314	.748	509	1788	17.7

Three-Point Field Goals: 1982-83, 34-for-76 (.447).

BOBBY JONES

NBA REGULAR SEASON RECORD

Sea.—Team	G.	Min.	FGA	FGM	Pct.	FTA	FTM	Pct.	Off.	Def.	Tot.	Ast.	PF	Dq.	Stl.	Blk.	Pts.	Avg.
									Rebounds									
84-85—Chicago	82	3144	1625	837	.515	746	630	.845	167	367	534	481	285	4	196	69	2313	28.2

Three-Point Field Goals: 1984-85, 9-for-52 (.173).

NBA PLAYOFF RECORD

Sea.—Team	G.	Min.	FGA	FGM	Pct.	FTA	FTM	Pct.	Off.	Def.	Tot.	Ast.	PF	Dq.	Stl.	Blk.	Pts.	Avg.
									Rebounds									
84-85—Chicago	4	171	78	34	.436	58	48	.828	7	16	23	34	15	0	11	4	117	29.3

Three-Point Field Goals: 1984-85, 1-for-8 (.125).

NBA ALL-STAR GAME RECORD

Season—Team	Min.	FGA	FGM	Pct.	FTA	FTM	Pct.	Off.	Def.	Tot.	Ast.	PF	Dq.	Stl.	Blk.	Pts.
								Rebounds								
1985—Chicago	22	9	2	.222	4	3	.750	3	3	6	2	4	0	3	1	7

Three-Point Field Goals: 1985, 0-for-1.

Named to All-NBA Second Team, 1985. . . . NBA Rookie of the Year, 1985. . . . NBA All-Rookie Team, 1985. . . . Recipient of Schick Pivotal Player Award, 1985. . . . Member of NCAA championship team, 1982. . . . Member of U.S. Olympic team, 1984. . . . Named THE SPORTING NEWS College Player of the Year, 1983 and 1984. . . . THE SPORTING NEWS All-America First Team, 1983 and 1984.

RICHARD RYLAND KELLEY
(Rich)

Born March 23, 1953 at San Mateo, Calif.   Height 7:00.   Weight 240.

High School—Woodside, Calif.

College—Stanford University, Stanford, Calif.

Drafted by New Orleans on first round, 1975 (7th pick).

Traded by Utah to New Jersey for Bernard King, John Gianelli and Jim Boylan, October 2, 1979.
Traded by New Jersey to Phoenix for two draft choices (1982 1st round and 1983 2nd round), February 15, 1980.
Traded by Phoenix to Denver for a 1982 1st round draft choice, June 21, 1982.
Traded by Denver to Utah for Danny Schayes and other considerations, February 7, 1983.

—COLLEGIATE RECORD—

Year	G.	Min.	FGA	FGM	Pct.	FTA	FTM	Pct.	Reb.	Pts.	Avg.
71-72†	17	....	241	112	.465	120	84	.700	284	308	18.1
72-73	25	....	330	171	.518	129	91	.705	331	433	17.3
73-74	25	....	358	167	.466	155	125	.806	313	459	18.4
74-75	26	....	371	188	.507	173	144	.832	300	520	20.0
Varsity Totals	76	....	1059	526	.497	457	360	.788	944	1412	18.6

NBA REGULAR SEASON RECORD

Sea.—Team	G.	Min.	FGA	FGM	Pct.	FTA	FTM	Pct.	Off.	Def.	Tot.	Ast.	PF	Dq.	Stl.	Blk.	Pts.	Avg.
									Rebounds									
75-76—N. Orleans	75	1346	379	184	.485	205	159	.776	193	335	528	155	209	5	52	60	527	7.0
76-77—N. Orleans	76	1505	386	184	.477	197	156	.792	210	377	587	208	244	7	45	63	524	6.9
77-78—N. Orleans	82	2119	602	304	.505	289	225	.779	249	510	759	233	293	6	89	129	833	10.2
78-79—N. Orleans	80	2705	870	440	.506	458	373	.814	303	723	1026	285	309	8	126	166	1253	15.7
79-80—N.J.-Phoe.	80	1839	484	229	.473	310	244	.787	200	315	515	178	273	5	78	96	702	8.8
80-81—Phoenix	81	1686	387	196	.506	231	175	.758	131	310	441	282	210	0	79	63	567	7.0
81-82—Phoenix	81	1892	505	236	.467	223	167	.749	168	329	497	293	292	14	64	71	639	7.9
82-83—Den.-Utah	70	1345	293	130	.444	175	142	.811	131	273	404	138	221	4	54	39	402	5.7
83-84—Utah	75	1674	264	132	.500	162	124	.765	140	350	490	157	273	6	55	29	388	5.2
84-85—Utah	77	1276	216	103	.477	112	84	.750	118	232	350	120	227	5	42	30	290	3.8
Totals	777	17387	4386	2138	.487	2362	1849	.783	1843	3754	5597	2049	2551	60	684	746	6125	7.9

Three-Point Field Goals: 1979-80, 0-for-3. 1980-81, 0-for-2. 1981-82, 0-for-1. 1984-85, 0-for-2. Totals, 0-for-8.

NBA PLAYOFF RECORD

Sea.—Team	G.	Min.	FGA	FGM	Pct.	FTA	FTM	Pct.	Off.	Def.	Tot.	Ast.	PF	Dq.	Stl.	Blk.	Pts.	Avg.
									Rebounds									
79-80—Phoenix	8	146	44	19	.432	10	9	.900	14	22	36	22	17	0	9	7	47	5.9
80-81—Phoenix	7	113	25	10	.400	14	9	.643	13	22	35	13	12	0	6	3	29	4.1
81-82—Phoenix	7	191	54	27	.500	20	14	.700	18	30	48	30	25	0	6	3	68	9.7
83-84—Utah	11	201	27	15	.556	29	25	.862	19	39	58	22	42	1	9	6	55	5.0
84-85—Utah	9	174	38	18	.474	15	13	.867	25	32	57	14	32	1	7	5	49	5.4
Totals	42	825	188	89	.473	88	70	.795	89	145	234	101	128	2	37	24	248	5.9

Three-Point Field Goals: 1979-80, 0-for-1. 1980-81, 0-for-1. Totals, 0-for-2.

MICHAEL JORDAN

CLARK CLIFTON KELLOGG

Born July 2, 1961 at Cleveland, O.   Height 6:07.   Weight 227.

High School—Cleveland, O., St. Joseph.

College—Ohio State University, Columbus, O.

Drafted by Indiana on first round as an undergraduate, 1982 (8th pick).

—COLLEGIATE RECORD—

Year	G.	Min.	FGA	FGM	Pct.	FTA	FTM	Pct.	Reb.	Pts.	Avg.
79-80	29	938	313	136	.435	79	63	.797	232	335	11.6
80-81	27	971	395	190	.481	112	88	.786	324	468	17.3
81-82	30	1102	404	213	.527	77	56	.727	316	482	16.1
Totals	86	3011	1112	539	.485	268	207	.772	872	1285	14.9

NBA REGULAR SEASON RECORD

Sea.—Team	G.	Min.	FGA	FGM	Pct.	FTA	FTM	Pct.	Off.	Def.	Tot.	Ast.	PF	Dq.	Stl.	Blk.	Pts.	Avg.
										—Rebounds—								
82-83—Indiana	81	2761	1420	680	.479	352	261	.741	340	520	860	223	298	6	141	43	1625	20.1
83-84—Indiana	79	2676	1193	619	.519	340	261	.768	230	489	719	234	242	2	121	28	1506	19.1
84-85—Indiana	77	2449	1112	562	.505	396	301	.760	224	500	724	244	247	2	86	26	1432	18.6
Totals	237	7886	3725	1861	.500	1088	823	.756	794	1509	2303	701	787	10	348	97	4563	19.3

Three-Point Field Goals: 1982-83, 4-for-18 (.222). 1983-84, 7-for-21 (.333). 1984-85, 7-for-14 (.500). Totals, 18-for-53 (.340).
Named to NBA All-Rookie Team, 1983.

GREGORY KELSER
(Greg)

Born September 17, 1957 at Panama City, Fla.   Height 6:07.   Weight 205.

High School—Detroit, Mich., Henry Ford.

College—Michigan State University, East Lansing, Mich.

Drafted by Detroit on first round, 1979 (4th pick).

Traded by Detroit to Seattle for Vinnie Johnson, November 23, 1981.
Traded by Seattle with James Donaldson, Mark Radford, a 1984 1st round draft choice and a 1985 2nd round draft choice to San Diego for Tom Chambers, Al Wood, a 1987 2nd round draft choice and a 1984 3rd round draft choice, August 18, 1983.
Signed by Indiana as Veteran Free Agent, March 25, 1985, to the first of consecutive 10-day contracts that expired, April 14, 1985.

—COLLEGIATE RECORD—

Year	G.	Min.	FGA	FGM	Pct.	FTA	FTM	Pct.	Reb.	Pts.	Avg.
75-76	27	....	263	136	.517	78	44	.564	260	316	11.7
76-77	26	....	441	217	.492	196	131	.668	280	565	21.7
77-78	30	....	362	221	.610	152	89	.586	274	531	17.7
78-79	32	1040	451	246	.545	164	110	.671	278	602	18.8
Totals	115	....	1517	820	.541	590	374	.634	1092	2014	17.5

NBA REGULAR SEASON RECORD

Sea.—Team	G.	Min.	FGA	FGM	Pct.	FTA	FTM	Pct.	Off.	Def.	Tot.	Ast.	PF	Dq.	Stl.	Blk.	Pts.	Avg.
										—Rebounds—								
79-80—Detroit	50	1231	593	280	.472	203	146	.719	124	152	276	108	176	5	60	34	709	14.2
80-81—Detroit	25	654	285	120	.421	106	68	.642	53	67	120	45	89	0	34	29	308	12.3
81-82—Det.-Sea.	60	741	271	116	.428	160	105	.656	80	113	193	57	131	0	18	21	337	5.6
82-83—Seattle	80	1507	450	247	.549	257	173	.673	158	245	403	97	243	5	52	35	667	8.3
83-84—San Diego	80	1783	603	313	.519	356	250	.702	188	203	391	91	249	3	68	31	878	11.0
84-85—Indiana	10	114	53	21	.396	28	20	.714	6	13	19	13	16	0	7	0	62	6.2
Totals	305	6030	2255	1097	.486	1110	762	.686	609	793	1402	411	904	13	239	150	2961	9.7

Three-Point Field Goals: 1979-80, 3-for-15 (.200). 1980-81, 0-for-2. 1981-82, 0-for-3, 1982-83, 0-for-3. 1983-84, 2-for-6 (.333). 1984-85, 0-for-1. Totals, 5-for-30 (.167).

NBA PLAYOFF RECORD

Sea.—Team	G.	Min.	FGA	FGM	Pct.	FTA	FTM	Pct.	Off.	Def.	Tot.	Ast.	PF	Dq.	Stl.	Blk.	Pts.	Avg.
										—Rebounds—								
81-82—Seattle	3	6	2	0	.000	4	4	1.000	1	2	3	1	2	0	0	0	4	1.3
82-83—Seattle	2	19	5	2	.400	0	0	.000	3	3	6	1	4	0	1	0	4	2.0
Totals	5	25	7	2	.286	4	4	1.000	4	5	9	2	6	0	1	0	8	1.6

Member of NCAA championship team, 1979.

JEROME KERSEY

Born June 26, 1962 at Clarksville, Va. Height 6:07. Weight 215.

High School—Clarksville, Va., Bluestone.

College—Longwood College, Farmville, Va.

Drafted by Portland on second round, 1984 (46th pick).

—COLLEGIATE RECORD—

Year	G.	Min.	FGA	FGM	Pct.	FTA	FTM	Pct.	Reb.	Pts.	Avg.
80-81	28	....	313	197	.629	133	78	.586	249	472	16.9
81-82	23	....	282	165	.585	98	62	.633	260	392	17.0
82-83	25	....	257	144	.560	125	76	.608	270	364	14.6
83-84	27	....	411	214	.521	165	100	.606	383	528	19.6
Totals	103	....	1263	720	.570	521	316	.607	1162	1756	17.0

NBA REGULAR SEASON RECORD

Sea.—Team	G.	Min.	FGA	FGM	Pct.	FTA	FTM	Pct.	Off.	Def.	Tot.	Ast.	PF	Dq.	Stl.	Blk.	Pts.	Avg.
84-85—Portland	77	958	372	178	.478	181	117	.646	95	111	206	63	147	1	49	29	473	6.1

Three-Point Field Goals: 1984-85, 0-for-3.

NBA PLAYOFF RECORD

Sea.—Team	G.	Min.	FGA	FGM	Pct.	FTA	FTM	Pct.	Off.	Def.	Tot.	Ast.	PF	Dq.	Stl.	Blk.	Pts.	Avg.
84-85—Portland	8	60	31	16	.516	8	6	.750	5	4	9	6	11	0	7	2	38	4.8

ALBERT KING

Born December 17, 1959 at Brooklyn, N. Y. Height 6:06. Weight 190.

High School—Brooklyn, N. Y., Fort Hamilton.

College—University of Maryland, College Park, Md.

Drafted by New Jersey on first round, 1981 (10th pick).

—COLLEGIATE RECORD—

Year	G.	Min.	FGA	FGM	Pct.	FTA	FTM	Pct.	Reb.	Pts.	Avg.
77-78	28	....	327	164	.502	82	53	.646	187	381	13.6
78-79	28	....	387	191	.494	81	62	.765	144	444	15.9
79-80	31	...	497	275	.553	151	124	.821	207	674	21.7
80-81	31	1075	462	232	.502	117	95	.812	177	559	18.0
Totals	118	....	1673	862	.515	531	334	.629	715	2058	17.4

NBA REGULAR SEASON RECORD

Sea.—Team	G.	Min.	FGA	FGM	Pct.	FTA	FTM	Pct.	Off.	Def.	Tot.	Ast.	PF	Dq.	Stl.	Blk.	Pts.	Avg.
81-82—New Jersey	76	1694	812	391	.482	171	133	.778	105	207	312	142	261	4	64	36	918	12.1
82-83—New Jersey	79	2447	1226	582	.475	227	176	.775	157	299	456	291	278	5	95	41	1346	17.0
83-84—New Jersey	79	2103	946	465	.492	295	232	.786	125	263	388	203	258	6	91	33	1165	14.7
84-85—New Jersey	42	860	460	226	.491	104	85	.817	70	89	159	58	110	0	41	9	537	12.8
Totals	276	7104	3444	1664	.483	797	626	.785	457	858	1315	694	907	15	291	119	3966	14.4

Three-Point Field Goals: 1981-82, 3-for-13 (.231). 1982-83, 6-for-23 (.261). 1983-84, 3-for-22 (.136). 1984-85, 0-for-8. Totals, 12-for-66 (.182).

NBA PLAYOFF RECORD

Sea.—Team	G.	Min.	FGA	FGM	Pct.	FTA	FTM	Pct.	Off.	Def.	Tot.	Ast.	PF	Dq.	Stl.	Blk.	Pts.	Avg.
81-82—New Jersey	2	58	33	18	.545	5	4	.800	3	5	8	6	8	0	5	1	40	20.0
82-83—New Jersey	2	68	38	18	.474	6	5	.833	4	4	8	3	12	2	2	0	42	21.0
83-84—New Jersey	11	295	128	53	.414	46	32	.696	25	33	58	25	32	0	10	4	138	12.5
84-85—New Jersey	3	105	57	28	.491	13	9	.692	4	19	23	5	14	0	7	2	66	22.0
Totals	18	526	256	117	.457	70	50	.714	36	61	97	39	66	2	24	7	286	15.9

Three-Point Field Goals: 1982-83, 1-for-2 (.500). 1983-84, 0-for-2. 1984-85, 1-for-1 (1.000). Totals, 2-for-5 (.400).

Named to THE SPORTING NEWS All-America First Team, 1981. . . . Brother of New York Knicks forward Bernard King.

—DID YOU KNOW—

That Dallas Owner Donald Carter drove in the antique car "Great American Race" from Hollywood, Calif., to New York last summer? Carter collects antique cars. He owns 10, including a 1911 Mitchell.

BERNARD KING

Born December 4, 1956 at Brooklyn, N. Y.   Height 6:07.   Weight 205.

High School—Brooklyn, N. Y., Fort Hamilton.

College—University of Tennessee, Knoxville, Tenn.

Drafted by New Jersey on first round as an undergraduate, 1977 (7th pick).

Traded by New Jersey with John Gianelli and Jim Boylan to Utah for Rich Kelley, October 2, 1979.
Traded by Utah to Golden State for Wayne Cooper and a 1981 2nd round draft choice, September 11, 1980.
Signed by New York as Veteran Free Agent, September 28, 1982; Golden State matched offer and traded King to New York for Micheal Ray Richardson and a 1984 5th round draft choice, October 22, 1982.

—COLLEGIATE RECORD—

Year	G.	Min.	FGA	FGM	Pct.	FTA	FTM	Pct.	Reb.	Pts.	Avg.
74-75	25	....	439	273	.622	147	115	.782	308	661	26.4
75-76	25	....	454	260	.573	163	109	.669	325	629	25.2
76-77	26	....	481	278	.578	163	116	.712	371	672	25.8
Totals	76	....	1374	811	.590	473	340	.719	1004	1962	25.8

NBA REGULAR SEASON RECORD

Sea.—Team	G.	Min.	FGA	FGM	Pct.	FTA	FTM	Pct.	Off.	Def.	Tot.	Ast.	PF	Dq.	Stl.	Blk.	Pts.	Avg.
77-78—New Jersey	79	3092	1665	798	.479	462	313	.677	265	486	751	193	302	5	122	36	1909	24.2
78-79—New Jersey	82	2859	1359	710	.522	619	349	.564	251	418	669	295	326	10	118	39	1769	21.6
79-80—Utah	19	419	137	71	.518	63	34	.540	24	64	88	52	66	3	7	4	176	9.3
80-81—Golden State	81	2914	1244	731	.588	437	307	.703	178	373	551	287	304	5	72	34	1771	21.9
81-82—Golden State	79	2861	1307	740	.566	499	352	.705	140	329	469	282	285	6	78	23	1833	23.2
82-83—New York	68	2207	1142	603	.528	388	280	.722	99	227	326	195	233	5	90	13	1486	21.9
83-84—New York	77	2667	1391	795	.572	561	437	.779	123	271	394	164	273	2	75	17	2027	26.3
84-85—New York	55	2063	1303	691	.530	552	426	.772	114	203	317	204	191	8	71	15	1809	32.9
Totals	540	19082	9548	5139	.538	3581	2498	.698	1194	2371	3565	1672	1980	39	633	181	12780	23.7

Three-Point Field Goals: 1980-81, 2-for-6 (.333). 1981-82, 1-for-5 (.200). 1982-83, 0-for-6. 1983-84, 0-for-4. 1984-85, 1-for-10 (.100). Totals, 4-for-31 (.129).

NBA PLAYOFF RECORD

Sea.—Team	G.	Min.	FGA	FGM	Pct.	FTA	FTM	Pct.	Off.	Def.	Tot.	Ast.	PF	Dq.	Stl.	Blk.	Pts.	Avg.
78-79—New Jersey	2	81	42	21	.500	24	10	.417	5	6	11	7	10	0	4	0	52	26.0
82-83—New York	6	184	97	56	.577	35	28	.800	8	16	24	13	16	0	2	0	141	23.5
83-84—New York	12	477	282	162	.574	123	93	.756	28	46	74	36	48	0	14	6	417	34.8
Totals	20	742	421	239	.568	182	131	.720	41	68	109	56	74	0	20	6	610	30.5

Three-Point Field Goals: 1982-83, 1-for-3 (.333). 1983-84, 0-for-1. Totals, 1-for-4 (.250).

NBA ALL-STAR GAME RECORD

Season—Team	Min.	FGA	FGM	Pct.	FTA	FTM	Pct.	Off.	Def.	Tot.	Ast.	PF	Dq.	Stl.	Blk.	Pts.
1982—Golden State	14	7	2	.286	2	2	1.000	0	4	4	1	2	0	3	1	6
1984—New York	22	13	8	.615	5	2	.400	2	1	3	4	2	0	0	0	18
1985—New York	22	10	6	.600	2	1	.500	4	3	7	1	5	0	0	0	13
Totals	58	30	16	.533	9	5	.556	6	8	14	6	9	0	3	1	37

Named to All-NBA First Team, 1984 and 1985.... Named to All-NBA Second Team, 1982.... Led NBA in scoring, 1985.... NBA All-Rookie Team, 1978.... NBA Comeback Player of the Year, 1981.... Shares NBA playoff game record for most points in one quarter, 23, vs. Detroit, April 19, 1984.... Named to THE SPORTING NEWS All-America Second Team, 1977.... Led NCAA in field-goal percentage, 1975.... Brother of New Jersey Nets forward Albert King.

REGINALD BIDDINGS KING
(Reggie)

Born February 14, 1957 at Birmingham, Ala.   Height 6:06.   Weight 230.

High School—Birmingham, Ala., Jackson-Olin.

College—University of Alabama, University, Ala.

Drafted by Kansas City on first round, 1979 (18th pick).

Traded by Kansas City to Seattle for a 1985 2nd round draft choice, October 26, 1983.

—COLLEGIATE RECORD—

Year	G.	Min.	FGA	FGM	Pct.	FTA	FTM	Pct.	Reb.	Pts.	Avg.
75-76	28	901	250	122	.488	113	62	.549	265	306	10.9
76-77	30	1024	386	213	.552	179	117	.654	328	543	18.1
77-78	27	966	371	218	.588	207	136	.657	359	572	21.2
78-79	33	1135	507	289	.570	236	169	.716	327	747	22.6
Totals	118	4026	1514	842	.556	735	484	.659	1279	2168	18.4

NBA REGULAR SEASON RECORD

Sea.—Team	G.	Min.	FGA	FGM	Pct.	FTA	FTM	Pct.	Off.	Def.	Tot.	Ast.	PF	Dq.	Stl.	Blk.	Pts.	Avg.
									Rebounds									
79-80—Kansas City	82	2052	499	257	.515	219	159	.726	184	382	566	106	230	2	69	31	673	8.2
80-81—Kansas City	81	2743	867	472	.544	386	264	.684	235	551	786	122	227	2	102	41	1208	14.9
81-82—Kansas City	80	2609	752	383	.509	285	201	.705	162	361	523	173	221	6	84	29	967	12.1
82-83—Kansas City	58	995	225	104	.462	96	73	.760	91	149	240	58	94	1	28	11	281	4.8
83-84—Seattle	77	2086	448	233	.520	206	136	.660	134	336	470	179	159	2	54	24	602	7.8
84-85—Seattle	60	860	149	63	.423	59	41	.695	44	78	122	53	74	1	28	11	167	2.8
Totals	438	11345	2940	1512	.514	1251	874	.699	850	1857	2707	691	1005	14	365	147	4545	10.4

Three-Point Field Goals: 1979-80, 0-for-1. 1983-84, 0-for-2. Totals, 0-for-3.

NBA PLAYOFF RECORD

Sea.—Team	G.	Min.	FGA	FGM	Pct.	FTA	FTM	Pct.	Off.	Def.	Tot.	Ast.	PF	Dq.	Stl.	Blk.	Pts.	Avg.
									Rebounds									
79-80—Kansas City	3	77	21	10	.476	9	5	.556	7	18	25	4	10	0	1	0	25	8.3
80-81—Kansas City	15	620	248	122	.492	102	75	.735	56	93	149	25	49	0	18	10	319	21.3
83-84—Seattle	5	91	12	5	.417	0	0	.000	6	11	17	6	14	0	2	3	10	2.0
Totals	23	788	281	137	.488	111	80	.721	69	122	191	35	73	0	21	13	354	15.4

Three-Point Field Goals: 1980-81, 0-for-1.

GREGORY FULLER KITE
(Greg)

Born August 5, 1961 at Houston, Tex.   Height 6:11.   Weight 250.

High School—Houston, Tex., Madison.

College—Brigham Young University, Provo, Utah.

Drafted by Boston on first round, 1983 (21st pick).

—COLLEGIATE RECORD—

Year	G.	Min.	FGA	FGM	Pct.	FTA	FTM	Pct.	Reb.	Pts.	Avg.
79-80	21	192	48	14	.292	25	12	.480	86	40	1.9
80-81	32	1002	221	108	.489	101	50	.495	272	266	8.3
81-82	30	853	169	79	.467	65	29	.446	234	187	6.2
82-83	29	896	206	90	.437	77	44	.571	255	224	7.7
Totals	112	2943	644	291	.452	268	135	.504	847	717	6.4

NBA REGULAR SEASON RECORD

Sea.—Team	G.	Min.	FGA	FGM	Pct.	FTA	FTM	Pct.	Off.	Def.	Tot.	Ast.	PF	Dq.	Stl.	Blk.	Pts.	Avg.
									Rebounds									
83-84—Boston	35	197	66	30	.455	16	5	.313	27	35	62	7	42	0	1	5	65	1.9
84-85—Boston	55	424	88	33	.375	32	22	.688	38	51	89	17	84	3	3	10	88	1.6
Totals	90	621	154	63	.409	48	27	.563	65	86	151	24	126	3	4	15	153	1.7

NBA PLAYOFF RECORD

Sea.—Team	G.	Min.	FGA	FGM	Pct.	FTA	FTM	Pct.	Off.	Def.	Tot.	Ast.	PF	Dq.	Stl.	Blk.	Pts.	Avg.
									Rebounds									
83-84—Boston	11	38	8	1	.125	6	5	.833	5	4	9	3	9	0	0	1	7	0.6
84-85—Boston	9	63	12	5	.417	2	1	.500	5	11	16	3	13	0	1	0	11	1.2
Totals	20	101	20	6	.300	8	6	.750	10	15	25	6	22	0	1	1	18	0.9

Member of NBA championship team, 1984.

WILLIAM R. KNIGHT
(Billy)

Born June 9, 1952 at Braddock, Pa.   Height 6:06.   Weight 195.

High School—Braddock, Pa.

College—University of Pittsburgh, Pittsburgh, Pa.

Drafted by Los Angeles on second round, 1974 (21st pick).

Selected by Indiana on first round of ABA draft, 1974.
Entered NBA with Indiana, 1976.
Traded by Indiana to Buffalo for Adrian Dantley and Mike Bantom, September 1, 1977.
Traded by San Diego with Nate Archibald, Marvin Barnes and two 2nd round draft choices (1981 and 1983) to Boston for Kevin Kunnert, Kermit Washington, Sidney Wicks and the draft rights to Freeman Williams, August 4, 1978.
Traded by Boston to Indiana for Rick Robey, January 16, 1979.
Traded by Indiana to New York for Vince Taylor and a 1984 1st round draft choice, September 17, 1983.
Traded by New York with cash to Kansas City for Ray Williams, September 17, 1983.
Traded by Kansas City to San Antonio for Mark McNamara, December 11, 1984.

Year 70-71†	G.	Min.	FGA	FGM	Pct.	FTA	FTM	Pct.	Reb.	Pts.	Avg.
					Did Not Play—Ineligible						
71-72	24	....	381	205	.538	131	95	.725	276	505	21.0
72-73	26	....	530	275	.519	89	67	.753	287	617	23.7
73-74	28	....	525	270	.514	89	69	.775	375	609	21.8
Totals	78	....	1436	750	.522	309	231	.748	938	1731	22.2

ABA REGULAR SEASON RECORD

Sea.—Team	G.	Min.	—2-Point—			—3-Point—								
			FGM	FGA	Pct.	FGM	FGA	Pct.	FTM	FTA	Pct.	Reb.	Ast.	Pts.	Avg.
74-75—Indiana	80	2559	576	1071	.538	4	16	.250	207	259	.799	632	168	1371	17.1
75-76—Indiana	70	2775	768	1552	.495	6	15	.400	415	501	.828	708	259	1969	28.1
Totals	150	5334	1344	2623	.512	10	31	.323	622	760	.818	1340	427	3340	22.3

ABA PLAYOFF RECORD

Sea.—Team	G.	Min.	—2-Point—			—3-Point—								
			FGM	FGA	Pct.	FGM	FGA	Pct.	FTM	FTA	Pct.	Reb.	Ast.	Pts.	Avg.
74-75—Indiana	18	763	176	308	.571	0	2	.000	82	97	.845	160	43	434	24.1
75-76—Indiana	3	143	41	73	.562	0	1	.000	19	22	.864	32	12	101	33.7
Totals	21	906	217	381	.570	0	3	.000	101	119	.849	192	55	535	25.5

ABA ALL-STAR GAME RECORD

Sea.—Team	Min.	—2-Point—			—3-Point—								
		FGM	FGA	Pct.	FGM	FGA	Pct.	FTM	FTA	Pct.	Reb.	Ast.	Pts.	Avg.
1976—Indiana	23	9	14	.643	0	1	.000	2	2	1.000	10	2	20	20.0

NBA REGULAR SEASON RECORD

Sea.—Team	G.	Min.	FGA	FGM	Pct.	FTA	FTM	Pct.	—Rebounds—			Ast.	PF	Dq.	Stl.	Blk.	Pts.	Avg.
									Off.	Def.	Tot.							
76-77—Indiana	78	3117	1687	831	.493	506	413	.816	223	359	582	260	197	0	117	19	2075	26.6
77-78—Buffalo	53	2155	926	457	.494	372	301	.809	126	257	383	161	137	0	82	13	1215	22.9
78-79—Boston-Ind.	79	2095	835	441	.528	296	249	.841	94	253	347	152	160	1	63	8	1131	14.3
79-80—Indiana	75	1910	722	385	.533	262	212	.809	136	225	361	155	96	0	82	9	986	13.2
80-81—Indiana	82	2385	1025	546	.533	410	341	.832	191	219	410	157	155	1	84	12	1436	17.5
81-82—Indiana	81	1803	764	378	.495	282	233	.826	97	160	257	118	132	0	63	14	998	12.3
82-83—Indiana	80	2262	984	512	.520	408	343	.841	152	172	324	192	143	0	66	8	1370	17.1
83-84—Kansas City	75	1885	729	358	.491	283	243	.859	89	166	255	160	122	0	54	6	963	12.8
84-85—K.C.-S.A.	68	800	354	156	.441	73	64	.877	50	68	118	80	62	0	16	2	387	5.7
Totals	671	18412	8026	4064	.506	2892	2399	.830	1158	1879	3037	1435	1204	2	627	91	10561	15.7

Three-Point Field Goals: 1979-80, 4-for-15 (.267). 1980-81, 3-for-19 (.158). 1981-82, 9-for-32 (.281). 1982-83, 3-for-19 (.158). 1983-84, 4-for-14 (.286). 1984-85, 11-for-25 (.440). Totals, 34-for-124 (.274).

NBA PLAYOFF RECORD

Sea.—Team	G.	Min.	FGA	FGM	Pct.	FTA	FTM	Pct.	—Rebounds—			Ast.	PF	Dq.	Stl.	Blk.	Pts.	Avg.
									Off.	Def.	Tot.							
80-81—Indiana	2	71	30	16	.533	8	5	.625	6	6	12	5	12	0	1	0	37	18.5
83-84—Kansas City	3	37	24	8	.333	2	2	1.000	2	1	3	2	2	0	0	0	18	6.0
84-85—San Antonio	5	45	15	8	.533	0	0	.000	3	3	6	3	2	0	2	0	16	3.2
Totals	10	153	69	32	.464	10	7	.700	11	10	21	10	9	0	3	0	71	7.1

Three-Point Field Goals: 1984-85, 0-for-4.

NBA ALL-STAR GAME RECORD

Season—Team	Min.	FGA	FGM	Pct.	FTA	FTM	Pct.	—Rebounds—			Ast.	PF	Dq.	Stl.	Blk.	Pts.
								Off.	Def.	Tot.						
1977—Indiana	12	5	1	.200	2	2	1.000	1	4	5	0	0	0	2	0	4

Named to ABA All-Star First Team, 1976.... ABA All-Rookie Team, 1975.... THE SPORTING NEWS All-America Second Team, 1974.

JOSEPH GERARD KOPICKI
(Joe)

Born June 12, 1960 at Warren, Mich. Height 6:09. Weight 240.

High School—Warren, Mich., Fitzgerald.

College—University of Detroit, Detroit, Mich.

Drafted by Atlanta on third round, 1982 (56th pick).

Waived by Atlanta, October 19, 1982; signed by Indiana as a free agent, October 22, 1982.
Waived by Indiana, October 27, 1982; signed by Washington as a free agent, March 9, 1983.
Waived by Washington, October 25, 1984; signed by Denver as a free agent, October 31, 1984.
Played in Continental Basketball Association with Wisconsin Flyers, 1982-83.

—COLLEGIATE RECORD—

Year	G.	Min.	FGA	FGM	Pct.	FTA	FTM	Pct.	Reb.	Pts.	Avg.
78-79	26	395	102	37	.363	39	23	.590	95	97	3.7
79-80	26	837	235	102	.434	92	70	.761	156	274	10.5
80-81	27	959	417	200	.480	176	137	.778	236	537	19.9
81-82	27	1007	366	186	.508	175	130	.743	284	502	18.6
Totals	106	3198	1120	525	.469	482	360	.747	771	1410	13.3

MINOR LEAGUE REGULAR SEASON RECORD

Sea.—Team	G.	Min.	—2-Point—			—3-Point—			FTM	FTA	Pct.	Reb.	Ast.	Pts.	Avg.
			FGM	FGA	Pct.	FGM	FGA	Pct.							
82-83—Wisconsin CBA	32	1169	237	480	.493	6	19	.316	188	241	.780	378	77	680	21.3

NBA REGULAR SEASON RECORD

Sea.—Team	G.	Min.	FGA	FGM	Pct.	FTA	FTM	Pct.	—Rebounds—			Ast.	PF	Dq.	Stl.	Blk.	Pts.	Avg.
									Off.	Def.	Tot.							
82-83—Washington	17	201	51	23	.451	25	21	.840	18	44	62	9	21	0	9	2	67	3.9
83-84—Washington	59	678	132	64	.485	112	91	.813	64	102	166	46	71	0	15	5	220	3.7
84-85—Denver	42	308	95	50	.526	54	43	.796	29	57	86	29	58	0	13	1	145	3.5
Totals	118	1187	278	137	.493	191	155	.812	111	203	314	84	150	0	37	8	432	3.7

Three-Point Field Goals: 1982-83, 0-for-1. 1983-84, 1-for-7 (.143). 1984-85, 2-for-3 (.667). Totals, 3-for-11 (.273).

NBA PLAYOFF RECORD

Sea.—Team	G.	Min.	FGA	FGM	Pct.	FTA	FTM	Pct.	—Rebounds—			Ast.	PF	Dq.	Stl.	Blk.	Pts.	Avg.
									Off.	Def.	Tot.							
83-84—Washington	3	25	6	3	.500	0	0	.000	0	5	5	1	6	0	0	0	6	2.0
84-85—Denver	7	32	16	6	.375	17	9	.529	2	11	13	3	5	0	1	1	21	3.0
Totals	10	57	22	9	.409	17	9	.529	2	16	18	4	11	0	1	1	27	2.7

MITCHELL KUPCHAK
(Mitch)

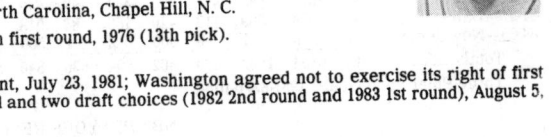

Born May 24, 1954 at Hicksville, N. Y.   Height 6:09.   Weight 230.

High School—Brentwood, N. Y.

College—University of North Carolina, Chapel Hill, N. C.

Drafted by Washington on first round, 1976 (13th pick).

Signed by Los Angeles as Veteran Free Agent, July 23, 1981; Washington agreed not to exercise its right of first refusal in exchange for Jim Chones, Brad Holland and two draft choices (1982 2nd round and 1983 1st round), August 5, 1981.

—COLLEGIATE RECORD—

Year	G.	Min.	FGA	FGM	Pct.	FTA	FTM	Pct.	Reb.	Pts.	Avg.
72-73	33	....	164	99	.604	95	56	.589	165	254	7.7
73-74	27	....	219	123	.562	70	44	.629	191	290	10.7
74-75	31	....	397	239	.602	150	97	.647	334	575	18.5
75-76	28	....	330	190	.576	150	112	.747	316	492	17.6
Totals	119	....	1110	651	.586	465	309	.665	1006	1611	13.5

NBA REGULAR SEASON RECORD

Sea.—Team	G.	Min.	FGA	FGM	Pct.	FTA	FTM	Pct.	—Rebounds—			Ast.	PF	Dq.	Stl.	Blk.	Pts.	Avg.
									Off.	Def.	Tot.							
76-77—Washington	82	1513	596	341	.572	246	170	.691	183	311	494	62	204	3	22	34	852	10.4
77-78—Washington	67	1759	768	393	.512	402	280	.697	162	298	460	71	196	1	28	42	1066	15.9
78-79—Washington	66	1604	685	369	.539	300	223	.743	152	278	430	88	141	0	23	23	961	14.6
79-80—Washington	40	451	160	67	.419	75	52	.693	32	73	105	16	49	1	8	8	186	4.7
80-81—Washington	82	1934	747	392	.525	340	240	.706	198	371	569	62	195	1	36	26	1024	12.5
81-82—Los Angeles	26	821	267	153	.573	98	65	.663	64	146	210	33	80	1	12	10	371	14.3
82-83—Los Angeles						(Did not play—injured)												
83-84—Los Angeles	34	324	108	41	.380	34	22	.647	35	52	87	7	46	0	4	6	104	3.1
84-85—L.A. Lakers	58	716	244	123	.504	91	60	.659	68	116	184	21	104	0	19	20	306	5.3
Totals	455	9122	3575	1879	.526	1586	1112	.701	894	1645	2539	360	1015	7	152	169	4870	10.7

Three-Point Field Goals: 1979-80, 0-for-2. 1980-81, 0-for-1. Totals, 0-for-3.

NBA PLAYOFF RECORD

Sea.—Team	G.	Min.	FGA	FGM	Pct.	FTA	FTM	Pct.	—Rebounds—			Ast.	PF	Dq.	Stl.	Blk.	Pts.	Avg.
									Off.	Def.	Tot.							
76-77—Washington	9	252	90	53	.589	59	40	.678	28	40	68	10	34	0	2	3	146	16.2
77-78—Washington	21	504	199	84	.422	69	45	.652	49	78	127	22	58	1	4	3	213	10.1
78-79—Washington	8	137	52	21	.404	15	10	.667	16	18	34	3	12	0	2	0	52	6.5
83-84—Los Angeles	9	69	17	5	.294	14	8	.571	12	17	29	2	12	0	1	2	18	2.0
84-85—L.A. Lakers	16	197	53	31	.585	22	13	.591	11	37	48	5	42	0	2	7	75	4.7
Totals	63	1159	411	194	.472	179	116	.648	116	190	306	42	158	1	11	15	504	8.0

Three-Point Field Goals: 1984-85, 0-for-1.

Named to NBA All-Rookie Team, 1977. . . . Member of NBA championship teams, 1978 and 1985. . . . Member of U. S. Olympic team, 1976.

THOMAS JOSEPH LAGARDE
(Tom)

Born February 10, 1955 at Detroit, Mich.   Height 6:10.   Weight 220.

High School—Detroit, Mich., Central Catholic.

College—University of North Carolina, Chapel Hill, N. C.

Drafted by Denver on first round, 1977 (9th pick).

Traded by Denver to Seattle for a 1978 1st round draft choice, June 9, 1978.
Selected from Seattle by Dallas in expansion draft, May 28, 1980.
Waived by Dallas, August 31, 1982; signed by New Jersey as a free agent, November 14, 1984.
Waived by New Jersey, December 18, 1984.
Played in Italy during 1982-83 and 1983-84 seasons.

—COLLEGIATE RECORD—

Year	G.	Min.	FGA	FGM	Pct.	FTA	FTM	Pct.	Reb.	Pts.	Avg.
73-74†	2	....	22	10	.455	13	11	.846	12	31	15.5
73-74	22	....	36	20	.556	19	9	.474	34	49	2.2
74-75	31	....	157	83	.529	98	72	.735	143	238	7.7
75-76	29	....	255	156	.612	131	106	.809	221	418	14.4
76-77	20	....	182	108	.593	110	86	.782	147	302	15.1
Varsity Totals	102	....	630	367	.583	358	273	.763	545	1007	9.9

NBA REGULAR SEASON RECORD

Sea.—Team	G.	Min.	FGA	FGM	Pct.	FTA	FTM	Pct.	Off.	Def.	Tot.	Ast.	PF	Dq.	Stl.	Blk.	Pts.	Avg.
77-78—Denver	77	868	237	96	.405	150	114	.760	75	139	214	47	146	1	17	17	306	4.0
78-79—Seattle	23	575	181	98	.541	95	57	.600	61	129	190	32	75	2	6	18	253	11.0
79-80—Seattle	82	1164	306	146	.477	137	90	.657	127	185	312	91	206	2	19	34	382	4.7
80-81—Dallas	82	2670	888	417	.470	444	288	.649	177	488	665	237	293	6	35	45	1122	13.7
81-82—Dallas	47	909	269	113	.420	166	86	.518	63	147	210	49	138	3	17	17	312	6.6
84-85—New Jersey	1	8	1	0	.000	2	1	.500	1	1	2	0	2	0	0	0	1	1.0
Totals	312	6194	1882	870	.462	994	636	.640	504	1089	1593	456	860	14	94	131	2376	7.6

Three-Point Field Goals: 1981-82, 0-for-2.

NBA PLAYOFF RECORD

Sea.—Team	G.	Min.	FGA	FGM	Pct.	FTA	FTM	Pct.	Off.	Def.	Tot.	Ast.	PF	Dq.	Stl.	Blk.	Pts.	Avg.
77-78—Denver	9	77	19	10	.526	7	5	.714	9	9	18	7	12	0	0	2	25	2.8
79-80—Seattle	14	163	46	17	.370	11	9	.818	13	27	40	12	25	0	2	0	43	3.1
Totals	23	240	65	27	.415	18	14	.778	22	36	58	19	37	0	2	2	68	3.0

Member of NBA championship team, 1979. . . . Named to THE SPORTING NEWS All-America Second Team, 1977. . . . Member of U. S. Olympic team, 1976.

WILLIAM LAIMBEER JR.
(Bill)

Born May 19, 1957 at Boston, Mass.   Height 6:11.   Weight 245.

High School—Palos Verdes, Calif.

Colleges—University of Notre Dame, Notre Dame, Ind.,
and Owens Technical College, Toledo, O.

Drafted by Cleveland on third round, 1979 (65th pick).

Traded by Cleveland with Kenny Carr to Detroit for Phil Hubbard, Paul Mokeski and two 1982 draft choices (1st and 2nd round), February 16, 1982.
Played in Italy during 1979-80 season.

—COLLEGIATE RECORD—
Notre Dame

Year	G.	Min.	FGA	FGM	Pct.	FTA	FTM	Pct.	Reb.	Pts.	Avg.
75-76	10	190	65	32	.492	23	18	.783	79	82	8.2

Owens Tech

Year	G.	Min.	FGA	FGM	Pct.	FTA	FTM	Pct.	Reb.	Pts.	Avg.
76-77					Did Not Play						

Year	G.	Min.	FGA	FGM	Pct.	FTA	FTM	Pct.	Reb.	Pts.	Avg.
77-78	29	654	175	97	.554	62	42	.677	190	236	8.1
78-79	30	614	145	78	.538	50	35	.700	164	191	6.4
Totals	69	1458	385	207	.538	135	95	.704	433	509	7.4

ITALIAN LEAGUE RECORD

Year	G.	Min.	FGA	FGM	Pct.	FTA	FTM	Pct.	Reb.	Pts.	Avg.
79-80—Brescia	29	....	465	258	.555	124	97	.782	363	613	21.1

NBA REGULAR SEASON RECORD

Sea.—Team	G.	Min.	FGA	FGM	Pct.	FTA	FTM	Pct.	Off.	Def.	Tot.	Ast.	PF	Dq.	Stl.	Blk.	Pts.	Avg.
80-81—Cleveland	81	2460	670	337	.503	153	117	.765	266	427	693	216	332	14	56	78	791	9.8
81-82—Clev.-Det.	80	1829	536	265	.494	232	184	.793	234	383	617	100	296	5	39	64	718	9.0
82-83—Detroit	82	2871	877	436	.497	310	245	.790	282	711	993	263	320	9	51	118	1119	13.6
83-84—Detroit	82	2864	1044	553	.530	365	316	.866	329	674	1003	149	273	4	49	84	1422	17.3
84-85—Detroit	82	2892	1177	595	.506	306	244	.797	295	718	1013	154	308	4	69	71	1438	17.5
Totals	407	12916	4304	2186	.508	1366	1106	.810	1406	2913	4319	882	1529	36	264	415	5488	13.5

Three-Point Field Goals: 1981-82, 4-for-13 (.308). 1982-83, 2-for-13 (.154). 1983-84, 0-for-11. 1984-85, 4-for-18 (.222). Totals, 10-for-55 (.182).

NBA PLAYOFF RECORD

Sea.—Team	G.	Min.	FGA	FGM	Pct.	FTA	FTM	Pct.	Off.	Def.	Tot.	Ast.	PF	Dq.	Stl.	Blk.	Pts.	Avg.
83-84—Detroit	5	165	51	29	.569	20	18	.900	14	48	62	12	23	2	4	3	76	15.2
84-85—Detroit	9	325	107	48	.449	51	36	.706	36	60	96	15	32	1	7	7	132	14.7
Totals	14	490	158	77	.487	71	54	.761	50	108	158	27	55	3	11	10	208	14.9

Three-Point Field Goals: 1984-85, 0-for-2.

NBA ALL-STAR GAME RECORD

Season—Team	Min.	FGA	FGM	Pct.	FTA	FTM	Pct.	Off.	Def.	Tot.	Ast.	PF	Dq.	Stl.	Blk.	Pts.
1983—Detroit	6	1	1	1.000	0	0	.000	1	0	1	0	1	0	0	0	2
1984—Detroit	17	8	6	.750	1	1	1.000	1	4	5	0	3	0	1	2	13
1985—Detroit	11	4	2	.500	2	1	.500	1	2	3	1	1	0	0	0	5
Totals	34	13	9	.692	3	2	.667	3	6	9	1	5	0	1	2	20

ALLEN FRAZIER LEAVELL

Born May 27, 1957 at Muncie, Ind. Height 6.01. Weight 190.

High School—Muncie, Ind., Central.

College—Oklahoma City University, Oklahoma City, Okla.

Drafted by Houston on fifth round, 1979 (104th pick).

—COLLEGIATE RECORD—

Year	G.	Min.	FGA	FGM	Pct.	FTA	FTM	Pct.	Reb.	Pts.	Avg.
75-76	24	....	80	34	.425	26	19	.731	40	87	3.6
76-77	18	....	125	61	.488	25	18	.720	20	140	7.8
77-78	27	....	494	248	.502	72	54	.750	107	550	20.4
78-79	21	....	404	192	.475	103	83	.806	67	467	22.2
Totals	90	....	1103	535	.485	236	174	.737	234	1244	13.8

NBA REGULAR SEASON RECORD

Sea.—Team	G.	Min.	FGA	FGM	Pct.	FTA	FTM	Pct.	Off.	Def.	Tot.	Ast.	PF	Dq.	Stl.	Blk.	Pts.	Avg.
79-80—Houston	77	2123	656	330	.503	221	180	.814	57	127	184	417	197	1	127	28	843	10.9
80-81—Houston	79	1686	548	258	.471	149	124	.832	30	104	134	384	160	1	97	15	642	8.1
81-82—Houston	79	2150	793	370	.467	135	115	.852	49	119	168	457	182	2	150	15	864	10.9
82-83—Houston	79	2602	1059	439	.415	297	247	.832	64	131	195	530	215	0	165	14	1167	14.8
83-84—Houston	82	2009	731	349	.477	286	238	.832	31	86	117	459	199	2	107	12	947	11.5
84-85—Houston	42	536	209	88	.421	57	44	.772	8	29	37	102	61	0	23	4	228	5.4
Totals	438	11106	3996	1834	.459	1145	948	.828	239	596	835	2349	1014	6	669	88	4691	10.7

Three-Point Field Goals: 1979-80, 3-for-19 (.158). 1980-81, 2-for-17 (.118). 1981-82, 9-for-31 (.290). 1982-83, 42-for-175 (.240). 1983-84, 11-for-71 (.155). 1984-85, 8-for-37 (.216). Totals, 75-for-350 (.214).

NBA PLAYOFF RECORD

Sea.—Team	G.	Min.	FGA	FGM	Pct.	FTA	FTM	Pct.	Off.	Def.	Tot.	Ast.	PF	Dq.	Stl.	Blk.	Pts.	Avg.
79-80—Houston	7	149	38	10	.263	21	19	.905	2	10	12	24	12	0	6	0	39	5.6
80-81—Houston	17	217	77	30	.390	17	15	.882	5	12	17	44	26	0	18	4	75	4.4
81-82—Houston	3	93	47	20	.426	2	2	1.000	1	4	5	10	9	0	3	1	42	14.0
84-85—Houston	5	16	6	2	.333	2	2	1.000	1	2	3	3	2	0	0	0	6	1.2
Totals	32	475	168	62	.369	42	38	.905	9	28	37	81	49	0	27	5	162	5.1

Three-Point Field Goals: 1979-80, 0-for-4. 1981-82, 0-for-1. 1984-85, 0-for-2. Totals, 0-for-7.

RONNIE LESTER

Born January 1, 1959 at Canton, Miss.   Height 6:02.   Weight 175.

High School—Chicago, Ill., Dunbar.

College—University of Iowa, Iowa City, Iowa.

Drafted by Portland on first round, 1980 (10th pick).

Draft rights traded by Portland with a 1981 1st round draft choice to Chicago for draft rights to Kelvin Ransey, June 10, 1980.

Waived by Chicago, November 16, 1984; signed by Los Angeles Lakers as a free agent, November 28, 1984.

—COLLEGIATE RECORD—

Year	G.	Min.	FGA	FGM	Pct.	FTA	FTM	Pct.	Reb.	Pts.	Avg.
76-77	27	....	312	140	.449	119	83	.697	66	363	13.4
77-78	27	....	423	202	.478	177	132	.746	68	536	19.9
78-79	28	....	401	194	.484	161	136	.845	63	524	18.7
79-80	17	....	185	86	.465	100	80	.800	29	252	14.8
Totals	99	....	1321	622	.471	557	431	.774	226	1675	16.9

NBA REGULAR SEASON RECORD

Sea.—Team	G.	Min.	FGA	FGM	Pct.	FTA	FTM	Pct.	Off.	Def.	Tot.	Ast.	PF	Dq.	Stl.	Blk.	Pts.	Avg.
80-81—Chicago	8	83	24	10	.417	11	10	.909	3	3	6	7	5	0	2	0	30	3.8
81-82—Chicago	75	2252	657	329	.501	256	208	.813	75	138	213	362	158	2	80	14	870	11.6
82-83—Chicago	65	1437	446	202	.453	171	124	.725	46	126	172	332	121	2	51	6	528	8.1
83-84—Chicago	43	687	188	78	.415	87	75	.862	20	26	46	168	59	1	30	6	232	5.4
84-85—L.A. Lakers	32	278	82	34	.415	31	21	.677	4	22	26	80	25	0	15	3	89	2.8
Totals	223	4737	1397	653	.467	556	438	.788	148	315	463	949	368	5	178	29	1749	7.8

Three-Point Field Goals: 1981-82, 4-for-8 (.500). 1982-83, 0-for-5. 1983-84, 1-for-5 (.200). 1984-85, 0-for-1. Totals, 5-for-19 (.263).

NBA PLAYOFF RECORD

Sea.—Team	G.	Min.	FGA	FGM	Pct.	FTA	FTM	Pct.	Off.	Def.	Tot.	Ast.	PF	Dq.	Stl.	Blk.	Pts.	Avg.
80-81—Chicago	5	42	18	7	.389	7	5	.714	5	1	6	4	4	0	2	0	19	3.8
84-85—L.A. Lakers	9	54	15	6	.400	9	7	.778	2	6	8	9	7	0	0	0	19	2.1
Totals	14	96	33	13	.394	16	12	.750	7	7	14	13	11	0	2	0	38	2.7

Three-Point Field Goals: 1980-81, 0-for-1.

Member of NBA championship team, 1985. . . . Named to THE SPORTING NEWS All-America Second Team, 1980.

LAFAYETTE LEVER
(Fat)

Born August 18, 1960 at Pine Bluff, Ark.   Height 6:03.   Weight 175.

High School—Tucson, Ariz., Pueblo.

College—Arizona State University, Tempe, Ariz.

Drafted by Portland on first round, 1982 (11th pick).

Traded by Portland with Calvin Natt, Wayne Cooper, a 1984 2nd round draft choice and a 1985 1st round draft choice to Denver for Kiki Vandeweghe, June 7, 1984.

—COLLEGIATE RECORD—

Year	G.	Min.	FGA	FGM	Pct.	FTA	FTM	Pct.	Reb.	Pts.	Avg.
78-79	29	377	92	38	.413	38	28	.737	44	104	3.6
79-80	29	974	220	98	.445	103	72	.699	125	268	9.2
80-81	28	1038	259	120	.463	116	84	.724	138	324	11.6
81-82	27	1032	357	162	.454	143	117	.818	146	441	16.3
Totals	113	3421	928	418	.450	400	301	.753	453	1137	10.1

NBA REGULAR SEASON RECORD

Sea.—Team	G.	Min.	FGA	FGM	Pct.	FTA	FTM	Pct.	Off.	Def.	Tot.	Ast.	PF	Dq.	Stl.	Blk.	Pts.	Avg.
82-83—Portland	81	2020	594	256	.431	116	159	.730	85	140	225	426	179	2	153	15	633	7.8
83-84—Portland	81	2010	701	313	.447	214	159	.743	96	122	218	372	178	1	135	31	788	9.7
84-85—Denver	82	2559	985	424	.430	256	197	.770	147	264	411	613	226	1	202	30	1051	12.8
Totals	244	6589	2280	993	.436	629	472	.750	328	526	854	1411	583	4	490	76	2472	10.1

Three-Point Field Goals: 1982-83, 5-for-15 (.333). 1983-84, 3-for-15 (.200). 1984-85, 6-for-24 (.250). Totals, 14-for-54 (.259).

LAFAYETTE LEVER

Sea.—Team	G.	Min.	FGA	FGM	Pct.	FTA	FTM	Pct.	Off.	Def.	Tot.	Ast.	PF	Dq.	Stl.	Blk.	Pts.	Avg.
										—Rebounds—								
82-83—Portland	7	134	42	19	.452	5	4	.800	3	11	14	31	13	0	7	0	42	6.0
83-84—Portland	5	75	30	8	.267	10	8	.800	10	5	15	9	6	0	4	0	26	5.2
84-85—Denver	11	342	122	49	.402	63	48	.762	23	48	71	93	33	0	26	2	146	13.3
Totals	23	551	194	76	.392	78	60	.769	36	64	100	133	52	0	37	2	214	9.3

Three-Point Field Goals: 1983-84, 2-for-3 (.667). 1984-85, 0-for-2. Totals, 2-for-5 (.400).

CLIFFORD EUGENE LEVINGSTON
(Cliff)

Born January 4, 1961 at San Diego, Calif.   Height 6:08.   Weight 220.

High School—San Diego, Calif., Morse.

College—Wichita State University, Wichita, Kan.

Drafted by Detroit on first round as an undergraduate, 1982 (9th pick).

Traded by Detroit with the draft rights to Antoine Carr and 1986 and 1987 2nd round draft choices to Atlanta for Dan Roundfield, June 18, 1984.

—COLLEGIATE RECORD—

Year	G.	Min.	FGA	FGM	Pct.	FTA	FTM	Pct.	Reb.	Pts.	Avg.
79-80	29	914	346	189	.546	127	79	.622	294	457	15.8
80-81	33	1108	452	246	.544	194	120	.619	376	612	18.5
81-82	29	902	312	162	.519	125	78	.624	295	402	13.9
Totals	91	2924	1110	597	.538	446	277	.621	965	1471	16.2

NBA REGULAR SEASON RECORD

Sea.—Team	G.	Min.	FGA	FGM	Pct.	FTA	FTM	Pct.	Off.	Def.	Tot.	Ast.	PF	Dq.	Stl.	Blk.	Pts.	Avg.
										—Rebounds—								
82-83—Detroit	62	879	270	131	.485	147	84	.571	104	128	232	52	125	2	23	36	346	5.6
83-84—Detroit	80	1746	436	229	.525	186	125	.672	234	311	545	109	281	7	44	78	583	7.3
84-85—Atlanta	74	2017	552	291	.527	222	145	.653	230	336	566	104	231	3	70	69	727	9.8
Totals	216	4642	1258	651	.517	555	354	.638	568	775	1343	265	637	12	137	183	1656	7.7

Three-Point Field Goals: 1982-83, 0-for-1. 1983-84, 0-for-3. 1984-85, 0-for-2. Totals, 0-for-6.

NBA PLAYOFF RECORD

Sea.—Team	G.	Min.	FGA	FGM	Pct.	FTA	FTM	Pct.	Off.	Def.	Tot.	Ast.	PF	Dq.	Stl.	Blk.	Pts.	Avg.
										—Rebounds—								
83-84—Detroit	5	101	19	15	.789	16	10	.625	11	13	24	1	15	0	1	2	40	8.0

ALTON LAVELLE LISTER

Born October 1, 1958 at Dallas, Tex.   Height 7:00.   Weight 240.

High School—Dallas, Tex., Woodrow Wilson.

Colleges—San Jacinto College, Pasadena, Tex., and Arizona State University, Tempe, Ariz.

Drafted by Milwaukee on first round, 1981 (21st pick).

—COLLEGIATE RECORD—

San Jacinto

Year	G.	Min.	FGA	FGM	Pct.	FTA	FTM	Pct.	Reb.	Pts.	Avg.
76-77	40	....	....	...	....	...	...	....	640	680	17.0

Arizona State

Year	G.	Min.	FGA	FGM	Pct.	FTA	FTM	Pct.	Reb.	Pts.	Avg.
77-78					Did Not Play—Redshirted						
78-79	29	584	209	104	.498	84	47	.560	194	255	8.8
79-80	27	793	264	133	.504	104	58	.558	231	324	12.0
80-81	26	845	282	158	.560	123	85	.691	251	401	15.4
Totals	82	2222	755	395	.523	311	190	.611	676	980	12.0

NBA REGULAR SEASON RECORD

Sea.—Team	G.	Min.	FGA	FGM	Pct.	FTA	FTM	Pct.	Off.	Def.	Tot.	Ast.	PF	Dq.	Stl.	Blk.	Pts.	Avg.
										—Rebounds—								
81-82—Milwaukee	80	1186	287	149	.519	123	64	.520	108	279	387	84	239	4	18	118	362	4.5
82-83—Milwaukee	80	1885	514	272	.529	242	130	.537	168	400	568	111	328	18	50	177	674	8.4
83-84—Milwaukee	82	1955	512	256	.500	182	114	.626	156	447	603	110	327	11	41	140	626	7.6
84-85—Milwaukee	81	2091	598	322	.538	262	154	.588	219	428	647	127	287	5	49	167	798	9.9
Totals	323	7117	1911	999	.523	809	462	.571	651	1554	2205	432	1181	38	158	602	2460	7.6

Three-Point Field Goals: 1982-83, 0-for-1. 1984-85, 0-for-1. Totals, 0-for-2.

Sea.—Team	G.	Min.	FGA	FGM	Pct.	FTA	FTM	Pct.	Off.	Def.	Tot.	Ast.	PF	Dq.	Stl.	Blk.	Pts.	Avg.
										—Rebounds—								
81-82—Milwaukee	6	112	24	14	.583	7	5	.714	6	21	27	5	23	0	2	15	33	5.5
82-83—Milwaukee	9	206	63	27	.429	5	4	.800	21	40	61	11	30	1	9	15	58	6.4
83-84—Milwaukee	16	368	78	39	.500	48	30	.625	26	70	96	10	63	2	5	24	108	6.8
84-85—Milwaukee	8	203	60	27	.450	32	15	.469	27	35	62	15	36	1	6	15	69	8.6
Totals	39	889	225	107	.476	92	54	.587	80	166	246	41	152	4	22	69	268	6.9

Member of U. S. Olympic team, 1980.

LEWIS KEVIN LLOYD

Born February 22, 1959 at Philadelphia, Pa.   Height 6:06.   Weight 215.

High School—Philadelphia, Pa., Overbrook.

Colleges—New Mexico Military Institute, Roswell, N. M.,
and Drake University, Des Moines, Iowa.

Drafted by Golden State on fourth round, 1981 (76th pick).

Signed by Houston as Veteran Free Agent, August 29, 1983; Golden State agreed not to exercise its right of first refusal in exchange for a 1985 2nd round draft choice.

—COLLEGIATE RECORD—

New Mexico Military

Year	G.	Min.	FGA	FGM	Pct.	FTA	FTM	Pct.	Reb.	Pts.	Avg.
77-78	22	....	411	244	.594	142	92	.648	295	580	26.4
78-79	30	....	580	377	.650	232	177	.763	377	931	31.0
JC Totals	52	....	991	621	.627	374	269	.719	672	1511	29.1

Drake

Year	G.	Min.	FGA	FGM	Pct.	FTA	FTM	Pct.	Reb.	Pts.	Avg.
79-80	27	1022	585	324	.554	236	167	.708	406	815	30.2
80-81	29	1044	548	298	.544	224	166	.741	291	762	26.3
Totals	56	2066	1133	622	.549	460	333	.724	697	1577	28.2

NBA REGULAR SEASON RECORD

Sea.—Team	G.	Min.	FGA	FGM	Pct.	FTA	FTM	Pct.	Off.	Def.	Tot.	Ast.	PF	Dq.	Stl.	Blk.	Pts.	Avg.
										—Rebounds—								
81-82—Golden State	16	95	45	25	.556	11	7	.636	9	7	16	6	20	0	5	1	57	3.6
82-83—Golden State	73	1350	566	293	.518	139	100	.719	77	183	260	130	109	0	61	31	687	9.4
83-84—Houston	82	2578	1182	610	.516	298	235	.789	128	167	295	321	211	4	102	44	1458	17.8
84-85—Houston	82	2128	869	457	.526	220	161	.732	98	133	231	280	196	1	73	28	1077	13.1
Totals	253	6151	2662	1385	.520	668	503	.753	312	490	802	737	536	5	241	104	3279	13.0

Three-Point Field Goals: 1982-83, 1-for-4 (.250). 1983-84, 3-for-13 (.231). 1984-85, 2-for-8 (.250). Totals, 6-for 25 (.240).

NBA PLAYOFF RECORD

Sea.—Team	G.	Min.	FGA	FGM	Pct.	FTA	FTM	Pct.	Off.	Def.	Tot.	Ast.	PF	Dq.	Stl.	Blk.	Pts.	Avg.
										—Rebounds—								
84-85—Houston	5	174	77	38	.494	14	10	.714	15	14	29	25	12	0	7	8	86	17.2

Brother of Daryl Lloyd, 6th round draft choice of Philadelphia 76ers in 1985 NBA draft.

JOHN EDDIE LONG

Born August 28, 1956 at Romulus, Mich.   Height 6:05.   Weight 200.

High School—Romulus, Mich.

College—University of Detroit, Detroit, Mich.

Drafted by Detroit on second round, 1978 (29th pick).

—COLLEGIATE RECORD—

Year	G.	Min.	FGA	FGM	Pct.	FTA	FTM	Pct.	Reb.	Pts.	Avg.
74-75	26	654	419	200	.477	58	45	.776	168	445	17.1
75-76	27	872	524	230	.439	95	72	.758	240	532	19.7
76-77	28	891	508	245	.482	102	78	.765	189	568	20.3
77-78	29	798	491	265	.540	114	92	.807	218	622	21.4
Totals	110	3215	1942	940	.484	369	287	.778	815	2167	19.7

NBA REGULAR SEASON RECORD

Sea.—Team	G.	Min.	FGA	FGM	Pct.	FTA	FTM	Pct.	Off.	Def.	Tot.	Ast.	PF	Dq.	Stl.	Blk.	Pts.	Avg.
										—Rebounds—								
78-79—Detroit	82	2498	1240	581	.469	190	157	.826	127	139	266	121	224	1	102	19	1319	16.1
79-80—Detroit	69	2364	1164	588	.505	194	160	.825	152	185	337	206	221	4	129	26	1337	19.4
80-81—Detroit	59	1750	957	441	.461	184	160	.870	95	102	197	106	164	3	95	22	1044	17.7

Sea.—Team	G.	Min.	FGA	FGM	Pct.	FTA	FTM	Pct.	Off.	Def.	Tot.	Ast.	PF	Dq.	Stl.	Blk.	Pts.	Avg.
									—Rebounds—									
81-82—Detroit	69	2211	1294	637	.492	275	238	.865	95	162	257	148	173	0	65	25	1514	21.9
82-83—Detroit	70	1485	692	312	.451	146	111	.760	56	124	180	105	130	1	44	12	737	10.5
83-84—Detroit	82	2514	1155	545	.472	275	243	.884	139	150	289	205	199	1	93	18	1334	16.3
84-85—Detroit	66	1820	885	431	.487	123	106	.862	81	109	190	130	139	0	71	14	973	14.7
Totals	497	14642	7387	3535	.479	1387	1175	.847	745	971	1716	1021	1250	10	599	136	8258	16.6

Three-Point Field Goals: 1979-80, 1-for-12 (083). 1980-81, 2-for-11 (.182). 1981-82, 2-for-15 (.133). 1982-83, 2-for-7 (.286). 1983-84, 1-for-5 (.200). 1984-85, 5-for-15 (.333). Totals, 13-for-65 (.200).

NBA PLAYOFF RECORD

Sea.—Team	G.	Min.	FGA	FGM	Pct.	FTA	FTM	Pct.	Off.	Def.	Tot.	Ast.	PF	Dq.	Stl.	Blk.	Pts.	Avg.
									—Rebounds—									
83-84—Detroit	5	149	55	20	.364	15	15	1.000	7	4	11	2	15	0	7	0	55	11.0
84-85—Detroit	9	255	105	48	.457	15	15	1.000	10	7	17	13	22	0	14	2	112	12.4
Totals	14	404	160	68	.425	30	30	1.000	17	11	28	15	37	0	21	2	167	11.9

Three-Point Field Goals: 1983-84, 0-for-1. 1984-85, 1-for-4 (.250). Totals, 1-for-5 (.200).

SIDNEY ROCHELL LOWE

Born January 21, 1960 at Washington, D. C.   Height 6:00.   Weight 195.

High School—Hyattsville, Md., DeMatha.

College—North Carolina State University, Raleigh, N. C.

Drafted by Chicago on second round, 1983 (25th pick).

Draft rights traded by Chicago with a 1984 2nd round draft choice to Indiana for draft rights to Mitchell Wiggins, June 28, 1983.
Waived by Indiana, October 4, 1984; signed by Detroit as a free agent, October 12, 1984.
Waived by Detroit, November 11, 1984; signed by Atlanta as a free agent, November 28, 1984.
Waived by Atlanta, December 18, 1984; re-signed by Atlanta to a 10-day contract that expired, December 30, 1984.
Re-signed by Atlanta to a 10-day contract that expired, January 26, 1985.
Played in Continental Basketball Association with Tampa Bay Thrillers, 1984-85.

—COLLEGIATE RECORD—

Year	G.	Min.	FGA	FGM	Pct.	FTA	FTM	Pct.	Reb.	Pts.	Avg.
79-80	28	....	97	43	.443	105	74	.705	53	160	5.7
80-81	24	....	148	67	.453	96	75	.781	80	209	8.7
81-82	32	....	188	97	.516	105	79	.752	85	273	8.5
82-83	36	....	295	136	.461	116	90	.776	134	406	11.3
Totals	120	....	728	343	.471	422	318	.754	352	1048	8.7

NBA REGULAR SEASON RECORD

Sea.—Team	G.	Min.	FGA	FGM	Pct.	FTA	FTM	Pct.	Off.	Def.	Tot.	Ast.	PF	Dq.	Stl.	Blk.	Pts.	Avg.
									—Rebounds—									
83-84—Indiana	78	1238	259	107	.413	139	108	.777	30	92	122	269	112	0	93	5	324	4.2
84-85—Det.-Atl.	21	190	27	10	.370	8	8	1.000	4	12	16	50	28	0	11	0	28	1.3
Totals	99	1428	286	117	.409	147	116	.789	34	104	138	319	140	0	104	5	352	3.6

Three-Point Field Goals: 1982-83, 44-for-115 (.383). 1984-85, 0-for-1. Totals, 2-for-19 (.105).

MINOR LEAGUE REGULAR SEASON RECORD

Sea.—Team	G.	Min.	FGM	FGA	Pct.	FGM	FGA	Pct.	FTM	FTA	Pct.	Reb.	Ast.	Pts.	Avg.
			——2-Point——			——3-Point——									
84-85—Tampa Bay CBA	18	494	33	70	.471	1	6	.167	30	37	.810	42	152	99	5.5

Member of NCAA championship team, 1983.

JOHN HARDING LUCAS JR.

Born October 31, 1953 at Durham, N. C.   Height 6:03.   Weight 185.

High School—Durham, N. C., Hillside.

College—University of Maryland, College Park, Md.

Drafted by Houston on first round, 1976 (1st pick).

Awarded from Houston with cash to Golden State as compensation for earlier signing of Veteran Free Agent Rick Barry, September 5, 1978.
Traded by Golden State to Washington for two 2nd round draft choices (1982 and 1984), October 19, 1981.
Waived by Washington, January 25, 1983; signed by Cleveland as a free agent, August 29, 1983.
Waived by Cleveland, September 21, 1983; signed by San Antonio as a free agent, December 4, 1983.
Traded by San Antonio with a 1985 3rd round draft choice to Houston for James Bailey, a 1985 2nd round draft choice and cash, October 4, 1984.
Waived by Houston, December 10, 1984; re-signed by Houston, February 19, 1985.
Played in Continental Basketball Association with Lancaster Lightning, 1983-84.

—COLLEGIATE RECORD—

Year	G.	Min.	FGA	FGM	Pct.	FTA	FTM	Pct.	Reb.	Pts.	Avg.
72-73	30	....	353	190	.538	64	45	.703	83	425	14.2
73-74	28	....	495	253	.511	77	58	.753	82	564	20.1
74-75	24	....	339	186	.549	116	97	.836	100	469	19.5
75-76	28	....	456	233	.511	117	91	.778	109	557	19.9
Totals	110	....	1643	862	.525	374	291	.778	374	2015	18.3

MINOR LEAGUE REGULAR SEASON RECORD

			—2-Point—			—3-Point—									
Sea.-Team	G.	Min.	FGM	FGA	Pct.	FGM	FGA	Pct.	FTM	FTA	Pct.	Reb.	Ast.	Pts.	Avg.
83-84—Lancaster CBA	2	48	11	17	.647	1	1	1.000	6	6	1.000	1	8	31	15.5

NBA REGULAR SEASON RECORD

									—Rebounds—									
Sea.—Team	G.	Min.	FGA	FGM	Pct.	FTA	FTM	Pct.	Off.	Def.	Tot.	Ast.	PF	Dq.	Stl.	Blk.	Pts.	Avg.
76-77—Houston	82	2531	814	388	.477	171	135	.789	55	164	219	463	174	0	125	19	911	11.1
77-78—Houston	82	2933	947	412	.435	250	193	.772	51	204	255	768	208	1	160	9	1017	12.4
78-79—Golden State	82	3095	1146	530	.462	321	264	.822	65	182	247	762	229	1	152	9	1324	16.1
79-80—Golden State	80	2763	830	388	.467	289	222	.768	61	159	220	602	196	2	138	3	1010	12.6
80-81—Golden State	66	1919	506	222	.439	145	107	.738	34	120	154	464	140	1	83	2	555	8.4
81-82—Washington	79	1940	618	263	.426	176	138	.784	40	126	166	551	105	0	95	6	666	8.4
82-83—Washington	35	386	131	62	.473	42	21	.500	8	21	29	102	18	0	25	1	145	4.1
83-84—San Antonio	63	1807	595	275	.462	157	120	.764	23	157	180	673	123	1	92	5	689	10.9
84-85—Houston	47	1158	446	206	.462	129	103	.798	21	64	85	318	78	0	62	2	536	11.4
Totals	616	18532	6033	2746	.455	1680	1303	.776	358	1197	1555	4703	1271	6	932	56	6853	11.1

Three-Point Field Goals: 1979-80, 12-for-42 (.286). 1980-81, 4-for-24 (.167). 1981-82, 2-for-22 (.091). 1982-83, 0-for-5. 1983-84, 19-for-69 (.275). 1984-85, 21-for-66 (.318). Totals, 58-for-228 (.254).

NBA PLAYOFF RECORD

									—Rebounds—									
Sea.—Team	G.	Min.	FGA	FGM	Pct.	FTA	FTM	Pct.	Off.	Def.	Tot.	Ast.	PF	Dq.	Stl.	Blk.	Pts.	Avg.
76-77—Houston	12	430	139	75	.540	34	26	.765	4	29	33	83	33	1	24	4	176	14.7
81-82—Washington	7	74	26	14	.538	3	2	.667	0	8	8	20	6	0	3	1	31	4.4
84-85—Houston	5	152	80	26	.325	22	14	.636	7	14	21	27	14	0	6	0	68	13.6
Totals	24	656	245	115	.469	59	42	.712	11	51	62	130	53	1	33	5	275	11.5

Three-Point Field Goals: 1981-82, 1-for-3 (.333). 1984-85, 2-for-14 (.143). Totals, 3-for-17 (.176).

Named to NBA All-Rookie Team, 1977. . . . Holds NBA record for most assists in one quarter, 14, vs. Denver, April 15, 1984. . . . Played World Team Tennis with Golden Gaters and New Orleans Nets, 1977 and 1978. . . . Named to THE SPORTING NEWS All-America First Team, 1975 and 1976. . . . THE SPORTING NEWS All-America Second Team, 1974.

MAURICE LUCAS

Born February 18, 1952 at Pittsburgh, Pa.   Height 6:09.   Weight 238.

High School—Pittsburgh, Pa., Schenley.

College—Marquette University, Milwaukee, Wis.

Drafted by Chicago on first round as hardship case, 1974 (14th pick).

Selected by Carolina on first round of ABA undergraduate draft, 1973; Carolina franchise transferred to St. Louis, 1974.

Traded by St. Louis to Kentucky for Caldwell Jones, December 17, 1975.

Selected by Portland NBA from Kentucky in ABA dispersal draft, August 5, 1976.

Traded by Portland with two 1st round draft choices (1980 and 1981) to New Jersey for Calvin Natt, February 8, 1980.

Traded by New Jersey to New York in exchange for the Knicks not exercising their right of first refusal on Ray Williams, October 25, 1981.

Traded by New York to Phoenix for Leonard (Truck) Robinson, July 7, 1982.

—COLLEGIATE RECORD—

Year	G.	Min.	FGA	FGM	Pct.	FTA	FTM	Pct.	Reb.	Pts.	Avg.
71-72†	17	....	345	203	.588	112	81	.723	286	487	28.6
72-73	29	....	374	186	.497	97	76	.784	315	448	15.4
73-74	31	....	429	211	.492	94	69	.734	328	491	15.8
Varsity Totals	60	....	803	397	.494	191	145	.759	643	939	15.7

ABA REGULAR SEASON RECORD

			—2-Point—			—3-Point—									
Sea.—Team	G.	Min.	FGM	FGA	Pct.	FGM	FGA	Pct.	FTM	FTA	Pct.	Reb.	Ast.	Pts.	Avg.
74-75—St. Louis	80	2464	436	928	.470	2	9	.222	180	229	.786	816	287	1058	13.2
75-76—St.L.-Ky.	86	2861	617	1328	.465	3	18	.167	217	283	.767	970	224	1460	17.0
Totals	166	5325	1053	2256	.467	5	27	.185	397	512	.775	1786	511	2518	15.2

ABA PLAYOFF RECORD

Sea.—Team	G.	Min.	2-Point FGM	FGA	Pct.	3-Point FGM	FGA	Pct.	FTM	FTA	Pct.	Reb.	Ast.	Pts.	Avg.
74-75—St. Louis	10	375	68	152	.447	0	1	.000	27	41	.659	147	50	163	16.3
75-76—Kentucky	10	330	75	152	.493	0	0	.000	15	19	.789	108	22	165	16.5
Totals	20	705	143	304	.470	0	1	.000	42	60	.700	255	72	328	16.4

ABA ALL-STAR GAME RECORD

Sea.—Team	Min.	2-Point FGM	FGA	Pct.	3-Point FGM	FGA	Pct.	FTM	FTA	Pct.	Reb.	Ast.	Pts.	Avg.
1976—Kentucky	14	2	5	.400	0	0	.000	1	1	1.000	5	3	5	5.0

NBA REGULAR SEASON RECORD

Sea.—Team	G.	Min.	FGA	FGM	Pct.	FTA	FTM	Pct.	Rebounds Off.	Def.	Tot.	Ast.	PF	Dq.	Stl.	Blk.	Pts.	Avg.
76-77—Portland	79	2863	1357	632	.466	438	335	.765	271	628	899	229	294	6	83	56	1599	20.2
77-78—Portland	68	2119	989	453	.458	270	207	.767	186	435	621	173	221	3	61	56	1113	16.4
78-79—Portland	69	2462	1208	568	.470	345	270	.783	192	524	716	215	254	3	66	81	1406	20.4
79-80—Port-N.J.	63	1884	813	371	.456	239	179	.749	143	394	537	208	223	2	42	62	923	14.7
80-81—New Jersey	68	2162	835	404	.484	254	191	.752	153	422	575	173	260	3	57	59	999	14.7
81-82—New York	80	2671	1001	505	.504	349	253	.725	274	629	903	179	309	4	68	70	1263	15.8
82-83—Phoenix	77	2586	1045	495	.474	356	278	.781	201	598	799	219	274	5	56	43	1269	16.5
83-84—Phoenix	75	2309	908	451	.497	383	293	.765	208	517	725	203	235	2	55	39	1195	15.9
84-85—Phoenix	63	1670	727	346	.476	200	150	.750	138	419	557	145	183	0	39	17	842	13.4
Totals	642	20726	8883	4225	.476	2834	2156	.761	1766	4566	6332	1744	2253	28	527	483	10609	16.5

Three-Point Field Goals: 1979-80, 2-for-9 (.222). 1980-81, 0-for-2. 1981-82, 0-for-3, 1982-83, 1-for-3 (.333). 1983-84, 0-for-5. 1984-85, 0-for-4. Totals, 3-for-26 (.115).

NBA PLAYOFF RECORD

Sea.—Team	G.	Min.	FGA	FGM	Pct.	FTA	FTM	Pct.	Rebounds Off.	Def.	Tot.	Ast.	PF	Dq.	Stl.	Blk.	Pts.	Avg.
76-77—Portland	19	731	316	164	.519	101	75	.743	43	145	188	79	79	3	28	23	403	21.2
77-78—Portland	6	233	108	46	.426	19	11	.579	19	56	75	15	28	0	4	2	103	17.2
78-79—Portland	3	104	41	14	.341	7	5	.714	2	30	32	18	12	0	3	1	33	11.0
82-83—Phoenix	2	57	21	12	.571	4	2	.500	5	7	12	8	5	0	3	0	26	13.0
83-84—Phoenix	17	570	227	116	.511	78	63	.808	42	127	169	61	66	2	12	8	295	17.4
84-85—Phoenix	3	84	47	22	.468	19	15	.789	12	21	33	10	12	0	2	2	59	19.7
Totals	50	1779	760	374	.492	228	171	.750	123	386	509	191	202	5	52	36	919	18.4

NBA ALL-STAR GAME RECORD

Season—Team	Min.	FGA	FGM	Pct.	FTA	FTM	Pct.	Rebounds Off.	Def.	Tot.	Ast.	PF	Dq.	Stl.	Blk.	Pts.
1977—Portland	11	9	3	.333	0	0	.000	2	2	4	2	2	0	1	1	6
1978—Portland	33	13	6	.462	0	0	.000	6	7	13	4	2	0	1	0	12
1979—Portland	19	10	4	.400	2	2	1.000	1	6	7	1	5	0	0	0	10
1983—Phoenix	27	8	3	.375	1	0	.000	1	6	7	1	1	0	0	0	6
Totals	90	40	16	.400	3	2	.667	10	21	31	8	10	0	2	1	34

Named to All-NBA Second Team, 1978.... NBA All-Defensive First Team, 1978.... NBA All-Defensive Second Team, 1979.... Member of NBA championship team, 1977.

KYLE ROBERT MACY

Born April 9, 1957 at Fort Wayne, Ind.   Height 6:03.   Weight 190.

High School—Peru, Ind.

Colleges—Purdue University, West Lafayette, Ind., and
University of Kentucky, Lexington, Ky.

Drafted by Phoenix on first round as junior eligible, 1979 (22nd pick).

—COLLEGIATE RECORD—

Purdue

Year	G.	Min.	FGA	FGM	Pct.	FTA	FTM	Pct.	Reb.	Pts.	Avg.
75-76	27	833	293	144	.491	99	85	.859	75	373	13.8

Kentucky

Year	G.	Min.	FGA	FGM	Pct.	FTA	FTM	Pct.	Reb.	Pts.	Avg.
76-77					Did Not Play—Transfer Student						
77-78	32	1097	267	143	.536	129	115	.891	76	401	12.5
78-79	31	1111	355	179	.504	129	112	.868	82	470	15.2
79-80	35	1182	415	218	.525	114	104	.912	85	540	15.4
Ky. Totals	98	3390	1037	540	.521	372	331	.890	243	1411	14.4
College Totals	125	4223	1330	684	.514	471	416	.883	318	1784	14.3

KYLE MACY

NBA REGULAR SEASON RECORD

Sea.—Team	G.	Min.	FGA	FGM	Pct.	FTA	FTM	Pct.	—Rebounds— Off.	Def.	Tot.	Ast.	PF	Dq.	Stl.	Blk.	Pts.	Avg.
80-81—Phoenix	82	1469	532	272	.511	119	107	.899	44	88	132	160	120	0	76	5	663	8.1
81-82—Phoenix	82	2845	945	486	.514	169	152	.899	78	183	261	384	185	1	143	9	1163	14.2
82-83—Phoenix	82	1836	634	328	.517	148	129	.872	41	124	165	278	138	0	64	8	808	9.9
83-84—Phoenix	82	2402	713	357	.501	114	95	.833	49	137	186	353	181	0	123	6	832	10.1
84-85—Phoenix	65	2018	582	282	.485	140	127	.907	33	146	179	380	128	0	85	3	714	11.0
Totals	393	10570	3406	1725	.506	690	610	.884	245	678	923	1555	752	1	491	31	4180	10.6

Three-Point Field Goals: 1980-81, 12-for-51 (.235). 1981-82, 39-for-100 (.390). 1982-83, 23-for-76 (.303). 1983-84, 23-for-70 (.329). 1984-85, 23-for-85 (.271). Totals, 120-for-382 (.314).

NBA PLAYOFF RECORD

Sea.—Team	G.	Min.	FGA	FGM	Pct.	FTA	FTM	Pct.	—Rebounds— Off.	Def.	Tot.	Ast.	PF	Dq.	Stl.	Blk.	Pts.	Avg.
80-81—Phoenix	7	102	36	19	.528	7	7	1.000	2	11	13	11	8	0	5	0	49	7.0
81-82—Phoenix	7	243	89	38	.427	16	15	.938	11	11	22	28	21	0	7	1	95	13.6
82-83—Phoenix	3	72	35	15	.429	7	5	.714	2	6	8	9	6	0	1	0	35	11.7
83-84—Phoenix	17	620	157	77	.490	16	12	.750	14	40	54	98	43	0	22	2	176	10.4
84-85—Phoenix	3	85	26	13	.500	5	4	.800	3	5	8	9	5	0	6	0	31	10.3
Totals	37	1122	343	162	.472	51	43	.843	32	73	105	155	83	0	41	2	386	10.4

Three-Point Field Goals: 1980-81, 4-for-8 (.500). 1981-82, 4-for-11 (.364). 1982-83, 0-for-3. 1983-84, 10-for-22 (.455). 1984-85, 1-for-4 (.250). Totals, 19-for-48 (.396).

Led NBA in free-throw percentage, 1982 and 1985. . . . Named to THE SPORTING NEWS All-America First Team, 1980. . . . Member of NCAA championship team, 1978.

DERRICK ALLEN MAHORN
(Ricky)

Born September 21, 1958 at Hartford, Conn. Height 6:10. Weight 240.

High School—Hartford, Conn., Weaver.

College—Hampton Institute, Hampton, Va.

Drafted by Washington on second round, 1980 (35th pick).

Traded by Washington with Mike Gibson to Detroit for Dan Roundfield, June 17, 1985.

—COLLEGIATE RECORD—

Year	G.	Min.	FGA	FGM	Pct.	FTA	FTM	Pct.	Reb.	Pts.	Avg.
76-77	28	....	159	65	.409	44	29	.659	168	159	5.7
77-78	30	....	570	291	.511	202	137	.678	377	719	24.0
78-79	30	....	489	274	.560	200	137	.685	430	685	22.8
79-80	31	1123	621	352	.567	220	151	.686	490	855	27.6
Totals	119	....	1839	982	.534	666	454	.682	1465	2418	20.3

NBA REGULAR SEASON RECORD

Sea.—Team	G.	Min.	FGA	FGM	Pct.	FTA	FTM	Pct.	—Rebounds— Off.	Def.	Tot.	Ast.	PF	Dq.	Stl.	Blk.	Pts.	Avg.
80-81—Washington	52	696	219	111	.507	40	27	.675	67	148	215	25	134	3	21	44	249	4.8
81-82—Washington	80	2664	816	414	.507	234	148	.632	149	555	704	150	349	12	57	138	976	12.2
82-83—Washington	82	3023	768	376	.490	254	146	.575	171	608	779	115	335	13	86	148	898	11.0
83-84—Washington	82	2701	605	307	.507	192	125	.651	169	569	738	131	358	14	62	123	739	9.0
84-85—Washington	77	2072	413	206	.499	104	71	.683	150	458	608	121	308	11	59	104	483	6.3
Totals	373	11156	2821	1414	.501	824	517	.627	706	2338	3044	542	1484	53	285	557	3345	9.0

Three-Point Field Goals: 1981-82, 0-for-3. 1982-83, 0-for-3. Totals, 0-for-6.

NBA PLAYOFF RECORD

Sea.—Team	G.	Min.	FGA	FGM	Pct.	FTA	FTM	Pct.	—Rebounds— Off.	Def.	Tot.	Ast.	PF	Dq.	Stl.	Blk.	Pts.	Avg.
81-82—Washington	7	242	73	32	.438	14	10	.714	14	47	61	13	30	1	10	5	74	10.6
83-84—Washington	4	154	25	15	.600	10	8	.800	7	36	43	6	19	0	1	6	38	9.5
84-85—Washington	4	41	8	4	.500	4	4	1.000	2	5	7	0	9	0	0	3	12	3.0
Totals	15	437	106	51	.481	28	22	.786	23	88	111	19	58	1	11	14	124	8.3

Three-Point Field Goals: 1983-84, 0-for-1.

Led NCAA Division II in rebounding average, 15.8, 1980.

JEFFREY NIGEL MALONE
(Jeff)

Born June 28, 1961 at Mobile, Ala. Height 6:04. Weight 205.

High School—Macon, Ga., Southwest.

College—Mississippi State University, Mississippi State, Miss.

Drafted by Washington on first round, 1983 (10th pick).

Year	G.	Min.	FGA	FGM	Pct.	FTA	FTM	Pct.	Reb.	Pts.	Avg.
79-80	27	781	303	139	.459	51	42	.824	90	320	11.9
80-81	27	999	447	219	.490	128	105	.820	113	543	20.1
81-82	27	1001	410	225	.549	70	52	.743	111	502	18.6
82-83	29	1070	608	323	.531	159	131	.824	106	777	26.8
Totals	110	3851	1768	906	.512	408	330	.809	420	2142	19.5

NBA REGULAR SEASON RECORD

Sea.—Team	G.	Min.	FGA	FGM	Pct.	FTA	FTM	Pct.	Off.	Def.	Tot.	Ast.	PF	Dq.	Stl.	Blk.	Pts.	Avg.
83-84—Washington	81	1976	918	408	.444	172	142	.826	57	98	155	151	162	1	23	13	982	12.1
84-85—Washington	76	2613	1213	605	.499	250	211	.844	60	146	206	184	176	1	52	9	1436	18.9
Totals	157	4589	2131	1013	.475	422	353	.836	117	244	361	335	338	2	75	22	2418	15.4

Three-Point Field Goals: 1983-84, 24-for-74 (.324). 1984-85, 15-for-72 (.208). Totals, 39-for-146 (.267).

NBA PLAYOFF RECORD

Sea.—Team	G.	Min.	FGA	FGM	Pct.	FTA	FTM	Pct.	Off.	Def.	Tot.	Ast.	PF	Dq.	Stl.	Blk.	Pts.	Avg.
83-84—Washington	4	71	26	12	.462	0	0	.000	2	3	5	2	6	0	1	0	24	6.0
84-85—Washington	4	126	56	27	.482	13	10	.769	3	3	6	8	14	1	5	0	65	16.3
Totals	8	197	82	39	.476	13	10	.769	5	6	11	10	20	1	6	0	89	11.1

Three-Point Field Goals: 1983-84, 0-for-1. 1984-85, 1-for-3 (.333). Totals, 1-for-4 (.250).

Named to NBA All-Rookie Team, 1984. . . . Named to THE SPORTING NEWS All-America First Team, 1983.

MOSES EUGENE MALONE

Born March 23, 1955 at Petersburg, Va.   Height 6:10.   Weight 255.

High School—Petersburg, Va.

Did not attend college.

Selected as an undergraduate by Utah on third round of ABA draft, 1974.
Sold by Utah to St. Louis, December 2, 1975.
Selected by Portland NBA from St. Louis in ABA dispersal draft, August 5, 1976.
Traded by Portland to Buffalo for 1978 1st round draft choice, October 18, 1976.
Traded by Buffalo to Houston for two 1st round draft choices (1977 and 1978), October 24, 1976.
Signed by Philadelphia as Veteran Free Agent, September 2, 1982; Houston matched offer and traded Malone to Philadelphia for Caldwell Jones and a 1983 1st round draft choice, September 15, 1982.

ABA REGULAR SEASON RECORD

Sea.—Team	G.	Min.	2-Point FGM	FGA	Pct.	3-Point FGM	FGA	Pct.	FTM	FTA	Pct.	Reb.	Ast.	Pts.	Avg.
74-75—Utah	83	3205	591	1034	.572	0	1	.000	375	635	.635	1209	89	1557	18.8
75-76—St. Louis	43	1168	251	488	.514	0	2	.000	112	183	.612	413	58	614	14.3
Totals	126	4373	842	1522	.553	0	3	.000	487	774	.629	1622	140	2171	17.2

ABA PLAYOFF RECORD

Sea.—Team	G.	Min.	2-Point FGM	FGA	Pct.	3-Point FGM	FGA	Pct.	FTM	FTA	Pct.	Reb.	Ast.	Pts.	Avg.
74-75—Utah	6	235	51	80	.638	0	0	.000	34	51	.667	195	9	136	22.7

ABA ALL-STAR GAME RECORD

Sea.—Team	Min.	2-Point FGM	FGA	Pct.	3-Point FGM	FGA	Pct.	FTM	FTA	Pct.	Reb.	Ast.	Pts.	Avg.
1975—Utah	20	2	3	.667	0	0	.000	2	5	.400	10	0	6	6.0

NBA REGULAR SEASON RECORD

Sea.—Team	G.	Min.	FGA	FGM	Pct.	FTA	FTM	Pct.	Off.	Def.	Tot.	Ast.	PF	Dq.	Stl.	Blk.	Pts.	Avg.
76-77—Buf-Hou	82	2506	810	389	.480	440	305	.693	437	635	1072	89	275	3	67	181	1083	13.2
77-78—Houston	59	2107	828	413	.499	443	318	.718	380	506	886	31	179	2	48	76	1144	19.4
78-79—Houston	82	3390	1325	716	.540	811	599	.739	587	857	1444	147	223	0	79	119	2031	24.8
79-80—Houston	82	3140	1549	778	.502	783	563	.719	573	617	1190	147	210	0	80	107	2119	25.8
80-81—Houston	80	3245	1545	806	.522	804	609	.757	474	706	1180	141	223	0	83	150	2222	27.8
81-82—Houston	81	3398	1822	945	.519	827	630	.762	558	630	1188	142	208	0	76	125	2520	31.1
82-83—Philadelphia	78	2922	1305	654	.501	788	600	.761	445	749	1194	101	206	0	89	157	1908	24.5
83-84—Philadelphia	71	2613	1101	532	.483	727	545	.750	352	598	950	96	188	0	71	110	1609	22.7
84-85—Philadelphia	79	2957	1284	602	.469	904	737	.815	385	646	1031	130	216	0	67	123	1941	24.6
Totals	694	26278	11569	5835	.504	6527	4906	.752	4191	5944	10135	1024	1928	5	660	1148	16577	23.9

Three-Point Field Goals: 1979-80, 0-for-6. 1980-81, 1-for-3 (.333). 1981-82, 0-for-6. 1982-83, 0-for-1. 1983-84, 0-for-4. 1984-85, 0-for-2. Totals, 1-for-22 (.045).

NBA PLAYOFF RECORD

Sea.—Team	G.	Min.	FGA	FGM	Pct.	FTA	FTM	Pct.	—Rebounds— Off.	Def.	Tot.	Ast.	PF	Dq.	Stl.	Blk.	Pts.	Avg.
76-77—Houston	12	518	162	81	.500	91	63	.692	84	119	203	7	42	0	13	21	225	18.8
78-79—Houston	2	78	41	18	.439	18	13	.722	25	16	41	2	5	0	1	8	49	24.5
79-80—Houston	7	275	138	74	.536	43	33	.767	42	55	97	7	18	0	4	16	181	25.9
80-81—Houston	21	955	432	207	.479	208	148	.711	125	180	305	35	54	0	13	34	562	26.8
81-82—Houston	3	136	67	29	.433	15	14	.933	28	23	51	10	8	0	2	2	72	24.0
82-83—Philadelphia	13	524	235	126	.536	120	86	.717	70	136	206	20	40	0	19	25	338	26.0
83-84—Philadelphia	5	212	83	38	.458	32	31	.969	20	49	69	7	15	0	3	11	107	21.4
84-85—Philadelphia	13	505	212	90	.425	103	82	.796	36	102	138	24	39	0	17	22	262	20.2
Totals	76	3203	1370	663	.484	630	470	.746	430	680	1110	112	221	0	72	139	1796	23.6

Three-Point Field Goals: 1979-80, 0-for-1. 1980-81, 0-for-2, 1982-83, 0-for-1. 1984-85, 0-for-1. Totals, 0-for-5.

NBA ALL-STAR GAME RECORD

Season—Team	Min.	FGA	FGM	Pct.	FTA	FTM	Pct.	—Rebounds— Off.	Def.	Tot.	Ast.	PF	Dq.	Stl.	Blk.	Pts.
1978—Houston	14	1	1	1.000	4	2	.500	1	3	4	1	1	0	1	0	4
1979—Houston	17	2	2	1.000	5	4	.800	2	5	7	1	0	0	1	0	8
1980—Houston	31	12	7	.583	12	6	.500	6	6	12	2	4	0	1	2	20
1981—Houston	22	8	3	.375	4	2	.500	2	4	6	3	3	0	1	0	8
1982—Houston	20	11	5	.455	6	2	.333	5	6	11	0	2	0	1	1	12
1983—Philadelphia	24	8	3	.375	6	4	.667	2	6	8	3	1	0	0	1	10
1984—Philadelphia					Selected but did not play											
1985—Philadelphia	33	10	2	.200	6	3	.500	5	7	12	1	4	0	0	0	7
Totals	161	52	23	.442	43	23	.535	23	37	60	11	15	0	5	4	69

Named NBA Most Valuable Player, 1979, 1982, 1983.... All-NBA First Team, 1979, 1982, 1983, 1985.... All-NBA Second Team, 1980, 1981, 1984.... NBA All-Defensive First Team, 1983.... NBA All-Defensive Second Team, 1979.... NBA Playoff MVP, 1983.... Member of NBA championship team, 1983.... Led NBA in rebounding, 1979, 1981, 1982, 1983, 1984, 1985.... Named to ABA All-Rookie Team, 1975.

PACE SHEWAN MANNION

Born September 22, 1960 at Salt Lake City, Utah.   Height 6:07.   Weight 190.

High School—Las Vegas, Nev., Chaparral.

College—University of Utah, Salt Lake City, Utah.

Drafted by Golden State on second round, 1983 (43rd pick).

Waived by Golden State, October 15, 1984; signed by Utah as a free agent, December 22, 1984.

—COLLEGIATE RECORD—

Year	G.	Min.	FGA	FGM	Pct.	FTA	FTM	Pct.	Reb.	Pts.	Avg.
79-80	28	457	82	31	.378	30	26	.867	53	88	3.1
80-81	28	902	163	73	.448	79	47	.595	93	193	6.9
81-82	28	1061	263	114	.433	97	64	.660	122	292	10.4
82-83	32	1195	344	166	.483	138	112	.812	147	444	13.9
Totals	116	3615	852	384	.451	344	249	.724	415	1017	8.8

NBA REGULAR SEASON RECORD

Sea.—Team	G.	Min.	FGA	FGM	Pct.	FTA	FTM	Pct.	—Rebounds— Off.	Def.	Tot.	Ast.	PF	Dq.	Stl.	Blk.	Pts.	Avg.
83-84—Golden State	57	469	126	50	.397	23	18	.783	23	36	59	47	63	0	25	2	121	2.1
84-85—Utah	34	190	63	27	.429	23	16	.696	12	11	23	27	17	0	16	3	70	2.1
Totals	91	659	189	77	.407	46	34	.739	35	47	82	74	80	0	41	5	191	2.1

Three-Point Field Goals: 1983-84, 3-for-13 (.231). 1984-85, 0-for-1. Totals, 3-for-14 (.214).

NBA PLAYOFF RECORD

Sea.—Team	G.	Min.	FGA	FGM	Pct.	FTA	FTM	Pct.	—Rebounds— Off.	Def.	Tot.	Ast.	PF	Dq.	Stl.	Blk.	Pts.	Avg.
84-85—Utah	8	41	12	4	.333	12	10	.833	3	4	7	4	5	0	1	2	18	2.3

Three Point Field Goals: 1984-85, 0-for-1.

WES JOEL MATTHEWS

Born August 24, 1959 at Sarasota, Fla.   Height 6:01.   Weight 170.

High School—Bridgeport, Conn., Harding.

College—University of Wisconsin, Madison, Wis.

Drafted by Washington on first round as an undergraduate, 1980 (14th pick).

Traded by Washington to Atlanta for Don Collins, January 17, 1981.

MOSES MALONE

Traded by Atlanta with Kevin Figaro to San Diego for a conditional 2nd round draft choice, October 6, 1983.
Waived by San Diego, October 17, 1983; signed by Atlanta to a 10-day contract that expired March 5, 1984.
Signed by Philadelphia, March 22, 1984, to the first of consecutive 10-day contracts that expired April 11, 1984.
Signed by Chicago as a free agent, October 26, 1984; Chicago relinquished right of first refusal, July 1, 1985.
Played in Continental Basketball Association with Ohio Mixers, 1983-84.

—COLLEGIATE RECORD—

Year	G.	Min.	FGA	FGM	Pct.	FTA	FTM	Pct.	Reb.	Pts.	Avg.
77-78	14	408	197	83	.421	52	37	.712	47	203	14.5
78-79	27	986	417	195	.468	139	109	.784	69	499	18.5
79-80	28	955	412	211	.512	143	127	.888	73	549	19.6
Totals	69	2349	1026	489	.477	334	273	.817	189	1251	18.1

NBA REGULAR SEASON RECORD

Sea.—Team	G.	Min.	FGA	FGM	Pct.	FTA	FTM	Pct.	Off.	Def.	Tot.	Ast.	PF	Dq.	Stl.	Blk.	Pts.	Avg.
80-81—Wash.-Atl.	79	2266	779	385	.494	252	202	.802	46	93	139	411	242	2	107	17	977	12.4
81-82—Atlanta	47	837	298	131	.440	79	60	.759	19	39	58	139	129	3	53	2	324	6.9
82-83—Atlanta	64	1187	424	171	.403	112	86	.768	25	66	91	249	129	0	60	8	442	6.9
83-84—Atl.-Phil.	20	388	131	61	.466	36	27	.750	7	20	27	83	45	0	16	3	150	7.5
84-85—Chicago	78	1523	386	191	.495	85	59	.694	16	51	67	354	133	0	73	12	443	5.7
Totals	288	6201	2018	939	.465	564	434	.770	113	269	382	1236	678	5	309	42	2336	8.1

Three-Point Field Goals: 1980-81, 5-for-21 (.238). 1981-82, 2-for-8 (.250). 1982-83, 14-for-48 (.292). 1983-84, 1-for-8 (.125). 1984-85, 2-for-16 (.125). Totals, 24-for-101 (.238).

NBA PLAYOFF RECORD

Sea.—Team	G.	Min.	FGA	FGM	Pct.	FTA	FTM	Pct.	Off.	Def.	Tot.	Ast.	PF	Dq.	Stl.	Blk.	Pts.	Avg.
81-82—Atlanta	2	28	10	2	.200	4	4	1.000	0	0	0	4	4	0	0	1	8	4.0
82-83—Atlanta	3	38	9	3	.333	5	4	.800	0	0	0	11	5	0	0	1	10	3.3
83-84—Philadelphia	4	23	8	4	.500	2	1	.500	0	0	0	4	4	0	1	0	10	2.5
84-85—Chicago	4	91	32	11	.344	9	7	.778	2	4	6	12	10	0	5	0	29	7.3
Totals	13	180	59	20	.339	20	16	.800	2	4	6	31	23	0	6	2	57	4.4

Three-Point Field Goals: 1982-83, 0-for-1. 1983-84, 1-for-2 (.500). 1984-85, 0-for-3. Totals, 1-for-6 (.167).

MINOR LEAGUE REGULAR SEASON RECORD

Sea.—Team	G.	Min.	2-Point			3-Point			FTM	FTA	Pct.	Reb.	Ast.	Pts.	Avg.
			FGM	FGA	Pct.	FGM	FGA	Pct.							
83-84—Ohio CBA	8	235	69	121	.570	1	10	.100	28	37	.756	21	66	169	21.1

CEDRIC BRYAN MAXWELL

Born November 21, 1955 at Kinston, N. C.   Height 6:08.   Weight 215.

High School—Kinston, N. C.

College—University of North Carolina at Charlotte, Charlotte, N. C.

Drafted by Boston on first round, 1977 (12th pick).

—COLLEGIATE RECORD—

Year	G.	Min.	FGA	FGM	Pct.	FTA	FTM	Pct.	Reb.	Pts.	Avg.
73-74	26	....	154	98	.636	77	41	.532	161	237	9.1
74-75	26	....	237	127	.535	88	64	.727	230	318	12.2
75-76	29	....	371	201	.541	215	177	.823	350	579	20.0
76-77	31	....	381	244	.640	263	202	.768	376	690	22.3
Totals	112	....	1143	670	.586	643	484	.753	1117	1824	16.3

NBA REGULAR SEASON RECORD

Sea.—Team	G.	Min.	FGA	FGM	Pct.	FTA	FTM	Pct.	Off.	Def.	Tot.	Ast.	PF	Dq.	Stl.	Blk.	Pts.	Avg.
77-78—Boston	72	1213	316	170	.538	250	188	.752	138	241	379	68	151	2	53	48	528	7.3
78-79—Boston	80	2969	808	472	.584	716	574	.802	272	519	791	228	266	4	98	74	1518	19.0
79-80—Boston	80	2744	750	457	.609	554	436	.787	284	420	704	199	266	6	76	61	1350	16.9
80-81—Boston	81	2730	750	441	.588	450	352	.782	222	303	525	219	256	5	79	68	1234	15.2
81-82—Boston	78	2590	724	397	.548	478	357	.747	218	281	499	183	263	6	79	49	1151	14.8
82-83—Boston	79	2252	663	331	.499	345	280	.812	185	237	422	186	202	3	65	39	942	11.9
83-84—Boston	80	2502	596	317	.532	425	320	.753	201	260	461	205	224	4	63	24	955	11.9
84-85—Boston	57	1495	377	201	.533	278	231	.831	98	144	242	102	140	2	36	15	633	11.1
Totals	607	18495	4984	2786	.559	3496	2738	.783	1618	2405	4023	1390	1768	32	549	378	8311	13.7

Three-Point Field Goals: 1980-81, 0-for-1. 1981-82, 0-for-3. 1982-83, 0-for-1. 1983-84, 1-for-6 (.167). 1984-85, 0-for-2. Totals, 1-for-13 (.077).

NBA PLAYOFF RECORD

Sea.—Team	G.	Min.	FGA	FGM	Pct.	FTA	FTM	Pct.	Off.	Def.	Tot.	Ast.	PF	Dq.	Stl.	Blk.	Pts.	Avg.
79-80—Boston	9	320	93	59	.634	61	46	.754	31	59	90	19	25	0	5	10	164	18.2
80-81—Boston	17	598	174	101	.580	88	72	.818	61	64	125	46	53	0	12	16	274	16.1
81-82—Boston	12	385	120	62	.517	70	50	.714	37	50	87	26	40	0	18	11	174	14.5
82-83—Boston	7	246	55	29	.527	38	32	.842	23	28	51	23	18	0	4	4	90	12.9
83-84—Boston	23	752	167	84	.503	136	106	.779	52	67	119	55	77	1	22	7	274	11.9
84-85—Boston	20	238	43	21	.488	43	34	.791	17	30	47	7	29	0	9	2	76	3.8
Totals	88	2539	652	356	.546	436	340	.780	221	298	519	176	242	1	70	50	1052	11.9

Three-Point Field Goals: 1983-84, 0-for-1.

Named NBA Playoff MVP, 1981. . . . Member of NBA championship teams, 1981 and 1984. . . . Led NBA in field-goal percentage, 1979 and 1980.

ROBERT ALLEN McADOO
(Bob)

Born September 25, 1951 at Greensboro, N. C.   Height 6:09.   Weight 225.

High School—Greensboro, N. C., Ben Smith.

Colleges—Vincennes University, Vincennes, Ind., and University of North Carolina, Chapel Hill, N. C.

Drafted by Buffalo on first round as hardship case, 1972 (2nd pick).

Traded by Buffalo with Tom McMillen to New York Knicks for John Gianelli and cash, December 9, 1976.

Traded by New York to Boston for three 1979 1st round draft choices and a player to be named later, February 12, 1979. New York acquired Tom Barker to complete the deal, February 14, 1979.

Acquired from Boston by Detroit for two 1980 1st round draft choices to complete compensation for Boston's earlier signing of Veteran Free Agent M. L. Carr, September 6, 1979.

Waived by Detroit, March 11, 1981; signed by New Jersey as a free agent, March 13, 1981.

Traded by New Jersey to Los Angeles for a 1983 2nd round draft choice and cash, December 24, 1981.

—COLLEGIATE RECORD—
Vincennes

Year	G.	Min.	FGA	FGM	Pct.	FTA	FTM	Pct.	Reb.	Pts.	Avg.
69-70	32	....	...	258	....	134	101	.754	320	617	19.3
70-71	27	....	...	273	....	164	129	.787	297	675	25.0
JC Totals.................	59	....	...	531	....	298	230	.772	617	1292	21.9

North Carolina

Year	G.	Min.	FGA	FGM	Pct.	FTA	FTM	Pct.	Reb.	Pts.	Avg.
71-72	31	....	471	243	.516	167	118	.707	312	604	19.5

NBA REGULAR SEASON RECORD

Sea.—Team	G.	Min.	FGA	FGM	Pct.	FTA	FTM	Pct.	Off.	Def.	Tot.	Ast.	PF	Dq.	Stl.	Blk.	Pts.	Avg.
72-73—Buffalo	80	2562	1293	585	.452	350	271	.774			728	139	256	6			1441	18.0
73-74—Buffalo	74	3185	1647	901	.547	579	459	.793	281	836	1117	170	252	3	88	246	2261	30.6
74-75—Buffalo	82	3539	2138	1095	.512	796	641	.805	307	848	1155	179	278	3	92	174	2831	34.5
75-76—Buffalo	78	3328	1918	934	.487	734	559	.762	241	724	965	315	298	5	93	160	2427	31.1
76-77—Buf-Knicks	72	2798	1445	740	.512	516	381	.738	199	727	926	205	262	3	77	99	1861	25.8
77-78—New York	79	3182	1564	814	.520	645	469	.727	236	774	1010	298	297	6	105	126	2097	26.5
78-79—N.Y.-Bos.	60	2231	1127	596	.529	450	295	.656	130	390	520	168	189	3	74	67	1487	24.8
79-80—Detroit	58	2097	1025	492	.480	322	235	.730	100	367	467	200	178	3	73	65	1222	21.1
80-81—Det.-N.J.	16	321	157	68	.433	41	29	.707	17	50	67	30	38	0	17	13	165	10.3
81-82—Los Angeles	41	746	330	151	.458	126	90	.714	45	114	159	32	109	1	22	36	392	9.6
82-83—Los Angeles	47	1019	562	292	.520	163	119	.730	76	171	247	39	153	2	40	40	703	15.0
83-84—Los Angeles	70	1456	748	352	.471	264	212	.803	82	207	289	74	182	0	42	50	916	13.1
84-85—L.A. Lakers	66	1254	546	284	.520	162	122	.753	79	216	295	67	170	0	18	53	690	10.5
Totals	823	27718	14500	7304	.504	5148	3882	.754			7945	1916	2662	35	741	1129	18493	22.5

Three-Point Field Goals: 1979-80, 3-for-24 (.125). 1980-81, 0-for-1. 1981-82, 0-for-5. 1982-83, 0-for-1. 1983-84, 0-for-5. 1984-85, 0-for-1. Totals, 3-for-37 (.081).

NBA PLAYOFF RECORD

Sea.—Team	G.	Min.	FGA	FGM	Pct.	FTA	FTM	Pct.	Off.	Def.	Tot.	Ast.	PF	Dq.	Stl.	Blk.	Pts.	Avg.
73-74—Buffalo	6	271	159	76	.478	47	38	.809	14	68	82	9	25	1	6	13	190	31.7
74-75—Buffalo	7	327	216	104	.481	73	54	.740	25	69	94	10	29	1	6	19	262	37.4
75-76—Buffalo	9	406	215	97	.451	82	58	.707	31	97	128	29	37	3	7	18	252	28.0
77-78—New York	6	238	126	61	.484	35	21	.600	11	47	58	23	19	0	7	12	143	23.8
81-82—Los Angeles	14	388	179	101	.564	47	32	.681	21	74	95	22	43	2	10	21	234	16.7
82-83—Los Angeles	8	166	84	37	.440	14	11	.786	15	31	46	5	23	0	11	10	87	10.9
83-84—Los Angeles	20	447	215	111	.516	81	57	.704	30	78	108	12	63	0	12	27	279	14.0
84-85—L.A. Lakers	19	398	193	91	.472	47	35	.745	25	61	86	15	66	2	9	26	217	11.4
Totals	89	2641	1387	678	.489	426	306	.718	172	525	697	125	305	9	68	146	1664	18.7

Three-Point Field Goals: 1982-83, 2-for-6 (.333). 1983-84, 0-for-1. 1984-85, 0-for-1. Totals, 2-for-8 (.250).

NBA ALL-STAR GAME RECORD

Season—Team	Min.	FGA	FGM	Pct.	FTA	FTM	Pct.	—Rebounds— Off.	Def.	Tot.	Ast.	PF	Dq.	Stl.	Blk.	Pts.
1974—Buffalo	13	4	3	.750	8	5	.625	1	2	3	1	4	0	0	1	11
1975—Buffalo	26	9	4	.444	3	3	1.000	4	2	6	2	4	0	0	0	11
1976—Buffalo	29	14	10	.714	4	2	.500	2	5	7	1	5	0	0	0	22
1977—Knicks	38	23	13	.565	4	4	1.000	3	7	10	2	3	0	3	1	30
1978—New York	20	14	7	.500	0	0	.000	3	1	4	0	2	0	1	0	14
Totals	126	64	37	.578	19	14	.737	13	17	30	6	18	0	4	2	88

Named NBA Most Valuable Player, 1975. . . . All-NBA First Team, 1975. . . . All-NBA Second Team, 1974. . . . NBA Rookie of the Year, 1973. . . . NBA All-Rookie Team, 1973. . . . Led NBA in scoring, 1974, 1975, 1976. . . . Led NBA in field-goal percentage, 1974. . . . Member of NBA championship teams, 1982 and 1985. . . . Named to THE SPORTING NEWS All-America First Team, 1972.

TIMOTHY DANIEL McCORMICK
(Tim)

Born March 10, 1962 at Detroit, Mich.   Height 6:11.   Weight 240.

High School—Clarkston, Mich.

College—University of Michigan, Ann Arbor, Mich.

Drafted by Cleveland on first round as an undergraduate, 1984 (12th pick).

Draft rights traded by Cleveland with Cliff Robinson and cash to Washington for the draft rights to Melvin Turpin, June 19, 1984.

Draft rights traded by Washington with Ricky Sobers to Seattle for Gus Williams, June 19, 1984.

—COLLEGIATE RECORD—

Year	G.	Min.	FGA	FGM	Pct.	FTA	FTM	Pct.	Reb.	Pts.	Avg.
80-81	30	524	106	54	.509	60	47	.783	106	155	5.2
81-82				Did Not Play—Knee Operations							
82-83	28	....	220	122	.555	134	109	.813	180	353	12.6
83-84	32	960	226	131	.580	186	124	.667	189	386	12.1
Totals	90	....	552	307	.556	380	280	.737	475	894	9.9

NBA REGULAR SEASON RECORD

Sea.—Team	G.	Min.	FGA	FGM	Pct.	FTA	FTM	Pct.	—Rebounds— Off.	Def.	Tot.	Ast.	PF	Dq.	Stl.	Blk.	Pts.	Avg.
1984-85—Seattle	78	1584	483	269	.557	263	188	.715	146	252	398	78	207	2	18	33	726	9.3

Three-Point Field Goals: 1984-85, 0-for-1.

CARLTON LAMONT McCRAY
(Scooter)

Born February 8, 1960 at Mt Vernon, N.Y.   Height 6:09.   Weight 215.

High School—Mt. Vernon, N.Y.

College—University of Louisville, Louisville, Ky.

Drafted by Seattle on second round, 1983 (36th pick).

Waived by Seattle, November 13, 1984.

—COLLEGIATE RECORD—

Year	G.	Min.	FGA	FGM	Pct.	FTA	FTM	Pct.	Reb.	Pts.	Avg.
78-79	32	954	256	123	.480	107	77	.720	209	323	10.1
79-80	3	58	11	5	.454	6	4	.667	11	14	4.7
80-81	30	682	217	92	.424	83	43	.518	168	227	7.6
81-82	30	472	96	37	.385	34	24	.706	101	98	3.3
82-83	36	1165	287	132	.460	98	65	.663	232	329	9.1
Totals	131	3331	867	389	.449	328	213	.649	721	991	7.6

(Suffered knee injury in 1979-80 season; granted extra season of eligibility.)

NBA REGULAR SEASON RECORD

Sea.—Team	G.	Min.	FGA	FGM	Pct.	FTA	FTM	Pct.	—Rebounds— Off.	Def.	Tot.	Ast.	PF	Dq.	Stl.	Blk.	Pts.	Avg.
1983-84—Seattle	47	520	121	47	.388	50	35	.700	45	70	115	44	73	1	11	19	129	2.7
1984-85—Seattle	6	93	10	6	.600	4	3	.750	6	11	17	7	13	0	1	3	15	2.5
Totals	53	613	131	53	.405	54	38	.704	51	81	132	51	86	1	12	22	144	2.7

NBA PLAYOFF RECORD

Sea.—Team	G.	Min.	FGA	FGM	Pct.	FTA	FTM	Pct.	—Rebounds— Off.	Def.	Tot.	Ast.	PF	Dq.	Stl.	Blk.	Pts.	Avg.
83-84—Seattle	4	38	6	4	.667	1	0	.000	3	3	6	3	8	0	1	0	8	2.0

Three-Point Field Goals: 1983-84, 0-for-1.

Brother of Houston Rockets forward Rodney McCray.

RODNEY McCRAY

RODNEY EARL McCRAY

Born August 29, 1961 at Mt. Vernon, N.Y.   Height 6:07.   Weight 220.

High School—Mt. Vernon, N.Y.

College—University of Louisville, Louisville, Ky.

Drafted by Houston on first round, 1983 (3rd pick).

—COLLEGIATE RECORD—

Year	G.	Min.	FGA	FGM	Pct.	FTA	FTM	Pct.	Reb.	Pts.	Avg.
79-80	36	1178	197	107	.543	102	66	.647	269	280	7.8
80-81	30	917	194	114	.588	90	60	.667	222	288	9.6
81-82	33	961	196	112	.571	84	59	.702	234	283	8.6
82-83	36	1197	259	152	.587	124	92	.742	304	396	11.0
Totals	135	4253	846	485	.573	400	277	.693	1029	1247	9.2

NBA REGULAR SEASON RECORD

Sea.—Team	G.	Min.	FGA	FGM	Pct.	FTA	FTM	Pct.	—Rebounds— Off.	Def.	Tot.	Ast.	PF	Dq.	Stl.	Blk.	Pts.	Avg.
83-84—Houston	79	2081	672	335	.499	249	182	.731	173	277	450	176	205	1	53	54	853	10.8
84-85—Houston	82	3001	890	476	.535	313	231	.738	201	338	539	355	215	2	90	75	1183	14.4
Totals	161	5082	1562	811	.519	562	413	.735	374	615	989	531	420	3	143	129	2036	12.6

Three-Point Field Goals: 1983-84, 1-for-4 (.250). 1984-85, 0-for-6. Totals, 1-for-10 (.100).

NBA PLAYOFF RECORD

Sea.—Team	G.	Min.	FGA	FGM	Pct.	FTA	FTM	Pct.	—Rebounds— Off.	Def.	Tot.	Ast.	PF	Dq.	Stl.	Blk.	Pts.	Avg.
84-85—Houston	5	181	34	19	.559	23	15	.652	9	21	30	11	17	0	6	1	53	10.6

Member of U.S. Olympic team, 1980. . . . Member of NCAA championship team, 1980. . . . Brother of former Seattle SuperSonics guard-forward Scooter McCray.

HANK LEIGH McDOWELL

Born November 13, 1959 at Memphis, Tenn.   Height 6:09.   Weight 215.

High School—Memphis, Tenn., Treadwell.

College—Memphis State University, Memphis, Tenn.

Drafted by Golden State on fifth round, 1981 (102nd pick).

Waived by Golden State and claimed by Portland on waivers, December 8, 1982.
Traded by Portland to Indiana for a 1986 3rd round draft choice, October 7, 1983.
Traded by Indiana to San Diego for a 1986 3rd round draft choice, October 26, 1983.
Traded by Los Angeles Clippers to Houston for a 1985 3rd round draft choice, August 29, 1984.

—COLLEGIATE RECORD—

Year	G.	Min.	FGA	FGM	Pct.	FTA	FTM	Pct.	Reb.	Pts.	Avg.
77-78†	12	....	....	....	....	....	....	....	130	162	13.5
77-78	14	88	14	9	.643	11	8	.727	15	26	1.9
78-79	28	637	171	80	.468	75	52	.693	145	212	7.6
79-80	27	900	237	107	.451	100	57	.570	203	271	10.0
80-81	27	934	226	112	.496	136	98	.721	206	322	11.9
Varsity Totals	96	2559	648	308	.475	322	215	.668	569	831	8.7

NBA REGULAR SEASON RECORD

Sea.—Team	G.	Min.	FGA	FGM	Pct.	FTA	FTM	Pct.	—Rebounds— Off.	Def.	Tot.	Ast.	PF	Dq.	Stl.	Blk.	Pts.	Avg.
81-82—Golden State	30	335	84	34	.405	41	27	.659	41	59	100	20	52	1	6	8	95	3.2
82-83—G.S.-Port.	56	505	126	58	.460	61	47	.770	54	65	119	24	84	0	8	11	163	2.9
83-84—San Diego	57	611	197	85	.431	56	38	.679	63	92	155	37	77	0	14	2	208	3.6
84-85—Houston	34	132	42	20	.476	10	7	.700	7	15	22	9	22	0	3	5	47	1.4
Totals	177	1583	449	197	.439	168	119	.708	165	231	396	90	235	1	31	26	513	2.9

Three-Point Field Goals: 1982-83, 0-for-2. 1983-84, 0-for-3. 1984-85, 0-for-1. Totals, 0-for-6.

NBA PLAYOFF RECORD

Sea.—Team	G.	Min.	FGA	FGM	Pct.	FTA	FTM	Pct.	—Rebounds— Off.	Def.	Tot.	Ast.	PF	Dq.	Stl.	Blk.	Pts.	Avg.
82-83—Portland	2	4	1	0	.000	0	0	.000	0	2	2	2	2	0	0	0	0	0.0

—DID YOU KNOW—

That draft-choice forwards Xavier McDaniel, first round by Seattle, and Tyrone Corbin, second round by San Antonio, were high school teammates in Columbia, S.C.?

MICHAEL RAY McGEE
(Mike)

Born July 29, 1959 at Tyler, Tex.   Height 6:05.   Weight 190.
High School—Omaha, Neb., North.
College—University of Michigan, Ann Arbor, Mich.
Drafted by Los Angeles on first round, 1981 (19th pick).

—COLLEGIATE RECORD—

Year	G.	Min.	FGA	FGM	Pct.	FTA	FTM	Pct.	Reb.	Pts.	Avg.
77-78	27	....	439	217	.494	122	97	.795	132	531	19.7
78-79	27	....	454	207	.456	146	97	.664	150	511	18.9
79-80	30	....	584	277	.474	159	111	.698	130	665	22.2
80-81	30	1070	600	309	.515	169	114	.675	118	732	24.4
Totals	114	....	2077	1010	.486	596	419	.703	530	2439	21.4

NBA REGULAR SEASON RECORD

Sea.—Team	G.	Min.	FGA	FGM	Pct.	FTA	FTM	Pct.	Off.	Def.	Tot.	Ast.	PF	Dq.	Stl.	Blk.	Pts.	Avg.
81-82—Los Angeles	39	352	172	80	.465	53	31	.585	34	15	49	16	59	0	18	3	191	4.9
82-83—Los Angeles	39	381	163	69	.423	23	17	.739	33	20	53	26	50	1	11	5	156	4.0
83-84—Los Angeles	77	1425	584	347	.594	113	61	.540	117	76	193	81	176	0	49	6	757	9.8
84-85—L.A. Lakers	76	1170	612	329	.538	160	94	.588	97	68	165	71	147	1	39	7	774	10.2
Totals	231	3328	1531	825	.539	349	203	.582	281	179	460	194	432	2	117	21	1878	8.1

Three-Point Field Goals: 1981-82, 0-for-4. 1982-83, 1-for-7 (.143). 1983-84, 2-for-13 (.154). 1984-85, 22-for-61 (.361). Totals, 25-for-85 (.294).

NBA PLAYOFF RECORD

Sea.—Team	G.	Min.	FGA	FGM	Pct.	FTA	FTM	Pct.	Off.	Def.	Tot.	Ast.	PF	Dq.	Stl.	Blk.	Pts.	Avg.
81-82—Los Angeles	4	10	13	6	.462	0	0	.000	3	0	3	0	1	0	0	0	12	3.0
82-83—Los Angeles	6	25	11	4	.364	4	3	.750	2	1	1	5	0	0	0	0	12	2.0
83-84—Los Angeles	17	370	157	90	.573	39	25	.641	22	12	34	23	52	0	11	1	211	12.4
84-85—L.A. Lakers	17	260	142	76	.535	42	29	.690	20	16	36	12	26	0	7	1	190	11.2
Totals	44	665	323	176	.545	85	57	.671	50	30	80	36	84	0	18	2	425	9.7

Three-Point Field Goals: 1981-82, 0-for-1. 1982-83, 1-for-1 (1.000). 1983-84, 6-for-17 (.353). 1984-85, 9-for-18 (.500). Totals, 16-for-37 (.432).

Member of NBA championship teams, 1982 and 1985. . . . Holds NBA record for highest field-goal percentage in a season by a guard, 1984.

KEVIN EDWARD McHALE

Born December 19, 1957 at Hibbing, Minn.   Height 6:10.   Weight 225.
High School—Hibbing, Minn.
College—University of Minnesota, Minneapolis, Minn.
Drafted by Boston on first round, 1980 (3rd pick).

—COLLEGIATE RECORD—

Year	G.	Min.	FGA	FGM	Pct.	FTA	FTM	Pct.	Reb.	Pts.	Avg.
76-77	27	....	241	133	.552	77	58	.753	218	324	12.0
77-78	26	....	242	143	.591	77	54	.701	192	340	13.1
78.79	27	....	391	202	.517	96	79	.823	259	483	17.9
79-80	32	....	416	236	.567	107	85	.794	281	557	17.4
Totals	112	....	1290	714	.553	357	276	.773	950	1704	15.2

NBA REGULAR SEASON RECORD

Sea.—Team	G.	Min.	FGA	FGM	Pct.	FTA	FTM	Pct.	Off.	Def.	Tot.	Ast.	PF	Dq.	Stl.	Blk.	Pts.	Avg.
80-81—Boston	82	1645	666	355	.533	159	108	.679	155	204	359	55	260	3	27	151	818	10.0
81-82—Boston	82	2332	875	465	.531	248	187	.754	191	365	556	91	264	1	30	185	1117	13.6
82-83—Boston	82	2345	893	483	.541	269	193	.717	215	338	553	104	241	3	34	192	1159	14.1
83-84—Boston	82	2577	1055	587	.556	439	336	.765	208	402	610	104	243	5	23	126	1511	18.4
84-85—Boston	79	2653	1062	605	.570	467	355	.760	229	483	712	141	234	3	28	120	1565	19.8
Totals	407	11552	4551	2495	.548	1582	1179	.745	998	1792	2790	495	1242	15	142	774	6170	15.2

Three-Point Field Goals: 1980-81, 0-for-2. 1982-83, 0-for-1. 1983-84, 1-for-3 (.333). 1984-85, 0-for-6. Totals, 1-for-12 (.083).

NBA PLAYOFF RECORD

Sea.—Team	G.	Min.	FGA	FGM	Pct.	FTA	FTM	Pct.	Off.	Def.	Tot.	Ast.	PF	Dq.	Stl.	Blk.	Pts.	Avg.
80-81—Boston	17	296	113	61	.540	36	23	.639	29	30	59	14	51	1	4	25	145	8.5
81-82—Boston	12	344	134	77	.575	53	40	.755	41	44	85	11	44	0	5	27	194	16.2

Sea.—Team	G.	Min.	FGA	FGM	Pct.	FTA	FTM	Pct.	Off.	Def.	Tot.	Ast.	PF	Dq.	Stl.	Blk.	Pts.	Avg.
									—Rebounds—									
82-83—Boston	7	177	62	34	.548	18	10	.556	15	27	42	5	16	0	3	7	78	11.1
83-84—Boston	23	702	244	123	.504	121	94	.777	62	81	143	27	75	1	3	35	340	14.8
84-85—Boston	21	837	303	172	.568	150	121	.807	74	134	208	32	73	3	13	46	465	22.1
Totals	80	2356	856	467	.546	378	288	.762	221	316	537	89	259	5	28	140	1222	15.3

Three-Point Field Goals: 1982-83, 0-for-1. 1983-84, 0-for-3. Totals, 0-for-4.

NBA ALL-STAR GAME RECORD

Season—Team	Min.	FGA	FGM	Pct.	FTA	FTM	Pct.	Off.	Def.	Tot.	Ast.	PF	Dq.	Stl.	Blk.	Pts.
								—Rebounds—								
1984—Boston............	11	7	3	.429	6	4	.667	2	3	5	0	1	0	0	0	10

Named to NBA All-Rookie Team, 1981. . . . Recipient of NBA Sixth Man Award, 1984 and 1985. . . . Member of NBA championship teams, 1981 and 1984. . . . NBA All-Defensive Second Team, 1983.

KEVIN ROBERT McKENNA

Born January 8, 1959 at St. Paul, Minn. Height 6:05. Weight 195.

High School—Palatine, Ill.

College—Creighton University, Omaha, Neb.

Drafted by Los Angeles on fourth round, 1981 (88th pick).

Waived by Los Angeles, October 8, 1982; signed by Indiana as a free agent, September 30, 1983.
Traded by Indiana to Houston for a 1985 5th round draft choice, September 17, 1984.
Waived by Houston, October 23, 1984; signed by New Jersey as a free agent, December 10, 1984.
Waived by New Jersey, December 18, 1984; re-signed by New Jersey, December 20, 1984.
Waived by New Jersey, April 15, 1985.
Played in Continental Basketball Association with Las Vegas-Albuquerque Silvers, 1982-83.

—COLLEGIATE RECORD—

Year	G.	Min.	FGA	FGM	Pct.	FTA	FTM	Pct.	Reb.	Pts.	Avg.
77-78	28	....	223	104	.466	51	36	.706	80	244	8.7
78-79	27	....	282	130	.461	82	59	.720	102	319	11.8
79-80	28	....	362	182	.503	124	99	.798	123	463	16.5
80-81	30	....	388	181	.466	135	112	.830	121	474	15.8
Totals	113		1255	597	.476	392	306	.781	426	1500	13.3

NBA REGULAR SEASON RECORD

Sea.—Team	G.	Min.	FGA	FGM	Pct.	FTA	FTM	Pct.	Off.	Def.	Tot.	Ast.	PF	Dq.	Stl.	Blk.	Pts.	Avg.
									—Rebounds—									
81-82—Los Angeles	36	237	87	28	.322	17	11	.647	18	11	29	14	45	0	10	2	67	1.9
83-84—Indiana	61	923	371	152	.410	98	80	.816	30	65	95	114	133	3	46	5	387	6.3
84-85—New Jersey	29	535	134	61	.455	43	38	.884	20	29	49	58	63	0	30	7	165	5.7
Totals	126	1695	592	241	.407	158	129	.816	68	105	173	186	241	3	86	14	619	4.9

Three-Point Field Goals: 1981-82, 0-for-2. 1983-84, 3-for-17 (.176). 1984-85, 5-for-13 (.385). Totals, 8-for-32 (.250).

MINOR LEAGUE REGULAR SEASON RECORD

Sea.—Team	G.	Min.	2-Point			3-Point			FTM	FTA	Pct.	Reb.	Ast.	Pts.	Avg.
			FGM	FGA	Pct.	FGM	FGA	Pct.							
82-83—L. Vegas-Albu. CBA .	42	1251	267	515	.518	1	21	.048	189	224	.843	154	96	726	17.3

CHARLES THOMAS McMILLEN
(Tom)

Born May 26, 1952 at Mansfield, Pa. Height 6:11. Weight 235.

High School—Mansfield, Pa.

College—University of Maryland, College Park, Md.

Drafted by Buffalo on first round, 1974 (9th pick).

Traded by Buffalo with Bob McAdoo to New York Knicks for John Gianelli and cash, December 9, 1976.
Traded by New York to Atlanta for a 1978 2nd round draft choice, November 14, 1977.
Traded by Atlanta with a 1984 2nd round draft choice to Washington for the draft rights to Randy Wittman, July 5, 1983.
Played in Italy during 1974-75 season.

—COLLEGIATE RECORD—

Year	G.	Min.	FGA	FGM	Pct.	FTA	FTM	Pct.	Reb.	Pts.	Avg.
70-71†	16	....	285	178	.625	125	113	.904	247	468	29.3
71-72	32	....	428	235	.549	241	197	.817	306	667	20.8
72-73	29	....	427	250	.585	145	116	.800	284	616	21.2
73-74	27	....	404	214	.530	126	96	.762	269	524	19.4
Varsity Totals	88	....	1259	699	.555	512	409	.799	859	1807	20.5

KEVIN McHALE

ITALIAN LEAGUE RECORD

Year	G.	Min.	FGA	FGM	Pct.	FTA	FTM	Pct.	Reb.	Pts.	Avg.
74-75—Bologna	28	....	302	156	.517	86	57	.663	192	369	13.2

NBA REGULAR SEASON RECORD

Sea.—Team	G.	Min.	FGA	FGM	Pct.	FTA	FTM	Pct.	Off.	Def.	Tot.	Ast.	PF	Dq.	Stl.	Blk.	Pts.	Avg.
75-76—Buffalo	50	708	222	96	.432	54	41	.759	64	122	186	69	87	1	7	6	233	4.7
76-77—Buf.-NYK	76	1492	563	274	.487	123	96	.780	114	275	389	67	163	0	11	6	644	8.5
77-78—Atlanta	68	1683	568	280	.493	145	116	.800	151	265	416	84	233	8	33	16	676	9.9
78-79—Atlanta	82	1392	498	232	.466	119	106	.891	131	201	332	69	211	2	15	32	570	7.0
79-80—Atlanta	53	1071	382	191	.500	107	81	.757	70	150	220	62	126	2	36	14	463	8.7
80-81—Atlanta	79	1564	519	253	.487	108	80	.741	96	199	295	72	165	0	23	25	587	7.4
81-82—Atlanta	73	1792	572	291	.509	170	140	.824	102	234	336	129	202	1	25	24	723	9.9
82-83—Atlanta	61	1364	424	198	.467	133	108	.812	57	160	217	76	143	2	17	24	504	8.3
83-84—Washington	62	1294	447	222	.497	156	127	.814	64	135	199	73	162	0	14	17	572	9.2
84-85—Washington	69	1547	534	252	.472	135	112	.830	64	146	210	52	163	3	8	17	616	8.9
Totals	673	13907	4729	2289	.484	1250	1007	.806	913	1887	2800	753	1655	19	190	181	5588	8.3

Three-Point Field Goals: 1979-80, 0-for-1. 1980-81, 1-for-6 (.167). 1981-82, 1-for-3 (.333). 1982-83, 0-for-1. 1983-84, 1-for-6 (.167). 1984-85, 0-for-5. Totals, 3-for-22 (.136).

NBA PLAYOFF RECORD

Sea.—Team	G.	Min.	FGA	FGM	Pct.	FTA	FTM	Pct.	Off.	Def.	Tot.	Ast.	PF	Dq.	Stl.	Blk.	Pts.	Avg.
75-76—Buffalo	1	3	2	1	.500	0	0	.000	1	0	1	0	1	0	0	0	2	2.0
77-78—Atlanta	2	75	23	13	.565	0	0	.000	7	15	22	1	9	0	1	0	26	13.0
78-79—Atlanta	9	163	46	20	.435	19	16	.842	14	20	34	7	21	1	2	1	56	6.2
81-82—Atlanta	2	47	13	8	.615	6	4	.667	0	7	7	1	5	0	3	0	20	10.0
82-83—Atlanta	3	39	12	4	.333	2	2	1.000	3	4	7	2	5	0	1	2	10	3.3
83-84—Washington	4	42	16	4	.250	2	1	.500	1	1	2	3	6	0	0	0	9	2.3
84-85—Washington	1	7	4	0	.000	0	0	.000	3	2	5	1	1	0	0	0	0	0.0
Totals	22	376	116	50	.431	29	23	.793	29	49	78	15	48	1	7	3	123	5.6

Three-Point Field Goals: 1984-85, 0-for-1.

Member of U. S. Olympic team, 1972.

MARK ROBERT McNAMARA

Born June 8, 1959 at San Jose, Calif. Height 6:11. Weight 235.

High School—San Jose, Calif., Del Mar.

Colleges—Santa Clara University, Santa Clara, Calif., and University of California, Berkeley, Calif.

Drafted by Philadelphia on first round, 1982 (22nd pick).

Traded by Philadelphia to San Antonio for a 1986 2nd round draft choice, November 4, 1983.
Traded by San Antonio to Kansas City for Billy Knight, December 11, 1984.

—COLLEGIATE RECORD—
Santa Clara

Year	G.	Min.	FGA	FGM	Pct.	FTA	FTM	Pct.	Reb.	Pts.	Avg.
77-78	29	....	229	143	.624	98	46	.469	197	332	11.4
78-79	25	652	266	153	.575	123	71	.577	167	377	15.1
SC Totals	54	....	495	296	.598	221	117	.529	364	709	13.1

California

Year	G.	Min.	FGA	FGM	Pct.	FTA	FTM	Pct.	Reb.	Pts.	Avg.
79-80				Did Not Play—Transfer Student							
80-81	26	....	295	182	.617	168	84	.500	272	448	17.2
81-82	27	....	329	231	.702	242	131	.541	341	593	22.0
Cal Totals	53	....	624	413	.662	410	215	.524	613	1041	19.6
College Totals	107	....	1119	709	.634	631	332	.526	977	1750	16.4

NBA REGULAR SEASON RECORD

Sea.—Team	G.	Min.	FGA	FGM	Pct.	FTA	FTM	Pct.	Off.	Def.	Tot.	Ast.	PF	Dq.	Stl.	Blk.	Pts.	Avg.
82-83—Philadelphia	36	182	64	29	.453	45	20	.444	34	42	76	7	42	1	3	3	78	2.2
83-84—San Antonio	70	1037	253	157	.621	157	74	.471	137	180	317	31	138	2	14	12	388	5.5
84-85—S.A.-K.C.	45	273	76	40	.526	62	32	.516	31	43	74	6	27	0	7	8	112	2.5
Totals	151	1492	393	226	.575	264	126	.477	202	265	467	44	207	3	24	23	578	3.8

NBA PLAYOFF RECORD

Sea.—Team	G.	Min.	FGA	FGM	Pct.	FTA	FTM	Pct.	Off.	Def.	Tot.	Ast.	PF	Dq.	Stl.	Blk.	Pts.	Avg.
82-83—Philadelphia	2	2	2	2	1.000	0	0	.000	0	1	1	0	0	0	0	0	4	2.0

Member of NBA championship team, 1983. . . . Led NCAA Division I in field-goal percentage, 1982.

JOE C. MERIWEATHER

Born October 26, 1953 at Phenix City, Ala.   Height 6:10.   Weight 218.

High School—Phenix City, Ala., Central.

College—Southern Illinois University, Carbondale, Ill.

Drafted by Houston on first round, 1975 (11th pick).

Traded by Houston with Gus Bailey and a 1976 1st round draft choice to Atlanta for Dwight Jones and a 1976 1st round draft choice, June 7, 1976.

Traded by Atlanta to New Orleans for a 1978 1st round draft choice, October 13, 1977.

Traded by New Orleans to New York for Spencer Haywood, January 5, 1979.

Traded by New York with a 1981 1st round draft choice to Kansas City in three-way deal with Cleveland, September 25, 1980 (Bill Robinzine went from Kansas City to Cleveland and Campy Russell went from Cleveland to New York).

—COLLEGIATE RECORD—

Year	G.	Min.	FGA	FGM	Pct.	FTA	FTM	Pct.	Reb.	Pts.	Avg.
71-72†	14	....	188	122	.649	88	57	.648	211	301	21.5
72-73	25	....	343	186	.542	98	56	.571	307	428	17.1
73-74	26	....	396	233	.588	114	85	.746	387	551	21.2
74-75	27	....	370	229	.619	154	99	.643	311	557	20.6
Varsity Totals	78	....	1109	648	.584	366	240	.656	1005	1536	19.7

NBA REGULAR SEASON RECORD

Sea.—Team	G.	Min.	FGA	FGM	Pct.	FTA	FTM	Pct.	Off.	Def.	Tot.	Ast.	PF	Dq.	Stl.	Blk.	Pts.	Avg.
75-76—Houston	81	2042	684	338	.494	239	154	.644	163	353	516	82	219	4	36	120	830	10.2
76-77—Atlanta	73	2068	607	319	.526	255	182	.714	216	380	596	82	324	21	41	82	820	11.2
77-78—N. Orleans	54	1277	411	194	.472	133	87	.654	135	237	372	58	188	8	18	118	475	8.8
78-79—NO-NY	77	1693	500	242	.484	187	126	.674	143	266	409	79	283	10	40	94	610	7.9
79-80—New York	65	1565	477	252	.528	121	78	.645	122	228	350	66	239	8	37	120	582	9.0
80-81—Kansas City	74	1514	415	206	.496	213	148	.695	126	267	393	77	219	4	27	80	560	7.6
81-82—Kansas City	18	380	91	47	.516	40	31	.775	25	63	88	17	68	1	13	21	125	6.9
82-83—Kansas City	78	1706	453	258	.570	163	102	.626	150	274	424	64	285	4	47	86	618	7.9
83-84—Kansas City	73	1501	363	193	.532	123	94	.764	111	242	353	51	247	8	35	61	480	6.6
84-85—Kansas City	76	1061	243	121	.498	124	96	.774	94	169	263	27	181	1	17	28	339	4.5
Totals	669	14807	4244	2170	.511	1598	1098	.687	1285	2479	3764	603	2253	69	311	810	5439	8.1

Three-Point Field Goals: 1979-80, 0-for-1. 1984-85, 1-for-2 (.500). Totals, 1-for-3 (.333).

NBA PLAYOFF RECORD

Sea.—Team	G.	Min.	FGA	FGM	Pct.	FTA	FTM	Pct.	Off.	Def.	Tot.	Ast.	PF	Dq.	Stl.	Blk.	Pts.	Avg.
80-81—Kansas City	10	199	49	24	.490	14	8	.571	12	19	31	5	31	1	5	7	56	5.6

Named to NBA All-Rookie Team, 1976. . . . THE SPORTING NEWS All-America Second Team, 1975.

LARRY WAYNE MICHEAUX

Born March 24, 1960 at Houston, Tex.   Height 6:09.   Weight 220.

High School—Houston, Tex., Worthing.

College—University of Houston, Houston, Tex.

Drafted by Chicago on second round, 1983 (29th pick).

Draft rights traded by Chicago with Mark Olberding to Kansas City for draft rights to Ennis Whatley and Chris McNealy and a 1984 2nd round draft choice, June 28, 1983.

Waived by Kansas City, October 15, 1984; signed by Milwaukee as a free agent, October 17, 1984.

Waived by Milwaukee, December 17, 1984; signed by Houston as a free agent, December 28, 1984.

—COLLEGIATE RECORD—

Year	G.	Min.	FGA	FGM	Pct.	FTA	FTM	Pct.	Reb.	Pts.	Avg.
79-80	27	468	117	61	.521	58	29	.500	115	151	5.6
80-81	29	860	205	123	.600	88	48	.545	191	294	10.1
81-82	33	1084	293	177	.604	95	55	.579	249	409	12.4
82-83	34	1006	328	193	.588	146	82	.562	232	468	13.8
Totals	123	3418	943	554	.587	387	214	.553	787	1322	10.7

NBA REGULAR SEASON RECORD

Sea.—Team	G.	Min.	FGA	FGM	Pct.	FTA	FTM	Pct.	Off.	Def.	Tot.	Ast.	PF	Dq.	Stl.	Blk.	Pts.	Avg.
83-84—Kansas City	39	332	90	49	.544	39	21	.538	40	73	113	19	46	0	21	11	119	3.1
84-85—Mil.-Hou.	57	565	157	91	.580	43	29	.674	62	81	143	30	75	0	20	21	211	3.7
Totals	96	897	247	140	.567	82	50	.610	102	154	256	49	121	0	41	32	330	3.4

Sea.—Team	G.	Min.	FGA	FGM	Pct.	FTA	FTM	Pct.	Off.	Def.	Tot.	Ast.	PF	Dq.	Stl.	Blk.	Pts.	Avg.
										—Rebounds—								
83-84—Kansas City	3	65	18	12	.667	10	6	.600	12	9	21	3	10	0	0	5	30	10.0
84-85—Houston	5	57	19	6	.316	10	4	.400	12	9	21	0	8	0	0	2	16	3.2
Totals	8	122	37	18	.486	20	10	.500	24	18	42	3	18	0	0	7	46	5.8

Three-Point Field Goals: 1984-85, 0-for-1.

MICHAEL ANTHONY MITCHELL
(Mike)

Born January 1, 1956 at Atlanta, Ga.   Height 6:07.   Weight 215.

High School—Atlanta, Ga., Price.

College—Auburn University, Auburn, Ala.

Drafted by Cleveland on first round, 1978 (15th pick).

Traded by Cleveland with Roger Phegley to San Antonio for Ron Brewer, Reggie Johnson and cash, December 23, 1981.

—COLLEGIATE RECORD—

Year	G.	Min.	FGA	FGM	Pct.	FTA	FTM	Pct.	Reb.	Pts.	Avg.
74-75	25	....	426	204	.479	98	53	.541	286	461	18.4
75-76	26	....	431	210	.487	96	66	.688	249	486	18.7
76-77	26	....	429	229	.534	69	47	.681	220	505	19.4
77-78	27	....	544	283	.520	135	105	.778	241	671	24.9
Totals	104	....	1830	926	.506	398	271	.681	996	2123	20.4

NBA REGULAR SEASON RECORD

Sea.—Team	G.	Min.	FGA	FGM	Pct.	FTA	FTM	Pct.	Off.	Def.	Tot.	Ast.	PF	Dq.	Stl.	Blk.	Pts.	Avg.
										—Rebounds—								
78-79—Cleveland	80	1576	706	362	.513	178	131	.736	127	202	329	60	215	6	51	29	855	10.7
79-80—Cleveland	82	2802	1482	775	.523	343	270	.787	206	385	591	93	259	4	70	77	1820	22.2
80-81—Cleveland	82	3194	1791	853	.476	385	302	.784	215	287	502	139	199	0	63	52	2012	24.5
81-82—Clev.-S.A.	84	3063	1477	753	.510	302	220	.728	244	346	590	82	277	4	60	43	1726	20.5
82-83—San Antonio	80	2803	1342	686	.511	289	219	.758	188	349	537	98	248	6	57	52	1591	19.9
83-84—San Antonio	79	2853	1597	779	.488	353	275	.779	188	382	570	93	251	6	62	73	1839	23.3
84-85—San Antonio	82	2853	1558	775	.497	346	269	.777	145	272	417	151	219	1	61	27	1824	22.2
Totals	569	19144	9953	4983	.501	2196	1686	.768	1313	2223	3536	716	1668	27	424	353	11667	20.5

Three-Point Field Goals: 1979-80, 0-for-6. 1980-81, 4-for-9 (.444). 1981-82, 0-for-7. 1982-83, 0-for-3. 1983-84, 6-for-14 (.429). 1984-85, 5-for-23 (.217). Totals, 15-for-62 (.242).

NBA PLAYOFF RECORD

Sea.—Team	G.	Min.	FGA	FGM	Pct.	FTA	FTM	Pct.	Off.	Def.	Tot.	Ast.	PF	Dq.	Stl.	Blk.	Pts.	Avg.
										—Rebounds—								
81-82—San Antonio	9	365	169	90	.533	57	43	.754	28	45	73	7	22	0	5	1	223	24.8
82-83—San Antonio	11	422	200	102	.501	33	25	.758	33	72	105	12	34	0	7	19	230	20.9
84-85—San Antonio	5	180	78	44	.564	24	21	.875	5	14	19	12	19	1	3	4	109	21.8
Totals	25	967	447	236	.528	114	89	.781	66	131	197	31	75	1	15	24	562	22.5

Three-Point Field Goals: 1982-83, 1-for-2 (.500). 1984-85, 0-for-1. Totals, 1-for-3 (.333).

NBA ALL-STAR GAME RECORD

Season—Team	Min.	FGA	FGM	Pct.	FTA	FTM	Pct.	Off.	Def.	Tot.	Ast.	PF	Dq.	Stl.	Blk.	Pts.
									—Rebounds—							
1981—Cleveland......	15	12	6	.500	2	2	1.000	4	0	4	2	2	0	1	0	14

PAUL KEEN MOKESKI

Born January 3, 1957 at Spokane, Wash.   Height 7:00.   Weight 250.

High School—Encino, Calif., Crespi Carmelite.

College—University of Kansas, Lawrence, Kan.

Drafted by Houston on second round, 1979 (42nd pick).

Traded by Houston to Detroit for a 1982 2nd round draft choice, October 7, 1980.
Traded by Detroit with Phil Hubbard and two 1982 draft choices (1st and 2nd round) to Cleveland for Kenny Carr and Bill Laimbeer, February 16, 1982.
Waived by Cleveland, December 20, 1982; signed by Milwaukee as a free agent, December 24, 1982.

—COLLEGIATE RECORD—

Year	G.	Min.	FGA	FGM	Pct.	FTA	FTM	Pct.	Reb.	Pts.	Avg.
75-76	18	474	170	82	.482	37	27	.730	115	191	10.6
76-77	14	250	96	38	.396	16	10	.625	86	86	6.1
77-78	28	653	220	114	.518	54	31	.574	237	259	9.3
78-79	29	974	323	161	.498	120	87	.725	242	409	14.1
Totals	89	2351	809	395	.488	227	155	.683	680	945	10.6

NBA REGULAR SEASON RECORD

Sea.—Team	G.	Min.	FGA	FGM	Pct.	FTA	FTM	Pct.	Off.	Def.	Tot.	Ast.	PF	Dq.	Stl.	Blk.	Pts.	Avg.
79-80—Houston	12	113	33	11	.333	9	7	.778	14	15	29	2	24	0	1	6	29	2.4
80-81—Detroit	80	1815	458	224	.489	200	120	.600	141	277	418	135	267	7	38	73	568	7.1
81-82—Det.-Clev.	67	868	193	84	.435	63	48	.762	59	149	208	35	171	2	33	40	216	3.2
82-83—Clev.-Milw.	73	1128	260	119	.458	68	50	.735	76	184	260	49	223	9	21	44	288	3.9
83-84—Milwaukee	68	838	213	102	.479	72	50	.694	51	115	166	44	168	1	11	29	255	3.8
84-85—Milwaukee	79	1586	429	205	.478	116	81	.698	107	303	410	99	266	6	28	35	491	6.2
Totals	379	6348	1586	745	.470	528	356	.674	448	1043	1491	364	1119	25	132	227	1847	4.9

Three-Point Field Goals: 1980-81, 0-for-1. 1981-82, 0-for-3. 1982-83, 0-for-1. 1983-84, 1-for-3 (.333). 1984-85, 0-for-2. Totals, 1-for-10 (.100).

NBA PLAYOFF RECORD

Sea.—Team	G.	Min.	FGA	FGM	Pct.	FTA	FTM	Pct.	Off.	Def.	Tot.	Ast.	PF	Dq.	Stl.	Blk.	Pts.	Avg.
82-83—Milwaukee	4	12	4	2	.500	0	0	.000	1	1	2	1	1	0	1	0	4	1.0
83-84—Milwaukee	16	322	63	34	.540	45	30	.667	20	68	88	6	62	0	9	11	98	6.1
84-85—Milwaukee	8	154	36	16	.444	12	12	1.000	8	26	34	12	28	1	2	4	44	5.5
Totals	28	488	103	52	.505	57	42	.737	29	95	124	19	91	1	12	15	146	5.2

Three-Point Field Goals: 1983-84, 0-for-2.

SIDNEY A. MONCRIEF

Born September 21, 1957 at Little Rock, Ark. Height 6:04. Weight 190.

High School—Little Rock, Ark., Hall.

College—University of Arkansas, Fayetteville, Ark.

Drafted by Milwaukee on first round, 1979 (5th pick).

—COLLEGIATE RECORD—

Year	G.	Min.	FGA	FGM	Pct.	FTA	FTM	Pct.	Reb.	Pts.	Avg.
75-76	28	....	224	149	.665	77	56	.727	213	354	12.6
76-77	28	997	242	157	.649	171	117	.684	235	431	15.4
77-78	36	1293	354	209	.590	256	203	.793	278	621	17.3
78-79	30	1157	400	224	.560	248	212	.855	289	660	22.0
Totals	122	....	1220	739	.606	752	588	.782	1015	2066	16.9

NBA REGULAR SEASON RECORD

Sea.—Team	G.	Min.	FGA	FGM	Pct.	FTA	FTM	Pct.	Off.	Def.	Tot.	Ast.	PF	Dq.	Stl.	Blk.	Pts.	Avg.
79-80—Milwaukee	77	1557	451	211	.468	292	232	.795	154	184	338	133	106	0	72	16	654	8.5
80-81—Milwaukee	80	2417	739	400	.541	398	320	.804	186	220	406	264	156	1	90	37	1122	14.0
81-82—Milwaukee	80	2980	1063	556	.523	573	468	.817	221	313	534	382	206	3	138	22	1581	19.8
82-83—Milwaukee	76	2710	1156	606	.524	604	499	.826	192	245	437	300	180	1	113	23	1712	22.5
83-84—Milwaukee	79	3075	1125	560	.498	624	529	.848	215	313	528	358	204	2	108	27	1654	20.9
84-85—Milwaukee	73	2734	1162	561	.483	548	454	.828	149	242	391	382	197	1	117	39	1585	21.7
Totals	465	15473	5696	2894	.508	3039	2502	.823	1117	1517	2634	1819	1049	8	638	164	8308	17.9

Three-Point Field Goals: 1979-80, 0-for-1. 1980-81, 2-for-9 (.222). 1981-82, 1-for-14 (.071). 1982-83, 1-for-10 (.100). 1983-84, 5-for-18 (.278). 1984-85, 9-for-33 (.273). Totals, 18-for-85 (.212).

NBA PLAYOFF RECORD

Sea.—Team	G.	Min.	FGA	FGM	Pct.	FTA	FTM	Pct.	Off.	Def.	Tot.	Ast.	PF	Dq.	Stl.	Blk.	Pts.	Avg.
79-80—Milwaukee	7	182	51	30	.588	31	27	.871	17	14	31	11	14	0	5	1	87	12.4
80-81—Milwaukee	7	277	69	30	.435	51	38	.745	19	28	47	20	24	0	12	3	98	14.0
81-82—Milwaukee	6	252	74	31	.419	38	30	.789	15	15	30	24	22	1	9	2	92	15.3
82-83—Milwaukee	9	377	142	62	.437	61	46	.754	28	32	60	33	25	1	18	3	170	18.9
83-84—Milwaukee	16	618	191	99	.518	134	106	.791	44	67	111	68	54	1	28	9	305	19.1
84-85—Milwaukee	8	319	99	55	.556	75	70	.933	10	24	34	40	26	0	5	4	184	23.0
Totals	53	2025	626	307	.490	390	317	.813	133	180	313	196	165	3	77	22	936	17.7

Three-Point Field Goals: 1981-82, 0-for-1. 1982-83, 0-for-1. 1983-84, 1-for-4 (.250). 1984-85, 4-for-10 (.400). Totals, 5-for-16 (.313).

NBA ALL-STAR GAME RECORD

Season—Team	Min.	FGA	FGM	Pct.	FTA	FTM	Pct.	Off.	Def.	Tot.	Ast.	PF	Dq.	Stl.	Blk.	Pts.
1982—Milwaukee....	22	11	3	.273	2	0	.000	3	1	4	1	2	0	1	0	6
1983—Milwaukee....	23	14	8	.571	5	4	.800	3	2	5	4	1	0	6	1	20
1984—Milwaukee....	26	6	3	.500	2	2	1.000	1	4	5	2	3	0	5	0	8
1985—Milwaukee....	22	5	1	.200	6	6	1.000	2	3	5	4	1	0	0	0	8
Totals	93	36	15	.417	15	12	.800	9	10	19	11	7	0	12	1	42

Named to All-NBA First Team, 1983. . . . All-NBA Second Team, 1982, 1984, 1985. . . . NBA Defensive Player of the Year, 1983 and 1984. . . . NBA All-Defensive First Team, 1983, 1984, 1985. . . . NBA All-Defensive Second Team, 1982. . . Named to THE SPORTING NEWS All-America Second Team, 1979. . . . Led NCAA in field-goal percentage, 1976.

SIDNEY MONCRIEF

JOHN BRIAN MOORE
(Johnny)

Born March 3, 1958 at Altoona, Pa. Height 6:02. Weight 185.

High School—Altoona, Pa.

College—University of Texas, Austin, Tex.

Drafted by Seattle on second round, 1979 (43rd pick).

Draft rights sold by Seattle to San Antonio, June 26, 1979.
Waived by San Antonio, October 12, 1979; re-signed by San Antonio, March 9, 1980.

—COLLEGIATE RECORD—

Year	G.	Min.	FGA	FGM	Pct.	FTA	FTM	Pct.	Reb.	Pts.	Avg.
75-76	26	....	353	154	.436	61	45	.738	61	353	13.6
76-77	26	....	387	168	.434	97	78	.804	97	414	15.9
77-78	31	....	344	168	.488	110	81	.736	159	417	13.5
78-79	29	....	254	119	.469	88	57	.648	129	295	10.2
Totals	112	....	1338	609	.455	356	261	.733	446	1479	13.2

NBA REGULAR SEASON RECORD

Sea.—Team	G.	Min.	FGA	FGM	Pct.	FTA	FTM	Pct.	Off.	Def.	Tot.	Ast.	PF	Dq.	Stl.	Blk.	Pts.	Avg.
80-81—San Antonio	82	1578	520	249	.479	172	105	.610	58	138	196	373	178	0	120	22	604	7.4
81-82—San Antonio	79	2294	667	309	.463	182	122	.670	62	213	275	762	254	6	163	12	741	9.4
82-83—San Antonio	77	2552	841	394	.468	199	148	.744	65	212	277	753	247	2	194	32	941	12.2
83-84—San Antonio	59	1650	518	231	.446	139	105	.755	37	141	178	566	168	2	123	20	595	10.1
84-85—San Antonio	82	2689	910	416	.457	248	189	.762	94	284	378	816	247	3	229	18	1046	12.8
Totals	379	10763	3456	1599	.463	940	669	.712	316	988	1304	3270	1094	13	829	104	3927	10.4

Three-Point Field Goals: 1980-81, 1-for-19 (.053). 1981-82, 1-for-21 (.048). 1982-83, 5-for-22 (.277). 1983-84, 28-for-87 (.322). 1984-85, 25-for-89 (.281). Totals, 60-for-238 (.252).

NBA PLAYOFF RECORD

Sea.—Team	G.	Min.	FGA	FGM	Pct.	FTA	FTM	Pct.	Off.	Def.	Tot.	Ast.	PF	Dq.	Stl.	Blk.	Pts.	Avg.
80-81—San Antonio	7	124	37	18	.486	8	6	.750	8	5	13	27	14	0	10	1	42	6.0
81-82—San Antonio	9	292	82	39	.476	27	16	.593	9	22	31	93	38	0	15	6	94	10.4
82-83—San Antonio	11	414	197	105	.533	35	28	.800	8	39	47	161	41	0	28	3	247	22.5
84-85—San Antonio	5	168	54	25	.463	23	15	.652	13	17	30	42	17	0	10	2	66	13.2
Totals	32	998	370	187	.505	93	65	.699	38	83	121	323	110	0	63	12	449	14.0

Three-Point Field Goals: 1980-81, 0-for-3. 1981-82, 0-for-3. 1982-83, 9-for-17 (.529). 1984-85, 1-for-3 (.333). Totals, 10-for-26 (.385).

Led NBA in assists, 1982.

JAY DENNIS MURPHY

Born June 26, 1962 at Meriden, Conn. Height 6:09. Weight 220.

High School—Meriden, Conn., Maloney.

College—Boston College, Chestnut Hill, Mass.

Drafted by Golden State on second round, 1984 (31st pick).

Draft rights traded by Golden State to Los Angeles Clippers for Jerome Whitehead, June 19, 1984.

—COLLEGIATE RECORD—

Year	G.	Min.	FGA	FGM	Pct.	FTA	FTM	Pct.	Reb.	Pts.	Avg.
80-81	30	676	210	108	.514	93	63	.677	132	279	9.3
81-82	31	735	236	126	.534	147	105	.714	153	357	11.5
82-83	32	957	455	224	.492	158	117	.741	260	565	17.7
83-84	30	958	481	227	.472	175	140	.800	218	594	19.8
Totals	123	3326	1382	685	.496	573	425	.742	763	1795	14.6

NBA REGULAR SEASON RECORD

Sea.—Team	G.	Min.	FGA	FGM	Pct.	FTA	FTM	Pct.	Off.	Def.	Tot.	Ast.	PF	Dq.	Stl.	Blk.	Pts.	Avg.
84-85—L.A. Clippers	23	149	50	8	.160	21	12	.571	6	35	41	4	21	0	1	2	28	1.2

Three-Point Field Goals: 1984-85, 0-for-1.

—DID YOU KNOW—

That the only coach other than current Coach Chuck Daly to post an overall winning record with the Detroit Pistons was Ray Scott? Daly is the 17th coach in the franchise's history.

LARRY DONELL NANCE

Born February 12, 1959 at Anderson, S. C.   Height 6:10.   Weight 215.

High School—Anderson, S. C., McDuffie.

College—Clemson University, Clemson, S. C.

Drafted by Phoenix on first round, 1981 (20th pick).

—COLLEGIATE RECORD—

Year	G.	Min.	FGA	FGM	Pct.	FTA	FTM	Pct.	Reb.	Pts.	Avg.
77-78	25	273	75	35	.467	17	8	.471	78	78	3.1
78-79	29	837	264	137	.519	77	49	.636	210	323	11.1
79-80	32	961	338	174	.515	164	98	.598	259	446	13.9
80-81	31	887	360	207	.575	116	80	.690	237	494	15.9
Totals	117	2958	1037	553	.533	374	235	.628	834	1341	11.5

NBA REGULAR SEASON RECORD

Sea.—Team	G.	Min.	FGA	FGM	Pct.	FTA	FTM	Pct.	Off.	Def.	Tot.	Ast.	PF	Dq.	Stl.	Blk.	Pts.	Avg.
81-82—Phoenix	80	1186	436	227	.521	117	75	.641	95	161	256	82	169	2	42	71	529	6.6
82-83—Phoenix	82	2914	1069	588	.550	287	193	.672	239	471	710	197	254	4	99	217	1370	16.7
83-84—Phoenix	82	2899	1044	601	.576	352	249	.707	227	451	678	214	274	5	86	174	1451	17.7
84-85—Phoenix	61	2202	877	515	.587	254	180	.709	195	341	536	159	185	2	88	104	1211	19.9
Totals	305	9201	3426	1931	.564	1010	697	.690	756	1424	2180	652	882	13	315	566	4561	15.0

Three-Point Field Goals: 1981-82, 0-for-1. 1982-83, 1-for-3 (.333). 1983-84, 0-for-7. 1984-85, 1-for-2 (.500). Totals, 2-for-13 (.154).

NBA PLAYOFF RECORD

Sea.—Team	G.	Min.	FGA	FGM	Pct.	FTA	FTM	Pct.	Off.	Def.	Tot.	Ast.	PF	Dq.	Stl.	Blk.	Pts.	Avg.
81-82—Phoenix	7	128	41	25	.610	8	4	.500	13	19	32	7	15	1	10	11	54	7.7
82-83—Phoenix	3	103	35	14	.400	10	8	.800	10	15	25	3	12	1	3	6	36	12.0
83-84—Phoenix	17	633	200	118	.590	76	51	.671	51	97	148	40	59	1	16	34	287	16.9
Totals	27	864	276	157	.569	94	63	.670	74	131	205	50	86	3	29	51	377	14.0

NBA ALL-STAR GAME RECORD

Season—Team	Min.	FGA	FGM	Pct.	FTA	FTM	Pct.	Off.	Def.	Tot.	Ast.	PF	Dq.	Stl.	Blk.	Pts.
1985—Phoenix	15	8	7	.875	2	2	1.000	1	4	5	0	5	0	0	2	16

CALVIN LEON NATT

Born January 8, 1957 at Monroe, La.   Height 6:06.   Weight 220.

High School—Bastrop, La.

College—Northeast Louisiana University, Monroe, La.

Drafted by New Jersey on first round, 1979 (8th pick).

Traded by New Jersey to Portland for Maurice Lucas and two 1st round draft choices (1980 and 1981), February 8, 1980.

Traded by Portland with Lafayette Lever, Wayne Cooper, a 1984 2nd round draft choice and a 1985 1st round draft choice to Denver for Kiki Vandeweghe, June 7, 1984.

—COLLEGIATE RECORD—

Year	G.	Min.	FGA	FGM	Pct.	FTA	FTM	Pct.	Reb.	Pts.	Avg.
75-76	25	....	371	207	.558	129	102	.791	274	516	20.6
76-77	27	....	493	307	.623	226	168	.743	340	782	29.0
77-78	27	....	401	220	.549	186	136	.731	356	576	21.3
78-79	29	....	506	283	.559	178	141	.792	315	707	24.4
Totals	108	....	1771	1017	.574	719	547	.761	1285	2581	23.9

NBA REGULAR SEASON RECORD

Sea.—Team	G.	Min.	FGA	FGM	Pct.	FTA	FTM	Pct.	Off.	Def.	Tot.	Ast.	PF	Dq.	Stl.	Blk.	Pts.	Avg.
79-80—N.J.-Port.	78	2857	1298	622	.479	419	306	.730	239	452	691	169	205	1	102	34	1553	19.9
80-81—Portland	74	2111	794	395	.497	283	200	.707	149	282	431	159	188	2	73	18	994	13.4
81-82—Portland	75	2599	894	515	.576	392	294	.750	193	420	613	150	175	1	62	36	1326	17.7
82-83—Portland	80	2879	1187	644	.543	428	339	.792	214	385	599	171	184	2	63	29	1630	20.4
83-84—Portland	79	2638	857	500	.583	345	275	.797	166	310	476	179	218	3	69	22	1277	16.2
84-85—Denver	78	2657	1255	685	.546	564	447	.793	209	401	610	238	182	1	75	33	1817	23.3
Totals	464	15741	6285	3361	.535	2431	1861	.766	1170	2250	3420	1066	1152	10	444	172	8597	18.5

Three-Point Field Goals: 1979-80, 3-for-9 (.333). 1980-81, 4-for-8 (.500). 1981-82, 2-for-8 (.250). 1982-83, 3-for-20 (.150). 1983-84, 2-for-17 (.118). 1984-85, 0-for-3. Totals, 14-for-65 (.215).

CALVIN NATT

NBA PLAYOFF RECORD

Sea.—Team	G.	Min.	FGA	FGM	Pct.	FTA	FTM	Pct.	—Rebounds— Off.	Def.	Tot.	Ast.	PF	Dq.	Stl.	Blk.	Pts.	Avg.
79-80—Portland	3	125	48	21	.438	10	6	.600	9	15	24	2	7	0	2	1	48	16.0
80-81—Portland	3	95	31	14	.452	8	4	.500	6	14	20	1	4	0	1	1	32	10.7
82-83—Portland	7	274	102	50	.490	48	31	.646	22	42	64	11	14	0	8	1	132	18.9
83-84—Portland	5	195	72	37	.514	36	25	.694	11	27	38	9	10	0	6	1	99	19.8
84-85—Denver	15	508	238	131	.550	89	72	.809	31	68	99	57	35	0	8	5	334	22.3
Totals	33	1197	491	253	.515	191	138	.723	79	166	245	80	70	0	25	9	645	19.5

Three-Point Field Goals: 1979-80, 0-for-2. 1982-83, 1-for-2 (.500). 1983-84, 0-for-3. Totals, 1-for-7 (.143).

NBA ALL-STAR GAME RECORD

Season—Team	Min.	FGA	FGM	Pct.	FTA	FTM	Pct.	—Rebounds— Off.	Def.	Tot.	Ast.	PF	Dq.	Stl.	Blk.	Pts.
1985—Denver	11	3	1	.333	2	1	.500	0	3	3	1	1	0	0	0	3

Named to NBA All-Rookie Team, 1980. . . . THE SPORTING NEWS All-America Second Team, 1979. . . . Brother of former NBA guard Kenny Natt.

KENNETH WAYNE NATT
(Kenny)

Born October 5, 1958 at Monroe, La.   Height 6:03.   Weight 185.

High School—Bastrop, La.

College—Northeast Louisiana University, Monroe, La.

Drafted by Indiana on second round, 1980 (30th pick).

Waived by Indiana, December 11, 1980; signed by San Antonio as a free agent, June 11, 1981.
Waived by San Antonio, October 21, 1981; signed by Utah as a free agent, February 24, 1983.
Waived by Utah, October 25, 1983; re-signed by Utah as a free agent, September 28, 1984.
Waived by Utah, November 8, 1984; signed by Kansas City as a free agent, December 14, 1984.
Waived by Kansas City, December 17, 1984; re-signed by Kansas City to a 10-day contract that expired, December 29, 1984.
Played in Continental Basketball Association with Alberta Dusters, Las Vegas-Albuquerque Silvers and Lancaster Lightning, 1981-82 through 1984-85 seasons.

—COLLEGIATE RECORD—

Year	G.	Min.	FGA	FGM	Pct.	FTA	FTM	Pct.	Reb.	Pts.	Avg.
76-77	27	....	174	68	.391	42	31	.738	62	167	6.2
77-78	26	....	131	59	.450	30	19	.633	52	137	5.3
78-79	28	....	112	50	.446	45	37	.822	47	137	4.9
79-80	28	....	435	237	.545	109	88	.807	99	562	20.1
Totals	109	....	852	414	.486	226	175	.774	260	1003	9.2

MINOR LEAGUE REGULAR SEASON RECORD

Sea.—Team	G.	Min.	2-Point FGM	FGA	Pct.	3-Point FGM	FGA	Pct.	FTM	FTA	Pct.	Reb.	Ast.	Pts.	Avg.
81-82—Alberta CBA	44	1507	337	653	.516	7	36	.194	124	167	.742	167	209	819	18.6
82-83—L.V.-Albu. CBA	38	1324	236	468	.504	14	33	.424	124	154	.805	161	165	638	16.8
83-84—Albu.-Lan. CBA.........	40	1183	237	503	.471	5	28	.179	133	173	.768	128	120	622	15.6
84-85—Lancaster CBA.........	37	1231	224	430	.520	16	43	.372	117	139	.841	116	113	613	16.6

NBA REGULAR SEASON RECORD

Sea.—Team	G.	Min.	FGA	FGM	Pct.	FTA	FTM	Pct.	—Rebounds— Off.	Def.	Tot.	Ast.	PF	Dq.	Stl.	Blk.	Pts.	Avg.
80-81—Indiana	19	149	77	25	.325	11	7	.636	9	6	15	10	18	0	5	1	59	3.1
82-83—Utah	22	210	73	38	.521	14	9	.643	6	16	22	28	36	0	5	0	85	3.9
84-85—Utah-K.C.	8	29	6	2	.333	4	2	.500	2	1	3	3	3	0	2	0	6	0.8
Totals	49	388	156	65	.417	29	18	.621	17	23	40	41	57	0	12	1	150	3.1

Three-Point Field Goals: 1980-81, 2-for-8 (.250). 1982-83, 0-for-2. Totals, 2-for-10 (.200).

Brother of Denver Nuggets forward Calvin Natt.

EDDIE CARL NEALY
(Ed)

Born February 19, 1960 at Pittsburg, Kan.   Height 6:07.   Weight 238.

High School—Bonner Springs, Kan.

College—Kansas State University, Manhattan, Kan.

Drafted by Kansas City on eighth round, 1982 (166th pick).

Waived by Kansas City, October 24, 1984; re-signed by Kansas City, February 27, 1985.
Played in Continental Basketball Association with Sarasota Stingers, 1984-85.

—COLLEGIATE RECORD—

Year	G.	Min.	FGA	FGM	Pct.	FTA	FTM	Pct.	Reb.	Pts.	Avg.
78-79	28	....	266	115	.432	71	56	.789	230	286	10.2
79-80	31	....	242	114	.471	105	76	.724	272	304	9.8
80-81	33	....	289	152	.526	82	59	.720	301	363	11.0
81-82	31	....	243	138	.568	122	75	.615	268	351	11.3
Totals	123	....	1040	519	.499	380	266	.700	1071	1304	10.6

NBA REGULAR SEASON RECORD

Sea.—Team	G.	Min.	FGA	FGM	Pct.	FTA	FTM	Pct.	Off.	Def.	Tot.	Ast.	PF	Dq.	Stl.	Blk.	Pts.	Avg.
82-83—Kansas City	82	1643	247	147	.595	114	70	.614	170	315	485	62	247	4	68	12	364	4.4
83-84—Kansas City	71	960	126	63	.500	60	48	.800	73	149	222	50	138	1	41	9	174	2.5
84-85—Kansas City	22	225	44	26	.591	19	10	.526	15	29	44	18	26	0	3	1	62	2.8
Totals	175	2828	417	236	.566	193	128	.663	258	493	751	130	411	5	112	22	600	3.4

NBA PLAYOFF RECORD

Sea.—Team	G.	Min.	FGA	FGM	Pct.	FTA	FTM	Pct.	Off.	Def.	Tot.	Ast.	PF	Dq.	Stl.	Blk.	Pts.	Avg.
83-84—Kansas City	2	19	2	2	1.000	2	2	1.000	2	4	6	2	1	0	0	0	6	3.0

MINOR LEAGUE REGULAR SEASON RECORD

Sea.—Team	G.	Min.	2-Point FGM	FGA	Pct.	3-Point FGM	FGA	Pct.	FTM	FTA	Pct.	Reb.	Ast.	Pts.	Avg.
84-85—Sarasota CBA	39	1350	156	267	.584	1	2	.500	113	142	.795	371	53	428	11.0

CHARLES GOODRICH NEVITT
(Chuck)

Born June 13, 1959 at Cortez, Colo. Height 7:05. Weight 237.

High School—Marietta, Ga., Sprayberry.

College—North Carolina State University, Raleigh, N. C.

Drafted by Houston on third round, 1982 (63rd pick).

Waived by Houston and claimed by Milwaukee on waivers, October 22, 1982.
Waived by Milwaukee, October 28, 1982; signed by Houston as a free agent, June 1, 1983.
Waived by Houston, November 29, 1983; signed by Los Angeles Lakers as a free agent, September 15, 1984.
Waived by Los Angeles Lakers, November 6, 1984; re-signed by Los Angeles Lakers, March 5, 1985, to the first of consecutive 10-day contracts that expired, March 24, 1985.
Re-signed by Los Angeles Lakers, March 25, 1985.

—COLLEGIATE RECORD—

Year	G.	Min.	FGA	FGM	Pct.	FTA	FTM	Pct.	Reb.	Pts.	Avg.
77-78					Did Not Play—Injured						
78-79	19	....	20	10	.500	15	4	.267	25	24	1.3
79-80	19	....	23	14	.609	10	2	.200	34	30	1.6
80-81	21	....	26	15	.577	23	10	.435	24	40	1.9
81-82	31	....	119	70	.588	57	32	.561	137	172	5.5
Totals	90	....	188	109	.580	105	48	.457	220	266	3.0

NBA REGULAR SEASON RECORD

Sea.—Team	G.	Min.	FGA	FGM	Pct.	FTA	FTM	Pct.	Off.	Def.	Tot.	Ast.	PF	Dq.	Stl.	Blk.	Pts.	Avg.
82-83—Houston	6	64	15	11	.733	4	1	.250	6	11	17	0	14	0	1	12	23	3.8
84-85—L.A. Lakers	11	59	17	5	.294	8	2	.250	5	15	20	3	20	0	0	15	12	1.1
Totals	17	123	32	16	.500	12	3	.250	11	26	37	3	34	0	1	27	35	2.1

NBA PLAYOFF RECORD

Sea.—Team	G.	Min.	FGA	FGM	Pct.	FTA	FTM	Pct.	Off.	Def.	Tot.	Ast.	PF	Dq.	Stl.	Blk.	Pts.	Avg.
84-85—L.A. Lakers	7	37	9	3	.333	8	4	.500	3	3	6	1	11	0	4	6	10	1.4

Member of NBA championship team, 1985.

KURT ALLEN NIMPHIUS

Born March 13, 1958 at Milwaukee, Wis. Height 6:10. Weight 218.

High School—South Milwaukee, Wis.

College—Arizona State University, Tempe, Ariz.

Drafted by Denver on third round, 1980 (47th pick).

Waived by Denver and signed same day by Dallas as a free agent, September 2, 1981.
Played in Continental Basketball Association with Alberta Dusters, 1980-81.
Played in Italy during 1980-81 season.

Year	G.	Min.	FGA	FGM	Pct.	FTA	FTM	Pct.	Reb.	Pts.	Avg.
76-77†	3	....	....	28	....	14	10	.714	44	66	22.0
76-77	18	76	19	10	.526	12	7	.583	28	27	1.5
77-78	27	670	176	98	.557	53	34	.642	166	230	8.5
78-79	30	576	180	105	.583	90	59	.656	150	269	9.0
79-80	29	977	304	185	.609	155	110	.710	277	480	16.6
Varsity Totals	104	2299	679	398	.586	310	210	.677	621	1006	9.7

MINOR LEAGUE REGULAR SEASON RECORD

Sea.—Team	G.	Min.	2-Point			3-Point			FTM	FTA	Pct.	Reb.	Ast.	Pts.	Avg.
			FGM	FGA	Pct.	FGM	FGA	Pct.							
80-81—Alberta CBA	18	498	92	181	.508	0	1	.000	53	67	.791	156	20	237	13.2

NBA REGULAR SEASON RECORD

Sea.—Team	G.	Min.	FGA	FGM	Pct.	FTA	FTM	Pct.	Rebounds			Ast.	PF	Dq.	Stl.	Blk.	Pts.	Avg.
									Off.	Def.	Tot.							
81-82—Dallas	63	1085	297	137	.461	108	63	.583	92	203	295	61	190	5	17	82	337	5.3
82-83—Dallas	81	1515	355	174	.490	140	77	.550	157	247	404	115	287	11	24	111	426	5.3
83-84—Dallas	82	2284	523	272	.520	162	101	.623	182	331	513	176	283	5	41	144	646	7.9
84-85—Dallas	82	2010	434	196	.452	140	108	.771	136	272	408	183	262	4	30	126	500	6.1
Totals	308	6894	1609	779	.484	550	349	.635	567	1053	1620	535	1022	25	112	463	1909	6.2

Three-Point Field Goals: 1982-83, 1-for-1 (1.000). 1983-84, 1-for-4 (.250). 1984-85, 0-for-6. Totals, 2-for-11 (.182).

NBA PLAYOFF RECORD

Sea.—Team	G.	Min.	FGA	FGM	Pct.	FTA	FTM	Pct.	Rebounds			Ast.	PF	Dq.	Stl.	Blk.	Pts.	Avg.
									Off.	Def.	Tot.							
83-84—Dallas	10	178	33	14	.424	17	14	.824	20	33	53	13	24	0	0	14	42	4.2
84-85—Dallas	4	50	6	3	.500	0	0	.000	3	3	6	3	10	0	1	1	6	1.5
Totals	14	228	39	17	.436	17	14	.824	23	36	59	16	34	0	1	15	48	3.4

NORMAN ELLARD NIXON
(Norm)

Born October 11, 1955 at Macon, Ga. Height 6:02. Weight 175.

High School—Macon, Ga., Southwest.

College—Duquesne University, Pittsburgh, Pa.

Drafted by Los Angeles on first round, 1977 (22nd pick).

Traded by Los Angeles with Eddie Jordan and 1986 and 1987 2nd round draft choices to San Diego for Swen Nater and the draft rights to Byron Scott, October 10, 1983.

—COLLEGIATE RECORD—

Year	G.	Min.	FGA	FGM	Pct.	FTA	FTM	Pct.	Reb.	Pts.	Avg.
73-74	24	....	257	113	.440	45	31	.689	99	257	10.7
74-75	25	....	282	147	.521	92	69	.750	88	363	14.5
75-76	25	....	434	214	.493	127	96	.756	105	524	21.0
76-77	30	1106	539	279	.518	138	103	.746	119	661	22.0
Totals	104	....	1512	753	.498	402	299	.744	411	1805	17.4

NBA REGULAR SEASON RECORD

Sea.—Team	G.	Min.	FGA	FGM	Pct.	FTA	FTM	Pct.	Rebounds			Ast.	PF	Dq.	Stl.	Blk.	Pts.	Avg.
									Off.	Def.	Tot.							
77-78—Los Angeles	81	2779	998	496	.497	161	115	.714	41	198	239	553	259	3	138	7	1107	13.7
78-79—Los Angeles	82	3145	1149	623	.542	204	158	.775	48	183	231	737	250	6	201	17	1404	17.1
79-80—Los Angeles	82	3226	1209	624	.516	253	197	.779	52	177	229	642	241	1	147	14	1446	17.6
80-81—Los Angeles	79	2962	1210	576	.476	252	196	.778	64	168	232	696	226	2	146	11	1350	17.1
81-82—Los Angeles	82	3024	1274	628	.493	224	181	.808	38	138	176	652	264	3	132	7	1440	17.6
82-83—Los Angeles	79	2711	1123	533	.475	168	125	.744	61	144	205	566	176	1	104	4	1191	15.1
83-84—San Diego	82	3053	1270	587	.462	271	206	.760	56	147	203	914	180	1	94	4	1391	17.0
84-85—L.A. Clippers	81	2894	1281	596	.465	218	170	.780	45	163	218	711	175	2	95	4	1395	17.2
Totals	648	23794	9514	4663	.490	1751	1348	.770	415	1318	1733	5471	1771	19	1057	68	10724	16.5

Three-Point Field Goals: 1979-80, 1-for-8 (.125). 1980-81, 2-for-12 (.167). 1981-82, 3-for-12 (.250). 1982-83, 0-for-13. 1983-84, 11-for-46 (.239). 1984-85, 33-for-99 (.333). Totals, 50-for-190 (.263).

NBA PLAYOFF RECORD

Sea.—Team	G.	Min.	FGA	FGM	Pct.	FTA	FTM	Pct.	Rebounds			Ast.	PF	Dq.	Stl.	Blk.	Pts.	Avg.
									Off.	Def.	Tot.							
77-78—Los Angeles	3	92	24	11	.458	3	2	.667	4	5	9	16	13	0	4	1	24	8.0
78-79—Los Angeles	8	327	119	56	.471	15	11	.733	6	22	28	94	37	1	11	0	123	15.4
79-80—Los Angeles	16	648	239	114	.477	51	41	.804	13	43	56	125	59	0	32	3	270	16.9
80-81—Los Angeles	3	133	49	25	.510	10	8	.800	1	10	11	26	9	0	1	1	58	19.3
81-82—Los Angeles	14	549	253	121	.478	57	43	.754	13	30	43	114	43	0	23	2	286	20.4
82-83—Los Angeles	14	538	237	113	.477	50	37	.740	13	35	48	89	40	0	18	1	266	19.0
Totals	58	2287	921	440	.478	186	142	.763	50	145	195	464	201	1	89	8	1027	17.7

Three-Point Field Goals: 1979-80, 1-for-5 (.200). 1981-82, 1-for-3 (.333). 1982-83, 3-for-7 (.429). Totals, 5-for-15 (.333).

Season—Team	Min.	FGA	FGM	Pct.	FTA	FTM	Pct.	—Rebounds— Off.	Def.	Tot.	Ast.	PF	Dq.	Stl.	Blk.	Pts.
1982—Los Angeles	19	14	7	.500	0	0	.000	0	0	0	2	0	0	1	0	14
1985—L.A. Clippers	19	7	5	.714	2	1	.500	0	2	2	8	0	0	1	0	11
Totals	38	21	12	.571	2	1	.500	0	2	2	10	0	0	2	0	25

Named to NBA All-Rookie Team, 1978.... Member of NBA championship teams, 1980 and 1982.... Holds NBA record for most minutes played in one game, 64, vs. Cleveland, January 29, 1980 (4 ot).

AUDIE JAMES NORRIS

Born December 18, 1960 at Jackson, Miss. Height 6:09. Weight 250.

High School—Jackson, Miss., Jim Hill.

College—Jackson State University, Jackson, Miss.

Drafted by Portland on second round, 1982 (37th pick).

—COLLEGIATE RECORD—

Year	G.	Min.	FGA	FGM	Pct.	FTA	FTM	Pct.	Reb.	Pts.	Avg.
78-79	27	....	270	148	.548	149	95	.638	235	391	14.5
79-80	28	948	339	190	.560	176	128	.727	285	508	18.1
80-81	29	925	287	166	.578	154	101	.656	325	433	14.9
81-82	28	935	314	172	.548	202	124	.614	341	468	16.7
Totals	112	....	1210	676	.559	681	448	.658	1186	1800	16.1

NBA REGULAR SEASON RECORD

Sea.—Team	G.	Min.	FGA	FGM	Pct.	FTA	FTM	Pct.	—Rebounds— Off.	Def.	Tot.	Ast.	PF	Dq.	Stl.	Blk.	Pts.	Avg.
82-83—Portland	30	311	63	26	.413	30	14	.467	25	44	69	24	61	0	13	2	66	2.2
83-84—Portland	79	1157	246	124	.504	149	104	.698	82	175	257	76	231	2	30	34	352	4.5
84-85—Portland	78	1117	245	133	.543	203	135	.665	90	160	250	47	221	7	42	33	401	5.1
Totals	187	2585	554	283	.511	382	253	.662	197	379	576	147	513	9	85	69	819	4.4

Three-Point Field Goals: 1984-85, 0-for-3.

NBA PLAYOFF RECORD

Sea.—Team	G.	Min.	FGA	FGM	Pct.	FTA	FTM	Pct.	—Rebounds— Off.	Def.	Tot.	Ast.	PF	Dq.	Stl.	Blk.	Pts.	Avg.
82-83—Portland	7	53	13	7	.538	2	1	.500	3	9	12	5	5	0	2	2	15	2.1
83-84—Portland	5	52	10	6	.600	8	5	.625	6	10	16	4	13	1	1	1	17	3.4
84-85—Portland	8	109	32	19	.594	22	9	.409	22	21	43	3	25	0	4	5	47	5.9
Totals	20	214	55	32	.582	32	15	.469	31	40	71	12	43	1	7	8	79	4.0

MICHAEL F. O'KOREN
(Mike)

Born February 7, 1958 at Jersey City, N. J. Height 6:07. Weight 217.

High School—Jersey City, N. J., Hudson Catholic.

College—University of North Carolina, Chapel Hill, N. C.

Drafted by New Jersey on first round, 1980 (6th pick).

—COLLEGIATE RECORD—

Year	G.	Min.	FGA	FGM	Pct.	FTA	FTM	Pct.	Reb.	Pts.	Avg.
76-77	33	....	298	172	.577	157	114	.726	217	458	13.9
77-78	27	....	269	173	.643	163	122	.748	180	468	17.3
78-79	28	....	259	135	.521	188	144	.766	202	414	14.8
79-80	29	....	298	163	.547	152	99	.651	216	425	14.7
Totals	117	....	1124	643	.572	660	479	.726	815	1765	15.1

NBA REGULAR SEASON RECORD

Sea.—Team	G.	Min.	FGA	FGM	Pct.	FTA	FTM	Pct.	—Rebounds— Off.	Def.	Tot.	Ast.	PF	Dq.	Stl.	Blk.	Pts.	Avg.
80-81—New Jersey	79	2473	751	365	.486	212	135	.637	179	299	478	252	243	8	86	27	870	11.0
81-82—New Jersey	80	2018	778	383	.492	189	135	.714	111	194	305	192	175	0	83	13	909	11.4
82-83—New Jersey	46	803	259	136	.525	48	34	.708	42	72	114	82	67	0	42	11	308	6.7
83-84—New Jersey	73	1191	385	186	.483	87	53	.609	71	104	175	95	148	3	34	11	430	5.9
84-85—New Jersey	43	1119	393	194	.494	67	42	.627	46	120	166	102	115	1	32	16	438	10.2
Totals	321	7604	2566	1264	.493	603	399	.662	449	789	1238	723	748	12	277	78	2955	9.2

Three-Point Field Goals: 1980-81, 5-for-18 (.278). 1981-82, 8-for-23 (.348). 1982-83, 2-for-9 (.222). 1983-84, 5-for-28 (.179). 1984-85, 8-for-21 (.381). Totals, 28-for-99 (.283).

NBA PLAYOFF RECORD

Sea.—Team	G.	Min.	FGA	FGM	Pct.	FTA	FTM	Pct.	Off.	Def.	Tot.	Ast.	PF	Dq.	Stl.	Blk.	Pts.	Avg.
81-82—New Jersey	2	44	11	3	.273	2	1	.500	0	8	8	3	8	1	1	0	7	3.5
82-83—New Jersey	2	18	8	2	.250	0	0	.000	1	5	6	3	3	0	0	0	4	2.0
83-84—New Jersey	11	216	59	25	.424	6	5	.833	18	17	35	21	37	1	3	4	55	5.0
84-85—New Jersey	3	34	7	3	.429	2	0	.000	1	9	10	4	6	0	0	0	6	2.0
Totals	18	312	85	33	.388	10	6	.600	20	39	59	31	54	2	4	4	72	4.0

Three-Point Field Goals: 1981-82, 0-for-1. 1983-84, 0-for-1. Totals, 0-for-2.

Named to THE SPORTING NEWS All-America First Team, 1979 and 1980.

AKEEM ABDUL OLAJUWON

Born January 23, 1963 at Lagos, Nigeria.   Height 7:00.   Weight 250.

High School—Lagos, Nigeria, Moslem Teachers College.

College—University of Houston, Houston, Tex.

Drafted by Houston on first round as an undergraduate, 1984 (1st pick).

—COLLEGIATE RECORD—

Year	G.	Min.	FGA	FGM	Pct.	FTA	FTM	Pct.	Reb.	Pts.	Avg.
80-81					Did Not Play						
81-82	29	529	150	91	.607	103	58	.563	179	240	8.3
82-83	34	932	314	192	.612	148	88	.595	388	472	13.9
83-84	37	1260	369	249	.675	232	122	.526	500	620	16.8
Totals	100	2721	833	532	.639	483	168	.555	1067	1332	13.3

NBA REGULAR SEASON RECORD

Sea.—Team	G.	Min.	FGA	FGM	Pct.	FTA	FTM	Pct.	Off.	Def.	Tot.	Ast.	PF	Dq.	Stl.	Blk.	Pts.	Avg.
84-85—Houston	82	2914	1258	677	.538	551	338	.613	440	534	974	111	344	10	99	220	1692	20.6

NBA PLAYOFF RECORD

Sea.—Team	G.	Min.	FGA	FGM	Pct.	FTA	FTM	Pct.	Off.	Def.	Tot.	Ast.	PF	Dq.	Stl.	Blk.	Pts.	Avg.
84-85—Houston	5	187	88	42	.477	46	22	.478	33	32	65	7	22	0	7	13	106	21.2

NBA ALL-STAR GAME RECORD

Season—Team	Min.	FGA	FGM	Pct.	FTA	FTM	Pct.	Off.	Def.	Tot.	Ast.	PF	Dq.	Stl.	Blk.	Pts.
1985—Houston	15	2	2	1.000	6	2	.333	2	3	5	1	1	0	0	2	6

Named to NBA All-Rookie Team, 1985. . . . NBA All-Defensive Second Team, 1985. . . . Named to THE SPORTING NEWS All-America First Team, 1984. . . . Led NCAA Division I in rebounding and blocked shots, 1984.

MARK ALLEN OLBERDING

Born April 21, 1956 at Melrose, Minn.   Height 6:08.   Weight 230.

High School—Melrose, Minn.

College—University of Minnesota, Minneapolis, Minn.

Never drafted by an NBA franchise.

Selected as an undergraduate by San Antonio on first round of ABA draft, 1975.
Draft rights sold by San Antonio to San Diego, August 20, 1975.
Selected by San Antonio from San Diego in dispersal draft, November 12, 1975.
Entered NBA with San Antonio, 1976.
Traded by San Antonio with Dave Corzine and cash to Chicago for Artis Gilmore, July 22, 1982.
Traded by Chicago with the rights to Larry Micheaux to Kansas City for the rights to Ennis Whatley and Chris McNealy and a 1984 2nd round draft choice, June 28, 1983.

—COLLEGIATE RECORD—

Year	G.	Min.	FGA	FGM	Pct.	FTA	FTM	Pct.	Reb.	Pts.	Avg.
74-75	26	....	296	156	.527	144	103	.715	214	415	16.0

ABA REGULAR SEASON RECORD

			——2-Point——			——3-Point——								
Sea.—Team	G.	Min.	FGM	FGA	Pct.	FGM	FGA	Pct.	FTM	FTA	Pct.	Reb.	Ast.	Pts.	Avg.
75-76—S.D.-S.A.	81	2055	302	607	.498	0	0	.000	191	247	.773	530	142	795	9.8

ABA PLAYOFF RECORD

			——2-Point——			——3-Point——								
Sea.—Team	G.	Min.	FGM	FGA	Pct.	FGM	FGA	Pct.	FTM	FTA	Pct.	Reb.	Ast.	Pts.	Avg.
1975-76—San Antonio	7	73	5	15	.333	0	0	.000	3	6	.500	22	3	13	1.9

AKEEM OLAJUWON

NBA REGULAR SEASON RECORD

Sea.—Team	G.	Min.	FGA	FGM	Pct.	FTA	FTM	Pct.	Off.	Def.	Tot.	Ast.	PF	Dq.	Stl.	Blk.	Pts.	Avg.
76-77—San Antonio	82	1949	598	301	.503	316	251	.794	162	287	449	119	277	6	59	29	853	10.4
77-78—San Antonio	79	1773	480	231	.481	227	184	.811	104	269	373	131	235	1	45	26	646	8.2
78-79—San Antonio	80	1885	551	261	.474	290	233	.803	96	333	429	211	282	2	53	18	755	9.4
79-80—San Antonio	75	2111	609	291	.478	264	210	.795	83	335	418	327	274	7	67	22	792	10.6
80-81—San Antonio	82	2408	685	348	.508	380	315	.829	146	325	471	277	307	6	75	31	1012	12.3
81-82—San Antonio	68	2098	705	333	.472	338	273	.808	118	321	439	202	253	5	57	29	941	13.8
82-83—Chicago	80	1817	522	251	.481	248	194	.782	108	250	358	131	246	3	50	9	698	8.7
83-84—Kansas City	81	2160	504	249	.494	318	261	.821	119	326	445	192	291	2	50	28	759	9.4
84-85—Kansas City	81	2277	528	265	.502	352	293	.832	139	374	513	243	298	8	56	11	823	10.2
Totals	708	18478	5182	2530	.488	2733	2214	.810	1075	2820	3895	1833	2463	40	512	203	7279	10.3

Three-Point Field Goals: 1979-80, 0-for-3. 1980-81, 1-for-7 (.143). 1981-82, 2-for-12 (.167). 1982-83, 2-for-12 (.167). 1983-84, 0-for-1. 1984-85, 0-for-3. Totals, 5-for-38 (.132).

NBA PLAYOFF RECORD

Sea.—Team	G.	Min.	FGA	FGM	Pct.	FTA	FTM	Pct.	Off.	Def.	Tot.	Ast.	PF	Dq.	Stl.	Blk.	Pts.	Avg.
76-77—San Antonio	2	42	9	5	.556	6	3	.500	2	5	7	2	8	0	0	1	13	6.5
77-78—San Antonio	6	152	51	25	.490	15	13	.867	9	21	30	14	23	0	6	6	63	10.5
78-79—San Antonio	14	359	103	41	.398	37	29	.784	12	57	69	33	53	2	12	5	111	7.9
79-80—San Antonio	3	97	23	13	.565	4	3	.750	5	17	22	11	14	1	2	1	29	9.7
80-81—San Antonio	7	254	105	58	.552	25	21	.840	11	30	41	30	31	1	4	0	138	19.7
81-82—San Antonio	9	328	120	53	.442	31	26	.839	20	38	58	32	39	1	9	6	132	14.7
83-84—Kansas City	3	60	15	6	.400	14	8	.571	4	11	15	6	6	0	0	0	20	6.7
Totals	44	1292	426	201	.472	132	103	.780	63	179	242	128	174	5	33	19	506	11.5

Three-Point Field Goals: 1980-81, 1-for-3 (.333). 1981-82, 0-for-1. Totals, 1-for-4 (.250).

Named to ABA All-Rookie Team, 1976.

JAWANN OLDHAM

Born July 4, 1957 at Seattle, Wash.   Height 7:00.   Weight 215.

High School—Seattle, Wash., Cleveland.

College—Seattle University, Seattle, Wash.

Drafted by Denver on second round, 1980 (41st pick).

Waived by Denver, October 21, 1980; signed by Houston as a free agent, August 28, 1981.
Waived by Houston, October 26, 1982; signed by Chicago as a free agent, February 16, 1983.
Played in Continental Basketball Association with Montana Golden Nuggets, 1980-81.

—COLLEGIATE RECORD—

Year	G.	Min.	FGA	FGM	Pct.	FTA	FTM	Pct.	Reb.	Pts.	Avg.
76-77	27	....	300	145	.483	51	31	.608	212	321	11.9
77-78	25	....	282	140	.496	74	32	.432	205	312	12.5
78-79	24	....	367	194	.529	73	42	.575	262	430	17.9
79-80	27	....	333	188	.565	143	81	.566	282	457	16.9
Totals	103	....	1282	667	.520	341	186	.545	961	1520	14.8

MINOR LEAGUE REGULAR SEASON RECORD

Sea.—Team	G.	Min.	2-Point FGM	FGA	Pct.	3-Point FGM	FGA	Pct.	FTM	FTA	Pct.	Reb.	Ast.	Pts.	Avg.
80-81—Montana CBA	7	172	36	83	.433	0	0	.000	7	15	.466	57	3	79	11.3

NBA REGULAR SEASON RECORD

Sea.—Team	G.	Min.	FGA	FGM	Pct.	FTA	FTM	Pct.	Off.	Def.	Tot.	Ast.	PF	Dq.	Stl.	Blk.	Pts.	Avg.
80-81—Denver	4	21	6	2	.333	0	0	.000	3	2	5	0	3	0	0	2	4	1.0
81-82—Houston	22	124	36	13	.361	14	8	.571	7	17	24	3	8	0	2	10	34	1.5
82-83—Chicago	16	171	58	31	.534	22	12	.545	18	29	47	5	30	1	5	13	74	4.6
83-84—Chicago	64	870	218	110	.505	66	39	.591	75	158	233	33	139	2	15	76	259	4.0
84-85—Chicago	63	993	192	89	.464	50	34	.680	79	157	236	31	166	3	11	127	212	3.4
Totals	169	2179	510	245	.480	152	93	.612	182	363	545	72	346	6	33	228	583	3.4

Three-Point Field Goals: 1984-85, 0-for-1.

NBA PLAYOFF RECORD

Sea.—Team	G.	Min.	FGA	FGM	Pct.	FTA	FTM	Pct.	Off.	Def.	Tot.	Ast.	PF	Dq.	Stl.	Blk.	Pts.	Avg.
84-85—Chicago	4	91	15	7	.467	0	0	.000	8	14	22	3	19	1	6	7	14	3.5

—DID YOU KNOW—

That Connie Simmons, a 6-7 center with no collegiate experience, led Boston in scoring during the Celtics' first season (1946-47) with a 10.3-point average?

LOUIS M. ORR

Born May 7, 1958 at Cincinnati, O.   Height 6:08.   Weight 195.

High School—Cincinnati, O., Withrow.

College—Syracuse University, Syracuse, N. Y.

Drafted by Indiana on second round, 1980 (29th pick).

Signed by New York as Veteran Free Agent, October 15, 1982; Indiana matched offer and traded Orr to New York for a 1983 2nd round draft choice and cash, October 22, 1982.

—COLLEGIATE RECORD—

Year	G.	Min.	FGA	FGM	Pct.	FTA	FTM	Pct.	Reb.	Pts.	Avg.
76-77	30	....	186	105	.565	96	72	.750	194	282	9.4
77-78	28	....	302	157	.520	59	43	.729	217	357	12.8
78-79	28	....	248	142	.573	117	85	.726	215	369	13.2
79-80	30	....	332	189	.569	119	101	.849	255	479	16.0
Totals	116	....	1068	593	.555	391	301	.770	881	1487	12.8

NBA REGULAR SEASON RECORD

Sea.—Team	G.	Min.	FGA	FGM	Pct.	FTA	FTM	Pct.	Off.	Def.	Tot.	Ast.	PF	Dq.	Stl.	Blk.	Pts.	Avg.
80-81—Indiana	82	1787	709	348	.491	202	163	.807	172	189	361	132	153	0	55	25	859	10.5
81-82—Indiana	80	1951	719	357	.497	254	203	.799	127	204	331	134	182	1	56	26	918	11.5
82-83—New York	82	1666	593	274	.462	175	140	.800	94	134	228	94	134	0	64	24	688	8.4
83-84—New York	78	1640	572	262	.458	211	173	.820	101	127	228	61	142	0	66	17	697	8.9
84-85—New York	79	2452	766	372	.486	334	262	.784	171	220	391	134	195	1	100	27	1007	12.7
Totals	401	9496	3359	1613	.480	1176	941	.800	665	874	1539	555	806	2	341	119	4169	10.4

Three-Point Field Goals: 1980-81, 0-for-6. 1981-82, 1-for-8 (.125). 1982-83, 0-for-2. 1984-85, 1-for-10 (.100). Totals, 2-for-26 (.077).

NBA PLAYOFF RECORD

Sea.—Team	G.	Min.	FGA	FGM	Pct.	FTA	FTM	Pct.	Off.	Def.	Tot.	Ast.	PF	Dq.	Stl.	Blk.	Pts.	Avg.
80-81—Indiana	2	56	25	9	.360	7	6	.857	6	4	10	4	4	0	5	1	24	12.0
82-83—New York	6	105	47	18	.383	10	10	1.000	8	13	21	3	10	0	5	4	46	7.7
83-84—New York	12	229	70	29	.414	19	15	.789	22	28	50	6	32	1	4	1	73	6.1
Totals	20	390	142	56	.394	36	31	.861	36	45	81	13	46	1	14	6	143	7.2

ROBERT L. PARISH

Born August 30, 1953 at Shreveport, La.   Height 7:00.   Weight 230.

High School—Shreveport, La., Woodlawn.

College—Centenary College, Shreveport, La.

Drafted by Golden State on first round, 1976 (8th pick).

Traded by Golden State with a 1980 1st round draft choice to Boston for two 1980 1st round draft choices, June 9, 1980.

—COLLEGIATE RECORD—

Year	G.	Min.	FGA	FGM	Pct.	FTA	FTM	Pct.	Reb.	Pts.	Avg.
72-73	27	885	492	285	.579	82	50	.610	505	620	23.0
73-74	25	841	428	224	.523	78	49	.628	382	497	19.9
74-75	29	900	423	237	.560	112	74	.660	447	548	18.9
75-76	27	939	489	288	.589	134	93	.694	486	669	24.8
Totals	108	3565	1832	1034	.564	406	266	.655	1820	2334	21.6

NBA REGULAR SEASON RECORD

Sea.—Team	G.	Min.	FGA	FGM	Pct.	FTA	FTM	Pct.	Off.	Def.	Tot.	Ast.	PF	Dq.	Stl.	Blk.	Pts.	Avg.
76-77—Golden State	77	1384	573	288	.503	171	121	.708	201	342	543	74	224	7	55	94	697	9.1
77-78—Golden State	82	1969	911	430	.472	264	165	.625	211	469	680	95	291	10	79	123	1025	12.5
78-79—Golden State	76	2411	1110	554	.499	281	196	.698	265	651	916	115	303	10	100	217	1304	17.2
79-80—Golden State	72	2119	1006	510	.507	284	203	.715	247	536	783	122	248	6	58	115	1223	17.0
80-81—Boston	82	2298	1166	635	.545	397	282	.710	245	532	777	144	310	9	81	214	1552	18.9
81-82—Boston	80	2534	1235	669	.542	355	252	.710	288	578	866	140	267	5	68	192	1590	19.9
82-83—Boston	78	2459	1125	619	.550	388	271	.698	260	567	827	141	222	4	79	148	1509	19.3
83-84—Boston	80	2867	1140	623	.546	368	274	.745	243	614	857	139	266	7	55	116	1520	19.0
84-85—Boston	79	2850	1016	551	.542	393	292	.743	263	577	840	125	223	2	56	101	1394	17.6
Totals	706	20891	9282	4879	.526	2901	2056	.709	2223	4866	7089	1095	2354	60	631	1320	11814	16.7

Three-Point Field Goals: 1979-80, 0-for-1. 1980-81, 0-for-1. 1982-83, 0-for-1. Totals, 0-for-3.

NBA PLAYOFF RECORD

Sea.—Team	G.	Min.	FGA	FGM	Pct.	FTA	FTM	Pct.	Off.	Def.	Tot.	Ast.	PF	Dq.	Stl.	Blk.	Pts.	Avg.
										—Rebounds—								
76-77—Golden State	10	239	108	52	.481	26	17	.654	43	60	103	11	42	1	7	11	121	12.1
80-81—Boston	17	492	219	108	.493	58	39	.672	50	96	146	19	74	2	21	39	255	15.0
81-82—Boston	12	426	209	102	.488	75	51	.680	43	92	135	18	47	1	5	48	255	21.3
82-83—Boston	7	249	89	43	.483	20	17	.850	21	53	74	9	18	0	5	9	103	14.7
83-84—Boston	23	869	291	139	.478	99	64	.646	76	172	248	27	100	6	23	41	342	14.9
84-85—Boston	21	803	276	136	.493	111	87	.784	57	162	219	31	68	0	21	34	359	17.1
Totals	90	3078	1192	580	.487	389	275	.707	290	635	925	115	349	10	82	182	1435	15.9

NBA ALL-STAR GAME RECORD

Season—Team	Min.	FGA	FGM	Pct.	FTA	FTM	Pct.	Off.	Def.	Tot.	Ast.	PF	Dq.	Stl.	Blk.	Pts.
										—Rebounds—						
1981—Boston...........	25	18	5	.278	6	6	1.000	6	4	10	2	3	0	0	2	16
1982—Boston...........	20	12	9	.750	4	3	.750	0	7	7	1	2	0	0	2	21
1983—Boston...........	18	6	5	.833	4	3	.750	0	3	3	0	2	0	1	1	13
1984—Boston...........	28	11	5	.455	4	2	.500	4	11	15	2	1	0	3	0	12
1985—Boston...........	10	5	2	.400	0	0	.000	3	3	6	1	0	0	0	0	4
Totals	101	52	26	.500	18	14	.778	13	28	41	6	8	0	4	5	66

Named to All-NBA Second Team, 1982. . . . Member of NBA championship teams, 1981 and 1984. . . . Named to THE SPORTING NEWS All-America First Team, 1976.

WILLIAM EDWARD PAULTZ
(Billy)

Born July 30, 1948 at River Edge, N. J.   Height 6:11.   Weight 255.

High School—River Edge, N. J., River Dell.

Colleges—Cameron College, Lawton, Okla., and
St. John's University, Jamaica, N.Y.

Drafted by San Diego on seventh round, 1970 (103rd pick).

Selected by Virginia on fifth round of ABA draft, 1970.
Sold by Virginia to New York, 1970.
Traded by New York to San Antonio for Rich Jones, Chuck Terry, Bob Warren and Kim Hughes, September 8, 1975.
Entered NBA with San Antonio, 1976.
Traded by San Antonio to Houston for John Shumate and a 1980 3rd round draft choice, January 17, 1980.
Waived by Houston, April 4, 1983; signed by San Antonio as a free agent, April 6, 1983.
Signed by Atlanta as Veteran Free Agent, September 29, 1983; San Antonio agreed not to exercise its right of first refusal in exchange for a 1985 3rd round draft choice.
Signed by Utah as Veteran Free Agent, September 28, 1984; Atlanta agreed not to exercise its right of first refusal.

—COLLEGIATE RECORD—
Cameron

Year	G.	Min.	FGA	FGM	Pct.	FTA	FTM	Pct.	Reb.	Pts.	Avg.
66-67	25	....	214	102	.477	40	34	.850	126	238	9.5

St. John's

Year	G.	Min.	FGA	FGM	Pct.	FTA	FTM	Pct.	Reb.	Pts.	Avg.
67-68				Did Not Play—Transfer Student							
68-69	28	....	176	88	.500	69	49	.710	185	225	8.0
69-70	29	....	377	181	.480	140	96	.686	417	458	15.8
Totals	57	....	553	269	.486	209	145	.694	602	683	12.0

ABA REGULAR SEASON RECORD

Sea.—Team	G.	Min.	FGM	FGA	Pct.	FGM	FGA	Pct.	FTM	FTA	Pct.	Reb.	Ast.	Pts.	Avg.
			——2-Point——			**——3-Point——**									
70-71—New York	83	2758	510	971	.525	0	2	.000	201	269	.747	940	160	1221	14.7
71-72—New York	83	2824	498	1018	.489	0	3	.000	207	299	.692	1035	128	1203	14.4
72-73—New York	81	2800	532	1025	.519	0	2	.000	287	405	.709	1015	189	1351	16.4
73-74—New York	77	2596	519	1050	.494	0	1	.000	222	308	.721	782	167	1260	16.4
74-75—New York	80	2826	524	1077	.487	0	3	.000	214	286	.748	772	179	1262	15.8
75-76—San Antonio	83	2958	566	1122	.504	0	2	.000	238	324	.735	862	340	1370	16.5
Totals............................	487	16762	3149	6263	.503	0	13	.000	1369	1891	.724	5406	1163	7667	15.7

ABA PLAYOFF RECORD

Sea.—Team	G.	Min.	FGM	FGA	Pct.	FGM	FGA	Pct.	FTM	FTA	Pct.	Reb.	Ast.	Pts.	Avg.
			——2-Point——			**——3-Point——**									
70-71—New York.................	6	239	44	75	.587	1	1	1.000	30	40	.750	90	18	121	20.2
71-72—New York.................	19	809	150	274	.607	0	2	.000	57	90	.633	288	29	337	17.7
72-73—New York.................	5	172	34	56	.607	0	0	.000	27	43	.628	55	10	95	19.0
73-74—New York.................	14	520	81	169	.479	0	0	.000	45	57	.789	132	28	207	14.8
74-75—New York.................	6	178	29	59	.492	0	0	.000	12	15	.800	45	11	70	14.0
75-76—San Antonio.................	7	254	43	97	.443	0	0	.000	35	40	.875	72	19	121	17.3
Totals	57	2172	381	730	.522	1	3	.333	206	285	.723	682	115	951	16.7

ABA ALL-STAR GAME RECORD

Sea.—Team	Min.	2-Point FGM	FGA	Pct.	3-Point FGM	FGA	Pct.	FTM	FTA	Pct.	Reb.	Ast.	Pts.	Avg.
1973—New York.........	15	1	3	.333	0	0	.000	1	1	1.000	3	3	3	3.0
1974—New York					Selected but did not play									
1975—New York.........	18	2	7	.286	0	0	.000	0	0	.000	4	4	4	4.0
1976—New York.........	20	4	6	.667	0	0	.000	2	2	1.000	2	1	10	10.0
Totals....................	53	7	16	.438	0	0	.000	3	3	1.000	11	8	17	5.7

NBA REGULAR SEASON RECORD

Sea.—Team	G.	Min.	FGA	FGM	Pct.	FTA	FTM	Pct.	—Rebounds— Off.	Def.	Tot.	Ast.	PF	Dq.	Stl.	Blk.	Pts.	Avg.
76-77—San Antonio	82	2694	1102	521	.473	320	238	.744	192	495	687	223	262	5	55	173	1280	15.6
77-78—San Antonio	80	2479	979	518	.529	306	230	.752	172	503	675	213	222	3	42	194	1266	15.8
78-79—San Antonio	79	2122	758	399	.526	194	114	.588	169	456	625	178	204	4	35	125	912	11.5
79-80—S.A.-Hou.	84	2193	673	327	.486	182	109	.599	187	399	586	188	213	3	69	84	763	9.1
80-81—Houston	81	1659	517	262	.507	153	75	.490	111	280	391	105	182	1	28	72	599	7.4
81-82—Houston	65	807	226	89	.394	65	34	.523	54	126	180	41	99	0	15	22	212	3.3
82-83—Hou-S.A.	64	820	227	101	.445	59	27	.458	64	136	200	61	109	0	17	18	229	3.6
83-84—Atlanta	40	486	88	36	.409	33	17	.515	35	78	113	18	57	0	8	7	89	2.2
84-85—Utah	62	370	87	32	.368	28	18	.643	24	72	96	16	51	0	6	11	82	1.3
Totals	637	13630	4657	2285	.491	1340	862	.643	1008	2545	3553	1043	1399	16	275	706	5432	8.5

NBA PLAYOFF RECORD

Sea.—Team	G.	Min.	FGA	FGM	Pct.	FTA	FTM	Pct.	—Rebounds— Off.	Def.	Tot.	Ast.	PF	Dq.	Stl.	Blk.	Pts.	Avg.
76-77—San Antonio	2	74	24	12	.500	13	10	.769	1	16	17	5	3	0	2	1	34	17.0
77-78—San Antonio	6	191	63	29	.460	17	11	.647	7	34	41	14	10	0	5	5	69	11.5
78-79—San Antonio	13	299	80	30	.375	33	22	.667	24	74	98	30	33	0	4	13	82	6.3
79-80—Houston	7	128	40	13	.325	7	4	.571	12	21	33	8	13	0	1	3	30	4.3
80-81—Houston	21	720	246	111	.451	48	32	.667	53	94	147	35	69	1	13	27	254	12.1
81-82—Houston	3	34	9	3	.333	3	1	.333	2	2	4	1	4	0	0	2	7	2.3
82-83—San Antonio	11	133	32	13	.406	4	4	1.000	11	21	32	11	18	0	4	2	30	2.7
83-84—Atlanta	2	7	3	1	.333	0	0	.000	0	0	0	0	0	0	0	0	2	1.0
84-85—Utah	5	30	8	3	.375	4	1	.250	3	5	8	2	7	0	1	1	7	1.4
Totals	70	1616	505	215	.426	129	85	.659	113	267	380	106	157	1	30	54	515	7.4

Three-Point Field Goals: 1980-81, 0-for-1.

Shares professional basketball record for most years in playoffs, 15. . . . Member of ABA championship team, 1974. . . . Led ABA in blocked shots, 1976.

JAMES JOSEPH PAXSON JR.
(Jim)

Born July 9, 1957 at Kettering, O.   Height 6:06.   Weight 200.

High School—Kettering, O., Alter.

College—University of Dayton, Dayton, O.

Drafted by Portland on first round, 1979 (12th pick).

—COLLEGIATE RECORD—

Year	G.	Min.	FGA	FGM	Pct.	FTA	FTM	Pct.	Reb.	Pts.	Avg.
75-76	27	1061	308	149	.484	73	55	.753	127	353	13.1
76-77	27	1012	401	219	.546	87	69	.793	157	507	18.8
77-78	29	1066	399	208	.521	115	89	.774	96	505	17.4
78-79	25	929	449	236	.526	134	108	.806	104	580	23.2
Totals	108	4068	1557	812	.521	409	321	.785	484	1945	18.0

NBA REGULAR SEASON RECORD

Sea.—Team	G.	Min.	FGA	FGM	Pct.	FTA	FTM	Pct.	—Rebounds— Off.	Def.	Tot.	Ast.	PF	Dq.	Stl.	Blk.	Pts.	Avg.
79-80—Portland	72	1270	460	189	.411	90	64	.711	25	84	109	144	97	0	48	5	443	6.2
80-81—Portland	79	2701	1092	585	.536	248	182	.734	74	137	211	299	172	1	140	9	1354	17.1
81-82—Portland	82	2756	1258	662	.526	287	220	.767	75	146	221	276	159	0	129	12	1552	18.9
82-83—Portland	81	2740	1323	682	.515	478	388	.812	68	106	174	231	160	0	140	17	1756	21.7
83-84—Portland	81	2686	1322	680	.514	410	345	.841	68	105	173	251	165	0	122	10	1722	21.3
84-85—Portland	68	2253	988	508	.514	248	196	.790	69	153	222	264	115	0	101	5	1218	17.9
Totals	463	14406	6443	3306	.513	1761	1395	.792	379	731	1110	1465	868	1	680	58	8045	17.4

Three-Point Field Goals: 1979-80, 1-for-22 (.045). 1980-81, 2-for-30 (.067). 1981-82, 8-for-35 (.229). 1982-83, 4-for-25 (.160). 1983-84, 17-for-59 (.288). 1984-85, 6-for-39 (.154). Totals, 38-for-210 (.181).

NBA PLAYOFF RECORD

Sea.—Team	G.	Min.	FGA	FGM	Pct.	FTA	FTM	Pct.	—Rebounds— Off.	Def.	Tot.	Ast.	PF	Dq.	Stl.	Blk.	Pts.	Avg.
79-80—Portland	3	44	16	5	.313	6	6	1.000	0	4	4	3	2	0	2	1	16	5.3
80-81—Portland	1	4	3	0	.000	0	0	.000	0	0	0	0	0	0	0	0	0	0.0
82-83—Portland	7	260	116	68	.586	33	25	.758	4	11	15	18	11	0	9	1	163	23.3

Sea.—Team	G.	Min.	FGA	FGM	Pct.	FTA	FTM	Pct.	Off.	Def.	Tot.	Ast.	PF	Dq.	Stl.	Blk.	Pts.	Avg.
83-84—Portland	5	172	78	40	.513	40	33	.825	11	8	19	12	13	0	2	0	114	22.8
84-85—Portland	9	212	101	47	.465	24	19	.792	6	14	20	21	16	0	6	0	116	12.9
Totals	25	692	314	160	.510	103	83	.806	21	37	58	54	42	0	19	2	409	16.4

Three-Point Field Goals: 1982-83, 2-for-4 (.500). 1983-84, 1-for-5 (.200). 1984-85, 3-for-10 (.300). Totals, 6-for-19 (.316).

NBA ALL-STAR GAME RECORD

Season—Team	Min.	FGA	FGM	Pct.	FTA	FTM	Pct.	Off.	Def.	Tot.	Ast.	PF	Dq.	Stl.	Blk.	Pts.
1983—Portland	17	7	5	.714	2	1	.500	0	0	0	1	0	0	2	0	11
1984—Portland	14	9	5	.556	0	0	.000	1	2	3	2	0	0	0	0	10
Totals	31	16	10	.625	2	1	.500	1	2	3	3	0	0	2	0	21

Named to All-NBA Second Team, 1984. . . . Son of Jim Paxson Sr., forward with Minneapolis Lakers (1956-57) and Cincinnati Royals (1957-58) and brother of San Antonio Spurs guard John Paxson.

JOHN MacBETH PAXSON

Born September 29, 1960 at Dayton, O.   Height 6:02.   Weight 185.

High School—Kettering, O., Archbishop Alter.

College—University of Notre Dame, Notre Dame, Ind.

Drafted by San Antonio on first round, 1983 (19th pick).

—COLLEGIATE RECORD—

Year	G.	Min.	FGA	FGM	Pct.	FTA	FTM	Pct.	Reb.	Pts.	Avg.
79-80	27	459	87	42	.483	55	41	.745	34	125	4.6
80-81	29	1062	218	113	.518	89	61	.685	53	287	9.9
81-82	27	1055	346	185	.535	93	72	.774	55	442	16.4
82-83	29	1082	411	219	.533	100	74	.740	63	512	17.7
Totals	112	3658	1062	559	.526	337	248	.736	205	1366	12.2

NBA REGULAR SEASON RECORD

Sea.—Team	G.	Min.	FGA	FGM	Pct.	FTA	FTM	Pct.	Off.	Def.	Tot.	Ast.	PF	Dq.	Stl.	Blk.	Pts.	Avg.
83-84—San Antonio	49	458	137	61	.445	26	16	.615	4	29	33	149	47	0	10	2	142	2.9
84-85—San Antonio	78	1259	385	196	.509	100	84	.840	19	49	68	215	117	0	45	3	486	6.2
Totals	127	1717	522	257	.492	126	100	.794	23	78	101	364	164	0	55	5	628	4.9

Three-Point Field Goals: 1983-84, 4-for-22 (.182). 1984-85, 10-for-34 (.294). Totals, 14-for-56 (.250).

NBA PLAYOFF RECORD

Sea.—Team	G.	Min.	FGA	FGM	Pct.	FTA	FTM	Pct.	Off.	Def.	Tot.	Ast.	PF	Dq.	Stl.	Blk.	Pts.	Avg.
84-85—San Antonio	5	114	42	21	.500	9	7	.778	0	5	5	21	9	0	5	0	51	10.2

Three-Point Field Goals: 1984-85, 2-for-9 (.222).

Brother of Portland Trail Blazers' guard Jim Paxson Jr.; son of Jim Paxson Sr., forward with Minneapolis Lakers (1956-57) and Cincinnati Royals (1957-58). . . . Named to THE SPORTING NEWS All-America Second Team, 1983.

SAMUEL BRUCE PERKINS
(Sam)

Born June 14, 1961 at Brooklyn, N. Y.   Height 6:09.   Weight 235.

High School—Latham, N. Y., Shaker.

College—University of North Carolina, Chapel Hill, N. C.

Drafted by Dallas on first round, 1984 (4th pick).

—COLLEGIATE RECORD—

Year	G.	Min.	FGA	FGM	Pct.	FTA	FTM	Pct.	Reb.	Pts.	Avg.
80-81	37	....	318	199	.626	205	152	.741	289	550	14.9
81-82	32	....	301	174	.578	142	109	.768	250	457	14.3
82-83	35	....	414	218	.527	177	145	.819	330	593	16.9
83-84	31	....	331	195	.589	181	155	.856	298	545	17.6
Totals	135	....	1364	786	.576	705	561	.796	1167	2145	15.9

Three-Point Field Goals: 1982-83, 12-for-28 (.429).

NBA REGULAR SEASON RECORD

Sea.—Team	G.	Min.	FGA	FGM	Pct.	FTA	FTM	Pct.	Off.	Def.	Tot.	Ast.	PF	Dq.	Stl.	Blk.	Pts.	Avg.
84-85—Dallas	82	2317	736	347	.471	244	200	.820	189	416	605	135	236	1	63	63	903	11.0

Three-Point Field Goals: 1984-85, 9-for-36 (.250).

SAM PERKINS

NBA PLAYOFF RECORD

Sea.—Team	G.	Min.	FGA	FGM	Pct.	FTA	FTM	Pct.	Off.	Def.	Tot.	Ast.	PF	Dq.	Stl.	Blk.	Pts.	Avg.
									—Rebounds—									
84-85—Dallas	4	169	49	24	.490	34	26	.765	16	35	51	11	13	1	2	1	75	18.8

Three-Point Field Goals: 1984-85, 1-for-4 (.250).

Named to NBA All-Rookie Team, 1985. . . . Member of NCAA championship team, 1982. . . . Member of U.S. Olympic team, 1984. . . . Named to THE SPORTING NEWS All-America First Team, 1984. . . . Named to THE SPORTING NEWS All-America Second Team, 1982 and 1983.

JAMES RICHARD PETERSEN
(Jim)

Born February 22, 1962 at Minneapolis, Minn. Height 6:10. Weight 235.

High School—St. Louis Park, Minn.

College—University of Minnesota, Minneapolis, Minn.

Drafted by Houston on third round, 1984 (51st pick).

—COLLEGIATE RECORD—

Year	G.	Min.	FGA	FGM	Pct.	FTA	FTM	Pct.	Reb.	Pts.	Avg.
80-81	22	....	26	13	.500	4	1	.250	22	27	1.2
81-82	21	....	52	24	.462	22	14	.636	43	62	3.0
82-83	29	....	149	82	.550	28	18	.643	155	182	6.3
83-84	24	....	180	115	.639	54	39	.722	166	269	11.2
Totals	96	....	407	234	.575	108	72	.667	386	540	5.6

NBA REGULAR SEASON RECORD

Sea.—Team	G.	Min.	FGA	FGM	Pct.	FTA	FTM	Pct.	Off.	Def.	Tot.	Ast.	PF	Dq.	Stl.	Blk.	Pts.	Avg.
									—Rebounds—									
84-85—Houston	60	714	144	70	.486	66	50	.758	44	103	147	29	125	1	14	32	190	3.2

NBA PLAYOFF RECORD

Sea.—Team	G.	Min.	FGA	FGM	Pct.	FTA	FTM	Pct.	Off.	Def.	Tot.	Ast.	PF	Dq.	Stl.	Blk.	Pts.	Avg.
									—Rebounds—									
84-85—Houston	3	8	1	1	1.000	0	0	.000	1	1	2	1	2	0	0	0	2	0.7

RICKY CHARLES PIERCE

Born August 19, 1959 at Dallas, Tex. Height 6:05. Weight 205.

High School—Garland Tex., South Garland.

Colleges—Walla Walla Community College, Walla Walla,
Wash., and Rice University, Houston, Tex.

Drafted by Detroit on first round, 1982 (18th pick).

Traded by Detroit to San Diego for 1986 and 1987 2nd round draft choices, October 17, 1983.
Traded by Los Angeles Clippers with Terry Cummings and Craig Hodges to Milwaukee for Marques Johnson, Harvey Catchings, Junior Bridgeman and cash, September 29, 1984.

—COLLEGIATE RECORD—
Walla Walla CC

Year	G.	Min.	FGA	FGM	Pct.	FTA	FTM	Pct.	Reb.	Pts.	Avg.
78-79	..	....	...	...	....	...	...	....	....	....	19.0

Rice

Year	G.	Min.	FGA	FGM	Pct.	FTA	FTM	Pct.	Reb.	Pts.	Avg.
79-80	26	878	421	202	.480	131	94	.718	214	498	19.2
80-81	26	901	444	230	.518	119	84	.706	181	544	20.9
81-82	30	1104	614	314	.511	223	177	.794	226	805	26.8
Totals	82	2883	1479	746	.504	473	355	.751	621	1847	22.5

NBA REGULAR SEASON RECORD

Sea.—Team	G.	Min.	FGA	FGM	Pct.	FTA	FTM	Pct.	Off.	Def.	Tot.	Ast.	PF	Dq.	Stl.	Blk.	Pts.	Avg.
									—Rebounds—									
82-83—Detroit	39	265	88	33	.375	32	18	.563	15	20	35	14	42	0	8	4	85	2.2
83-84—San Diego	69	1280	570	268	.470	173	149	.861	59	76	135	60	143	1	27	13	685	9.9
84-85—Milwaukee	44	882	307	165	.537	124	102	.823	49	68	117	94	117	0	34	5	433	9.8
Totals	152	2427	965	466	.483	329	269	.818	123	164	287	168	302	1	69	22	1203	7.9

Three-Point Field Goals: 1982-83, 1-for-7 (.143). 1983-84, 0-for-9. 1984-85, 1-for-4 (.250). Totals, 1-for-20 (.050).

NBA PLAYOFF RECORD

Sea.—Team	G.	Min.	FGA	FGM	Pct.	FTA	FTM	Pct.	Off.	Def.	Tot.	Ast.	PF	Dq.	Stl.	Blk.	Pts.	Avg.
									—Rebounds—									
84-85—Milwaukee	8	198	73	36	.493	9	7	.778	8	10	18	15	26	0	3	1	79	9.9

Three-Point Field Goals: 1984-85, 0-for-2.

CHARLES E. PITTMAN

Born March 23, 1958 at Rocky Mount, N. C.   Height 6:08.   Weight 220.

High School—Rocky Mount, N. C., Northern Nash.

Colleges—Merced College, Merced, Calif., and University of Maryland, College Park, Md.

Drafted by Phoenix on third round, 1982 (61st pick).

Waived by Phoenix, October 28, 1982; re-signed by Phoenix, February 7, 1983.
Played in Continental Basketball Association with Billings Volcanos, 1982-83.

—COLLEGIATE RECORD—

Year	G.	Min.	FGA	FGM	Pct.	FTA	FTM	Pct.	Reb.	Pts.	Avg.
78-79	35	....	307	188	.612	111	72	.649	252	448	12.8
79-80	27	....	230	142	.617	107	76	.710	213	360	13.3
J.C. Totals	62	....	557	330	.592	218	148	.679	465	808	13.0

Maryland

Year	G.	Min.	FGA	FGM	Pct.	FTA	FTM	Pct.	Reb.	Pts.	Avg.
80-81	31	553	94	63	.670	50	32	.640	115	158	5.1
81-82	24	828	167	102	.611	117	83	.709	174	287	12.0
Md. Totals	55	1381	261	165	.632	167	115	.689	289	445	8.1

MINOR LEAGUE REGULAR SEASON RECORD

Sea.—Team	G.	Min.	2-Point FGM	FGA	Pct.	3-Point FGM	FGA	Pct.	FTM	FTA	Pct.	Reb.	Ast.	Pts.	Avg.
82-83—Billings CBA	30	1042	140	238	.588	0	1	.000	125	152	.822	240	38	405	13.5

NBA REGULAR SEASON RECORD

Sea.—Team	G.	Min.	FGA	FGM	Pct.	FTA	FTM	Pct.	Off.	Def.	Tot.	Ast.	PF	Dq.	Stl.	Blk.	Pts.	Avg.
82-83—Phoenix	28	170	40	19	.475	37	25	.676	13	18	31	7	41	0	2	7	63	2.3
83-84—Phoenix	69	989	209	126	.603	101	69	.683	76	138	214	70	129	1	16	22	321	4.7
84-85—Phoenix	68	1001	227	107	.471	146	109	.747	90	137	227	69	144	1	20	21	323	4.8
Totals	165	2160	476	252	.529	284	203	.715	179	293	472	146	314	2	38	50	707	4.3

Three-Point Field Goals: 1982-83, 0-for-1. 1983-84, 0-for-2. 1984-85, 0-for-2. Totals 0-for-5.

NBA PLAYOFF RECORD

Sea.—Team	G.	Min.	FGA	FGM	Pct.	FTA	FTM	Pct.	Off.	Def.	Tot.	Ast.	PF	Dq.	Stl.	Blk.	Pts.	Avg.
82-83—Phoenix	1	1	0	0	.000	0	0	.000	0	0	0	0	0	0	0	0	0	0.0
83-84—Phoenix	17	253	51	28	.549	29	18	.621	25	39	64	12	31	0	5	5	74	4.4
84-85—Phoenix	3	82	23	14	.609	17	12	.706	6	13	19	9	10	0	0	3	40	13.3
Totals	21	336	74	42	.568	46	30	.652	31	52	83	21	41	0	5	8	114	5.4

Three-Point Field Goals: 1983-84, 0-for-1.

GARY PLUMMER

Born February 21, 1962 at Highland Park, Mich.   Height 6:09.   Weight 21⁵.

High School—Detroit, Mich., Osborn.

College—Boston University, Boston, Mass.

Drafted by Golden State on second round, 1984 (45th pick).

—COLLEGIATE RECORD—

Year	G.	Min.	FGA	FGM	Pct.	FTA	FTM	Pct.	Reb.	Pts.	Avg.
80-81	26	311	75	37	.493	41	30	.732	47	104	4.0
81-82	10	254	106	55	.519	28	15	.536	61	125	12.5
82-83	27	800	379	176	.464	108	89	.824	213	441	16.3
83-84	27	840	348	174	.500	145	111	.766	282	459	17.0
Totals	90	2205	908	442	.487	322	245	.761	603	1129	12.5

NBA REGULAR SEASON RECORD

Sea.—Team	G.	Min.	FGA	FGM	Pct.	FTA	FTM	Pct.	Off.	Def.	Tot.	Ast.	PF	Dq.	Stl.	Blk.	Pts.	Avg.
84-85—Golden State	66	702	232	92	.397	92	65	.707	54	80	134	26	127	1	15	14	250	3.8

Three-Point Field Goals: 1984-85, 1-for-4 (.250).

—DID YOU KNOW—

That former UCLA and Los Angeles Lakers player Keith Erickson was a member of the U.S. Olympic volleyball team in 1964? Erickson is now a broadcaster for the Lakers.

DAVID POPE

Born April 15, 1962 at Newport News, Va. Height 6:07. Weight 220.
High School—Newport News, Va., Menchville.
College—Norfolk State University, Norfolk, Va.
Drafted by Utah on third round, 1984 (62nd pick).

Waived by Utah, October 24, 1984; signed by Kansas City as a free agent, December 8, 1984.
Waived by Kansas City, February 27, 1985.
Played in Continental Basketball Association with Albuquerque Silvers, 1984-85.

—COLLEGIATE RECORD—

Year	G.	Min.	FGA	FGM	Pct.	FTA	FTM	Pct.	Reb.	Pts.	Avg.
80-81	28	937	478	268	.561	98	75	.765	265	611	21.8
81-82	25	858	346	165	.477	98	67	.684	202	397	15.9
82-83	29	993	474	235	.496	175	133	.760	329	603	20.8
83-84	31	1114	503	282	.561	216	161	.745	374	725	23.4
Totals	113	3902	1801	950	.527	587	436	.743	1170	2339	20.7

NBA REGULAR SEASON RECORD

Sea.—Team	G.	Min.	FGA	FGM	Pct.	FTA	FTM	Pct.	Off.	Def.	Tot.	Ast.	PF	Dq.	Stl.	Blk.	Pts.	Avg.
84-85—Kansas City	22	129	53	17	.321	13	7	.538	9	9	18	5	30	0	3	3	41	1.9

Three-Point Field Goals: 1984-85, 0-for-1.

MINOR LEAGUE REGULAR SEASON RECORD

			2-Point			3-Point							
Sea.—Team	G.	Min.	FGM	FGA	Pct.	FGM	FGA	Pct.	FTM	FTA	Pct.	Reb.	Ast.	Pts.	Avg.
84-85—Albuquerque CBA	1	28	2	3	.667	0	0	.000	2	4	.500	2	1	6	6.0

BENEDICT JAY POQUETTE
(Ben)

Born May 7, 1955 at Ann Arbor, Mich. Height 6:09. Weight 235.
High School—East Lansing, Mich.
College—Central Michigan University, Mt. Pleasant, Mich.
Drafted by Detroit on second round, 1977 (36th pick).

Signed by Utah as Veteran Free Agent, June 28, 1979; Utah also received cash and a 1980 2nd round draft choice as compensation for Veteran Free Agent James McElroy, who signed with Detroit.
Traded by Utah to Cleveland for cash, October 14, 1983.

—COLLEGIATE RECORD—

Year	G.	Min.	FGA	FGM	Pct.	FTA	FTM	Pct.	Reb.	Pts.	Avg.
73-74	25	....	130	61	.469	41	22	.537	138	144	5.8
74-75	19	....	138	60	.435	38	19	.500	129	139	7.3
75-76	26	....	293	143	.488	92	65	.706	237	351	13.5
76-77	28	....	369	179	.485	132	103	.780	309	461	16.5
Totals	98	....	930	443	.476	303	209	.690	813	1095	11.1

NBA REGULAR SEASON RECORD

Sea.—Team	G.	Min.	FGA	FGM	Pct.	FTA	FTM	Pct.	Off.	Def.	Tot.	Ast.	PF	Dq.	Stl.	Blk.	Pts.	Avg.
77-78—Detroit	52	626	225	95	.422	60	42	.700	50	95	145	20	69	1	10	22	232	4.5
78-79—Detroit	76	1337	464	198	.427	142	111	.782	99	237	336	57	198	4	38	98	507	6.7
79-80—Utah	82	2349	566	296	.523	167	139	.832	124	436	560	131	283	8	45	162	731	8.9
80-81—Utah	82	2808	614	324	.528	162	126	.778	160	469	629	161	342	18	67	174	777	9.5
81-82—Utah	82	1698	428	220	.514	120	97	.808	117	294	411	94	235	4	51	65	540	6.6
82-83—Utah	75	2331	697	329	.472	221	166	.751	155	366	521	168	264	5	64	116	825	11.0
83-84—Cleveland	51	858	171	75	.439	43	34	.791	57	125	182	49	114	1	20	33	185	3.6
84-85—Cleveland	79	1656	457	210	.460	137	109	.796	148	325	473	79	220	3	47	58	532	6.7
Totals	579	13663	3622	1747	.482	1052	824	.783	910	2347	3257	759	1725	44	342	728	4329	7.5

Three-Point Field Goals: 1979-80, 0-for-2. 1980-81, 3-for-6 (.500). 1981-82, 3-for-10 (.300). 1982-83, 1-for-5 (.200). 1983-84, 1-for-5 (.200). 1984-85, 3-for-17 (.176). Totals, 11-for-45 (.244).

NBA PLAYOFF RECORD

Sea.—Team	G.	Min.	FGA	FGM	Pct.	FTA	FTM	Pct.	Off.	Def.	Tot.	Ast.	PF	Dq.	Stl.	Blk.	Pts.	Avg.
84-85—Cleveland	4	91	21	13	.619	5	4	.800	4	10	14	1	16	2	2	6	30	7.5

PAUL MATTHEW PRESSEY

Born December 24, 1958 at Richmond, Va.   Height 6:05.   Weight 185.

High School—Richmond, Va., George Wythe.

Colleges—Western Texas College, Snyder, Tex., and University of Tulsa, Tulsa, Okla.

Drafted by Milwaukee on first round, 1982 (20th pick).

—COLLEGIATE RECORD—
Western Texas

Year	G.	Min.	FGA	FGM	Pct.	FTA	FTM	Pct.	Reb.	Pts.	Avg.
78-79	33	....	286	191	.668	103	78	.757	262	460	13.9
79-80	37	....	327	213	.651	122	93	.762	291	519	14.0
J.C. Totals	70	....	613	404	.659	225	171	.760	553	979	14.0

Tulsa

Year	G.	Min.	FGA	FGM	Pct.	FTA	FTM	Pct.	Reb.	Pts.	Avg.
80-81	33	1050	288	137	.476	114	66	.579	178	340	10.3
81-82	30	973	275	154	.560	131	87	.664	192	395	13.2
Totals	63	2023	563	291	.517	245	153	.624	370	735	11.7

NBA REGULAR SEASON RECORD

Sea.—Team	G.	Min.	FGA	FGM	Pct.	FTA	FTM	Pct.	Off.	Def.	Tot.	Ast.	PF	Dq.	Stl.	Blk.	Pts.	Avg.
82-83—Milwaukee	79	1528	466	213	.457	176	105	.597	83	198	281	207	174	2	99	47	532	6.7
83-84—Milwaukee	81	1730	528	276	.523	200	120	.600	102	180	282	252	241	6	86	50	674	8.3
84-85—Milwaukee	80	2876	928	480	.517	418	317	.758	149	280	429	543	258	4	129	56	1284	16.1
Totals	240	6134	1922	969	.504	794	542	.683	334	658	992	1002	673	12	314	153	2490	10.4

Three-Point Field Goals: 1982-83, 1-for-9 (.111). 1983-84, 2-for-9 (.222). 1984-85, 7-for-20 (.350). Totals, 10-for-38 (.263).

NBA PLAYOFF RECORD

Sea.—Team	G.	Min.	FGA	FGM	Pct.	FTA	FTM	Pct.	Off.	Def.	Tot.	Ast.	PF	Dq.	Stl.	Blk.	Pts.	Avg.
82-83—Milwaukee	9	150	47	19	.404	20	8	.400	14	19	33	14	23	0	9	6	46	5.1
83-84—Milwaukee	16	351	100	52	.520	56	38	.679	17	42	59	50	53	1	22	9	142	8.9
84-85—Milwaukee	8	296	88	45	.511	38	31	.816	15	33	48	61	27	1	18	5	122	15.3
Totals	33	797	235	116	.494	114	77	.675	46	94	140	125	103	2	49	20	310	9.4

Three-Point Field Goals: 1982-83, 0-for-1. 1983-84, 0-for-3. 1984-85, 1-for-3 (.333). Totals, 1-for-7 (.143).

Named to NBA All-Defensive First Team, 1985.

DARRELL KURT RAMBIS
(Known by middle name.)

Born February 25, 1958 at Cupertino, Calif.   Height 6:08.   Weight 220.

High School—Cupertino, Calif.

College—University of Santa Clara, Santa Clara, Calif.

Drafted by New York on third round, 1980 (58th pick).

Waived by New York, September 18, 1980; signed by New York to 10-day contract that expired January 30, 1981.
Signed by Los Angeles as a free agent, September 13, 1981.
Played in Greece during 1980-81 season.

—COLLEGIATE RECORD—

Year	G.	Min.	FGA	FGM	Pct.	FTA	FTM	Pct.	Reb.	Pts.	Avg.
76-77	27	....	317	167	.527	125	70	.560	313	404	15.0
77-78	27	....	268	136	.507	143	99	.692	231	371	13.7
78-79	27	763	336	172	.512	109	78	.716	226	422	15.6
79-80	27	860	395	211	.534	168	107	.637	267	529	19.6
Totals	108	....	1316	686	.521	545	354	.650	1037	1726	16.0

NBA REGULAR SEASON RECORD

Sea.—Team	G.	Min.	FGA	FGM	Pct.	FTA	FTM	Pct.	Off.	Def.	Tot.	Ast.	PF	Dq.	Stl.	Blk.	Pts.	Avg.
81-82—Los Angeles	64	1131	228	118	.518	117	59	.504	116	232	348	56	167	2	60	76	295	4.6
82-83—Los Angeles	78	1806	413	235	.569	166	114	.687	164	367	531	90	233	2	105	63	584	7.5
83-84—Los Angeles	47	743	113	63	.558	66	42	.636	82	184	266	34	108	0	30	14	168	3.6
84-85—L.A. Lakers	82	1617	327	181	.554	103	68	.660	164	364	528	69	211	0	82	47	430	5.2
Totals	271	5297	1081	597	.552	452	283	.626	526	1147	1673	249	719	4	277	200	1477	5.5

Three-Point Field Goals: 1981-82, 0-for-1. 1982-83, 0-for-2. Totals, 0-for-3.

PAUL PRESSEY

NBA PLAYOFF RECORD

Sea.—Team	G.	Min.	FGA	FGM	Pct.	FTA	FTM	Pct.	Off.	Def.	Tot.	Ast.	PF	Dq.	Stl.	Blk.	Pts.	Avg.
									Rebounds									
81-82—Los Angeles	14	279	64	33	.516	26	16	.615	32	54	86	11	47	0	8	12	82	5.9
82-83—Los Angeles	15	377	79	45	.570	35	23	.657	27	63	90	19	51	0	13	16	113	7.5
83-84—Los Angeles	21	428	92	60	.652	33	21	.636	33	88	121	14	57	0	10	10	141	6.7
84-85—L.A. Lakers	19	375	81	48	.593	28	19	.679	42	87	129	17	52	0	18	9	115	6.1
Totals	69	1459	316	186	.589	122	79	.648	134	292	426	61	207	0	49	47	451	6.5

Member of NBA championship teams, 1982 and 1985. . . . Brother of Randy Rambis, pitcher in Cleveland Indians' organization, 1978 through 1980.

KELVIN RANSEY

Born May 3, 1958 at Toledo, O.   Height 6:01.   Weight 180.

High School—Toledo, O., Macomber.

College—Ohio State University, Columbus, O.

Drafted by Chicago on first round, 1980 (4th pick).

Draft rights traded by Chicago to Portland for a 1981 1st round draft choice and draft rights to Ronnie Lester, June 10, 1980.

Traded by Portland to Dallas for Wayne Cooper and a 1985 1st round draft choice, June 28, 1982.

Traded by Dallas to New Jersey for Clarence (Foots) Walker, a 1984 2nd round draft choice and a 1985 1st round draft choice, August 12, 1983.

—COLLEGIATE RECORD—

Year	G.	Min.	FGA	FGM	Pct.	FTA	FTM	Pct.	Reb.	Pts.	Avg.
76-77	25	789	365	149	.408	37	29	.784	84	327	13.1
77-78	27	948	420	207	.493	81	60	.741	100	474	17.6
78-79	31	1163	516	282	.547	132	100	.758	112	664	21.4
79-80	29	1069	387	189	.488	109	91	.835	121	469	16.2
Totals	112	3969	1688	827	.490	359	280	.780	417	1934	17.3

NBA REGULAR SEASON RECORD

Sea.—Team	G.	Min.	FGA	FGM	Pct.	FTA	FTM	Pct.	Off.	Def.	Tot.	Ast.	PF	Dq.	Stl.	Blk.	Pts.	Avg.
									Rebounds									
80-81—Portland	80	2431	1162	525	.452	219	164	.749	42	153	195	555	201	1	88	9	1217	15.2
81-82—Portland	78	2418	1095	504	.460	318	242	.761	39	147	186	555	169	1	97	4	1253	16.1
82-83—Dallas	76	1607	746	343	.460	199	152	.764	44	103	147	280	109	1	58	4	840	11.1
83-84—New Jersey	80	1937	700	304	.434	183	145	.792	28	99	127	483	182	2	91	6	760	9.5
84-85—New Jersey	81	1689	654	300	.459	142	122	.859	40	90	130	355	134	0	87	7	724	8.9
Totals	395	10082	4357	1976	.454	1061	825	.778	193	592	785	2228	795	5	421	30	4794	12.1

Three-Point Field Goals: 1980-81, 3-for-31 (.097). 1981-82, 3-for-38 (.079). 1982-83, 2-for-16 (.125). 1983-84, 7-for-32 (.219). 1984-85, 2-for-11 (.182). Totals, 17-for-128 (.133).

NBA PLAYOFF RECORD

Sea.—Team	G.	Min.	FGA	FGM	Pct.	FTA	FTM	Pct.	Off.	Def.	Tot.	Ast.	PF	Dq.	Stl.	Blk.	Pts.	Avg.
									Rebounds									
80-81—Portland	3	131	65	23	.354	6	3	.500	5	7	12	25	8	0	6	1	49	16.3
83-84—New Jersey	5	44	14	6	.429	0	0	.000	0	1	1	10	6	0	0	1	13	2.6
84-85—New Jersey	3	63	16	6	.375	5	5	1.000	0	5	5	17	10	0	2	1	17	5.7
Totals	11	238	95	35	.368	11	8	.727	5	13	18	52	24	0	8	3	79	7.2

Three-Point Field Goals: 1980-81, 0-for-1. 1983-84, 1-for-1 (1.000). Totals, 1-for-2 (.500).

Named to NBA All-Rookie Team, 1981. . . . THE SPORTING NEWS All-America Second Team, 1980.

LEO R. RAUTINS

Born March 20, 1960 at Toronto, Ontario.   Height 6:08.   Weight 215.

High School—Toronto, Ontario, St. Michael's.

Colleges—University of Minnesota, Minneapolis, Minn., and Syracuse University, Syracuse, N. Y.

Drafted by Philadelphia on first round, 1983 (17th pick).

Traded by Philadelphia to Indiana for a 1987 3rd round draft choice, September 14, 1984.

Waived by Indiana, October 4, 1984; signed by Atlanta as a free agent, October 15, 1984.

Waived by Atlanta, November 5, 1984.

—COLLEGIATE RECORD—
Minnesota

Year	G.	Min.	FGA	FGM	Pct.	FTA	FTM	Pct.	Reb.	Pts.	Avg.
78-79	27	....	245	96	.392	42	33	.786	110	225	8.3

Year	G.	Min.	FGA	FGM	Pct.	FTA	FTM	Pct.	Reb.	Pts.	Avg.
					Syracuse						
79-80			Did Not Play—Transfer Student								
80-81	32	....	255	127	.498	57	45	.789	173	299	9.3
81-82	22	....	245	121	.494	66	51	.773	129	293	13.3
82-83	31	987	350	182	.520	100	75	.750	227	439	14.2
Syracuse Totals	85	....	850	430	.506	223	171	.787	529	1031	12.1
College Totals	112	....	1095	526	.480	265	204	.770	639	1256	11.2

NBA REGULAR SEASON RECORD

Sea.—Team	G.	Min.	FGA	FGM	Pct.	FTA	FTM	Pct.	Off.	Def.	Tot.	Ast.	PF	Dq.	Stl.	Blk.	Pts.	Avg.
										—Rebounds—								
83-84—Philadelphia	28	196	58	21	.362	10	6	.600	9	24	33	29	31	0	9	2	48	1.7
84-85—Atlanta	4	12	2	0	.000	0	0	.000	1	1	2	3	3	0	0	0	0	0.0
Totals	32	208	60	21	.350	10	6	.600	10	25	35	32	34	0	9	2	48	1.5

NBA PLAYOFF RECORD

Sea.—Team	G.	Min.	FGA	FGM	Pct.	FTA	FTM	Pct.	Off.	Def.	Tot.	Ast.	PF	Dq.	Stl.	Blk.	Pts.	Avg.
										—Rebounds—								
83-84—Philadelphia	3	5	3	1	.333	0	0	.000	2	0	2	1	2	0	1	0	3	1.0

ROBERT KEITH REID

Born August 30, 1955 at Atlanta, Ga.   Height 6:08.   Weight 205.

High School—Schertz, Tex., Samuel Clemens.

College—St. Mary's University, San Antonio, Tex.

Drafted by Houston on second round, 1977 (40th pick).

Sat out 1982-83 season for religious reasons.

—COLLEGIATE RECORD—

Year	G.	Min.	FGA	FGM	Pct.	FTA	FTM	Pct.	Reb.	Pts.	Avg.
73-74	19	....	30	14	.467	21	11	.524	14	39	2.1
74-75	33	....	368	197	.535	73	53	.726	286	447	13.5
75-76	28	....	458	237	.517	85	74	.871	288	548	19.6
76-77	29	....	405	196	.484	115	83	.722	244	475	16.4
Totals	109	...	1261	644	.511	294	221	.752	832	1509	13.8

NBA REGULAR SEASON RECORD

Sea.—Team	G.	Min.	FGA	FGM	Pct.	FTA	FTM	Pct.	Off.	Def.	Tot.	Ast.	PF	Dq.	Stl.	Blk.	Pts.	Avg.
										—Rebounds—								
77-78—Houston	80	1849	574	261	.455	96	63	.656	111	248	359	121	277	8	67	51	585	7.3
78-79—Houston	82	2259	777	382	.492	186	131	.704	129	354	483	230	302	7	75	48	895	10.9
79-80—Houston	76	2304	861	419	.487	208	153	.736	140	301	441	244	281	2	132	57	991	13.0
80-81—Houston	82	2963	1113	536	.482	303	229	.756	164	419	583	344	325	4	163	66	1301	15.9
81-82—Houston	77	2913	958	437	.456	214	160	.748	175	336	511	314	297	2	115	48	1035	13.4
83-84—Houston	64	1936	857	406	.474	122	81	.659	97	244	341	217	243	5	88	30	895	14.0
84-85—Houston	82	1763	648	312	.481	126	88	.698	81	192	273	171	196	1	48	22	713	8.7
Totals	543	15987	5788	2753	.476	1256	905	.721	897	2094	2991	1641	1921	29	688	322	6415	11.8

Three-Point Field Goals: 1979-80, 0-for-3. 1980-81, 0-for-4. 1981-82, 1-for-10 (.100). 1983-84, 2-for-8 (.250). 1984-85, 1-for-16 (.063). Totals, 4-for-41 (.098).

NBA PLAYOFF RECORD

Sea.—Team	G.	Min.	FGA	FGM	Pct.	FTA	FTM	Pct.	Off.	Def.	Tot.	Ast.	PF	Dq.	Stl.	Blk.	Pts.	Avg.
										—Rebounds—								
78-79—Houston	2	45	17	7	.412	9	6	.667	5	4	9	2	7	0	1	2	20	10.0
79-80—Houston	7	266	102	52	.510	26	22	.846	14	41	55	26	28	0	6	7	126	18.0
80-81—Houston	21	868	303	139	.459	92	61	.663	56	86	142	98	80	2	50	24	339	16.1
81-82—Houston	3	115	31	15	.484	5	4	.800	9	17	26	9	10	0	5	2	34	11.3
84-85—Houston	5	87	45	19	.422	0	0	.000	3	14	17	5	22	0	4	2	38	7.6
Totals	38	1381	498	232	.466	132	93	.705	87	162	249	140	147	2	66	37	557	14.7

Three-Point Field Goals: 1979-80, 0-for-1. 1980-81, 0-for-2. 1984-85, 0-for-4. Totals, 0-for-7.

CLINT DEWITT RICHARDSON

Born August 7, 1956 at Seattle, Wash.   Height 6:03.   Weight 195.

High School—Seattle, Wash., O'Dea.

College—Seattle University, Seattle, Wash.

Drafted by Philadelphia on second round, 1979 (36th pick).

—COLLEGIATE RECORD—

Year	G.	Min.	FGA	FGM	Pct.	FTA	FTM	Pct.	Reb.	Pts.	Avg.
75-76	26	....	416	205	.493	101	71	.703	192	481	18.5
76-77	24	....	338	163	.482	89	61	.685	180	387	16.1
77-78	27	....	398	203	.510	79	58	.734	169	464	17.2
78-79	26	....	367	187	.510	133	95	.714	193	469	18.0
Totals	103	....	1529	758	.496	402	285	.709	734	1801	17.5

NBA REGULAR SEASON RECORD

Sea.—Team	G.	Min.	FGA	FGM	Pct.	FTA	FTM	Pct.	Off.	Def.	Tot.	Ast.	PF	Dq.	Stl.	Blk.	Pts.	Avg.
79-80—Philadelphia	52	988	348	159	.457	45	28	.622	55	68	123	107	97	0	24	15	347	6.7
80-81—Philadelphia	77	1313	464	227	.489	108	84	.778	83	93	176	152	102	0	36	10	538	7.0
81-82—Philadelphia	77	1040	310	140	.452	88	69	.784	55	63	118	109	109	0	36	9	351	4.6
82-83—Philadelphia	77	1755	559	259	.463	111	71	.640	98	149	247	168	164	0	71	18	589	7.6
83-84—Philadelphia	69	1571	473	221	.467	103	79	.767	62	103	165	155	145	0	49	23	521	7.6
84-85—Philadelphia	74	1531	404	183	.453	89	76	.854	60	95	155	157	143	0	37	15	443	6.0
Totals	426	8198	2558	1189	.465	544	407	.748	413	571	984	848	760	0	253	90	2789	6.5

Three-Point Field Goals: 1979-80, 1-for-3 (.333). 1980-81, 0-for-1. 1981-82, 2-for-2. 1982-83, 0-for-6. 1983-84, 0-for-4. 1984-85, 1-for-3 (.333). Totals, 4-for-19 (.211).

NBA PLAYOFF RECORD

Sea.—Team	G.	Min.	FGA	FGM	Pct.	FTA	FTM	Pct.	Off.	Def.	Tot.	Ast.	PF	Dq.	Stl.	Blk.	Pts.	Avg.
79-80—Philadelphia	3	3	3	1	.333	0	0	.000	0	0	0	0	0	0	1	0	2	0.7
80-81—Philadelphia	13	181	38	20	.526	17	9	.529	9	12	21	12	15	0	6	3	49	3.8
81-82—Philadelphia	21	415	104	47	.452	30	17	.567	29	40	69	40	48	0	13	5	111	5.3
82-83—Philadelphia	13	319	83	37	.446	17	14	.824	14	25	39	23	37	0	15	3	88	6.8
83-84—Philadelphia	5	115	23	13	.565	12	11	.917	4	12	16	10	17	0	3	1	37	7.4
84-85—Philadelphia	13	281	94	53	.564	10	9	.900	14	24	38	27	23	0	10	2	115	8.8
Totals	68	1314	345	171	.496	86	60	.698	70	113	183	112	140	0	48	14	402	5.9

Three-Point Field Goals: 1979-80, 0-for-2.

Member of NBA championship team, 1983.

MICHEAL RAY RICHARDSON
(Sugar Ray)

Born April 11, 1955 at Lubbock, Tex.   Height 6:05.   Weight 195.

High School—Denver, Colo., Manual.

College—University of Montana, Missoula, Mont.

Drafted by New York on first round, 1978 (4th pick).

Traded by New York with a 1984 5th round draft choice to Golden State for Bernard King, October 22, 1982.
Traded by Golden State to New Jersey for Eric Floyd and Mickey Johnson, February 6, 1983.
Waived by New Jersey, October 11, 1983; reinstated by New Jersey, December 21, 1983.

—COLLEGIATE RECORD—

Year	G.	Min.	FGA	FGM	Pct.	FTA	FTM	Pct.	Reb.	Pts.	Avg.
74-75†	11	....	139	73	.525	50	38	.760	182	184	16.7
74-75	29	....	188	92	.489	58	34	.586	104	218	7.5
75-76	25	....	356	187	.525	113	82	.726	157	456	18.2
76-77	26	....	466	221	.474	96	58	.604	224	500	19.2
77-78	27	....	567	272	.480	159	109	.686	185	653	24.2
Varsity Totals	107	....	1577	772	.490	426	283	.664	670	1827	17.1

NBA REGULAR SEASON RECORD

Sea.—Team	G.	Min.	FGA	FGM	Pct.	FTA	FTM	Pct.	Off.	Def.	Tot.	Ast.	PF	Dq.	Stl.	Blk.	Pts.	Avg.
78-79—New York	72	1218	483	200	.414	128	69	.539	78	155	233	213	188	2	100	18	469	6.5
79-80—New York	82	3060	1063	502	.472	338	223	.660	151	388	539	832	260	3	265	35	1254	15.3
80-81—New York	79	3175	1116	523	.469	338	224	.663	173	372	545	627	258	2	232	35	1293	16.4
81-82—New York	82	3044	1343	619	.461	303	212	.700	177	388	565	572	317	3	213	41	1469	17.9
82-83—G.S.-N.J.	64	2076	815	346	.425	163	106	.650	113	182	295	432	240	4	182	24	806	12.6
83-84—New Jersey	48	1285	528	243	.460	108	76	.704	56	116	172	214	156	4	103	20	576	12.0
84-85—New Jersey	82	3127	1470	690	.469	313	240	.767	156	301	457	669	277	3	243	22	1649	20.1
Totals	509	16985	6818	3123	.458	1691	1150	.680	904	1902	2806	3559	1696	21	1338	195	7516	14.8

Three-Point Field Goals: 1979-80, 27-for-110 (.245). 1980-81, 23-for-102 (.225). 1981-82, 19-for-101 (.188). 1982-83, 8-for-51 (.157). 1983-84, 14-for-48 (.241). 1984-85, 29-for-115 (.252). Totals, 120-for-537 (.223).

NBA PLAYOFF RECORD

Sea.—Team	G.	Min.	FGA	FGM	Pct.	FTA	FTM	Pct.	Off.	Def.	Tot.	Ast.	PF	Dq.	Stl.	Blk.	Pts.	Avg.
80-81—New York	2	86	33	8	.242	12	7	.583	6	13	19	11	8	0	7	0	23	11.5
82-83—New Jersey	2	58	21	8	.381	5	3	.600	2	6	8	5	3	0	5	0	19	9.5

Sea.—Team	G.	Min.	FGA	FGM	Pct.	FTA	FTM	Pct.	Off.	Def.	Tot.	Ast.	PF	Dq.	Stl.	Blk.	Pts.	Avg.
										—Rebounds—								
83-84—New Jersey	11	443	169	69	.408	56	41	.732	20	34	54	79	40	1	34	4	185	16.8
84-85—New Jersey	3	125	57	23	.404	14	9	.643	4	14	18	34	12	0	4	0	55	18.3
Totals	18	712	280	108	.386	87	60	.690	32	67	99	129	63	1	50	4	282	15.7

Three-Point Field Goals: 1980-81, 0-for-4. 1982-83, 0-for-1. 1983-84, 6-for-22 (.273). 1984-85, 0-for-2. Totals, 6-for-29 (.207).

NBA ALL-STAR GAME RECORD

Season—Team	Min.	FGA	FGM	Pct.	FTA	FTM	Pct.	Off.	Def.	Tot.	Ast.	PF	Dq.	Stl.	Blk.	Pts.
									—Rebounds—							
1980—New York.....	13	7	3	.429	0	0	.000	1	0	1	2	2	0	1	0	6
1981—New York.....	24	7	5	.714	2	1	.500	2	3	5	3	3	0	4	0	11
1982—New York.....	20	10	5	.500	0	0	.000	0	2	2	4	1	0	2	0	10
1985—New Jersey..	13	8	2	.250	2	1	.500	2	0	2	1	3	0	2	0	5
Totals	70	32	15	.563	4	2	.500	5	5	10	10	9	0	9	0	32

Three-Point Field Goals: 1981, 0-for-1. 1985, 0-for-2. Totals, 0-for-3.

Named to NBA All-Defensive First Team, 1980 and 1981.... Named NBA Comeback Player of the Year, 1985.... Led NBA in steals, 1980, 1983, 1985.... Led NBA in assists, 1980.

GLENN ANTON RIVERS
(Doc)

Born October 13, 1961 at Maywood, Ill. Height 6:04. Weight 185.

High School—Maywood, Ill., Proviso East.

College—Marquette University, Milwaukee, Wis.

Drafted by Atlanta on second round as an undergraduate, 1983 (31st pick).

—COLLEGIATE RECORD—

Year	G.	Min.	FGA	FGM	Pct.	FTA	FTM	Pct.	Reb.	Pts.	Avg.
80-81	31	....	329	182	.553	119	70	.588	99	434	14.0
81-82	29	....	382	173	.453	108	70	.648	99	416	14.3
82-83	29	....	373	163	.437	95	58	.611	94	384	13.2
Totals	89	....	1084	518	.478	322	198	.615	292	1234	13.9

NBA REGULAR SEASON RECORD

Sea.—Team	G.	Min.	FGA	FGM	Pct.	FTA	FTM	Pct.	Off.	Def.	Tot.	Ast.	PF	Dq.	Stl.	Blk.	Pts.	Avg.
										—Rebounds—								
83-84—Atlanta	81	1938	541	250	.462	325	255	.785	72	148	220	314	286	8	127	30	757	9.3
84-85—Atlanta	69	2126	701	334	.476	378	291	.770	66	148	214	410	250	7	163	53	974	14.1
Totals	150	4064	1242	584	.470	703	546	.777	138	296	434	724	536	15	290	83	1731	11.5

Three-Point Field Goals: 1983-84, 2-for-12 (.167). 1984-85, 15-for-36 (.417). Totals, 17-for-48 (.354).

NBA PLAYOFF RECORD

Sea.—Team	G.	Min.	FGA	FGM	Pct.	FTA	FTM	Pct.	Off.	Def.	Tot.	Ast.	PF	Dq.	Stl.	Blk.	Pts.	Avg.
										—Rebounds—								
83-84—Atlanta	5	130	32	16	.500	41	36	.878	7	3	10	16	16	0	12	4	68	13.6

Three-Point Field Goals: 1983-84, 0-for-3.

Nephew of former NBA forward Jim Brewer.... Cousin of former major league outfielder Ken Singleton.

FREDERICK CLARK ROBERTS
(Fred)

Born August 14, 1960 at Provo, Utah. Height 6:10. Weight 220.

High School—Riverton, Utah, Bingham.

College—Brigham Young University, Provo, Utah.

Drafted by Milwaukee on second round, 1982 (27th pick).

Draft rights traded by Milwaukee with Mickey Johnson to New Jersey for Phil Ford and a 1983 2nd round draft choice, November 10, 1982.

Draft rights traded by New Jersey with a 1983 2nd round draft choice and cash to San Antonio in exchange for the Spurs' relinquishing their rights to Coach Stan Albeck, June 7, 1983.

Traded by San Antonio to Utah for 1986 and 1988 2nd round draft choices, December 18, 1984.

Played in Italian League during 1982-83 season.

—COLLEGIATE RECORD—

Year	G.	Min.	FGA	FGM	Pct.	FTA	FTM	Pct.	Reb.	Pts.	Avg.
78-79	28	861	291	158	.543	106	83	.783	191	399	14.3
79-80	29	891	257	151	.588	98	71	.724	177	373	12.9
80-81	32	1188	373	216	.579	220	171	.777	255	603	18.8
81-82	30	1118	338	162	.479	178	142	.798	215	466	15.5
Totals	119	4058	1259	687	.546	602	467	.776	838	1841	15.5

ITALIAN LEAGUE RECORD

Year	G.	Min.	FGA	FGM	Pct.	FTA	FTM	Pct.	Reb.	Pts.	Avg.
82-83—Fort. Bologna .	30	1114	462	233	.504	148	106	.716	258	572	19.1

NBA REGULAR SEASON RECORD

Sea.—Team	G.	Min.	FGA	FGM	Pct.	FTA	FTM	Pct.	Off.	Def.	Tot.	Ast.	PF	Dq.	Stl.	Blk.	Pts.	Avg.
83-84—San Antonio	79	1531	399	214	.536	172	144	.837	102	202	304	98	219	4	52	38	573	7.3
84-85—S.A.-Utah	74	1178	418	208	.498	182	150	.824	78	108	186	87	141	0	28	22	567	7.7
Totals	153	2709	817	422	.517	354	294	.831	180	310	490	185	360	4	80	60	1140	7.5

Three-Point Field Goals: 1983-84, 1-for-4 (.250). 1984-85, 1-for-1. Totals, 2-for-5 (.400).

NBA PLAYOFF RECORD

Sea.—Team	G.	Min.	FGA	FGM	Pct.	FTA	FTM	Pct.	Off.	Def.	Tot.	Ast.	PF	Dq.	Stl.	Blk.	Pts.	Avg.
84-85—Utah	10	130	43	19	.442	20	16	.800	6	11	17	9	16	0	7	3	54	5.4

ALVIN CYRRALE ROBERTSON

Born July 22, 1962 at Barberton, O.   Height 6:03.   Weight 185.

High School—Barberton, O.

Colleges—Crowder Junior College, Neosho, Mo., and
University of Arkansas, Fayetteville, Ark.

Drafted by San Antonio on first round, 1984 (7th pick).

—COLLEGIATE RECORD—

Crowder JC

Year	G.	Min.	FGA	FGM	Pct.	FTA	FTM	Pct.	Reb.	Pts.	Avg.
80-81	34	....	470	269	.572	112	73	.652	284	611	18.0

Arkansas

Year	G.	Min.	FGA	FGM	Pct.	FTA	FTM	Pct.	Reb.	Pts.	Avg.
81-82	28	495	159	84	.528	58	35	.603	62	203	7.3
82-83	28	915	294	161	.548	115	76	.661	137	398	14.2
83-84	32	1109	375	187	.499	182	122	.670	175	496	15.5
Ark. Totals............	88	2519	828	432	.522	355	233	.656	374	1097	12.5

NBA REGULAR SEASON RECORD

Sea.—Team	G.	Min.	FGA	FGM	Pct.	FTA	FTM	Pct.	Off.	Def.	Tot.	Ast.	PF	Dq.	Stl.	Blk.	Pts.	Avg.
84-85—San Antonio	79	1685	600	299	.498	169	124	.734	116	149	265	275	217	1	127	24	726	9.2

Three-Point Field Goals: 1984-85, 4-for-11 (.364).

Member of U.S. Olympic team, 1984.

FREDRICK ROBERT ROBEY
(Rick)

Born January 30, 1956 at Coral Gables, Fla.   Height 6:11.   Weight 230.

High School—New Orleans, La., Brother Martin.

College—University of Kentucky, Lexington, Ky.

Drafted by Indiana on first round, 1978 (3rd pick).

Traded by Indiana to Boston for Billy Knight, January 16, 1979.
Traded by Boston with two 1983 2nd round draft choices to Phoenix for Dennis Johnson and 1983 1st and 3rd round draft choices, June 27, 1983.

—COLLEGIATE RECORD—

Year	G.	Min.	FGA	FGM	Pct.	FTA	FTM	Pct.	Reb.	Pts.	Avg.
74-75	31	616	248	135	.544	63	51	.810	214	321	10.4
75-76	12	357	130	73	.562	56	41	.732	90	187	15.6
76-77	30	823	276	158	.572	161	111	.689	273	427	14.2
77-78	32	915	263	167	.635	175	126	.720	261	460	14.4
Totals	105	2711	917	533	.581	455	329	.723	838	1395	13.3

NBA REGULAR SEASON RECORD

Sea.—Team	G.	Min.	FGA	FGM	Pct.	FTA	FTM	Pct.	Off.	Def.	Tot.	Ast.	PF	Dq.	Stl.	Blk.	Pts.	Avg.
78-79—Ind-Bos	79	1763	673	322	.478	224	174	.777	168	345	513	132	232	4	48	15	818	10.4
79-80—Boston	82	1918	727	379	.521	269	184	.684	209	321	530	92	244	2	53	15	942	11.5
80-81—Boston	82	1569	547	298	.545	251	144	.574	132	258	390	126	204	0	38	19	740	9.0
81-82—Boston	80	1186	375	185	.493	157	84	.535	114	181	295	68	183	2	27	14	454	5.7
82-83—Boston	59	855	214	100	.467	78	45	.577	79	140	219	65	131	1	13	8	245	4.2
83-84—Phoenix	61	856	257	140	.545	88	61	.693	80	118	198	65	120	0	20	14	342	5.6
84-85—Phoenix	4	48	9	2	.222	2	1	.500	3	5	8	5	7	0	2	0	5	1.3
Totals	447	8195	2802	1426	.509	1069	693	.648	785	1368	2153	553	1121	9	201	85	3546	7.9

Three-Point Field Goals: 1979-80, 0-for-1. 1980-81, 0-for-1. 1981-82, 0-for-2. 1983-84, 1-for-1 (1.000). Totals, 1-for-5 (.200).

Sea.—Team	G.	Min.	FGA	FGM	Pct.	FTA	FTM	Pct.	—Rebounds— Off.	Def.	Tot.	Ast.	PF	Dq.	Stl.	Blk.	Pts.	Avg.
79-80—Boston	9	151	53	24	.453	14	7	.500	13	19	32	10	27	0	7	3	55	6.1
80-81—Boston	17	265	81	35	.432	35	16	.457	19	41	60	12	44	0	2	5	86	5.1
81-82—Boston	12	122	40	21	.525	17	13	.765	13	16	29	4	27	0	2	3	55	4.6
82-83—Boston	5	29	4	0	.000	4	2	.500	3	5	8	1	4	0	0	0	2	0.4
83-84—Phoenix	10	43	16	7	.438	8	4	.500	7	3	10	2	5	0	2	0	18	1.8
Totals	53	610	194	87	.448	78	42	.538	55	84	139	29	107	0	13	11	216	4.1

Three-Point Field Goals: 1979-80, 0-for-1. 1982-83, 0-for-1. 1983-84, 0-for-1. Totals, 0-for-3.

Member of NBA championship team, 1981. . . . Named to THE SPORTING NEWS All-America Second Team, 1978. . . . Member of NCAA championship team, 1978.

CLIFFORD TRENT ROBINSON
(Cliff)

Born March 13, 1960 at Oakland, Calif.   Height 6:09.   Weight 230.

High School—Oakland, Calif., Castlemont.

College—University of Southern California, Los Angeles, Calif.

Drafted by New Jersey on first round as an undergraduate, 1979 (11th pick).

Traded by New Jersey to Kansas City for Otis Birdsong and a 1981 2nd round draft choice, June 8, 1981.
Traded by Kansas City to Cleveland for Reggie Johnson, February 16, 1982.
Traded by Cleveland with the draft rights to Tim McCormick and cash to Washington for the draft rights to Melvin Turpin, June 19, 1984.

—COLLEGIATE RECORD—

Year	G.	Min.	FGA	FGM	Pct.	FTA	FTM	Pct.	Reb.	Pts.	Avg.
77-78	24	724	367	191	.520	100	60	.600	231	442	18.4
78-79	21	670	338	159	.470	107	76	.710	243	394	18.8
Totals	45	1394	705	350	.496	207	136	.657	474	836	18.6

NBA REGULAR SEASON RECORD

Sea.—Team	G.	Min.	FGA	FGM	Pct.	FTA	FTM	Pct.	—Rebounds— Off.	Def.	Tot.	Ast.	PF	Dq.	Stl.	Blk.	Pts.	Avg.
79-80—New Jersey	70	1661	833	391	.469	242	168	.694	174	332	506	98	178	1	61	34	951	13.6
80-81—New Jersey	63	1822	1070	525	.491	248	178	.718	120	361	481	105	216	6	58	52	1229	19.5
81-82—K.C.-Clev.	68	2175	1143	518	.453	313	222	.709	174	435	609	120	222	4	88	103	1258	18.5
82-83—Cleveland	77	2601	1230	587	.477	301	213	.708	190	666	856	145	272	7	61	58	1387	18.0
83-84—Cleveland	73	2402	1185	533	.450	334	234	.701	156	597	753	185	195	2	51	32	1301	17.8
84-85—Washington	60	1870	896	422	.471	213	158	.742	141	405	546	149	187	4	51	47	1003	16.7
Totals	411	12531	6357	2976	.468	1651	1173	.710	955	2796	3751	802	1270	24	370	326	7129	17.3

Three-Point Field Goals: 1979-80, 1-for-4 (.250). 1980-81, 1-for-1. 1981-82, 0-for-4. 1982-83, 0-for-5. 1983-84, 1-for-2 (.500). 1984-85, 1-for-2 (.500). Totals, 4-for-18 (.222).

NBA PLAYOFF RECORD

Sea.—Team	G.	Min.	FGA	FGM	Pct.	FTA	FTM	Pct.	—Rebounds— Off.	Def.	Tot.	Ast.	PF	Dq.	Stl.	Blk.	Pts.	Avg.
84-85—Washington	4	123	56	25	.446	12	9	.750	12	18	30	4	14	0	4	2	59	14.8

LEONARD EUGENE ROBINSON
(Truck)

Born October 4, 1951 at Jacksonville, Fla.   Height 6:07.   Weight 225.

High School—Jacksonville, Fla., Raines.

College—Tennessee State University, Nashville, Tenn.

Drafted by Washington on second round, 1974 (22nd pick).

Traded by Washington with a 1977 1st round draft choice to Atlanta for Tom Henderson and a 1977 1st round draft choice, January 20, 1977.
Signed by New Orleans as Veteran Free Agent, August 5, 1977; Atlanta acquired Ron Behagen and cash as compensation.
Traded by New Orleans to Phoenix for Ron Lee, Marty Byrnes, two 1st round draft choices (1979 and 1980) and cash, January 12, 1979.
Traded by Phoenix to New York for Maurice Lucas, July 7, 1982.

—COLLEGIATE RECORD—

Year	G.	Min.	FGA	FGM	Pct.	FTA	FTM	Pct.	Reb.	Pts.	Avg.
70-71	26	....	253	131	.518	96	55	.573	228	317	12.2
71-72	27	....	376	189	.503	137	93	.679	267	471	17.4
72-73	30	....	601	309	.514	226	152	.673	528	770	25.7
73-74	28	....	527	287	.545	188	117	.622	478	691	24.7
Totals	111	....	1757	916	.521	647	417	.645	1501	2249	20.3

NBA REGULAR SEASON RECORD

Sea.—Team	G.	Min.	FGA	FGM	Pct.	FTA	FTM	Pct.	Off.	Def.	Tot.	Ast.	PF	Dq.	Stl.	Blk.	Pts.	Avg.
74-75—Washington	76	995	393	191	.486	115	60	.522	94	207	301	40	132	0	36	32	442	5.8
75-76—Washington	82	2055	779	354	.454	314	211	.672	139	418	557	113	239	3	42	107	919	11.2
76-77—Wash.-Atl.	77	2777	1200	574	.478	430	314	.730	252	576	828	142	253	3	66	38	1462	19.0
77-78—N. Orleans	82	3638	1683	748	.444	572	366	.640	298	990	1288	171	265	5	73	79	1862	22.7
78-79—N.O.-Phoe.	69	2537	1152	566	.491	462	324	.701	195	607	802	113	206	2	46	75	1456	21.1
79-80—Phoenix	82	2710	1064	545	.512	487	325	.667	213	557	770	142	262	2	58	59	1415	17.3
80-81—Phoenix	82	3088	1280	647	.505	396	249	.629	216	573	789	206	220	1	68	38	1543	18.8
81-82—Phoenix	74	2745	1128	579	.513	371	255	.687	202	519	721	179	215	2	42	28	1414	19.1
82-83—New York	81	2426	706	326	.462	201	118	.587	199	458	657	145	241	4	57	24	770	9.5
83-84—New York	65	2135	581	284	.489	206	133	.646	171	374	545	94	217	6	43	27	701	10.8
84-85—New York	2	35	5	2	.400	2	0	.000	6	3	9	3	3	0	2	3	4	2.0
Totals	772	25141	9971	4816	.483	3556	2355	.662	1985	5282	7267	1348	2253	28	533	510	11988	15.5

Three-Point Field Goals: 1981-82, 1-for-1 (1.000).

NBA PLAYOFF RECORD

Sea.—Team	G.	Min.	FGA	FGM	Pct.	FTA	FTM	Pct.	Off.	Def.	Tot.	Ast.	PF	Dq.	Stl.	Blk.	Pts.	Avg.
74-75—Washington	17	130	42	14	.333	14	7	.500	11	29	40	6	21	0	6	10	35	2.1
75-76—Washington	7	137	37	16	.432	21	17	.810	8	25	33	5	27	0	5	8	49	7.0
78-79—Phoenix	15	392	139	56	.403	69	45	.652	38	83	121	10	52	0	6	12	157	10.5
79-80—Phoenix	3	64	16	6	.375	7	5	.714	5	15	20	4	6	0	3	2	17	5.7
80-81—Phoenix	7	233	77	27	.351	34	20	.588	23	52	75	13	15	0	5	2	74	10.6
81-82—Phoenix	7	213	80	45	.563	10	3	.300	14	39	53	19	17	0	5	1	93	13.3
82-83—New York	6	205	73	39	.534	28	16	.571	21	45	66	13	25	1	10	2	94	15.7
83-84—New York	12	362	74	38	.514	15	9	.600	31	66	97	7	41	2	7	9	85	7.1
Totals	74	1736	538	241	.448	198	122	.616	151	354	505	77	204	3	47	46	604	8.2

NBA ALL-STAR GAME RECORD

Season—Team	Min.	FGA	FGM	Pct.	FTA	FTM	Pct.	Off.	Def.	Tot.	Ast.	PF	Dq.	Stl.	Blk.	Pts.
1978—N. Orleans....	24	7	3	.429	2	1	.500	2	4	6	1	2	0	0	0	7
1981—Phoenix.........	21	6	3	.500	0	0	.000	2	3	5	2	4	0	0	0	6
Totals	45	13	6	.462	2	1	.500	4	7	11	3	6	0	0	0	13

Named to All-NBA First Team, 1978.... Led NBA in rebounding, 1978.

WAYNE MONTE ROLLINS
(Tree)

Born June 16, 1955 at Winter Haven, Fla.   Height 7:01.   Weight 235.

High School—Cordele, Ga., Crisp County.

College—Clemson University, Clemson, S. C.

Drafted by Atlanta on first round, 1977 (14th pick).

—COLLEGIATE RECORD—

Year	G.	Min.	FGA	FGM	Pct.	FTA	FTM	Pct.	Reb.	Pts.	Avg.
73-74	26	....	265	144	.543	54	34	.630	316	322	12.4
74-75	28	....	326	162	.497	67	40	.597	328	364	13.0
75-76	28	....	313	170	.543	76	43	.566	308	383	13.7
76-77	28	....	288	167	.580	95	60	.632	359	394	14.1
Totals	110	....	1192	643	.539	292	177	.606	1311	1463	13.3

NBA REGULAR SEASON RECORD

Sea.—Team	G.	Min.	FGA	FGM	Pct.	FTA	FTM	Pct.	Off.	Def.	Tot.	Ast.	PF	Dq.	Stl.	Blk.	Pts.	Avg.
77-78—Atlanta	80	1795	520	253	.487	148	104	.703	179	373	552	79	326	16	57	218	610	7.6
78-79—Atlanta	81	1900	555	297	.535	141	89	.631	219	369	588	49	328	19	46	254	683	8.4
79-80—Atlanta	82	2123	514	287	.558	220	157	.714	283	491	774	76	322	12	54	244	731	8.9
80-81—Atlanta	40	1044	210	116	.552	57	46	.807	102	184	286	35	151	7	29	117	278	7.0
81-82—Atlanta	79	2018	346	202	.584	129	79	.612	168	443	611	59	285	4	35	224	483	6.1
82-83—Atlanta	80	2472	512	261	.510	135	98	.726	210	533	743	75	294	7	49	343	620	7.8
83-84—Atlanta	77	2351	529	274	.518	190	118	.621	200	393	593	62	297	9	35	277	666	8.6
84-85—Atlanta	70	1750	339	186	.549	93	67	.720	113	329	442	52	213	6	35	167	439	6.3
Totals	589	15453	3525	1876	.532	1113	758	.681	1474	3115	4589	487	2216	80	340	1844	4510	7.7

Three-Point Field Goals: 1980-81, 0-for-1. 1982-83, 0-for-1. Totals, 0-for-2.

NBA PLAYOFF RECORD

Sea.—Team	G.	Min.	FGA	FGM	Pct.	FTA	FTM	Pct.	Off.	Def.	Tot.	Ast.	PF	Dq.	Stl.	Blk.	Pts.	Avg.
77-78—Atlanta	2	51	12	7	.583	8	2	.250	3	6	9	1	8	1	4	16	16	8.0
78-79—Atlanta	9	212	51	21	.412	13	9	.692	19	52	71	5	29	1	3	24	51	5.7
79-80—Atlanta	5	134	31	18	.581	10	6	.600	18	20	38	3	25	3	2	14	42	8.4

Sea.—Team	G.	Min.	FGA	FGM	Pct.	FTA	FTM	Pct.	Off.	Def.	Tot.	Ast.	PF	Dq.	Stl.	Blk.	Pts.	Avg.
81-82—Atlanta	2	65	6	2	.333	4	3	.750	5	3	8	2	8	1	0	6	7	3.5
82-83—Atlanta	3	118	27	13	.481	9	3	.333	10	20	30	3	12	1	1	10	29	9.7
83-84—Atlanta	5	152	25	10	.400	8	5	.625	10	24	34	1	23	1	2	10	25	5.0
Totals	26	732	152	71	.467	52	28	.538	65	125	190	15	105	8	9	68	170	6.5

Led NBA in blocked shots, 1983. . . . Named to NBA All-Defensive First Team, 1984. . . . Named to NBA All-Defensive Second Team, 1983.

LORENZO ROMAR

Born November 13, 1958 at South Gate, Calif.   Height 6:01.   Weight 180.

High School—Downey, Calif., Pius X.

Colleges—Cerritos College, Norwalk, Calif., and
University of Washington, Seattle, Wash.

Drafted by Golden State on seventh round, 1980 (141st pick).

Waived by Golden State, November 10, 1983; signed by Milwaukee as a free agent, November 23, 1983.
Waived by Milwaukee, November 5, 1984; signed by Detroit as a free agent, November 8, 1984.
Waived by Detroit, November 27, 1984.
Played in Continental Basketball Association with Evansville Thunder and Tampa Bay Thrillers, 1984-85.

—COLLEGIATE RECORD—

Cerritos

Year	G.	Min.	FGA	FGM	Pct.	FTA	FTM	Pct.	Reb.	Pts.	Avg.
76-77	23	....	163	75	.460	47	36	.766	60	186	8.1
77-78	29	....	296	150	.507	132	107	.811	63	407	14.0
JC Totals................	52	....	459	225	.490	179	143	.799	123	593	11.4

Washington

Year	G.	Min.	FGA	FGM	Pct.	FTA	FTM	Pct.	Reb.	Pts.	Avg.
78-79	27	535	130	66	.508	43	31	.721	38	163	6.0
79-80	28	753	219	107	.489	59	45	.763	52	259	9.3
Totals	55	1288	349	173	.496	102	76	.745	90	422	7.7

NBA REGULAR SEASON RECORD

Sea.—Team	G.	Min.	FGA	FGM	Pct.	FTA	FTM	Pct.	Off.	Def.	Tot.	Ast.	PF	Dq.	Stl.	Blk.	Pts.	Avg.
80-81—Golden State	53	726	211	87	.412	63	43	.683	10	46	56	136	64	0	27	3	219	4.1
81-82—Golden State	79	1259	403	203	.504	96	79	.823	12	86	98	226	103	0	60	13	488	6.2
82-83—Golden State	82	2130	572	266	.465	105	78	.743	23	138	138	455	142	0	98	5	620	7.6
83-84—G.S.-Mil.	68	1022	351	161	.459	94	67	.713	21	72	93	193	77	0	55	8	393	5.8
84-85—Mil.-Det.	9	51	16	3	.188	5	5	1.000	0	0	0	12	7	0	4	0	11	1.2
Totals	291	5188	1553	720	.464	363	272	.749	66	319	385	1022	393	0	244	29	1731	5.9

Three-Point Field Goals: 1980-81, 2-for-6 (.333). 1981-82, 3-for-15 (.200). 1982-83, 10-for-33 (.303). 1983-84, 4-for-33 (.121). 1984-85, 0-for-3. Totals, 19-for-90 (.211).

NBA PLAYOFF RECORD

Sea.—Team	G.	Min.	FGA	FGM	Pct.	FTA	FTM	Pct.	Off.	Def.	Tot.	Ast.	PF	Dq.	Stl.	Blk.	Pts.	Avg.
83-84—Milwaukee	13	67	20	9	.450	11	7	.636	0	3	3	15	9	0	0	0	25	1.9

Three-Point Field Goals: 1983-84, 0-for-3.

MINOR LEAGUE REGULAR SEASON RECORD

Sea.—Team	G.	Min.	2-Point			3-Point			FTM	FTA	Pct.	Reb.	Ast.	Pts.	Avg.
			FGM	FGA	Pct.	FGM	FGA	Pct.							
84-85—Evan.-T.B. CBA........	23	366	51	99	.515	2	6	.333	38	47	.808	20	86	146	6.3

DANNY THOMAS ROUNDFIELD

Born May 26, 1953 at Detroit, Mich.   Height 6:08.   Weight 215.

High School—Detroit, Mich., Chadsey.

College—Central Michigan University, Mt. Pleasant, Mich.

Drafted by Cleveland on second round, 1975 (28th pick).

Selected by Indiana in first round of ABA draft, 1975.
Entered NBA with Indiana, 1976.
Signed by Atlanta as Veteran Free Agent, June 9, 1978; Indiana received cash and a 1979 1st round draft choice as compensation, July 28, 1978.
Traded by Atlanta to Detroit for Cliff Levingston, the draft rights to Antoine Carr, and 1986 and 1987 2nd round draft choices, June 18, 1984.
Traded by Detroit to Washington for Rick Mahorn and Mike Gibson, June 17, 1985.

—COLLEGIATE RECORD—

Year	G.	Min.	FGA	FGM	Pct.	FTA	FTM	Pct.	Reb.	Pts.	Avg.
71-72†	16	....	19?	133	.693	81	45	.556	202	311	19.4
72-73	25	....	305	147	.482	105	64	.610	346	358	14.3
73-74	26	....	342	179	.523	107	70	.654	357	428	16.5
74-75	28	....	353	216	.612	159	100	.629	328	532	19.0
Varsity Totals	79	...	1000	542	.542	371	234	.631	1031	1318	16.7

ABA REGULAR SEASON RECORD

Sea.—Team	G.	Min.	2-Point FGM	FGA	Pct.	3-Point FGM	FGA	Pct.	FTM	FTA	Pct.	Reb.	Ast.	Pts.	Avg.
75-76—Indiana	67	767	131	307	.427	0	2	.000	77	122	.631	259	35	339	5.1

ABA PLAYOFF RECORD

Sea.—Team	G.	Min.	2-Point FGM	FGA	Pct.	3-Point FGM	FGA	Pct.	FTM	FTA	Pct.	Reb.	Ast.	Pts.	Avg.
75-76—Indiana	2	25	7	12	.583	0	0	.000	8	9	.889	10	0	22	11.0

NBA REGULAR SEASON RECORD

Sea.—Team	G.	Min.	FGA	FGM	Pct.	FTA	FTM	Pct.	Rebounds Off.	Def.	Tot.	Ast.	PF	Dq.	Stl.	Blk.	Pts.	Avg.
76-77—Indiana	61	1645	734	342	.466	239	164	.686	179	339	518	69	243	8	61	131	848	13.9
77-78—Indiana	79	2423	861	421	.489	300	218	.727	275	527	802	196	297	4	81	149	1060	13.4
78-79—Atlanta	80	2539	916	462	.504	420	300	.714	326	539	865	131	358	16	87	176	1224	15.3
79-80—Atlanta	81	2588	1007	502	.499	465	330	.710	293	544	837	184	317	6	101	139	1334	16.5
80-81—Atlanta	63	2128	808	426	.527	355	256	.721	231	403	634	161	258	8	76	119	1108	17.6
81-82—Atlanta	61	2217	910	424	.466	375	285	.760	227	494	721	162	210	3	64	93	1134	18.6
82-83—Atlanta	77	2811	1193	561	.470	450	337	.749	259	621	880	225	239	1	60	115	1464	19.0
83-84—Atlanta	73	2610	1038	503	.485	486	374	.770	206	515	721	184	221	2	61	74	1380	18.9
84-85—Detroit	56	1492	505	236	.467	178	139	.781	175	278	453	102	147	0	26	54	611	10.9
Totals	631	20453	7972	3877	.486	3268	2403	.735	2171	4260	6431	1414	2290	48	617	1050	10163	16.1

Three-Point Field Goals: 1979-80, 0-for-4. 1980-81, 0-for-1. 1981-82, 1-for-5 (.200). 1982-83, 5-for-27 (.185). 1983-84, 0-for-11. 1984-85, 0-for-2. Totals, 6-for-50 (.120).

NBA PLAYOFF RECORD

Sea.—Team	G.	Min.	FGA	FGM	Pct.	FTA	FTM	Pct.	Rebounds Off.	Def.	Tot.	Ast.	PF	Dq.	Stl.	Blk.	Pts.	Avg.
78-79—Atlanta	9	338	133	61	.459	45	36	.800	44	62	106	25	44	3	8	23	158	17.6
79-80—Atlanta	5	174	69	32	.464	35	22	.629	25	33	58	11	22	1	4	8	86	17.2
81-82—Atlanta	2	85	36	17	.472	14	8	.571	6	16	22	2	8	0	2	4	42	21.0
82-83—Atlanta	3	124	50	24	.480	11	5	.455	6	36	42	10	5	0	4	4	53	17.7
83-84—Atlanta	5	191	69	30	.435	35	25	.714	12	32	44	8	16	1	2	7	86	17.2
84-85—Detroit	9	215	68	33	.485	17	16	.941	19	41	60	15	21	0	4	6	82	9.1
Totals	33	1127	425	197	.464	157	112	.713	112	220	332	71	116	5	24	52	507	15.4

Three-Point Field Goals: 1979-80, 0-for-1. 1982-83, 0-for-1. 1983-84, 1-for-1 (1.000). Totals, 1-for-3 (.333).

NBA ALL-STAR GAME RECORD

Season—Team	Min.	FGA	FGM	Pct.	FTA	FTM	Pct.	Rebounds Off.	Def.	Tot.	Ast.	PF	Dq.	Stl.	Blk.	Pts.
1980—Atlanta	27	15	7	.467	9	4	.444	9	4	13	0	2	0	1	1	18

Named to All-NBA Second Team, 1980. . . . NBA All-Defensive First Team, 1980, 1982, 1983. . . . NBA All-Defensive Second Team, 1981 and 1984.

JEFFREY ALAN RULAND
(Jeff)

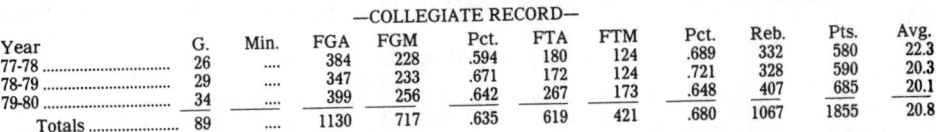

Born December 16, 1958 at Bayshore, N. Y.   Height 6:10.   Weight 240.

High School—Lake Ronkonkoma, N. Y., Sachem.

College—Iona College, New Rochelle, N. Y.

Drafted by Golden State on second round as an undergraduate, 1980 (25th pick).

Draft rights traded by Golden State to Washington for a 1981 2nd round draft choice, June 10, 1980.
Played with pro team in Barcelona, Spain during 1980-81 season (averaged 21 points and 11 rebounds per game).

—COLLEGIATE RECORD—

Year	G.	Min.	FGA	FGM	Pct.	FTA	FTM	Pct.	Reb.	Pts.	Avg.
77-78	26	....	384	228	.594	180	124	.689	332	580	22.3
78-79	29	....	347	233	.671	172	124	.721	328	590	20.3
79-80	34	....	399	256	.642	267	173	.648	407	685	20.1
Totals	89	....	1130	717	.635	619	421	.680	1067	1855	20.8

NBA REGULAR SEASON RECORD

Sea.—Team	G.	Min.	FGA	FGM	Pct.	FTA	FTM	Pct.	Rebounds Off.	Def.	Tot.	Ast.	PF	Dq.	Stl.	Blk.	Pts.	Avg.
81-82—Washington	82	2214	749	420	.561	455	342	.752	253	509	762	134	319	7	44	58	1183	14.4

Sea.—Team	G.	Min.	FGA	FGM	Pct.	FTA	FTM	Pct.	—Rebounds— Off.	Def.	Tot.	Ast.	PF	Dq.	Stl.	Blk.	Pts.	Avg.
82-83—Washington	79	2862	1051	580	.552	544	375	.689	293	578	871	234	312	12	74	77	1536	19.4
83-84—Washington	75	3082	1035	599	.579	636	466	.733	265	657	922	296	285	8	68	72	1665	22.2
84-85—Washington	37	1436	439	250	.569	292	200	.685	127	283	410	162	128	2	31	27	700	18.9
Totals	273	9594	3274	1849	.565	1927	1383	.718	938	2027	2965	826	1044	29	217	234	5084	18.6

Three-Point Field Goals: 1981-82, 1-for-3 (.333). 1982-83, 1-for-3 (.333). 1983-84, 1-for-7 (.143). 1984-85, 0-for-2. Totals, 3-for-15 (.200).

NBA PLAYOFF RECORD

Sea.—Team	G.	Min.	FGA	FGM	Pct.	FTA	FTM	Pct.	—Rebounds— Off.	Def.	Tot.	Ast.	PF	Dq.	Stl.	Blk.	Pts.	Avg.
81-82—Washington	7	237	79	38	.481	56	43	.768	29	37	66	5	24	1	3	4	119	17.0
83-84—Washington	4	187	71	37	.521	27	22	.815	16	35	51	31	15	0	2	3	96	24.0
84-85—Washington	4	162	47	28	.596	20	14	.700	12	22	34	21	15	0	9	4	70	17.5
Totals	15	586	197	103	.523	103	79	.767	57	94	151	57	54	1	14	11	285	19.0

Three-Point Field Goals: 1981-82, 0-for-1. 1983-84, 0-for-1. 1984-85, 0-for-2. Totals, 0-for-4.

NBA ALL-STAR GAME RECORD

Season—Team	Min.	FGA	FGM	Pct.	FTA	FTM	Pct.	—Rebounds— Off.	Def.	Tot.	Ast.	PF	Dq.	Stl.	Blk.	Pts.
1984—Washington .	13	3	2	.667	2	2	1.000	1	3	4	2	2	0	1	0	6

Named to NBA All-Rookie Team, 1982.

MICHAEL CAMPANELLA RUSSELL
(Campy)

Born January 12, 1952 at Jackson, Tenn.   Height 6:08.   Weight 215.

High School—Pontiac, Mich., Central.

College—University of Michigan, Ann Arbor, Mich.

Drafted by Cleveland on first round as hardship case, 1974 (8th pick).

Traded by Cleveland to New York in three-way deal with Kansas City, September 25, 1980 (Joe C. Meriweather and a 1981 1st round draft choice went from New York to Kansas City and Bill Robinzine went from Kansas City to Cleveland).

Traded by New York to Cleveland for a conditional 1985 2nd round draft choice, September 29, 1984.

Waived by Cleveland, November 5, 1985.

Played in Continental Basketball Association with Detroit Spirits, 1984-85.

—COLLEGIATE RECORD—

Year	G.	Min.	FGA	FGM	Pct.	FTA	FTM	Pct.	Reb.	Pts.	Avg.
71-72†	12	....	284	148	.521	102	66	.647	151	362	30.2
72-73	24	....	404	177	.438	121	88	.727	231	442	18.4
73-74	27	....	542	254	.469	171	132	.772	300	640	23.7
Varsity Totals	51	....	946	431	.456	292	220	.753	531	1082	21.2

NBA REGULAR SEASON RECORD

Sea.—Team	G.	Min.	FGA	FGM	Pct.	FTA	FTM	Pct.	—Rebounds— Off.	Def.	Tot.	Ast.	PF	Dq.	Stl.	Blk.	Pts.	Avg.
74-75—Cleveland	68	754	365	150	.411	165	124	.752	43	109	152	45	100	0	21	3	424	6.2
75-76—Cleveland	82	1961	1003	483	.482	344	266	.773	134	211	345	107	231	5	69	10	1232	15.0
76-77—Cleveland	70	2109	1003	435	.434	370	288	.778	144	275	419	189	196	3	70	24	1158	16.5
77-78—Cleveland	72	2520	1168	523	.448	469	352	.751	154	304	458	278	193	3	88	12	1398	19.4
78-79—Cleveland	74	2859	1268	603	.476	523	417	.797	147	356	503	348	222	2	98	25	1623	21.9
79-80—Cleveland	41	1331	630	284	.451	239	178	.745	76	149	225	173	113	1	72	20	747	18.2
80-81—New York	79	2865	1095	508	.464	343	268	.781	109	244	353	257	248	2	99	8	1292	16.4
81-82—New York	77	2358	858	410	.478	294	228	.776	86	150	236	284	221	1	77	12	1073	13.9
82-83—New York						(Did Not Play—Injured)												
84-85—Cleveland	3	24	7	2	.286	3	2	.667	0	5	5	3	3	0	0	0	6	2.0
Totals	566	16781	7397	3398	.459	2750	2123	.772	893	1803	2696	1684	1527	17	594	114	8953	15.8

Three-Point Field Goals: 1979-80, 1-for-9 (.111). 1980-81, 8-for-26 (.308). 1981-82, 25-for-57 (.439). 1984-85, 0-for-1. Totals, 34-for-93 (.366).

NBA PLAYOFF RECORD

Sea.—Team	G.	Min.	FGA	FGM	Pct.	FTA	FTM	Pct.	—Rebounds— Off.	Def.	Tot.	Ast.	PF	Dq.	Stl.	Blk.	Pts.	Avg.
75-76—Cleveland	13	328	161	65	.404	55	47	.855	25	46	71	14	51	0	8	7	177	13.6
76-77—Cleveland	3	100	54	21	.389	15	11	.733	10	16	26	10	10	0	3	1	53	17.7
77-78—Cleveland	2	88	39	19	.487	21	17	.810	7	8	15	11	9	0	3	1	55	27.5
80-81—New York	2	89	34	15	.441	17	16	.941	1	8	9	9	9	0	4	1	46	23.0
Totals	20	605	288	120	.417	108	91	.843	43	78	121	44	79	0	18	10	331	16.6

Three-Point Field Goals: 1980-81, 0-for-2.

NBA ALL-STAR GAME RECORD

Season—Team	Min.	FGA	FGM	Pct.	FTA	FTM	Pct.	Rebounds— Off.	Def.	Tot.	Ast.	PF	Dq.	Stl.	Blk.	Pts.
1979—Cleveland......	13	8	2	.250	0	0	.000	1	0	1	0	0	0	0	0	4

MINOR LEAGUE REGULAR SEASON RECORD

Sea.—Team	G.	Min.	2-Point FGM	FGA	Pct.	3-Point FGM	FGA	Pct.	FTM	FTA	Pct.	Reb.	Ast.	Pts.	Avg.
84-85—Detroit CBA..............	36	1175	170	337	.504	19	51	.373	152	187	.812	210	156	549	15.3

Led NBA in three-point field goal percentage, 1982.

WALKER D. RUSSELL

Born October 26, 1960 at Pontiac, Mich.   Height 6:05.   Weight 195.

High School—Pontiac, Mich., Central.

Colleges—Oakland Community College, Union Lake, Mich.; University of Houston, Houston, Tex., and Western Michigan University, Kalamazoo, Mich.

Drafted by Detroit on fourth round, 1982 (78th pick).

Waived by Detroit, December 20, 1983; signed by Atlanta as a free agent, July 11, 1984.
Waived by Atlanta, December 18, 1984.
Played in Continental Basketball Association with Detroit Spirits, 1983-84.

—COLLEGIATE RECORD—
Oakland CC

Year	G.	Min.	FGA	FGM	Pct.	FTA	FTM	Pct.	Reb.	Pts.	Avg.
78-79	..	....	...	...	....	...	...	....	....	....	20.4

Houston

Year	G.	Min.	FGA	FGM	Pct.	FTA	FTM	Pct.	Reb.	Pts.	Avg.
79-80	8	186	73	34	.466	20	10	.500	19	78	9.8

Western Michigan

Year	G.	Min.	FGA	FGM	Pct.	FTA	FTM	Pct.	Reb.	Pts.	Avg.
80-81	17	....	243	110	.453	69	52	.754	82	272	16.0
81-82	29	....	471	230	.488	139	116	.835	102	576	19.9
WMU Totals	46	....	714	340	.476	208	168	.808	184	848	18.4
College Totals	54	...	787	374	.475	228	178	.781	203	926	17.1

MINOR LEAGUE REGULAR SEASON RECORD

Sea.—Team	G.	Min.	2-Point FGM	FGA	Pct.	3-Point FGM	FGA	Pct.	FTM	FTA	Pct.	Reb.	Ast.	Pts.	Avg.
83-84—Detroit CBA	30	951	182	349	.521	2	17	.117	83	96	.864	116	270	453	15.1

NBA REGULAR SEASON RECORD

Sea.—Team	G.	Min.	FGA	FGM	Pct.	FTA	FTM	Pct.	Rebounds— Off.	Def.	Tot.	Ast.	PF	Dq.	Stl.	Blk.	Pts.	Avg.
82-83—Detroit	68	757	184	67	.364	58	47	.810	19	54	73	131	71	0	16	1	183	2.7
83-84—Detroit	16	119	42	14	.333	13	12	.923	6	13	19	22	25	0	4	0	41	2.6
84-85—Atlanta	21	377	63	34	.540	17	14	.824	8	32	40	66	37	1	17	4	83	4.0
Totals	105	1253	289	115	.398	88	73	.830	33	99	132	219	133	1	37	5	307	2.9

Three-Point Field Goals: 1982-83, 2-for-18 (.111). 1983-84, 1-for-2 (.500). 1984-85, 1-for-1. (1.000). Totals, 4-for-21 (.190).

Led CBA in assists, 1984. . . . Brother of former NBA forward Campy Russell and Frank Russell, guard with the Chicago Bulls, 1972-73.

RALPH LEE SAMPSON

Born July 7, 1960 at Harrisonburg, Va.   Height 7:04.   Weight 228.

High School—Harrisonburg, Va.

College—University of Virginia, Charlottesville, Va.

Drafted by Houston on first round, 1983 (1st pick).

—COLLEGIATE RECORD—

Year	G.	Min.	FGA	FGM	Pct.	FTA	FTM	Pct.	Reb.	Pts.	Avg.
79-80	34	1017	404	221	.547	94	66	.702	381	508	14.9
80-81	33	1056	413	230	.557	198	125	.631	378	585	17.7
81-82	32	1002	353	198	.561	179	110	.615	366	506	15.8
82-83	33	995	414	250	.604	179	126	.704	386	629	19.1
Totals	132	4070	1584	899	.568	650	427	.657	1511	2228	16.9

Sea.—Team	G.	Min.	FGA	FGM	Pct.	FTA	FTM	Pct.	—Rebounds— Off.	Def.	Tot.	Ast.	PF	Dq.	Stl.	Blk.	Pts.	Avg.
83-84—Houston	82	2693	1369	716	.523	434	287	.661	293	620	913	163	339	16	70	197	1720	21.0
84-85—Houston	82	3086	1499	753	.502	448	303	.676	227	626	853	224	306	10	81	168	1809	22.1
Totals	164	5779	2868	1469	.512	882	590	.669	520	1246	1766	387	645	26	151	365	3529	21.5

Three-Point Field Goals: 1983-84, 1-for-4 (.250). 1984-85, 0-for-6. Totals, 1-for-10 (.100).

NBA PLAYOFF RECORD

Sea.—Team	G.	Min.	FGA	FGM	Pct.	FTA	FTM	Pct.	—Rebounds— Off.	Def.	Tot.	Ast.	PF	Dq.	Stl.	Blk.	Pts.	Avg.
84-85—Houston	5	193	100	43	.430	37	19	.514	25	58	83	7	23	2	2	8	106	21.2

Three-Point Field Goals: 1984-85, 1-for-1. (1.000).

NBA ALL-STAR GAME RECORD

Season—Team	Min.	FGA	FGM	Pct.	FTA	FTM	Pct.	—Rebounds— Off.	Def.	Tot.	Ast.	PF	Dq.	Stl.	Blk.	Pts.
1984—Houston	16	7	4	.571	2	1	.500	1	4	5	0	4	0	0	0	9
1985—Houston	29	15	10	.667	6	4	.667	3	7	10	1	5	0	0	1	24
Totals	45	22	14	.636	8	5	.625	4	11	15	1	9	0	0	1	33

Named to All-NBA Second Team, 1985.... NBA All-Star Game MVP, 1985.... NBA Rookie of the Year, 1984.... NBA All-Rookie Team, 1984.... THE SPORTING NEWS College Player of the Year, 1982.... THE SPORTING NEWS All-America First Team, 1981, 1982, 1983.

MICHAEL ANTHONY SANDERS
(Mike)

Born May 7, 1960 at Vidalia, La.   Height 6:06.   Weight 210.

High School—DeRidder, La.

College—University of California at Los Angeles, Los Angeles, Calif.

Drafted by Kansas City on fourth round, 1982 (74th pick).

Waived by Kansas City, October 4, 1982; signed by San Antonio as a free agent, February 9, 1983.
Waived by San Antonio, October 17, 1983; signed by Phoenix as a free agent, December 19, 1983.
Played in Continental Basketball Association with Montana Golden Nuggets, 1982-83, and Sarasota Stingers, 1983-84.

—COLLEGIATE RECORD—

Year	G.	Min.	FGA	FGM	Pct.	FTA	FTM	Pct.	Reb.	Pts.	Avg.
78-79	23	138	38	16	.421	16	11	.688	35	43	1.9
79-80	32	805	248	142	.573	96	76	.792	190	360	11.3
80-81	27	814	287	161	.561	124	95	.766	179	417	15.4
81-82	27	943	299	150	.502	116	90	.776	173	390	14.4
Totals	109	2700	872	469	.538	352	272	.773	577	1210	11.1

MINOR LEAGUE REGULAR SEASON RECORD

Sea.—Team	G.	Min.	—2-Point— FGM	FGA	Pct.	—3-Point— FGM	FGA	Pct.	FTM	FTA	Pct.	Reb.	Ast.	Pts.	Avg.
82-83—Montana CBA	30	1036	273	473	.577	0	0	....	123	149	.825	247	42	669	22.3
83-84—Sarasota CBA	7	295	69	126	.547	0	1	.000	56	65	.861	52	8	194	27.7

NBA REGULAR SEASON RECORD

Sea.—Team	G.	Min.	FGA	FGM	Pct.	FTA	FTM	Pct.	—Rebounds— Off.	Def.	Tot.	Ast.	PF	Dq.	Stl.	Blk.	Pts.	Avg.
82-83—San Antonio	26	393	157	76	.484	43	31	.721	31	63	94	19	57	0	18	6	183	7.0
83-84—Phoenix	50	586	203	97	.478	42	29	.690	40	63	103	44	101	0	23	12	223	4.5
84-85—Phoenix	21	418	175	85	.486	59	45	.763	38	51	89	29	59	0	23	4	215	10.2
Totals	97	1397	535	258	.482	144	105	.729	109	177	286	92	217	0	64	22	621	6.4

Three-Point Field Goals: 1982-83, 0-for-2.

NBA PLAYOFF RECORD

Sea.—Team	G.	Min.	FGA	FGM	Pct.	FTA	FTM	Pct.	—Rebounds— Off.	Def.	Tot.	Ast.	PF	Dq.	Stl.	Blk.	Pts.	Avg.
82-83—San Antonio	6	25	13	7	.538	0	0	.000	2	7	9	4	3	0	0	0	14	2.3
83-84—Phoenix	15	152	46	22	.478	17	16	.941	10	10	20	7	31	0	6	4	60	4.0
84-85—Phoenix	3	91	37	22	.595	10	8	.800	8	7	15	10	8	0	5	0	52	17.3
Totals	24	268	96	51	.531	27	24	.889	20	24	44	21	42	0	11	4	126	5.3

Named to CBA All-Star First Team, 1983.... CBA All-Defensive Second Team, 1983.

—DID YOU KNOW—

That the 45 points Chicago's Michael Jordan scored against San Antonio last season were the most by a rookie since Golden State's Joe Barry Carroll had 46 against San Diego in 1981? Wilt Chamberlain holds the all-time rookie record, twice scoring 58.

RALPH SAMPSON

WAYNE SAPPLETON

Born November 17, 1960 at Kingston, Jamaica.   Height 6:09.   Weight 230.

High School—Kingston, Jamaica, Ardenne.

College—Loyola University, Chicago, Ill.

Drafted by Golden State on second round, 1982 (38th pick).

Draft rights traded by Golden State to New Jersey for a 1983 2nd round draft choice, June 19, 1982. Played in Italy during 1982-83 and 1983-84 seasons.

—COLLEGIATE RECORD—

Year	G.	Min.	FGA	FGM	Pct.	FTA	FTM	Pct.	Reb.	Pts.	Avg.
78-79	7	....	9	3	.333	3	1	.333	8	7	1.0
79-80	29	....	153	78	.510	58	40	.690	219	196	6.8
80-81	28	1069	405	203	.501	174	126	.724	374	532	19.0
81-82	29	1115	443	238	.537	220	162	.736	376	638	22.0
Totals	93	....	1010	522	.517	455	329	.723	977	1373	14.8

NBA REGULAR SEASON RECORD

Sea.—Team	G.	Min.	FGA	FGM	Pct.	FTA	FTM	Pct.	—Rebounds— Off.	Def.	Tot.	Ast.	PF	Dq.	Stl.	Blk.	Pts.	Avg.
84-85—New Jersey	33	298	87	41	.471	34	14	.412	28	47	75	7	50	0	7	4	96	2.9

DANIEL LESLIE SCHAYES
(Dan)

Born May 10, 1959 at Syracuse, N. Y.   Height 6:11.   Weight 245.

High School—DeWitt, N. Y., Jamesville-DeWitt.

College—Syracuse University, Syracuse, N. Y.

Drafted by Utah on first round, 1981 (13th pick).

Traded by Utah with other considerations to Denver for Rich Kelley, February 7, 1983.

—COLLEGIATE RECORD—

Year	G.	Min.	FGA	FGM	Pct.	FTA	FTM	Pct.	Reb.	Pts.	Avg.
77-78	24	....	69	39	.565	45	34	.756	96	112	4.7
78-79	29	....	117	62	.530	66	55	.833	121	179	6.2
79-80	30	....	116	59	.509	78	60	.769	134	178	5.9
80-81	34	....	285	165	.579	202	166	.822	284	496	14.6
Totals	117	....	587	325	.554	391	315	.806	635	965	8.2

NBA REGULAR SEASON RECORD

Sea.—Team	G.	Min.	FGA	FGM	Pct.	FTA	FTM	Pct.	—Rebounds— Off.	Def.	Tot.	Ast.	PF	Dq.	Stl.	Blk.	Pts.	Avg.
81-82—Utah	82	1623	524	252	.481	185	140	.757	131	296	427	146	292	4	46	72	644	7.9
82-83—Utah-Den.	82	2284	749	342	.457	295	228	.773	200	435	635	205	325	8	54	98	912	11.1
83-84—Denver	82	1420	371	183	.493	272	215	.790	145	288	433	91	308	5	32	60	581	7.1
84-85—Denver	56	542	129	60	.465	97	79	.814	48	96	144	38	98	2	20	25	199	3.6
Totals	302	5869	1773	837	.472	849	662	.780	524	1115	1639	480	1023	19	152	255	2336	7.7

Three-Point Field Goals: 1981-82, 0-for-1. 1982-83, 0-for-1. 1983-84, 0-for-2. Totals, 0-for-4.

NBA PLAYOFF RECORD

Sea.—Team	G.	Min.	FGA	FGM	Pct.	FTA	FTM	Pct.	—Rebounds— Off.	Def.	Tot.	Ast.	PF	Dq.	Stl.	Blk.	Pts.	Avg.
82-83—Denver	8	163	43	21	.488	15	15	1.000	11	29	40	14	25	0	2	5	57	7.1
83-84—Denver	5	81	18	11	.611	8	6	.750	3	21	24	4	20	0	4	3	28	5.6
84-85—Denver	9	118	26	11	.423	20	14	.700	8	22	30	12	22	0	3	4	36	4.0
Totals	22	362	87	43	.494	43	35	.814	22	72	94	30	67	0	9	12	121	5.5

Son of Dolph Schayes, former NBA forward, former NBA Supervisor of Referees and a member of the Naismith Memorial Basketball Hall of Fame.

THOMAS MARK SCHEFFLER
(Tom)

Born September 27, 1954 at St. Joseph, Mich.   Height 6:11.   Weight 240.

High School—St. Joseph, Mich.

College—Purdue University, West Lafayette, Ind.

Drafted by Indiana on sixth round, 1977 (117th pick).

Signed by Portland as a free agent, July 25, 1984.

Played in Italy during 1977-78, 1978-79, 1979-80 and 1980-81 seasons.
Played in Switzerland during 1981-82 and 1982-83 seasons.
Played in France during 1983-84 season.

—COLLEGIATE RECORD—

Year	G.	Min.	FGA	FGM	Pct.	FTA	FTM	Pct.	Reb.	Pts.	Avg.
73-74	29	393	117	58	.496	56	42	.750	92	158	5.4
74-75	28	344	102	49	.480	53	41	.774	113	139	5.0
75-76	25	588	139	77	.554	80	62	.775	190	216	8.6
76-77	28	532	158	84	.532	75	57	.760	133	225	8.0
Totals	110	1857	516	268	.519	264	202	.765	528	738	6.7

ITALIAN LEAGUE RECORD

Year	G.	Min.	FGA	FGM	Pct.	FTA	FTM	Pct.	Reb.	Pts.	Avg.
77-78—Scav. Pesaro	36	....	430	235	.547	80	59	.738	411	529	14.7
78-79—Scav. Pesaro	27	931	276	152	.551	54	34	.630	285	338	12.5
79-80—Lib. Treviso	26	886	254	141	.555	72	43	.597	246	325	12.5
80-81—Lib. Treviso	35	1190	295	173	.586	96	53	.552	306	399	11.4

NBA REGULAR SEASON RECORD

Sea.—Team	G.	Min.	FGA	FGM	Pct.	FTA	FTM	Pct.	Off.	Def.	Tot.	Ast.	PF	Dq.	Stl.	Blk.	Pts.	Avg.
									\-\-Rebounds\-\-									
84-85—Portland	39	268	51	21	.412	20	10	.500	18	58	76	11	48	0	8	11	52	1.3

NBA PLAYOFF RECORD

Sea.—Team	G.	Min.	FGA	FGM	Pct.	FTA	FTM	Pct.	Off.	Def.	Tot.	Ast.	PF	Dq.	Stl.	Blk.	Pts.	Avg.
									\-\-Rebounds\-\-									
84-85—Portland	3	10	3	2	.667	4	3	.750	3	2	5	0	0	0	1	0	7	2.3

JOHN ELWOOD SCHWEITZ

Born April 19, 1960 at Waterloo, N. Y.   Height 6:06.   Weight 210.

High School—Waterloo, N. Y.

College—University of Richmond, Richmond, Va.

Drafted by Boston on sixth round, 1982 (138th pick).

Waived by Boston, October 26, 1982; re-signed by Boston, June 8, 1983.
Waived by Boston, October 25, 1983; signed by Seattle as a free agent, September 21, 1984.
Played in Continental Basketball Association with Maine Lumberjacks, 1982-83, and Albany Patroons, 1983-84.

—COLLEGIATE RECORD—

Year	G.	Min.	FGA	FGM	Pct.	FTA	FTM	Pct.	Reb.	Pts.	Avg.
78-79	26	492	199	94	.472	60	45	.750	67	233	9.0
79-80	27	817	370	200	.541	94	77	.819	134	477	17.7
80-81	27	961	398	211	.530	97	84	.866	138	506	18.7
81-82	29	1029	405	215	.531	100	77	.770	143	507	17.5
Totals	109	3299	1372	720	.525	351	283	.806	482	1723	15.8

MINOR LEAGUE REGULAR SEASON RECORD

Sea.—Team	G.	Min.	2-Point			3-Point			FTM	FTA	Pct.	Reb.	Ast.	Pts.	Avg.
			FGM	FGA	Pct.	FGM	FGA	Pct.							
82-83—Maine CBA	42	1471	280	650	.430	47	130	.362	161	181	.889	158	133	862	20.5
83-84—Albany CBA	37	864	181	402	.450	20	60	.333	113	126	.896	125	82	535	14.5

NBA REGULAR SEASON RECORD

Sea.—Team	G.	Min.	FGA	FGM	Pct.	FTA	FTM	Pct.	Off.	Def.	Tot.	Ast.	PF	Dq.	Stl.	Blk.	Pts.	Avg.
									\-\-Rebounds\-\-									
84-85—Seattle	19	110	74	25	.338	10	7	.700	6	15	21	18	12	0	0	1	57	3.0

Three-Point Field Goals: 1984-85, 0-for-4.

Led CBA in three-point field goals, 1983.

ALVIN LEROY SCOTT

Born September 14, 1955 at Cleveland, Tenn.   Height 6:07.   Weight 215.

High School—Cleveland, Tenn., Bradley.

College—Oral Roberts University, Tulsa, Okla.

Drafted by Phoenix on seventh round, 1977 (136th pick).

Year†	G.	Min.	FGA	FGM	Pct.	FTA	FTM	Pct.	Reb.	Pts.	Avg.
73-74†	17	....	219	107	.489	29	19	.655	240	233	13.7
73-74	4	....	4	1	.250	4	3	.750	6	5	1.3
74-75	28	....	89	41	.461	38	25	.658	125	107	3.8
75-76	26	....	147	85	.578	36	27	.750	183	197	7.6
76-77	28	....	248	116	.468	62	37	.597	267	269	9.6
Varsity Totals	86	....	488	243	.498	140	92	.657	581	578	6.7

NBA REGULAR SEASON RECORD

Sea.—Team	G.	Min.	FGA	FGM	Pct.	FTA	FTM	Pct.	Off.	Def.	Tot.	Ast.	PF	Dq.	Stl.	Blk.	Pts.	Avg.
77-78—Phoenix	81	1538	369	180	.488	191	132	.691	135	222	357	88	158	0	52	40	492	6.1
78-79—Phoenix	81	1737	396	212	.535	168	120	.714	104	256	360	126	139	2	80	62	544	6.7
79-80—Phoenix	79	1303	301	127	.422	122	95	.779	89	139	228	98	101	0	47	53	350	4.4
80-81—Phoenix	82	1423	348	173	.497	127	97	.764	101	167	268	114	124	0	60	70	444	5.4
81-82—Phoenix	81	1740	380	189	.497	148	108	.730	97	197	294	149	169	0	59	70	486	6.0
82-83—Phoenix	81	1139	259	124	.479	110	81	.736	60	164	224	97	133	0	48	31	329	4.1
83-84—Phoenix	65	735	124	55	.444	72	56	.778	29	71	100	48	85	0	19	20	167	2.6
84-85—Phoenix	77	1238	259	111	.429	74	53	.716	46	115	161	127	125	0	39	25	276	3.6
Totals	627	10853	2436	1171	.481	1012	742	.733	661	1331	1992	847	1034	2	404	371	3088	4.9

Three-Point Field Goals: 1979-80, 1-for-3 (.333). 1980-81, 1-for-6 (.167). 1981-82, 0-for-2. 1982-83, 0-for-2. 1983-84, 1-for-2 (.500). 1984-85, 1-for-5 (.200). Totals, 4-for-20 (.200).

NBA PLAYOFF RECORD

Sea.—Team	G.	Min.	FGA	FGM	Pct.	FTA	FTM	Pct.	Off.	Def.	Tot.	Ast.	PF	Dq.	Stl.	Blk.	Pts.	Avg.
77-78—Phoenix	2	37	8	4	.500	6	5	.833	2	4	6	3	3	0	2	0	13	6.5
78-79—Phoenix	15	217	52	20	.385	21	13	.619	14	28	42	22	20	0	6	16	53	3.5
79-80—Phoenix	8	140	33	17	.515	8	4	.500	8	14	22	10	8	0	4	5	38	4.8
80-81—Phoenix	7	120	30	14	.467	15	10	.667	8	11	19	7	6	0	4	6	38	5.4
81-82—Phoenix	7	127	32	14	.438	8	4	.500	8	8	16	14	12	0	8	13	32	4.6
82-83—Phoenix	3	62	13	6	.462	2	2	1.000	4	8	12	5	6	0	2	5	14	4.7
83-84—Phoenix	16	111	26	10	.385	6	4	.667	10	14	24	7	14	0	2	2	25	1.6
84-85—Phoenix	3	64	12	3	.250	6	5	.833	3	5	8	10	8	0	1	4	11	3.7
Totals	61	878	206	88	.427	72	47	.653	57	92	149	78	77	0	29	51	224	3.7

Three-Point Field Goals: 1979-80, 0-for-2. 1981-82, 0-for-4. 1983-84, 1-for-1 (1.000). 1984-85, 0-for-1. Totals, 1-for-8 (.125).

BYRON ANTOM SCOTT

Born March 28, 1961 at Ogden, Utah.   Height 6:03.   Weight 195.

High School—Inglewood, Calif., Morningside.

College—Arizona State University, Tempe, Ariz.

Drafted by San Diego on first round as an undergraduate, 1983 (4th pick).

Draft rights traded by San Diego with Swen Nater to Los Angeles for Norm Nixon and Eddie Jordan and 1986 and 1987 2nd round draft choices, October 10, 1983.

—COLLEGIATE RECORD—

Year	G.	Min.	FGA	FGM	Pct.	FTA	FTM	Pct.	Reb.	Pts.	Avg.
79-80	29	936	332	166	.500	86	63	.733	79	395	13.6
80-81	28	1003	390	197	.505	101	70	.693	106	464	16.6
81-82				Did Not Play—Academic and Personal Reasons							
82-83	33	1206	552	283	.513	188	147	.782	177	713	21.6
Totals	90	3145	1274	646	.507	375	280	.747	362	1572	17.5

NBA REGULAR SEASON RECORD

Sea.—Team	G.	Min.	FGA	FGM	Pct.	FTA	FTM	Pct.	Off.	Def.	Tot.	Ast.	PF	Dq.	Stl.	Blk.	Pts.	Avg.
83-84—Los Angeles	74	1637	690	334	.484	139	112	.806	50	114	164	177	174	0	81	19	788	10.6
84-85—L.A. Lakers	81	2305	1003	541	.539	228	187	.820	57	153	210	244	197	1	100	17	1295	16.0
Totals	155	3942	1693	875	.517	367	299	.815	107	267	374	421	371	1	181	36	2083	13.4

Three-Point Field Goals: 1983-84, 8-for-34 (.235). 1984-85, 26-for-60 (.433). Totals, 34-for-94 (.362).

NBA PLAYOFF RECORD

Sea.—Team	G.	Min.	FGA	FGM	Pct.	FTA	FTM	Pct.	Off.	Def.	Tot.	Ast.	PF	Dq.	Stl.	Blk.	Pts.	Avg.
83-84—Los Angeles	20	404	161	74	.460	35	21	.600	11	26	37	34	39	1	18	2	171	8.6
84-85—L.A. Lakers	19	585	267	138	.517	44	35	.795	16	36	52	50	47	0	41	4	321	16.9
Totals	39	989	428	212	.495	79	56	.709	27	62	89	84	86	1	59	6	492	12.6

Three-Point Field Goals: 1983-84, 2-for-10 (.200). 1984-85, 10-for-21 (.476). Totals, 12-for-31 (.387).

Named to NBA All-Rookie Team, 1984. . . . Member of NBA championship team, 1985. . . . Led NBA in three-point field goal percentage, 1985.

BYRON SCOTT

TOM SEWELL

Born March 11, 1962 at Pensacola, Fla.   Height 6:05.   Weight 185.

High School—Pensacola, Fla., Booker T. Washington.

Colleges—Amarillo Junior College, Amarillo, Tex., and
Lamar University, Beaumont, Tex.

Drafted by Philadelphia on first round, 1984 (22nd pick).

Draft rights traded by Philadelphia to Washington for a 1988 1st round draft choice, June 19, 1984.

—COLLEGIATE RECORD—
Amarillo JC

Year	G.	Min.	FGA	FGM	Pct.	FTA	FTM	Pct.	Reb.	Pts.	Avg.
80-81	....	....	....	....	.605	....	....	.718	....	....	17.0

Lamar

Year	G.	Min.	FGA	FGM	Pct.	FTA	FTM	Pct.	Reb.	Pts.	Avg.
81-82	29	659	205	108	.527	43	30	.698	85	246	8.5
82-83	29	883	448	232	.518	103	76	.738	85	540	18.6
83-84	31	1091	532	287	.539	165	136	.824	145	710	22.9
Lamar Totals	89	2633	1185	627	.529	311	242	.778	315	1496	16.8

NBA REGULAR SEASON RECORD

Sea.—Team	G.	Min.	FGA	FGM	Pct.	FTA	FTM	Pct.	Off.	Def.	Tot.	Ast.	PF	Dq.	Stl.	Blk.	Pts.	Avg.
										Rebounds								
84-85—Washington	21	87	36	9	.250	4	2	.500	2	2	4	6	13	0	3	1	20	1.0

Three-Point Field Goals: 1984-85, 0-for-2.

LONNIE JEWEL SHELTON

Born October 19, 1955 at Bakersfield, Calif.   Height 6:08.   Weight 255.

High School—Bakersfield, Calif., Foothill.

College—Oregon State University, Corvallis, Ore.

Drafted by New York on second round as hardship case, 1976 (25th pick).

Awarded from New York with a 1979 1st round draft choice and cash to Seattle as compensation for earlier signing of Veteran Free Agent Marvin Webster, September 29, 1978; New York subsequently received a 1981 1st round draft choice and cash from Seattle as part of transaction.

Traded by Seattle to Cleveland for a 1983 2nd round draft choice and cash, June 27, 1983.

—COLLEGIATE RECORD—

Year	G.	Min.	FGA	FGM	Pct.	FTA	FTM	Pct.	Reb.	Pts.	Avg.
73-74	26	....	260	135	.519	75	48	.640	204	318	12.2
74-75	31	....	439	235	.535	132	96	.727	292	566	18.3
75-76	23	....	296	167	.564	111	76	.685	178	410	17.8
Totals	80	....	995	537	.540	328	220	.671	674	1294	16.2

NBA REGULAR SEASON RECORD

Sea.—Team	G.	Min.	FGA	FGM	Pct.	FTA	FTM	Pct.	Off.	Def.	Tot.	Ast.	PF	Dq.	Stl.	Blk.	Pts.	Avg.
										Rebounds								
76-77—N.Y. Knicks	82	2104	836	398	.476	225	159	.707	220	413	633	149	363	10	125	98	955	11.6
77-78—New York	82	2319	988	508	.514	276	203	.736	204	376	580	195	350	11	109	112	1219	14.9
78-79—Seattle	76	2158	859	446	.519	189	131	.693	182	286	468	110	266	7	76	75	1023	13.5
79-80—Seattle	76	2243	802	425	.530	241	184	.763	199	383	582	145	292	11	92	79	1035	13.6
80-81—Seattle	14	440	174	73	.420	55	36	.655	31	47	78	35	48	0	22	3	182	13.0
81-82—Seattle	81	2667	1046	508	.486	240	188	.783	161	348	509	252	317	12	99	43	1204	14.9
82-83—Seattle	82	2572	915	437	.478	187	141	.754	158	337	495	237	310	8	75	72	1016	12.4
83-84—Cleveland	79	2101	779	371	.476	140	107	.764	140	241	381	179	279	9	76	55	850	10.8
84-85—Cleveland	57	1244	363	158	.435	77	51	.662	82	185	267	96	187	3	44	18	367	6.4
Totals	629	17848	6762	3324	.492	1630	1200	.736	1377	2616	3993	1398	2412	71	718	555	7851	12.5

Three-Point Field Goals: 1979-80, 1-for-5 (.200). 1981-82, 0-for-8. 1982-83, 1-for-6 (.167). 1983-84, 1-for-5 (.200). 1984-85, 0-for-5. Totals, 3-for-29 (.103).

NBA PLAYOFF RECORD

Sea.—Team	G.	Min.	FGA	FGM	Pct.	FTA	FTM	Pct.	Off.	Def.	Tot.	Ast.	PF	Dq.	Stl.	Blk.	Pts.	Avg.
										Rebounds								
77-78—New York	6	151	56	30	.536	8	6	.750	18	26	44	17	29	1	2	5	66	11.0
78-79—Seattle	17	566	209	101	.483	26	18	.692	61	81	142	34	80	4	19	18	220	12.9
79-80—Seattle	15	469	146	74	.507	51	32	.627	35	90	125	25	54	0	23	12	180	12.0
81-82—Seattle	8	266	85	40	.471	32	22	.688	24	35	59	16	38	3	5	7	102	12.8
82-83—Seattle	2	53	23	4	.174	5	2	.400	13	8	21	5	7	0	1	0	10	5.0
84-85—Cleveland	4	106	34	19	.559	10	8	.800	6	16	22	4	20	2	2	1	46	11.5
Totals	52	1611	553	268	.485	132	88	.667	157	256	413	101	228	10	52	43	624	12.0

Three-Point Field Goals: 1979-80, 0-for-1.

NBA ALL-STAR GAME RECORD

Season—Team	Min.	FGA	FGM	Pct.	FTA	FTM	Pct.	Off.	Def.	Tot.	Ast.	PF	Dq.	Stl.	Blk.	Pts.
								—Rebounds—								
1982—Seattle............	20	3	3	1.000	2	1	.500	4	5	9	1	4	0	1	0	7

Named to NBA All-Defensive Second Team, 1982.... Member of NBA championship team, 1979.

PURVIS SHORT

Born July 2, 1957 at Hattiesburg, Miss.   Height 6:07.   Weight 220.

High School—Hattiesburg, Miss., Blair.

College—Jackson State University, Jackson, Miss.

Drafted by Golden State on first round, 1978 (5th pick).

—COLLEGIATE RECORD—

Year	G.	Min.	FGA	FGM	Pct.	FTA	FTM	Pct.	Reb.	Pts.	Avg.
74-75	28	....	325	190	.585	66	44	.667	218	424	15.1
75-76	28	....	635	324	.510	91	66	.725	283	714	25.5
76-77	26	....	541	288	.532	92	70	.761	218	646	24.8
77-78	22	....	535	285	.532	111	80	.721	250	650	29.5
Totals	104	....	2036	1087	.534	360	260	.722	969	2434	23.4

NBA REGULAR SEASON RECORD

Sea.—Team	G.	Min.	FGA	FGM	Pct.	FTA	FTM	Pct.	Off.	Def.	Tot.	Ast.	PF	Dq.	Stl.	Blk.	Pts.	Avg.
									—Rebounds—									
78-79—Golden State	75	1703	771	369	.479	85	57	.671	127	220	347	97	233	6	54	12	795	10.6
79-80—Golden State	62	1636	916	461	.503	165	134	.812	119	197	316	123	186	4	63	9	1056	17.0
80-81—Golden State	79	2309	1157	549	.475	205	168	.820	151	240	391	249	244	3	78	19	1269	16.1
81-82—Golden State	76	1782	935	456	.488	221	177	.801	123	143	266	209	220	3	65	10	1095	14.4
82-83—Golden State	67	2397	1209	589	.487	308	255	.828	145	209	354	228	242	3	94	14	1437	21.4
83-84—Golden State	79	2945	1509	714	.473	445	353	.793	184	254	438	246	252	2	103	11	1803	22.8
84-85—Golden State	78	3081	1780	819	.460	613	501	.817	157	241	398	234	255	4	116	27	2186	28.0
Totals	516	15853	8277	3957	.478	2042	1645	.806	1006	1504	2510	1386	1632	25	573	102	9641	18.7

Three-Point Field Goals: 1979-80, 0-for-6. 1980-81, 3-for-17 (.176). 1981-82, 6-for-28 (.214). 1982-83, 4-for-15 (.267). 1983-84, 22-for-72 (.306). 1984-85, 47-for-150 (.313). Totals, 82-for-288 (.285).

Brother of former NBA forward Eugene Short.

JERRY LEE SICHTING

Born November 29, 1956 at Martinsville, Ind.   Height 6:01.   Weight 178.

High School—Martinsville, Ind.

College—Purdue University, West Lafayette, Ind.

Drafted by Golden State on fourth round, 1979 (82nd pick).

Waived by Golden State, October 4, 1979; signed by Indiana as a free agent, October 9, 1980.

—COLLEGIATE RECORD—

Year	G.	Min.	FGA	FGM	Pct.	FTA	FTM	Pct.	Reb.	Pts.	Avg.
75-76	27	436	123	67	.545	38	31	.816	42	165	6.1
76-77	28	536	131	71	.542	69	61	.884	36	203	7.3
77-78	27	975	233	120	.515	90	78	.867	67	318	11.8
78-79	35	1202	367	186	.507	118	103	.873	97	475	13.6
Totals	117	3149	854	444	.520	315	273	.867	242	1161	9.9

NBA REGULAR SEASON RECORD

Sea.—Team	G.	Min.	FGA	FGM	Pct.	FTA	FTM	Pct.	Off.	Def.	Tot.	Ast.	PF	Dq.	Stl.	Blk.	Pts.	Avg.
									—Rebounds—									
80-81—Indiana	47	450	95	34	.358	32	25	.781	11	32	43	70	38	0	23	1	93	2.0
81-82—Indiana	51	800	194	91	.469	38	29	.763	14	41	55	117	63	0	33	1	212	4.2
82-83—Indiana	78	2435	661	316	.478	107	92	.860	33	122	155	433	185	0	104	2	727	9.3
83-84—Indiana	80	2497	746	397	.532	135	117	.867	44	127	171	457	179	0	90	8	917	11.5
84-85—Indiana	70	1808	624	325	.521	128	112	.875	24	90	114	264	116	0	47	4	771	11.0
Totals	326	7990	2320	1163	.501	440	375	.852	126	412	538	1341	581	0	297	16	2720	8.3

Three-Point Field Goals: 1980-81, 0-for-5. 1981-82, 1-for-9 (.111). 1982-83, 3-for-18 (.167). 1983-84, 6-for-20 (.300). 1984-85, 9-for-37 (.243). Totals, 19-for-89 (.213).

NBA PLAYOFF RECORD

Sea.—Team	G.	Min.	FGA	FGM	Pct.	FTA	FTM	Pct.	Off.	Def.	Tot.	Ast.	PF	Dq.	Stl.	Blk.	Pts.	Avg.
									—Rebounds—									
80-81—Indiana	1	1	0	0	.000	0	0	.000	0	0	0	0	0	0	1	0	0	0.0

PURVIS SHORT

JACK WAYNE SIKMA

Born November 14, 1955 at Kankakee, Ill.   Height 6:11.   Weight 250.

High School—St. Anne, Ill.

College—Illinois Wesleyan University, Bloomington, Ill.

Drafted by Seattle on first round, 1977 (8th pick).

—COLLEGIATE RECORD—

Year	G.	Min.	FGA	FGM	Pct.	FTA	FTM	Pct.	Reb.	Pts.	Avg.
73-74	21	....	306	148	.484	37	28	.757	223	324	15.4
74-75	30	....	537	265	.493	112	80	.714	415	610	20.3
75-76	25	....	385	204	.530	126	93	.738	290	501	20.0
76-77	31	....	302	324	.528	235	189	.804	477	837	27.0
Totals	107	....	1530	941	.514	510	390	.765	1405	2272	21.2

NBA REGULAR SEASON RECORD

Sea.—Team	G.	Min.	FGA	FGM	Pct.	FTA	FTM	Pct.	—Rebounds— Off.	Def.	Tot.	Ast.	PF	Dq.	Stl.	Blk.	Pts.	Avg.
77-78—Seattle	82	2238	752	342	.455	247	192	.777	196	482	678	134	300	6	68	40	876	10.7
78-79—Seattle	82	2958	1034	476	.460	404	329	.814	232	781	1013	261	295	4	82	67	1281	15.6
79-80—Seattle	82	2793	989	470	.475	292	235	.805	198	710	908	279	232	5	68	77	1175	14.3
80-81—Seattle	82	2920	1311	595	.454	413	340	.823	184	668	852	248	282	5	78	93	1530	18.7
81-82—Seattle	82	3049	1212	581	.479	523	447	.855	223	815	1038	277	268	5	102	107	1611	19.6
82-83—Seattle	75	2564	1043	484	.464	478	400	.837	213	645	858	233	263	4	87	65	1368	18.2
83-84—Seattle	82	2993	1155	576	.499	480	411	.856	225	686	911	327	301	6	95	92	1563	19.1
84-85—Seattle	68	2402	943	461	.489	393	335	.852	164	559	723	285	239	1	83	91	1259	18.5
Totals	635	21917	8439	3985	.472	3230	2689	.833	1635	5346	6981	2044	2180	36	663	632	10663	16.8

Three-Point Field Goals: 1979-80, 0-for-1. 1980-81, 0-for-5. 1981-82, 2-for-13 (.154). 1982-83, 0-for-8. 1983-84, 0-for-2. 1984-85, 2-for-10 (.200). Totals, 4-for-39 (.103).

NBA PLAYOFF RECORD

Sea.—Team	G.	Min.	FGA	FGM	Pct.	FTA	FTM	Pct.	—Rebounds— Off.	Def.	Tot.	Ast.	PF	Dq.	Stl.	Blk.	Pts.	Avg.
77-78—Seattle	22	701	247	115	.466	91	71	.780	50	128	178	27	101	7	18	11	301	13.7
78-79—Seattle	17	655	224	103	.460	61	48	.787	39	160	199	43	70	2	16	24	254	14.9
79-80—Seattle	15	534	163	65	.399	54	46	.852	30	96	126	55	55	1	17	5	176	11.7
81-82—Seattle	8	315	128	57	.445	58	50	.862	21	76	97	24	34	1	9	8	164	20.5
82-83—Seattle	2	75	31	11	.355	12	8	.667	6	20	26	11	7	0	2	2	30	15.0
83-84—Seattle	5	193	98	49	.500	14	12	.857	11	40	51	5	22	1	3	7	110	22.0
Totals	69	2473	891	400	.449	290	235	.810	157	520	677	165	289	12	65	57	1035	15.0

Three-Point Field Goals: 1979-80, 0-for-2. 1982-83, 0-for-1. 1983-84, 0-for-1. Totals, 0-for-4.

NBA ALL-STAR GAME RECORD

Season—Team	Min.	FGA	FGM	Pct.	FTA	FTM	Pct.	—Rebounds— Off.	Def.	Tot.	Ast.	PF	Dq.	Stl.	Blk.	Pts.
1979—Seattle	18	5	4	.800	0	0	.000	1	3	4	0	1	0	0	0	8
1980—Seattle	28	10	4	.400	0	0	.000	2	6	8	4	5	0	2	3	8
1981—Seattle	21	5	2	.400	2	2	1.000	1	3	4	4	5	0	1	1	6
1982—Seattle	21	11	5	.455	0	0	.000	2	7	9	1	2	0	2	1	10
1983—Seattle	17	6	4	.667	0	0	.000	1	2	3	1	2	0	1	1	5
1984—Seattle	30	12	5	.417	6	5	.833	5	7	12	1	4	0	3	0	15
1985—Seattle	12	2	0	.000	0	0	.000	0	2	2	0	1	0	0	1	0
Totals	147	51	24	.471	8	7	.875	12	30	42	11	20	0	9	7	52

Three-Point Field Goals: 1980, 0-for-1. 1981, 0-for-1. Totals, 0-for-2.

Named to NBA All-Defensive Second Team, 1982. . . . Named to NBA All-Rookie Team, 1978. . . . Member of NBA championship team, 1979.

CHARLES E. SITTON
(Charlie)

Born July 3, 1962 at McMinnville, Ore.   Height 6:08.   Weight 210.

High School—McMinnville, Ore.

College—Oregon State University, Corvallis, Ore.

Drafted by Dallas on second round, 1984 (38th pick).

—COLLEGIATE RECORD—

Year	G.	Min.	FGA	FGM	Pct.	FTA	FTM	Pct.	Reb.	Pts.	Avg.
80-81	28	697	146	80	.548	31	19	.613	92	179	6.4
81-82	30	899	249	149	.598	108	88	.815	129	386	12.9
82-83	30	998	346	199	.575	208	165	.793	157	563	18.8
83-84	29	960	272	154	.566	169	125	.740	124	433	14.9
Totals	117	3554	1013	582	.575	516	397	.769	502	1561	13.3

Sea.—Team	G.	Min.	FGA	FGM	Pct.	FTA	FTM	Pct.	Off.	Def.	Tot.	Ast.	PF	Dq.	Stl.	Blk.	Pts.	Avg.
									— Rebounds —									
84-85—Dallas	43	304	94	39	.415	25	13	.520	24	36	60	26	50	0	7	6	91	2.1

Three-Point Field Goals: 1984-85, 0-for-2.

TOM GRIFFIN SLUBY

Born February 18, 1962 at Washington, D. C.   Height 6:04.   Weight 200.

High School—Washington, D. C., Gonzaga.

College—University of Notre Dame, Notre Dame, Ind.

Drafted by Dallas on second round, 1984 (41st pick).

Waived by Dallas, May 8, 1985.

—COLLEGIATE RECORD—

Year	G.	Min.	FGA	FGM	Pct.	FTA	FTM	Pct.	Reb.	Pts.	Avg.
80-81	27	377	70	36	.514	21	14	.667	38	86	3.2
81-82	11	357	86	35	.407	33	16	.485	23	86	7.8
82-83	27	494	110	57	.518	26	22	.846	47	136	5.0
83-84	33	1099	505	254	.503	166	108	.651	90	616	18.7
Totals	98	2327	771	382	.495	246	160	.650	198	924	9.4

NBA REGULAR SEASON RECORD

Sea.—Team	G.	Min.	FGA	FGM	Pct.	FTA	FTM	Pct.	Off.	Def.	Tot.	Ast.	PF	Dq.	Stl.	Blk.	Pts.	Avg.
									— Rebounds —									
84-85—Dallas	31	151	58	30	.517	21	13	.619	5	7	12	16	18	0	3	0	73	2.4

Three-Point Field Goals: 1984-85, 0-for-2.

DEREK ERVIN SMITH

Born November 1, 1961 at Hogansville, Ga.   Height 6:07.   Weight 215.

High School—Hogansville, Ga.

College—University of Louisville, Louisville, Ky.

Drafted by Golden State on second round, 1982 (35th pick).

Waived by Golden State, September 8, 1983; signed by San Diego as a free agent, September 13, 1983.

—COLLEGIATE RECORD—

Year	G.	Min.	FGA	FGM	Pct.	FTA	FTM	Pct.	Reb.	Pts.	Avg.
78-79	32	622	185	117	.632	123	79	.642	153	313	9.8
79-80	36	1222	372	213	.573	150	105	.700	299	531	14.8
80-81	30	964	348	188	.540	135	89	.659	233	465	15.5
81-82	33	950	346	204	.590	162	109	.673	199	517	15.7
Totals	131	3758	1251	722	.577	570	382	.670	884	1826	13.9

NBA REGULAR SEASON RECORD

Sea.—Team	G.	Min.	FGA	FGM	Pct.	FTA	FTM	Pct.	Off.	Def.	Tot.	Ast.	PF	Dq.	Stl.	Blk.	Pts.	Avg.
									— Rebounds —									
82-83—Golden State	27	154	51	21	.412	25	17	.680	10	28	38	2	40	0	0	4	59	2.2
83-84—San Diego	61	1297	436	238	.546	163	123	.755	54	116	170	82	165	2	33	22	600	9.8
84-85—L.A. Clippers	80	2762	1271	682	.537	504	400	.794	174	253	427	216	317	8	77	52	1767	22.1
Totals	168	4213	1758	941	.535	692	540	.780	238	397	635	300	522	10	110	78	2426	14.4

Three-Point Field Goals: 1982-83, 0-for-2. 1983-84, 1-for-6 (.167). 1984-85, 3-for-19 (.158). Totals, 4-for-27 (.148).

LARRY SMITH

Born January 18, 1958 at Rolling Fork, Miss.   Height 6:08.   Weight 225.

High School—Hollandale, Miss., Simmons.

College—Alcorn State University, Lorman, Miss.

Drafted by Golden State on second round, 1980 (24th pick).

—COLLEGIATE RECORD—

Year	G.	Min.	FGA	FGM	Pct.	FTA	FTM	Pct.	Reb.	Pts.	Avg.
76-77	34	....	402	212	.526	124	74	.596	222	498	14.6
77-78	22	....	231	137	.593	74	45	.608	222	319	14.5

LARRY SMITH

Year	G.	Min.	FGA	FGM	Pct.	FTA	FTM	Pct.	Reb.	Pts.	Avg.
78-79	29	....	360	216	.600	142	81	.570	398	513	17.7
79-80	26	849	342	198	.579	182	126	.692	392	522	20.1
Totals	111	....	1335	763	.572	522	326	.625	1234	1852	16.7

NBA REGULAR SEASON RECORD

Sea.—Team	G.	Min.	FGA	FGM	Pct.	FTA	FTM	Pct.	Off.	Def.	Tot.	Ast.	PF	Dq.	Stl.	Blk.	Pts.	Avg.
80-81—Golden State	82	2578	594	304	.512	301	177	.588	433	561	994	93	316	10	70	63	785	9.6
81-82—Golden State	74	2213	412	220	.534	159	88	.553	279	534	813	83	291	7	65	54	528	7.1
82-83—Golden State	49	1433	306	180	.588	99	53	.535	209	276	485	46	186	5	36	20	413	8.4
83-84—Golden State	75	2091	436	244	.560	168	94	.560	282	390	672	72	274	6	61	22	582	7.8
84-85—Golden State	80	2497	690	366	.530	256	155	.605	405	464	869	96	285	5	78	54	887	11.1
Totals	360	10812	2438	1314	.539	983	567	.577	1608	2225	3833	390	1352	33	310	213	3195	8.9

Three-Point Field Goals: 1981-82, 0-for-1.

Named to NBA All-Rookie Team, 1981.... Led NCAA in rebounding, 1980.

ROBERT LEROY SMITH

Born March 10, 1955 at Los Angeles, Calif.   Height 5:11.   Weight 170.

High School—Los Angeles, Calif., Crenshaw.

Colleges—Arizona Western College, Yuma, Ariz., and
University of Nevada at Las Vegas, Las Vegas, Nev.

Drafted by Denver on third round, 1977 (65th pick).

Waived by Denver, January 30, 1978; re-signed by Denver, February 8, 1978.
Traded by Denver to Utah for two draft choices (1980 3rd round and 1981 2nd round), October 9, 1979.
Waived by Utah, October 25, 1979; signed by New Jersey as a free agent, November 13, 1979.
Waived by New Jersey, September 25, 1980; signed by Cleveland as a free agent, October 1, 1980.
Waived by Cleveland, October 14, 1980; signed by Kansas City as a free agent, October 1, 1981.
Waived by Kansas City, October 19, 1981; signed by Milwaukee as a free agent, March 17, 1982.
Traded by Milwaukee to San Diego for a 1983 6th round draft choice, October 15, 1982.
Waived by San Diego, November 17, 1982; signed by San Antonio as a free agent, March 23, 1983.
Waived by San Antonio, October 14, 1983; signed by Cleveland as a free agent, September, 1984.
Waived by Cleveland, November 26, 1984.
Played in Continental Basketball Association with Montana Golden Nuggets, 1981-82 and 1982-83, and Toronto Tornados, 1983-84 and 1984-85.

—COLLEGIATE RECORD—
Arizona Western

Year	G.	Min.	FGA	FGM	Pct.	FTA	FTM	Pct.	Reb.	Pts.	Avg.
73-74	31	....	...	...	.520	...	...	.840	....	....	12.9

Nevada-Las Vegas

Year	G.	Min.	FGA	FGM	Pct.	FTA	FTM	Pct.	Reb.	Pts.	Avg.
74-75	29	....	213	110	.516	66	54	.818	36	274	9.4
75-76	32	....	221	104	.471	74	64	.865	58	272	8.5
76-77	32	....	318	155	.487	106	98	.925	79	408	12.8
Totals	93	....	752	369	.491	246	216	.878	173	954	10.3

MINOR LEAGUE REGULAR SEASON RECORD

Sea.—Team	G.	Min.	2-Point			3-Point			FTM	FTA	Pct.	Reb.	Ast.	Pts.	Avg.
			FGM	FGA	Pct.	FGM	FGA	Pct.							
81-82—Montana CBA	34	1177	237	431	.549	10	24	.417	204	219	.932	112	200	708	20.8
82-83—Montana CBA	44	1611	333	621	.536	9	23	.391	290	310	.935	97	414	983	22.3
83-84—Toronto CBA	44	1653	328	615	.533	18	63	.286	231	248	.931	144	361	941	21.4
84-85—Toronto CBA	35	1268	253	507	.499	57	125	.456	191	205	.931	111	292	868	24.8

NBA REGULAR SEASON RECORD

Sea.—Team	G.	Min.	FGA	FGM	Pct.	FTA	FTM	Pct.	Off.	Def.	Tot.	Ast.	PF	Dq.	Stl.	Blk.	Pts.	Avg.
77-78—Denver	45	378	97	50	.515	24	21	.875	6	30	36	39	52	0	18	3	121	2.7
78-79—Denver	82	1479	436	184	.422	180	159	.883	41	105	146	208	165	1	58	13	527	6.4
79-80—Utah-NJ	65	809	269	118	.439	92	80	.870	20	59	79	92	105	1	26	4	324	5.0
80-81—Cleveland	1	20	5	2	.400	4	4	1.000	1	2	3	3	6	1	0	0	8	8.0
81-82—Milwaukee	17	316	110	52	.473	12	10	.833	1	13	14	44	35	0	10	1	116	6.8
82-83—S.D.-S.A.	12	68	24	7	.292	10	9	.900	1	5	6	8	13	0	5	0	23	1.9
84-85—Cleveland	7	48	17	4	.235	10	8	.800	0	4	4	7	6	0	2	0	16	2.3
Totals	229	3118	958	417	.435	332	291	.877	70	218	288	401	382	3	119	21	1135	5.0

Three-Point Field Goals: 1979-80, 8-for-26 (.308). 1981-82, 2-for-10 (.200). 1982-83, 0-for-2. 1984-85, 0-for-4. Totals, 10-for-42 (.238).

Sea.—Team	G.	Min.	FGA	FGM	Pct.	FTA	FTM	Pct.	—Rebounds— Off.	Def.	Ast.	PF	Dq.	Stl.	Blk.	Pts.	Avg.
77-78—Denver	11	96	26	17	.654	7	5	.714	5	4	9	17	13	0	6	0	39	3.5
78-79—Denver	3	25	7	0	.000	2	2	1.000	1	1	2	4	2	0	2	0	2	0.7
81-82—Milwaukee	6	68	26	10	.385	8	7	.875	1	6	7	12	8	0	1	0	29	4.8
82-83—San Antonio	6	19	9	4	.444	2	2	1.000	3	2	5	6	2	0	1	0	10	1.7
Totals	26	208	68	31	.456	19	16	.842	10	13	23	39	25	0	10	0	80	3.1

Note: columns are G. Min. FGA FGM Pct. FTA FTM Pct. Off. Def. Ast. PF Dq. Stl. Blk. Pts. Avg.

Three-Point Field Goals: 1981-82, 2-for-7 (.286). 1982-83, 0-for-1. Totals, 2-for-8 (.250).

Named CBA Most Valuable Player, 1983.... CBA All-Star First Team, 1983 and 1985.... CBA All-Star Second Team, 1982.... CBA All-Defensive Second Team, 1985........ Led CBA in free-throw percentage, 1983 and 1985.... Led CBA in assists, 1983.... Led NCAA Division I in free-throw percentage, 1977.

RICKY BRAD SOBERS

Born January 15, 1953 at Bronx, N. Y.   Height 6:03.   Weight 198.

High School—Bronx, N. Y., DeWitt Clinton (Did Not Play).

Colleges—College of Southern Idaho, Twins Falls, Idaho, and University of Nevada at Las Vegas, Las Vegas, Nev.

Drafted by Phoenix on first round, 1975 (16th pick).

Traded by Phoenix to Indiana for Don Buse, September 6, 1977.
Awarded from Indiana to Chicago as compensation for earlier signing of Veteran Free Agent Mickey Johnson, August 28, 1979.
Signed by Washington as Veteran Free Agent, January 24, 1983; Chicago agreed not to exercise its right of first refusal in exchange for two 2nd round draft choices (1983 and 1985).
Traded by Washington with the draft rights to Tim McCormick to Seattle for Gus Williams, June 19, 1984.

—COLLEGIATE RECORD—
Southern Idaho

Year	G.	Min.	FGA	FGM	Pct.	FTA	FTM	Pct.	Reb.	Pts.	Avg.
71-72	....	....	....	....	....	....	....	....	....	....	....
72-73	....	....	....	....	....	....	....	....	....	....	19.7

Nevada—Las Vegas

Year	G.	Min.	FGA	FGM	Pct.	FTA	FTM	Pct.	Reb.	Pts.	Avg.
73-74	25	....	303	140	.462	67	52	.776	95	332	13.3
74-75	29	....	431	209	.496	127	105	.827	108	523	18.0
Totals	54	....	734	349	.475	194	157	.809	203	855	15.8

NBA REGULAR SEASON RECORD

Sea.—Team	G.	Min.	FGA	FGM	Pct.	FTA	FTM	Pct.	—Rebounds— Off.	Def.	Tot.	Ast.	PF	Dq.	Stl.	Blk.	Pts.	Avg.
75-76—Phoenix	78	1898	623	280	.449	192	158	.823	80	179	259	215	253	6	106	7	718	9.2
76-77—Phoenix	79	2005	834	414	.496	289	243	.841	82	152	234	238	258	3	93	14	1071	13.6
77-78—Indiana	79	3019	1221	553	.453	400	330	.825	92	235	327	327	308	10	170	23	1436	18.2
78-79—Indiana	81	2825	1194	553	.463	338	298	.882	118	183	301	450	315	8	138	23	1404	17.3
79-80—Chicago	82	2673	1002	470	.469	239	200	.837	75	167	242	426	294	4	136	17	1161	14.2
80-81—Chicago	71	1803	769	355	.462	247	231	.935	46	98	144	284	225	3	98	17	958	13.5
81-82—Chicago	80	1938	801	363	.453	254	195	.768	37	105	142	301	238	6	73	18	940	11.8
82-83—Washington	41	1438	534	234	.438	185	154	.832	35	67	102	218	158	3	61	14	645	15.7
83-84—Washington	81	2624	1115	508	.456	264	221	.837	51	128	179	377	278	10	117	17	1266	15.6
84-85—Seattle	71	1490	628	280	.446	162	132	.815	27	76	103	252	156	0	49	9	700	9.9
Totals	743	21713	8721	4010	.460	2570	2162	.841	643	1390	2033	3345	2483	53	1041	159	10299	13.9

Three-Point Field Goals: 1979-80, 21-for-68 (.309). 1980-81, 17-for-66 (.258). 1981-82, 19-for-76 (.250). 1982-83, 23-for-55 (.418). 1983-84, 29-for-111 (.261). 1984-85, 8-for-28 (.286). Totals, 117-for-404 (.290).

NBA PLAYOFF RECORD

Sea.—Team	G.	Min.	FGA	FGM	Pct.	FTA	FTM	Pct.	—Rebounds— Off.	Def.	Tot.	Ast.	PF	Dq.	Stl.	Blk.	Pts.	Avg.
75-76—Phoenix	19	563	205	96	.468	66	55	.833	20	43	63	79	77	3	18	6	247	13.0
80-81—Chicago	6	162	81	35	.432	9	8	.889	3	8	11	22	26	1	4	0	79	13.2
83-84—Washington	4	150	57	25	.439	10	8	.800	2	3	5	16	19	1	5	2	61	15.3
Totals	29	875	343	156	.455	85	71	.835	25	54	79	117	122	5	27	8	387	13.3

Three-Point Field Goals: 1980-81, 1-for-6 (.167). 1983-84, 3-for-10 (.300). Totals, 4-for-16 (.250).

RORY DARNELL SPARROW

Born June 12, 1958 at Suffolk, Va.   Height 6:02.   Weight 195.

High School—Paterson, N. J., Eastside.

College—Villanova University, Villanova, Pa.

Drafted by New Jersey on fourth round, 1980 (75th pick).

Waived by New Jersey, October 7, 1980; re-signed by New Jersey to a 10-day contract that expired December 29, 1980.

Re-signed by New Jersey, February 18, 1981.
Traded by New Jersey to Atlanta for a 1982 4th round draft choice, August 12, 1981.
Traded by Atlanta to New York for Scott Hastings and cash, February 12, 1983.
Played in Continental Basketball Association with Scranton Aces, 1980-81.

—COLLEGIATE RECORD—

Year	G.	Min.	FGA	FGM	Pct.	FTA	FTM	Pct.	Reb.	Pts.	Avg.
76-77	33	....	193	99	.513	42	34	.810	69	232	7.0
77-78	32	1036	213	109	.512	79	57	.722	74	275	8.6
78-79	28	877	282	145	.514	61	50	.820	60	340	12.1
79-80	31	937	243	136	.560	77	64	.831	75	336	10.8
Totals	124	....	931	489	.525	259	205	.792	278	1183	9.5

MINOR LEAGUE REGULAR SEASON RECORD

Sea.—Team	G.	Min.	2-Point			3-Point			FTM	FTA	Pct.	Reb.	Ast.	Pts.	Avg.
			FGM	FGA	Pct.	FGM	FGA	Pct.							
80-81—Scranton CBA	20	827	196	388	.505	2	8	.250	83	107	.775	82	180	481	24.1

NBA REGULAR SEASON RECORD

Sea.—Team	G.	Min.	FGA	FGM	Pct.	FTA	FTM	Pct.	Off.	Def.	Tot.	Ast.	PF	Dq.	Stl.	Blk.	Pts.	Avg.
80-81—New Jersey	15	212	63	22	.349	16	12	.750	7	11	18	32	15	0	13	3	56	3.7
81-82—Atlanta	82	2610	730	366	.501	148	124	.838	53	171	224	424	240	2	87	13	857	10.5
82-83—Atl.-N.Y.	81	2428	810	392	.484	199	147	.739	61	169	230	397	255	4	107	5	936	11.6
83-84—New York	79	2436	738	350	.474	131	108	.824	48	141	189	539	230	4	100	8	818	10.4
84-85—New York	79	2292	662	326	.492	141	122	.865	38	131	169	557	200	2	81	9	781	9.9
Totals	336	9978	3003	1456	.485	635	513	.808	207	623	830	1949	940	12	388	38	3448	10.3

Three-Point Field Goals: 1981-82, 1-for-15 (.067). 1982-83, 5-for-22 (.227). 1983-84, 10-for-39 (.256). 1984-85, 7-for-31 (.226). Totals, 23-for-107 (.215).

NBA PLAYOFF RECORD

Sea.—Team	G.	Min.	FGA	FGM	Pct.	FTA	FTM	Pct.	Off.	Def.	Tot.	Ast.	PF	Dq.	Stl.	Blk.	Pts.	Avg.
81-82—Atlanta	2	69	12	5	.417	4	4	1.000	2	6	8	11	7	0	2	0	14	7.0
82-83—New York	6	202	71	30	.423	21	17	.810	3	10	13	42	18	1	7	0	78	13.0
83-84—New York	12	389	121	54	.446	30	24	.800	10	16	26	86	41	2	12	1	134	11.2
Totals	20	660	204	89	.436	55	45	.818	15	32	47	139	66	3	21	1	226	11.3

Three-Point Field Goals: 1981-82, 0-for-1. 1982-83, 1-for-5 (.200). 1983-84, 2-for-6 (.333). Totals, 3-for-12 (.250).

LARRY MICHAEL SPRIGGS

Born September 8, 1959 at Cheverly, Md.   Height 6:07.   Weight 230.

High School—North Brentwood, Md., Northwestern.

Colleges—San Jacinto College, Pasadena, Tex., and
Howard University, Washington, D. C.

Drafted by Houston on fourth round, 1981 (81st pick).

Waived by Houston, October 28, 1981; re-signed by Houston, March 9, 1982.
Waived by Houston, October 20, 1982; signed by Chicago as a free agent, March 2, 1983.
Signed by Los Angeles as a free agent, August 24, 1983.
Played in Continental Basketball Association with Rochester Zeniths, Las Vegas Silvers and Albany Patroons, 1981-82 and 1982-83.

—COLLEGIATE RECORD—
San Jacinto

Year	G.	Min.	FGA	FGM	Pct.	FTA	FTM	Pct.	Reb.	Pts.	Avg.
77-78				Statistics Unavailable							

Howard University

Year	G.	Min.	FGA	FGM	Pct.	FTA	FTM	Pct.	Reb.	Pts.	Avg.
78-79	28	....	369	178	.482	115	79	.687	272	435	15.5
79-80	26	....	298	163	.547	95	58	.611	180	384	14.8
80-81	27	....	328	177	.540	108	63	.583	270	417	15.4
Totals	81	....	995	518	.521	318	200	.629	722	1236	15.3

MINOR LEAGUE REGULAR SEASON RECORD

Sea.—Team	G.	Min.	2-Point			3-Point			FTM	FTA	Pct.	Reb.	Ast.	Pts.	Avg.
			FGM	FGA	Pct.	FGM	FGA	Pct.							
81-82—Rochester CBA	42	1737	433	779	.555	0	2	.000	198	264	.750	519	133	1064	25.3
82-83—L. V.-Albany CBA	41	1544	376	715	.525	0	3	.000	206	262	.786	338	186	958	23.4

NBA REGULAR SEASON RECORD

Sea.—Team	G.	Min.	FGA	FGM	Pct.	FTA	FTM	Pct.	Off.	Def.	Tot.	Ast.	PF	Dq.	Stl.	Blk.	Pts.	Avg.
81-82—Houston	4	37	11	7	.636	2	0	.000	2	4	6	4	7	0	2	0	14	3.5

Sea.—Team	G.	Min.	FGA	FGM	Pct.	FTA	FTM	Pct.	Off.	Def.	Tot.	Ast.	PF	Dq.	Stl.	Blk.	Pts.	Avg.
82-83—Chicago	9	39	20	8	.400	7	5	.714	2	7	9	3	3	0	1	2	21	2.3
83-84—Los Angeles	38	363	82	44	.537	50	36	.720	16	45	61	30	55	0	12	4	124	3.3
84-85—L.A. Lakers	75	1292	354	194	.548	146	112	.767	77	150	227	132	195	2	47	13	500	6.7
Totals	126	1731	467	253	.542	205	153	.746	97	206	303	169	260	2	62	19	659	5.2

Three-Point Field Goals: 1983-84, 0-for-2. 1984-85, 0-for-3. Totals, 0-for-5.

NBA PLAYOFF RECORD

Sea.—Team	G.	Min.	FGA	FGM	Pct.	FTA	FTM	Pct.	Off.	Def.	Tot.	Ast.	PF	Dq.	Stl.	Blk.	Pts.	Avg.
81-82—Houston	2	9	4	3	.750	1	0	.000	0	1	1	2	3	0	0	0	6	3.0
83-84—Los Angeles	9	45	19	7	.368	11	11	1.000	4	5	9	3	11	0	0	1	25	2.8
84-85—L.A. Lakers	16	230	77	40	.519	29	18	.621	16	35	51	33	36	0	4	5	98	6.1
Totals	27	284	100	50	.500	41	29	.707	20	41	61	38	50	0	4	6	129	4.8

Three-Point Field Goals: 1984-85, 0-for-2.

Member of NBA championship team, 1985. . . . Named to CBA All-Star First Team, 1982. . . . CBA All-Star Second Team, 1983. . . . CBA All-Star Game MVP, 1983. . . . CBA Rookie of the Year, 1982.

TERENCE R. STANSBURY

Born February 27, 1961 at Los Angeles, Calif.   Height 6:05.   Weight 170.

High Schools—Los Angeles, Calif., Washington (Sophomore)
and Newark, Del. (Junior-Senior).

College—Temple University, Philadelphia, Pa.

Drafted by Dallas on first round, 1984 (15th pick).

Traded by Dallas with Bill Garnett to Indiana for a future 1st round draft choice, October 22, 1984.

—COLLEGIATE RECORD—

Year	G.	Min.	FGA	FGM	Pct.	FTA	FTM	Pct.	Reb.	Pts.	Avg.
80-81	28	....	125	67	.536	63	42	.667	42	176	6.3
81-82	27	....	258	133	.516	108	79	.731	102	345	12.8
82-83	29	....	601	248	.413	218	168	.771	109	713	24.6
83-84	31	1216	482	221	.459	169	135	.799	140	577	18.6
Totals	115	....	1466	669	.456	558	424	.760	393	1811	15.7

Three-Point Field Goals: 1982-83, 49-for-123 (.398).

NBA REGULAR SEASON RECORD

Sea.—Team	G.	Min.	FGA	FGM	Pct.	FTA	FTM	Pct.	Off.	Def.	Tot.	Ast.	PF	Dq.	Stl.	Blk.	Pts.	Avg.
84-85—Indiana	74	1278	458	210	.459	126	102	.810	39	75	114	127	205	2	47	12	526	7.1

Three-Point Field Goals: 1984-85, 4-for-25 (.160).

MICHAEL HOLBROOK STEPPE
(Brook)

Born November 7, 1959 at Chapel Hill, N. C.   Height 6:05.   Weight 195.

High School—Atlanta, Ga., North Springs.

Colleges—DeKalb Central Community College, Clarkston, Ga.,
and Georgia Tech, Atlanta, Ga.

Drafted by Kansas City on first round, 1982 (17th pick).

Traded by Kansas City to Indiana for a 1984 2nd round draft choice, September 17, 1983.
Waived by Indiana, October 15, 1984; signed by Detroit as a free agent, November 24, 1984.

—COLLEGIATE RECORD—
DeKalb Central CC

Year	G.	Min.	FGA	FGM	Pct.	FTA	FTM	Pct.	Reb.	Pts.	Avg.
77-78	30	....	425	245	.576	183	148	.809	137	638	22.0

Georgia Tech

Year	G.	Min.	FGA	FGM	Pct.	FTA	FTM	Pct.	Reb.	Pts.	Avg.
78-79	26	346	113	57	.504	67	55	.821	35	169	6.5
79-80	26	904	352	178	.506	168	135	.804	111	491	18.9
80-81			Did Not Play—Academically Ineligible								
81-82	25	....	329	175	.532	129	95	.736	136	445	17.8
Totals	77	....	794	410	.516	364	285	.783	282	1105	14.4

NBA REGULAR SEASON RECORD

Sea.—Team	G.	Min.	FGA	FGM	Pct.	FTA	FTM	Pct.	Off.	Def.	Tot.	Ast.	PF	Dq.	Stl.	Blk.	Pts.	Avg.
										—Rebounds—								
82-83—Kansas City	62	606	176	84	.477	100	76	.760	25	48	73	68	92	0	26	3	245	4.0
83-84—Indiana	61	857	314	148	.471	161	134	.832	43	79	122	79	93	0	34	6	430	7.0
84-85—Detroit	54	486	178	83	.466	104	87	.837	25	32	57	36	61	0	16	4	253	4.7
Totals	177	1949	668	315	.472	365	297	.814	93	159	252	183	246	0	76	13	928	5.2

Three-Point Field Goals: 1982-83, 1-for-7 (.143). 1983-84, 0-for-3. 1984-85, 0-for-1. Totals, 1-for-11 (.091).

NBA PLAYOFF RECORD

Sea.—Team	G.	Min.	FGA	FGM	Pct.	FTA	FTM	Pct.	Off.	Def.	Tot.	Ast.	PF	Dq.	Stl.	Blk.	Pts.	Avg.
										—Rebounds—								
84-85—Detroit	4	20	7	2	.286	6	4	.667	1	2	3	2	3	0	0	0	8	2.0

Three-Point Field Goals: 1984-85, 0-for-1.

STEPHEN SAMUEL STIPANOVICH
(Steve)

Born November 17, 1960 at St. Louis, Mo.   Height 6:11.   Weight 245.

High School—Creve Coeur, Mo., DeSmet.

College—University of Missouri, Columbia, Mo.

Drafted by Indiana on first round, 1983 (2nd pick).

—COLLEGIATE RECORD—

Year	G.	Min.	FGA	FGM	Pct.	FTA	FTM	Pct.	Reb.	Pts.	Avg.
79-80	31	1034	301	180	.598	127	85	.669	199	445	14.4
80-81	32	970	286	143	.500	162	120	.741	237	406	12.7
81-82	31	956	278	140	.504	104	79	.760	248	359	11.6
82-83	34	1264	454	246	.542	187	134	.717	300	626	18.4
Totals	128	4224	1319	709	.538	580	418	.721	984	1836	14.3

NBA REGULAR SEASON RECORD

Sea.—Team	G.	Min.	FGA	FGM	Pct.	FTA	FTM	Pct.	Off.	Def.	Tot.	Ast.	PF	Dq.	Stl.	Blk.	Pts.	Avg.
										—Rebounds—								
83-84—Indiana	81	2426	816	392	.480	243	183	.753	116	446	562	170	303	4	73	67	970	12.0
84-85—Indiana	82	2315	871	414	.475	372	297	.798	141	473	614	199	265	4	71	78	1126	13.7
Totals	163	4741	1687	806	.478	615	480	.780	257	919	1176	369	568	8	144	145	2096	12.9

Three-Point Field Goals: 1983-84, 3-for-16 (.188). 1984-85, 1-for-11 (.091). Totals, 4-for-27 (.148).

Named to NBA All-Rookie Team, 1984. . . . Named to THE SPORTING NEWS All-America Second Team, 1983.

JOHN HOUSTON STOCKTON

Born March 26, 1962 at Spokane, Wash.   Height 6:01.   Weight 170.

High School—Spokane, Wash., Gonzaga Prep.

College—Gonzaga University, Spokane, Wash.

Drafted by Utah on first round, 1984 (16th pick).

—COLLEGIATE RECORD—

Year	G.	Min.	FGA	FGM	Pct.	FTA	FTM	Pct.	Reb.	Pts.	Avg.
80-81	25	235	45	26	.578	35	26	.743	11	78	3.1
81-82	27	1054	203	117	.576	102	69	.676	67	303	11.2
82-83	27	1036	274	142	.518	115	91	.791	87	375	13.9
83-84	28	1053	397	229	.577	182	126	.692	66	584	20.9
Totals	107	3378	919	514	.559	434	312	.719	231	1340	12.5

NBA REGULAR SEASON RECORD

Sea.—Team	G.	Min.	FGA	FGM	Pct.	FTA	FTM	Pct.	Off.	Def.	Tot.	Ast.	PF	Dq.	Stl.	Blk.	Pts.	Avg.
										—Rebounds—								
84-85—Utah	82	1490	333	157	.471	193	142	.736	26	79	105	415	203	3	109	11	458	5.6

Three-Point Field Goals: 1984-85, 2-for-11 (.182).

NBA PLAYOFF RECORD

Sea.—Team	G.	Min.	FGA	FGM	Pct.	FTA	FTM	Pct.	Off.	Def.	Tot.	Ast.	PF	Dq.	Stl.	Blk.	Pts.	Avg.
										—Rebounds—								
84-85—Utah	10	186	45	21	.467	35	26	.743	7	21	28	43	30	0	11	2	68	6.8

Three-Point Field Goals: 1984-85, 0-for-2.

—DID YOU KNOW—

That backup center Mark McNamara was a stand-in for Chewbacca in the movie "Return of the Jedi?"

JOHN STOCKTON

JON THOMAS SUNDVOLD

Born July 2, 1961 at Sioux Falls, S. D.   Height 6:02.   Weight 170.

High School—Blue Springs, Mo.

College—University of Missouri, Columbia, Mo.

Drafted by Seattle on first round, 1983 (16th pick).

—COLLEGIATE RECORD—

Year	G.	Min.	FGA	FGM	Pct.	FTA	FTM	Pct.	Reb.	Pts.	Avg.
79-80	31	790	169	76	.450	59	44	.746	52	196	6.3
80-81	32	1134	350	178	.509	99	85	.859	54	441	13.8
81-82	31	1062	307	149	.485	93	81	.871	66	379	12.2
82-83	34	1303	447	225	.503	151	131	.868	82	581	17.1
Totals	128	4289	1273	628	.493	402	341	.848	254	1597	12.5

NBA REGULAR SEASON RECORD

| | | | | | | | | | —Rebounds— | | | | | | | | |
Sea.—Team	G.	Min.	FGA	FGM	Pct.	FTA	FTM	Pct.	Off.	Def.	Tot.	Ast.	PF	Dq.	Stl.	Blk.	Pts.	Avg.
83-84—Seattle	73	1284	488	217	.445	72	64	.889	23	68	91	239	81	0	29	1	507	6.9
84-85—Seattle	73	1150	400	170	.425	59	48	.814	17	53	70	206	87	0	36	1	400	5.5
Totals	146	2434	888	387	.436	131	112	.855	40	121	161	445	168	0	65	2	907	6.2

Three-Point Field Goals: 1983-84, 9-for-37 (.243). 1984-85, 12-for-38 (.316). Totals, 21-for-75 (.280).

NBA PLAYOFF RECORD

| | | | | | | | | | —Rebounds— | | | | | | | | |
Sea.—Team	G.	Min.	FGA	FGM	Pct.	FTA	FTM	Pct.	Off.	Def.	Tot.	Ast.	PF	Dq.	Stl.	Blk.	Pts.	Avg.
83-84—Seattle	3	22	8	3	.375	2	2	1.000	1	1	2	5	1	0	0	0	8	2.7

Three-Point Field Goals: 1983-84, 0-for-3.

DANE SUTTLE

Born August 9, 1961, at Los Angeles, Calif.   Height 6:03.   Weight 190.

High School—Los Angeles, Calif., Fremont.

College—Pepperdine University, Malibu, Calif.

Drafted by Kansas City on seventh round, 1983 (152nd pick).

Waived by Kansas City, October 24, 1983, resigned by Kansas City as a free agent, October 28, 1983.
Waived by Kansas City, December 6, 1984.

—COLLEGIATE RECORD—

Year	G.	Min.	FGA	FGM	Pct.	FTA	FTM	Pct.	Reb.	Pts.	Avg.
79-80	20	259	91	46	.505	46	36	.783	37	128	6.4
80-81	28	790	330	180	.545	80	63	.788	69	423	15.1
81-82	28	929	351	186	.530	123	100	.813	76	472	16.9
82-83	29	1019	497	266	.535	170	142	.835	62	679	23.4
Totals	105	2997	1269	678	.534	419	341	.814	244	1702	16.2

Three-Point Field Goals: 1982-83, 5.

NBA REGULAR SEASON RECORD

| | | | | | | | | | —Rebounds— | | | | | | | | |
Sea.—Team	G.	Min.	FGA	FGM	Pct.	FTA	FTM	Pct.	Off.	Def.	Tot.	Ast.	PF	Dq.	Stl.	Blk.	Pts.	Avg.
83-84—Kansas City	40	469	214	109	.509	47	40	.851	21	25	46	46	46	0	20	0	258	6.5
84-85—Kansas City	6	24	13	6	.462	2	2	1.000	0	3	3	2	3	0	1	0	14	2.3
Totals	46	493	227	115	.507	49	42	.857	21	28	49	48	49	0	21	0	272	5.9

Three-Point Field Goals: 1983-84, 0-for-3. 1984-85, 0-for-1. Totals, 0-for-4.

TERRY MICHAEL TEAGLE

Born April 10, 1960 at Broaddus, Tex.   Height 6:05.   Weight 195.

High School—Broaddus, Tex.

College—Baylor University, Waco, Tex.

Drafted by Houston on first round, 1982 (16th pick).

Waived by Houston, October 23, 1984; signed by Detroit as a free agent, November 7, 1984.
Waived by Detroit, November 20, 1984; signed by Golden State as a free agent, March 11, 1985.
Played in Continental Basketball Association with Detroit Spirits, 1984-85.

—COLLEGIATE RECORD—

Year	G.	Min.	FGA	FGM	Pct.	FTA	FTM	Pct.	Reb.	Pts.	Avg.
78-79	28	....	310	164	.529	113	80	.708	183	408	14.6
79-80	27	....	440	239	.543	171	142	.830	222	620	23.0

Year	G.	Min.	FGA	FGM	Pct.	FTA	FTM	Pct.	Reb.	Pts.	Avg.
80-81	27	....	399	214	.536	151	111	.735	190	539	20.0
81-82	28	....	479	259	.541	144	104	.722	210	622	22.2
Totals	110	....	1628	876	.538	579	437	.755	805	2189	19.9

NBA REGULAR SEASON RECORD

Sea.—Team	G.	Min.	FGA	FGM	Pct.	FTA	FTM	Pct.	—Rebounds— Off.	Def.	Tot.	Ast.	PF	Dq.	Stl.	Blk.	Pts.	Avg.
82-83—Houston	73	1708	776	332	.428	125	87	.696	74	120	194	150	171	0	53	18	761	10.4
83-84—Houston	68	616	315	148	.470	44	37	.841	28	50	78	63	81	1	13	4	340	5.0
84-85—Det.-G.S.	21	349	137	74	.540	35	25	.714	22	21	43	14	36	0	13	5	175	8.3
Totals	162	2673	1228	554	.451	204	149	.730	124	191	315	227	288	1	79	27	1276	7.9

Three-Point Field Goals: 1982-83, 10-for-29 (.345). 1983-84, 7-for-27 (.259). 1984-85, 2-for-4 (.500). Totals, 19-for-60 (.317).

MINOR LEAGUE REGULAR SEASON RECORD

Sea.—Team	G.	Min.	——2-Point—— FGM	FGA	Pct.	——3-Point—— FGM	FGA	Pct.	FTM	FTA	Pct.	Reb.	Ast.	Pts.	Avg.
84-85—Detroit CBA	40	1146	294	532	.552	2	14	.143	187	222	.842	171	67	781	19.5

REGGIE WAYNE THEUS

Born October 13, 1957 at Inglewood, Calif.   Height 6:06.   Weight 205.

High School—Inglewood, Calif.

College—University of Nevada at Las Vegas, Las Vegas, Nev.

Drafted by Chicago on first round as an undergraduate, 1978 (9th pick).

Traded by Chicago to Kansas City for Steve Johnson, a 1984 2nd round draft choice and two 1985 2nd round draft choices, February 15, 1984.

—COLLEGIATE RECORD—

Year	G.	Min.	FGA	FGM	Pct.	FTA	FTM	Pct.	Reb.	Pts.	Avg.
75-76	31	....	163	68	.417	60	48	.800	53	184	5.9
76-77	32	....	358	178	.497	132	108	.818	145	464	14.5
77-78	28	....	389	181	.465	207	167	.807	191	529	18.9
Totals	91	....	910	427	.469	399	323	.810	389	1177	12.9

NBA REGULAR SEASON RECORD

Sea.—Team	G.	Min.	FGA	FGM	Pct.	FTA	FTM	Pct.	—Rebounds— Off.	Def.	Tot.	Ast.	PF	Dq.	Stl.	Blk.	Pts.	Avg.
78-79—Chicago	82	2753	1119	537	.480	347	264	.761	92	136	228	429	270	2	93	18	1338	16.3
79-80—Chicago	82	3029	1172	566	.483	597	500	.838	143	186	329	515	262	4	114	20	1660	20.2
80-81—Chicago	82	2820	1097	543	.495	550	445	.809	124	163	287	426	258	1	122	20	1549	18.9
81-82—Chicago	82	2838	1194	560	.469	449	363	.808	115	197	312	476	243	1	87	16	1508	18.4
82-83—Chicago	82	2856	1567	749	.478	542	434	.801	91	209	300	484	281	6	143	17	1953	23.8
83-84—Chi.-K.C.	61	1498	625	262	.419	281	214	.762	50	79	129	352	171	3	50	12	745	12.2
84-85—Kansas City	82	2543	1029	501	.487	387	334	.863	106	164	270	656	250	0	95	18	1341	16.4
Totals	553	18337	7803	3718	.476	3153	2554	.810	721	1134	1855	3338	1735	17	704	121	10094	18.3

Three-Point Field Goals: 1979-80, 28-for-105 (.267). 1980-81, 18-for-90 (.200). 1981-82, 25-for-100 (.250). 1982-83, 21-for-91 (.231). 1983-84, 7-for-42 (.167). 1984-85, 5-for-38 (.132). Totals, 104-for-466 (.223).

NBA PLAYOFF RECORD

Sea.—Team	G.	Min.	FGA	FGM	Pct.	FTA	FTM	Pct.	—Rebounds— Off.	Def.	Tot.	Ast.	PF	Dq.	Stl.	Blk.	Pts.	Avg.
80-81—Chicago	6	232	90	40	.444	43	37	.860	7	14	21	38	22	0	9	0	119	19.8
83-84—Kansas City	3	81	43	17	.395	10	9	.900	4	7	11	16	9	0	5	0	43	14.3
Totals	9	313	133	57	.429	53	46	.868	11	21	32	54	31	0	14	0	162	18.0

Three-Point Field Goals: 1980-81, 2-for-9 (.222). 1983-84, 0-for-3. Totals, 2-for-12 (.167).

NBA ALL-STAR GAME RECORD

Season—Team	Min.	FGA	FGM	Pct.	FTA	FTM	Pct.	—Rebounds— Off.	Def.	Tot.	Ast.	PF	Dq.	Stl.	Blk.	Pts.
1981—Chicago	19	7	4	.571	0	0	.000	0	1	1	3	0	0	2	0	8
1983—Chicago	8	5	0	.000	0	0	.000	1	0	1	1	1	0	0	0	0
Totals	27	12	4	.333	0	0	.000	1	1	2	4	1	0	2	0	8

Named to NBA All-Rookie Team, 1979.

PETER THIBEAUX

Born October 3, 1961 at Los Angeles, Calif.   Height 6:07.   Weight 210.

High School—Oakland, Calif., Skyline.

College—St. Mary's College, Moraga, Calif.

Drafted by Golden State on fourth round, 1983 (77th pick).

Waived by Golden State, October 25, 1983; re-signed by Golden State, May 9, 1984.
Played in Continental Basketball Association with Toronto, Tornados, 1983-84.

—COLLEGIATE RECORD—

Year	G.	Min.	FGA	FGM	Pct.	FTA	FTM	Pct.	Reb.	Pts.	Avg.
79-80	27	....	171	82	.480	50	35	.700	93	199	7.4
80-81	27	....	245	133	.543	77	55	.714	173	321	11.9
81-82	27	....	336	194	.577	117	86	.735	193	474	17.6
82-83	25	....	315	192	.610	152	112	.737	191	496	19.8
Totals	106	....	1067	601	.563	396	288	.727	650	1490	14.1

MINOR LEAGUE REGULAR SEASON RECORD

			—2-Point—			—3-Point—								
Sea.—Team	G.	Min.	FGM	FGA	Pct.	FGM	FGA	Pct.	FTM	FTA	Pct.	Reb.	Ast.	Pts.	Avg.
83-84—Toronto CBA	44	1236	220	407	.540	0	1	.000	80	109	.733	245	48	520	11.8

NBA REGULAR SEASON RECORD

									—Rebounds—								
Sea.—Team	G.	Min.	FGA	FGM	Pct.	FTA	FTM	Pct.	Off.	Def.	Tot.	Ast.	PF	Dq.	Stl.	Blk.	Pts.	Avg.
84-85—Golden State	51	461	195	94	.482	67	43	.642	29	40	69	17	85	1	11	17	231	4.5

Three-Point Field Goals: 1984-85, 0-for-2.

DAVID THIRDKILL

Born April 12, 1960 at St. Louis, Mo.   Height 6:07.   Weight 215.

High School—St. Louis, Mo., Soldan.

Colleges—College of Southern Idaho, Twin Falls, Idaho, and
Bradley University, Peoria, Ill.

Drafted by Phoenix on first round, 1982 (15th pick).

Traded by Phoenix to Detroit for 1986 and 1987 2nd round draft choices, October 17, 1983.
Waived by Detroit, November 29, 1984; signed by Milwaukee, February 12, 1985, to the first of consecutive contracts that expired, March 6, 1985.
Signed by San Antonio as a free agent, April 9, 1985.
Waived by San Antonio, July 16, 1985.

—COLLEGIATE RECORD—
Southern Idaho

Year	G.	Min.	FGA	FGM	Pct.	FTA	FTM	Pct.	Reb.	Pts.	Avg.
78-79	31	....	638	278	.436	209	152	.727	206	708	22.8

Bradley

Year	G.	Min.	FGA	FGM	Pct.	FTA	FTM	Pct.	Reb.	Pts.	Avg.
79-80	33	1112	427	181	.424	123	78	.634	165	440	13.3
80-81	26	....	255	143	.561	111	71	.640	121	357	13.7
81-82	35	....	296	164	.554	193	136	.705	242	464	13.3
Totals	94	....	978	488	.499	427	285	.667	528	1261	13.4

NBA REGULAR SEASON RECORD

									—Rebounds—								
Sea.—Team	G.	Min.	FGA	FGM	Pct.	FTA	FTM	Pct.	Off.	Def.	Tot.	Ast.	PF	Dq.	Stl.	Blk.	Pts.	Avg.
82-83—Phoenix	49	521	170	74	.435	78	45	.577	28	44	72	36	93	1	19	4	194	4.0
83-84—Detroit	46	291	72	31	.431	31	15	.484	9	22	31	27	44	0	10	3	77	1.7
84-85—Dt.-Ml-SA	18	183	38	20	.526	19	11	.579	10	7	17	4	22	0	5	3	51	2.8
Totals	113	995	280	125	.446	128	71	.555	47	73	120	67	159	1	34	10	322	2.8

Three-Point Field Goals: 1982-83, 1-for-7 (.143). 1983-84, 0-for-1. 1984-85, 0-for-1. Totals, 1-for-9 (.111).

NBA PLAYOFF RECORD

									—Rebounds—								
Sea.—Team	G.	Min.	FGA	FGM	Pct.	FTA	FTM	Pct.	Off.	Def.	Tot.	Ast.	PF	Dq.	Stl.	Blk.	Pts.	Avg.
84-85—San Antonio	5	22	4	1	.250	4	2	.500	0	2	2	2	4	0	0	0	4	0.8

Three-Point Field Goals: 1984-85, 0-for-2.

ISIAH LORD THOMAS III

Born April 30, 1961 at Chicago, Ill.   Height 6:01.   Weight 185.

High School—Westchester, Ill., St. Joseph's.

College—Indiana University, Bloomington, Ind.

Drafted by Detroit on first round as an undergraduate, 1981 (2nd pick).

Year	G.	Min.	FGA	FGM	Pct.	FTA	FTM	Pct.	Reb.	Pts.	Avg.
79-80	29	....	302	154	.510	149	115	.772	116	423	14.6
80-81	34	....	383	212	.554	163	121	.742	105	545	16.0
Totals	63	....	685	366	.534	312	236	.756	221	968	15.4

NBA REGULAR SEASON RECORD

Sea.—Team	G.	Min.	FGA	FGM	Pct.	FTA	FTM	Pct.	Off.	Def.	Tot.	Ast.	PF	Dq.	Stl.	Blk.	Pts.	Avg.
81-82—Detroit	72	2433	1068	453	.424	429	302	.704	57	152	209	565	253	2	150	17	1225	17.0
82-83—Detroit	81	3093	1537	725	.472	518	368	.710	105	223	328	634	318	8	199	29	1854	22.9
83-84—Detroit	82	3007	1448	669	.462	529	388	.733	103	224	327	914	324	8	204	33	1748	21.3
84-85—Detroit	81	3089	1410	646	.458	493	399	.809	114	247	361	1123	288	8	187	25	1720	21.2
Totals	316	11622	5463	2493	.456	1969	1457	.740	379	846	1225	3236	1183	26	740	104	6547	20.7

Three-Point Field Goals: 1981-82, 17-for-59 (.288). 1982-83, 36-for-125 (.288). 1983-84, 22-for-65 (.338). 1984-85, 29-for-113 (.257). Totals, 104-for-362 (.287).

NBA PLAYOFF RECORD

Sea.—Team	G.	Min.	FGA	FGM	Pct.	FTA	FTM	Pct.	Off.	Def.	Tot.	Ast.	PF	Dq.	Stl.	Blk.	Pts.	Avg.
83-84—Detroit	5	198	83	39	.470	35	27	.771	7	12	19	55	22	1	13	6	107	21.4
84-85—Detroit	9	355	166	83	.500	62	47	.758	11	36	47	101	39	2	19	4	219	24.3
Totals	14	553	249	122	.490	97	74	.763	18	48	66	156	61	3	32	10	326	23.3

Three-Point Field Goals: 1983-84, 2-for-6 (.333). 1984-85, 6-for-15 (.400). Totals, 8-for-21 (.381).

NBA ALL-STAR GAME RECORD

Season—Team	Min.	FGA	FGM	Pct.	FTA	FTM	Pct.	Off.	Def.	Tot.	Ast.	PF	Dq.	Stl.	Blk.	Pts.
1982—Detroit	17	7	5	.714	4	2	.500	1	0	1	4	1	0	3	0	12
1983—Detroit	29	14	9	.643	1	1	1.000	3	1	4	7	0	0	4	0	19
1984—Detroit	39	17	9	.529	3	3	1.000	3	2	5	15	4	0	4	0	21
1985—Detroit	25	14	9	.643	1	1	1.000	1	1	2	5	2	0	2	0	22
Totals	110	52	32	.615	9	7	.778	8	4	12	31	7	0	13	0	74

Three-Point Field Goals: 1984, 0-for-2. 1985, 3-for-4 (.750). Totals, 3-for-6 (.500).

Named to All-NBA First Team, 1984 and 1985. . . . All-NBA Second Team, 1983. . . . NBA All-Rookie Team, 1982. . . . NBA All-Star Game MVP, 1984. . . . Holds NBA record for most assists in one season, 1985. . . . Named to THE SPORTING NEWS All-America First Team, 1981. . . . NCAA Division I Tournament Most Outstanding Player, 1981. . . . Member of NCAA championship team, 1981. . . . Member of U.S. Olympic team, 1980.

JAMES EDWARD THOMAS
(Jim)

Born October 19, 1960 at Lakeland, Fla.   Height 6:03.   Weight 190.

High School—Ft. Lauderdale, Fla., Nova.

College—Indiana University, Bloomington, Ind.

Drafted by Indiana on second round, 1983 (40th pick).

—COLLEGIATE RECORD—

Year	G.	Min.	FGA	FGM	Pct.	FTA	FTM	Pct.	Reb.	Pts.	Avg.
79-80	21	....	44	20	.455	26	16	.615	34	56	2.7
80-81	33	....	95	47	.495	35	27	.771	105	121	3.7
81-82	29	....	200	104	.520	69	59	.855	181	267	9.2
82-83	30	....	235	123	.523	81	61	.753	159	307	10.2
Totals	113	....	574	294	.512	211	163	.773	479	751	6.6

NBA REGULAR SEASON RECORD

Sea.—Team	G.	Min.	FGA	FGM	Pct.	FTA	FTM	Pct.	Off.	Def.	Tot.	Ast.	PF	Dq.	Stl.	Blk.	Pts.	Avg.
83-84—Indiana	72	1219	403	187	.464	110	80	.727	59	90	149	130	115	1	60	6	455	6.3
84-85—Indiana	80	2059	726	347	.478	234	183	.782	74	187	261	234	195	2	76	5	885	11.1
Totals	152	3278	1129	534	.473	344	263	.765	133	277	410	364	310	3	136	11	1340	8.8

Three-Point Field Goals: 1983-84, 1-for-11 (.091). 1984-85, 8-for-42 (.190). Totals, 9-for-53 (.170).

Member of NCAA championship team, 1981. . . . Drafted by Green Bay Packers in 10th round of 1983 National Football League draft. . . . Drafted by Boston Breakers in 20th round of 1983 United States Football League draft.

BERNARD THOMPSON

Born August 30, 1962 at Phoenix, Ariz.   Height 6:06.   Weight 215.

High School—Phoenix, Ariz., South Mountain.

College—Fresno State University, Fresno, Calif.

Drafted by Portland on first round, 1984 (19th pick).

Traded by Portland to Phoenix for a 1987 2nd round draft choice, June 14, 1985.

—COLLEGIATE RECORD—

Year	G.	Min.	FGA	FGM	Pct.	FTA	FTM	Pct.	Reb.	Pts.	Avg.
80-81	23	259	53	28	.528	48	34	.708	45	90	3.9
81-82	30	837	177	103	.582	92	71	.772	115	277	9.2
82-83	35	1211	363	214	.590	187	138	.738	207	566	16.2
83-84	33	1151	338	192	.568	174	135	.776	193	519	15.7
Totals	121	3458	931	537	.577	501	378	.754	560	1452	12.0

NBA REGULAR SEASON RECORD

Sea.—Team	G.	Min.	FGA	FGM	Pct.	FTA	FTM	Pct.	—Rebounds— Off.	Def.	Tot.	Ast.	PF	Dq.	Stl.	Blk.	Pts.	Avg.
84-85—Portland	59	535	212	79	.373	51	39	.765	37	39	76	52	79	0	31	10	197	3.3

Three-Point Field Goals: 1984-85, 0-for-8.

NBA PLAYOFF RECORD

Sea.—Team	G.	Min.	FGA	FGM	Pct.	FTA	FTM	Pct.	—Rebounds— Off.	Def.	Tot.	Ast.	PF	Dq.	Stl.	Blk.	Pts.	Avg.
84-85—Portland	2	10	5	0	.000	2	2	1.000	1	2	3	2	1	0	0	1	2	1.0

DAVID O'NEIL THOMPSON

Born July 13, 1954 at Shelby, N. C.   Height 6:04.   Weight 195.

High School—Shelby, N. C., Crest.

College—North Carolina State University, Raleigh, N. C.

Drafted by Atlanta on first round, 1975 (1st pick).

Selected by Virginia on first round of ABA draft, 1975.
ABA draft rights traded by Virginia with George Irvine to Denver for Mack Calvin, Mike Green and Jan van Breda Kolff, July 14, 1975.
Entered NBA with Denver, 1976.
Traded by Denver to Seattle for rights to free agent Wally Walker and a 1982 1st round draft choice, June 16, 1982. Seattle traded Bill Hanzlik to Denver when Walker's rights were ruled non-transferable by an arbitrator, July 20, 1982.
Did not play during 1984-85 season.

—COLLEGIATE RECORD—

Year	G.	Min.	FGA	FGM	Pct.	FTA	FTM	Pct.	Reb.	Pts.	Avg.
71-72†	16	....	386	214	.554	179	141	.788	217	569	35.6
72-73	27	....	469	267	.569	160	132	.825	220	666	24.7
73-74	31	....	594	325	.547	208	155	.745	245	805	26.0
74-75	28	....	635	347	.546	197	144	.731	229	838	29.9
Varsity Totals	86	....	1698	939	.553	565	431	.763	694	2309	26.8

ABA REGULAR SEASON RECORD

Sea.—Team	G.	Min.	2-Point FGM	FGA	Pct.	3-Point FGM	FGA	Pct.	FTM	FTA	Pct.	Reb.	Ast.	Pts.	Avg.
75-76—Denver	83	3101	804	1548	.519	3	19	.158	541	681	.794	525	308	2158	26.0

ABA PLAYOFF RECORD

Sea.—Team	G.	Min.	2-Point FGM	FGA	Pct.	3-Point FGM	FGA	Pct.	FTM	FTA	Pct.	Reb.	Ast.	Pts.	Avg.
75-76—Denver	13	508	126	233	.541	1	4	.250	88	105	.838	83	39	343	26.4

ABA ALL-STAR GAME RECORD

Sea.—Team	Min.	2-Point FGM	FGA	Pct.	3-Point FGM	FGA	Pct.	FTM	FTA	Pct.	Reb.	Ast.	Pts.	Avg.
1976—Denver	34	9	18	.500	0	0	.000	11	13	.846	8	2	29	29.0

NBA REGULAR SEASON RECORD

Sea.—Team	G.	Min.	FGA	FGM	Pct.	FTA	FTM	Pct.	—Rebounds— Off.	Def.	Tot.	Ast.	PF	Dq.	Stl.	Blk.	Pts.	Avg.
76-77—Denver	82	3001	1626	824	.507	623	477	.766	138	196	334	337	236	1	114	53	2125	25.9
77-78—Denver	80	3025	1584	826	.521	668	520	.778	156	234	390	362	213	1	92	99	2172	27.2
78-79—Denver	76	2670	1353	693	.512	583	439	.753	109	165	274	225	180	2	70	82	1825	24.0
79-80—Denver	39	1239	617	289	.468	335	254	.758	56	118	174	124	106	0	39	38	839	21.5
80-81—Denver	77	2620	1451	734	.506	615	489	.795	107	180	287	231	231	3	53	60	1967	25.5
81-82—Denver	61	1246	644	313	.486	339	276	.814	57	91	148	117	149	1	34	29	906	14.9
82-83—Seattle	75	2155	925	445	.481	380	298	.784	96	174	270	222	142	0	47	33	1190	15.9
83-84—Seattle	19	349	165	89	.539	73	62	.849	18	26	44	13	30	0	10	13	240	12.6
Totals	509	16305	8365	4213	.504	3616	2815	.778	737	1184	1921	1631	1287	8	459	407	11264	22.1

Three-Point Field Goals: 1979-80, 7-for-19 (.368). 1980-81, 10-for-39 (.256). 1981-82, 4-for-14 (.286). 1982-83, 2-for-10 (.200). 1983-84, 0-for-1. Totals, 23-for-83 (.277).

NBA PLAYOFF RECORD

Sea.—Team	G.	Min.	FGA	FGM	Pct.	FTA	FTM	Pct.	Off.	Def.	Tot.	Ast.	PF	Dq.	Stl.	Blk.	Pts.	Avg.
76-77—Denver	6	237	121	56	.463	53	36	.679	13	18	31	24	22	1	9	4	148	24.7
77-78—Denver	13	481	291	131	.450	80	66	.825	18	35	53	52	34	0	9	21	328	25.2
78-79—Denver	3	122	69	38	.551	11	8	.727	7	14	21	12	12	0	4	1	84	28.0
81-82—Denver	3	66	33	15	.455	7	4	.571	4	6	10	6	8	0	1	0	35	11.7
82-83—Seattle	2	65	25	9	.360	10	6	.600	0	0	0	7	7	0	1	1	24	12.0
Totals	27	971	539	249	.462	161	120	.745	42	73	115	101	83	1	24	27	619	22.9

Three-Point Field Goals: 1981-82, 1-for-3 (.333).

NBA ALL-STAR GAME RECORD

Season—Team	Min.	FGA	FGM	Pct.	FTA	FTM	Pct.	Off.	Def.	Tot.	Ast.	PF	Dq.	Stl.	Blk.	Pts.
1977—Denver	29	9	7	.778	6	4	.667	0	7	7	3	3	0	3	0	18
1978—Denver	35	16	10	.625	4	2	.500	0	3	3	3	4	0	1	0	22
1979—Denver	34	17	11	.647	7	3	.429	3	2	5	2	4	0	1	1	25
1983—Seattle	17	7	5	.714	0	0	.000	0	1	1	2	2	0	1	0	10
Totals	115	49	33	.673	17	9	.529	3	13	16	10	13	0	6	1	75

Named to All-NBA First Team, 1977 and 1978. . . . Holds NBA record for most field goals made in one quarter, 13, vs. Detroit, April 9, 1978. . . . NBA All-Star Game MVP, 1979. . . . Named to ABA All-Star Second Team, 1976. . . . ABA Rookie of the Year, 1976. . . . ABA All-Rookie Team, 1976. . . . ABA All-Star Game MVP, 1976. . . . Named THE SPORTING NEWS College Player of the Year, 1975. . . . THE SPORTING NEWS All-America First Team, 1973, 1974, 1975. . . . NCAA Tournament Most Outstanding Player, 1974. . . . Member of NCAA championship team, 1974.

LaSALLE THOMPSON III

Born June 23, 1961 at Cincinnati, O.   Height 6:10.   Weight 248.

High School—Cincinnati, O., Withrow.

College—University of Texas, Austin, Tex.

Drafted by Kansas City on first round as an undergraduate, 1982 (5th pick).

—COLLEGIATE RECORD—

Year	G.	Min.	FGA	FGM	Pct.	FTA	FTM	Pct.	Reb.	Pts.	Avg.
79-80	30	971	274	153	.558	103	77	.748	292	383	12.8
80-81	30	1106	411	235	.572	147	107	.728	370	577	19.2
81-82	27	1042	371	196	.528	164	111	.677	365	503	18.6
Totals	87	3119	1056	584	.553	414	295	.713	1027	1463	16.8

NBA REGULAR SEASON RECORD

Sea.—Team	G.	Min.	FGA	FGM	Pct.	FTA	FTM	Pct.	Off.	Def.	Tot.	Ast.	PF	Dq.	Stl.	Blk.	Pts.	Avg.
82-83—Kansas City	71	987	287	147	.512	137	89	.650	133	242	375	33	186	1	40	61	383	5.4
83-84—Kansas City	80	1915	637	333	.523	223	160	.717	260	449	709	86	327	8	71	145	826	10.3
84-85—Kansas City	82	2458	695	369	.531	315	227	.721	274	580	854	130	328	4	98	128	965	11.8
Totals	233	5360	1619	849	.524	675	476	.705	667	1271	1938	249	841	13	209	334	2174	9.3

Three-Point Field Goals: 1982-83, 0-for-1.

NBA PLAYOFF RECORD

Sea.—Team	G.	Min.	FGA	FGM	Pct.	FTA	FTM	Pct.	Off.	Def.	Tot.	Ast.	PF	Dq.	Stl.	Blk.	Pts.	Avg.
83-84—Kansas City	3	93	40	18	.450	11	9	.818	11	19	30	4	14	0	3	4	45	15.0

Led NCAA Division I in rebounding, 1982.

MYCHAL GEORGE THOMPSON

Born January 30, 1955 at Nassau, Bahamas.   Height 6:10.   Weight 226.

High School—Miami, Fla., Jackson.

College—University of Minnesota, Minneapolis, Minn.

Drafted by Portland on first round, 1978 (1st pick).

—COLLEGIATE RECORD—

Year	G.	Min.	FGA	FGM	Pct.	FTA	FTM	Pct.	Reb.	Pts.	Avg.
74-75	23	....	215	114	.530	78	59	.756	176	287	12.5
75-76	25	....	461	264	.573	171	119	.696	312	647	25.9
76-77	27	....	414	251	.606	132	93	.705	240	595	22.0
77-78	21	....	362	194	.536	119	75	.630	228	463	22.0
Totals	96	....	1452	823	.567	500	346	.692	956	1992	20.8

NBA REGULAR SEASON RECORD

Sea.—Team	G.	Min.	FGA	FGM	Pct.	FTA	FTM	Pct.	Off.	Def.	Tot.	Ast.	PF	Dq.	Stl.	Blk.	Pts.	Avg.
									—Rebounds—									
78-79—Portland	73	2144	938	460	.490	269	154	.572	198	406	604	176	270	10	67	134	1074	14.7
79-80—Portland						Missed Entire Season—Fractured Leg												
80-81—Portland	79	2790	1151	569	.494	323	207	.641	223	463	686	284	260	5	62	170	1345	17.0
81-82—Portland	79	3129	1303	681	.523	446	280	.628	258	663	921	319	233	2	69	107	1642	20.8
82-83—Portland	80	3017	1033	505	.489	401	249	.621	183	570	753	380	213	1	68	110	1259	15.7
83-84—Portland	79	2648	929	487	.524	399	266	.667	235	453	688	308	237	2	84	108	1240	15.7
84-85—Portland	79	2616	1111	572	.515	449	307	.684	211	407	618	205	216	0	78	104	1451	18.4
Totals	469	16344	6465	3274	.506	2287	1463	.640	1308	2962	4270	1672	1429	20	428	733	8011	17.1

Three-Point Field Goals: 1980-81, 0-for-1. 1982-83, 0-for-1. 1983-84, 0-for-2. Totals, 0-for-4.

NBA PLAYOFF RECORD

Sea.—Team	G.	Min.	FGA	FGM	Pct.	FTA	FTM	Pct.	Off.	Def.	Tot.	Ast.	PF	Dq.	Stl.	Blk.	Pts.	Avg.
									—Rebounds—									
78-79—Portland	3	121	54	27	.500	10	5	.500	9	22	31	6	11	0	2	5	59	19.7
80-81—Portland	3	132	51	31	.608	18	13	.722	5	18	23	4	10	0	3	9	75	25.0
82-83—Portland	7	284	85	40	.471	38	25	.658	16	40	56	39	24	0	6	8	105	15.0
83-84—Portland	4	121	44	22	.500	22	17	.773	9	20	29	15	11	0	5	3	61	15.3
84-85—Portland	9	250	102	50	.490	49	33	.673	25	47	72	14	32	2	7	12	133	14.8
Totals	26	908	336	170	.506	137	93	.679	64	147	211	78	88	2	23	37	433	16.7

Named to NBA All-Rookie Team, 1979. . . . THE SPORTING NEWS All-America First Team, 1978. . . . THE SPORTING NEWS All-America Second Team, 1977.

PAUL STANFORD THOMPSON

Born May 25, 1961, at Smyrna, Tenn.   Height 6:06.   Weight 210.

High School—Alexandria, La., Peabody.

College—Tulane University, New Orleans, La.

Drafted by Cleveland on third round, 1983 (50th pick).

Traded by Cleveland to Milwaukee for 1985 and 1987 2nd round draft choices, February 12, 1985.

—COLLEGIATE RECORD—

Year	G.	Min.	FGA	FGM	Pct.	FTA	FTM	Pct.	Reb.	Pts.	Avg.
79-80	26	811	355	164	.462	90	63	.700	212	391	15.0
80-81	27	965	445	199	.447	133	107	.805	255	505	18.7
81-82	28	951	349	172	.493	87	68	.782	206	412	14.7
82-83	31	1129	431	219	.508	132	105	.795	230	543	17.5
Totals	112	3856	1580	754	.477	442	343	.776	903	1851	16.5

NBA REGULAR SEASON RECORD

Sea.—Team	G.	Min.	FGA	FGM	Pct.	FTA	FTM	Pct.	Off.	Def.	Tot.	Ast.	PF	Dq.	Stl.	Blk.	Pts.	Avg.
									—Rebounds—									
83-84—Cleveland	82	1731	662	309	.467	149	115	.772	120	192	312	122	192	2	70	37	742	9.0
84-85—Clev.-Mil.	49	942	459	189	.412	87	69	.793	57	101	158	78	119	1	56	25	453	9.2
Totals	131	2673	1121	498	.444	236	184	.780	177	293	470	200	311	3	126	62	1195	9.1

Three-Point Field Goals: 1983-84, 9-for-39 (.231). 1984-85, 6-for-30 (.200). Totals, 15-for-69 (.217).

NBA PLAYOFF RECORD

Sea.—Team	G.	Min.	FGA	FGM	Pct.	FTA	FTM	Pct.	Off.	Def.	Tot.	Ast.	PF	Dq.	Stl.	Blk.	Pts.	Avg.
									—Rebounds—									
84-85—Milwaukee	3	34	12	5	.417	5	3	.600	1	4	5	2	3	0	4	1	13	4.3

Three-Point Field Goals: 1984-85, 0-for-2.

OTIS THORPE

Born August 5, 1962 at Boynton Beach, Fla.   Height 6:09.   Weight 225.

High School—Lake Worth, Fla.

College—Providence College, Providence, R.I.

Drafted by Kansas City on first round, 1984 (9th pick).

—COLLEGIATE RECORD—

Year	G.	Min.	FGA	FGM	Pct.	FTA	FTM	Pct.	Reb.	Pts.	Avg.
80-81	26	668	194	100	.515	76	50	.658	137	250	9.6
81-82	27	942	283	153	.541	115	74	.643	216	380	14.1
82-83	31	1041	321	204	.636	138	91	.659	249	499	16.1
83-84	29	1051	288	167	.580	248	162	.653	300	496	17.1
Totals	113	3702	1086	624	.575	577	377	.653	902	1625	14.4

MYCHAL THOMPSON

NBA REGULAR SEASON RECORD

									—Rebounds—								
Sea.—Team	G.	Min.	FGA	FGM	Pct.	FTA	FTM	Pct.	Off.	Def.	Tot.	Ast.	PF	Dq.	Stl.	Blk.	Pts.	Avg.
84-85—Kansas City	82	1918	685	411	.600	371	230	620	187	369	556	111	256	2	34	37	1052	12.8

Three-Point Field Goals: 1984-85, 0-for-2.

SEDALE THREATT

Born September 10, 1961, at Atlanta, Ga. Height 6:02. Weight 175.

High School—Atlanta, Ga., Therrell.

College—West Virginia Institute of Technology, Montgomery, W. Va.

Drafted by Philadelphia on sixth round, 1983 (139th pick).

—COLLEGIATE RECORD—

Year	G.	Min.	FGA	FGM	Pct.	FTA	FTM	Pct.	Reb.	Pts.	Avg.
79-80	28	....	424	204	.481	126	90	.714	97	498	17.8
80-81	31	....	524	237	.452	104	74	.712	122	548	17.7
81-82	34	....	598	299	.500	214	156	.729	118	754	22.2
82-83	27	951	510	284	.557	164	120	.732	104	688	25.5
Totals	120	....	2056	1024	.498	608	440	.724	441	2488	20.7

NBA REGULAR SEASON RECORD

									—Rebounds—								
Sea.—Team	G.	Min.	FGA	FGM	Pct.	FTA	FTM	Pct.	Off.	Def.	Tot.	Ast.	PF	Dq.	Stl.	Blk.	Pts.	Avg.
83-84—Philadelphia	45	464	148	62	.419	28	23	.821	17	23	40	41	65	1	13	2	148	3.3
84-85—Philadelphia	82	1304	416	188	.452	90	66	.733	21	78	99	175	171	2	80	16	446	5.4
Totals	127	1768	564	250	.443	118	89	.754	38	101	139	216	236	3	93	18	594	4.7

Three-Point Field Goals: 1983-84, 1-for-8 (.125). 1984-85, 4-for-22 (.182). Totals, 5-for-30 (.167).

NBA PLAYOFF RECORD

									—Rebounds—								
Sea.—Team	G.	Min.	FGA	FGM	Pct.	FTA	FTM	Pct.	Off.	Def.	Tot.	Ast.	PF	Dq.	Stl.	Blk.	Pts.	Avg.
83-84—Philadelphia	3	6	3	1	.333	0	0	.000	1	1	2	1	0	0	1	0	2	0.7
84-85—Philadelphia	4	28	7	2	.286	0	0	.000	1	0	1	5	2	0	1	0	4	1.0
Totals	7	34	10	3	.300	0	0	.000	2	1	3	6	2	0	2	0	6	0.9

Three-Point Field Goals: 1983-84, 0-for-2.

ANDREW TONEY

Born November 23, 1957 at Birmingham, Ala. Height 6:03. Weight 188.

High School—Birmingham, Ala., Glenn.

College—University of Southwestern Louisiana, Lafayette, La.

Drafted by Philadelphia on first round, 1980 (8th pick).

—COLLEGIATE RECORD—

Year	G.	Min.	FGA	FGM	Pct.	FTA	FTM	Pct.	Reb.	Pts.	Avg.
76-77	29	933	489	253	.517	133	102	.767	89	608	21.0
77-78	27	885	468	262	.560	179	137	.765	71	661	24.5
78-79	27	900	500	242	.484	193	146	.756	90	630	23.3
79-80	24	809	425	239	.562	185	149	.805	90	627	26.1
Totals	107	3527	1882	996	.529	690	534	.774	340	2526	23.6

NBA REGULAR SEASON RECORD

									—Rebounds—								
Sea.—Team	G.	Min.	FGA	FGM	Pct.	FTA	FTM	Pct.	Off.	Def.	Tot.	Ast.	PF	Dq.	Stl.	Blk.	Pts.	Avg.
80-81—Philadelphia	75	1768	806	399	.495	226	161	.712	32	111	143	273	234	5	59	10	968	12.9
81-82—Philadelphia	77	1909	979	511	.522	306	227	.742	43	91	134	283	269	5	64	17	1274	16.5
82-83—Philadelphia	81	2474	1250	626	.501	411	324	.788	42	183	225	365	255	0	80	17	1588	20.4
83-84—Philadelphia	78	2556	1125	593	.527	465	390	.839	57	136	193	373	251	1	70	23	1588	20.4
84-85—Philadelphia	70	2237	914	450	.492	355	306	.862	35	142	177	363	211	1	65	24	1245	17.8
Totals	381	10944	5074	2579	.508	1763	1408	.799	209	663	872	1657	1220	12	338	91	6673	17.5

Three-Point Field Goals: 1980-81, 9-for-29 (.310). 1981-82, 25-for-59 (.424). 1982-83, 22-for-76 (.289). 1983-84, 12-for-38 (.316). 1984-85, 39-for-105 (.371). Totals, 107-for-307 (.349).

NBA PLAYOFF RECORD

									—Rebounds—								
Sea.—Team	G.	Min.	FGA	FGM	Pct.	FTA	FTM	Pct.	Off.	Def.	Tot.	Ast.	PF	Dq.	Stl.	Blk.	Pts.	Avg.
80-81—Philadelphia	16	356	180	77	.428	81	66	.815	10	27	37	54	50	0	11	7	221	13.8
81-82—Philadelphia	21	707	365	185	.507	103	82	.796	20	31	51	102	86	1	18	2	457	21.8
82-83—Philadelphia	12	357	185	87	.470	69	52	.754	11	17	28	55	43	1	11	1	226	18.8
83-84—Philadelphia	5	180	77	40	.519	30	23	.767	5	6	11	19	24	0	4	1	103	20.6
84-85—Philadelphia	13	442	174	83	.477	61	47	.770	8	24	32	66	46	0	12	5	219	16.8
Totals	67	2042	981	472	.481	344	270	.785	54	105	159	296	249	2	56	16	1226	18.3

ANDREW TONEY

Three-Point Field Goals: 1980-81, 1-for-9 (.111). 1981-82, 5-for-15 (.333). 1982-83, 0-for-5. 1983-84, 0-for-5. 1984-85, 6-for-14 (.429). Totals, 12-for-48 (.250).

NBA ALL-STAR GAME RECORD

Season—Team	Min.	FGA	FGM	Pct.	FTA	FTM	Pct.	Off.	Def.	Tot.	Ast.	PF	Dq.	Stl.	Blk.	Pts.
								—Rebounds—								
1983—Philadelphia	18	5	4	.800	0	0	.000	0	1	1	7	3	0	2	0	8
1984—Philadelphia	22	11	6	.545	1	1	1.000	0	0	0	3	0	0	2	0	13
Totals	40	16	10	.625	1	1	1.000	0	1	1	10	3	0	4	0	21

Three-Point Field Goals: 1983, 0-for-1.

Member of NBA championship team, 1983.

LINTON RODNEY TOWNES

Born November 30, 1959 at Richmond, Va.   Height 6:07.   Weight 195.

High School—Covington, Va.

College—James Madison University, Harrisonburg, Va.

Drafted by Portland on second round, 1982 (33rd pick).

Traded by Portland to Cleveland for a 1987 2nd round draft choice, September 6, 1983.
Waived by Cleveland, October 25, 1983; signed by Milwaukee as a free agent, November 8, 1983.
Waived by Milwaukee, November 16, 1983; signed by San Diego, December 23, 1983, to first of consecutive 10-day contracts that expired January 11, 1984.
Signed by Los Angeles Clippers, September 13, 1984.
Waived by Los Angeles Clippers, October 24, 1984; signed by San Antonio as a free agent, April 12, 1985.
Waived by San Antonio, July 16, 1985.
Played in Continental Basketball Association with Lancaster Lightning, 1983-84, and Tampa Bay Thrillers, 1984-85.

—COLLEGIATE RECORD—

Year	G.	Min.	FGA	FGM	Pct.	FTA	FTM	Pct.	Reb.	Pts.	Avg.
78-79	26	765	245	138	.563	35	26	.743	109	302	11.6
79-80	10	322	120	67	.558	18	12	.667	52	146	14.6
80-81	29	944	351	196	.558	71	51	.718	168	443	15.3
81-82	30	1065	386	213	.552	79	63	.797	178	489	16.3
Totals	95	3096	1102	614	.557	203	152	.749	507	1380	14.5

MINOR LEAGUE REGULAR SEASON RECORD

Sea.—Team	G.	Min.	2-Point FGM	FGA	Pct.	3-Point FGM	FGA	Pct.	FTM	FTA	Pct.	Reb.	Ast.	Pts.	Avg.
83-84—Lancaster CBA..........	31	876	192	373	.514	9	21	.428	72	83	.867	138	55	483	15.6
84-85—Tampa Bay CBA	46	1894	403	784	.514	37	84	.440	193	227	.850	299	107	1110	24.1

NBA REGULAR SEASON RECORD

Sea.—Team	G.	Min.	FGA	FGM	Pct.	FTA	FTM	Pct.	Off.	Def.	Tot.	Ast.	PF	Dq.	Stl.	Blk.	Pts.	Avg.
									—Rebounds—									
82-83—Portland	55	516	234	105	.449	38	28	.737	30	35	65	31	81	0	19	5	247	4.5
83-84—Mil.-S.D.	4	19	8	4	.500	0	0	.000	0	1	1	1	4	0	1	2	8	2.0
84-85—San Antonio	1	8	6	0	.000	2	2	1.000	1	0	1	0	1	0	0	0	2	2.0
Totals	60	543	248	109	.440	40	30	.750	31	36	67	32	86	0	20	7	257	4.3

Three-Point Field Goals: 1982-83, 9-for-25 (.360).

NBA PLAYOFF RECORD

Sea.—Team	G.	Min.	FGA	FGM	Pct.	FTA	FTM	Pct.	Off.	Def.	Tot.	Ast.	PF	Dq.	Stl.	Blk.	Pts.	Avg.
									—Rebounds—									
82-83—Portland	6	60	27	13	.481	7	6	.857	2	1	3	5	11	0	0	0	33	5.5
84-85—San Antonio	2	6	8	4	.500	0	0	.000	2	1	3	0	1	0	0	0	8	4.0
Totals	8	66	35	17	.486	7	6	.857	4	2	6	5	12	0	0	0	41	5.1

Three-Point Field Goals: 1-for-3 (.333). 1984-85, 0-for-1. Totals, 1-for-4 (.250).

Named to CBA All-Defensive Second Team, 1985.

PETER KELLY TRIPUCKA

(Known by middle name.)

Born February 16, 1959 at Glen Ridge, N. J.   Height 6:06.   Weight 220.

High School—Bloomfield, N. J.

College—University of Notre Dame, Notre Dame, Ind.

Drafted by Detroit on first round, 1981 (12th pick).

Year	G.	Min.	FGA	FGM	Pct.	FTA	FTM	Pct.	Reb.	Pts.	Avg.
77-78	31	643	247	141	.571	108	80	.741	161	362	11.7
78-79	29	807	277	143	.516	151	129	.854	125	415	14.3
79-80	23	691	270	150	.556	151	115	.762	151	415	18.0
80-81	29	919	354	195	.551	168	137	.815	169	527	18.2
Totals	112	3060	1148	629	.548	578	461	.798	606	1719	15.3

NBA REGULAR SEASON RECORD

Sea.—Team	G.	Min.	FGA	FGM	Pct.	FTA	FTM	Pct.	Off.	Def.	Tot.	Ast.	PF	Dq.	Stl.	Blk.	Pts.	Avg.
81-82—Detroit	82	3077	1281	636	.496	621	495	.797	219	224	443	270	241	0	89	16	1772	21.6
82-83—Detroit	58	2252	1156	565	.489	464	392	.845	126	138	264	237	157	0	67	20	1536	26.5
83-84—Detroit	76	2493	1296	595	.459	523	426	.815	119	187	306	228	190	0	65	17	1618	21.3
84-85—Detroit	55	1675	831	396	.477	288	255	.885	66	152	218	135	118	1	49	14	1049	19.1
Totals	271	9497	4564	2192	.480	1896	1568	.827	530	701	1231	870	706	1	270	67	5975	22.0

Three-Point Field Goals: 1981-82, 5-for-22 (.227). 1982-83, 14-for-37 (.378). 1983-84, 2-for-17 (.118). 1984-85, 2-for-5 (.400). Totals, 23-for-81 (.284).

NBA PLAYOFF RECORD

Sea.—Team	G.	Min.	FGA	FGM	Pct.	FTA	FTM	Pct.	Off.	Def.	Tot.	Ast.	PF	Dq.	Stl.	Blk.	Pts.	Avg.
83-84—Detroit	5	208	102	48	.471	51	41	.804	10	13	23	15	22	1	11	0	137	27.4
84-85—Detroit	9	288	118	49	.415	40	35	.875	19	20	39	29	22	0	4	3	133	14.8
Totals	14	496	220	97	.441	91	76	.835	29	33	62	44	44	1	15	3	270	19.3

Three-Point Field Goals: 1983-84, 0-for-1. 1984-85, 0-for-1. Totals, 0-for-2.

NBA ALL-STAR GAME RECORD

Season—Team	Min.	FGA	FGM	Pct.	FTA	FTM	Pct.	Off.	Def.	Tot.	Ast.	PF	Dq.	Stl.	Blk.	Pts.
1982—Detroit	15	7	3	.429	0	0	.000	0	1	1	2	0	0	0	0	6
1984—Detroit	6	0	0	.000	2	1	.500	0	0	0	2	1	0	1	0	1
Totals	21	7	3	.429	2	1	.500	0	1	1	4	1	0	1	0	7

Named to NBA All-Rookie Team, 1982.

KELVIN TRENT TUCKER

(Known by middle name.)

Born December 20, 1959 at Tarboro, N. C.   Height 6:05.   Weight 193.

High School—Flint, Mich., Northwestern.

College—University of Minnesota, Minneapolis, Minn.

Drafted by New York on first round, 1982 (6th pick).

Year	G.	Min.	FGA	FGM	Pct.	FTA	FTM	Pct.	Reb.	Pts.	Avg.
78-79	25	....	239	114	.477	32	19	.594	85	247	9.9
79-80	32	....	310	152	.490	46	34	.739	103	338	10.6
80-81	29	....	362	187	.517	69	56	.812	102	430	14.8
81-82	29	....	353	178	.504	90	74	.822	103	430	14.8
Totals	115	....	1264	631	.499	237	183	.772	393	1445	12.6

NBA REGULAR SEASON RECORD

Sea.—Team	G.	Min.	FGA	FGM	Pct.	FTA	FTM	Pct.	Off.	Def.	Tot.	Ast.	PF	Dq.	Stl.	Blk.	Pts.	Avg.
82-83—New York	78	1830	647	299	.462	64	43	.672	75	141	216	195	235	1	56	6	655	8.4
83-84—New York	63	1228	450	225	.500	33	25	.758	43	87	130	138	124	0	63	8	481	7.6
84-85—New York	77	1819	606	293	.483	48	38	.792	74	114	188	199	195	0	75	15	653	8.5
Totals	218	4877	1703	817	.480	145	106	.731	192	342	534	532	554	1	194	29	1789	8.2

Three-Point Field Goals: 1982-83, 14-for-30 (.467). 1983-84, 6-for-16 (.375). 1984-85, 29-for-72 (.403). Totals, 49-for-118 (.415).

NBA PLAYOFF RECORD

Sea.—Team	G.	Min.	FGA	FGM	Pct.	FTA	FTM	Pct.	Off.	Def.	Tot.	Ast.	PF	Dq.	Stl.	Blk.	Pts.	Avg.
82-83—New York	6	85	15	9	.600	10	7	.700	2	7	9	5	7	0	2	0	26	4.3
83-84—New York	12	254	84	42	.500	10	6	.600	6	12	18	27	32	0	11	3	91	7.6
Totals	18	339	99	51	.515	20	13	.650	8	19	27	32	39	0	13	3	117	6.5

Three-Point Field Goals: 1982-83, 1-for-2 (.500). 1983-84, 1-for-5 (.200). Totals, 13-for-20 (.650).

Named to THE SPORTING NEWS All-America First Team, 1982.

ELSTON HOWARD TURNER

Born June 10, 1959 at Knoxville, Tenn.   Height 6:05.   Weight 220.

High School—Knoxville, Tenn., Austin-East.

College—University of Mississippi, University, Miss.

Drafted by Dallas on second round, 1981 (43rd pick).

Signed offer sheet with Denver, August 3, 1984; Dallas received Howard Carter for agreement of not matching offer sheet, August 23, 1984.

—COLLEGIATE RECORD—

Year	G.	Min.	FGA	FGM	Pct.	FTA	FTM	Pct.	Reb.	Pts.	Avg.
77-78	27	936	268	113	.422	65	43	.662	210	269	10.0
78-79	27	1035	366	183	.500	83	64	.771	173	430	15.9
79-80	30	1070	388	212	.546	110	84	.764	209	508	16.9
80-81	29	1068	473	246	.520	161	106	.658	236	598	20.6
Totals	113	4109	1495	754	.504	419	297	.709	828	1805	16.0

NBA REGULAR SEASON RECORD

Sea.—Team	G.	Min.	FGA	FGM	Pct.	FTA	FTM	Pct.	Off.	Def.	Tot.	Ast.	PF	Dq.	Stl.	Blk.	Pts.	Avg.
81-82—Dallas	80	1996	639	282	.441	138	97	.703	143	158	301	189	182	1	75	2	661	8.3
82-83—Dallas	59	879	238	96	.403	30	20	.667	68	84	152	88	75	0	47	0	214	3.6
83-84—Dallas	47	536	150	54	.360	34	28	.824	42	51	93	59	40	0	26	0	137	2.9
84-85—Denver	81	1491	388	181	.466	65	51	.785	88	128	216	158	152	0	96	7	414	5.1
Totals	267	4902	1415	613	.433	267	196	.734	341	421	762	494	449	1	244	9	1426	5.3

Three-Point Field Goals: 1981-82, 0-for-4. 1982-83, 2-for-3 (.667). 1983-84, 1-for-9 (.111). 1984-85, 1-for-6 (.167). Totals, 4-for-22 (.182).

NBA PLAYOFF RECORD

Sea.—Team	G.	Min.	FGA	FGM	Pct.	FTA	FTM	Pct.	Off.	Def.	Tot.	Ast.	PF	Dq.	Stl.	Blk.	Pts.	Avg.
83-84—Dallas	8	53	20	7	.350	0	0	.000	5	5	10	8	4	0	6	1	14	1.8
84-85—Denver	15	358	102	50	.490	19	12	.632	30	43	73	46	42	0	17	1	114	7.6
Totals	23	411	122	57	.467	19	12	.632	35	48	83	54	46	0	23	2	128	5.6

Three-Point Field Goals: 1984-85, 2-for-2 (1.000).

JEFFREY STEVEN TURNER
(Jeff)

Born April 9, 1962 at Bangor, Maine.   Height 6:09.   Weight 230.

High School—Brandon, Fla.

College—Vanderbilt University, Nashville, Tenn.

Drafted by New Jersey on first round, 1984 (17th pick).

—COLLEGIATE RECORD—

Year	G.	Min.	FGA	FGM	Pct.	FTA	FTM	Pct.	Reb.	Pts.	Avg.
80-81	28	586	96	40	.417	31	20	.645	84	100	3.6
81-82	27	772	189	99	.524	71	52	.732	145	250	9.3
82-83	33	1008	366	180	.492	98	75	.765	182	435	13.2
83-84	29	953	375	200	.533	102	86	.843	213	486	16.8
Totals	117	3319	1026	519	.506	302	233	.772	624	1271	10.9

NBA REGULAR SEASON RECORD

Sea.—Team	G.	Min.	FGA	FGM	Pct.	FTA	FTM	Pct.	Off.	Def.	Tot.	Ast.	PF	Dq.	Stl.	Blk.	Pts.	Avg.
84-85—New Jersey	72	1429	377	171	.454	92	79	.859	88	130	218	108	243	8	29	7	421	5.8

Three-Point Field Goals: 1984-85, 0-for-3.

NBA PLAYOFF RECORD

Sea.—Team	G.	Min.	FGA	FGM	Pct.	FTA	FTM	Pct.	Off.	Def.	Tot.	Ast.	PF	Dq.	Stl.	Blk.	Pts.	Avg.
84-85—New Jersey	3	21	5	2	.400	0	0	.000	2	2	4	2	6	0	0	0	4	1.3

Member of U.S. Olympic team, 1984.

—DID YOU KNOW—

That Wilt Chamberlain was the last non-guard to lead the NBA in assists? Chamberlain accomplished the feat in 1967-68.

MELVIN TURPIN

MELVIN HARRISON TURPIN

Born December 28, 1960 at Lexington, Ky.   Height 6:11.   Weight 240.

High School—Lexington, Ky., Bryan Station.

Prep School—Fork Union Military Academy, Fork Union, Va.

College—University of Kentucky, Lexington, Ky.

Drafted by Washington on first round, 1984 (6th pick).

Draft rights traded by Washington to Cleveland for Cliff Robinson, the draft rights to Tim McCormick and cash, June 19, 1984.

—COLLEGIATE RECORD—

Year	G.	Min.	FGA	FGM	Pct.	FTA	FTM	Pct.	Reb.	Pts.	Avg.
80-81	28	380	95	50	.526	44	31	.705	106	131	4.7
81-82	30	912	275	160	.582	106	72	.679	212	392	13.1
82-83	31	962	311	192	.617	125	84	.672	195	468	15.1
83-84	34	1071	378	224	.593	94	70	.745	217	518	15.2
Totals	123	3325	1059	626	.591	369	257	.696	730	1509	12.3

NBA REGULAR SEASON RECORD

Sea.—Team	G.	Min.	FGA	FGM	Pct.	FTA	FTM	Pct.	—Rebounds— Off.	Def.	Tot.	Ast.	PF	Dq.	Stl.	Blk.	Pts.	Avg.
84-85—Cleveland	79	1949	711	363	.511	139	109	.784	155	297	452	36	211	3	38	87	835	10.6

NBA PLAYOFF RECORD

Sea.—Team	G.	Min.	FGA	FGM	Pct.	FTA	FTM	Pct.	—Rebounds— Off.	Def.	Tot.	Ast.	PF	Dq.	Stl.	Blk.	Pts.	Avg.
84-85—Cleveland	4	45	19	12	.632	2	1	.500	3	5	8	0	3	0	4	1	25	6.3

TERRY CHRISTOPHER TYLER

Born October 30, 1956 at Detroit, Mich.   Height 6:07.   Weight 220.

High School—Detroit, Mich., Northwestern.

College—University of Detroit, Detroit, Mich.

Drafted by Detroit on second round, 1978 (23rd pick).

—COLLEGIATE RECORD—

Year	G.	Min.	FGA	FGM	Pct.	FTA	FTM	Pct.	Reb.	Pts.	Avg.
74-75	26	629	184	98	.533	47	24	.511	182	220	8.5
75-76	27	804	358	197	.550	108	70	.648	298	464	17.2
76-77	29	901	360	212	.589	109	81	.743	319	505	17.4
77-78	28	912	336	195	.580	98	70	.714	352	460	16.4
Totals	110	3246	1238	702	.567	362	245	.677	1151	1649	15.0

NBA REGULAR SEASON RECORD

Sea.—Team	G.	Min.	FGA	FGM	Pct.	FTA	FTM	Pct.	—Rebounds— Off.	Def.	Tot.	Ast.	PF	Dq.	Stl.	Blk.	Pts.	Avg.
78-79—Detroit	82	2560	946	456	.482	219	144	.658	211	437	648	89	254	3	104	201	1056	12.9
79-80—Detroit	82	2672	925	430	.465	187	143	.765	228	399	627	129	237	3	107	220	1005	12.3
80-81—Detroit	82	2549	895	476	.532	250	148	.592	198	369	567	136	215	2	112	180	1100	13.4
81-82—Detroit	82	1989	643	336	.523	192	142	.740	154	339	493	126	182	1	77	160	815	9.9
82-83—Detroit	82	2543	880	421	.478	196	146	.745	180	360	540	157	221	3	103	160	990	12.1
83-84—Detroit	82	1602	691	313	.453	132	94	.712	104	181	285	76	151	1	63	59	722	8.8
84-85—Detroit	82	2004	855	422	.494	148	106	.716	148	275	423	63	192	0	49	90	950	11.6
Totals	574	15919	5835	2854	.489	1324	923	.697	1223	2360	3583	776	1452	13	615	1070	6638	11.6

Three-Point Field Goals: 1979-80, 2-for-12 (.167). 1980-81, 0-for-8. 1981-82, 1-for-4 (.250). 1982-83, 2-for-15 (.133). 1983-84, 2-for-13 (.154). 1984-85, 0-for-8. Totals, 7-for-60 (.117).

NBA PLAYOFF RECORD

Sea.—Team	G.	Min.	FGA	FGM	Pct.	FTA	FTM	Pct.	—Rebounds— Off.	Def.	Tot.	Ast.	PF	Dq.	Stl.	Blk.	Pts.	Avg.
83-84—Detroit	5	42	24	10	.417	9	5	.556	5	2	7	1	4	0	0	3	25	5.0
84-85—Detroit	9	179	100	49	.490	27	22	.815	15	25	40	3	17	0	6	4	120	13.3
Totals	14	221	124	59	.476	36	27	.750	20	27	47	4	21	0	6	7	145	10.4

Three-Point Field Goals: 1984-85, 0-for-1.

Named to NBA All-Rookie Team, 1979.

—DID YOU KNOW—

That Los Angeles Dodgers Manager Tommy Lasorda once was a referee in the Continental Basketball Association?

DARNELL TERRELL VALENTINE

Born February 3, 1959 at Chicago, Ill.   Height 6:02.   Weight 185.

High School—Wichita, Kan., Wichita Heights.

College—University of Kansas, Lawrence, Kan.

Drafted by Portland on first round, 1981 (16th pick).

—COLLEGIATE RECORD—

Year	G.	Min.	FGA	FGM	Pct.	FTA	FTM	Pct.	Reb.	Pts.	Avg.
77-78	29	761	297	143	.481	143	106	.741	82	392	13.5
78-79	29	1008	375	166	.443	200	136	.680	133	468	16.1
79-80	28	951	322	155	.481	197	153	.777	89	463	16.5
80-81	32	1186	350	176	.503	214	146	.682	118	498	15.6
Totals	118	3906	1344	640	.476	754	541	.718	408	1821	15.4

NBA REGULAR SEASON RECORD

Sea.—Team	G.	Min.	FGA	FGM	Pct.	FTA	FTM	Pct.	Off.	Def.	Tot.	Ast.	PF	Dq.	Stl.	Blk.	Pts.	Avg.
81-82—Portland	82	1387	453	187	.413	200	152	.760	48	101	149	270	187	1	94	3	526	6.4
82-83—Portland	47	1298	460	209	.454	213	169	.793	34	83	117	293	139	1	101	5	587	12.5
83-84—Portland	68	1893	561	251	.447	246	194	.789	49	78	127	395	179	1	107	6	696	10.2
84-85—Portland	75	2278	679	321	.473	290	230	.793	54	165	219	522	189	1	143	5	872	11.6
Totals	272	6856	2153	968	.450	949	745	.785	185	427	612	1480	694	4	445	19	2681	9.9

Three-Point Field Goals: 1981-82, 0-for-9. 1982-83, 0-for-1. 1983-84, 0-for-3. 1984-85, 0-for-2. Totals, 0-for-15.

NBA PLAYOFF RECORD

Sea.—Team	G.	Min.	FGA	FGM	Pct.	FTA	FTM	Pct.	Off.	Def.	Tot.	Ast.	PF	Dq.	Stl.	Blk.	Pts.	Avg.
82-83—Portland	7	205	80	34	.425	21	16	.762	5	10	15	61	21	0	10	3	85	12.1
83-84—Portland	5	178	60	30	.500	35	32	.914	3	8	11	42	23	2	9	1	92	18.4
84-85—Portland	9	244	88	43	.489	31	29	.935	6	11	17	58	28	1	16	0	115	12.8
Totals	21	627	228	107	.469	87	77	.885	14	29	43	161	72	3	35	4	292	13.9

Three-Point Field Goals: 1982-83, 1-for-2 (.500).

Named to THE SPORTING NEWS All-America Second Team, 1979 and 1981. . . . Member of U. S. Olympic team, 1980.

ERNEST MAURICE VANDEWEGHE
(Kiki)

Born August 1, 1958 at Weisbaden, Germany.   Height 6:08.   Weight 220.

High School—Pacific Palisades, Calif., Palisades.

College—University of California at Los Angeles, Los Angeles, Calif.

Drafted by Dallas on first round, 1980 (11th pick).

Traded by Dallas with a 1986 1st round draft choice to Denver for two 1st round draft choices (1981 and 1985), December 3, 1980.

Traded by Denver to Portland for Lafayette Lever, Calvin Natt, Wayne Cooper, a 1984 2nd round draft choice and a 1985 1st round draft choice, June 7, 1984.

—COLLEGIATE RECORD—

Year	G.	Min.	FGA	FGM	Pct.	FTA	FTM	Pct.	Reb.	Pts.	Avg.
76-77	23	230	70	35	.500	17	12	.706	41	82	3.6
77-78	28	592	184	101	.549	67	46	.687	123	248	8.9
78-79	30	916	267	166	.622	117	95	.812	189	427	14.2
79-80	32	1081	420	234	.557	196	155	.791	216	623	19.5
Totals	113	2819	941	536	.570	397	308	.776	569	1380	12.2

NBA REGULAR SEASON RECORD

Sea.—Team	G.	Min.	FGA	FGM	Pct.	FTA	FTM	Pct.	Off.	Def.	Tot.	Ast.	PF	Dq.	Stl.	Blk.	Pts.	Avg.
80-81—Denver	51	1376	537	229	.426	159	130	.818	86	184	270	94	116	0	29	24	588	11.5
81-82—Denver	82	2775	1260	706	.560	405	347	.857	149	312	461	247	217	1	52	29	1760	21.5
82-83—Denver	82	2909	1537	841	.547	559	489	.875	124	313	437	203	198	0	66	38	2186	26.7
83-84—Denver	78	2734	1603	895	.558	580	494	.852	84	289	373	238	187	1	53	50	2295	29.4
84-85—Portland	72	2502	1158	618	.534	412	369	.896	74	154	228	106	116	0	37	22	1616	22.4
Totals	365	12296	6095	3289	.540	2115	1829	.865	517	1252	1769	888	834	2	237	163	8445	23.1

Three-Point Field Goals: 1980-81, 0-for-7. 1981-82, 1-for-13 (.077). 1982-83, 15-for-51 (.294). 1983-84, 11-for-30 (.367). 1984-85, 11-for-33 (.333). Totals, 38-for-134 (.284).

NBA PLAYOFF RECORD

Sea.—Team	G.	Min.	FGA	FGM	Pct.	FTA	FTM	Pct.	Off.	Def.	Tot.	Ast.	PF	Dq.	Stl.	Blk.	Pts.	Avg.
81-82—Denver	3	109	43	25	.581	18	18	1.000	4	14	18	9	7	0	2	4	68	22.7

KIKI VANDEWEGHE

Sea.—Team	G.	Min.	FGA	FGM	Pct.	FTA	FTM	Pct.	Off.	Def.	Tot.	Ast.	PF	Dq.	Stl.	Blk.	Pts.	Avg.
82-83—Denver	8	317	160	87	.544	50	40	.800	6	46	52	32	16	0	4	7	214	26.8
83-84—Denver	5	180	96	49	.510	28	27	.964	6	17	23	20	14	1	9	5	127	25.4
84-85—Portland	9	311	158	85	.538	33	31	.939	14	13	27	17	23	0	8	3	202	22.4
Totals	25	917	457	246	.538	129	116	.899	30	90	120	78	60	1	23	19	611	24.4

Three-Point Field-Goals: 1982-83, 0-for-4. 1983-84, 2-for-5 (.400). 1984-85, 1-for-7 (.143). Totals, 3-for-16 (.188).

NBA ALL-STAR GAME RECORD

Season—Team	Min.	FGA	FGM	Pct.	FTA	FTM	Pct.	Off.	Def.	Tot.	Ast.	PF	Dq.	Stl.	Blk.	Pts.
1983—Denver	14	4	3	.750	2	1	.500	0	3	3	1	0	0	1	0	7
1984—Denver	26	13	7	.538	0	0	.000	1	2	3	1	2	0	0	0	14
Totals	40	17	10	.588	2	1	.500	1	5	6	2	2	0	1	0	21

Son of former NBA forward-guard Ernie Vandeweghe and nephew of former NBA forward-center Mel Hutchins.

PETER GERARD VERHOEVEN
(Pete)

Born February 15, 1959 at Hanford, Calif.   Height 6:09.   Weight 215.

High School—Hanford, Calif.

College—Fresno State University, Fresno, Calif.

Drafted by Portland on fourth round, 1981 (85th pick).

Waived by Portland, October 23, 1984; signed by Kansas City as a free agent, November 2, 1984.

—COLLEGIATE RECORD—

Year	G.	Min.	FGA	FGM	Pct.	FTA	FTM	Pct.	Reb.	Pts.	Avg.
77-78	20	....	26	11	.423	12	8	.750	23	30	1.5
78-79	28	....	114	64	.561	31	23	.742	79	151	5.4
79-80	22	....	130	75	.577	40	31	.775	104	181	8.2
80-81	29	878	190	108	.568	65	48	.738	151	264	9.1
Totals	99	....	460	258	.561	148	110	.743	357	626	6.3

NBA REGULAR SEASON RECORD

Sea.—Team	G.	Min.	FGA	FGM	Pct.	FTA	FTM	Pct.	Off.	Def.	Tot.	Ast.	PF	Dq.	Stl.	Blk.	Pts.	Avg.
81-82—Portland	71	1207	296	149	.503	72	51	.708	106	148	254	52	215	4	42	22	349	4.9
82-83—Portland	48	527	171	87	.509	31	21	.677	44	52	96	32	95	2	18	9	195	4.1
83-84—Portland	43	327	100	50	.500	25	17	.680	27	34	61	20	75	0	22	11	117	2.7
84-85—Kansas City	54	366	108	51	.472	25	21	.840	28	35	63	17	85	1	15	7	123	2.3
Totals	216	2427	675	337	.499	153	110	.719	205	269	474	121	470	7	97	49	784	3.6

Three-Point Field Goals: 1982-83, 0-for-1. 1983-84, 0-for-1. Totals, 0-for-2.

NBA PLAYOFF RECORD

Sea.—Team	G.	Min.	FGA	FGM	Pct.	FTA	FTM	Pct.	Off.	Def.	Tot.	Ast.	PF	Dq.	Stl.	Blk.	Pts.	Avg.
83-84—Portland	3	19	0	0	.000	2	2	1.000	0	0	0	0	10	0	1	0	2	0.7

Brother of former major league pitcher John Verhoeven.

JAY FLETCHER VINCENT

Born June 10, 1959 at Kalamazoo, Mich.   Height 6:08.   Weight 225.

High School—Lansing, Mich., Eastern.

College—Michigan State University, East Lansing, Mich.

Drafted by Dallas on second round, 1981 (24th pick).

—COLLEGIATE RECORD—

Year	G.	Min.	FGA	FGM	Pct.	FTA	FTM	Pct.	Reb.	Pts.	Avg.
77-78	29	....	239	137	.573	86	55	.640	110	329	11.3
78-79	31	939	343	170	.496	93	54	.581	161	394	12.7
79-80	27	965	451	233	.517	161	116	.720	209	582	21.6
80-81	27	1001	522	259	.496	141	91	.645	229	609	22.6
Totals	114	....	1555	799	.514	481	316	.657	709	1914	16.8

NBA REGULAR SEASON RECORD

Sea.—Team	G.	Min.	FGA	FGM	Pct.	FTA	FTM	Pct.	Off.	Def.	Tot.	Ast.	PF	Dq.	Stl.	Blk.	Pts.	Avg.
81-82—Dallas	81	2626	1448	719	.497	409	293	.716	182	383	565	176	308	8	89	22	1732	21.4
82-83—Dallas	81	2726	1272	622	.489	343	269	.784	217	375	592	212	295	4	70	45	1513	18.7
83-84—Dallas	61	1421	579	252	.435	215	168	.781	81	166	247	114	159	1	30	10	672	11.0
84-85—Dallas	79	2543	1138	545	.479	420	351	.836	185	519	704	169	226	0	48	22	1441	18.2
Totals	302	9316	4437	2138	.482	1387	1081	.779	665	1443	2108	671	988	13	237	99	5358	17.7

Three-Point Field Goals: 1981-82, 1-for-4 (.250). 1982-83, 0-for-3. 1983-84, 0-for-1. 1984-85, 0-for-4. Totals, 1-for-12 (.083).

Sea.—Team	G.	Min.	FGA	FGM	Pct.	FTA	FTM	Pct.	Off.	Def.	Tot.	Ast.	PF	Dq.	Stl.	Blk.	Pts.	Avg.
										Rebounds								
83-84—Dallas	10	353	124	48	.387	62	56	.903	29	41	70	19	36	1	7	1	152	15.2
84-85—Dallas	4	134	56	20	.357	29	22	.759	9	13	22	3	16	0	6	3	62	15.5
Totals	14	487	180	68	.378	91	78	.857	38	54	92	22	52	1	13	4	214	15.3

Three-Point Field Goals: 1983-84, 0-for-1.

Named to NBA All-Rookie Team, 1982. . . . Member of NCAA championship team, 1979. . . . Brother of Sam Vincent, 1st round draft choice of Boston Celtics in 1985 NBA draft.

DANIEL LaDREW VRANES
(Danny)

Born October 29, 1958 at Salt Lake City, Utah. Height 6:07. Weight 210.

High School—Salt Lake City, Utah, Skyline.

College—University of Utah, Salt Lake City, Utah.

Drafted by Seattle on first round, 1981 (5th pick).

—COLLEGIATE RECORD—

Year	G.	Min.	FGA	FGM	Pct.	FTA	FTM	Pct.	Reb.	Pts.	Avg.
77-78	29	851	265	145	.547	113	65	.575	210	355	12.2
78-79	28	867	292	180	.616	148	101	.682	283	455	16.3
79-80	24	760	242	138	.570	141	105	.745	228	380	15.8
80-81	30	977	304	181	.595	206	164	.796	230	526	17.5
Totals	111	3455	1103	644	.584	608	435	.715	951	1716	15.5

NBA REGULAR SEASON RECORD

Sea.—Team	G.	Min.	FGA	FGM	Pct.	FTA	FTM	Pct.	Off.	Def.	Tot.	Ast.	PF	Dq.	Stl.	Blk.	Pts.	Avg.
										Rebounds								
81-82—Seattle	77	1075	262	143	.546	148	89	.601	71	127	198	56	150	0	28	21	375	4.9
82-83—Seattle	82	2054	429	226	.527	209	115	.550	117	248	425	120	254	2	53	49	567	6.9
83-84—Seattle	80	2174	495	258	.521	236	153	.648	150	245	395	132	263	4	51	54	669	8.4
84-85—Seattle	76	2163	402	186	.463	127	67	.528	154	282	436	152	256	4	76	57	440	5.8
Totals	315	7466	1588	813	.512	720	424	.589	492	902	1454	460	923	10	208	181	2051	6.5

Three-Point Field Goals: 1981-82, 0-for-1. 1982-83, 0-for-1. 1983-84, 0-for-1. 1984-85, 1-for-4 (.250). Totals, 1-for-7 (.143).

NBA PLAYOFF RECORD

Sea.—Team	G.	Min.	FGA	FGM	Pct.	FTA	FTM	Pct.	Off.	Def.	Tot.	Ast.	PF	Dq.	Stl.	Blk.	Pts.	Avg.
										Rebounds								
81-82—Seattle	6	29	5	1	.200	2	1	.500	1	1	2	0	2	0	1	0	3	0.5
82-83—Seattle	2	56	17	6	.353	0	0	.000	9	10	19	1	7	0	0	1	12	6.0
83-84—Seattle	5	147	39	16	.410	7	4	.571	16	22	38	11	24	1	3	6	36	7.2
Totals	13	232	61	23	.377	9	5	.556	26	33	59	12	33	1	4	7	51	3.9

Three-Point Field Goals: 1983-84, 0-for-1.

Named to NBA All-Defensive Second Team, 1985. . . . Named to THE SPORTING NEWS All-America Second Team, 1981. . . . Member of U. S. Olympic team, 1980.

GRANVILLE S. WAITERS

Born January 8, 1961 at Columbus, O. Height 6:11. Weight 225.

High School—Columbus, O., East.

College—Ohio State University, Columbus, O.

Drafted by Portland on second round, 1983 (39th pick).

Draft rights traded by Portland to Indiana for a 1984 2nd round draft choice, August 18, 1983.

—COLLEGIATE RECORD—

Year	G.	Min.	FGA	FGM	Pct.	FTA	FTM	Pct.	Reb.	Pts.	Avg.
79-80	17	49	11	6	.545	0	0	.000	14	12	0.7
80-81	26	232	50	27	.540	10	3	.300	39	57	2.2
81-82	31	941	166	93	.560	53	35	.660	156	221	7.1
82-83	30	993	246	131	.533	68	49	.721	225	311	10.4
Totals	104	2215	473	257	.543	131	87	.664	434	601	5.8

NBA REGULAR SEASON RECORD

Sea.—Team	G.	Min.	FGA	FGM	Pct.	FTA	FTM	Pct.	Off.	Def.	Tot.	Ast.	PF	Dq.	Stl.	Blk.	Pts.	Avg.
										Rebounds								
83-84—Indiana	78	1040	238	123	.517	51	31	.608	64	163	227	60	164	2	24	85	277	3.6
84-85—Indiana	62	703	190	85	.447	50	29	.580	57	113	170	30	107	2	16	44	199	3.2
Totals	140	1743	428	208	.486	101	60	.594	121	276	397	90	271	4	40	129	476	3.4

Three-Point Field Goals: 1983-84, 0-for-1. 1984-85, 0-for-1. Totals, 0-for-2.

DANNY VRANES

DARRELL WALKER

Born March 9, 1961 at Chicago, Ill.   Height 6:04.   Weight 180.

High School—Chicago, Ill., Corliss.

Colleges—Westark Community College, Fort Smith, Ark., and University of Arkansas, Fayetteville, Ark.

Drafted by New York on first round, 1983 (12th pick).

—COLLEGIATE RECORD—
Westark CC

Year	G.	Min.	FGA	FGM	Pct.	FTA	FTM	Pct.	Reb.	Pts.	Avg.
79-80	37	1332	472	255	.540	178	117	.657	259	627	16.9

Arkansas

Year	G.	Min.	FGA	FGM	Pct.	FTA	FTM	Pct.	Reb.	Pts.	Avg.
80-81	31	926	269	137	.509	125	75	.600	139	349	11.3
81-82	29	1039	316	162	.513	161	106	.658	152	430	14.8
82-83	30	1105	374	197	.527	238	152	.639	172	546	18.2
Totals	90	3070	959	496	.517	524	333	.635	463	1325	14.7

NBA REGULAR SEASON RECORD

Sea.—Team	G.	Min.	FGA	FGM	Pct.	FTA	FTM	Pct.	Off.	Def.	Tot.	Ast.	PF	Dq.	Stl.	Blk.	Pts.	Avg.
83-84—New York	82	1324	518	216	.417	263	208	.791	74	93	167	284	202	1	127	15	644	7.9
84-85—New York	82	2489	989	430	.435	347	243	.700	128	150	278	408	244	2	167	21	1103	13.5
Totals	164	3813	1507	646	.429	610	451	.739	202	243	445	692	446	3	294	36	1747	10.7

(Header spanning Off./Def./Tot.: —Rebounds—)

Three-Point Field Goals: 1983-84, 4-for-15 (.267). 1984-85, 0-for-17. Totals, 4-for-32 (.125).

NBA PLAYOFF RECORD

Sea.—Team	G.	Min.	FGA	FGM	Pct.	FTA	FTM	Pct.	Off.	Def.	Tot.	Ast.	PF	Dq.	Stl.	Blk.	Pts.	Avg.
83-84—New York	12	195	73	27	.370	46	28	.609	20	15	35	20	29	0	24	2	82	6.8

(Header spanning Off./Def./Tot.: —Rebounds—)

Named to NBA All-Rookie Team, 1984.

WILLIAM THEODORE WALTON
(Bill)

Born November 5, 1952 at La Mesa, Calif.   Height 6:11.   Weight 225.

High School—La Mesa, Calif., Helix.

College—University of California at Los Angeles, Los Angeles, Calif.

Drafted by Portland on first round, 1974 (1st pick).

Signed by San Diego as Veteran Free Agent, May 13, 1979; Portland received Kevin Kunnert, Kermit Washington, cash and a 1980 1st round draft choice as compensation, August 15, 1980.

—COLLEGIATE RECORD—

Year	G.	Min.	FGA	FGM	Pct.	FTA	FTM	Pct.	Reb.	Pts.	Avg.
70-71†	20	....	266	155	.686	82	52	.634	321	362	18.1
71-72	30	....	372	238	.640	223	157	.704	466	633	21.1
72-73	30	....	426	277	.650	102	59	.569	506	612	20.4
73-74	27	....	349	232	.665	100	58	.580	398	522	19.3
Varsity Totals	87	....	1147	747	.651	425	273	.642	1370	1767	20.3

NBA REGULAR SEASON RECORD

Sea.—Team	G.	Min.	FGA	FGM	Pct.	FTA	FTM	Pct.	Off.	Def.	Tot.	Ast.	PF	Dq.	Stl.	Blk.	Pts.	Avg.
74-75—Portland	35	1153	345	177	.513	137	94	.686	92	349	441	167	115	4	29	94	448	12.8
75-76—Portland	51	1687	732	345	.471	228	133	.583	132	549	681	220	144	3	49	82	823	16.1
76-77—Portland	65	2264	930	491	.528	327	228	.697	211	723	934	245	174	5	66	211	1210	18.6
77-78—Portland	58	1929	882	460	.522	246	177	.720	118	648	766	291	145	3	60	146	1097	18.9
78-79—Portland					Missed Entire Season—Foot Injury													
79-80—San Diego	14	337	161	81	.503	54	32	.593	28	98	126	34	37	0	8	38	194	13.9
80-81—San Diego					Missed Entire Season—Foot Injury													
81-82—San Diego					Missed Entire Season—Foot Injury													
82-83—San Diego	33	1099	379	200	.528	117	65	.556	75	248	323	120	113	0	34	119	465	14.1
83-84—San Diego	55	1476	518	288	.556	154	92	.597	132	345	477	183	153	1	45	88	668	12.1
84-85—L.A. Clippers	67	1647	516	269	.521	203	138	.680	168	432	600	156	184	0	50	140	676	10.1
Totals	378	11592	4463	2311	.518	1466	959	.654	956	3392	4348	1416	1065	16	341	918	5581	14.8

(Header spanning Off./Def./Tot.: —Rebounds—)

Three-Point Field Goals: 1983-84, 0-for-2. 1984-85, 0-for-2. Totals, 0-for-4.

BILL WALTON

Sea.—Team	G.	Min.	FGA	FGM	Pct.	FTA	FTM	Pct.	—Rebounds— Off.	Def.	Tot.	Ast.	PF	Dq.	Stl.	Blk.	Pts.	Avg.
76-77—Portland	19	755	302	153	.507	57	39	.684	56	232	288	104	80	3	20	64	345	18.2
77-78—Portland	2	49	18	11	.611	7	5	.714	5	17	22	4	1	0	3	3	27	13.5
Totals..............	21	804	320	164	.513	64	44	.688	61	249	310	108	81	3	23	67	372	17.7

NBA ALL-STAR GAME RECORD

Season—Team	Min.	FGA	FGM	Pct.	FTA	FTM	Pct.	—Rebounds— Off.	Def.	Tot.	Ast.	PF	Dq.	Stl.	Blk.	Pts.
1977—Portland........						Selected—Injured, Did Not Play										
1978—Portland	31	14	6	.429	3	3	1.000	2	8	10	2	3	0	3	2	15

Named NBA Most Valuable Player, 1978.... All-NBA First Team, 1978.... All-NBA Second Team, 1977.... NBA All-Defensive First Team, 1977 and 1978.... NBA Playoff MVP, 1977.... Member of NBA championship team, 1977.. .. Holds NBA championship series game record for most blocked shots, 8, vs. Philadelphia, June 5, 1977.... Led NBA in blocked shots and rebounding, 1977.... THE SPORTING NEWS College Player of the Year, 1972, 1973, 1974.. ..Named to THE SPORTING NEWS All-America First Team, 1972, 1973, 1974.... NCAA Division I Tournament Most Outstanding Player, 1972 and 1973.... Member of NCAA championship teams, 1972 and 1973.... Holds NCAA tournament record for highest field-goal percentage in one year (minimum of 25 made), 76.3 percent (45-of-59), 1973. ... Holds NCAA tournament record for highest field-goal percentage in career (minimum of 60 made), 68.6 percent (109-of-159), 1972 through 1974.... Brother of former National Football League tackle Bruce Walton.

BRYAN ANTHONY WARRICK

Born July 22, 1959 at Moses Lake, Wash.   Height 6:05.   Weight 195.

High School—Burlington, N. J., Township.

College—Saint Joseph's University, Philadelphia, Pa.

Drafted by Washington on second round, 1982 (25th pick).

Waived by Washington, October 26, 1983; re-signed by Washington, November 17, 1983.
Traded by Washington to Los Angeles Clippers for a 1985 3rd round draft choice, September 25, 1984.
Waived by Los Angeles Clippers, March 8, 1985.

—COLLEGIATE RECORD—

Year	G.	Min.	FGA	FGM	Pct.	FTA	FTM	Pct.	Reb.	Pts.	Avg.
78-79	24	217	77	31	.403	24	16	.667	23	78	3.3
79-80	30	1031	298	141	.473	102	75	.735	81	357	11.9
80-81	29	967	355	160	.451	104	71	.683	79	391	13.5
81-82	30	1057	345	175	.507	125	97	.776	97	447	14.9
Totals	113	3272	1075	507	.472	355	259	.730	280	1273	11.3

NBA REGULAR SEASON RECORD

Sea.—Team	G.	Min.	FGA	FGM	Pct.	FTA	FTM	Pct.	—Rebounds— Off.	Def.	Tot.	Ast.	PF	Dq.	Stl.	Blk.	Pts.	Avg.
82-83—Washington	43	727	171	65	.380	57	42	.737	15	54	69	126	103	5	21	8	172	4.0
83-84—Washington	32	254	66	27	.409	16	8	.500	5	17	22	43	37	0	9	3	63	2.0
84-85—L.A. Clippers	58	713	173	85	.491	57	44	.772	10	48	58	153	85	0	23	6	215	3.7
Totals	133	1694	410	177	.432	130	94	.723	30	119	149	322	225	5	53	17	450	3.4

Three-Point Field Goals: 1982-83, 0-for-5. 1983-84, 1-for-3 (.333). 1984-85, 1-for-4 (.250). Totals, 2-for-12 (.167).

MARVIN NATHANIEL WEBSTER

Born April 13, 1952 at Baltimore, Md.   Height 7:01.   Weight 240.

High School—Baltimore, Md., Edmondson.

College—Morgan State University, Baltimore, Md.

Drafted by Atlanta on first round, 1975 (3rd pick).

Selected by Denver as bonus choice (first pick in ABA draft), 1975.
Entered NBA with Denver, 1976.
Traded by Denver with Paul Silas and Willie Wise to Seattle for Tom Burleson, Bob Wilkerson and a 1977 2nd round draft choice, May 24, 1977.
Signed by New York as Veteran Free Agent, August 28, 1978; Seattle received Lonnie Shelton, a 1979 1st round draft choice and cash as compensation, September 29, 1978. Seattle subsequently conveyed a 1981 1st round draft choice and cash to New York as part of transaction.
Missed entire 1984-85 season due to illness.

—COLLEGIATE RECORD—

Year	G.	Min.	FGA	FGM	Pct.	FTA	FTM	Pct.	Reb.	Pts.	Avg.
71-72	26	....	276	125	.453	134	92	.687	419	342	13.2
72-73	28	....	387	199	.514	175	120	.686	650	518	18.5
73-74	33	....	501	273	.545	231	161	.697	740	707	21.4
74-75	27	....	331	186	.562	104	51	.490	458	423	15.7
Totals	114	....	1495	783	.524	644	424	.658	2267	1990	17.5

ABA REGULAR SEASON RECORD

Sea.—Team	G.	Min.	2-Point FGM	FGA	Pct.	3-Point FGM	FGA	Pct.	FTM	FTA	Pct.	Reb.	Ast.	Pts.	Avg.
75-76—Denver	38	398	55	119	.462	0	1	.000	55	78	.705	174	30	165	4.3

ABA PLAYOFF RECORD

Sea.—Team	G.	Min.	2-Point FGM	FGA	Pct.	3-Point FGM	FGA	Pct.	FTM	FTA	Pct.	Reb.	Ast.	Pts.	Avg.
75-76—Denver	13	155	21	50	.420	0	0	.000	15	28	.536	71	9	57	4.4

NBA REGULAR SEASON RECORD

Sea.—Team	G.	Min.	FGA	FGM	Pct.	FTA	FTM	Pct.	Off.	Def.	Tot.	Ast.	PF	Dq.	Stl.	Blk.	Pts.	Avg.
76-77—Denver	80	1276	400	198	.495	220	143	.650	152	332	484	62	149	2	23	118	539	6.7
77-78—Seattle	82	2910	851	427	.502	461	290	.629	361	674	1035	203	262	8	48	162	1144	14.0
78-79—New York	60	2027	558	264	.473	262	150	.573	198	457	655	172	183	6	24	112	678	11.3
79-80—New York	20	298	79	38	.481	16	12	.750	28	52	80	9	39	1	3	11	88	4.4
80-81—New York	82	1708	341	159	.466	163	104	.638	162	303	465	72	187	2	27	97	423	5.2
81-82—New York	82	1883	405	199	.491	170	108	.635	184	306	490	99	211	2	22	91	506	6.2
82-83—New York	82	1472	331	168	.508	180	106	.589	176	267	443	49	210	3	35	131	442	5.4
83-84—New York	76	1290	239	112	.469	117	66	.564	146	220	366	53	187	2	34	100	290	3.8
Totals	564	12864	3204	1565	.488	1589	979	.616	1407	2611	4018	719	1428	26	216	822	4110	7.3

Three-Point Field Goals: 1980-81, 1-for-4 (.250). 1982-83, 0-for-1. Totals, 1-for-5 (.200).

NBA PLAYOFF RECORD

Sea.—Team	G.	Min.	FGA	FGM	Pct.	FTA	FTM	Pct.	Off.	Def.	Tot.	Ast.	PF	Dq.	Stl.	Blk.	Pts.	Avg.
76-77—Denver	6	96	26	13	.500	6	4	.667	14	26	40	3	12	0	2	11	30	5.0
77-78—Seattle	22	904	280	137	.489	120	81	.675	95	194	289	58	76	2	6	58	355	16.1
80-81—New York	2	63	12	6	.500	4	0	.000	4	6	10	1	6	0	0	1	12	6.0
82-83—New York	6	115	18	7	.389	22	14	.636	13	15	28	3	18	0	0	7	28	4.7
83-84—New York	12	204	29	14	.483	15	9	.600	24	32	56	3	32	0	4	17	37	3.1
Totals	48	1382	365	177	.485	167	108	.647	150	273	423	68	144	2	12	94	462	9.6

NCAA Division II Tournament Most Outstanding Player, 1974. . . . Member of NCAA Division II championship team, 1974.

SCOTT DEAN WEDMAN

Born July 29, 1952 at Harper, Kan.   Height 6:07.   Weight 235.

High School—Denver, Colo., Mullen.

College—University of Colorado, Boulder, Colo.

Drafted by Kansas City-Omaha on first round, 1974 (6th pick).

Signed by Cleveland as Veteran Free Agent, June 2, 1981; Kansas City agreed not to exercise its right of first refusal and traded a 1981 2nd round draft choice to Cleveland for a 1981 1st round draft choice, June 8, 1981. Traded by Cleveland to Boston for Darren Tillis, a 1983 1st round draft choice and cash, January 14, 1983.

—COLLEGIATE RECORD—

Year	G.	Min.	FGA	FGM	Pct.	FTA	FTM	Pct.	Reb.	Pts.	Avg.
70-71†	10	....	...	66	....	53	46	.768	....	175	17.5
71-72	26	....	291	132	.454	103	68	.660	228	332	12.8
72-73	26	....	383	185	.483	111	90	.811	242	460	17.7
73-74	23	....	372	199	.535	97	61	.629	214	459	20.0
Varsity Totals	75	....	1046	516	.493	311	219	.704	684	1251	16.7

NBA REGULAR SEASON RECORD

Sea.—Team	G.	Min.	FGA	FGM	Pct.	FTA	FTM	Pct.	Off.	Def.	Tot.	Ast.	PF	Dq.	Stl.	Blk.	Pts.	Avg.
74-75—K.C.-Oma.	80	2554	806	375	.465	170	139	.818	202	288	490	129	270	2	81	27	889	11.1
75-76—Kansas City	82	2968	1181	538	.456	245	191	.780	199	407	606	199	280	8	103	36	1267	15.5
76-77—Kansas City	81	2743	1133	521	.460	241	206	.855	187	319	506	227	226	3	100	23	1248	15.4
77-78—Kansas City	81	2961	1192	607	.509	254	221	.870	144	319	463	201	242	2	99	30	1435	17.7
78-79—Kansas City	73	2498	1050	561	.534	271	216	.797	135	251	386	144	239	4	76	30	1338	18.3
79-80—Kansas City	68	2347	1112	569	.512	181	145	.801	114	272	386	145	230	1	84	45	1290	19.0
80-81—Kansas City	81	2902	1437	685	.477	204	140	.686	128	305	433	226	294	4	97	46	1535	19.0
81-82—Cleveland	54	1638	589	260	.441	90	66	.733	128	176	304	133	189	4	73	14	591	10.9
82-83—Clev.-Bos.	75	1793	788	374	.475	107	85	.794	98	184	282	117	228	6	43	17	843	11.2
83-84—Boston	68	916	333	148	.444	35	29	.829	41	98	139	67	107	0	27	7	327	4.8
84-85—Boston	78	1127	460	220	.478	55	42	.764	57	102	159	94	111	0	23	10	499	6.4
Totals	821	24447	10081	4858	.482	1853	1480	.799	1433	2721	4154	1682	2416	34	806	277	11262	13.7

Three-Point Field Goals: 1979-80, 7-for-22 (.318). 1980-81, 25-for-77 (.325). 1981-82, 5-for-23 (.217). 1982-83, 10-for-32 (.313). 1983-84, 2-for-13 (.154). 1984-85, 17-for-34 (.500). Totals, 66-for-201 (.328).

Sea.—Team	G.	Min.	FGA	FGM	Pct.	FTA	FTM	Pct.	—Rebounds— Off.	Def.	Tot.	Ast.	PF	Dq.	Stl.	Blk.	Pts.	Avg.
74-75—K.C.-Oma.	6	230	68	27	.397	18	12	.667	10	25	35	16	17	0	6	3	66	11.0
78-79—Kansas City	5	174	78	36	.462	32	24	.750	13	24	37	9	17	0	6	3	66	19.2
79-80—Kansas City	3	116	64	29	.453	11	8	.727	6	15	21	9	9	0	1	3	68	22.7
80-81—Kansas City	15	657	297	129	.434	56	40	.714	16	71	87	58	51	0	18	8	307	20.5
82-83—Boston	6	66	24	14	.583	2	1	.500	3	11	14	0	11	0	1	0	29	4.8
83-84—Boston	17	226	96	40	.417	10	5	.500	24	23	47	17	19	0	6	0	89	5.2
84-85—Boston	21	350	134	73	.545	38	26	.684	22	37	59	33	50	1	13	0	182	8.7
Totals	73	1819	761	348	.457	167	116	.694	94	206	300	142	175	1	54	17	837	11.5

Three-Point Field Goals: 1979-80, 2-for-3 (.667). 1980-81, 9-for-32 (.281). 1982-83, 0-for-2. 1983-84, 4-for-7 (.571). 1984-85, 10-for-22 (.455). Totals, 25-for-66 (.379).

NBA ALL-STAR GAME RECORD

Season—Team	Min.	FGA	FGM	Pct.	FTA	FTM	Pct.	—Rebounds— Off.	Def.	Tot.	Ast.	PF	Dq.	Stl.	Blk.	Pts.
1976—Kansas City	20	5	4	.800	0	0	.000	0	6	6	2	2	0	1	0	8

Named to NBA All-Defensive Second Team, 1980. . . . NBA All-Rookie Team, 1975. . . . Member of NBA championship team, 1984. . . . Holds NBA championship series game record for highest field-goal percentage, 1.000, vs. Los Angeles Lakers, May 27, 1985.

MARK ANDRE WEST

Born November 5, 1960 at Petersburg, Va.   Height 6:10.   Weight 230.

High School—Petersburg, Va.

College—Old Dominion University, Norfolk, Va.

Drafted by Dallas on second round, 1983 (30th pick).

Waived by Dallas, October 23, 1984; signed by Milwaukee as a free agent, November 6, 1984.
Waived by Milwaukee, November 12, 1984; signed by Cleveland as a free agent, November 23, 1984.

—COLLEGIATE RECORD—

Year	G.	Min.	FGA	FGM	Pct.	FTA	FTM	Pct.	Reb.	Pts.	Avg.
79-80	30	679	141	67	.475	27	10	.370	212	144	4.8
80-81	28	845	243	128	.527	83	48	.578	287	304	10.9
81-82	30	1007	323	197	.610	147	78	.531	300	472	15.7
82-83	29	1005	297	169	.569	163	80	.491	314	418	14.4
Totals	117	3536	1004	561	.559	420	216	.514	1113	1338	11.4

NBA REGULAR SEASON RECORD

Sea.—Team	G.	Min.	FGA	FGM	Pct.	FTA	FTM	Pct.	—Rebounds— Off.	Def.	Tot.	Ast.	PF	Dq.	Stl.	Blk.	Pts.	Avg.
83-84—Dallas	34	202	42	15	.357	22	7	.318	19	27	46	13	55	0	1	15	37	1.1
84-85—Mil.-Clev.	66	888	194	106	.546	87	43	.494	90	161	251	15	197	7	13	49	255	3.9
Totals	100	1090	236	121	.513	109	50	.459	109	188	297	28	252	7	14	64	292	2.9

Three-Point Field Goals: 1984-85, 0-for-1.

NBA PLAYOFF RECORD

Sea.—Team	G.	Min.	FGA	FGM	Pct.	FTA	FTM	Pct.	—Rebounds— Off.	Def.	Tot.	Ast.	PF	Dq.	Stl.	Blk.	Pts.	Avg.
83-84—Dallas	4	32	9	5	.556	3	2	.667	0	7	7	3	11	1	0	3	12	3.0
84-85—Cleveland	4	68	5	3	.600	5	2	.400	5	13	18	4	19	0	2	0	8	2.0
Totals	8	100	14	8	.571	8	4	.500	5	20	25	7	30	1	2	3	20	2.5

Led NCAA Division I in blocked shots, 1981 and 1982.

ENNIS WHATLEY

Born August 11, 1962 at Birmingham, Ala.   Height 6:03.   Weight 177.

High School—Birmingham, Ala., Phillips.

College—University of Alabama, University, Ala.

Drafted by Kansas City on first round as an undergraduate, 1983 (13th pick).

Draft rights traded by Kansas City with draft rights to Chris McNealy and a 1984 2nd round draft choice to Chicago for Mark Olberding and draft rights to Larry Micheaux, June 28, 1983.
Traded by Chicago with draft rights to Keith Lee to Cleveland for draft rights to Charles Oakley and Calvin Duncan, June 18, 1985.

—COLLEGIATE RECORD—

Year	G.	Min.	FGA	FGM	Pct.	FTA	FTM	Pct.	Reb.	Pts.	Avg.
81-82	31	996	285	141	.495	129	93	.721	76	375	12.1
82-83	32	1109	366	183	.500	157	121	.771	128	487	15.2
Totals	63	2105	651	324	.498	286	214	.748	204	862	13.7

Sea.—Team	G.	Min.	FGA	FGM	Pct.	FTA	FTM	Pct.	Off.	Def.	Tot.	Ast.	PF	Dq.	Stl.	Blk.	Pts.	Avg.
83-84—Chicago	80	2159	556	261	.469	200	146	.730	63	134	197	662	223	4	119	17	668	8.4
84-85—Chicago	70	1385	313	140	.447	86	68	.791	34	67	101	381	141	1	66	10	349	5.0
Totals	150	3544	869	401	.461	286	214	.748	97	201	298	1043	364	5	185	27	1017	6.8

Three-Point Field Goals: 1983-84, 0-for-2. 1984-85, 1-for-9 (.111). Totals, 1-for-11 (.091).

Named to THE SPORTING NEWS All-America Second Team, 1983.

RORY WILBUR WHITE

Born August 16, 1959 at Tuskegee, Ala.   Height 6:08.   Weight 210.

High School—Tuskegee, Ala.

College—University of South Alabama, Mobile, Ala.

Drafted by Phoenix on fourth round, 1983 (86th pick).

Waived by Phoenix, December 20, 1983; signed by Milwaukee, January 5, 1984, to first of consecutive 10-day contracts that expired January 24, 1984.

Signed by San Diego as a free agent, March 9, 1984.

Played in Continental Basketball Association with Wyoming Wildcatters and Albuquerque Silvers, 1983-84.

—COLLEGIATE RECORD—

Year	G.	Min.	FGA	FGM	Pct.	FTA	FTM	Pct.	Reb.	Pts.	Avg.
77-78	28	538	180	97	.539	52	33	.635	122	227	8.1
78-79	27	856	400	221	.553	106	71	.670	226	513	19.0
79-80	2	10	4	3	.750	2	0	.000	1	6	6.0
80-81	31	1031	367	216	.589	104	75	.721	205	507	16.4
81-82	28	939	347	195	.562	118	83	.703	183	473	16.9
Totals	115	3374	1298	732	.564	382	262	.686	737	1726	15.0

(Suffered knee injury in first game of 1979-80 season; granted extra year of eligibility.)

MINOR LEAGUE REGULAR SEASON RECORD

			—2-Point—			—3-Point—								
Sea.—Team	G.	Min.	FGM	FGA	Pct.	FGM	FGA	Pct.	FTM	FTA	Pct.	Reb.	Ast.	Pts.	Avg.
83-84—Wyoming-Albu. CBA	11	288	64	123	.520	0	0	.000	38	53	.716	59	9	166	15.1

NBA REGULAR SEASON RECORD

Sea.—Team	G.	Min.	FGA	FGM	Pct.	FTA	FTM	Pct.	Off.	Def.	Tot.	Ast.	PF	Dq.	Stl.	Blk.	Pts.	Avg.
82-83—Phoenix	65	626	234	127	.543	109	70	.642	47	58	105	30	54	0	16	2	324	5.0
83-84—Phoe-Mil-SD	36	372	170	80	.471	47	26	.553	37	37	74	15	31	0	15	3	186	5.2
84-85—L.A. Clippers	80	1106	279	144	.516	130	90	.692	94	101	195	34	115	0	35	20	378	4.7
Totals	181	2104	683	351	.514	286	186	.650	178	196	374	79	200	0	66	25	888	4.9

Three-Point Field Goals: 1982-83, 0-for-1.

NBA PLAYOFF RECORD

Sea.—Team	G.	Min.	FGA	FGM	Pct.	FTA	FTM	Pct.	Off.	Def.	Tot.	Ast.	PF	Dq.	Stl.	Blk.	Pts.	Avg.
82-83—Phoenix	3	40	14	7	.500	4	2	.500	1	9	10	0	4	0	0	0	16	5.3

Three-Point Field Goals: 1982-83, 0-for-1.

WILLIE WHITE

Born August 20, 1962 at Memphis, Tenn.   Height 6:03.   Weight 195.

High School—Memphis, Tenn., Carver.

College—University of Tennessee at Chattanooga, Chattanooga, Tenn.

Drafted by Denver on second round, 1984 (42nd pick).

—COLLEGIATE RECORD—

Year	G.	Min.	FGA	FGM	Pct.	FTA	FTM	Pct.	Reb.	Pts.	Avg.
80-81	30	....	309	154	.498	42	36	.857	124	353	11.8
81-82	31	....	377	200	.531	107	85	.794	133	491	15.8
82-83	30	....	437	227	.519	93	75	.806	120	553	18.4
83-84	31	1127	443	216	.488	143	124	.867	122	575	18.5
Totals	122	....	1566	797	.509	385	320	.831	499	1972	16.2

Three-Point Field Goals: 1980-81, 9-for-24 (.375). 1981-82, 6-for-11 (.545). 1982-83, 24-for-64 (.375). 1983-84, 19-for-40 (.475). Totals, 58-for-139 (.417).

NBA REGULAR SEASON RECORD

Sea.—Team	G.	Min.	FGA	FGM	Pct.	FTA	FTM	Pct.	Off.	Def.	Tot.	Ast.	PF	Dq.	Stl.	Blk.	Pts.	Avg.
84-85—Denver	39	234	124	52	.419	31	21	.677	15	21	36	29	24	0	5	2	129	3.3

Three-Point Field Goals: 1984-85, 4-for-11 (.364).

Sea.—Team	G.	Min.	FGA	FGM	Pct.	FTA	FTM	Pct.	—Rebounds— Off.	Def.	Tot.	Ast.	PF	Dq.	Stl.	Blk.	Pts.	Avg.
84-85—Denver	10	123	57	27	.474	12	7	.583	9	8	17	17	6	0	5	0	63	6.3

Three Point-Field Goals: 1984-85, 2-for-3 (.667).

JEROME CLAY WHITEHEAD

Born September 30, 1956 at Waukegan, Ill. Height 6:10. Weight 225.

High School—Waukegan, Ill.

Colleges—Riverside City College, Riverside, Calif., and
Marquette University, Milwaukee, Wis.

Drafted by Buffalo on second round, 1978 (41st pick).

Waived by San Diego, December 4, 1979; signed by Utah as a free agent, January 18, 1980.
Selected from Utah by Dallas in expansion draft, May 28, 1980.
Traded by Dallas with Richard Washington to Cleveland for Bill Robinzine and two 1st round draft choices (1983 and 1986), October 30, 1980.
Waived by Cleveland, November 17, 1980; signed by San Diego as a free agent, January 9, 1981.
Traded by Los Angeles Clippers to Golden State for the draft rights to Jay Murphy, June 19, 1984.

—COLLEGIATE RECORD—
Riverside City

Year	G.	Min.	FGA	FGM	Pct.	FTA	FTM	Pct.	Reb.	Pts.	Avg.
74-75	..	....	...	...	....	...	...	....	....	....	21.0

Marquette

Year	G.	Min.	FGA	FGM	Pct.	FTA	FTM	Pct.	Reb.	Pts.	Avg.
75-76	29	766	211	111	.526	56	37	.661	186	259	8.9
76-77	32	1022	290	150	.517	62	36	.581	266	336	10.5
77-78	28	884	276	165	.598	97	62	.639	232	392	14.0
Totals	89	2672	777	426	.548	215	135	.628	684	987	11.1

NBA REGULAR SEASON RECORD

Sea.—Team	G.	Min.	FGA	FGM	Pct.	FTA	FTM	Pct.	—Rebounds— Off.	Def.	Tot.	Ast.	PF	Dq.	Stl.	Blk.	Pts.	Avg.
78-79—San Diego	31	152	34	15	.441	18	8	.444	16	34	50	7	29	0	3	4	38	1.2
79-80—SD-Utah	50	553	114	58	.509	35	10	.286	56	111	167	24	97	3	8	17	126	2.5
80-81—Dal-Cle-SD	48	688	180	83	.461	56	28	.500	58	156	214	26	122	2	20	9	194	4.0
81-82—San Diego	72	2214	726	406	.559	241	184	.763	231	433	664	102	290	16	48	44	996	13.8
82-83—San Diego	46	905	306	164	.536	87	72	.828	105	156	261	42	139	2	21	15	400	8.7
83-84—San Diego	70	921	294	144	.490	107	88	.822	94	151	245	19	159	2	17	12	376	5.4
84-85—Golden State	79	2536	825	421	.510	235	184	.783	219	403	622	53	322	8	45	43	1026	13.0
Totals	396	7969	2479	1291	.521	779	574	.737	779	1444	2223	273	1158	33	162	144	3156	8.0

Three-Point Field Goals: 1980-81, 0-for-1.
Member of NCAA championship team, 1977.

MITCHELL WIGGINS

Born September 28, 1959 at Lenoir County, N. C. Height 6:04. Weight 185.

High School—La Grange, N. C., North Lenoir.

Colleges—Truett-McConnell College, Cleveland, Ga.; Clemson University,
Clemson, S. C., and Florida State University, Tallahassee, Fla.

Drafted by Indiana on first round, 1983 (23rd pick).

Draft rights traded by Indiana to Chicago for draft rights to Sidney Lowe and a 1984 2nd round draft choice, June 28, 1983.
Traded by Chicago with 1985 2nd and 3rd round draft choices to Houston for Caldwell Jones, August 10, 1984.

—COLLEGIATE RECORD—
Truett-McConnell

Year	G.	Min.	FGA	FGM	Pct.	FTA	FTM	Pct.	Reb.	Pts.	Avg.
78-79											25.2

Clemson

Year	G.	Min.	FGA	FGM	Pct.	FTA	FTM	Pct.	Reb.	Pts.	Avg.
79-80	32	537	162	76	.469	45	25	.556	96	177	5.5

Florida State

Year	G.	Min.	FGA	FGM	Pct.	FTA	FTM	Pct.	Reb.	Pts.	Avg.
80-81				Did Not Play—Transfer Student							
81-82	22	808	388	223	.574	102	77	.755	213	523	23.8
82-83	24	873	410	216	.527	147	112	.762	196	544	22.7
FSU Totals	46	1681	798	439	.550	249	189	.759	409	1067	23.2
College Totals	78	2218	960	515	.536	294	214	.728	505	1244	15.9

NBA REGULAR SEASON RECORD

Sea.—Team	G.	Min.	FGA	FGM	Pct.	FTA	FTM	Pct.	Rebounds—Off.	Def.	Tot.	Ast.	PF	Dq.	Stl.	Blk.	Pts.	Avg.
83-84—Chicago	82	2123	890	399	.448	287	213	.742	138	190	328	187	278	8	106	11	1018	12.4
84-85—Houston	82	1575	657	318	.484	131	96	.733	110	125	235	119	195	1	83	13	738	9.0
Totals	164	3698	1547	717	.463	418	309	.739	248	315	563	306	473	9	189	24	1756	10.7

Three-Point Field Goals: 1983-84, 7-for-29 (.241). 1984-85, 6-for-23 (.261). Totals, 13-for-52 (.250).

NBA PLAYOFF RECORD

Sea.—Team	G.	Min.	FGA	FGM	Pct.	FTA	FTM	Pct.	Rebounds—Off.	Def.	Tot.	Ast.	PF	Dq.	Stl.	Blk.	Pts.	Avg.
84-85—Houston	5	45	18	9	.500	0	0	.000	3	1	4	1	6	0	4	0	18	3.6

JAMAAL WILKES

(Formerly Jackson Keith Wilkes and known by middle name.)

Born May 2, 1953 at Berkeley, Calif. Height 6:06. Weight 190.

High Schools—Ventura, Calif. (Junior) and Santa Barbara, Calif. (Senior).

College—University of California at Los Angeles, Los Angeles, Calif.

Drafted by Golden State on first round, 1974 (11th pick).

Signed by Los Angeles as Veteran Free Agent, July 11, 1977; Golden State received cash and a 1978 1st round draft choice as compensation, September 14, 1977.

—COLLEGIATE RECORD—

Year	G.	Min.	FGA	FGM	Pct.	FTA	FTM	Pct.	Reb.	Pts.	Avg.
70-71†	20	....	267	166	.622	95	68	.716	242	400	20.0
71-72	30	....	322	171	.531	92	64	.696	245	406	13.5
72-73	30	....	381	200	.525	66	43	.652	220	443	14.8
73-74	30	....	426	209	.491	94	82	.872	198	500	16.7
Varsity Totals	90	....	1129	580	.514	252	189	.750	663	1349	15.0

NBA REGULAR SEASON RECORD

Sea.—Team	G.	Min.	FGA	FGM	Pct.	FTA	FTM	Pct.	Rebounds—Off.	Def.	Tot.	Ast.	PF	Dq.	Stl.	Blk.	Pts.	Avg.
74-75—Golden State	82	2515	1135	502	.442	218	160	.734	203	468	671	183	222	0	107	22	1164	14.2
75-76—Golden State	82	2716	1334	617	.463	294	227	.772	193	527	720	167	222	0	102	31	1461	17.8
76-77—Golden State	76	2579	1147	548	.478	310	247	.797	155	423	578	211	222	1	127	16	1343	17.7
77-78—Los Angeles	51	1490	630	277	.440	148	106	.716	113	267	380	182	162	1	77	22	660	12.9
78-79—Los Angeles	82	2915	1242	626	.504	362	272	.751	164	445	609	227	275	2	134	27	1524	18.6
79-80—Los Angeles	82	3111	1358	726	.535	234	189	.808	176	349	525	250	220	1	129	28	1644	20.0
80-81—Los Angeles	81	3028	1495	786	.526	335	254	.758	146	289	435	235	223	1	121	29	1827	22.6
81-82—Los Angeles	82	2906	1417	744	.525	336	246	.732	153	240	393	143	240	1	89	24	1734	21.1
82-83—Los Angeles	80	2552	1290	684	.530	268	203	.757	146	197	343	182	221	0	65	17	1571	19.6
83-84—Los Angeles	75	2507	1055	542	.514	280	208	.743	130	210	340	214	205	0	72	41	1294	17.3
84-85—L.A. Lakers	42	761	303	148	.488	66	51	.773	35	59	94	41	65	0	19	3	347	8.3
Totals	815	27080	12406	6200	.500	2851	2163	.759	1614	3474	5088	2035	2277	7	1042	260	14569	17.9

Three-Point Field Goals: 1979-80, 3-for-17 (.176). 1980-81, 1-for-13 (.077). 1981-82, 0-for-4. 1982-83, 0-for-6. 1983-84, 2-for-8 (.250). 1984-85, 0-for-1. Totals, 6-for-49 (.122).

NBA PLAYOFF RECORD

Sea.—Team	G.	Min.	FGA	FGM	Pct.	FTA	FTM	Pct.	Rebounds—Off.	Def.	Tot.	Ast.	PF	Dq.	Stl.	Blk.	Pts.	Avg.
74-75—Golden State	17	503	249	111	.446	47	33	.702	30	89	119	28	53	1	26	14	255	15.0
75-76—Golden State	13	450	200	86	.430	45	35	.778	25	78	103	29	33	1	12	8	207	15.9
76-77—Golden State	10	346	154	66	.429	28	23	.821	18	62	80	16	23	0	16	6	155	15.5
77-78—Los Angeles	3	108	32	15	.469	11	6	.545	9	17	26	8	14	1	3	1	36	12.0
78-79—Los Angeles	8	307	128	61	.477	37	25	.676	20	48	68	16	21	0	15	2	147	18.4
79-80—Los Angeles	16	652	294	140	.476	54	44	.815	53	75	128	48	51	0	24	5	324	20.3
80-81—Los Angeles	3	113	48	21	.438	18	12	.667	4	4	8	4	10	0	1	1	54	18.0
81-82—Los Angeles	14	535	241	121	.502	49	38	.776	40	30	70	37	43	0	16	3	280	20.0
82-83—Los Angeles	15	589	273	136	.498	44	27	.614	42	48	90	51	51	0	20	11	299	19.9
83-84—Los Angeles	14	196	70	28	.400	11	7	.636	10	16	26	9	27	0	4	2	63	4.5
Totals	113	3799	1689	785	.465	344	250	.727	251	467	718	246	326	3	137	53	1820	16.1

Three-Point Field Goals: 1979-80, 0-for-1. 1980-81, 0-for-1. 1981-82, 0-for-1. 1982-83, 0-for-2. 1983-84, 0-for-1. Totals, 0-for-6.

NBA ALL-STAR GAME RECORD

Season—Team	Min.	FGA	FGM	Pct.	FTA	FTM	Pct.	Rebounds—Off.	Def.	Tot.	Ast.	PF	Dq.	Stl.	Blk.	Pts.
1976—Golden State	14	9	3	.333	2	2	1.000	3	1	4	2	0	0	1	0	8
1981—Los Angeles	25	12	6	.500	3	3	1.000	2	6	8	3	3	0	2	0	15
1983—Los Angeles	15	6	4	.667	2	2	1.000	1	1	2	2	0	0	1	0	10
Totals	54	27	13	.481	7	7	1.000	6	8	14	7	3	0	4	0	33

Named NBA Rookie of the Year, 1975. . . . NBA All-Rookie Team, 1975. . . . NBA All-Defensive Second Team, 1976 and 1977. . . . Member of NBA championship teams, 1975, 1980, 1982, 1985. . . . Named to THE SPORTING NEWS All-America Second Team, 1974. . . . Member of NCAA championship teams, 1972 and 1973.

JACQUE DOMINIQUE WILKINS
(Known by middle name.)

Born January 12, 1960 at Paris, France.   Height 6:07.   Weight 200.

High School—Washington, N. C.

College—University of Georgia, Athens, Ga.

Drafted by Utah on first round as an undergraduate, 1982 (3rd pick).

Draft rights traded by Utah to Atlanta for John Drew, Freeman Williams and cash, September 2, 1982.

—COLLEGIATE RECORD—

Year	G.	Min.	FGA	FGM	Pct.	FTA	FTM	Pct.	Reb.	Pts.	Avg.
79-80	16	508	257	135	.525	37	27	.730	104	297	18.6
80-81	31	1157	582	310	.533	149	112	.752	234	732	23.6
81-82	31	1083	526	278	.529	160	103	.644	250	659	21.3
Totals	78	2748	1365	723	.530	346	242	.699	588	1688	21.6

NBA REGULAR SEASON RECORD

Sea.—Team	G.	Min.	FGA	FGM	Pct.	FTA	FTM	Pct.	—Rebounds— Off.	Def.	Tot.	Ast.	PF	Dq.	Stl.	Blk.	Pts.	Avg.
82-83—Atlanta	82	2697	1220	601	.493	337	230	.682	226	252	478	129	210	1	84	63	1434	17.5
83-84—Atlanta	81	2961	1429	684	.479	496	382	.770	254	328	582	126	197	1	117	87	1750	21.6
84-85—Atlanta	81	3023	1891	853	.451	603	486	.806	226	331	557	200	170	0	135	54	2217	27.4
Totals	244	8681	4540	2138	.471	1436	1098	.765	706	911	1617	455	577	2	336	204	5401	22.1

Three-Point Field Goals: 1982-83, 2-for-11 (.182). 1983-84, 0-for-11. 1984-85, 25-for-81 (.309). Totals, 27-for-103 (.262).

NBA PLAYOFF RECORD

Sea.—Team	G.	Min.	FGA	FGM	Pct.	FTA	FTM	Pct.	—Rebounds— Off.	Def.	Tot.	Ast.	PF	Dq.	Stl.	Blk.	Pts.	Avg.
82-83—Atlanta	3	109	42	17	.405	14	12	.887	8	7	15	1	9	0	2	1	47	15.7
83-84—Atlanta	5	197	84	35	.417	31	26	.839	21	20	41	11	13	0	12	1	96	19.2
Totals	8	306	126	52	.413	45	38	.844	29	27	56	12	22	0	14	2	143	17.9

Three-Point Field Goals: 1982-83, 1-for-1 (1.000). 1983-84, 0-for-1. Totals, 1-for-2 (.500).

Named to NBA All-Rookie Team, 1983. . . . THE SPORTING NEWS All-America Second Team, 1981 and 1982. . . . Brother of Gerald Wilkins, 2nd round draft choice of New York Knicks in 1985 NBA draft.

EDDIE LEE WILKINS

Born May 7, 1962 at Cartersville, Ga.   Height 6:10.   Weight 220.

High School—Cartersville, Ga., Cass.

College—Gardner-Webb College, Boiling Springs, N. C.

Drafted by New York on sixth round, 1984 (133rd pick).

—COLLEGIATE RECORD—

Year	G.	Min.	FGA	FGM	Pct.	FTA	FTM	Pct.	Reb.	Pts.	Avg.
80-81	36	....	296	166	.561	163	104	.638	242	436	12.1
81-82	29	....	350	217	.620	211	142	.673	257	576	19.9
82-83	32	....	463	295	.637	284	203	.715	340	793	24.8
83-84	29	....	376	214	.569	209	128	.612	264	556	19.2
Totals	126	....	1485	892	.601	867	577	.666	1103	2361	18.7

NBA REGULAR SEASON RECORD

Sea.—Team	G.	Min.	FGA	FGM	Pct.	FTA	FTM	Pct.	—Rebounds— Off.	Def.	Tot.	Ast.	PF	Dq.	Stl.	Blk.	Pts.	Avg.
84-85—New York	54	917	233	116	.498	122	66	.541	86	176	262	16	155	3	21	16	298	5.5

Three-Point Field Goals: 1984-85, 0-for-2.

—DID YOU KNOW—

That three of the defending-champion Lakers' 1984-85 starters came to the NBA from NCAA champions? Magic Johnson played for Michigan State in 1979, James Worthy was at North Carolina in 1982 and Kareem Abdul-Jabbar led UCLA to the 1967, 1968 and 1969 championships.

JEFFREY WILKINS
(Jeff)

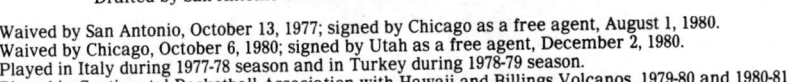

Born March 9, 1955 at Chicago, Ill.   Height 6:11.   Weight 240.

High School—Elgin, Ill.

Colleges—Black Hawk College, Moline, Ill., and
Illinois State University, Normal, Ill.

Drafted by San Antonio on second round, 1977 (37th pick).

Waived by San Antonio, October 13, 1977; signed by Chicago as a free agent, August 1, 1980.
Waived by Chicago, October 6, 1980; signed by Utah as a free agent, December 2, 1980.
Played in Italy during 1977-78 season and in Turkey during 1978-79 season.
Played in Continental Basketball Association with Hawaii and Billings Volcanos, 1979-80 and 1980-81.

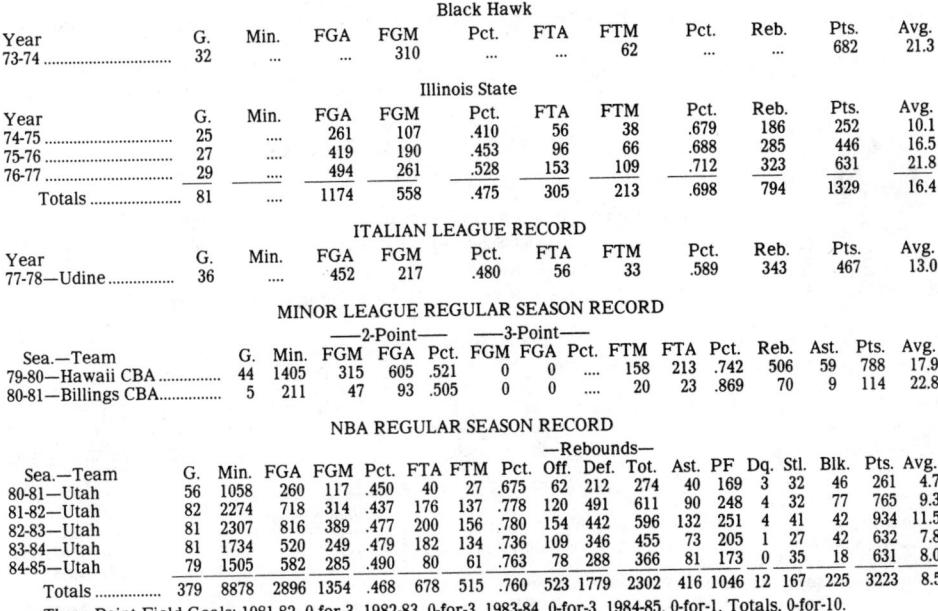

Black Hawk

Year	G.	Min.	FGA	FGM	Pct.	FTA	FTM	Pct.	Reb.	Pts.	Avg.
73-74	32	...	...	310	...	...	62	...	...	682	21.3

Illinois State

Year	G.	Min.	FGA	FGM	Pct.	FTA	FTM	Pct.	Reb.	Pts.	Avg.
74-75	25	....	261	107	.410	56	38	.679	186	252	10.1
75-76	27	....	419	190	.453	96	66	.688	285	446	16.5
76-77	29	....	494	261	.528	153	109	.712	323	631	21.8
Totals	81	....	1174	558	.475	305	213	.698	794	1329	16.4

ITALIAN LEAGUE RECORD

Year	G.	Min.	FGA	FGM	Pct.	FTA	FTM	Pct.	Reb.	Pts.	Avg.
77-78—Udine	36	....	452	217	.480	56	33	.589	343	467	13.0

MINOR LEAGUE REGULAR SEASON RECORD

Sea.—Team	G.	Min.	2-Point FGM	FGA	Pct.	3-Point FGM	FGA	Pct.	FTM	FTA	Pct.	Reb.	Ast.	Pts.	Avg.
79-80—Hawaii CBA	44	1405	315	605	.521	0	0	....	158	213	.742	506	59	788	17.9
80-81—Billings CBA	5	211	47	93	.505	0	0	....	20	23	.869	70	9	114	22.8

NBA REGULAR SEASON RECORD

Sea.—Team	G.	Min.	FGA	FGM	Pct.	FTA	FTM	Pct.	Off.	Def.	Tot.	Ast.	PF	Dq.	Stl.	Blk.	Pts.	Avg.
80-81—Utah	56	1058	260	117	.450	40	27	.675	62	212	274	40	169	3	32	46	261	4.7
81-82—Utah	82	2274	718	314	.437	176	137	.778	120	491	611	90	248	4	32	77	765	9.3
82-83—Utah	81	2307	816	389	.477	200	156	.780	154	442	596	132	251	4	41	42	934	11.5
83-84—Utah	81	1734	520	249	.479	182	134	.736	109	346	455	73	205	1	27	42	632	7.8
84-85—Utah	79	1505	582	285	.490	80	61	.763	78	288	366	81	173	0	35	18	631	8.0
Totals	379	8878	2896	1354	.468	678	515	.760	523	1779	2302	416	1046	12	167	225	3223	8.5

Three-Point Field Goals: 1981-82, 0-for-3. 1982-83, 0-for-3. 1983-84, 0-for-3. 1984-85, 0-for-1. Totals, 0-for-10.

NBA PLAYOFF RECORD

Sea.—Team	G.	Min.	FGA	FGM	Pct.	FTA	FTM	Pct.	Off.	Def.	Tot.	Ast.	PF	Dq.	Stl.	Blk.	Pts.	Avg.
83-84—Utah	11	205	57	30	.526	22	17	.773	10	39	49	5	32	0	0	5	77	7.0
84-85—Utah	10	257	118	51	.432	35	27	.771	13	50	63	13	27	0	4	5	129	12.9
Totals	21	462	175	81	.463	57	44	.772	23	89	112	18	59	0	4	10	206	9.8

Three-Point Field Goals: 1984-85, 0-for-1.

Named to CBA All-Star Second Team, 1980.

DALE WAYNE WILKINSON

Born March 18, 1960 at Pocatello, Ida.   Height 6:10.   Weight 220.

High School—Pocatello, Ida., Highland.

College—Idaho State University, Pocatello, Ida.

Drafted by Phoenix on tenth round, 1982 (221st pick).

Signed by Los Angeles as a free agent, September 27, 1983.
Waived by Los Angeles, October 17, 1983; signed by Cleveland as a free agent, September 1984.
Waived by Cleveland, October 22, 1984; signed by Detroit as a free agent, October 24, 1984.
Waived by Detroit, November 6, 1984; signed by Los Angeles Clippers to a 10-day contract that expired, March 10, 1985.
Signed by Los Angeles Clippers, March 11, 1985.
Played in Continental Basketball Association with Billings Volcanos, 1982-83; Sarasota Stingers and Wisconsin Flyers, 1983-84, and Wisconsin Flyers, 1984-85.

—COLLEGIATE RECORD—

Year	G.	Min.	FGA	FGM	Pct.	FTA	FTM	Pct.	Reb.	Pts.	Avg.
78-79	19	83	16	5	.313	10	5	.500	11	15	0.8
79-80	25	430	116	53	.457	55	41	.745	87	147	5.9
80-81	26	935	299	167	.559	62	50	.806	175	384	14.8
81-82	26	684	183	87	.475	50	45	.900	119	219	8.4
Totals	96	2132	614	312	.508	177	141	.797	392	765	8.0

MINOR LEAGUE REGULAR SEASON RECORD

Sea.—Team	G.	Min.	2-Point			3-Point			FTM	FTA	Pct.	Reb.	Ast.	Pts.	Avg.
			FGM	FGA	Pct.	FGM	FGA	Pct.							
82-83—Billings CBA	44	1105	216	402	.537	1	10	.100	94	108	.870	195	64	529	12.0
83-84—Sar.-Wisc. CBA	40	1214	246	451	.545	1	4	.250	66	96	.687	217	101	561	14.0
84-85—Wisconsin CBA	41	1522	304	582	.522	2	6	.333	140	160	.875	276	190	754	18.4

NBA REGULAR SEASON RECORD

Sea.—Team	G.	Min.	FGA	FGM	Pct.	FTA	FTM	Pct.	Off.	Def.	Tot.	Ast.	PF	Dq.	Stl.	Blk.	Pts.	Avg.
84-85—Det.-L.A.C.	12	45	16	4	.250	7	6	.857	1	3	4	2	10	0	0	0	14	1.2

Three-Point Field Goals: 1984-85, 0-for-1.

CHARLES LINWOOD WILLIAMS
(Buck)

Born March 8, 1960 at Rocky Mount, N. C.   Height 6:08.   Weight 215.

High School—Rocky Mount, N. C.

College—University of Maryland, College Park, Md.

Drafted by New Jersey on first round as an undergraduate, 1981 (3rd pick).

—COLLEGIATE RECORD—

Year	G.	Min.	FGA	FGM	Pct.	FTA	FTM	Pct.	Reb.	Pts.	Avg.
78-79	30	....	206	120	.583	109	60	.550	323	300	10.0
79-80	24	....	236	143	.606	128	85	.664	242	371	15.5
80-81	31	1080	283	183	.647	182	116	.637	363	482	15.5
Totals	85	....	725	446	.615	419	261	.623	928	1153	13.6

NBA REGULAR SEASON RECORD

Sea.—Team	G.	Min.	FGA	FGM	Pct.	FTA	FTM	Pct.	Off.	Def.	Tot.	Ast.	PF	Dq.	Stl.	Blk.	Pts.	Avg.
81-82—New Jersey	82	2825	881	513	.582	388	242	.624	347	658	1005	107	285	5	84	84	1268	15.5
82-83—New Jersey	82	2961	912	536	.588	523	324	.620	365	662	1027	125	270	4	91	110	1396	17.0
83-84—New Jersey	81	3003	926	495	.535	498	284	.570	355	645	1000	130	298	3	81	125	1274	15.7
84-85—New Jersey	82	3182	1089	577	.530	538	336	.625	323	682	1005	167	293	7	63	110	1491	18.2
Totals	327	11971	3808	2121	.557	1947	1186	.609	1390	2647	4037	529	1146	19	319	429	5429	16.6

Three-Point Field Goals: 1981-82, 0-for-1. 1982-83, 0-for-4. 1983-84, 0-for-4. 1984-85, 1-for-4 (.250). Totals, 1-for-13 (.077).

NBA PLAYOFF RECORD

Sea.—Team	G.	Min.	FGA	FGM	Pct.	FTA	FTM	Pct.	Off.	Def.	Tot.	Ast.	PF	Dq.	Stl.	Blk.	Pts.	Avg.
81-82—New Jersey	2	79	26	14	.538	15	7	.467	11	10	21	3	7	0	1	2	35	17.5
82-83—New Jersey	2	85	22	11	.500	20	16	.800	9	14	23	4	12	2	2	2	38	19.0
83-84—New Jersey	11	473	130	63	.485	81	45	.556	57	98	155	16	44	2	15	17	171	15.5
84-85—New Jersey	3	123	40	26	.650	30	22	.733	14	18	32	1	12	0	3	5	74	24.7
Totals	18	760	218	114	.523	146	90	.616	91	140	231	24	75	4	21	26	318	17.7

NBA ALL-STAR GAME RECORD

Season—Team	Min.	FGA	FGM	Pct.	FTA	FTM	Pct.	Off.	Def.	Tot.	Ast.	PF	Dq.	Stl.	Blk.	Pts.
1982—New Jersey	22	7	2	.286	2	0	.000	1	9	10	1	3	0	0	2	4
1983—New Jersey	19	4	3	.750	4	2	.500	3	4	7	1	0	0	1	0	8
Totals	41	11	5	.455	6	2	.333	4	13	17	2	3	0	1	2	12

Named to All-NBA Second Team, 1983. . . . NBA Rookie of the Year, 1982. . . . NBA All-Rookie Team, 1982. . . . Member of U.S. Olympic team, 1980.

—DID YOU KNOW—

That New York's Bernard King and Milwaukee's Sidney Moncrief were freshmen when they led the NCAA in field-goal percentage in 1974-75 and 1975-76, respectively? King shot 62.2 percent from the floor for Tennessee and Moncrief hit 66.5 percent of his shots for Arkansas the next season.

GUS WILLIAMS

Born October 10, 1953 at Mt. Vernon, N. Y.   Height 6:02.   Weight 175.

High School—Mt. Vernon, N. Y.

College—University of Southern California, Los Angeles, Calif.

Drafted by Golden State on second round, 1975 (20th pick).

Signed by Seattle as Veteran Free Agent, October 17, 1977; Golden State received cash as compensation.
Traded by Seattle to Washington for Ricky Sobers and the draft rights to Tim McCormick, June 19, 1984.

—COLLEGIATE RECORD—

Year	G.	Min.	FGA	FGM	Pct.	FTA	FTM	Pct.	Reb.	Pts.	Avg.
71-72†	19	....	246	113	.459	69	46	.667	78	272	14.3
72-73	28	....	324	141	.435	72	54	.750	126	336	12.0
73-74	29	....	394	191	.485	105	67	.638	100	449	15.5
74-75	25	....	460	220	.478	120	89	.742	116	529	21.2
Varsity Totals	82	....	1178	552	.469	297	210	.707	342	1314	16.0

NBA REGULAR SEASON RECORD

Sea.—Team	G.	Min.	FGA	FGM	Pct.	FTA	FTM	Pct.	Off.	Def.	Tot.	Ast.	PF	Dq.	Stl.	Blk.	Pts.	Avg.
75-76—Golden State	77	1728	853	365	.428	233	173	.742	62	97	159	240	143	2	140	26	903	11.7
76-77—Golden State	82	1930	701	325	.464	150	112	.747	72	161	233	292	218	4	121	19	762	9.3
77-78—Seattle	79	2572	1335	602	.451	278	227	.817	83	173	256	294	198	2	185	41	1431	18.1
78-79—Seattle	76	2266	1224	606	.495	316	245	.775	111	134	245	307	162	3	158	29	1457	19.2
79-80—Seattle	82	2969	1533	739	.482	420	331	.788	127	148	275	397	160	1	200	37	1816	22.1
80-81—Seattle							Missed Entire Season—Contract Dispute											
81-82—Seattle	80	2876	1592	773	.486	436	320	.734	92	152	244	549	163	0	172	36	1875	23.4
82-83—Seattle	80	2761	1384	660	.477	370	278	.751	72	133	205	643	117	0	182	26	1600	20.0
83-84—Seattle	80	2818	1306	598	.458	396	297	.750	67	137	204	675	151	0	189	25	1497	18.7
84-85—Washington	79	2960	1483	638	.430	346	251	.725	72	123	195	608	159	1	178	32	1578	20.0
Totals	715	22880	11411	5306	.465	2945	2234	.759	758	1258	2016	4005	1471	13	1525	271	12919	18.1

Three-Point Field Goals: 1979-80, 7-for-36 (.194). 1981-82, 9-for-40 (.225). 1982-83, 2-for-43 (.047). 1983-84, 4-for-25 (.160). 1984-85, 51-for-176 (.290). Totals, 73-for-320 (.228).

NBA PLAYOFF RECORD

Sea.—Team	G.	Min.	FGA	FGM	Pct.	FTA	FTM	Pct.	Off.	Def.	Tot.	Ast.	PF	Dq.	Stl.	Blk.	Pts.	Avg.
75-76—Golden State	11	178	85	30	.353	21	14	.667	5	9	14	26	22	0	11	0	74	6.7
76-77—Golden State	10	184	70	35	.500	21	18	.857	9	6	15	25	30	1	8	1	88	8.8
77-78—Seattle	22	701	342	163	.477	106	77	.726	30	56	86	88	70	2	45	12	403	18.1
78-79—Seattle	17	609	382	181	.474	127	90	.709	36	34	70	63	42	1	34	11	452	26.6
79-80—Seattle	15	564	284	146	.514	86	62	.721	30	30	60	84	38	0	34	7	355	23.7
81-82—Seattle	8	315	186	82	.441	56	44	.786	12	14	26	65	13	0	13	5	210	26.3
82-83—Seattle	2	81	47	26	.553	15	13	.867	4	3	7	8	5	0	5	0	65	32.5
83-84—Seattle	5	215	98	50	.510	21	15	.714	2	10	12	57	7	0	8	3	117	23.4
84-85—Washington	4	159	71	30	.423	12	9	.750	4	4	8	20	5	0	5	1	72	18.0
Totals	94	3006	1565	743	.475	465	342	.735	132	166	298	436	232	4	163	40	1836	19.5

Three-Point Field Goals: 1979-80, 1-for-5 (.200). 1981-82, 2-for-6 (.333). 1982-83, 0-for-2. 1983-84, 2-for-6 (.333). 1984-85, 3-for-10 (.300). Totals, 8-for-29 (.276).

NBA ALL-STAR RECORD

Season—Team	Min.	FGA	FGM	Pct.	FTA	FTM	Pct.	Off.	Def.	Tot.	Ast.	PF	Dq.	Stl.	Blk.	Pts.
1982—Seattle	26	19	9	.474	4	4	1.000	2	0	2	9	1	0	1	0	22
1983—Seattle	15	9	3	.333	0	0	.000	1	0	1	4	1	0	1	0	6
Totals	41	28	12	.429	4	4	1.000	3	0	3	13	2	0	2	0	28

Three-Point Field Goals: 1981-82, 0-for-1.

Named to All-NBA First Team, 1982. . . . All-NBA Second Team, 1980. . . . NBA All-Rookie Team, 1976. . . . Member of NBA championship team, 1979. . . . Named NBA Comeback Player of the Year, 1982. . . . Holds all-time NBA record for most steals. . . . Shares NBA playoff game records for most field goals made in one half, 14, and most points in one quarter, 23, vs. Dallas, April 17, 1984. . . . Named to THE SPORTING NEWS All-America Second Team, 1975. . . . Brother of Boston Celtics guard Ray Williams.

GUY BERNARD WILLIAMS

Born July 1, 1960 at Los Angeles, Calif.   Height 6:09.   Weight 200.

High School—Oakland, Calif., Bishop O'Dowd.

Colleges—University of San Francisco, San Francisco, Calif., and
Washington State University, Pullman, Wash.

Drafted by Washington on second round, 1983 (34th pick).

GUS WILLIAMS

San Francisco

Year	G.	Min.	FGA	FGM	Pct.	FTA	FTM	Pct.	Reb.	Pts.	Avg.
78-79	26	664	254	118	.465	46	24	.522	75	260	10.0
79-80	29	....	325	142	.437	78	47	.603	126	331	11.4
USF Totals	55	....	579	260	.449	124	71	.573	201	591	10.7

Washington State

Year	G.	Min.	FGA	FGM	Pct.	FTA	FTM	Pct.	Reb.	Pts.	Avg.
80-81	Did Not Play—Transfer Student										
81-82	29	900	316	140	.443	66	43	.652	165	323	11.1
82-83	15	481	210	119	.567	60	44	.733	134	282	18.8
WSU Totals	44	1381	526	259	.492	126	87	.690	299	605	13.8
College Totals	99	....	1105	519	.470	250	158	.632	500	1196	12.1

NBA REGULAR SEASON RECORD

Sea.—Team	G.	Min.	FGA	FGM	Pct.	FTA	FTM	Pct.	Off.	Def.	Tot.	Ast.	PF	Dq.	Stl.	Blk.	Pts.	Avg.
84-85—Washington	21	119	63	29	.460	5	2	.400	15	12	27	9	17	0	5	2	61	2.9

Three-Point Field Goals: 1984-85, 1-for-4 (.250).

HERBERT L. WILLIAMS
(Herb)

Born February 16, 1958 at Columbus, O.   Height 6:10.   Weight 242.

High School—Columbus, O., Marion Franklin.

College—Ohio State University, Columbus, O.

Drafted by Indiana on first round, 1981 (14th pick).

—COLLEGIATE RECORD—

Year	G.	Min.	FGA	FGM	Pct.	FTA	FTM	Pct.	Reb.	Pts.	Avg.
77-78	27	992	407	196	.482	91	60	.659	308	452	16.7
78-79	31	1212	483	253	.524	166	111	.669	325	617	19.9
79-80	29	1069	415	206	.496	147	97	.660	263	509	17.6
80-81	27	1020	368	179	.486	109	75	.688	215	433	16.0
Totals	114	4293	1673	834	.499	513	343	.669	1111	2011	17.6

NBA REGULAR SEASON RECORD

Sea.—Team	G.	Min.	FGA	FGM	Pct.	FTA	FTM	Pct.	Off.	Def.	Tot.	Ast.	PF	Dq.	Stl.	Blk.	Pts.	Avg.
81-82—Indiana	82	2277	854	407	.477	188	126	.670	175	430	605	139	200	0	53	178	942	11.5
82-83—Indiana	78	2513	1163	580	.499	220	155	.705	151	432	583	262	230	4	54	171	1315	16.9
83-84—Indiana	69	2279	860	411	.478	295	207	.702	154	400	554	215	193	4	60	108	1029	14.9
84-85—Indiana	75	2557	1211	575	.475	341	224	.657	154	480	634	252	218	1	54	134	1375	18.3
Totals	304	9626	4088	1973	.483	1044	712	.682	634	1742	2376	868	841	9	221	591	4661	15.3

Three-Point Field Goals: 1981-82, 2-for-7 (.286). 1982-83, 0-for-7. 1983-84, 0-for-4. 1984-85, 1-for-9 (.111). Totals, 3-for-27 (.111).

KEVIN EUGENE WILLIAMS

Born September 11, 1961 at New York, N. Y.   Height 6:03.   Weight 175.

High School—New York, N. Y., Charles E. Hughes.

College—St. John's University, Jamaica, N. Y.

Drafted by San Antonio on second round, 1983 (46th pick).

Waived by San Antonio, December 12, 1983; signed by Cleveland as a free agent, December 20, 1984.
Played in Continental Basketball Association with Ohio Mixers in 1983-84 and Bay State Bombardiers in 1984-85.

—COLLEGIATE RECORD—

Year	G.	Min.	FGA	FGM	Pct.	FTA	FTM	Pct.	Reb.	Pts.	Avg.
79-80	12	65	29	13	.448	26	21	.808	18	47	3.9
80-81	27	348	104	54	.519	52	35	.673	31	143	5.3
81-82	30	431	136	69	.507	78	64	.821	41	202	6.7
82-83	33	727	217	123	.567	92	71	.772	64	317	9.6
Totals	102	1571	486	259	.533	248	191	.770	154	709	7.0

MINOR LEAGUE REGULAR SEASON RECORD

Sea.—Team	G.	Min.	2-Point			3-Point			FTM	FTA	Pct.	Reb.	Ast.	Pts.	Avg.
			FGM	FGA	Pct.	FGM	FGA	Pct.							
83-84—Ohio CBA	32	895	210	410	.512	1	4	.250	187	229	.816	134	136	610	19.1
84-85—Bay State CBA	8	322	93	187	.497	1	4	.250	65	77	.844	40	46	254	31.8

NBA REGULAR SEASON RECORD

Sea.—Team	G.	Min.	FGA	FGM	Pct.	FTA	FTM	Pct.	—Rebounds—Off.	Def.	Tot.	Ast.	PF	Dq.	Stl.	Blk.	Pts.	Avg.
83-84—San Antonio	19	200	58	25	.431	32	25	.781	4	9	13	43	42	1	8	4	75	3.9
84-85—Cleveland	46	413	134	58	.433	64	47	.734	19	44	63	61	86	1	22	4	163	3.5
Totals	65	613	192	83	.432	96	72	.750	23	53	76	104	128	2	30	8	238	3.7

Three-Point Field Goals: 1983-84, 0-for-1. 1984-85, 0-for-5. Totals, 0-for-6.

NBA PLAYOFF RECORD

Sea.—Team	G.	Min.	FGA	FGM	Pct.	FTA	FTM	Pct.	—Rebounds—Off.	Def.	Tot.	Ast.	PF	Dq.	Stl.	Blk.	Pts.	Avg.
84-85—Cleveland	2	7	2	1	.500	0	0	.000	0	0	0	1	1	0	0	0	2	1.0

SAMUEL KEITH WILLIAMS
(Sam)

Born March 7, 1959 at Los Angeles, Calif.   Height 6:08.   Weight 215.

High School—Los Angeles, Calif., Westchester.

Colleges—Pasadena City College, Pasadena, Calif., and
Arizona State University, Tempe, Ariz.

Drafted by Golden State on second round, 1981 (33rd pick).

Traded by Golden State to Philadelphia for a 1984 2nd round draft choice and cash, November 12, 1983.

—COLLEGIATE RECORD—
Pasadena

Year	G.	Min.	FGA	FGM	Pct.	FTA	FTM	Pct.	Reb.	Pts.	Avg.
77-78	33	....	262	150	.573	131	73	.557	297	373	11.3

Arizona State

Year	G.	Min.	FGA	FGM	Pct.	FTA	FTM	Pct.	Reb.	Pts.	Avg.
78-79	30	500	133	67	.504	67	36	.537	167	170	5.7
79-80	27	781	240	140	.583	93	55	.591	161	335	12.4
80-81	28	880	270	150	.556	114	69	.605	193	369	13.2
Totals	85	2161	643	357	.555	274	160	.584	521	874	10.3

NBA REGULAR SEASON RECORD

Sea.—Team	G.	Min.	FGA	FGM	Pct.	FTA	FTM	Pct.	—Rebounds—Off.	Def.	Tot.	Ast.	PF	Dq.	Stl.	Blk.	Pts.	Avg.
81-82—Golden State	59	1073	277	154	.556	89	49	.551	91	217	308	38	156	0	45	76	357	6.1
82-83—Golden State	75	1533	479	252	.526	171	123	.719	153	240	393	45	244	4	71	89	627	8.4
83-84—GS-Phil.	77	1434	431	204	.473	140	92	.657	121	218	339	62	209	3	68	106	500	6.5
84-85—Philadelphia	46	488	148	58	.392	47	28	.596	38	68	106	11	92	1	26	26	144	3.1
Totals	257	4528	1335	668	.500	447	292	.653	403	743	1146	156	701	8	310	297	1628	6.3

Three-Point Field Goals: 1982-83, 0-for-1. 1983-84, 0-for-1. 1984-85, 0-for-1. Totals, 0-for-3.

NBA PLAYOFF RECORD

Sea.—Team	G.	Min.	FGA	FGM	Pct.	FTA	FTM	Pct.	—Rebounds—Off.	Def.	Tot.	Ast.	PF	Dq.	Stl.	Blk.	Pts.	Avg.
83-84—Philadelphia	4	55	8	2	.250	2	1	.500	1	5	6	3	7	0	2	6	5	1.3
84-85—Philadelphia	5	26	6	1	.167	10	3	.300	4	8	12	0	2	0	0	0	5	1.0
Totals	9	81	14	3	.214	12	4	.333	5	13	18	3	9	0	2	6	10	1.1

SYLVESTER WILLIAMS
(Sly)

Born January 26, 1958 at New Haven, Conn.   Height 6:07.   Weight 215.

High School—New Haven, Conn., Lee.

College—University of Rhode Island, Kingston, R. I.

Drafted by New York on first round as an undergraduate, 1979 (21st pick).

Traded by New York with cash to Atlanta for Rudy Macklin, June 29, 1983.

—COLLEGIATE RECORD—

Year	G.	Min.	FGA	FGM	Pct.	FTA	FTM	Pct.	Reb.	Pts.	Avg.
76-77	26	919	496	212	.427	135	96	.711	210	520	20.0
77-78	29	906	416	225	.541	168	114	.679	255	564	19.4
78-79	29	1025	532	279	.524	186	135	.726	244	693	23.9
Totals	84	2850	1444	716	.496	489	345	.706	709	1777	21.2

NBA REGULAR SEASON RECORD

Sea.—Team	G.	Min.	FGA	FGM	Pct.	FTA	FTM	Pct.	Off.	Def.	Tot.	Ast.	PF	Dq.	Stl.	Blk.	Pts.	Avg.
79-80—New York	57	556	267	104	.390	90	58	.644	65	56	121	36	73	0	19	8	266	4.7
80-81—New York	67	1976	708	349	.493	268	185	.690	159	257	416	180	199	0	116	18	885	13.2
81-82—New York	60	1521	628	349	.556	173	131	.757	100	127	227	142	153	0	77	16	831	13.9
82-83—New York	68	1385	647	314	.485	259	176	.680	94	196	290	133	166	3	73	3	806	11.9
83-84—Atlanta	13	258	114	34	.298	46	36	.783	19	31	50	16	33	0	14	1	105	8.1
84-85—Atlanta	34	867	380	167	.439	123	79	.642	45	123	168	94	83	1	28	8	417	12.3
Totals	299	6563	2744	1317	.480	959	665	.693	482	790	1272	601	707	4	327	54	3310	11.1

Three-Point Field Goals: 1979-80, 0-for-4. 1980-81, 2-for-8 (.250). 1981-82, 2-for-9 (.222). 1982-83, 2-for-19 (.105). 1983-84, 1-for-9 (.111). 1984-85, 4-for-15 (.267). Totals, 11-for-64 (.172).

NBA PLAYOFF RECORD

Sea.—Team	G.	Min.	FGA	FGM	Pct.	FTA	FTM	Pct.	Off.	Def.	Tot.	Ast.	PF	Dq.	Stl.	Blk.	Pts.	Avg.
80-81—New York	2	56	18	13	.722	0	0	.000	4	5	9	5	7	0	3	0	26	13.0
82-83—New York	5	82	41	16	.390	3	3	1.000	10	11	21	6	4	0	3	1	36	7.2
Totals	7	138	59	29	.492	3	3	1.000	14	16	30	11	11	0	6	1	62	8.9

Three-Point Field Goals: 1982-83, 1-for-1.

THOMAS RAY WILLIAMS

(Known by middle name.)

Born October 14, 1954 at Mt. Vernon, N. Y. Height 6:03. Weight 195.

High School—Mt. Vernon, N. Y.

Colleges—San Jacinto College, Pasadena, Tex., and University of Minnesota, Minneapolis, Minn.

Drafted by New York Knicks on first round, 1977 (10th pick).

Signed by New Jersey as Veteran Free Agent, October 25, 1981; New York agreed not to exercise its right of first refusal in exchange for Maurice Lucas.
Traded by New Jersey to Kansas City for Phil Ford, June 29, 1982.
Traded by Kansas City to New York for Billy Knight and cash, September 17, 1983.
Signed by Boston as Veteran Free Agent, February 21, 1985; New York agreed not to exercise its right of first refusal in exchange for a 1985 2nd round draft choice.

—COLLEGIATE RECORD—
San Jacinto

Year	G.	Min.	FGA	FGM	Pct.	FTA	FTM	Pct.	Reb.	Pts.	Avg.
73-74	38	....	410	280	.683	130	81	.623	276	641	16.9
74-75	37	....	596	353	.592	146	96	.658	326	802	21.7
JC Totals	75	....	1006	633	.629	276	177	.641	602	1443	19.2

Minnesota

Year	G.	Min.	FGA	FGM	Pct.	FTA	FTM	Pct.	Reb.	Pts.	Avg.
75-76	25	....	414	195	.471	145	107	.738	141	497	19.9
76-77	27	....	395	187	.473	142	112	.789	203	486	18.0
Totals	52	....	809	382	.472	287	219	.763	344	983	18.9

NBA REGULAR SEASON RECORD

Sea.—Team	G.	Min.	FGA	FGM	Pct.	FTA	FTM	Pct.	Off.	Def.	Tot.	Ast.	PF	Dq.	Stl.	Blk.	Pts.	Avg.
77-78—New York	81	1550	689	305	.443	207	146	.705	85	124	209	363	211	4	108	15	756	9.3
78-79—New York	81	2370	1257	575	.457	313	251	.802	104	187	291	504	274	4	128	19	1401	17.3
79-80—New York	82	2582	1384	687	.496	423	333	.787	149	263	412	512	295	5	167	24	1714	20.9
80-81—New York	79	2742	1335	616	.461	382	312	.817	122	199	321	432	270	4	185	37	1560	19.7
81-82—New Jersey	82	2732	1383	639	.462	465	387	.832	117	208	325	488	302	9	199	43	1674	20.4
82-83—Kansas City	72	2170	1068	419	.392	333	256	.769	93	234	327	569	248	3	120	26	1109	15.4
83-84—New York	76	2230	939	418	.445	318	263	.827	67	200	267	449	274	5	162	26	1124	14.8
84-85—Boston	23	459	143	55	.385	46	31	.674	16	41	57	90	56	1	30	5	147	6.4
Totals	576	16835	8198	3714	.453	2487	1979	.796	753	1456	2209	3407	1930	35	1099	195	9485	16.5

Three-Point Field Goals: 1979-80, 7-for-37 (.189). 1980-81, 16-for-68 (.235). 1981-82, 9-for-54 (.167). 1982-83, 15-for-74 (.203). 1983-84, 25-for-81 (.309). 1984-85, 6-for-23 (.261). Totals, 78-for-337 (.231).

NBA PLAYOFF RECORD

Sea.—Team	G.	Min.	FGA	FGM	Pct.	FTA	FTM	Pct.	Off.	Def.	Tot.	Ast.	PF	Dq.	Stl.	Blk.	Pts.	Avg.
77-78—New York	6	140	78	41	.526	26	23	.885	6	9	15	31	25	0	6	0	105	17.5
80-81—New York	2	84	41	18	.439	11	6	.545	3	5	8	9	10	1	4	0	43	21.5
81-82—New Jersey	2	77	47	14	.298	5	4	.800	8	4	12	14	10	0	4	0	34	17.0
83-84—New York	11	310	130	46	.354	39	29	.744	8	31	39	88	39	1	17	1	123	11.2
84-85—Boston	19	278	116	47	.405	25	24	.960	14	22	36	60	44	0	12	1	120	6.3
Totals	40	889	412	166	.403	106	86	.811	39	71	110	202	128	2	43	2	425	10.6

Three-Point Field Goals: 1980-81, 1-for-3 (.333). 1981-82, 2-for-5 (.400). 1983-84, 2-for-12 (.167). 1984-85, 2-for-15 (.133). Totals, 7-for-35 (.200).

Named to THE SPORTING NEWS All-America Second Team, 1977. . . . Brother of Washington Bullets guard Gus Williams.

KEVIN ANDRE WILLIS

Born September 6, 1962 at Los Angeles, Calif.   Height 7:00.   Weight 220.

High School—Detroit, Mich., Pershing.

Colleges—Jackson Community College, Jackson, Mich., and
Michigan State University, East Lansing, Mich.

Drafted by Atlanta on first round, 1984 (11th pick).

—COLLEGIATE RECORD—
Jackson CC

Year	G.	Min.	FGA	FGM	Pct.	FTA	FTM	Pct.	Reb.	Pts.	Avg.
80-81	....	....	....	....	....	....	....	....	....	....	19.0

Michigan State

Year	G.	Min.	FGA	FGM	Pct.	FTA	FTM	Pct.	Reb.	Pts.	Avg.
81-82	27	518	154	73	.474	30	17	.567	113	163	6.0
82-83	27	865	272	162	.596	70	36	.514	258	360	13.3
83-84	25	738	240	118	.492	59	39	.661	192	275	11.0
MSU Totals	79	2121	666	353	.530	159	92	.579	563	798	10.1

Three-Point Field Goals: 1982-83, 0-for-1.

NBA REGULAR SEASON RECORD

Sea.—Team	G.	Min.	FGA	FGM	Pct.	FTA	FTM	Pct.	Off.	Def.	Tot.	Ast.	PF	Dq.	Stl.	Blk.	Pts.	Avg.
									|—Rebounds—|									
84-85—Atlanta	82	1785	690	322	.467	181	119	.657	177	345	522	36	226	4	31	49	765	9.3

Three-Point Field Goals: 1984-85, 2-for-9 (.222).

COATLEN OTHELL WILSON
(Known by middle name.)

Born October 26, 1961 at Alexandria, Va.   Height 6:00.   Weight 190.

High Schools—Woodbridge, Va., Woodbridge (Freshman-Junior), and
Woodbridge, Va., Gar-Field (Senior).

College—University of Virginia, Charlottesville, Va.

Drafted by Golden State on second round, 1984 (35th pick).

—COLLEGIATE RECORD—

Year	G.	Min.	FGA	FGM	Pct.	FTA	FTM	Pct.	Reb.	Pts.	Avg.
80-81	32	703	164	78	.476	71	55	.775	71	211	6.6
81-82	32	920	270	149	.552	91	67	.736	80	365	11.4
82-83	34	1051	347	178	.513	148	107	.723	113	492	14.5
83-84	29	973	337	166	.493	96	69	.719	111	401	13.8
Totals	127	3647	1118	571	.511	406	298	.734	375	1469	11.6

Three-Point Field Goals: 1982-83, 29-for-54 (.537).

NBA REGULAR SEASON RECORD

Sea.—Team	G.	Min.	FGA	FGM	Pct.	FTA	FTM	Pct.	Off.	Def.	Tot.	Ast.	PF	Dq.	Stl.	Blk.	Pts.	Avg.
									|—Rebounds—|									
84-85—Golden State	74	1260	291	134	.460	76	54	.711	35	96	131	217	122	0	77	12	325	4.4

Three-Point Field Goals: 1984-85, 3-for-16 (.188).

MICHAEL WILSON

Born September 15, 1959 at Memphis, Tenn.   Height 6:04.   Weight 180.

High School—Memphis, Tenn., Manassas.

College—Marquette University, Milwaukee, Wis.

Drafted by Cleveland on third round, 1982 (47th pick).

Waived by Cleveland, October 1982; signed by Washington as a free agent, October 1983.
Waived by Washington, November 17, 1983; signed by New Jersey as a free agent, September 27, 1984.
Waived by New Jersey, November 14, 1984; claimed off waivers by Cleveland, November 16, 1984.
Waived by Cleveland, December 14, 1984; signed by New Jersey to a 10-day contract that expired, January 5, 1985.
Played in Continental Basketball Association with Wisconsin Flyers and Sarasota Stingers, 1982-83 and 1983-84.

—COLLEGIATE RECORD—

Year	G.	Min.	FGA	FGM	Pct.	FTA	FTM	Pct.	Reb.	Pts.	Avg.
78-79	29	....	170	70	.412	44	28	.636	70	168	5.8
79-80	27	....	216	97	.449	49	36	.735	100	230	8.5
80-81	31	....	289	158	.547	89	69	.775	110	385	12.4
81-82	32	....	395	201	.509	159	114	.717	141	516	16.1
Totals	119	....	1070	526	.492	341	247	.724	421	1299	10.9

MINOR LEAGUE REGULAR SEASON RECORD

Sea.—Team	G.	Min.	2-Point			3-Point			FTM	FTA	Pct.	Reb.	Ast.	Pts.	Avg.
			FGM	FGA	Pct.	FGM	FGA	Pct.							
82-83—Wisconsin CBA	32	855	186	370	.502	1	8	.125	165	209	.789	107	98	540	16.9
83-84—Wisc.-Sarasota CBA	41	1526	305	606	.503	1	5	.200	371	448	.828	182	176	984	24.0

NBA REGULAR SEASON RECORD

Sea.—Team	G.	Min.	FGA	FGM	Pct.	FTA	FTM	Pct.	Rebounds			Ast.	PF	Dq.	Stl.	Blk.	Pts.	Avg.
									Off.	Def.	Tot.							
83-84—Washington	6	26	2	0	.000	2	1	.500	1	0	1	3	5	0	0	0	1	0.2
84-85—Clev.-N.J.	19	267	77	36	.468	36	27	.750	14	17	31	35	21	0	14	5	99	5.2
Totals	25	293	79	36	.456	38	28	.737	15	17	32	38	26	0	14	5	100	4.0

Three-Point Field Goals: 1983-84, 0-for-1.

RANDY SCOTT WITTMAN

Born October 28, 1959 at Indianapolis, Ind. Height 6:06. Weight 210.

High School—Indianapolis, Ind., Ben Davis.

College—Indiana University, Bloomington, Ind.

Drafted by Washington on first round, 1983 (22nd pick).

Draft rights traded by Washington to Atlanta for Tom McMillen and a 1984 2nd round draft choice, July 5, 1983.

—COLLEGIATE RECORD—

Year	G.	Min.	FGA	FGM	Pct.	FTA	FTM	Pct.	Reb.	Pts.	Avg.
78-79	34	....	190	101	.532	53	39	.736	90	241	7.1
79-80	5	....	28	13	.464	4	3	.750	7	29	5.8
80-81	35	....	286	155	.542	69	53	.768	79	363	10.4
81-82	29	....	299	144	.482	78	59	.756	94	347	12.0
82-83	30	....	435	236	.543	108	89	.824	135	569	19.0
Totals	133	....	1238	649	.524	312	243	.779	405	1549	11.6

Three-Point Field Goals: 1982-83, 8-for-18 (.444).
(Suffered stress fracture of right ankle in 1979-80 season; granted extra year of eligibility.)

NBA REGULAR SEASON RECORD

Sea.—Team	G.	Min.	FGA	FGM	Pct.	FTA	FTM	Pct.	Rebounds			Ast.	PF	Dq.	Stl.	Blk.	Pts.	Avg.
									Off.	Def.	Tot.							
83-84—Atlanta	78	1071	318	160	.503	46	28	.609	14	57	71	71	82	0	17	0	350	4.5
84-85—Atlanta	41	1168	352	187	.531	41	30	.732	16	57	73	125	58	0	28	7	406	9.9
Totals	119	2239	670	347	.518	87	58	.667	30	114	144	196	140	0	45	7	756	6.4

Three-Point Field Goals: 1983-84, 2-for-5 (.400). 1984-85, 2-for-7 (.286). Totals, 4-for-12 (.333).

NBA PLAYOFF RECORD

Sea.—Team	G.	Min.	FGA	FGM	Pct.	FTA	FTM	Pct.	Rebounds			Ast.	PF	Dq.	Stl.	Blk.	Pts.	Avg.
									Off.	Def.	Tot.							
83-84—Atlanta	5	96	37	20	.541	0	0	.000	5	4	9	11	5	0	1	0	40	8.0

Member of NCAA championship team, 1981.

MARTIN ALPHONZO WOOD
(Al)

Born June 2, 1958 at Gray, Ga. Height 6:06. Weight 193.

High School—Gray, Ga., Jones County.

College—University of North Carolina, Chapel Hill, N. C.

Drafted by Atlanta on first round, 1981 (4th pick).

Traded by Atlanta with Charlie Criss to San Diego for Freeman Williams, January 20, 1982.
Traded by San Diego with Tom Chambers, a 1987 2nd round draft choice and a 1984 3rd round draft choice to Seattle for James Donaldson, Greg Kelser, Mark Radford, a 1984 1st round draft choice and a 1985 2nd round draft choice, August 18, 1983.

—COLLEGIATE RECORD—

Year	G.	Min.	FGA	FGM	Pct.	FTA	FTM	Pct.	Reb.	Pts.	Avg.
77-78	31	....	207	125	.604	43	31	.721	121	281	9.1
78-79	29	....	367	210	.572	125	95	.760	119	515	17.8
79-80	29	....	378	216	.571	154	118	.766	151	550	19.0
80-81	37	....	522	274	.525	156	121	.776	233	669	18.1
Totals	126	....	1474	825	.560	478	365	.764	624	2015	16.0

NBA REGULAR SEASON RECORD

Sea.—Team	G.	Min.	FGA	FGM	Pct.	FTA	FTM	Pct.	—Rebounds— Off.	Def.	Tot.	Ast.	PF	Dq.	Stl.	Blk.	Pts.	Avg.
81-82—Atl.-S.D.	48	930	381	179	.470	119	93	.782	51	83	134	58	108	4	31	9	454	9.5
82-83—San Diego	76	1822	740	343	.464	161	124	.770	96	140	236	134	188	5	55	36	825	10.9
83-84—Seattle	81	2236	945	467	.494	271	223	.823	94	181	275	166	207	1	64	32	1160	14.3
84-85—Seattle	80	2545	1061	515	.485	214	166	.776	99	180	279	236	187	3	84	52	1203	15.0
Totals	285	7533	3127	1504	.481	765	606	.792	340	584	924	594	690	13	234	129	3642	12.8

Three-Point Field Goals: 1981-82, 3-for-24 (.125). 1982-83, 15-for-50 (.300). 1983-84, 3-for-21 (.143). 1984-85, 7-for-33 (.212). Totals, 28-for-128 (.219).

NBA PLAYOFF RECORD

Sea.—Team	G.	Min.	FGA	FGM	Pct.	FTA	FTM	Pct.	—Rebounds— Off.	Def.	Tot.	Ast.	PF	Dq.	Stl.	Blk.	Pts.	Avg.
83-84—Seattle	5	157	56	26	.464	12	8	.667	7	27	34	10	16	0	1	1	60	12.0

Three-Point Field Goals: 1983-84, 0-for-1.
Member of U. S. Olympic team, 1980.

OSIE LEON WOOD III
(Known by middle name.)

Born March 25, 1962 at Columbia S. C.   Height 6:03.   Weight 185.

High School—Santa Monica, Calif., St. Monica.

Colleges—University of Arizona, Tucson, Ariz., and California State University at Fullerton, Fullerton, Calif.

Drafted by Philadelphia on first round, 1984 (10th pick).

—COLLEGIATE RECORD—
Arizona

Year	G.	Min.	FGA	FGM	Pct.	FTA	FTM	Pct.	Reb.	Pts.	Avg.
79-80	25	221	111	43	.387	26	19	.731	6	105	4.2

Cal State-Fullerton

Year	G.	Min.	FGA	FGM	Pct.	FTA	FTM	Pct.	Reb.	Pts.	Avg.
80-81			Did Not Play—Transfer Student								
81-82	32	1263	448	222	.496	229	187	.817	57	631	19.7
82-83	29	1076	378	178	.471	180	142	.789	72	526	18.1
83-84	30	1170	540	254	.470	257	211	.821	78	719	24.0
CSF Totals	91	3509	1366	654	.479	666	540	.811	207	1876	20.6
College Totals	116	3730	1477	697	.472	692	559	.808	213	1981	17.1

Three-Point Field Goals: 1982-83, 28-for-63 (.444).

NBA REGULAR SEASON RECORD

Sea.—Team	G.	Min.	FGA	FGM	Pct.	FTA	FTM	Pct.	—Rebounds— Off.	Def.	Tot.	Ast.	PF	Dq.	Stl.	Blk.	Pts.	Avg.
84-85—Philadelphia	38	269	134	50	.373	26	18	.692	3	15	18	45	17	0	8	0	122	3.2

Three-Point Field Goals: 1984-85, 4-for-30 (.133).

NBA PLAYOFF RECORD

Sea.—Team	G.	Min.	FGA	FGM	Pct.	FTA	FTM	Pct.	—Rebounds— Off.	Def.	Tot.	Ast.	PF	Dq.	Stl.	Blk.	Pts.	Avg.
84-85—Philadelphia	5	15	9	4	.444	8	6	.750	0	1	1	2	0	0	0	0	14	2.8

Three-Point Field Goals: 1984-85, 0-for-1.
Member of U.S. Olympic team, 1984. . . . Named to THE SPORTING NEWS All-America First Team, 1984.

MICHAEL WOODSON
(Mike)

Born March 24, 1958 at Indianapolis, Ind.   Height 6:05.   Weight 198.

High School—Indianapolis, Ind., Broad Ripple.

College—Indiana University, Bloomington, Ind.

Drafted by New York on first round, 1980 (12th pick).

Traded by New York to New Jersey for Mike Newlin, June 10, 1981.
Traded by New Jersey with a 1982 1st round draft choice to Kansas City for Sam Lacey, November 12, 1981.

—COLLEGIATE RECORD—

Year	G.	Min.	FGA	FGM	Pct.	FTA	FTM	Pct.	Reb.	Pts.	Avg.
76-77	27	....	407	212	.521	96	76	.792	182	500	18.5
77-78	29	....	462	242	.524	121	93	.769	157	577	19.9
78-79	34	....	532	265	.498	241	184	.763	193	714	21.0
79-80	14	....	225	102	.453	79	66	.835	49	270	19.3
Totals	104	....	1626	821	.505	537	419	.780	581	2061	19.8

MIKE WOODSON

NBA REGULAR SEASON RECORD

Sea.—Team	G.	Min.	FGA	FGM	Pct.	FTA	FTM	Pct.	Off.	Def.	Tot.	Ast.	PF	Dq.	Stl.	Blk.	Pts.	Avg.
80-81—New York	81	949	373	165	.442	64	49	.766	33	64	97	75	95	0	36	12	380	4.7
81-82—N.J.-K.C.	83	2331	1069	538	.503	286	221	.773	102	145	247	222	220	3	142	35	1304	15.7
82-83—Kansas City	81	2426	1154	584	.506	377	298	.790	84	164	248	254	203	0	137	59	1473	18.2
83-84—Kansas City	71	1838	816	389	.477	302	247	.818	62	113	175	175	174	2	83	28	1027	14.5
84-85—Kansas City	78	1998	1068	530	.496	330	264	.800	69	129	198	143	216	1	117	28	1329	17.0
Totals	394	9542	4480	2206	.492	1359	1079	.794	350	615	965	869	908	6	515	162	5513	14.0

Three-Point Field Goals: 1980-81, 1-for-5 (.200). 1981-82, 7-for-25 (.280). 1982-83, 7-for-33 (.212). 1983-84, 2-for-8 (.250). 1984-85, 5-for-21 (.238). Totals, 22-for-92 (.239).

NBA PLAYOFF RECORD

Sea.—Team	G.	Min.	FGA	FGM	Pct.	FTA	FTM	Pct.	Off.	Def.	Tot.	Ast.	PF	Dq.	Stl.	Blk.	Pts.	Avg.
80-81—New York	2	8	3	1	.333	2	2	1.000	2	0	2	0	3	0	0	0	4	2.0
83-84—Kansas City	3	87	44	18	.409	15	13	.867	4	4	8	9	11	0	2	0	49	16.3
Totals	5	95	47	19	.404	17	15	.882	6	4	10	9	14	0	2	0	53	10.6

Three-Point Field Goals: 1983-84, 0-for-1.

ORLANDO VERNADA WOOLRIDGE

Born December 16, 1959 at Bernice, La.   Height 6:09.   Weight 215.

High Schools—Pelican, La., All Saints (Freshman, Sophomore and Junior) and Mansfield, La. (Senior).

College—University of Notre Dame, Notre Dame, Ind.

Drafted by Chicago on first round, 1981 (6th pick).

—COLLEGIATE RECORD—

Year	G.	Min.	FGA	FGM	Pct.	FTA	FTM	Pct.	Reb.	Pts.	Avg.
77-78	24	230	78	41	.526	33	16	.485	51	98	4.1
78-79	30	752	253	145	.573	56	41	.732	145	331	11.0
79-80	27	835	212	124	.585	117	81	.692	186	329	12.2
80-81	28	924	240	156	.650	135	90	.667	168	402	14.4
Totals	109	2741	783	466	.595	341	228	.669	550	1160	10.6

NBA REGULAR SEASON RECORD

Sea.—Team	G.	Min.	FGA	FGM	Pct.	FTA	FTM	Pct.	Off.	Def.	Tot.	Ast.	PF	Dq.	Stl.	Blk.	Pts.	Avg.
81-82—Chicago	75	1188	394	202	.513	206	144	.699	82	145	227	81	152	1	23	24	548	7.3
82-83—Chicago	57	1627	622	361	.580	340	217	.638	122	176	298	97	177	1	38	44	939	16.5
83-84—Chicago	75	2544	1086	570	.525	424	303	.715	130	239	369	136	253	6	71	60	1444	19.3
84-85—Chicago	77	2816	1225	679	.554	521	409	.785	158	277	435	135	185	0	58	38	1767	22.9
Totals	284	8175	3327	1812	.545	1491	1073	.720	492	837	1329	449	767	8	190	166	4698	16.5

Three-Point Field Goals: 1981-82, 0-for-3. 1982-83, 0-for-3. 1983-84, 1-for-2 (.500). 1984-85, 0-for-5. Totals, 1-for-13 (.077).

NBA PLAYOFF RECORD

Sea.—Team	G.	Min.	FGA	FGM	Pct.	FTA	FTM	Pct.	Off.	Def.	Tot.	Ast.	PF	Dq.	Stl.	Blk.	Pts.	Avg.
84-85—Chicago	4	167	68	34	.500	18	14	.778	6	7	13	8	19	1	6	1	82	20.5

Named to THE SPORTING NEWS All-America Second Team, 1981.

JAMES AGER WORTHY

Born February 27, 1961 at Gastonia, N. C.   Height 6:09.   Weight 225.

High School—Gastonia, N. C., Ashbrook.

College—University of North Carolina, Chapel Hill, N. C.

Drafted by Los Angeles on first round as an undergraduate, 1982 (1st pick).

—COLLEGIATE RECORD—

Year	G.	Min.	FGA	FGM	Pct.	FTA	FTM	Pct.	Reb.	Pts.	Avg.
79-80	14	....	126	74	.587	45	27	.600	104	175	12.5
80-81	36	....	416	208	.500	150	96	.640	301	512	14.2
81-82	34	....	354	203	.573	187	126	.674	215	532	15.6
Totals	84	....	896	485	.541	382	249	.652	620	1219	14.5

NBA REGULAR SEASON RECORD

Sea.—Team	G.	Min.	FGA	FGM	Pct.	FTA	FTM	Pct.	Off.	Def.	Tot.	Ast.	PF	Dq.	Stl.	Blk.	Pts.	Avg.
82-83—Los Angeles	77	1970	772	447	.579	221	138	.624	157	242	399	132	221	2	91	64	1033	13.4
83-84—Los Angeles	82	2415	890	495	.556	257	195	.759	157	358	515	207	244	5	77	70	1185	14.5
84-85—L.A. Lakers	80	2696	1066	610	.572	245	190	.776	169	342	511	201	196	0	87	67	1410	17.6
Totals	239	7081	2728	1552	.569	723	523	.723	483	942	1425	540	661	7	255	201	3628	15.2

Three-Point Field Goals: 1982-83, 1-for-4 (.250). 1983-84, 0-for-6. 1984-85, 0-for-7. Totals, 1-for-17 (.059).

Sea.—Team	G.	Min.	FGA	FGM	Pct.	FTA	FTM	Pct.	Off.	Def.	Tot.	Ast.	PF	Dq.	Stl.	Blk.	Pts.	Avg.
										—Rebounds—								
83-84—Los Angeles	21	708	274	164	.599	69	42	.609	36	69	105	56	57	0	27	11	371	17.7
84-85—L.A. Lakers	19	626	267	166	.622	111	75	.676	35	61	96	41	53	1	17	13	408	21.5
Totals	40	1334	541	330	.610	180	117	.650	71	130	201	97	110	1	44	24	779	19.5

Three-Point Field Goals: 1983-84, 1-for-2 (.500). 1984-85, 1-for-2 (.500). Totals, 2-for-4 (.500).

Named to NBA All-Rookie Team, 1983. . . . Member of NBA championship team, 1985. . . . THE SPORTING NEWS All-America First Team, 1982. . . . NCAA Division I Tournament Most Outstanding Player, 1982. . . . Member of NCAA championship team, 1982.

DANNY YOUNG

Born July 26, 1962 at Raleigh, N.C.   Height 6:03.   Weight 175.

High School—Raleigh, N. C., Enloe.

College—Wake Forest University, Winston-Salem, N. C.

Drafted by Seattle on second round, 1984 (39th pick).

Waived by Seattle, November 13, 1984.
Played in Continental Basketball Association with Wyoming Wildcatters, 1984-85.

—COLLEGIATE RECORD—

Year	G.	Min.	FGA	FGM	Pct.	FTA	FTM	Pct.	Reb.	Pts.	Avg.
80-81	29	491	117	58	.496	48	33	.688	38	149	5.1
81-82	30	946	254	129	.508	84	60	.714	74	318	10.6
82-83	31	999	315	144	.457	115	82	.713	66	397	12.8
83-84	32	1043	272	124	.456	82	58	.707	59	306	9.6
Totals	122	3479	958	455	.475	329	233	.708	237	1170	9.6

Three-Point Field Goals: 1982-83, 27-for-73 (.370).

NBA REGULAR SEASON RECORD

Sea.—Team	G.	Min.	FGA	FGM	Pct.	FTA	FTM	Pct.	Off.	Def.	Tot.	Ast.	PF	Dq.	Stl.	Blk.	Pts.	Avg.
										—Rebounds—								
84-85—Seattle	3	26	10	2	.200	0	0	.000	0	3	3	2	2	0	3	0	4	1.3

Three-Point Field Goals: 1984-85, 0-for-1.

MINOR LEAGUE REGULAR SEASON RECORD

Sea.—Team	G.	Min.	FGM	FGA	Pct.	FGM	FGA	Pct.	FTM	FTA	Pct.	Reb.	Ast.	Pts.	Avg.
			—2-Point—			—3-Point—									
84-85—Wyoming CBA...........	26	489	77	156	.493	4	12	.333	59	61	.967	34	95	225	8.7

MICHAEL WAYNE YOUNG

Born January 2, 1961 at Houston, Tex.   Height 6:07.   Weight 220.

High School—Houston, Tex., Yates.

College—University of Houston, Houston, Tex.

Drafted by Boston on first round, 1984 (24th pick).

Waived by Boston, October 25, 1984; signed by Phoenix as a free agent, November 27, 1984.
Waived by Phoenix, December 10, 1984.
Played in Continental Basketball Association with Detroit Spirits, 1984-85.

—COLLEGIATE RECORD—

Year	G.	Min.	FGA	FGM	Pct.	FTA	FTM	Pct.	Reb.	Pts.	Avg.
80-81	30	1049	319	157	.492	84	47	.560	190	361	12.0
81-82	33	979	358	158	.441	64	44	.688	179	360	10.9
82-83	34	1116	519	266	.513	88	56	.636	195	588	17.3
83-84	37	1354	637	319	.501	149	96	.644	231	734	19.8
Totals	134	4498	1833	900	.491	385	243	.631	795	2043	15.2

NBA REGULAR SEASON RECORD

Sea.—Team	G.	Min.	FGA	FGM	Pct.	FTA	FTM	Pct.	Off.	Def.	Tot.	Ast.	PF	Dq.	Stl.	Blk.	Pts.	Avg.
										—Rebounds—								
84-85—Phoenix	2	11	6	2	.333	0	0	.000	1	1	2	0	0	0	0	0	4	2.0

Three-Point Field Goals 1984-85, 0-for-1.

MINOR LEAGUE REGULAR SEASON RECORD

Sea.—Team	G.	Min.	FGM	FGA	Pct.	FGM	FGA	Pct.	FTM	FTA	Pct.	Reb.	Ast.	Pts.	Avg.
			—2-Point—			—3-Point—									
84-85—Detroit CBA..............	43	1308	313	586	.534	9	31	.290	79	119	.663	256	85	732	17.0

Named to THE SPORTING NEWS All-America Second Team, 1984.

INDIVIDUAL CAREER HIGHS

REGULAR SEASON

Player	FGM	FGA	FTM	FTA	Reb.	Ast.	Pts.
Kareem Abdul-Jabbar	24	39	20	25	34	14	55
Alvan Adams	18	31	14	17	19	13	47
Mark Aguirre	21	40	14	20	13	16	49
Danny Ainge	11	20	9	10	10	13	26
Chuck Aleksinas	6	13	4	6	12	3	15
Mitchell Anderson	8	17	7	10	16	6	21
Ron Anderson	11	19	7	9	13	6	27
John Bagley	16	20	8	12	11	19	35
James Bailey	13	22	12	14	21	6	34
Thurl Bailey	12	23	10	11	16	9	27
Greg Ballard	16	28	11	12	20	10	38
Gene Banks	19	22	11	12	17	8	44
Ken Bannister	10	18	5	10	14	2	24
Charles Barkley	12	18	12	16	19	8	29
Kent Benson	12	23	10	13	22	9	28
Larry Bird	22	36	16	17	21	17	60
Otis Birdsong	20	31	12	17	11	11	49
Rolando Blackman	18	27	20	21	11	10	43
Cory Blackwell	5	11	5	7	6	3	11
Sam Bowie	11	16	10	13	20	7	26
Dudley Bradley	11	16	10	13	8	10	22
Mike Bratz	12	22	9	11	8	14	28
Randy Breuer	7	12	8	10	9	3	18
Ron Brewer	19	28	11	14	9	8	44
Frank Brickowski	10	21	6	8	12	7	22
Junior Bridgeman	16	25	12	13	12	10	41
Michael Brooks	16	27	11	13	17	12	37
Rickey Brown	10	17	6	8	18	4	21
Tony Brown	11	17	10	12	11	7	25
Wallace Bryant	8	13	2	4	17	5	18
Quinn Buckner	19	25	8	10	10	18	40
Steve Burtt	6	14	4	6	4	3	14
Don Buse	11	17	8	10	12	17	23
Michael Cage	10	13	6	10	16	5	22
Tony Campbell	6	14	5	6	6	3	17
Rick Carlisle	4	10	2	3	3	7	8
Antoine Carr	7	15	9	9	11	8	17
Kenny Carr	15	21	12	16	20	7	32
M.L. Carr	15	24	11	13	18	9	36
Joe Barry Carroll	22	34	14	18	21	7	52
Butch Carter	17	30	10	14	8	11	42
Howard Carter	10	25	6	6	6	6	25
Bill Cartwright	16	26	14	18	18	6	38
Harvey Catchings	7	13	8	10	19	7	16
Ron Cavenall	2	6	3	4	12	2	7
Tom Chambers	15	29	17	18	18	7	39
Maurice Cheeks	14	18	10	12	10	21	32
Carlos Clark	6	10	7	8	5	5	12
Don Collins	15	20	11	17	14	8	32
Steve Colter	14	20	9	10	8	12	35
Lester Conner	10	17	11	13	9	12	24
Darwin Cook	14	21	9	11	13	15	35
Jeff Cook	8	15	9	10	16	6	18
Joe Cooper	6	12	3	4	11	4	14
Michael Cooper	13	22	9	10	13	17	31
Wayne Cooper	13	21	12	14	19	7	30
Dave Corzine	15	29	17	19	22	8	35
Charlie Criss	13	25	12	13	8	13	34
Pat Cummings	14	23	10	13	20	6	34
Terry Cummings	17	29	13	20	24	9	39
Earl Cureton	11	17	5	6	15	5	23
Quintin Dailey	17	26	15	17	10	9	44
Adrian Dantley	24	36	28	31	19	11	55
Brad Davis	14	17	11	14	8	17	32
Charles Davis	15	22	5	7	11	5	33
Johnny Davis	14	26	13	14	8	17	35

Player	FGM	FGA	FTM	FTA	Reb.	Ast.	Pts.
Walter Davis	19	33	19	21	13	12	43
Darryl Dawkins	14	25	12	19	19	7	36
Darren Daye	10	14	10	10	9	10	21
James Donaldson	12	17	9	11	19	7	29
John Drew	21	34	21	28	25	8	50
Larry Drew	13	27	15	18	8	17	33
Clyde Drexler	15	25	9	12	13	13	37
Mike Dunleavy	19	30	12	15	7	17	48
T.R. Dunn	10	18	11	14	17	8	23
Devin Durrant	7	14	7	9	6	6	17
Mark Eaton	8	18	10	12	20	7	20
Jerry Eaves	11	19	13	14	6	8	35
Kent Edelin	1	3	2	2	6	3	2
Franklin Edwards	8	14	5	6	5	12	18
James Edwards	16	25	13	18	17	7	39
Craig Ehlo	7	14	4	4	6	4	14
Dale Ellis	12	23	7	8	12	4	31
Chris Engler	6	9	4	4	9	2	14
Alex English	22	37	15	17	20	16	47
Julius Erving	20	32	19	20	18	12	45
Mike Evans	15	20	12	12	6	10	38
Kenny Fields	9	13	3	4	7	4	21
Vern Fleming	12	20	11	13	10	9	29
Eric Floyd	13	26	14	17	11	17	35
Phil Ford	15	28	18	22	7	22	38
Rod Foster	11	19	7	9	7	11	27
World B. Free	21	33	22	29	11	13	49
Bill Garnett	9	12	8	10	18	11	21
George Gervin	24	49	18	22	18	11	63
Mike Gibson	3	8	4	4	13	2	8
Artis Gilmore	16	26	20	25	28	9	42
Mike Glenn	13	19	9	9	6	8	31
Mike Gminski	12	23	15	16	20	6	31
Lancaster Gordon	10	20	4	6	3	7	22
Stewart Granger	6	10	6	6	4	9	16
Butch Graves	1	3	1	4	2	1	3
Stuart Gray	3	7	6	7	11	3	7
Rickey Green	16	25	13	17	9	20	45
Sidney Green	8	14	6	8	15	3	18
David Greenwood	14	26	12	13	22	9	35
Kevin Grevey	15	26	13	15	10	10	43
Darrell Griffith	19	32	10	12	12	10	41
Ernie Grunfeld	13	19	9	13	13	12	30
Bob Hansen	10	17	7	10	6	9	22
Bill Hanzlik	10	15	10	12	11	11	25
Derek Harper	9	16	6	9	9	10	22
Scott Hastings	8	16	8	8	17	6	16
Steve Hayes	7	10	4	6	10	4	15
Gerald Henderson	12	20	9	12	8	16	31
Rod Higgins	9	18	9	12	12	9	25
Roy Hinson	13	24	9	13	17	5	32
Craig Hodges	11	23	6	8	9	12	24
Lionel Hollins	20	31	12	14	10	15	43
Mike Holton	10	17	7	7	6	10	25
Phil Hubbard	15	22	14	19	21	7	37
Jay Humphries	11	18	7	9	6	11	26
Geoff Huston	13	25	9	12	6	27	31
Marc Iavaroni	7	11	7	9	19	7	19
Dan Issel	17	29	19	23	21	10	47
Ralph Jackson	1	3	0	0	1	4	2
Clemon Johnson	11	22	9	10	18	7	22
Dennis Johnson	14	29	16	18	12	17	39
Eddie Johnson	16	30	14	18	9	17	40
Eddie A. Johnson	18	31	10	12	15	10	40
Frank Johnson	12	23	18	19	8	15	36
George L. Johnson	12	21	8	12	16	8	32
George T. Johnson	11	20	7	10	30	7	25
Magic Johnson	18	26	17	21	18	23	41
Marques Johnson	18	32	14	18	18	11	40
Mickey Johnson	16	33	17	21	22	15	41
Steve Johnson	14	23	11	15	18	7	33
Vinnie Johnson	13	21	11	12	11	15	33

Player	FGM	FGA	FTM	FTA	Reb.	Ast.	Pts.
Bobby Jones	12	21	13	15	18	9	33
Caldwell Jones	12	22	13	14	27	7	29
Charles Jones	6	9	5	6	13	3	15
Charles A. Jones	9	15	13	15	14	8	27
Earl Jones	0	1	0	0	0	0	0
Edgar Jones	10	19	13	16	25	5	27
Major Jones	10	19	7	11	16	6	21
Ozell Jones	8	12	3	8	13	4	19
Michael Jordan	20	33	14	17	15	16	49
Rich Kelley	12	28	21	25	25	12	33
Clark Kellogg	17	27	15	18	21	9	37
Greg Kelser	14	26	15	15	17	6	37
Jerome Kersey	9	15	7	10	9	5	21
Albert King	14	29	12	12	14	11	31
Bernard King	20	34	22	26	18	13	60
Reggie King	15	22	12	18	20	10	33
Greg Kite	6	9	6	7	10	2	14
Billy Knight	20	32	17	18	16	9	52
Joe Kopicki	7	10	7	9	11	5	19
Mitch Kupchak	13	21	14	19	20	6	32
Tom LaGarde	14	20	9	13	17	9	32
Bill Laimbeer	16	27	12	13	23	11	35
Allen Leavell	15	26	14	17	8	22	42
Ronnie Lester	10	20	13	15	8	14	27
Lafayette Lever	11	20	11	14	9	18	28
Cliff Levingston	9	17	9	14	17	7	24
Alton Lister	13	16	8	12	20	6	30
Lewis Lloyd	16	26	12	14	13	12	36
John Long	18	31	13	15	13	12	41
Sidney Lowe	4	9	5	8	7	11	11
John Lucas	15	26	11	15	11	24	35
Maurice Lucas	19	32	15	19	26	10	46
Kyle Macy	15	21	11	11	10	15	31
Rick Mahorn	12	23	10	15	19	7	28
Jeff Malone	16	28	12	12	7	9	40
Moses Malone	20	35	21	26	37	7	53
Pace Mannion	5	9	3	4	5	5	14
Wes Matthews	13	20	12	13	7	18	27
Cedric Maxwell	13	20	19	22	19	9	35
Bob McAdoo	22	37	18	22	29	10	52
Tim McCormick	12	18	10	15	15	5	29
Rodney McCray	12	21	12	14	15	12	28
Scooter McCray	5	9	6	9	9	7	13
Hank McDowell	6	13	9	12	10	4	15
Mike McGee	18	25	9	12	9	5	41
Kevin McHale	22	28	12	16	16	6	56
Kevin McKenna	8	15	7	8	6	7	21
Tom McMillen	15	26	9	10	19	6	37
Mark McNamara	9	12	5	8	12	2	22
Joe C. Meriweather	14	27	11	15	20	6	29
Larry Micheaux	6	13	4	6	17	4	16
Mike Mitchell	20	36	12	15	19	6	47
Paul Mokeski	9	16	9	10	13	6	21
Sidney Moncrief	16	26	18	21	15	12	43
Johnny Moore	12	22	10	11	11	20	29
Jay Murphy	2	6	4	4	6	2	6
Larry Nance	19	29	13	16	17	11	44
Calvin Natt	16	29	16	22	19	7	39
Kenny Natt	6	15	4	4	5	5	16
Ed Nealy	6	10	6	8	13	4	16
Chuck Nevitt	4	6	1	4	6	1	8
Kurt Nimphius	10	20	7	9	15	10	24
Norm Nixon	18	28	13	13	9	21	39
Audie Norris	7	10	10	18	14	6	20
Mike O'Koren	12	19	11	14	16	10	28
Akeem Olajuwon	18	25	13	18	25	5	42
Mark Olberding	13	21	14	17	17	12	30
Jawann Oldham	6	13	5	8	11	3	17
Louis Orr	12	24	14	17	12	6	28
Robert Parish	16	31	13	18	32	7	40
Billy Paultz	14	22	11	16	19	8	31
Jim Paxson	18	33	13	15	8	9	41

Player	FGM	FGA	FTM	FTA	Reb.	Ast.	Pts.
John Paxson	12	16	6	7	5	12	25
Sam Perkins	11	16	11	12	16	6	29
Jim Petersen	5	10	7	10	12	3	13
Ricky Pierce	11	20	9	10	12	6	30
Charles Pittman	9	15	9	10	11	6	20
Gary Plummer	6	12	7	10	10	2	16
David Pope	4	7	5	7	4	2	11
Ben Poquette	13	19	9	11	18	6	30
Paul Pressey	13	23	13	18	15	13	30
Kurt Rambis	10	14	8	9	17	5	21
Kelvin Ransey	16	30	11	13	9	17	35
Leo Rautins	6	11	2	2	5	5	13
Robert Reid	15	26	12	13	16	12	32
Clint Richardson	11	17	7	8	12	8	24
Micheal Ray Richardson	16	29	16	17	16	19	36
Glenn Rivers	11	19	13	16	7	15	30
Fred Roberts	10	17	9	12	15	7	25
Alvin Robertson	13	18	8	10	10	14	27
Rick Robey	13	27	11	13	21	7	28
Cliff Robinson	19	29	14	20	23	8	45
Truck Robinson	20	33	16	18	27	8	51
Wayne Rollins	11	20	8	9	23	6	26
Lorenzo Romar	10	20	7	8	6	14	22
Dan Roundfield	15	28	15	21	26	11	38
Jeff Ruland	16	27	18	22	24	12	38
Campy Russell	16	29	15	21	16	12	41
Walker Russell	6	10	6	6	10	8	16
Ralph Sampson	19	31	15	17	23	8	43
Mike Sanders	9	15	7	10	13	7	21
Wayne Sappleton	4	9	3	6	11	1	9
Danny Schayes	10	18	14	16	24	11	28
Tom Scheffler	4	8	2	4	9	2	10
John Schweitz	5	11	3	4	4	4	11
Alvin Scott	7	11	7	10	12	8	18
Byron Scott	13	20	10	11	9	10	32
Tom Sewell	2	6	2	2	2	2	4
Lonnie Shelton	17	32	12	13	19	10	41
Purvis Short	24	38	16	18	15	14	59
Jerry Sichting	12	18	10	11	7	16	29
Jack Sikma	15	28	21	23	25	10	39
Charlie Sitton	4	9	2	6	5	4	8
Tom Sluby	4	8	3	4	2	3	8
Derek Smith	14	25	13	17	11	7	41
Larry Smith	11	19	8	14	31	5	25
Robert Smith	7	12	11	12	11	9	19
Ricky Sobers	14	26	14	15	12	16	34
Rory Sparrow	13	23	10	12	10	15	30
Larry Spriggs	9	15	8	10	9	7	20
Terence Stansbury	9	19	7	8	5	6	25
Brook Steppe	7	15	9	10	8	6	21
Steve Stipanovich	14	23	11	12	16	8	34
John Stockton	7	13	9	10	4	12	19
Jon Sundvold	9	16	6	8	6	13	24
Dane Suttle	9	16	8	8	5	4	26
Terry Teagle	16	25	7	10	9	7	34
Reggie Theus	18	33	16	18	17	16	46
Peter Thibeaux	10	14	5	6	6	2	22
David Thirdkill	7	12	4	6	6	5	15
Isiah Thomas	19	34	15	19	12	25	47
Jim Thomas	10	20	12	12	9	8	26
Bernard Thompson	6	11	5	8	7	4	13
David Thompson	28	38	20	22	11	12	73
LaSalle Thompson	12	18	12	13	20	5	28
Mychal Thompson	17	28	12	20	22	11	38
Paul Thompson	11	26	6	7	13	6	26
Otis Thorpe	13	20	10	11	19	5	31
Sedale Threatt	7	15	5	8	6	9	19
Andrew Toney	21	29	15	18	11	13	46
Linton Townes	8	13	3	4	7	3	20
Kelly Tripucka	19	30	20	22	14	11	56
Trent Tucker	12	21	5	6	9	8	27
Elston Turner	9	16	7	8	11	7	19

Player	FGM	FGA	FTM	FTA	Reb.	Ast.	Pts.
Jeff Turner	6	14	4	6	8	5	14
Mel Turpin	11	18	7	7	17	3	24
Terry Tyler	14	25	10	12	18	8	32
Darnell Valentine	13	18	13	15	8	15	26
Kiki Vandeweghe	21	30	16	19	13	10	51
Peter Verhoeven	12	15	8	11	12	4	28
Jay Vincent	17	33	17	20	17	8	41
Danny Vranes	10	15	9	12	15	8	24
Granville Waiters	6	11	5	8	10	3	14
Darrell Walker	13	25	10	12	9	15	31
Bill Walton	17	31	12	17	26	14	36
Bryan Warrick	8	12	6	8	6	14	18
Marvin Webster	11	18	11	15	29	8	26
Scott Wedman	19	31	11	16	18	11	45
Mark West	8	12	4	8	14	2	16
Ennis Whatley	9	14	9	11	8	22	21
Rory White	9	15	7	8	10	4	18
Willie White	9	13	4	6	4	4	21
Jerome Whitehead	13	20	13	14	23	6	31
Mitchell Wiggins	10	23	11	12	10	9	28
Jamaal Wilkes	17	28	14	17	19	10	36
Dominique Wilkins	18	38	14	16	15	7	48
Eddie Wilkins	9	15	6	11	15	3	24
Jeff Wilkins	15	23	9	12	20	8	37
Dale Wilkinson	2	2	6	6	2	1	8
Buck Williams	14	22	14	19	24	7	33
Gus Williams	19	35	13	15	10	20	42
Guy Williams	6	7	1	2	7	2	13
Herb Williams	15	26	17	20	17	8	34
Kevin Williams	5	13	6	10	9	9	13
Ray Williams	21	34	16	20	12	18	52
Sam Williams	10	17	10	10	18	5	26
Sly Williams	13	21	13	16	15	8	34
Kevin Willis	10	19	6	8	16	4	24
Mike Wilson	5	10	4	6	6	4	13
Othell Wilson	7	12	5	6	6	7	15
Randy Wittman	14	22	4	6	6	7	28
Al Wood	14	24	10	11	11	9	35
Leon Wood	6	14	4	5	4	5	16
Mike Woodson	22	26	12	15	8	9	48
Orlando Woolridge	15	23	13	16	16	7	37
James Worthy	14	24	11	11	17	8	37
Danny Young	2	6	0	0	3	1	4
Michael Young	2	3	0	0	2	0	4

PLAYOFFS

Player	FGM	FGA	FTM	FTA	Reb.	Ast.	Pts.
Kareem Abdul-Jabbar	20	37	13	18	31	11	46
Alvan Adams	14	27	8	10	20	12	33
Mark Aguirre	15	26	9	10	17	7	39
Danny Ainge	12	22	7	8	6	11	25
Mitchell Anderson	2	2	0	0	1	0	4
Ron Anderson	0	2	0	0	2	0	0
John Bagley	11	19	4	6	7	15	22
James Bailey	6	11	5	7	7	1	13
Thurl Bailey	11	20	8	9	14	6	26
Greg Ballard	8	19	7	11	15	6	20
Gene Banks	11	20	6	8	11	7	24
Charles Barkley	10	20	7	8	20	4	23
Kent Benson	8	12	5	5	14	3	18
Larry Bird	17	33	14	15	21	12	43
Otis Birdsong	14	24	7	12	9	7	30
Rolando Blackman	19	33	13	14	10	8	43
Sam Bowie	5	11	6	12	20	5	12
Dudley Bradley	4	7	2	2	4	6	10
Mike Bratz	9	17	8	8	5	10	25
Randy Breuer	4	7	6	8	6	2	12
Ron Brewer	11	24	6	8	7	5	27
Junior Bridgeman	12	20	8	9	10	8	32

Player	FGM	FGA	FTM	FTA	Reb.	Ast.	Pts.
Rickey Brown	4	8	3	3	7	1	11
Wallace Bryant	0	1	2	2	6	1	2
Quinn Buckner	8	17	5	7	6	10	19
Don Buse	8	12	8	8	9	9	17
Tony Campbell	1	3	0	0	2	1	2
Kenny Carr	9	17	6	6	12	3	24
M.L. Carr	9	18	6	7	10	5	23
Howard Carter	3	6	0	0	3	2	6
Bill Cartwright	10	19	11	13	14	2	29
Harvey Catchings	4	6	2	3	12	3	10
Tom Chambers	12	18	6	9	9	4	30
Maurice Cheeks	12	19	11	14	8	14	33
Carlos Clark	2	5	2	2	1	3	4
Don Collins	8	16	2	2	8	2	17
Steve Colter	11	15	3	5	4	8	26
Darwin Cook	7	18	7	10	5	6	15
Jeff Cook	7	12	5	7	12	4	17
Michael Cooper	9	16	10	12	8	12	23
Wayne Cooper	10	18	4	8	14	7	23
Dave Corzine	9	16	5	7	13	7	23
Charlie Criss	8	16	9	10	5	7	18
Pat Cummings	8	16	4	4	14	3	16
Terry Cummings	15	25	13	16	13	4	41
Earl Cureton	5	15	3	5	9	2	12
Quintin Dailey	12	20	4	4	5	5	25
Adrian Dantley	16	27	15	20	14	7	46
Brad Davis	8	10	5	6	4	10	18
Charles Davis	4	9	3	4	4	2	9
Johnny Davis	11	21	7	8	6	14	25
Walter Davis	14	28	11	13	10	13	34
Darryl Dawkins	14	25	16	18	16	6	32
Darren Daye	7	10	5	10	5	9	19
James Donaldson	7	12	5	6	16	2	16
John Drew	11	26	11	14	13	4	29
Larry Drew	4	9	3	3	3	7	11
Clyde Drexler	9	18	9	10	11	14	21
Mike Dunleavy	11	22	6	6	4	10	28
T.R. Dunn	5	9	4	4	12	6	11
Mark Eaton	4	8	3	4	12	4	10
Jerry Eaves	9	15	2	2	3	3	19
Franklin Edwards	5	10	8	8	3	3	11
James Edwards	10	18	9	10	9	4	23
Craig Ehlo	1	1	2	2	0	0	4
Dale Ellis	8	14	2	2	10	2	16
Chris Engler	1	1	0	0	2	0	2
Alex English	17	31	13	14	11	12	42
Julius Erving	17	29	12	16	15	10	40
Mike Evans	9	18	7	8	8	11	23
Phil Ford	7	17	5	8	6	13	20
Rod Foster	3	11	4	6	2	3	10
World B. Free	13	27	11	13	6	9	32
Bill Garnett	7	13	4	4	7	2	14
George Gervin	19	32	14	17	15	9	46
Artis Gilmore	11	19	9	13	20	3	27
Mike Glenn	5	10	3	3	4	3	13
Mike Gminski	7	13	10	12	9	2	20
Rickey Green	12	24	8	10	10	16	29
Sidney Green	7	14	3	6	9	2	17
David Greenwood	11	18	5	6	13	3	24
Kevin Grevey	15	24	11	13	7	6	41
Darrell Griffith	11	21	7	10	10	8	28
Ernie Grunfeld	11	19	11	12	8	8	27
Bob Hansen	1	5	3	4	3	2	4
Bill Hanzlik	6	12	7	9	8	7	14
Derek Harper	6	10	4	5	4	8	14
Scott Hastings	1	3	2	2	4	1	2
Gerald Henderson	10	17	5	7	6	9	22
Rod Higgins	0	0	0	0	0	0	0
Roy Hinson	10	17	8	13	11	2	24
Craig Hodges	5	15	2	2	4	8	13
Lionel Hollins	15	28	9	13	9	13	35
Mike Holton	5	7	4	4	2	5	10

Player	FGM	FGA	FTM	FTA	Reb.	Ast.	Pts.
Phil Hubbard	10	15	7	8	7	1	23
Jay Humphries	7	11	7	7	2	8	21
Marc Iavaroni	5	8	8	10	11	4	15
Dan Issel	13	23	14	15	18	6	36
Clemon Johnson	5	9	4	7	13	2	10
Dennis Johnson	13	27	13	17	12	17	33
Eddie Johnson	12	22	7	8	6	8	26
Eddie A. Johnson	11	19	4	4	4	6	25
Frank Johnson	9	22	7	9	7	11	26
George L. Johnson	4	6	0	0	2	1	9
George T. Johnson	8	11	5	7	15	5	18
Magic Johnson	14	23	16	17	18	24	42
Marques Johnson	16	26	11	16	17	9	36
Mickey Johnson	13	25	14	14	15	7	34
Steve Johnson	1	4	2	2	3	1	4
Vinnie Johnson	16	21	8	9	8	5	34
Bobby Jones	10	20	11	14	11	7	25
Caldwell Jones	8	15	8	11	26	5	24
Charles Jones	5	9	3	6	9	1	11
Charles A. Jones	3	3	6	6	3	2	12
Edgar Jones	7	15	6	10	11	6	19
Major Jones	5	7	3	3	9	3	11
Ozell Jones	3	4	1	4	8	2	6
Michael Jordan	12	26	17	20	8	12	35
Rich Kelley	7	12	6	8	12	7	18
Greg Kelser	2	5	2	2	6	1	4
Jerome Kersey	6	10	6	8	3	2	18
Albert King	12	22	5	8	9	4	28
Bernard King	19	35	12	15	12	5	46
Reggie King	13	24	10	13	16	6	31
Greg Kite	3	5	2	2	5	2	7
Billy Knight	10	18	5	7	7	4	25
Joe Kopicki	3	7	3	4	6	1	6
Mitch Kupchak	14	18	8	10	16	6	32
Tom LaGarde	4	12	4	4	8	6	10
Bill Laimbeer	10	18	13	13	17	4	31
Allen Leavell	9	20	6	6	4	8	20
Ronnie Lester	4	8	2	3	3	3	10
Lafayette Lever	8	16	12	12	16	18	22
Cliff Levingston	6	8	5	8	8	1	17
Alton Lister	8	14	9	13	14	3	17
Lewis Lloyd	12	20	3	4	8	6	27
John Long	9	17	7	7	5	3	20
John Lucas	10	20	7	12	10	14	24
Maurice Lucas	14	24	12	14	17	9	29
Kyle Macy	9	21	4	5	7	12	22
Rick Mahorn	7	14	6	6	15	4	16
Jeff Malone	13	20	4	5	3	3	30
Moses Malone	16	34	18	20	26	6	42
Pace Mannion	3	5	3	4	2	2	9
Wes Matthews	4	10	4	5	3	5	11
Cedric Maxwell	10	16	14	17	15	8	28
Bob McAdoo	21	40	12	14	22	6	50
Rodney McCray	6	8	5	6	7	3	16
Scooter McCray	3	5	0	1	4	1	6
Hank McDowell	0	1	0	0	2	2	0
Mike McGee	12	19	6	8	7	4	27
Kevin McHale	12	22	11	14	17	5	32
Tom McMillen	7	14	5	7	14	2	19
Mark McNamara	2	2	0	0	1	0	4
Joe C. Meriweather	6	12	4	8	8	2	13
Larry Micheaux	7	11	3	5	10	2	16
Mike Mitchell	17	30	11	12	16	4	37
Paul Mokeski	7	10	6	8	12	6	17
Sidney Moncrief	10	21	14	16	13	8	30
Johnny Moore	16	24	8	10	10	20	39
Larry Nance	12	22	9	13	15	6	29
Calvin Natt	13	23	12	17	11	10	30
Ed Nealy	2	2	2	2	6	2	6
Chuck Nevitt	2	5	2	2	2	1	6
Kurt Nimphius	3	6	4	4	10	3	9
Norm Nixon	17	25	8	9	7	19	36

Player	FGM	FGA	FTM	FTA	Reb.	Ast.	Pts.
Audie Norris	7	8	6	10	10	3	15
Mike O'Koren	5	9	2	2	6	3	10
Akeem Olajuwon	12	20	8	15	16	3	32
Mark Olberding	14	20	7	11	13	8	34
Jawann Oldham	3	5	0	0	9	2	6
Louis Orr	7	17	4	4	8	3	16
Robert Parish	13	25	11	15	18	6	33
Billy Paultz	10	16	8	11	14	6	20
Jim Paxson	13	21	8	12	6	5	32
John Paxson	5	10	5	7	2	7	16
Sam Perkins	9	16	11	13	19	3	26
Jim Petersen	1	1	0	0	2	1	2
Ricky Pierce	7	12	3	4	4	3	15
Charles Pittman	9	12	4	8	8	4	22
Ben Poquette	5	8	2	3	5	1	10
Paul Pressey	10	16	8	12	10	16	25
Kurt Rambis	7	11	5	7	15	3	17
Kelvin Ransey	12	26	4	4	7	10	26
Leo Rautins	1	2	0	0	2	1	3
Robert Reid	12	24	11	14	14	10	33
Clint Richardson	11	12	7	8	10	5	22
Micheal Ray Richardson	12	26	9	10	13	14	32
Glenn Rivers	6	11	15	16	3	6	21
Fred Roberts	4	7	6	6	5	5	11
Rick Robey	7	14	5	7	10	4	19
Cliff Robinson	10	21	4	4	11	2	24
Truck Robinson	11	20	10	13	20	6	23
Wayne Rollins	8	14	6	10	17	3	18
Lorenzo Romar	4	4	3	4	1	4	8
Dan Roundfield	11	23	10	13	20	7	29
Jeff Ruland	13	22	15	17	20	10	33
Campy Russell	13	25	13	14	11	6	32
Ralph Sampson	10	25	7	14	24	2	26
Mike Sanders	8	17	6	6	8	4	20
Danny Schayes	4	8	4	6	9	4	12
Tom Scheffler	2	2	2	2	2	0	5
Alvin Scott	5	11	6	7	7	6	12
Byron Scott	13	19	7	12	7	7	31
Lonnie Shelton	10	17	11	14	15	6	25
Jerry Sichting	0	0	0	0	0	0	0
Jack Sikma	12	24	14	15	17	8	33
Robert Smith	4	8	2	3	3	4	10
Ricky Sobers	11	22	7	8	8	11	25
Rory Sparrow	8	16	8	8	8	11	22
Larry Spriggs	7	10	11	11	10	5	16
Brook Steppe	2	4	2	4	3	2	6
John Stockton	5	8	9	10	5	10	13
Jon Sundvold	2	4	2	2	1	2	4
Reggie Theus	10	18	17	18	8	11	37
David Thirdkill	1	2	1	2	1	2	4
Isiah Thomas	13	28	13	17	12	16	37
Bernard Thompson	0	3	2	2	2	2	2
David Thompson	16	30	12	14	8	7	40
LaSalle Thompson	9	19	5	5	14	2	23
Mychal Thompson	15	23	10	12	17	8	40
Paul Thompson	3	7	2	4	2	1	7
Sedale Threatt	1	3	0	0	2	3	2
Andrew Toney	14	25	13	14	7	11	39
Linton Townes	5	7	2	2	2	3	13
Kelly Tripucka	15	25	11	14	11	6	40
Trent Tucker	9	12	3	4	6	6	18
Elston Turner	9	12	4	6	11	10	18
Jeff Turner	2	4	0	0	4	1	4
Mel Turpin	5	9	1	2	3	0	10
Terry Tyler	9	19	11	12	11	3	23
Darnell Valentine	9	16	15	16	5	15	29
Kiki Vandeweghe	17	24	12	12	14	7	37
Peter Verhoeven	0	0	2	2	0	0	2
Jay Vincent	8	20	10	14	11	5	23
Danny Vranes	6	16	2	3	18	4	12
Darrell Walker	8	15	7	10	6	7	18
Bill Walton	12	22	6	7	24	10	28

Player	FGM	FGA	FTM	FTA	Reb.	Ast.	Pts.
Marvin Webster	11	19	12	17	23	7	28
Scott Wedman	14	25	7	9	11	9	32
Mark West	2	6	2	3	6	2	5
Rory White	4	7	2	2	6	0	8
Willie White	6	12	2	3	6	5	15
Mitchell Wiggins	4	7	0	0	2	1	8
Jamaal Wilkes	16	30	10	13	18	7	37
Dominique Wilkins	10	20	9	10	13	4	22
Jeff Wilkins	10	24	8	9	12	3	22
Buck Williams	10	16	10	12	18	5	28
Gus Williams	17	33	12	16	8	15	38
Kevin Williams	1	1	0	0	0	1	2
Ray Williams	10	28	8	11	9	12	24
Sam Williams	1	5	1	4	6	2	3
Sly Williams	9	12	2	2	6	3	18
Randy Wittman	6	11	0	0	3	3	12
Al Wood	8	17	4	4	9	5	18
Leon Wood	2	4	6	7	1	1	10
Mike Woodson	9	16	5	6	4	5	22
Orlando Woolridge	11	20	8	8	4	4	28
James Worthy	14	22	7	11	13	6	33

Promising Newcomers

MARK RICHARD ACRES

Born November 15, 1962 at Inglewood, Calif.   Height 6:11.   Weight 220.

High School—Palos Verdes Estates, Calif., Palos Verdes.

College—Oral Roberts University, Tulsa, Okla.

Drafted by Dallas on second round, 1985 (40th pick).

—COLLEGIATE RECORD—

Year	G.	Min.	FGA	FGM	Pct.	FTA	FTM	Pct.	Reb.	Pts.	Avg.
81-82	22	702	186	109	.586	143	104	.727	178	322	14.6
82-83	28	976	368	203	.552	167	120	.719	269	526	18.8
83-84	31	...	482	266	.552	159	114	.717	324	646	20.8
84-85	29	959	380	221	.582	163	102	.626	280	544	18.8
Totals	110	....	1416	799	.564	632	440	.696	1051	2038	18.5

LEONARD BENOIT BENJAMIN

(Known by middle name.)

Born November 22, 1964 at Monroe, La.   Height 7:00.   Weight 250.

High School—Monroe, La., Carroll.

College—Creighton University, Omaha, Neb.

Drafted by Los Angeles Clippers on first round as an undergraduate, 1985 (3rd pick).

—COLLEGIATE RECORD—

Year	G.	Min.	FGA	FGM	Pct.	FTA	FTM	Pct.	Reb.	Pts.	Avg.
82-83	27	871	292	162	.555	116	76	.655	259	400	14.8
83-84	30	1112	350	190	.543	144	107	.743	295	487	16.2
84-85	32	1193	443	258	.582	233	172	.738	451	688	21.5
Totals	89	3176	1085	610	.562	493	355	.720	1005	1575	17.7

UWE KONSTATINE BLAB

Born March 26, 1962 at Munich, West Germany.   Height 7:02.   Weight 255.

High School—Effingham, Ill.

College—Indiana University, Bloomington, Ind.

Drafted by Dallas on first round, 1985 (17th pick).

—COLLEGIATE RECORD—

Year	G.	Min.	FGA	FGM	Pct.	FTA	FTM	Pct.	Reb.	Pts.	Avg.
81-82	24	....	124	69	.556	70	41	.586	89	179	7.5
82-83	30	....	220	114	.518	97	55	.567	148	283	9.4
83-84	31	....	284	150	.528	104	66	.635	190	366	11.8
84-85	33	....	375	212	.565	147	105	.714	207	529	16.0
Totals	118	....	1003	545	.543	418	267	.639	634	1357	11.5

Member of West German Olympic team, 1984.

MANUTE BOL

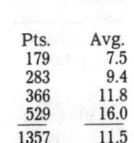

Born in Gogrial, Sudan (date unknown).   Height 7:06.   Weight 200.

High School—Attended Case Western Reserve English Language School, Cleveland, O.

College—University of Bridgeport, Bridgeport, Conn.

Drafted by San Diego on fifth round, 1983 (97th pick).

Drafted by Washington on second round as an undergraduate, 1985 (31st pick).

Played in United States Basketball League with Rhode Island Gulls, 1985.

—COLLEGIATE RECORD—

Year	G.	Min.	FGA	FGM	Pct.	FTA	FTM	Pct.	Reb.	Pts.	Avg.
84-85	31	....	496	303	.611	153	91	.595	419	697	22.5

ADRIAN FRANCIS BRANCH

Born November 17, 1963 at Washington, D.C.   Height 6:08.   Weight 185.

High School—Hyattsville, Md., DeMatha.

College—University of Maryland, College Park, Md.

Drafted by Chicago on second round, 1985 (46th pick).

Year	G.	Min.	FGA	FGM	Pct.	FTA	FTM	Pct.	Reb.	Pts.	Avg.
81-82	29	976	346	164	.474	149	114	.765	125	442	15.2
82-83	29	1043	420	197	.469	165	118	.715	150	541	18.7
83-84	28	862	284	136	.479	121	91	.752	89	363	13.0
84-85	37	1298	529	270	.510	172	131	.762	182	671	18.1
Totals	123	4179	1579	767	.486	607	454	.748	546	2017	16.4

Three-Point Field Goals: 1982-83, 29-for-81 (.358).

MICHAEL JAMES BRITTAIN
(Mike)

Born June 21, 1963 at Clearwater, Fla.   Height 7:00.   Weight 235.

High School—Clearwater, Fla.

College—University of South Carolina, Columbia, S.C.

Drafted by San Antonio on second round, 1985 (29th pick).

—COLLEGIATE RECORD—

Year	G.	Min.	FGA	FGM	Pct.	FTA	FTM	Pct.	Reb.	Pts.	Avg.
81-82	29	412	113	46	.407	41	30	.732	91	122	4.2
82-83	29	334	85	42	.494	51	45	.882	67	129	4.4
83-84	27	717	240	109	.454	63	45	.714	173	263	9.7
84-85	24	633	220	97	.441	96	56	.583	174	250	10.4
Totals	109	2096	658	294	.447	251	176	.701	505	764	7.0

TERRY DEWAYNE CATLEDGE

Born August 22, 1963 at Houston, Miss.   Height 6:08.   Weight 220.

High School—Houston, Miss.

Colleges—Itawamba Junior College, Fulton, Miss., and
University of South Alabama, Mobile, Ala.

Drafted by Philadelphia on first round, 1985 (21st pick).

—COLLEGIATE RECORD—

Itawamba

Year	G.	Min.	FGA	FGM	Pct.	FTA	FTM	Pct.	Reb.	Pts.	Avg.
81-82				Transferred before basketball season.							

South Alabama

Year	G.	Min.	FGA	FGM	Pct.	FTA	FTM	Pct.	Reb.	Pts.	Avg.
81-82				Did Not Play—Transfer Student							
82-83	28	911	387	216	.558	171	119	.696	278	551	19.7
83-84	30	1032	373	220	.590	219	157	.717	332	597	19.9
84-85	28	1038	536	285	.532	250	148	.592	322	718	25.6
Totals	86	2981	1296	721	.556	640	424	.663	932	1866	21.7

LORENZO EMILE CHARLES

Born November 25, 1963 at Brooklyn, N.Y.   Height 6:07.   Weight 225.

High School—Brooklyn, N.Y., Tech.

College—North Carolina State University, Raleigh, N.C.

Drafted by Atlanta on second round, 1985 (41st pick).

—COLLEGIATE RECORD—

Year	G.	Min.	FGA	FGM	Pct.	FTA	FTM	Pct.	Reb.	Pts.	Avg.
81-82	24	....	32	16	.500	32	20	.625	28	52	2.2
82-83	36	....	201	109	.542	109	73	.670	215	291	8.1
83-84	33	1156	411	222	.540	206	151	.733	275	595	18.0
84-85	33	1104	411	236	.574	178	125	.702	212	597	18.1
Totals	126	....	1055	583	.553	525	369	.703	730	1535	12.2

Member of NCAA championship team, 1983.

BEN COLEMAN

Born November 14, 1961 at Minneapolis, Minn.   Height 6:09.   Weight 235.

High School—Minneapolis, Minn., North.

Colleges—University of Minnesota, Minneapolis, Minn., and
University of Maryland, College Park, Md.

Drafted by Chicago on second round, 1984 (37th pick).

Draft rights traded by Chicago with draft rights to Ken Johnson to Portland for draft rights to Mike Smrek, June 18, 1985.

Played in Italy during 1984-85 season, averaging 25.7 points in 30 games.

—COLLEGIATE RECORD—

Minnesota

Year	G.	Min.	FGA	FGM	Pct.	FTA	FTM	Pct.	Reb.	Pts.	Avg.
79-80	17	....	38	14	.369	8	3	.375	21	31	1.8
80-81	23	....	190	85	.447	35	23	.657	118	193	8.4
Minn. Totals	40	....	228	99	.434	43	26	.605	139	224	5.6

Maryland

Year	G.	Min.	FGA	FGM	Pct.	FTA	FTM	Pct.	Reb.	Pts.	Avg.
81-82					Did Not Play-Transfer Student						
82-83	30	995	319	192	.571	138	90	.652	242	454	15.1
83-84	32	1094	319	194	.608	144	103	.715	269	491	15.3
Md. Totals	62	2089	638	376	.589	282	193	.684	511	945	15.2
Col. Totals	102	....	866	475	.548	325	219	.674	650	1169	11.5

TYRONE CORBIN

Born December 31, 1962 at Columbia, S.C.   Height 6:06.   Weight 210.

High School—Columbia, S.C., A.C. Flora.

College—DePaul University, Chicago, Ill.

Drafted by San Antonio on second round, 1985 (35th pick).

—COLLEGIATE RECORD—

Year	G.	Min.	FGA	FGM	Pct.	FTA	FTM	Pct.	Reb.	Pts.	Avg.
81-82	28	602	103	43	.417	78	56	.718	172	142	5.1
82-83	33	1060	263	124	.471	132	102	.773	262	350	10.6
83-84	30	1070	316	166	.525	125	93	.744	223	425	14.2
84-85	29	1004	354	189	.534	102	83	.814	236	461	15.8
Totals	120	3736	1036	522	.504	437	334	.764	893	1378	11.5

JOE DUMARS III

Born May 24, 1963 at Shreveport, La.   Height 6:03.   Weight 190.

High School—Natchitoches, La., Central.

College—McNeese State University, Lake Charles, La.

Drafted by Detroit on first round, 1985 (18th pick).

—COLLEGIATE RECORD—

Year	G.	Min.	FGA	FGM	Pct.	FTA	FTM	Pct.	Reb.	Pts.	Avg.
81-82	29	....	464	206	.444	160	115	.719	64	527	18.2
82-83	29	....	487	212	.435	197	140	.711	128	569	19.6
83-84	31	....	586	276	.471	324	267	.824	164	819	26.4
84-85	27	....	501	248	.495	236	201	.852	132	697	25.8
Totals	116	....	2038	942	.462	917	723	.788	488	2612	22.5

Three-Point Field Goals: 1982-83, 5-for-8 (.625).

Named to THE SPORTING NEWS All-America Second Team, 1985.

CALVIN ANTHONY DUNCAN

Born March 21, 1961 at South Boston, Va.   Height 6:04.   Weight 195.

High School—Linden, N.J.

Prep School—Mouth of Wilson, Va., Oak Hill Academy.

College—Virginia Commonwealth University, Richmond, Va.

Drafted by Cleveland on second round, 1985 (30th pick).

Draft rights traded by Cleveland with draft rights to Charles Oakley to Chicago for Ennis Whatley and draft rights to Keith Lee, June 18, 1985.

—COLLEGIATE RECORD—

Year	G.	Min.	FGA	FGM	Pct.	FTA	FTM	Pct.	Reb.	Pts.	Avg.
81-82	28	629	179	74	.413	77	65	.844	84	213	7.6
82-83	31	1051	376	189	.503	174	145	.833	162	539	17.4
83-84	29	965	322	141	.438	140	111	.793	120	393	13.6
84-85	32	1140	379	183	.483	147	119	.810	161	485	15.2
Totals	120	3785	1256	587	.467	538	440	.818	527	1630	13.6

Three-Point Field Goals: 1982-83, 16-for-28 (.571).

PATRICK ALOYSIUS EWING

Born August 5, 1962 at Kingston, Jamaica.   Height 7:00.   Weight 240.

High School—Cambridge, Mass., Rindge & Latin.

College—Georgetown University, Washington, D.C.

Drafted by New York on first round, 1985 (1st pick).

—COLLEGIATE RECORD—

Year	G.	Min.	FGA	FGM	Pct.	FTA	FTM	Pct.	Reb.	Pts.	Avg.
81-82	37	1064	290	183	.631	167	103	.617	279	469	12.7
82-83	32	1024	372	212	.570	224	141	.629	325	565	17.7
83-84	37	1179	368	242	.658	189	124	.656	371	608	16.4
84-85	37	1132	352	220	.625	160	102	.638	341	542	14.6
Totals	143	4399	1382	857	.620	740	470	.635	1316	2184	15.3

Member of NCAA championship team, 1984. . . . Named NCAA Division I Tournament Most Outstanding Player, 1984. . . . Member of U.S. Olympic team, 1984. . . . THE SPORTING NEWS College Player of the Year, 1985. . . . THE SPORTING NEWS All-America First Team, 1985. . . . THE SPORTING NEWS All-America Second Team, 1983 and 1984.

A. C. GREEN JR.

Born October 4, 1963 at Portland, Ore.   Height 6:09.   Weight 220.

High School—Portland, Ore., Benson.

College—Oregon State University, Corvallis, Ore.

Drafted by Los Angeles Lakers on first round, 1985 (23rd pick).

—COLLEGIATE RECORD—

Year	G.	Min.	FGA	FGM	Pct.	FTA	FTM	Pct.	Reb.	Pts.	Avg.
81-82	30	895	161	99	.615	100	61	.610	158	259	8.6
82-83	31	1113	290	162	.559	161	111	.689	235	435	14.0
83-84	23	853	204	134	.657	183	141	.770	201	409	17.8
84-85	31	1191	362	217	.599	231	157	.680	286	591	19.1
Totals	115	4052	1017	612	.602	675	470	.696	880	1694	14.7

KENNETH LEROY GREEN
(Kenny)

Born October 11, 1964 at Eustis, Fla.   Height 6:06.   Weight 210.

High School—Eustis, Fla.

College—Wake Forest University, Winston-Salem, N.C.

Drafted by Washington on first round as an undergraduate, 1985 (12th pick).

—COLLEGIATE RECORD—

Year	G.	Min.	FGA	FGM	Pct.	FTA	FTM	Pct.	Reb.	Pts.	Avg.
82-83	25	455	166	92	.554	65	41	.631	110	225	9.0
83-84	31	1060	397	229	.577	136	94	.691	211	552	17.8
84-85	28	1028	402	203	.505	107	69	.645	233	475	17.0
Totals	84	2543	965	524	.543	308	204	.662	554	1252	14.9

STEVEN DWAYNE HARRIS
(Steve)

Born October 15, 1963 at Kansas City, Mo.   Height 6:05.   Weight 195.

High School—Blue Springs, Mo.

College—University of Tulsa, Tulsa, Okla.

Drafted by Houston on first round, 1985 (19th pick).

—COLLEGIATE RECORD—

Year	G.	Min.	FGA	FGM	Pct.	FTA	FTM	Pct.	Reb.	Pts.	Avg.
81-82	29	587	239	127	.531	67	57	.851	60	311	10.7
82-83	31	1119	443	233	.526	119	104	.874	130	574	18.5
83-84	31	1043	468	271	.579	142	113	.796	104	655	21.1
84-85	31	1069	499	273	.547	215	186	.865	134	732	23.6
Totals	122	3818	1649	904	.548	543	460	.847	428	2272	18.6

PATRICK EWING

ALFREDRICK HUGHES

Born July 19, 1962 at Chicago, Ill.   Height 6:05.   Weight 215.

High School—Chicago, Ill., Robeson.

College—Loyola University, Chicago, Ill.

Drafted by San Antonio on first round, 1985 (14th pick).

—COLLEGIATE RECORD—

Year	G.	Min.	FGA	FGM	Pct.	FTA	FTM	Pct.	Reb.	Pts.	Avg.
81-82	29	1019	538	216	.401	109	70	.642	177	502	17.3
82-83	29	1038	711	318	.447	188	108	.574	254	744	25.7
83-84	29	1151	655	326	.498	209	148	.708	237	800	27.6
84-85	33	1251	756	366	.484	195	136	.697	314	868	26.3
Totals	120	4459	2660	1226	.461	701	462	.659	982	2914	24.3

BOBBY LEE HURT

Born December 6, 1961 at Huntsville, Ala.   Height 6:09.   Weight 240.

High School—Huntsville, Ala., Butler.

College—University of Alabama, University, Ala.

Drafted by Golden State on second round, 1985 (42nd pick).

—COLLEGIATE RECORD—

Year	G.	Min.	FGA	FGM	Pct.	FTA	FTM	Pct.	Reb.	Pts.	Avg.
81-82	31	793	204	126	.618	110	65	.591	171	317	10.2
82-83	32	1133	311	190	.611	160	111	.694	285	491	15.3
83-84	30	1084	253	168	.664	182	131	.720	273	467	15.6
84-85	33	1172	256	162	.633	165	98	.594	283	422	12.8
Totals	126	4182	1024	646	.631	617	405	.656	1012	1697	13.5

KENNETH H. JOHNSON
(Ken)

Born November 7, 1962 at Tuskegee, Ala.   Height 6:08.   Weight 240.

High Schools—Montgomery, Ala., Carver; Montgomery, Ala.,
Lanier; La Jolla, Calif.

Colleges—University of Southern California, Los Angeles, Calif., and
Michigan State University, East Lansing, Mich.

Drafted by Chicago on second round, 1985 (28th pick).

Draft rights traded by Chicago with draft rights to Ben Coleman to Portland for draft rights to Mike Smrek, June 18, 1985.

—COLLEGIATE RECORD—

Year	G.	Min.	FGA	FGM	Pct.	FTA	FTM	Pct.	Reb.	Pts.	Avg.
81-82	28	....	223	111	.498	76	44	.579	220	266	9.5
82-83	1	30	6	1	.167	1	0	.000	9	2	2.0
USC Totals	29	....	229	112	.489	77	44	.571	229	268	9.2

Michigan State

Year	G.	Min.	FGA	FGM	Pct.	FTA	FTM	Pct.	Reb.	Pts.	Avg.
82-83				Did Not Play—Transfer Student							
83-84	19	475	132	65	.492	51	32	.627	132	162	8.5
84-85	28	990	212	128	.604	99	45	.455	285	301	10.8
MSU Totals	47	1465	344	193	.561	150	77	.513	417	463	9.9
College Totals	76	....	573	305	.532	227	121	.533	646	731	9.6

YVON JOSEPH

Born October 31, 1957 at Cap-Haitian, Haiti.   Height 6:11.   Weight 245.

High School—Port-au-Prince, Haiti, Notre Dame.

Colleges—Miami-Dade Community College North, Miami, Fla., and
Georgia Tech, Atlanta, Ga.

Drafted by New Jersey on second round, 1985 (36th pick).

Miami-Dade North

Year	G.	Min.	FGA	FGM	Pct.	FTA	FTM	Pct.	Reb.	Pts.	Avg.
0-81	30	....	159	83	.522	64	40	.625	161	206	6.9
4-82	34	....	327	191	.584	128	86	.672	354	466	13.7
JC Totals	64	....	486	274	.564	192	126	.656	515	672	10.5

Georgia Tech

Year	G.	Min.	FGA	FGM	Pct.	FTA	FTM	Pct.	Reb.	Pts.	Avg.
2-83	2	32	17	8	.471	6	4	.667	14	20	10.0
3-84	29	851	240	129	.538	128	87	.680	208	345	11.9
4-85	34	1051	268	151	.563	123	91	740	224	393	11.6
Totals	65	1934	525	288	.549	257	182	.708	426	758	11.7

(Suffered back injury in 1982-83 season; granted extra year of eligibility.)

JOSEPH WILLIAM KLEINE
(Joe)

Born January 4, 1962 at Colorado Springs, Colo.   Height 6:11.   Weight 255.

High School—Slater, Mo.

Colleges—University of Notre Dame, Notre Dame, Ind., and
University of Arkansas, Fayetteville, Ark.

Drafted by Sacramento on first round, 1985 (6th pick).

Notre Dame

Year	G.	Min.	FGA	FGM	Pct.	FTA	FTM	Pct.	Reb.	Pts.	Avg.
0-81	29	291	50	32	.640	16	12	.750	71	76	2.6

Arkansas

Year	G.	Min.	FGA	FGM	Pct.	FTA	FTM	Pct.	Reb.	Pts.	Avg.
1-82			Did Not Play—Transfer Student								
2-83	30	950	307	165	.537	109	69	.633	219	399	13.3
3-84	32	1173	351	209	.595	211	163	.773	293	581	18.2
4-85	35	1289	484	294	.607	257	185	.720	294	773	22.1
Ark. Totals	97	3412	1142	668	.585	577	417	.723	806	1753	18.1
College Totals	126	3703	1192	700	.587	593	429	.723	877	1829	14.5

Member of U.S. Olympic team, 1984.

JON FRANCIS KONCAK

Born May 17, 1963 at Cedar Rapids, Ia.   Height 7:00.   Weight 250.

High School—Kansas City, Mo., Center.

College—Southern Methodist University, Dallas, Tex.

Drafted by Atlanta on first round, 1985 (5th pick).

Year	G.	Min.	FGA	FGM	Pct.	FTA	FTM	Pct.	Reb.	Pts.	Avg.
31-82	27	745	232	107	.461	92	57	.620	155	271	10.0
32-83	30	980	334	176	.527	123	85	.691	282	437	14.6
33-84	33	1162	340	211	.621	145	88	.607	378	510	15.5
34-85	33	1084	370	219	.592	192	128	.667	354	566	17.2
Totals	123	3971	1276	713	.559	552	358	.649	1169	1784	14.5

Member of U.S. Olympic team, 1984. . . . Named to THE SPORTING NEWS All-America Second Team, 1985.

KEITH DEYWANE LEE

Born December 28, 1962 at West Memphis, Ark.   Height 6:10.   Weight 215.

High School—West Memphis, Ark.

College—Memphis State University, Memphis, Tenn.

Drafted by Chicago on first round, 1985 (11th pick).

Draft rights traded by Chicago with Ennis Whatley to Cleveland for draft rights to Charles Oakley and Calvin Duncan, June 18, 1985.

Year	G.	Min.	FGA	FGM	Pct.	FTA	FTM	Pct.	Reb.	Pts.	Avg.
31-82	29	1041	370	199	.538	178	134	.753	320	532	18.3
32-83	31	1109	438	220	.502	172	141	.820	336	581	18.7

Year	G.	Min.	FGA	FGM	Pct.	FTA	FTM	Pct.	Reb.	Pts.	Avg.
83-84	33	1139	453	245	.541	151	117	.775	357	607	18.4
84-85	35	1141	536	266	.496	200	156	.780	323	688	19.7
Totals	128	4430	1797	930	.518	701	548	.782	1336	2408	18.8

Named to THE SPORTING NEWS All-America First Team, 1983 and 1985.

KARL MALONE

Born July 24, 1963 at Summerfield, La.   Height 6:09.   Weight 250.

High School—Summerfield, La.

College—Louisiana Tech University, Ruston, La.

Drafted by Utah on first round as an undergraduate, 1985 (13th pick).

—COLLEGIATE RECORD—

Year	G.	Min.	FGA	FGM	Pct.	FTA	FTM	Pct.	Reb.	Pts.	Avg.
81-82			Did Not Play—Scholastically Ineligible								
82-83	28	....	373	217	.583	244	152	.623	289	586	20.9
83-84	32	....	382	220	.576	236	161	.682	282	601	18.8
84-85	32	....	399	216	.541	170	97	.571	288	529	16.5
Totals	92	....	1154	653	.566	650	410	.631	859	1716	18.7

FERNANDO MARTIN

Born March 25, 1962 at Madrid, Spain.   Height 6:09.   Weight 220.

High School—Madrid, Spain, Estudiantes.

Did not attend college.

Drafted by New Jersey on second round, 1985 (38th pick).

Played for Real Madrid team during 1984-85 season, averaging 19.4 points, 8.9 rebounds and 1.5 blocked shots with a .585 field goal percentage.

Member of Spanish Olympic team, 1984.

WILLIAM MARTIN
(Bill)

Born August 16, 1962 at Washington, D.C.   Height 6:07.   Weight 215.

High School—Washington, D.C., McKinley.

College—Georgetown University, Washington, D.C.

Drafted by Indiana on second round, 1985 (26th pick).

—COLLEGIATE RECORD—

Year	G.	Min.	FGA	FGM	Pct.	FTA	FTM	Pct.	Reb.	Pts.	Avg.
81-82	35	468	126	63	.500	74	46	.622	84	172	4.9
82-83	32	917	260	131	.504	102	78	.765	203	340	10.6
83-84	37	800	232	118	.509	132	93	.705	219	329	8.9
84-85	38	1147	361	196	.543	117	76	.650	234	468	12.3
Totals	142	3332	979	508	.519	425	293	.689	740	1309	9.2

Member of NCAA championship team, 1984.

DWAYNE EDWARD McCLAIN

Born February 7, 1963 at Worcester, Mass.   Height 6:06.   Weight 185.

High School—Worcester, Mass., Holy Name.

College—Villanova University, Villanova, Pa.

Drafted by Indiana on second round, 1985 (27th pick).

—COLLEGIATE RECORD—

Year	G.	Min.	FGA	FGM	Pct.	FTA	FTM	Pct.	Reb.	Pts.	Avg.
81-82	30	828	229	138	.603	54	37	.685	71	313	10.4
82-83	29	744	245	130	.531	65	47	.723	95	307	10.6
83-84	31	973	286	169	.591	93	68	.731	129	406	13.1
84-85	35	1114	359	206	.574	137	106	.774	143	518	14.8
Totals	125	3659	1119	643	.575	349	258	.739	438	1544	12.4

Member of NCAA championship team, 1985.

—DID YOU KNOW—

That Detroit General Manager Jack McCloskey was the Continental Basketball Association's MVP in 1953 and 1954?

XAVIER MAURICE McDANIEL

Born June 4, 1963 at Columbia, S.C.   Height 6:08.   Weight 205.

High School—Columbia, S.C., A.C. Flora.

College—Wichita State University, Wichita, Kan.

Drafted by Seattle on first round, 1985 (4th pick).

—COLLEGIATE RECORD—

Year	G.	Min.	FGA	FGM	Pct.	FTA	FTM	Pct.	Reb.	Pts.	Avg.
81-82	28	378	135	68	.504	43	27	.628	103	163	5.8
82-83	28	987	376	223	.593	148	80	.541	403	526	18.8
83-84	30	1130	445	251	.564	172	117	.680	393	619	20.6
84-85	31	1143	628	351	.559	224	142	.634	460	844	27.2
Totals	117	3638	1584	893	.564	587	366	.624	1359	2152	18.4

Led NCAA Division I in scoring, 1985. . . . Led NCAA Division I in rebounding, 1983 and 1985.

GEORGE WASHINGTON MONTGOMERY

Born April 26, 1962 at Chicago, Ill.   Height 6:09.   Weight 235.

High School—Chicago, Ill., Corliss.

College—University of Illinois, Champaign, Ill.

Drafted by Portland on second round, 1985 (39th pick).

—COLLEGIATE RECORD—

Year	G.	Min.	FGA	FGM	Pct.	FTA	FTM	Pct.	Reb.	Pts.	Avg.
81-82	28	463	83	41	.494	40	20	.500	104	102	3.6
82-83	32	643	143	72	.503	78	40	.513	146	184	5.8
83-84	31	967	226	124	.549	103	53	.515	224	301	9.7
84-85	23	586	171	86	.503	104	64	.615	168	236	10.3
Totals	114	2659	623	323	.518	325	177	.545	642	823	7.2

CHRISTOPHER PAUL MULLIN
(Chris)

Born July 30, 1963 at New York, N.Y.   Height, 6:06.   Weight 200.

High School—Brooklyn, N.Y., Xaverian.

College—St. John's University, Jamaica, N.Y.

Drafted by Golden State on first round, 1985 (7th pick).

—COLLEGIATE RECORD—

Year	G.	Min.	FGA	FGM	Pct.	FTA	FTM	Pct.	Reb.	Pts.	Avg.
81-82	30	1061	328	175	.534	187	148	.791	97	498	16.6
82-83	33	1210	395	228	.577	197	173	.878	123	629	19.1
83-84	27	1070	394	225	.571	187	169	.904	120	619	22.9
84-85	35	1327	482	251	.521	233	192	.824	169	694	19.8
Totals	125	4668	1599	879	.550	804	682	.848	509	2440	19.5

Member of U.S. Olympic team, 1984. . . . Named to THE SPORTING NEWS All-America First Team, 1985. . . . THE SPORTING NEWS All-America Second Team, 1984.

CHARLES OAKLEY

Born December 18, 1963 at Cleveland, O.   Height 6:08.   Weight 225.

High School—Cleveland, O., John Hay.

College—Virginia Union University, Richmond, Va.

Drafted by Cleveland on first round, 1985 (9th pick).

Draft rights traded by Cleveland with draft rights to Calvin Duncan to Chicago for Ennis Whatley and draft rights to Keith Lee, June 18, 1985.

—COLLEGIATE RECORD—

Year	G.	Min.	FGA	FGM	Pct.	FTA	FTM	Pct.	Reb.	Pts.	Avg.
81-82			Statistics Unavailable								
82-83	28	....	378	220	.582	170	100	.588	365	540	19.3
83-84	30	....	418	256	.612	...	139	....	393	651	21.7
84-85	31		453	283	.625	266	178	.669	535	744	24.0

Led NCAA Division II in rebounding, 1985.

—DID YOU KNOW—
That Chet Forte, who directed NFL Monday Night Football for ABC television, once played in the Continental Basketball Association?

EDWARD LEWIS PINCKNEY
(Ed)

Born March 27, 1963 at Bronx, N.Y.   Height 6:09.   Weight 195.

High School—Bronx, N.Y., Adlai Stevenson.

College—Villanova University, Villanova, Pa.

Drafted by Phoenix on first round, 1985 (10th pick).

—COLLEGIATE RECORD—

Year	G.	Min.	FGA	FGM	Pct.	FTA	FTM	Pct.	Reb.	Pts.	Avg.
81-82	32	1083	264	169	.640	161	115	.714	249	453	14.2
82-83	31	1029	227	129	.568	171	130	.760	301	388	12.5
83-84	31	1068	268	162	.604	222	154	.694	246	478	15.4
84-85	35	1186	295	177	.600	263	192	.730	311	546	15.6
Totals	129	4366	1054	637	.604	817	591	.723	1107	1865	14.5

Member of NCAA championship team, 1985. . . . Named NCAA Division I Tournament Most Outstanding Player, 1985.

TERRY PORTER

Born April 8, 1963 at Milwaukee, Wis.   Height 6:03.   Weight 195.

High School—Milwaukee, Wis., South Division.

College—University of Wisconsin at Stevens Point,
Stevens Point, Wisc.

Drafted by Portland on first round, 1985 (24th pick).

—COLLEGIATE RECORD—

Year	G.	Min.	FGA	FGM	Pct.	FTA	FTM	Pct.	Reb.	Pts.	Avg.
81-82	25	273	57	21	.368	13	9	.692	13	51	2.0
82-83	30	949	229	140	.611	89	62	.697	117	342	11.4
83-84	32	1040	392	244	.622	135	112	.830	165	600	18.8
84-85	30	1042	405	233	.575	151	126	.834	155	592	19.7
Totals	117	3304	1083	638	.589	388	309	.796	450	1585	13.5

BLAIR ALLEN RASMUSSEN

Born November 13, 1962 at Auburn, Wash.   Height 7:00.   Weight 250.

High School—Auburn, Wash.

College—University of Oregon, Eugene, Ore.

Drafted by Denver on first round, 1985 (15th pick).

—COLLEGIATE RECORD—

Year	G.	Min.	FGA	FGM	Pct.	FTA	FTM	Pct.	Reb.	Pts.	Avg.
81-82	27	521	141	67	.475	53	39	.736	129	173	6.4
82-83	27	819	296	160	.540	116	80	.690	146	400	14.8
83-84	29	1017	377	196	.520	112	90	.804	176	482	16.6
84-85	31	1081	381	195	.512	151	109	.722	222	499	16.1
Totals	114	3438	1195	618	.517	432	318	.736	673	1554	13.6

JERRY REYNOLDS

Born December 23, 1962 at Brooklyn, N.Y.   Height 6:08.   Weight 200.

High School—Brooklyn, N.Y., Alexander Hamilton.

Colleges—Madison Area Technical College, Madison, Wisc., and
Louisiana State University, Baton Rouge, La.

Drafted by Milwaukee on first round as an undergraduate, 1985 (22nd pick).

—COLLEGIATE RECORD—
Madison Tech

Year	G.	Min.	FGA	FGM	Pct.	FTA	FTM	Pct.	Reb.	Pts.	Avg.
81-82					Did Not Play						

LSU

Year	G.	Min.	FGA	FGM	Pct.	FTA	FTM	Pct.	Reb.	Pts.	Avg.
82-83	32	888	236	126	.534	142	88	.620	198	340	10.6
83-84	29	899	307	162	.528	158	85	.538	239	409	14.1
84-85	29	803	255	128	.502	107	64	.598	176	320	11.0
Totals	90	2590	798	416	.521	407	237	.582	613	1069	11.9

DETLEF SCHREMPF

Born January 21, 1963 at Leverkusen, West Germany.   Height 6:09.   Weight 220.

High School—Centralia, Wash.

College—University of Washington, Seattle, Wash.

Drafted by Dallas on first round, 1985 (8th pick).

—COLLEGIATE RECORD—

Year	G.	Min.	FGA	FGM	Pct.	FTA	FTM	Pct.	Reb.	Pts.	Avg.
81-82	28	314	73	33	.452	47	26	.553	56	92	3.3
82-83	31	958	266	124	.466	113	81	.717	211	329	10.6
83-84	31	1186	362	195	.539	178	131	.736	230	521	16.8
84-85	32	1180	342	191	.558	175	125	.714	255	507	15.8
Totals	122	3638	1043	543	.521	513	363	.708	752	1449	11.9

Member of West German Olympic team, 1984. . . . Named to THE SPORTING NEWS All-America Second Team, 1985.

CAREY SCURRY

Born December 4, 1962 at Brooklyn, N.Y.   Height 6:09.   Weight 205.

High School—Brooklyn, N.Y., Alexander Hamilton.

Colleges—Northeastern Oklahoma A&M College, Miami, Okla.,
and Long Island University, Brooklyn, N.Y.

Drafted by Utah on second round, 1985 (37th pick).

—COLLEGIATE RECORD—
Northeastern Oklahoma A&M

Year	G.	Min.	FGA	FGM	Pct.	FTA	FTM	Pct.	Reb.	Pts.	Avg.
81-82	12	....	127	69	.543	23	13	.565	79	151	12.6

Long Island

Year	G.	Min.	FGA	FGM	Pct.	FTA	FTM	Pct.	Reb.	Pts.	Avg.
82-83	20	....	191	99	.518	69	47	.681	201	245	12.3
83-84	31	....	417	226	.542	175	126	.720	418	578	18.6
84-85	28	....	413	224	.542	200	142	.710	394	590	21.1
LIU Totals	79	....	1021	549	.538	444	315	.709	1013	1413	17.9

AUBREY DWIGHT SHERROD

Born November 6, 1962 at Wichita, Kan.   Height 6:04.   Weight 195.

High School—Wichita, Kan., Wichita Heights.

College—Wichita State University, Wichita, Kan.

Drafted by Chicago on second round, 1985 (34th pick).

—COLLEGIATE RECORD—

Year	G.	Min.	FGA	FGM	Pct.	FTA	FTM	Pct.	Reb.	Pts.	Avg.
81-82	29	769	270	137	.507	57	44	.772	47	318	11.0
82-83	27	866	338	167	.494	76	56	.737	76	413	15.3
83-84	30	1059	420	195	.464	102	69	.676	95	459	15.3
84-85	31	1143	470	240	.511	111	95	.856	101	575	18.5
Totals	117	3837	1498	739	.493	346	264	.763	319	1765	15.1

Three-Point Field Goals: 1982-83, 23-for-59 (.390).

MICHAEL FRANK SMREK
(Mike)

Born August 31, 1962 at Welland, Ontario.   Height 7:00.   Weight 250.

High School—Port Robinson, Ontario, Eastdale.

College—Canisius College, Buffalo, N.Y.

Drafted by Portland on second round, 1985 (25th pick).

Draft rights traded by Portland to Chicago for draft rights to Ben Coleman and Ken Johnson, June 18, 1985.

—COLLEGIATE RECORD—

Year	G.	Min.	FGA	FGM	Pct.	FTA	FTM	Pct.	Reb.	Pts.	Avg.
81-82	22	311	54	24	.444	14	7	.500	68	55	2.5

Year	G.	Min.	FGA	FGM	Pct.	FTA	FTM	Pct.	Reb.	Pts.	Avg.
82-83	28	560	106	49	.462	52	27	.519	131	125	4.5
83-84	30	829	242	153	.632	96	56	.583	175	362	12.1
84-85	28	812	286	172	.601	148	97	.655	192	441	15.8
Totals	108	2512	688	398	.578	310	187	.603	566	983	9.1

BARRY STEVENS

Born November 7, 1963 at Flint, Mich.   Height 6:05.   Weight 190.

High School—Flint, Mich., Northwestern.

College—Iowa State University, Ames, Iowa.

Drafted by Denver on second round, 1985 (43rd pick).

—COLLEGIATE RECORD—

Year	G.	Min.	FGA	FGM	Pct.	FTA	FTM	Pct.	Reb.	Pts.	Avg.
81-82	26	767	287	132	.460	97	74	.763	116	338	13.0
82-83	28	917	409	190	.465	116	89	.767	145	469	16.8
83-84	29	1059	544	257	.472	171	130	.760	145	644	22.2
84-85	34	1211	607	301	.496	171	137	.801	138	738	21.7
Totals	117	3954	1847	880	.476	555	430	.775	544	2190	18.7

GREGORY LEWIS STOKES
(Greg)

Born August 5, 1963 at New Haven, Conn.   Height 6:10.   Weight 220.

High School—Hamilton, Ohio.

College—University of Iowa, Iowa City, Iowa.

Drafted by Philadelphia on second round, 1985 (33rd pick).

—COLLEGIATE RECORD—

Year	G.	Min.	FGA	FGM	Pct.	FTA	FTM	Pct.	Reb.	Pts.	Avg.
81-82	29	....	128	61	.477	77	43	.558	123	165	5.7
82-83	31	....	403	219	.543	173	110	.636	223	548	17.7
83-84	28	1013	284	163	.574	134	91	.679	193	417	14.9
84-85	32	1148	479	262	.547	170	114	.671	268	638	19.9
Totals	120	....	1294	705	.545	554	358	.646	807	1768	14.7

WAYMAN LAWRENCE TISDALE

Born June 9, 1964 at Tulsa, Okla.   Height 6:09.   Weight 250.

High School—Tulsa, Okla., Washington.

College—University of Oklahoma, Norman, Okla.

Drafted by Indiana on first round as an undergraduate, 1985 (2nd pick).

—COLLEGIATE RECORD—

Year	G.	Min.	FGA	FGM	Pct.	FTA	FTM	Pct.	Reb.	Pts.	Avg.
82-83	33	1138	583	338	.580	211	134	.635	341	810	24.5
83-84	34	1232	639	369	.577	283	181	.640	329	919	27.0
84-85	37	1283	640	370	.578	273	192	.703	378	932	25.2
Totals	104	3653	1862	1077	.578	767	507	.661	1048	2661	25.6

Member of U.S. Olympic team, 1984. . . . Named to THE SPORTING NEWS All-America First Team, 1984 and 1985. . . . THE SPORTING NEWS All-America Second Team, 1983.

ERIC CLIFTON TURNER

Born February 7, 1963 at Elkhart, Ind.   Height 6:03.   Weight 175.

High School—Flint, Mich., Central.

College—University of Michigan, Ann Arbor, Mich.

Drafted by Detroit on second round as an undergraduate, 1984 (32nd pick).

Waived by Detroit, October 18, 1984; signed by Houston as a free agent, May 14, 1985.

Played in Continental Basketball Association with Detroit Spirits, 1984-85.

—COLLEGIATE RECORD—

Year	G.	Min.	FGA	FGM	Pct.	FTA	FTM	Pct.	Reb.	Pts.	Avg.
81-82	27	....	343	163	.475	113	72	.637	57	398	14.7

WAYMAN TISDALE

Year	G.	Min.	FGA	FGM	Pct.	FTA	FTM	Pct.	Reb.	Pts.	Avg.
82-83	27	....	401	193	.481	159	104	.654	87	519	19.2
83-84	31	1020	292	123	.421	113	88	.779	65	334	10.8
Totals	85	....	1036	479	.462	385	264	.686	209	1251	14.7

Three-Point Field Goals: 1982-83, 29-for-68 (.426).

MINOR LEAGUE REGULAR SEASON RECORD

Sea.—Team	G.	Min.	2-Point			3-Point			FTM	FTA	Pct.	Reb.	Ast.	Pts.	Avg.
			FGM	FGA	Pct.	FGM	FGA	Pct.							
84-85—Detroit CBA	47	1785	280	537	.521	3	16	.188	254	310	.819	173	400	823	17.5

Named CBA Rookie of the Year, 1985.

NICHOLAS VANOS
(Nick)

Born April 13, 1963 at San Mateo, Calif.   Height 7:01.   Weight 255.

High School—San Mateo, Calif., Hillsdale.

College—University of Santa Clara, Santa Clara, Calif.

Drafted by Phoenix on second round, 1985 (32nd pick).

—COLLEGIATE RECORD—

Year	G.	Min.	FGA	FGM	Pct.	FTA	FTM	Pct.	Reb.	Pts.	Avg.
81-82	24	251	79	39	.494	30	12	.400	62	90	3.8
82-83	28	509	225	111	.493	103	55	.534	185	277	9.9
83-84	32	1034	414	213	.514	182	118	.648	317	544	17.0
84-85	29	1002	373	193	.517	165	102	.618	312	488	16.8
Totals	113	2796	1091	556	.510	480	287	.598	876	1399	12.4

JAMES SAMUEL VINCENT
(Sam)

Born May 18, 1963 at Lansing, Mich.   Height 6:02.   Weight 185.

High School—Lansing, Mich., Eastern.

College—Michigan State University, Lansing, Mich.

Drafted by Boston on first round, 1985 (20th pick).

—COLLEGIATE RECORD—

Year	G.	Min.	FGA	FGM	Pct.	FTA	FTM	Pct.	Reb.	Pts.	Avg.
81-82	28	965	282	130	.461	91	68	.747	78	328	11.7
82-83	30	1066	401	180	.449	172	133	.773	79	498	16.6
83-84	23	740	261	130	.498	122	99	.811	62	359	15.6
84-85	29	1093	450	245	.544	208	176	.846	112	666	23.0
Totals	110	3864	1394	685	.491	593	476	.803	331	1851	16.8

Three-Point Field Goals: 1982-83, 5-for-11 (.455).

Named to THE SPORTING NEWS All-America First Team, 1985. . . . Brother of Dallas Mavericks forward Jay Vincent.

WILLIAM PERCEY WENNINGTON
(Bill)

Born December 26, 1964 at Montreal, Can.   Height 7:00.   Weight 245.

High School—Brookville, N.Y., Long Island Lutheran.

College—St. John's University, Jamaica, N.Y.

Drafted by Dallas on first round, 1985 (16th pick).

—COLLEGIATE RECORD—

Year	G.	Min.	FGA	FGM	Pct.	FTA	FTM	Pct.	Reb.	Pts.	Avg.
81-82	30	505	85	37	.435	34	23	.676	126	97	3.2
82-83	33	656	114	69	.605	63	44	.698	146	182	5.5
83-84	26	735	209	124	.593	83	56	.675	148	304	11.7
84-85	35	1099	279	168	.602	125	102	.816	224	438	12.5
Totals	124	2995	687	398	.579	305	225	.738	644	1021	8.2

Member of Canadian Olympic team, 1984.

—DID YOU KNOW—

That Seattle forward Danny Vranes' grandfather was Dallas Coach Dick Motta's high school coach at Midvale, Utah?

GERALD WILKINS

Born September 11, 1963 at Atlanta, Ga.   Height 6:06.   Weight 185.

High School—Atlanta, Ga., Mays Academy.

Colleges—Moberly Area Junior College, Moberly, Mo., and University of Tennessee-Chattanooga, Chattanooga, Tenn.

Drafted by New York on second round, 1985 (47th pick).

—COLLEGIATE RECORD—

Moberly

Year	G.	Min.	FGA	FGM	Pct.	FTA	FTM	Pct.	Reb.	Pts.	Avg.
81-82	39	1340	566	312	.551	126	97	.770	229	721	18.5

Tennessee-Chattanooga

Year	G.	Min.	FGA	FGM	Pct.	FTA	FTM	Pct.	Reb.	Pts.	Avg.
82-83	30	....	350	169	.483	62	41	.661	113	379	12.6
83-84	23	737	297	161	.542	105	73	.695	92	398	17.3
84-85	32	1188	532	276	.519	190	120	.632	147	672	21.0
UTC Totals	85	....	1179	606	.514	357	234	.655	352	1449	17.0

Three-Point Field Goals: 1982-83, 0-for-2 (.000). 1983-84, 3-for-10 (.300).

Brother of Atlanta Hawks forward Dominique Wilkins.

JOHN WILLIAMS

Born August 9, 1961 at Sorrento, La.   Height 6:10.   Weight 215.

High School—Sorrento, La., St. Amant.

College—Tulane University, New Orleans, La.

Drafted by Cleveland on second round, 1985 (45th pick).

—COLLEGIATE RECORD—

Year	G.	Min.	FGA	FGM	Pct.	FTA	FTM	Pct.	Reb.	Pts.	Avg.
81-82	28	932	279	163	.584	133	88	.662	202	414	14.8
82-83	31	996	317	151	.476	118	83	.703	166	385	12.4
83-84	28	1038	355	202	.569	184	140	.761	222	544	19.4
84-85	28	1006	334	189	.566	155	120	.774	219	498	17.8
Totals	115	3972	1285	705	.549	590	431	.731	809	1841	16.0

VOISE LEE WINTERS

Born October 12, 1962 at Chicago, Ill.   Height 6:08.   Weight 200.

High School—Chicago, Ill., Gage Park.

College—Bradley University, Peoria, Ill.

Drafted by Philadelphia on second round, 1985 (44th pick).

—COLLEGIATE RECORD—

Year	G.	Min.	FGA	FGM	Pct.	FTA	FTM	Pct.	Reb.	Pts.	Avg.
81-82	34	....	228	102	.447	37	19	.514	130	223	6.6
82-83	29	1025	395	195	.494	72	52	.722	183	448	15.4
83-84	27	919	344	172	.500	94	71	.755	179	415	15.4
84-85	30	1132	496	262	.528	142	104	.732	194	628	20.9
Totals	120	....	1463	731	.500	345	246	.713	686	1714	14.3

Three-Point Field Goals: 1982-83, 6.

NBA Head Coaches

CHARLES STANLEY ALBECK
(Stan)
Chicago Bulls

Born May 17, 1931 at Chenoa, Ill.

High School—Chenoa, Ill.

College—Bradley University, Peoria, Ill.

—COLLEGIATE PLAYING RECORD—

Year	G.	Min.	FGA	FGM	Pct.	FTA	FTM	Pct.	Reb.	Pts.	Avg.
49-50†					Statistics Unavailable						
50-51	18	....	...	22	...	...	7	....	....	51	2.8
51-52	11	....	34	15	.441	1	0	.000	7	30	2.7
54-55	25	....	175	56	.320	74	44	.595	....	156	6.2
Varsity Totals	54	....	...	93	...	...	51	....	....	237	4.4

NOTE: In military service during 1952-53 and 1953-54 seasons.

COLLEGIATE COACHING RECORD

Sea. Club	W.	L.	Pct.	Sea. Club	W.	L.	Pct.
1956-57—Adrian College..	16	5	.762	1964-65—No. Michigan.....	19	6	.760
1957-58—No. Michigan.....	15	3	.833	1965-66—No. Michigan.....	16	6	.727
1958-59—No. Michigan.....	16	8	.667	1966-67—No. Michigan.....	14	10	.583
1959-60—No. Michigan.....	13	5	.722	1967-68—No. Michigan.....	16	8	.667
1960-61—No. Michigan.....	24	3	.889	1968-69—Denver	2	24	.077
1961-62—No. Michigan.....	14	9	.609	1969-70—Denver	5	13	.278
1962-63—No. Michigan.....	19	8	.704	Totals (14 seasons)	201	119	.628
1963-64—No. Michigan.....	12	11	.522				

ABA COACHING RECORD

Sea. Club	Regular Season				Playoffs	
	W.	L.	Pct.	Pos.	W.	L.
1970-71—Denver	27	44	.380	4T†	0	1

NBA COACHING RECORD

Sea. Club	Regular Season				Playoffs	
	W.	L.	Pct.	Pos.	W.	L.
1979-80—Cleveland............	37	45	.451	4T‡	..	..
1980-81—San Antonio........	52	30	.634	1§	3	4
1981-82—San Antonio........	48	34	.585	1§	4	5
1982-83—San Antonio........	53	29	.646	1§	6	5
1983-84—New Jersey........	45	37	.549	4x	5	6
1984-85—New Jersey........	42	40	.512	3x	0	3
Totals (6 seasons)	277	215	.563		18	23

†Western Division. ‡Central Division. §Midwest Division. xAtlantic Division.

JOHN WILLIAM BACH
Golden State Warriors

Born July 10, 1925 at Brooklyn, N. Y.   Height 6:02.   Weight 180.

High School—Brooklyn, N. Y., St. John's Prep.

Colleges—Fordham University, Bronx, N. Y.; Brown University, Providence, R. I., and University of Rochester, Rochester, N. Y.

Drafted by Boston on fifth round, 1948 BAA draft.

Played in American Basketball League with Hartford, 1949-50.

—COLLEGIATE PLAYING RECORD—

Fordham

Year	G.	Min.	FGA	FGM	Pct.	FTA	FTM	Pct.	Reb.	Pts.	Avg.
42-43					Statistics Unavailable						
47-48	23	....	...	123	...	...	96	....	...	342	14.9

Rochester

Year	G.	Min.	FGA	FGM	Pct.	FTA	FTM	Pct.	Reb.	Pts.	Avg.
43-44	14	....	...	....	....	...	...	....	....	172	12.3

Brown

Year	G.	Min.	FGA	FGM	Pct.	FTA	FTM	Pct.	Reb.	Pts.	Avg.
43-44	5	....	...	32	....	...	9	....	....	73	14.6
44-45	15	....	...	...	....	...	...	....	....	...	15.7

BAA REGULAR SEASON RECORD

Sea.—Team	G.	Min.	FGA	FGM	Pct.	FTA	FTM	Pct.	Reb.	Ast.	PF	Disq.	Pts.	Avg.
48-49—Boston	34	....	119	34	.286	75	51	.680	..	25	24	..	119	3.5

ABL RECORD

Year	G.	Min.	FGA	FGM	Pct.	FTA	FTM	Pct.	Reb.	Pts.	Avg.
49-50—Hartford	37	....	429	164	.382	235	171	.728	25	499	13.5

COLLEGIATE COACHING RECORD

Sea. Club	W.	L.	Pct.	Sea. Club	W.	L.	Pct.
1950-51—Fordham	19	8	.704	1966-67—Fordham	14	11	.560
1951-52—Fordham	20	8	.714	1967-68—Fordham	19	8	.704
1952-53—Fordham	18	8	.692	1968-69—Penn State	13	9	.591
1953-54—Fordham	18	6	.750	1969-70—Penn State	13	11	.542
1954-55—Fordham	18	9	.667	1970-71—Penn State	10	12	.455
1955-56—Fordham	11	14	.440	1971-72—Penn State	17	8	.680
1956-57—Fordham	16	10	.615	1972-73—Penn State	15	8	.652
1957-58—Fordham	16	9	.640	1973-74—Penn State	14	12	.538
1958-59—Fordham	17	8	.680	1974-75—Penn State	11	12	.478
1959-60—Fordham	8	18	.308	1975-76—Penn State	10	15	.400
1960-61—Fordham	7	16	.304	1976-77—Penn State	11	15	.423
1961-62—Fordham	10	14	.417	1977-78—Penn State	8	19	.296
1962-63—Fordham	18	8	.692	Tot. Fordham (18 sea.)	263	193	.577
1963-64—Fordham	9	11	.450	Tot. Penn St. (10 sea.)	122	121	.502
1964-65—Fordham	15	12	.556	Totals (28 seasons)	385	314	.551
1965-66—Fordham	10	15	.400				

NOTE: Fordham participated in the NIT in 1958, 1959, 1963, 1965 and 1968.

NBA COACHING RECORD

Sea. Club	Regular Season				Playoffs	
	W.	L.	Pct.	Pos.	W.	L.
1983-84—Golden State	37	45	.451	5†		
1984-85—Golden State	22	60	.268	6†	—	—
Totals (2 seasons)	59	105	.360			

†Pacific Division.

Named to ABL All-Star second team, 1950.

BERNARD T. BICKERSTAFF
(Bernie)
Seattle SuperSonics

Born February 11, 1944 at Benham, Ky.

High School—East Benham, Ky.

Colleges—Rio Grande College, Rio Grande, O., and
University of San Diego, San Diego, Calif.

—COLLEGIATE PLAYING RECORD—

Played with 1964-65 and 1965-66 University of San Diego teams; statistics unavailable.

—COLLEGIATE COACHING RECORD—

Sea. Club	W.	L.	Pct.
1969-70—San Diego U.	14	12	.538
1970-71—San Diego U.	10	14	.417
1971-72—San Diego U.	12	14	.462
1972-73—San Diego U.	19	9	.679
Totals (4 seasons)	55	49	.529

Assistant coach, San Diego University, 1967-68 and 1968-69.
Also served as coach of National Puerto Rican team, winning Caribbean Tournament championship in 1975-76 and finishing second in 1976-77.

NBA COACHING RECORD

Served as assistant coach with Capital Bullets, 1973-74, and Washington Bullets, 1974-75 through 1984-85 seasons.

—DID YOU KNOW—

That the oldest rookie in NBA history was Matt Guokas Sr., who broke in with the Philadelphia Warriors in 1946-47, the NBA's first season? Guokas, father of new Philadelphia Coach Matt Guokas, turned 32 in November of 1946.

HUBERT JUDE BROWN
(Hubie)
New York Knicks

Born September 25, 1933 at Elizabeth, N. J.   Height 6:00.   Weight 160.
High School—Elizabeth, N. J., St. Mary's.
College—Niagara University, Niagara University, N. Y.

Played in Eastern Basketball League with Rochester, 1958-59.

COLLEGIATE PLAYING RECORD

Year	G.	Min.	FGA	FGM	Pct.	FTA	FTM	Pct.	Reb.	Pts.	Avg.
51-52	8	....	...	3	....	5	4	.800	....	10	1.3
52-53	21	....	...	15	....	...	15	....	....	45	2.1
53-54	30	....	...	24	....	...	27	....	....	75	3.5
54-55	23	....	...	63	....	...	66	....	....	192	8.3
Totals	82	....		105	....	...	112	....	....	322	3.9

MINOR LEAGUE REGULAR SEASON RECORD

Year	G.	Min.	FGA	FGM	Pct.	FTA	FTM	Pct.	Reb.	Pts.	Avg.
58-59—Roch. EBL	8	....	....	49	....	....	12	....	....	110	13.8

ABA COACHING RECORD

Sea. Club	Regular Season W.	L.	Pct.	Pos.	Playoffs W.	L.
1974-75—Kentucky*	58	26	.690	1T†	12	3
1975-76—Kentucky	46	38	.548	4	5	5
Totals (2 seasons)	104	64	.619		17	8

NBA COACHING RECORD

Sea. Club	Regular Season W.	L.	Pct.	Pos.	Playoffs W.	L.
1976-77—Atlanta	31	51	.378	6‡	..	..
1977-78—Atlanta	41	41	.500	4‡	0	2
1978-79—Atlanta	46	36	.561	3‡	5	4
1979-80—Atlanta	50	32	.610	1‡	1	4
1980-81—Atlanta	31	48	.392	4‡	..	..
1982-83—New York	44	38	.537	4§	2	4
1983-84—New York	47	35	.573	3§	6	6
1984-85—New York	24	58	.293	5§	..	..
Totals (8 seasons)	314	339	.481		14	20

*Won ABA championship.   †Eastern Division.   ‡Central Division.   §Atlantic Division.
NBA Coach of the Year, 1978.

DON CHANEY
Los Angeles Clippers

Born March 22, 1946 at Baton Rouge, La.   Height 6:05.   Weight 210.
High School—Baton Rouge, La., McKinley.
College—University of Houston, Houston, Tex.
Drafted by Boston on first round, 1968 (12th pick).

Signed by St. Louis ABA, September 27, 1974, for 1975-76 season.
Played out option with Boston, September 1, 1975; signed by Los Angeles as a free agent, September 22, 1976.
Traded by Los Angeles with Kermit Washington and a 1978 1st round draft choice to Boston for Charlie Scott, December 27, 1977.

—COLLEGIATE RECORD—

Year	G.	Min.	FGA	FGM	Pct.	FTA	FTM	Pct.	Reb.	Pts.	Avg.
64-65j	21	....	421	186	.442	123	84	.683	183	456	21.7
65-66	26	627	243	105	.432	38	21	.553	124	231	8.9
66-67	31	1038	448	197	.440	116	80	.690	160	474	15.3
67-68	33	1010	431	189	.439	84	50	.595	191	428	13.0
Varsity Totals	90	2675	1122	491	.438	238	151	.634	475	1133	12.6

ABA REGULAR SEASON RECORD

Sea.—Team	G.	Min.	2-Point FGM	FGA	Pct.	3-Point FGM	FGA	Pct.	FTM	FTA	Pct.	Reb.	Ast.	Pts.	Avg.
75-76—St. Louis	48	1475	190	453	.419	1	4	.250	64	82	.780	234	169	447	9.3

NBA REGULAR SEASON RECORD

Sea.—Team	G.	Min.	FGA	FGM	Pct.	FTA	FTM	Pct.	Off.	Def.	Tot.	Ast.	PF	Dq.	Stl.	Blk.	Pts.	Avg.
68-69—Boston	20	209	113	36	.319	20	8	.400			46	19	32	0			80	4.0
69-70—Boston	63	839	320	115	.359	109	82	.752			152	72	118	0			312	5.0
70-71—Boston	81	2289	766	348	.454	313	234	.748			463	235	288	11			930	11.5
71-72—Boston	79	2275	786	373	.475	255	197	.773			395	202	295	7			943	11.9
72-73—Boston	79	2488	859	414	.482	267	210	.787			449	221	276	6			1038	13.1
73-74—Boston	81	2258	750	348	.464	180	149	.828	210	168	378	176	247	7	83	62	845	10.4
74-75—Boston	82	2208	750	321	.428	165	133	.806	171	199	370	181	244	5	122	66	775	9.5
76-77—Los Angeles	81	2408	522	213	.408	94	70	.745	120	210	330	308	224	4	140	33	496	6.1
77-78—L.A.-Bos.	51	835	269	104	.387	45	38	.844	40	76	116	66	107	0	44	13	246	4.8
78-79—Boston	65	1074	414	174	.420	42	36	.857	63	78	141	75	167	3	72	11	384	5.9
79-80—Boston	60	523	189	67	.354	42	32	.762	31	42	73	38	80	1	31	11	167	2.8
Totals	742	17406	5738	2513	.438	1532	1189	.776			2913	1593	2078	44	492	196	6216	8.4

Three-Point Field Goals: 1979-80, 1-for-6 (.167).

NBA PLAYOFF RECORD

Sea.—Team	G.	Min.	FGA	FGM	Pct.	FTA	FTM	Pct.	Off.	Def.	Tot.	Ast.	PF	Dq.	Stl.	Blk.	Pts.	Avg.
68-69—Boston	7	25	6	1	.167	4	3	.750			4	0	7	0			5	0.7
71-72—Boston	11	271	81	41	.506	20	15	.750			39	22	39	0			97	8.8
72-73—Boston	12	288	82	39	.476	17	12	.706			40	25	41	1			90	7.5
73-74—Boston	18	545	141	65	.461	50	41	.820	37	40	77	40	64	0	24	9	171	9.5
74-75—Boston	11	294	105	48	.457	29	23	.793	24	14	38	21	46	2	21	5	119	10.8
76-77—Los Angeles	11	412	96	36	.375	22	16	.727	24	28	52	48	32	0	21	3	88	8.0
Totals	70	1835	511	230	.450	142	110	.775			250	156	229	3	66	17	570	8.1

NBA COACHING RECORD

		Regular Season				Playoffs	
Sea.	Club	W.	L.	Pct.	Pos.	W.	L.
1984-85—L.A. Clippers		9	12	.429	..		

Named interim coach of Los Angeles Clippers, March 6, 1985.

Member of NBA championship teams, 1969 and 1974. . . . Named to NBA All-Defensive Second Team, 1972, 1973, 1974, 1975, 1977.

CHARLES JOSEPH DALY
(Chuck)
Detroit Pistons

Born July 20, 1930 at St. Mary's, Pa. Height 6:02. Weight 180.

High School—Kane, Pa.

Colleges—St. Bonaventure University, Olean, N. Y.;
Bloomsburg State College, Bloomsburg, Pa., and graduate work at
Penn State University, University Park, Pa.

COLLEGIATE PLAYING RECORD
St. Bonaventure

Year	G.	Min.	FGA	FGM	Pct.	FTA	FTM	Pct.	Reb.	Pts.	Avg.
48-49†				Statistics Unavailable							

Bloomsburg State

Year	G.	Min.	FGA	FGM	Pct.	FTA	FTM	Pct.	Reb.	Pts.	Avg.
49-50				Did Not Play—Transfer Student							
50-51	16	....	...	...	...	...	...	....	....	215	13.4
51-52	16	....	...	...	...	...	...	....	....	203	12.7
Totals	32	....	...	...	...	...	...	....	....	418	13.1

COLLEGIATE COACHING RECORD

Sea.	Club	W.	L.	Pct.	Pos.	Sea.	Club	W.	L.	Pct.	Pos.
1969-70—Boston College		11	13	.458	..	1975-76—Penn		17	9	.654	2
1970-71—Boston College		15	11	.577	..	1976-77—Penn		18	8	.692	2
1971-72—Penn		25	3	.893	1	Totals B. C. (2 sea.)		26	24	.520	
1972-73—Penn		21	7	.750	1	Totals Penn (6 sea.)		125	38	.767	
1973-74—Penn		21	6	.778	1	Totals (8 seasons)		151	62	.709	
1974-75—Penn		23	5	.821	1						

Assistant coach, Duke University, 1963 to 1969.

NBA COACHING RECORD

		Regular Season				Playoffs	
Sea.	Club	W.	L.	Pct.	Pos.	W.	L.
1981-82—Cleveland		9	32	.220	..	..	..
1983-84—Detroit		49	33	.598	2†	2	3
1984-85—Detroit		46	36	.561	2†	5	4
Totals (3 seasons)		104	101	.507		7	7

†Central Division.

WILLIAM CHARLES FITCH
(Bill)
Houston Rockets

Born May 19, 1934 at Davenport, Iowa.
High School—Cedar Rapids, Iowa.
College—Coe College, Cedar Rapids, Iowa.

—COLLEGIATE PLAYING RECORD—

Year	G.	Min.	FGA	FGM	Pct.	FTA	FTM	Pct.	Reb.	Pts.	Avg.
50-51					Statistics Unavailable						
51-52	20	....	...	63	....	...	50	....	....	176	8.8
52-53	19	....	...	83	....	...	72	....	....	238	12.5
53-54	22	....	...	123	....	...	92	....	....	338	15.4

COLLEGIATE COACHING RECORD

Sea.	Club	W.	L.	Pct.	Pos.	Sea.	Club	W.	L.	Pct.	Pos.
1958-59	Coe College	11	9	.550	6	1965-66	North Dakota	24	5	.828	
1959-60	Coe College	12	9	.571	5T	1966-67	North Dakota	20	6	.769	
1960-61	Coe College	10	12	.455	4T	1967-68	Bowl. Green	18	7	.720	
1961-62	Coe College	11	10	.524	6T	1968-69	Minnesota	12	12	.500	5T
1962-63	North Dakota	14	13	.519		1969-70	Minnesota	13	11	.542	5
1963-64	North Dakota	10	16	.385		Totals (12 seasons)		181	115	.611	
1964-65	North Dakota	26	5	.839							

NBA COACHING RECORD

Sea.	Club	Regular Season				Playoffs		Sea.	Club	Regular Season				Playoffs	
		W.	L.	Pct.	Pos.	W.	L.			W.	L.	Pct.	Pos.	W.	L.
1970-71	Cleveland	15	67	.183	4†	..	..	1978-79	Cleveland	30	52	.366	4T†	..	..
1971-72	Cleveland	23	59	.280	4†	..	..	1979-80	Boston	61	21	.744	1‡	5	4
1972-73	Cleveland	32	50	.390	4†	..	..	1980-81	Boston*	62	20	.756	1T‡	12	5
1973-74	Cleveland	29	53	.354	4†	..	..	1981-82	Boston	63	19	.768	1‡	7	5
1974-75	Cleveland	40	42	.488	3†	..	..	1982-83	Boston	56	26	.683	2‡	2	5
1975-76	Cleveland	49	33	.598	1†	6	7	1983-84	Houston	29	53	.354	6§	..	..
1976-77	Cleveland	43	39	.524	4†	1	2	1984-85	Houston	48	34	.585	2§	2	3
1977-78	Cleveland	43	39	.524	3†	0	2	Totals (15 seasons)		623	607	.507		35	33

*Won NBA championship. †Central Division. ‡Atlantic Division. §Midwest Division.
NBA Coach of the Year, 1976 and 1980.... Coach of NBA championship team, 1981.

LOWELL FITZSIMMONS
(Cotton)
San Antonio Spurs

Born October 7, 1931 at Hannibal, Mo.
High School—Bowling Green, Mo.
Colleges—Hannibal-LaGrange College, Hannibal, Mo.,
and Midwestern State University, Wichita Falls, Tex.

—COLLEGIATE PLAYING RECORD—
Hannibal-LaGrange

Year	G.	Min.	FGA	FGM	Pct.	FTA	FTM	Pct.	Reb.	Pts.	Avg.
52-53	33	....	...	...	....	...	...	....	....	838	25.4

Midwestern State

Year	G.	Min.	FGA	FGM	Pct.	FTA	FTM	Pct.	Reb.	Pts.	Avg.
53-54	27	....	161	53	.329	173	128	.740	....	234	8.7
54-55	27	....	258	118	.457	210	162	.771	....	398	14.7
55-56	28	....	319	148	.464	223	164	.735	....	460	16.4
Totals	82	....	738	319	.432	606	454	.749	....	1092	13.3

COLLEGIATE COACHING RECORD

Sea.	Club	W.	L.	Pct.	Pos.	Sea.	Club	W.	L.	Pct.	Pos.
1958-59	Moberly J.C.	16	15	.516	..	1965-66	Moberly J.C.	29	5	.853	..
1959-60	Moberly J.C.	19	8	.704	..	1966-67	Moberly J.C.	31	2	.939	..
1960-61	Moberly J.C.	26	5	.839	..	1968-69	Kansas State	14	12	.538	2T*
1961-62	Moberly J.C.	26	9	.743	..	1969-70	Kansas State	20	8	.714	1*
1962-63	Moberly J.C.	26	6	.813	..	Totals (JC)		222	60	.787	
1963-64	Moberly J.C.	24	5	.828	..	Totals (College)		34	20	.630	
1964-65	Moberly J.C.	25	5	.833	..						

Assistant coach at Kansas State, 1967-68.   *Big Eight Conference.

NBA COACHING RECORD

Sea. Club	Regular Season W.	L.	Pct.	Pos.	Playoffs W.	L.	Sea. Club	Regular Season W.	L.	Pct.	Pos.	Playoffs W.	L.
1970-71—Phoenix	48	34	.585	3†	..	..	1979-80—Kansas City	47	35	.573	2†	1	2
1971-72—Phoenix	49	33	.598	3†	..	..	1980-81—Kansas City	40	42	.488	2T†	7	8
1972-73—Atlanta	46	36	.561	2‡	2	4	1981-82—Kansas City	30	52	.366	4†	..	..
1973-74—Atlanta	35	47	.427	2‡	..	..	1982-83—Kansas City	45	37	.549	2T†	..	..
1974-75—Atlanta	31	51	.378	4‡	..	..	1983-84—Kansas City	38	44	.463	3T†	0	3
1975-76—Atlanta	28	46	.378	5‡	..	..	1984-85—San Antonio	41	41	.500	4T†	2	3
1977-78—Buffalo	27	55	.329	4§	..	..	Totals (14 seasons)	553	581	.488		13	24
1978-79—Kansas City	48	34	.585	1†	1	4							

†Midwest Division. ‡Central Division. §Atlantic Division.

NBA Coach of the Year, 1979. . . . Father of Gary Fitzsimmons, scout-assistant coach for San Antonio Spurs.

MICHAEL ROBERT FRATELLO
(Mike)
Atlanta Hawks

Born February 24, 1947 at Hackensack, N. J.   Height 5:07.   Weight 150.

High School—Hackensack, N. J.

Colleges—Montclair State College, Montclair, N. J., and
graduate work at University of Rhode Island, Kingston, R. I.

—COLLEGIATE PLAYING RECORD—

Played with 1965-66 Montclair State team; statistics unavailable.

COLLEGIATE COACHING RECORD

Assistant, Rhode Island (1971), James Madison (1972 through 1975), and Villanova (1976 through 1978).

NBA COACHING RECORD

Sea. Club	Regular Season W.	L.	Pct.	Pos.	Playoffs W.	L.
1983-84—Atlanta	40	42	.488	3†	2	3
1984-85—Atlanta	33	49	.402	5†	..	..
Totals (2 seasons)	73	91	.445		2	3

†Central Division.
Assistant, Atlanta (1978-79 through 1981-82) and New York (1982-83).

MATTHEW GEORGE GUOKAS JR.
(Matt)
Philadelphia 76ers

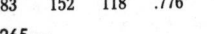

Born February 25, 1944 at Philadelphia, Pa.   Height 6:06.   Weight 195.

High School—Philadelphia, Pa., St. Joseph's.

Colleges—University of Miami, Coral Gables, Fla., and
St. Joseph's University, Philadelphia, Pa.

Drafted by Philadelphia on first round, 1966.

Traded by Philadelphia to Chicago for a draft choice, October 16, 1970.
Traded by Chicago with a draft choice to Cincinnati for Charlie Paulk, May 14, 1971.
Traded by Kansas City-Omaha to Houston for Jimmy Walker, October 29, 1973.
Traded by Houston with Jack Marin to Buffalo for Kevin Kunnert and Dave Wohl, February 1, 1974.
Traded by Buffalo with a draft choice to Chicago for Bob Weiss, September 4, 1974.
Traded by Chicago to Kansas City for draft choices, December 8, 1975.
Waived by Kansas City, July 29, 1976.

—COLLEGIATE RECORD—

Miami

Year	G.	Min.	FGA	FGM	Pct.	FTA	FTM	Pct.	Reb.	Pts.	Avg.
62-63					Freshman Team Statistics Unavailable						

St. Joseph's

Year	G.	Min.	FGA	FGM	Pct.	FTA	FTM	Pct.	Reb.	Pts.	Avg.
63-64					Did Not Play—Transfer Student						
64-65	29	....	342	157	.459	98	71	.724	195	385	13.3
65-66	29	....	413	207	.501	122	94	.770	72	508	17.5
Varsity Totals	58		755	364	.482	220	165	.750	267	893	15.4

NBA REGULAR SEASON RECORD

Sea.—Team	G.	Min.	FGA	FGM	Pct.	FTA	FTM	Pct.	Reb.	Ast.	PF	Disq.	Pts.	Avg.
66-67—Philadelphia	69	808	203	79	.389	81	49	.605	83	105	82	0	207	3.0
67-68—Philadelphia	82	1612	393	190	.483	152	118	.776	185	191	172	0	498	6.1

Sea.—Team	G.	Min.	FGA	FGM	Pct.	FTA	FTM	Pct.	Reb.	Ast.	PF	Disq.	Pts.	Avg.
68-69—Philadelphia	72	838	216	92	.426	81	54	.667	94	104	121	1	238	3.3
69-70—Philadelphia	80	1558	416	189	.454	149	106	.711	216	222	201	0	484	6.1
70-71—Phil.-Chicago	79	2213	418	206	.493	138	101	.732	158	342	189	1	513	6.5
71-72—Cincinnati	61	1975	385	191	.496	83	64	.771	142	321	150	0	446	7.3
72-73—K.C.-Omaha	79	2846	565	322	.570	90	74	.822	245	403	190	0	718	9.1

Sea.—Team	G.	Min.	FGA	FGM	Pct.	FTA	FTM	Pct.	—Rebounds— Off.	Def.	Tot.	Ast.	PF	Dq.	Stl.	Blk.	Pts.	Avg.
73-74—KC-O-Ho-Bu	75	1871	396	195	.492	60	39	.650	31	90	121	238	150	3	54	21	429	5.7
74-75—Chicago	82	2089	500	255	.510	103	78	.757	24	115	139	178	154	1	45	17	588	7.2
75-76—Chi.-K.C.	56	793	173	73	.422	27	18	.667	22	41	63	70	76	0	18	3	164	2.9
Totals	735	16603	3665	1792	.489	964	701	.727			1446	2174	1485	6	117	41	4285	5.8

NBA PLAYOFF RECORD

Sea.—Team	G.	Min.	FGA	FGM	Pct.	FTA	FTM	Pct.	Reb.	Ast.	PF	Disq.	Pts.	Avg.
66-67—Philadelphia	15	252	64	26	.406	17	13	.765	30	23	33	0	65	4.3
67-68—Philadelphia	13	327	79	30	.380	27	20	.741	43	30	39	0	80	6.2
68-69—Philadelphia	5	100	27	11	.407	5	4	.800	12	8	12	0	26	5.2
69-70—Philadelphia	2	23	8	6	.750	1	1	1.000	3	1	1	0	13	6.5
70-71—Chicago	6	83	14	8	.571	5	4	.800	8	12	8	0	20	3.3

Sea.—Team	G.	Min.	FGA	FGM	Pct.	FTA	FTM	Pct.	—Rebounds— Off.	Def.	Tot.	Ast.	PF	Dq.	Stl.	Blk.	Pts.	Avg.
73-74—Buffalo	6	85	15	8	.533	4	3	.750	3	5	8	13	8	0	0	1	19	3.2
74-75—Chicago	13	202	35	12	.343	8	7	.875	4	10	14	11	20	0	7	1	31	2.4
Totals	60	1072	242	101	.417	67	52	.776			118	98	121	0	7	2	254	4.2

Member of NBA championship team, 1967. . . . Son of Matt Guokas Sr., forward with Philadelphia Warriors, 1946-47.

GEORGE R. IRVINE
Indiana Pacers

Born February 1, 1948 at Seattle, Wash.   Height 6:06.   Weight 200.

High School—Seattle, Wash., Ballard.

College—University of Washington, Seattle, Wash.

Drafted by Seattle on eighth round, 1970 (125th pick).

Drafted by Washington on third round of American Basketball Association draft, 1970.

Washington franchise transferred to Virginia, 1970.
Traded by Virginia to Denver with draft rights to David Thompson for Mike Green, Mack Calvin and Jan van Breda Kolff, July 14, 1975.
Entered NBA with Denver, 1976.
Waived by Denver, 1976.

—COLLEGIATE RECORD—

Year	G.	Min.	FGA	FGM	Pct.	FTA	FTM	Pct.	Reb.	Pts.	Avg.
66-67†	22	....	267	150	.562	112	89	.795	162	389	17.7
67-68	26	....	255	144	.565	139	102	.734	197	390	15.0
68-69	26	....	302	161	.533	120	82	.683	196	404	15.5
69-70	26	....	337	194	.576	166	132	.795	175	520	20.0
Varsity Totals	78	....	894	499	.558	425	316	.744	568	1314	16.8

ABA REGULAR SEASON RECORD

Sea.—Team	G.	Min.	2-Point FGM	FGA	Pct.	3-Point FGM	FGA	Pct.	FTM	FTA	Pct.	Reb.	Ast.	Pts.	Avg.
70-71—Virginia	34	338	81	141	.574	2	8	.250	26	35	.743	65	25	194	5.7
71-72—Virginia	75	1362	197	387	.509	3	10	.300	54	75	.720	217	70	457	6.1
72-73—Virginia	79	2075	417	772	.540	7	33	.212	169	203	.833	296	149	1024	13.0
73-74—Virginia	75	1140	242	470	.515	12	46	.261	120	138	.870	177	76	640	8.5
74-75—Virginia	59	1522	298	552	.540	13	37	.351	138	164	.841	203	108	774	13.1
Totals	322	6437	1235	2322	.532	37	134	.276	508	615	.826	958	428	3089	9.6

ABA PLAYOFF RECORD

Sea.—Team	G.	Min.	2-Point FGM	FGA	Pct.	3-Point FGM	FGA	Pct.	FTM	FTA	Pct.	Reb.	Ast.	Pts.	Avg.
70-71—Virginia	7	25	3	4	.750	0	2	.000	1	1	1.000	5	2	7	1.0
71-72—Virginia	11	285	56	85	.659	0	1	.000	25	31	.806	27	10	137	12.5
72-73—Virginia	5	53	6	15	.400	0	0	.000	5	5	1.000	5	5	17	3.4
73-74—Virginia	5	109	23	48	.479	1	7	.142	10	10	1.000	11	10	59	11.8
Totals	28	472	88	152	.579	1	10	.100	41	47	.872	48	27	220	7.9

NBA COACHING RECORD

Sea. Club	Regular Season W.	L.	Pct.	Pos.	Playoffs W.	L.
1984-85—Indiana	23	59	.280	6†	..	..

†Central Division.

PHILIP DONALD JOHNSON
(Phil)
Sacramento Kings

Born September 6, 1941, at Grace, Ida. Height 6:05. Weight 180.

High School—Grace, Ida.

Colleges—Utah State University, Logan, Utah, and Weber
Junior College, Ogden, Utah.

—COLLEGIATE RECORD—
Utah State

Year	G.	Min.	FGA	FGM	Pct.	FTA	FTM	Pct.	Reb.	Pts.	Avg.
59-60†	12	....	...	...	....	...	...	....	....	....	11.8

Weber J. C.

Year	G.	Min.	FGA	FGM	Pct.	FTA	FTM	Pct.	Reb.	Pts.	Avg.
60-61					Statistics Unavailable						

Utah State

Year	G.	Min.	FGA	FGM	Pct.	FTA	FTM	Pct.	Reb.	Pts.	Avg.
61-62	28	....	252	104	.413	100	60	.600	222	268	9.6
62-63	20	....	213	101	.474	65	44	.677	143	246	12.3
Varsity Totals	48	....	465	205	.441	165	104	.630	365	514	10.7

COLLEGIATE COACHING RECORD

Sea.	Club	W.	L.	Pct.	Pos.
1968-69	Weber State	27	3	.900	1‡
1969-70	Weber State	20	7	.741	1‡
1970-71	Weber State	21	6	.778	1‡
	Totals (3 seasons)	68	16	.810	

‡Big Sky Conference.

NBA COACHING RECORD

		Regular Season				Playoffs	
Sea.	Club	W.	L.	Pct.	Pos.	W.	L.
1973-74	K. C.-Omaha	27	30	.474	..	..	..
1974-75	K. C.-Omaha	44	38	.537	2†	2	4
1975-76	Kansas City	31	51	.378	3†	..	..
1976-77	Kansas City	40	42	.488	4†	..	..
1977-78	Kansas City	13	24	.351	..	..	..
1984-85	Kansas City	30	43	.411	..	..	..
	Totals (6 seasons)	185	228	.448		2	4

†Midwest Division.

Assistant coach, Chicago Bulls, 1971-72 through 1973-74; 1979-80 through 1981-82 seasons.
Assistant coach, Utah Jazz, 1982-83 through 1984-85 seasons.

Named NBA Coach of the Year, 1975.

K.C. JONES
Boston Celtics

Born May 25, 1932 at San Francisco, Calif. Height 6:01. Weight 200.

High School—San Francisco, Calif., Commerce.

College—University of San Francisco, San Francisco, Calif.

Drafted by Boston on second round, 1956.

In military service, 1956-57 and 1957-58; played at Fort Leonard Wood, Mo.; named to Amateur Athletic Union
All-America team as a member of 1957-58 Fort Leonard Wood team.

—COLLEGIATE PLAYING RECORD—

Year	G.	Min.	FGA	FGM	Pct.	FTA	FTM	Pct.	Reb.	Pts.	Avg.
51-52	24	....	128	44	.344	64	46	.719	....	134	5.6
52-53	23	....	159	163	.396	149	81	.544	....	207	9.0
53-54	1	....	12	3	.250	2	2	1.000	3	8	8.0
54-55	29	....	293	105	.358	144	97	.674	148	307	10.6
55-56	25	....	208	76	.365	142	93	.655	130	245	9.8
Totals	102	....	800	291	.364	501	319	.637		901	8.8

(Jones underwent an appendectomy after one game of the 1953-54 season and was granted an extra year of
eligibility by the University of San Francisco; however, he was ineligible for the 1955-56 NCAA tournament because he
was playing his fifth season of college basketball.)

NBA REGULAR SEASON RECORD

Sea.—Team	G.	Min.	FGA	FGM	Pct.	FTA	FTM	Pct.	Reb.	Ast.	PF	Disq.	Pts.	Avg.
58-59—Boston	49	609	192	65	.339	68	41	.603	127	70	58	0	171	3.5
59-60—Boston	74	1274	414	169	.408	170	128	.752	199	189	109	1	466	6.3

Sea.—Team	G.	Min.	FGA	FGM	Pct.	FTA	FTM	Pct.	Reb.	Ast.	PF	Disq.	Pts.	Avg.
60-61—Boston	78	1607	601	203	.337	320	186	.581	279	253	200	3	592	7.6
61-62—Boston	79	2023	707	289	.409	231	145	.628	291	339	204	2	723	9.1
62-63—Boston	79	1945	591	230	.389	177	112	.633	263	317	221	3	572	7.2
63-64—Boston	80	2424	722	283	.392	168	88	.524	372	407	253	0	654	8.2
64-65—Boston	78	2434	639	253	.396	227	143	.630	318	437	263	5	649	8.3
65-66—Boston	80	2710	619	240	.388	303	209	.690	304	503	243	4	689	8.6
66-67—Boston	78	2446	459	182	.397	189	110	.630	239	389	273	7	483	6.2
Totals	675	17472	4944	1914	.387	1853	1171	.632	2392	2904	1824	25	4999	7.4

NBA PLAYOFF RECORD

Sea.—Team	G.	Min.	FGA	FGM	Pct.	FTA	FTM	Pct.	Reb.	Ast.	PF	Disq.	Pts.	Avg.
58-59—Boston	8	75	20	5	.250	5	5	1.000	12	10	8	0	15	1.9
59-60—Boston	13	232	80	27	.337	22	17	.773	45	14	28	0	71	5.522
60-61—Boston	9	103	30	9	.300	14	7	.500	19	15	17	0	25	2.8
61-62—Boston	14	329	102	44	.431	53	38	.717	56	55	50	1	126	9.0
62-63—Boston	13	250	64	19	.297	30	21	.700	36	37	42	1	59	4.5
63-64—Boston	10	312	72	25	.347	25	13	.520	37	68	40	0	63	6.3
64-65—Boston	12	396	104	43	.413	45	35	.778	39	74	49	1	121	10.1
65-66—Boston	17	543	109	45	.413	57	39	.684	52	75	65	0	129	7.6
66-67—Boston	9	254	75	24	.320	18	11	.611	24	48	36	1	59	6.6
Totals	105	2494	656	241	.367	269	186	.691	320	396	335	4	668	6.4

NBA COACHING RECORD

Sea.	Club	Regular Season W.	L.	Pct.	Pos.	Playoffs W.	L.
1973-74—Capital		47	35	.573	1†	3	4
1974-75—Washington		60	22	.732	1†	8	9
1975-76—Washington		48	34	.585	2†	3	4
1983-84—Boston*		62	20	.756	1‡	15	8
1984-85—Boston		63	19	.768	1‡	13	8
Totals (5 seasons)		280	130	.683		42	33

*Won NBA championship. †Central Division. ‡Atlantic Division.

Member of 1956 U.S. Olympic team. . . . Member of 1955 NCAA championship team. . . . Member of NBA championship teams, 1959, 1960, 1961, 1962, 1963, 1964, 1965, 1966. . . . Coach of NBA championship team, 1984. . . . Drafted by Los Angeles Rams in 30th round of 1955 National Football League draft.

GEORGE MATTHEW KARL
Cleveland Cavaliers

Born May 12, 1951 at Penn Hills, Pa.   Height 6:02.   Weight 190.

High School—Penn Hills, Pa.

College—University of North Carolina, Chapel Hill, N. C.

Signed as a free agent by San Antonio, ABA, 1973.
Entered NBA with San Antonio, 1976.

—COLLEGIATE RECORD—

Year	G.	Min.	FGA	FGM	Pct.	FTA	FTM	Pct.	Reb.	Pts.	Avg.
69-70†	6	....	97	56	.577	23	20	.870	29	132	22.0
70-71	32	....	286	150	.524	115	92	.800	104	392	12.3
71-72	29	....	241	125	.519	113	89	.788	72	339	11.7
72-73	33	....	437	219	.501	163	124	.761	103	562	17.0
Varsity Totals	94	....	964	494	.512	391	305	.780	279	1293	13.8

ABA REGULAR SEASON RECORD

Sea.—Team	G.	Min.	2-Point FGM	FGA	Pct.	3-Point FGM	FGA	Pct.	FTM	FTA	Pct.	Reb.	Ast.	Pts.	Avg.
73-74—San Antonio	74	1339	228	480	.475	8	22	.364	94	113	.832	126	160	574	7.7
74-75—San Antonio	82	1629	257	511	.503	4	23	.174	137	177	.774	155	334	663	8.1
75-76—San Antonio	75	1200	150	325	.462	0	9	.000	81	106	.764	66	250	381	5.1
Totals	231	4168	635	1316	.483	12	54	.222	312	396	.788	347	744	1618	7.0

ABA PLAYOFF RECORD

Sea.—Team	G.	Min.	2-Point FGM	FGA	Pct.	3-Point FGM	FGA	Pct.	FTM	FTA	Pct.	Reb.	Ast.	Pts.	Avg.
73-74—San Antonio	7	141	13	27	.481	0	1	.000	2	5	.400	15	23	28	4.0
74-75—San Antonio	4	40	1	7	.142	0	1	.000	3	4	.750	3	5	5	1.3
75-76—San Antonio	6	64	10	21	.476	0	1	.000	6	9	.667	4	17	26	4.3
Totals	17	245	24	55	.436	0	3	.000	11	18	.611	22	45	59	3.5

NBA REGULAR SEASON RECORD

Sea.—Team	G.	Min.	FGA	FGM	Pct.	FTA	FTM	Pct.	Rebounds—Off.	Def.	Tot.	Ast.	PF	Dq.	Stl.	Blk.	Pts.	Avg.
76-77—San Antonio	29	251	73	25	.342	42	29	.690	4	13	17	46	36	0	10	0	79	2.7
77-78—San Antonio	4	30	6	2	.333	2	2	1.000	0	5	5	5	6	0	1	0	6	1.5
Totals	33	281	79	27	.342	44	31	.705	4	18	22	51	42	0	11	0	85	2.6

NBA PLAYOFF RECORD

Sea.—Team	G.	Min.	FGA	FGM	Pct.	FTA	FTM	Pct.	Rebounds—Off.	Def.	Tot.	Ast.	PF	Dq.	Stl.	Blk.	Pts.	Avg.
76-77—San Antonio	1	1	0	0	.000	0	0	.000	0	0	0	0	0	0	0	0	0	0.0

NBA COACHING RECORD

Sea. Club	Regular Season W.	L.	Pct.	Pos.	Playoffs W.	L.
1984-85—Cleveland............	36	46	.439	4‡	1	3

‡Central Division.

CBA COACHING RECORD

Sea. Club	Regular Season W.	L.	Pct.	Pos.	Playoffs W.	L.
1980-81—Montana..............	27	15	.643	1†	5	5
1981-82—Montana..............	30	16	.652	2†	2	3
1982-83—Montana..............	33	11	.750	1†	6	5
Totals (3 seasons)	90	42	.682		13	13

†Western Division.
Named CBA Coach of the Year, 1981 and 1983.

FRANCIS P. LAYDEN
(Frank)
Utah Jazz

Born January 5, 1932 at Brooklyn, N. Y. Height 6:01. Weight 212.

High School—Brooklyn, N. Y., Fort Hamilton.

College—Niagara University, Niagara Falls, N. Y.

COLLEGIATE PLAYING RECORD

Year	G.	Min.	FGA	FGM	Pct.	FTA	FTM	Pct.	Reb.	Pts.	Avg.
51-52	5	....	...	0	....	6	3	.500	....	3	0.6
52-53	13	....	...	14	....	...	...	....	....	33	2.5
53-54						Did Not Play—Freshman Coach					
54-55						Did Not Play—Freshman Coach					
Totals	18	....	...	14	....	...	8	....	....	36	2.0

COLLEGIATE COACHING RECORD

Sea. Club	W.	L.	Pct.	Sea. Club	W.	L.	Pct.
1968-69—Niagara..............	11	13	.458	1973-74—Niagara	12	14	.462
1969-70—Niagara..............	22	7	.759	1974-75—Niagara	13	14	.481
1970-71—Niagara..............	14	12	.538	1975-76—Niagara	17	12	.586
1971-72—Niagara..............	21	9	.700	Totals	119	97	.551
1972-73—Niagara..............	9	16	.360				

NOTE: Niagara posted a 1-2 record in 1970 NCAA tournament and was runner-up in 1972 NIT.

NBA COACHING RECORD

Sea. Club	Regular Season W.	L.	Pct.	Pos.	Playoffs W.	L.
1981-82—Utah	17	45	.274	6†	..	..
1982-83—Utah	30	52	.366	5†	..	..
1983-84—Utah	45	37	.549	1†	5	6
1984-85—Utah	41	41	.500	T4†	4	6
Totals (4 seasons)	133	175	.432		9	12

†Midwest Division.
Assistant coach, Atlanta Hawks, 1976-77 through 1978-79.

NBA Coach of the Year, 1984. . . . NBA Executive of the Year, 1984. . . . Father of Scott Layden, an assistant coach with Utah Jazz.

—DID YOU KNOW—

That when Bob Lanier signed his first Pistons contract in 1970, he was in a wheelchair because of torn ligaments suffered when his St. Bonaventure team played Villanova in the NCAA playoffs?

JOHN MATTHEW MacLEOD
Phoenix Suns

Born October 3, 1937 at New Albany, Ind.   Height 6:00.   Weight 170.

High School—Clarksville, Ind., New Providence.

College—Bellarmine College, Louisville, Ky.

—COLLEGIATE PLAYING RECORD—

Year	G.	Min.	FGA	FGM	Pct.	FTA	FTM	Pct.	Reb.	Pts.	Avg.
55-56					Statistics Unavailable						
56-57	10	....	...	0	....	...	1	....	....	1	0.1
57-58	8	....	...	2	....	10	3	.300	....	7	0.8
58-59	5	....	...	2	....	....	4	....	....	8	1.6

COLLEGIATE COACHING RECORD

Sea.	Club	W.	L.	Pct.	Pos.
1967-68—Oklahoma		13	13	.500	3T§
1968-69—Oklahoma		7	19	.269	8§
1969-70—Oklahoma		9	19	.321	3§
1970-71—Oklahoma		19	8	.704	2§
1971-72—Oklahoma		14	12	.538	3§
1972-73—Oklahoma		18	8	.692	4§
Totals (6 seasons)		80	79	.503	

Assistant coach at Oklahoma, 1966-67. §Big Eight Conference.

NBA COACHING RECORD

Sea.	Club	Regular Season W.	L.	Pct.	Pos.	Playoffs W.	L.	Sea.	Club	Regular Season W.	L.	Pct.	Pos.	Playoffs W.	L.
1973-74—Phoenix		30	52	.366	4†	..	..	1980-81—Phoenix		57	25	.695	1†	3	4
1974-75—Phoenix		32	50	.390	4†	..	..	1981-82—Phoenix		46	36	.561	3†	2	5
1975-76—Phoenix		42	40	.512	3†	10	9	1982-83—Phoenix		53	29	.646	2†	1	2
1976-77—Phoenix		34	48	.415	5†	..	..	1983-84—Phoenix		41	41	.500	4†	9	8
1977-78—Phoenix		49	33	.598	2†	0	2	1984-85—Phoenix		36	46	.439	3†	0	3
1978-79—Phoenix		50	32	.610	2†	9	6	Totals (12 seasons)		525	459	.534		37	44
1979-80—Phoenix		55	27	.671	3†	3	5								

†Pacific Division.

Son-in-law of Pat McGroder, Executive Vice President of Buffalo Bills.

DOUGLAS EDWIN MOE
(Doug)
Denver Nuggets

Born September 21, 1938 at Brooklyn, N. Y.   Height 6:05.   Weight 220.

High School—Brooklyn, N. Y., Erasmus Hall.

Prep School—Silver Springs, Md., Bullis.

Colleges—University of North Carolina, Chapel Hill, N. C.

and Elon College, Elon College, N.C.

Signed by New Orleans ABA, 1967.

Traded by New Orleans with Larry Brown to Oakland for Steve Jones, Ron Franz and Barry Leibowitz, June 18, 1968.

Traded by Oakland to Carolina in three-team deal that sent Stew Johnson from Carolina to Pittsburgh and Frank Card from Pittsburgh to Oakland, June 12, 1969.

Traded by Carolina to Washington for Gary Bradds and Ira Harge, July 24, 1970.

Washington franchise transferred to Virginia, 1970.

Played with Padua, Italy, during 1965-66 and 1966-67 seasons.

—COLLEGIATE PLAYING RECORD—

Year	G.	Min.	FGA	FGM	Pct.	FTA	FTM	Pct.	Reb.	Pts.	Avg.
57-58†					Statistics Unavailable						
58-59	25	....	265	106	.400	164	104	.634	179	316	12.6
59-60	12	....	144	60	.417	113	82	.726	135	202	16.8
60-61	23	....	401	163	.406	207	143	.691	321	469	20.4
Varsity Totals	60	....	810	329	.406	484	329	.680	635	987	16.5

ABA REGULAR SEASON RECORD

Sea.—Team	G.	Min.	2-Point FGM	FGA	Pct.	3-Point FGM	FGA	Pct.	FTM	FTA	Pct.	Reb.	Ast.	Pts.	Avg.
67-68—New Orleans	78	3113	662	1588	.417	3	22	.136	551	693	.795	795	202	1884	24.2
68-69—Oakland	75	2528	524	1213	.432	5	14	.357	360	444	.811	614	151	1423	19.0
69-70—Carolina	80	2671	527	1220	.432	8	34	.235	304	399	.762	437	425	1382	17.2
70-71—Virginia	78	2297	395	861	.459	2	10	.200	221	259	.853	473	270	1017	13.0
71-72—Virginia	67	1472	174	406	.429	1	9	.111	104	129	.806	241	149	455	6.8
Totals	378	12081	2282	5288	.432	19	89	.213	1540	1924	.800	2560	1197	6161	16.3

ABA PLAYOFF RECORD

Sea.—Team	G.	Min.	FGM	FGA	Pct.	FGM	FGA	Pct.	FTM	FTA	Pct.	Reb.	Ast.	Pts.	Avg.
			2-Point			3-Point									
67-68—New Orleans	17	715	140	335	.418	4	11	.364	107	149	.718	169	40	399	23.5
68-69—Oakland	16	593	115	280	.411	0	4	.000	87	111	.784	124	31	317	19.8
69-70—Carolina	4	168	25	72	.347	0	4	.000	12	16	.750	26	25	62	15.5
70-71—Virginia	12	421	89	174	.511	1	3	.333	31	41	.756	57	37	212	17.7
71-72—Virginia	11	245	37	84	.440	0	1	.000	22	25	.880	43	27	96	8.7
Totals	60	2142	406	945	.430	5	23	.217	259	342	.757	419	160	1086	18.1

ABA ALL-STAR GAME RECORD

Sea.—Team	Min.	FGM	FGA	Pct.	FGM	FGA	Pct.	FTM	FTA	Pct.	Reb.	Ast.	Pts.	Avg.
		2-Point			3-Point									
1968—New Orleans	29	7	12	.583	0	1	.000	3	5	.600	7	5	17	17.0
1969—Oakland	26	6	13	.462	0	0	.000	5	8	.625	6	6	17	17.0
1970—Carolina	36	0	5	.000	0	0	.000	2	3	.667	8	6	2	2.0
Totals	91	13	30	.433	0	1	.000	10	16	.625	21	17	36	12.0

NBA COACHING RECORD

Sea. Club	Regular Season W.	L.	Pct.	Pos.	Playoffs W.	L.	Sea. Club	Regular Season W.	L.	Pct.	Pos.	Playoffs W.	L.
1976-77—San Antonio	44	38	.537	3†	0	2	1981-82—Denver	46	36	.561	2T‡	1	2
1977-78—San Antonio	52	30	.634	1†	2	4	1982-83—Denver	45	37	.549	2T‡	3	5
1978-79—San Antonio	48	34	.585	1†	7	7	1983-84—Denver	38	44	.463	3T‡	2	3
1979-80—San Antonio	33	33	.500	2T†	..	..	1984-85—Denver	52	30	.634	1‡	8	7
1980-81—Denver	26	25	.510	4‡	..	..	Totals (9 seasons)	384	307	.556		23	30

†Central Division. ‡Midwest Division.

Named to ABA All-Star First Team, 1968.... ABA All-Star Second Team, 1969.... Member of ABA championship team, 1969.... Named to THE SPORTING NEWS All-America Second Team, 1959 and 1961.

JOHN RICHARD MOTTA
(Dick)
Dallas Mavericks

Born September 3, 1931 at Medvale, Utah. Height 5:10. Weight 170.

High School—Jordan, Utah (did not play varsity basketball).

College—Utah State University, Logan, Utah (did not play basketball).

—COLLEGIATE COACHING RECORD—

Sea. Club	W.	L.	Pct.	Pos.	Sea. Club	W.	L.	Pct.	Pos.
1962-63—Weber State	22	4	.846	..	1966-67—Weber State	18	7	.720	3
1963-64—Weber State	17	8	.680	2	1967-68—Weber State	21	6	.778	1
1964-65—Weber State	22	3	.880	1	Totals (6 seasons)	120	33	.784	
1965-66—Weber State	20	5	.800	1T					

NBA COACHING RECORD

Sea. Club	Regular Season W.	L.	Pct.	Pos.	Playoffs W.	L.	Sea. Club	Regular Season W.	L.	Pct.	Pos.	Playoffs W.	L.
1968-69—Chicago	33	49	.402	5†	..	..	1977-78—Washington	44	38	.537	2§	14	7
1969-70—Chicago	39	43	.476	3T†	1	4	1978-79—Washington	54	28	.659	1x	9	10
1970-71—Chicago	51	31	.622	2‡	3	4	1979-80—Washington	39	43	.476	3†	0	2
1971-72—Chicago	57	25	.695	2‡	0	4	1980-81—Dallas	15	67	.183	6‡	..	..
1972-73—Chicago	51	31	.622	2‡	3	4	1981-82—Dallas	28	54	.341	5‡	..	..
1973-74—Chicago	54	28	.659	2‡	4	7	1982-83—Dallas	38	44	.463	4‡	..	..
1974-75—Chicago	47	35	.573	1‡	7	6	1983-84—Dallas	43	39	.524	2‡	4	6
1975-76—Chicago	24	58	.293	4‡	..	..	1984-85—Dallas	44	38	.537	3‡	1	3
1976-77—Washington	48	34	.585	2§	4	5	Totals (17 seasons)	709	685	.509		50	62

*Won NBA championship. †Western Division. ‡Midwest Division. §Central Division. xAtlantic Division.
NBA Coach of the Year, 1971.... Coach of NBA championship team, 1978.

DONALD ARVID NELSON
(Don)
Milwaukee Bucks

Born May 15, 1940 at Muskegon, Mich. Height 6:06. Weight 210.

High School—Rock Island, Ill.

College—University of Iowa, Iowa City, Iowa.

Drafted by Chicago on third round, 1962 (19th pick).

Sold by Chicago (Baltimore) to Los Angeles, September 6, 1963.

Waived by Los Angeles, October 21, 1965; signed by Boston as a free agent, October 28, 1965.

—COLLEGIATE PLAYING RECORD—

Year	G.	Min.	FGA	FGM	Pct.	FTA	FTM	Pct.	Reb.	Pts.	Avg.
58-59†					(Freshman team did not play intercollegiate schedule.)						
59-60	24	....	320	140	.438	155	100	.645	241	380	15.8
60-61	24	....	377	197	.523	268	176	.657	258	570	23.8
61-62	24	....	348	193	.555	264	186	.705	285	572	23.8
Varsity Totals	72	....	1045	530	.507	687	462	.672	784	1522	21.1

NBA REGULAR SEASON RECORD

Sea.—Team	G.	Min.	FGA	FGM	Pct.	FTA	FTM	Pct.	Reb.	Ast.	PF	Disq.	Pts.	Avg.
62-63—Chicago	62	1071	293	129	.440	221	161	.729	279	72	136	3	419	6.8
63-64—Los Angeles	80	1406	323	135	.418	201	149	.741	323	76	181	1	419	5.2
64-65—Los Angeles	39	238	85	36	.424	26	20	.769	73	24	40	1	92	2.4
65-66—Boston	75	1765	618	271	.439	326	223	.684	403	79	187	1	765	10.2
66-67—Boston	79	1202	509	227	.446	190	141	.742	295	65	143	0	595	7.5
67-68—Boston	82	1498	632	312	.494	268	195	.728	431	103	178	1	819	10.0
68-69—Boston	82	1773	771	374	.485	259	201	.776	458	92	198	2	949	11.6
69-70—Boston	82	2224	920	461	.501	435	337	.775	601	148	238	3	1259	15.4
70-71—Boston	82	2254	881	412	.468	426	317	.744	565	153	232	2	1141	13.9
71-72—Boston	82	2086	811	389	.480	452	356	.788	453	192	220	3	1134	13.8
72-73—Boston	72	1425	649	309	.476	188	159	.846	315	102	155	1	777	10.8

Sea.—Team	G.	Min.	FGA	FGM	Pct.	FTA	FTM	Pct.	Off.	Def.	Tot.	Ast.	PF	Dq.	Stl.	Blk.	Pts.	Avg.
										—Rebounds—								
73-74—Boston	82	1748	717	364	.508	273	215	.788	90	255	345	162	189	1	19	13	943	11.5
74-75—Boston	79	2052	785	423	.539	318	263	.827	127	342	469	181	239	2	32	15	1109	14.0
75-76—Boston	75	943	379	175	.462	161	127	.789	56	126	182	77	115	0	14	7	477	6.4
Totals	1053	21685	8373	4017	.480	3744	2864	.765			5192	1526	2451	21	65	35	10898	10.3

NBA PLAYOFF RECORD

Sea.—Team	G.	Min.	FGA	FGM	Pct.	FTA	FTM	Pct.	Reb.	Ast.	PF	Disq.	Pts.	Avg.
63-64—Los Angeles	5	56	13	7	.538	3	3	1.000	13	2	11	1	17	3.4
64-65—Los Angeles	11	212	53	24	.453	25	19	.760	59	19	31	0	67	6.1
65-66—Boston	17	316	118	50	.424	52	42	.808	85	13	50	0	142	8.4
66-67—Boston	9	142	59	27	.458	17	10	.588	42	9	12	0	64	7.1
67-68—Boston	19	468	175	91	.520	74	55	.743	143	32	49	0	237	12.5
68-69—Boston	18	348	168	87	.518	60	50	.833	83	21	51	0	224	12.4
71-72—Boston	11	308	99	52	.525	48	41	.854	61	21	30	0	145	13.2
72-73—Boston	13	303	101	47	.465	56	49	.875	38	15	29	0	143	11.0

Sea.—Team	G.	Min.	FGA	FGM	Pct.	FTA	FTM	Pct.	Off.	Def.	Tot.	Ast.	PF	Dq.	Stl.	Blk.	Pts.	Avg.
										—Rebounds—								
73-74—Boston	18	467	164	82	.500	53	41	.774	25	72	97	35	54	2	8	3	205	11.4
74-75—Boston	11	274	117	66	.564	41	37	.902	18	27	45	26	36	1	2	2	169	15.4
75-76—Boston	18	315	108	52	.481	69	60	.870	17	36	53	17	46	1	3	2	164	9.1
Totals	150	3209	1175	585	.498	498	407	.817			719	210	399	5	13	7	1577	10.5

NBA COACHING RECORD

Sea. Club	Regular Season W.	L.	Pct.	Pos.	Playoffs W.	L.	Sea. Club	Regular Season W.	L.	Pct.	Pos.	Playoffs W.	L.
1976-77—Milwaukee	27	37	.422	6†	...	...	1981-82—Milwaukee	55	27	.671	1‡	2	4
1977-78—Milwaukee	44	38	.537	2†	5	4	1982-83—Milwaukee	51	31	.622	1‡	5	4
1978-79—Milwaukee	38	44	.463	4†	...	...	1983-84—Milwaukee	50	32	.610	1‡	8	8
1979-80—Milwaukee	49	33	.598	1†	3	4	1984-85—Milwaukee	59	23	.720	1‡	3	5
1980-81—Milwaukee	60	22	.732	1‡	3	4	Totals (9 seasons)	433	287	.601		29	33

†Midwest Division. ‡Central Division.

Led NBA in field-goal percentage, 1975. . . . Member of NBA championship teams, 1966, 1968, 1969, 1974, 1976. . . . NBA Coach of the Year, 1983 and 1985.

JOHN T. RAMSAY
(Jack)
Portland Trail Blazers

Born February 21, 1925 at Philadelphia, Pa. Height 6:01. Weight 180.
High School—Upper Darby, Pa.
Colleges—St. Joseph's University, Philadelphia, Pa.,
and Villanova University, Villanova, Pa.

Played with San Diego Dons, an Amateur Athletic Union Team, during 1945-46 season.
Played in Eastern Basketball League with Harrisburg and Sunbury, 1949 through 1955.

—COLLEGIATE PLAYING RECORD—
St. Joseph's

Year	G.	Min.	FGA	FGM	Pct.	FTA	FTM	Pct.	Reb.	Pts.	Avg.
42-43					Statistics Unavailable						
46-47	21	....	214	72	.336	32	20	.625	....	164	7.8

Year	G.	Min.	FGA	FGM	Pct.	FTA	FTM	Pct.	Reb.	Pts.	Avg.
47-48	14	....	....	60	....	...	38	....	....	158	11.3
48-49	23	....	...	75	....	...	52	....	....	202	8.8

NOTE: In military service (Navy) during 1943-44, 1944-45 and 1945-46 seasons.

COLLEGIATE COACHING RECORD

Sea. Club	W.	L.	Pct.	Pos.	Sea. Club	W.	L.	Pct.	Pos.
1955-56—St. Joseph's	23	6	.793	..	1961-62—St. Joseph's	18	10	.643	1
1956-57—St. Joseph's	17	7	.708	..	1962-63—St. Joseph's	23	5	.821	2
1957-58—St. Joseph's	18	9	.667	..	1963-64—St. Joseph's	18	10	.643	2
1958-59—St. Joseph's	22	5	.815	..	1964-65—St. Joseph's	26	3	.897	1
1959-60—St. Joseph's	20	7	.741	1	1965-66—St. Joseph's	24	5	.828	1
1960-61—St. Joseph's	25	5	.833	1	Totals (11 seasons)	234	72	.765	

NBA COACHING RECORD

	Regular Season				Playoffs			Regular Season				Playoffs	
Sea. Club	W.	L.	Pct.	Pos.	W.	L.	Sea. Club	W.	L.	Pct.	Pos.	W.	L.
1968-69—Philadelphia	55	27	.671	2†	1	4	1977-78—Portland..............	58	24	.707	1§	2	4
1969-70—Philadelphia	42	40	.512	4†	1	4	1978-79—Portland..............	45	37	.549	4§	1	2
1970-71—Philadelphia	47	35	.573	2‡	3	4	1979-80—Portland..............	38	44	.463	4§	1	2
1971-72—Philadelphia	30	52	.366	3‡	..	..	1980-81—Portland..............	45	37	.549	3§	1	2
1972-73—Buffalo................	21	61	.256	3‡	..	..	1981-82—Portland..............	42	40	.512	5§	..	..
1973-74—Buffalo................	42	40	.512	3‡	2	4	1982-83—Portland..............	46	36	.561	4§	3	4
1974-75—Buffalo................	49	33	.598	3‡	3	4	1983-84—Portland..............	48	34	.585	2§	2	3
1975-76—Buffalo................	46	36	.561	2T‡	4	5	1984-85—Portland..............	42	40	.512	2§	4	5
1976-77—Portland*............	49	33	.598	2§	14	5	Totals (17 seasons)	745	649	.534		42	52

*Won NBA championship. †Eastern Division. ‡Atlantic Division. §Pacific Division.

Coach of NBA championship team, 1977.

PATRICK JAMES RILEY
(Pat)
Los Angeles Lakers

Born March 20, 1945 at Rome, N. Y. Height 6:04. Weight 205.

High School—Schenectady, N. Y., Linton.

College—University of Kentucky, Lexington, Ky.

Drafted by San Diego on first round, 1967 (7th pick).

Selected from San Diego by Portland in expansion draft, May 11, 1970.
Sold by Portland to Los Angeles, October 9, 1970.
Traded by Los Angeles to Phoenix for draft rights to John Roche and a 1976 2nd round draft choice, November 3, 1975.

—COLLEGIATE RECORD—

Year	G.	Min.	FGA	FGM	Pct.	FTA	FTM	Pct.	Reb.	Pts.	Avg.
63-64†	16	....	259	120	.463	146	93	.637	235	333	20.8
64-65	25	825	370	160	.432	89	55	.618	212	375	15.0
65-66	29	1078	514	265	.516	153	107	.699	259	637	22.0
66-67	26	953	373	165	.442	156	122	.782	201	452	17.4
Varsity Totals	80	2856	1257	590	.469	398	284	.714	672	1464	18.3

NBA REGULAR SEASON RECORD

Sea.—Team	G.	Min.	FGA	FGM	Pct.	FTA	FTM	Pct.	Reb.	Ast.	PF	Disq.	Pts.	Avg.
67-68—San Diego	80	1263	660	250	.379	202	128	.634	177	138	205	1	628	7.9
68-69—San Diego	56	1027	498	202	.406	134	90	.672	112	136	146	1	494	8.8
69-70—San Diego	36	474	180	75	.417	55	40	.727	57	85	68	0	190	5.3
70-71—Los Angeles	54	506	254	105	.413	87	56	.644	54	72	84	0	266	4.9
71-72—Los Angeles	67	926	441	197	.447	74	55	.743	127	75	110	0	449	6.7
72-73—Los Angeles	55	801	390	167	.428	82	65	.793	65	81	126	0	399	7.3

| | | | | | | | —Rebounds— | | | | | | | | |
Sea.—Team	G.	Min.	FGA	FGM	Pct.	FTA	FTM	Pct.	Off.	Def.	Tot.	Ast.	PF	Dq.	Stl.	Blk.	Pts.	Avg.
73-74—Los Ang.	72	1361	667	287	.430	144	110	.764	38	90	128	148	173	1	54	3	684	9.5
74-75—Los Ang.	46	1016	523	219	.419	93	69	.742	25	60	85	121	128	0	36	4	507	11.0
75-76—LA-Phoe.	62	813	301	117	.389	77	55	.714	16	34	50	57	112	0	22	6	289	4.7
Totals	528	8187	3914	1619	.414	948	668	.705			855	913	1152	3	112	13	3906	7.4

NBA PLAYOFF RECORD

Sea.—Team	G.	Min.	FGA	FGM	Pct.	FTA	FTM	Pct.	Reb.	Ast.	PF	Disq.	Pts.	Avg.
68-69—San Diego	5	76	37	16	.432	6	5	.833	11	2	13	0	37	7.4
70-71—Los Angeles	7	135	69	29	.420	11	8	.727	15	14	12	0	66	9.4
71-72—Los Angeles	15	244	99	33	.333	16	12	.750	29	14	37	0	78	5.2
72-73—Los Angeles	7	53	27	9	.333	0	0	.000	5	7	10	0	18	2.6

Sea.—Team	G.	Min.	FGA	FGM	Pct.	FTA	FTM	Pct.	Off.	Def.	Tot.	Ast.	PF	Dq.	Stl.	Blk.	Pts.	Avg.
									—Rebounds—									
73-74—Los Ang.	5	106	50	18	.360	4	3	.750	3	3	6	10	11	0	4	0	39	7.8
75-76—Phoe.	5	27	15	6	.400	1	1	1.000	0	0	0	5	3	0	0	0	13	2.6
Totals	44	641	297	111	.374	38	29	.763				66	52	86	0	4	0	251	5.7

NBA COACHING RECORD

		Regular Season				Playoffs	
Sea.	Club	W.	L.	Pct.	Pos.	W.	L.
1981-82—Los Angeles*		50	21	.704	1†	12	2
1982-83—Los Angeles		58	24	.707	1†	8	7
1983-84—Los Angeles		54	28	.659	1†	14	7
1984-85—L.A. Lakers*		62	20	.756	1†	15	4
Totals (4 seasons)		224	93	.707		49	20

*Won NBA championship. †Pacific Division.

Member of NBA championship team, 1972. . . . Coach of NBA championship teams, 1982 and 1985. . . . Son of former major league catcher and minor league manager Leon Riley. . . . Brother of former National Football League defensive back Lee Riley. . . . Drafted by Dallas Cowboys in 11th round of 1967 NFL draft.

EUGENE WILLIAM SHUE
(Gene)
Washington Bullets

Born December 18, 1931 at Baltimore, Md.   Height 6:02.   Weight 175.

High School—Towson, Md., Catholic.

College—University of Maryland, College Park, Md.

Drafted by Philadelphia on first round, 1954 (3rd pick).

Sold by Philadelphia to New York, November 29, 1954.
Traded by New York to Fort Wayne for rights to Ron Sobieszczyk, April 30, 1956.
Fort Wayne franchise transferred to Detroit, 1957.
Traded by Detroit to New York for Darrell Imhoff and cash, August 29, 1962.
Traded with Paul Hogue by New York to Baltimore for Bill McGill, October 30, 1963.

—COLLEGIATE PLAYING RECORD—

Year	G.	Min.	FGA	FGM	Pct.	FTA	FTM	Pct.	Reb.	Pts.	Avg.
50-51†	14	....	....	....	....	....	....	....	....	181	12.9
51-52	22	....	243	91	.374	75	53	.707	....	235	10.7
52-53	23	....	375	176	.469	223	156	.700	....	508	22.1
53-54	30	....	469	237	.505	228	180	.789	....	654	21.8
Varsity Totals	75	....	1087	504	.464	526	389	.740	....	1397	18.6

NBA REGULAR SEASON RECORD

Sea.—Team	G.	Min.	FGA	FGM	Pct.	FTA	FTM	Pct.	Reb.	Ast.	PF	Disq.	Pts.	Avg.
54-55—Phila.-N. Y.	62	947	289	100	.346	78	59	.756	154	89	64	0	259	4.2
55-56—New York	72	1750	625	240	.384	237	181	.764	212	179	111	0	661	9.2
56-57—Fort Wayne	72	2470	710	273	.385	316	241	.763	421	238	137	0	787	10.9
57-58—Detroit	63	2333	919	353	.384	327	276	.844	333	172	150	1	982	15.6
58-59—Detroit	72	2745	1197	464	.388	421	338	.803	335	231	129	1	1266	17.6
59-60—Detroit	75	3338	1501	620	.413	541	472	.872	409	295	146	2	1712	22.8
60-61—Detroit	78	3361	1545	650	.421	543	465	.856	334	530	207	1	1765	22.6
61-62—Detroit	80	3143	1422	580	.408	447	362	.810	372	465	192	1	1522	19.0
62-63—New York	78	2288	894	354	.396	302	208	.689	191	259	171	0	916	11.7
63-64—Baltimore	47	963	276	81	.293	61	36	.590	94	150	98	2	198	4.2
Totals	699	23338	9378	3715	.396	3273	2638	.806	2855	2608	1405	8	10068	14.4

NBA PLAYOFF RECORD

Sea.—Team	G.	Min.	FGA	FGM	Pct.	FTA	FTM	Pct.	Reb.	Ast.	PF	Disq.	Pts.	Avg.
54-55—New York	3	49	17	8	.471	7	6	.857	12	4	5	0	22	7.3
56-57—Fort Wayne	2	79	27	14	.519	4	4	1.000	7	8	3	0	32	16.0
57-58—Detroit	7	281	123	45	.366	43	40	.930	46	33	15	0	130	18.6
58-59—Detroit	3	118	60	28	.467	33	27	.818	14	10	7	0	83	27.7
59-60—Detroit	2	89	38	15	.395	20	18	.900	12	6	5	0	48	24.0
60-61—Detroit	5	186	72	35	.486	29	23	.793	12	22	11	0	93	18.6
61-62—Detroit	10	369	151	62	.410	48	37	.771	30	49	29	0	161	16.1
Totals	32	1171	488	207	.424	184	155	.842	133	132	75	0	569	17.8

NBA ALL-STAR GAME RECORD

Season—Team	Min.	FGA	FGM	Pct.	FTA	FTM	Pct.	Reb.	Ast.	PF	Disq.	Pts.
1958—Detroit........................	25	11	8	.727	3	2	.667	2	0	3	0	18
1959—Detroit........................	31	12	6	.500	2	1	.500	4	3	4	0	13
1960—Detroit........................	34	13	6	.462	2	1	.500	6	6	0	0	13
1961—Detroit........................	23	10	6	.600	4	3	.750	3	6	1	0	15
1962—Detroit........................	17	6	3	.500	1	1	1.000	5	4	3	0	7
Totals	130	52	29	.558	12	8	.667	20	19	11	0	66

PAT RILEY

NBA COACHING RECORD

Sea.	Club	Regular Season				Playoffs	
		W.	L.	Pct.	Pos.	W.	L.
1966-67	Baltimore	16	40	.286	5†	...	...
1967-68	Baltimore	36	46	.439	6†	...	...
1968-69	Baltimore	57	25	.695	1†	0	4
1969-70	Baltimore	50	32	.610	3†	3	4
1970-71	Baltimore	42	40	.512	1‡	8	10
1971-72	Baltimore	38	44	.463	1‡	2	4
1972-73	Baltimore	52	30	.634	1‡	1	4
1973-74	Philadelphia	25	57	.305	4§	...	...
1974-75	Philadelphia	34	48	.415	4§	...	...
1975-76	Philadelphia	46	36	.561	2T§	1	2
1976-77	Philadelphia	50	32	.610	1§	10	9
1977-78	Philadelphia	2	4	.333	...§	...	...
1978-79	San Diego	43	39	.524	5x	...	...
1979-80	San Diego	35	47	.427	5x	...	...
1980-81	Washington	39	43	.476	4§	...	...
1981-82	Washington	43	39	.524	4§	3	4
1982-83	Washington	42	40	.512	5§	..	..
1983-84	Washington	35	47	.427	5§	1	3
1984-85	Washington	40	42	.488	4§	1	3
Totals (19 seasons)		725	731	.498		30	47

†Eastern Division.   ‡Central Division.   §Atlantic Division.   xPacific Division.

Named to All-NBA First Team, 1960. . . . All-NBA Second Team, 1961. . . . NBA Coach of the Year, 1969 and 1982.

ALL-TIME GREATS

Included are coaches and non-active players who reached one or more of the following plateaus: 17,000 points; 10,000 rebounds; 5,000 assists and 10,000 points; named to either the 25th or 35th NBA Anniversary All-Time Teams; NBA Most Valuable Player; four-time First or Second Team NBA All-Star; six NBA All-Star Games; career scoring average of 23 points per game; 420 regular-season coaching victories in NBA with winning percentage of .520.

PLAYERS

NATHANIEL ARCHIBALD
(Tiny or Nate)

Born September 2, 1948 at New York, N. Y.   Height 6:01.   Weight 160.

High School—Bronx, N. Y., DeWitt Clinton.

Colleges—Arizona Western College, Yuma, Ariz., and
University of Texas-El Paso, El Paso, Tex.

Drafted by Cincinnati on second round, 1970 (19th pick).

Traded by Kansas City to New York Nets for Brian Taylor, Jim Eakins and two 1st round draft choices (1977 and 1978), September 10, 1976.

Traded by New Jersey to Buffalo for George Johnson and a 1979 1st round draft choice, September 1, 1977.

Traded by San Diego with Marvin Barnes, Billy Knight and two 2nd round draft choices (1981 and 1983) to Boston for Kermit Washington, Kevin Kunnert, Sidney Wicks and the draft rights to Freeman Williams, August 4, 1978.

Waived by Boston, July 22, 1983; signed by Milwaukee as a free agent, August 1, 1983.

—COLLEGIATE RECORD—
Arizona Western

Year	G.	Min.	FGA	FGM	Pct.	FTA	FTM	Pct.	Reb.	Pts.	Avg.
66-67	27	....	....	303	....	....	190	....	....	796	29.5

Texas-El Paso

Year	G.	Min.	FGA	FGM	Pct.	FTA	FTM	Pct.	Reb.	Pts.	Avg.
67-68	23	....	281	131	.466	140	102	.729	81	364	15.8
68-69	25	....	374	199	.532	194	161	.830	69	559	22.4
69-70	25	....	351	180	.512	225	176	.782	66	536	21.4
Totals	73	....	1006	510	.507	559	439	.785	216	1459	20.0

NBA REGULAR SEASON RECORD

Sea.—Team	G.	Min.	FGA	FGM	Pct.	FTA	FTM	Pct.	Reb.	Ast.	PF	Disq.	Pts.	Avg.
70-71—Cincinnati	82	2867	1095	486	.444	444	336	.757	242	450	218	2	1308	16.0
71-72—Cincinnati	76	3272	1511	734	.486	824	677	.822	222	701	198	3	2145	28.2
72-73—K.C.-Omaha	80	3681	2106	1028	.488	783	663	.847	223	910	207	2	2719	34.0

									—Rebounds—								
Sea.—Team	G.	Min.	FGA	FGM	Pct.	FTA	FTM	Pct.	Off.	Def.	Tot.	Ast.	PF	Dq.	Stl.	Blk.	Pts.	Avg.
73-74—KC-Omaha	35	1272	492	222	.451	211	173	.820	21	64	85	266	76	0	56	7	617	17.6
74-75—KC-Omaha	82	3244	1664	759	.456	748	652	.872	48	174	222	557	187	0	119	7	2170	26.5
75-76—Kan. City	78	3184	1583	717	.453	625	501	.802	67	146	213	615	169	0	126	15	1935	24.8
76-77—NY Nets	34	1277	560	250	.446	251	197	.785	22	58	80	254	77	1	59	11	697	20.5
77-78—Buffalo					Injured—Torn Achilles Tendon													
78-79—Boston	69	1662	573	259	.452	307	242	.788	25	78	103	324	132	2	55	6	760	11.0
79-80—Boston	80	2864	794	383	.482	435	361	.830	59	138	197	671	218	2	106	10	1131	14.1
80-81—Boston	80	2820	766	382	.499	419	342	.816	36	140	176	618	201	1	75	18	1106	13.8
81-82—Boston	68	2167	652	308	.472	316	236	.747	25	91	116	541	131	1	52	3	858	12.6
82-83—Boston	66	1811	553	235	.425	296	220	.743	25	66	91	409	110	1	38	4	695	10.5
83-84—Milwaukee	46	1038	279	136	.487	101	64	.634	16	60	76	160	78	0	33	0	340	7.4
Totals	876	31159	12628	5899	.467	5760	4664	.810			2046	6476	2002	15	719	81	16481	18.8

Three-Point Field Goals: 1979-80, 4-for-18 (.222). 1980-81, 0-for-9. 1981-82, 6-for-16 (.375). 1982-83, 5-for-24 (.208). 1983-84, 4-for-18 (.222). Totals, 19-for-85 (.224).

NBA PLAYOFF RECORD

									—Rebounds—								
Sea.—Team	G.	Min.	FGA	FGM	Pct.	FTA	FTM	Pct.	Off.	Def.	Tot.	Ast.	PF	Dq.	Stl.	Blk.	Pts.	Avg.
74-75—KC-Omaha	6	242	118	43	.364	43	35	.814	2	9	11	32	18	0	4	0	121	20.2
79-80—Boston	9	332	89	45	.506	42	37	.881	3	8	11	71	28	1	10	0	128	14.2
80-81—Boston	17	630	211	95	.450	94	76	.809	6	22	28	107	39	0	13	0	266	15.6
81-82—Boston	8	277	70	30	.429	28	25	.893	1	16	17	52	21	0	5	2	85	10.6
82-83—Boston	7	161	68	22	.324	29	22	.759	3	7	10	44	12	0	2	0	67	9.6
Totals	47	1642	556	235	.423	236	195	.826	15	62	77	306	118	1	34	2	667	14.2

Three-Point Field Goals: 1979-80, 1-for-2 (.500). 1980-81, 0-for-5. 1981-82, 0-for-4. 1982-83, 1-for-6. (.167). Totals, 2-for-17 (.118).

NBA ALL-STAR GAME RECORD

Season—Team	Min.	FGA	FGM	Pct.	FTA	FTM	Pct.	Off.	Def.	Tot.	Ast.	PF	Dq.	Stl.	Blk.	Pts.
								—Rebounds—								
1973—K.C.-Omaha ..	27	12	6	.500	5	5	1.000			1	5	1	0			17
1975—K.C.-Omaha ..	36	15	10	.667	8	7	.875	1	1	2	6	2	0	3	1	27
1976—Kansas City ..	30	13	5	.385	3	3	1.000	2	3	5	7	0	0	2	0	13
1980—Boston............	21	8	0	.000	3	2	.667	1	2	3	6	1	0	2	0	2
1981—Boston............	25	7	4	.571	3	1	.333	0	5	5	9	3	0	3	0	9
1982—Boston............	23	5	2	.400	2	2	1.000	1	1	2	7	3	0	1	0	6
Totals	162	60	27	.450	24	20	.833	5	13	18	40	10	0	11	1	74

Named to All-NBA First Team, 1973, 1975, 1976. . . . All-NBA Second Team, 1972 and 1981. . . . Member of NBA championship team, 1981. . . . Led NBA in scoring, 1973. . . . Led NBA in assists, 1973. . . . NBA All-Star Game MVP, 1981.

PAUL JOSEPH ARIZIN

Born April 9, 1928 at Philadelphia, Pa.   Height 6:04.   Weight 200.

High School—Philadelphia, Pa., La Salle (Did not play varsity basketball).

College—Villanova University, Villanova, Pa.

Drafted by Philadelphia on first round, 1950.

Played in Eastern Basketball League with Camden Bullets, 1962-63 through 1964-65.

—COLLEGIATE RECORD—

Year	G.	Min.	FGA	FGM	Pct.	FTA	FTM	Pct.	Reb.	Pts.	Avg.
46-47						Did Not Play					
47-48	24	....	...	101	....	...	65	....	...	267	11.1
48-49	27	....	...	210	....	233	174	.747	...	594	22.0
49-50	29	....	527	260	.493	277	215	.776	...	735	25.3
Totals	80	....		571	....		454	....	...	1596	20.0

NBA REGULAR SEASON RECORD

Sea.—Team	G.	Min.	FGA	FGM	Pct.	FTA	FTM	Pct.	Reb.	Ast.	PF	Disq.	Pts.	Avg.
50-51—Philadelphia	65	....	864	352	.407	526	417	.793	640	138	284	18	1121	17.2
51-51—Philadelphia	66	2939	1222	548	.448	707	578	.818	745	170	250	5	1674	25.4
52-53—Philadelphia						Did Not Play—Military Service								
53-54—Philadelphia						Did Not Play—Military Service								
54-55—Philadelphia	72	2953	1325	529	.399	585	454	.776	675	210	270	5	1512	21.0
55-56—Philadelphia	72	2724	1378	617	.448	626	507	.810	539	189	282	11	1741	24.2
56-57—Philadelphia	71	2767	1451	613	.422	713	591	.829	561	150	274	13	1817	25.6
57-58—Philadelphia	68	2377	1229	483	.393	544	440	.809	503	135	235	7	1406	20.7
58-59—Philadelphia	70	2799	1466	632	.431	722	587	.813	637	119	264	7	1851	26.4
59-60—Philadelphia	72	2618	1400	593	.423	526	420	.798	621	165	263	6	1606	22.3
60-61—Philadelphia	79	2905	1529	650	.425	639	532	.832	681	188	335	11	1832	23.2
61-62—Philadelphia	78	2785	1490	611	.410	601	484	.805	527	201	307	18	1706	21.9
Totals	713	....	13354	5628	.421	6189	5010	.810	6129	1665	2764	101	16266	22.8

NBA PLAYOFF RECORD

Sea.—Team	G.	Min.	FGA	FGM	Pct.	FTA	FTM	Pct.	Reb.	Ast.	PF	Disq.	Pts.	Avg.
50-51—Philadelphia	2	....	27	14	.519	16	13	.813	20	3	10	1	41	20.5
51-52—Philadelphia	3	120	53	24	.453	33	29	.879	38	8	17	2	77	25.7
55-56—Philadelphia	10	409	229	103	.450	99	83	.838	84	29	31	1	289	28.9
56-57—Philadelphia	2	22	8	3	.375	5	3	.600	8	1	3	0	9	4.5
57-58—Philadelphia	8	309	169	66	.391	72	56	.778	62	16	26	1	188	23.5
59-60—Philadelphia	9	371	195	84	.431	79	69	.873	86	33	29	0	237	26.3
60-61—Philadelphia	3	125	67	22	.328	33	23	.697	26	12	17	2	67	22.3
61-62—Philadelphia	12	459	253	95	.375	102	88	.863	80	26	44	1	278	23.2
Totals	49	....	1001	411	.411	439	364	.829	404	128	177	8	1186	24.2

NBA ALL-STAR GAME RECORD

Season—Team	Min.	FGA	FGM	Pct.	FTA	FTM	Pct.	Reb.	Ast.	PF	Disq.	Pts.
1951—Philadelphia	..	12	7	.583	2	1	.500	7	0	2	0	15
1952—Philadelphia	32	13	9	.692	8	8	1.000	6	0	1	0	26
1955—Philadelphia	23	9	4	.444	2	1	.500	2	2	5	0	9
1956—Philadelphia	28	13	5	.385	5	3	.600	7	1	6	1	13
1957—Philadelphia	26	13	6	.462	2	1	.500	5	0	2	0	13
1958—Philadelphia	29	17	11	.647	2	2	1.000	8	2	3	0	24
1959—Philadelphia	30	15	4	.267	9	8	.889	8	0	2	0	16
1960—Philadelphia					Selected—Injured, Did Not Play							
1961—Philadelphia	17	12	6	.500	5	5	1.000	2	1	4	0	17
1962—Philadelphia	21	12	2	.167	0	0	.000	2	0	4	0	4
Totals (9 games)	...	116	54	.466	35	29	.829	47	6	29	1	137

MINOR LEAGUE REGULAR SEASON RECORD

Sea.—Team	G.	Min.	2-Point FGM	FGA	Pct.	3-Point FGM	FGA	Pct.	FTM	FTA	Pct.	Reb.	Ast.	Pts.	Avg.
62-63—Camden	28	....	264	...	...	...	...	...	196	249	.787	203	42	724	27.4
63-64—Camden	27	....	261	...	...	...	...	...	174	218	.798	226	52	696	25.8
64-65—Camden	28	....	226	...	...	3	...	...	196	244	.803	164	50	657	23.5

Named to NBA 25th Anniversary All-Time Team, 1970. . . . Elected to Naismith Memorial Basketball Hall of Fame, 1977. . . . Named to NBA All-Star First Team, 1952, 1956, 1957. . . . NBA All-Star Second Team, 1959. . . . NBA All-Star Game MVP, 1952. . . . Member of NBA championship team, 1956. . . . Led NBA in field-goal percentage, 1952. . . . Led NBA in scoring, 1952 and 1957. . . . Eastern Basketball League MVP, 1963. . . . Named to EBL All-Star First Team, 1963, 1964. . . . EBL All-Star Second Team, 1965. . . . Led NCAA Division I in scoring, 1950. . . . THE SPORTING NEWS College Player of the Year, 1950. . . . Named to THE SPORTING NEWS All-America First Team, 1950.

RICHARD BARRY
(Rick)

Born March 28, 1944 at Elizabeth, N. J.   Height 6:07.   Weight 220.

High School—Roselle Park, N. J.

College—University of Miami, Coral Gables, Fla.

Drafted by San Francisco on first round, 1965.

Signed as free agent by Oakland ABA for 1968-69 season (sat out option season with San Francisco NBA, 1967-68). Oakland franchise transferred to Washington, 1969.
Washington franchise transferred to Virginia, 1970.
Traded by Virginia to New York for cash and a 1st round draft choice, August, 1970.
Returned to NBA with Golden State, 1972.
Completed contract with Golden State; signed by Houston as Veteran Free Agent, June 17, 1978. Golden State received John Lucas and cash as compensation.

—COLLEGIATE RECORD—

Year	G.	Min.	FGA	FGM	Pct.	FTA	FTM	Pct.	Reb.	Pts.	Avg.
61-62†	17	....		208			73			489	28.8
62-63	24	....	341	162	.475	158	131	.829	351	455	19.0
63-64	27	....	572	314	.549	287	242	.843	448	870	32.2
64-65	26	....	651	340	.522	341	293	.859	475	973	37.4
Varsity Totals	77	....	1564	816	.522	786	666	.847	1274	2298	29.8

ABA REGULAR SEASON RECORD

Sea.—Team	G.	Min.	2-Point FGM	FGA	Pct.	3-Point FGM	FGA	Pct.	FTM	FTA	Pct.	Reb.	Ast.	Pts.	Avg.
67-68					Did Not Play—Sat Out Option Year										
68-69—Oakland	35	1361	389	757	.514	3	10	.300	403	454	.888	329	136	1190	34.0
69-70—Washington	52	1849	509	907	.511	8	39	.205	400	463	.864	363	178	1442	27.7
70-71—New York	59	2502	613	1262	.486	19	86	.221	451	507	.890	401	294	1734	29.4
71-72—New York	80	3616	829	1732	.479	73	237	.308	641	730	.878	602	327	2518	31.5
Totals	226	9328	2340	4748	.493	103	374	.275	1895	2154	.880	1695	935	6884	30.5

ABA PLAYOFF RECORD

Sea.—Team	G.	Min.	2-Point FGM	FGA	Pct.	3-Point FGM	FGA	Pct.	FTM	FTA	Pct.	Reb.	Ast.	Pts.	Avg.
69-70—Washington	7	302	105	194	.541	3	9	.333	62	68	.912	70	23	281	40.1
70-71—New York	6	287	46	108	.426	14	27	.519	48	59	.814	66	17	202	33.7
71-72—New York	18	749	180	368	.489	23	66	.348	125	146	.856	117	69	554	30.7
Totals	31	1338	331	670	.494	40	102	.392	235	273	.861	253	109	1037	33.5

ABA ALL-STAR GAME RECORD

Sea.—Team	Min.	2-Point FGM	FGA	Pct.	3-Point FGM	FGA	Pct.	FTM	FTA	Pct.	Reb.	Ast.	Pts.	Avg.
68-69—Oakland	12	3	9	.333	0	0	.000	4	5	.800	3	1	10	10.0
69-70—Washington	27	7	12	.583	0	0	.000	2	2	1.000	7	7	16	16.0
70-71—New York	17	4	6	.667	0	0	.000	6	6	1.000	2	2	14	14.0
71-72—New York	26	2	10	.200	0	0	.000	0	1	.000	12	8	4	4.0
Totals	82	16	37	.432	0	0	.000	12	14	.857	24	18	44	11.0

NBA REGULAR SEASON RECORD

Sea.—Team	G.	Min.	FGA	FGM	Pct.	FTA	FTM	Pct.	Reb.	Ast.	PF	Disq.	Pts.	Avg.
65-66—San Fran.	80	2990	1698	745	.439	660	569	.862	850	173	297	2	2059	25.7
66-67—San Fran.	78	3175	2240	1011	.451	852	753	.884	714	282	258	1	2775	35.6
72-73—Golden St.	82	3075	1630	737	.452	397	358	.902	728	399	245	2	1832	22.3

Sea.—Team	G.	Min.	FGA	FGM	Pct.	FTA	FTM	Pct.	Rebounds Off.	Def.	Tot.	Ast.	PF	Dq.	Stl.	Blk.	Pts.	Avg.
73-74—Golden St.	80	2918	1746	796	.456	464	417	.899	103	437	540	484	265	4	169	40	2009	25.1
74-75—Golden St.	80	3235	2217	1028	.464	436	394	.904	92	364	456	492	225	0	228	33	2450	30.6
75-76—Golden St.	81	3122	1624	707	.435	311	287	.923	74	422	496	496	215	1	202	27	1701	21.0
76-77—Golden St.	79	2904	1551	682	.440	392	359	.916	73	349	422	475	194	2	172	58	1723	21.8

RICK BARRY

Sea.—Team	G.	Min.	FGA	FGM	Pct.	FTA	FTM	Pct.	Off.	Def.	Tot.	Ast.	PF	Dq.	Stl.	Blk.	Pts.	Avg.
										—Rebounds—								
77-78—Golden St.	82	3024	1686	760	.451	409	378	.924	75	374	449	446	188	1	158	45	1898	23.1
78-79—Houston	80	2566	1000	461	.461	169	160	.947	40	237	277	502	195	0	95	38	1082	13.5
79-80—Houston	72	1816	771	325	.422	153	143	.935	53	183	236	268	182	0	80	28	866	12.0
Totals	794	28825	16163	7252	.449	4243	3818	.900			5168	4017	2264	13	1104	269	18395	23.2

Three-Point Field Goals: 1979-70, 73-for-221 (.330).

NBA PLAYOFF RECORD

Sea.—Team	G.	Min.	FGA	FGM	Pct.	FTA	FTM	Pct.	Reb.	Ast.	PF	Disq.	Pts.	Avg.
66-67—San Fran.	15	614	489	197	.403	157	127	.809	113	58	49	0	521	34.7
72-73—Golden St.	11	292	164	65	.396	55	50	.909	54	24	41	1	180	16.4

Sea.—Team	G.	Min.	FGA	FGM	Pct.	FTA	FTM	Pct.	Off.	Def.	Tot.	Ast.	PF	Dq.	Stl.	Blk.	Pts.	Avg.
										—Rebounds—								
74-75—Golden St.	17	726	426	189	.444	110	101	.918	22	72	94	103	51	1	50	15	479	28.2
75-76—Golden St.	13	532	289	126	.436	68	60	.882	20	64	84	84	40	1	38	14	312	24.0
76-77—Golden St.	10	415	262	122	.466	44	40	.909	25	34	59	47	32	0	17	7	284	28.4
78-79—Houston	2	65	25	8	.320	8	8	1.000	2	6	8	9	8	0	0	2	24	12.0
79-80—Houston	6	79	33	12	.364	6	6	1.000	0	6	6	15	11	0	1	1	33	5.5
Totals	74	2723	1688	719	.426	448	392	.875			418	340	232	3	106	39	1833	24.8

Three-Point Field Goals: 1979-80, 3-for-12 (.250).

NBA ALL-STAR GAME RECORD

Season—Team	Min.	FGA	FGM	Pct.	FTA	FTM	Pct.	Reb.	Ast.	PF	Disq.	Pts.
1966—San Francisco	17	10	4	.400	4	2	.500	2	2	6	1	10
1967—San Francisco	34	27	16	.593	8	6	.750	6	3	5	0	38
1973—Golden State					Selected—Injured, Did Not Play							

Season—Team	Min.	FGA	FGM	Pct.	FTA	FTM	Pct.	Off.	Def.	Tot.	Ast.	PF	Dq.	Stl.	Blk.	Pts.
									—Rebounds—							
1974—Golden St......	19	6	3	.500	2	2	1.000	1	3	4	3	3	0	1	0	8
1975—Golden St......	38	20	11	.550	0	0	.000	1	4	5	8	4	0	8	1	22
1976—Golden St......	28	15	6	.400	5	5	1.000	2	2	4	2	5	0	2	0	17
1977—Golden St......	29	16	7	.438	4	4	1.000	1	3	4	8	1	0	2	0	18
1978—Golden St......	30	17	7	.412	1	1	1.000	2	2	4	5	6	1	3	0	15
Totals..............	195	111	54	.486	24	20	.833			29	31	30	2	16	1	128

Named to NBA All-Star First Team, 1966, 1967, 1974, 1975, 1976.... NBA All-Star Second Team, 1973.... NBA Rookie of the Year, 1966.... NBA All-Rookie Team, 1966.... NBA Playoff MVP, 1975.... Shares NBA record for most free throws made in one quarter, 14, vs. New York, December 6, 1966.... NBA all-time leader in free-throw percentage.... NBA All-Star Game MVP, 1967.... Holds NBA All-Star Game record for most field goals attempted in one game, 27, in 1967.... Shares NBA All-Star Game record for most free throws made in one half, 10, in 1967.... Holds NBA record for most field-goal attempts in championship series game, 48, and shares record for most field goals, 22, vs. Philadelphia, April 18, 1967. . . . Shares NBA record for most free throws in one half of championship series game, 12, vs. Philadelphia, April 24, 1967.... Holds NBA record for most field-goal attempts in one quarter of championship series game, 17, vs. Philadelphia, April 14, 1967. . . . Shares NBA record for most three-point field goals, 8, vs. Utah, February 9, 1980.... Member of NBA championship team, 1975.... Led NBA in scoring, 1967.... Led NBA in steals, 1975.... Led NBA in free-throw percentage, 1973, 1975, 1976, 1978, 1979, 1980.... ABA All-Star First Team, 1969, 1970, 1971, 1972.... Led ABA in scoring, 1969.... Led ABA in free-throw percentage, 1969, 1971, 1972.... Named to THE SPORTING NEWS All-America Second Team, 1965.

ELGIN GAY BAYLOR

Born September 16, 1934 at Washington, D. C. Height 6:05. Weight 225.

High Schools—Washington, D. C., Phelps Vocational (Fr.-Jr.) and Spingarn (Sr.).

Colleges—The College of Idaho, Caldwell, Idaho, and
Seattle University, Seattle, Wash.

Drafted by Minneapolis on first round as junior eligible, 1958.

—COLLEGIATE RECORD—

College of Idaho

Year	G.	Min.	FGA	FGM	Pct.	FTA	FTM	Pct.	Reb.	Pts.	Avg.
54-55	26	....	651	332	.510	232	150	.647	492	814	31.3

Seattle

Year	G.	Min.	FGA	FGM	Pct.	FTA	FTM	Pct.	Reb.	Pts.	Avg.
55-56			Did Not Play—Transfer Student								
56-57	25	....	555	271	.488	251	201	.801	508	743	29.7
57-58	29	....	697	353	.506	308	237	.769	559	943	32.5
Totals	54	....	1252	624	.498	559	438	.784	1067	1686	31.2
College Totals	80	....	1903	956	.502	791	588	.743	1559	2500	31.3

NOTE: 1954-55 rebound figures are for 24 games. Baylor played for Westside Ford, an AAU team in Seattle, during 1955-56 season (averaged 34 points per game).

ELGIN BAYLOR

NBA REGULAR SEASON RECORD

Sea.—Team	G.	Min.	FGA	FGM	Pct.	FTA	FTM	Pct.	Reb.	Ast.	PF	Disq.	Pts.	Avg.
58-59—Minneapolis	70	2855	1482	605	.408	685	532	.777	1050	287	270	4	1742	24.9
59-60—Minneapolis	70	2873	1781	755	.424	770	564	.732	1150	243	234	2	2074	29.6
60-61—Los Angeles	73	3133	2166	931	.430	863	676	.783	1447	371	279	3	2538	34.8
61-62—Los Angeles	48	2129	1588	680	.428	631	476	.754	892	222	155	1	1836	38.3
62-63—Los Angeles	80	3370	2273	1029	.453	790	661	.837	1146	386	226	1	2719	34.0
63-64—Los Angeles	78	3164	1778	756	.425	586	471	.804	936	347	235	1	1983	25.4
64-65—Los Angeles	74	3056	1903	763	.401	610	483	.792	950	280	235	0	2009	27.1
65-66—Los Angeles	65	1975	1034	415	.401	337	249	.739	621	224	157	0	1079	16.6
66-67—Los Angeles	70	2706	1658	711	.429	541	440	.813	898	215	211	1	1862	26.6
67-68—Los Angeles	77	3029	1709	757	.443	621	488	.786	941	355	232	0	2002	26.0
68-69—Los Angeles	76	3064	1632	730	.447	567	421	.743	805	408	204	0	1881	24.8
69-70—Los Angeles	54	2213	1051	511	.486	357	276	.773	559	292	132	1	1298	24.0
70-71—Los Angeles	2	57	19	8	.421	6	4	.667	11	2	6	0	20	10.0
71-72—Los Angeles	9	239	97	42	.433	27	22	.815	57	18	20	0	106	11.8
Totals	846	33863	20171	8693	.431	7391	5763	.780	11463	3650	2596	14	23149	27.4

NBA PLAYOFF RECORD

Sea.—Team	G.	Min.	FGA	FGM	Pct.	FTA	FTM	Pct.	Reb.	Ast.	PF	Disq.	Pts.	Avg.
58-59—Minneapolis	13	556	303	122	.403	113	87	.770	156	43	52	0	331	25.5
59-60—Minneapolis	9	408	234	111	.474	94	79	.840	128	31	38	0	301	33.4
60-61—Los Angeles	12	540	362	170	.470	142	117	.824	183	55	44	1	457	38.1
61-62—Los Angeles	13	571	425	186	.428	168	130	.774	230	47	45	1	502	38.6
62-63—Los Angeles	13	562	362	160	.442	126	104	.825	177	58	58	0	424	32.6
63-64—Los Angeles	5	221	119	45	.378	40	31	.775	58	28	17	0	121	24.2
64-65—Los Angeles	1	5	2	0	.000	0	0	.000	0	1	0	0	0	0.0
65-66—Los Angeles	14	586	328	145	.442	105	85	.810	197	52	38	0	375	26.8
66-67—Los Angeles	3	121	76	28	.368	20	15	.750	39	9	6	0	71	23.7
67-68—Los Angeles	15	633	376	176	.468	112	76	.679	218	60	41	0	428	28.5
68-69—Los Angeles	18	640	278	107	.385	100	63	.630	166	74	56	0	277	15.4
69-70—Los Angeles	18	667	296	138	.466	81	60	.741	173	83	50	1	336	18.7
Totals	134	5510	3161	1388	.439	1101	847	.769	1725	541	445	3	3623	27.0

NBA ALL-STAR GAME RECORD

Season—Team	Min.	FGA	FGM	Pct.	FTA	FTM	Pct.	Reb.	Ast.	PF	Disq.	Pts.
1959—Minneapolis	32	20	10	.500	5	4	.800	11	1	3	0	24
1960—Minneapolis	28	18	10	.556	7	5	.714	13	3	4	0	25
1961—Los Angeles	27	11	3	.273	10	9	.900	10	4	5	0	15
1962—Los Angeles	37	23	10	.435	14	12	.857	9	4	2	0	32
1963—Los Angeles	36	15	4	.267	13	9	.692	14	7	0	0	17
1964—Los Angeles	29	15	5	.333	11	5	.455	8	5	1	0	15
1965—Los Angeles	27	13	5	.385	8	8	1.000	7	0	4	0	18
1967—Los Angeles	20	14	8	.571	4	4	1.000	5	5	2	0	20
1968—Los Angeles	27	13	8	.615	7	6	.857	6	1	5	0	22
1969—Los Angeles	32	13	5	.385	12	11	.917	9	5	2	0	21
1970—Los Angeles	26	9	2	.222	7	5	.714	7	3	3	0	9
Totals	321	164	70	.427	98	78	.796	99	38	31	0	218

NBA COACHING RECORD

		Regular Season			
Sea.	Club	W.	L.	Pct.	Pos.
1974-75—New Orleans		0	1	.000	...†
1976-77—New Orleans		21	35	.375	5†
1977-78—New Orleans		39	43	.476	5†
1978-79—New Orleans		26	56	.317	6†
Totals (4 seasons)		86	135	.389	

†Central Division.

Named to NBA 35th Anniversary All-Time Team, 1980. . . . Elected to Naismith Memorial Basketball Hall of Fame, 1976. . . . Named to NBA All-Star First Team, 1959, 1960, 1961, 1962, 1963, 1964, 1965, 1967, 1968, 1969. . . . NBA Rookie of the Year, 1959. . . . Holds NBA record for most points in playoff game, 61, vs. Boston, April 14, 1962. . . . Shares NBA record for most field goals in championship series game, 22, vs. Boston, April 14, 1962. . . . Holds NBA records for most points, 33, and most field-goal attempts, 25, in one half of championship series game, vs. Boston, April 14, 1962. . . . NBA All-Star Game co-MVP, 1959. . . . Holds NBA All-Star Game records for most career free throws made and most field goals attempted in one half, 15, in 1959. . . . Shares NBA All-Star Game records for most career free throws attempted and most free throws made in one game, 12, in 1962. . . . Led NCAA Division I in rebounding, 1957. . . . NCAA University Division tournament MVP, 1958. . . . Named to THE SPORTING NEWS All-America First Team, 1958.

WALTER BELLAMY
(Walt)

Born July 24, 1939 at New Bern, N. C.   Height 6:11.   Weight 245.

High School—New Bern, N. C., J. T. Barber.

College—Indiana University, Bloomington, Ind.

Drafted by Chicago on first round, 1961.

Chicago franchise moved to Baltimore, 1963.

Traded by Baltimore to New York for John Green, John Egan, Jim Barnes and cash, November 2, 1965.
Traded by New York with Howard Komives to Detroit for Dave DeBusschere, December 19, 1968.
Traded by Detroit to Atlanta for a player to be designated, February 1, 1970. Detroit received John Arthurs from Milwaukee as part of deal.
Selected from Atlanta by New Orleans in expansion draft, May 20, 1974.
Waived by New Orleans, October 18, 1974.

—COLLEGIATE RECORD—

Year	G.	Min.	FGA	FGM	Pct.	FTA	FTM	Pct.	Reb.	Pts.	Avg.
57-58†			(Freshman team did not play intercollegiate schedule.)								
58-59	22	....	289	148	.512	141	86	.610	335	382	17.4
59-60	24	....	396	212	.535	161	113	.702	324	537	22.4
60-61	24	....	389	195	.501	204	132	.647	428	522	21.8
Varsity Totals	70	....	1074	555	.517	506	331	.654	1087	1441	20.6

NBA REGULAR SEASON RECORD

Sea.—Team	G.	Min.	FGA	FGM	Pct.	FTA	FTM	Pct.	Reb.	Ast.	PF	Disq.	Pts.	Avg.
61-62—Chicago	79	3344	1875	973	.519	853	549	.644	1500	210	281	6	2495	31.6
62-63—Chicago	80	3306	1595	840	.527	821	553	.674	1309	233	283	7	2233	27.9
63-64—Baltimore	80	3394	1582	811	.513	825	537	.651	1361	126	300	7	2159	27.0
64-65—Baltimore	80	3301	1441	733	.509	752	515	.685	1166	191	260	2	1981	24.8
65-66—Balt.-N.Y.	80	3352	1373	695	.506	689	430	.624	1254	235	294	9	1820	22.8
66-67—New York	79	3010	1084	565	.521	580	369	.637	1064	206	275	5	1499	19.0
67-68—New York	82	2695	944	511	.541	529	350	.662	961	164	259	3	1372	16.7
68-69—N.Y.-Det.	88	3159	1103	563	.510	618	401	.649	1101	176	320	5	1527	17.4
69-70—Det.-Atl.	79	2028	671	351	.523	373	215	.576	707	143	260	5	917	11.6
70-71—Atlanta	82	2908	879	433	.493	556	336	.604	1060	230	271	4	1202	14.7
71-72—Atlanta	82	3187	1089	593	.544	581	340	.585	1049	262	255	2	1526	18.6
72-73—Atlanta	74	2802	901	455	.505	526	283	.538	964	179	244	1	1193	16.1

| | | | | | | | —Rebounds— | | | | | | | | | |
Sea.—Team	G.	Min.	FGA	FGM	Pct.	FTA	FTM	Pct.	Off.	Def.	Tot.	Ast.	PF	Dq.	Stl.	Blk.	Pts.	Avg.
73-74—Atlanta	77	2440	801	389	.486	383	233	.608	264	476	740	189	232	2	52	48	1011	13.1
74-75—N. O.	1	14	2	2	1.000	2	2	1.000	0	5	5	0	2	0	0	0	6	6.0
Totals	1043	38940	15340	7914	.516	8088	5113	.632			14241	2544	3536	58	52	48	20941	20.1

NBA PLAYOFF RECORD

Sea.—Team	G.	Min.	FGA	FGM	Pct.	FTA	FTM	Pct.	Reb.	Ast.	PF	Disq.	Pts.	Avg.
64-65—Baltimore	10	427	158	74	.468	92	61	.663	151	34	38	0	209	20.9
66-67—New York	4	157	54	28	.519	29	17	.586	66	12	15	0	73	18.3
67-68—New York	6	277	107	45	.421	48	30	.625	96	21	22	0	120	20.0
69-70—Atlanta	9	368	126	59	.468	46	33	.717	140	35	32	0	151	16.8
70-71—Atlanta	5	216	69	41	.594	29	22	.759	72	10	16	0	104	20.8
71-72—Atlanta	6	247	86	42	.488	43	27	.628	82	11	20	0	111	18.5
72-73—Atlanta	6	247	86	34	.395	31	14	.452	73	13	17	0	82	13.7
Totals	46	1939	686	323	.471	318	204	.642	680	136	160	0	850	18.5

NBA ALL-STAR GAME RECORD

Season—Team	Min.	FGA	FGM	Pct.	FTA	FTM	Pct.	Reb.	Ast.	PF	Disq.	Pts.
1962—Chicago	29	18	10	.556	8	3	.375	17	1	6	1	23
1963—Chicago	14	4	1	.250	2	0	.000	1	2	3	0	2
1964—Baltimore	23	11	4	.364	5	3	.600	7	0	3	0	11
1965—Baltimore	17	5	4	.800	4	4	1.000	5	1	3	0	12
Totals	83	38	19	.500	19	10	.526	30	4	15	1	48

NBA Rookie of the Year, 1962.... Led NBA in field-goal percentage, 1962.... Holds NBA record for most games played in one season, 1969. . . . Member of U.S. Olympic Team, 1960. . . . Named to THE SPORTING NEWS All-America Second Team, 1961.

DAVID BING
(Dave)

Born November 24, 1943 at Washington, D. C. Height 6:03. Weight 185.

High School—Washington, D. C., Spingarn.

College—Syracuse University, Syracuse, N. Y.

Drafted by Detroit on first round, 1966 (1st pick).

Traded by Detroit with a 1977 1st round draft choice to Washington for Kevin Porter, August 28, 1975.
Waived by Washington, September 20, 1977; signed by Boston as a free agent, September 28, 1977.

—COLLEGIATE RECORD—

Year	G.	Min.	FGA	FGM	Pct.	FTA	FTM	Pct.	Reb.	Pts.	Avg.
62-63†	17	....	341	170	.499	131	97	.740	192	437	25.7
63-64	25	....	460	215	.467	172	126	.733	206	556	22.2
64-65	23	....	444	206	.464	162	121	.747	277	533	23.2
65-66	28	....	569	308	.541	222	178	.802	303	794	28.4
Varsity Totals	76	....	1473	729	.495	556	425	.764	786	1883	24.8

DAVE BING

NBA REGULAR SEASON RECORD

Sea.—Team	G.	Min.	FGA	FGM	Pct.	FTA	FTM	Pct.	Reb.	Ast.	PF	Disq.	Pts.	Avg.
66-67—Detroit	80	2762	1522	664	.436	370	273	.738	359	330	217	2	1601	20.6
67-68—Detroit	79	3209	1893	835	.441	668	472	.707	373	509	254	2	2142	27.1
68-69—Detroit	77	3039	1594	678	.425	623	444	.713	382	546	256	3	1800	23.4
69-70—Detroit	70	2334	1295	575	.444	580	454	.783	299	418	196	0	1604	22.9
70-71—Detroit	82	3065	1710	799	.467	772	615	.797	364	408	228	4	2213	27.0
71-72—Detroit	45	1936	891	369	.414	354	278	.785	186	317	138	3	1016	22.6
72-73—Detroit	82	3361	1545	692	.448	560	456	.814	298	637	229	1	1840	22.4

Sea.—Team	G.	Min.	FGA	FGM	Pct.	FTA	FTM	Pct.	Off.	Def.	Tot.	Ast.	PF	Dq.	Stl.	Blk.	Pts.	Avg.
73-74—Detroit	81	3124	1336	582	.436	438	356	.813	108	173	281	555	216	1	109	17	1520	18.0
74-75—Detroit	79	3222	1333	578	.434	424	343	.809	86	200	286	610	222	3	116	26	1499	19.0
75-76—Wash.	82	2945	1113	497	.447	422	332	.787	94	143	237	492	262	0	118	23	1326	16.2
76-77—Wash.	64	1516	597	271	.454	176	136	.773	54	89	143	275	150	1	61	5	678	10.6
77-78—Boston	80	2256	940	422	.449	296	244	.824	76	136	212	300	247	2	79	18	1088	13.6
Totals	901	32769	15769	6962	.441	5683	4403	.775			3420	5397	2615	22	483	89	18327	20.3

NBA PLAYOFF RECORD

Sea.—Team	G.	Min.	FGA	FGM	Pct.	FTA	FTM	Pct.	Off.	Def.	Tot.	Ast.	PF	Dq.	Stl.	Blk.	Pts.	Avg.
67-68—Detroit	6	254	166	68	.410	45	33	.763			24	29	21	0			169	28.2
73-74—Detroit	7	312	131	55	.420	30	22	.733	6	20	26	42	20	0	3	1	132	18.9
74-75—Detroit	3	134	47	20	.426	13	8	.615	3	8	11	29	12	0	5	0	48	16.0
75-76—Wash.	7	209	76	34	.447	35	28	.800	6	12	18	28	18	0	7	2	96	13.7
76-77—Wash.	8	55	32	14	.438	4	4	1.000	3	3	6	5	5	0	0	1	32	4.0
Totals	31	964	452	191	.423	127	95	.748			85	133	76	0	15	4	477	15.4

NBA ALL-STAR GAME RECORD

Season—Team	Min.	FGA	FGM	Pct.	FTA	FTM	Pct.	Reb.	Ast.	PF	Disq.	Pts.
1968—Detroit	20	7	4	.571	1	1	1.000	2	4	3	0	9
1969—Detroit	13	3	1	.333	1	1	1.000	0	3	0	0	3
1971—Detroit	19	7	2	.286	0	0	.000	2	2	1	0	4
1973—Detroit	19	4	0	.000	2	2	1.000	3	0	1	0	2

Season—Team	Min.	FGA	FGM	Pct.	FTA	FTM	Pct.	Off.	Def.	Tot.	Ast.	PF	Dq.	Stl.	Blk.	Pts.
1974—Detroit	16	9	2	.222	1	1	1.000	1	5	6	2	1	0	0	0	5
1975—Detroit	12	2	0	.000	2	2	1.000	0	0	0	1	0	0	0	0	2
1976—Washington	26	11	7	.636	2	2	1.000	1	2	3	4	1	0	0	0	16
Totals	125	43	16	.372	9	9	1.000			16	16	7	0	0	0	41

Named to NBA All-Star First Team, 1968 and 1971.... NBA All-Star Second Team, 1974.... NBA Rookie of the Year, 1967.... NBA All-Rookie Team, 1967.... Led NBA in scoring, 1968.... NBA All-Star Game MVP, 1976.... Named to THE SPORTING NEWS All-America First Team, 1965.

RON BOONE

Born September 6, 1946 at Oklahoma City, Okla. Height 6:02. Weight 200.

High School—Omaha, Neb., Tech.

Colleges—Iowa Western Community College, Clarinda, Iowa, and Idaho State University, Pocatello, Idaho.

Drafted by Phoenix on eleventh round, 1968 (147th pick).

Selected by Dallas on eighth round of ABA draft, 1968.
Traded by Dallas with Glen Combs to Utah for Donnie Freeman and Wayne Hightower, January 8, 1971.
Sold by Utah to St. Louis, December 2, 1975.
Selected by Kansas City NBA from St. Louis for $250,000 in ABA dispersal draft, August 5, 1976.
Traded by Kansas City with a 1979 2nd round draft choice to Denver for Darnell Hillman and the draft rights to Mike Evans, June 26, 1978.
Traded by Denver with two 1979 2nd round draft choices to Los Angeles for Charlie Scott, June 26, 1978.
Traded by Los Angeles to Utah for a 1981 3rd round draft choice, October 25, 1979.
Waived by Utah, January 26, 1981.

—COLLEGIATE RECORD—
Iowa Western CC

Year	G.	Min.	FGA	FGM	Pct.	FTA	FTM	Pct.	Reb.	Pts.	Avg.
64-65	9	....	....	....	....	....	....	....	....	227	25.2

Idaho State

Year	G.	Min.	FGA	FGM	Pct.	FTA	FTM	Pct.	Reb.	Pts.	Avg.
65-66	10	....	119	46	.387	26	17	.654	95	109	10.9
66-67	25	....	416	199	.478	215	160	.744	128	558	22.3
67-68	26	....	519	223	.430	159	108	.679	110	554	21.3
Totals	61	....	1054	468	.444	400	285	.713	333	1221	20.0

ABA REGULAR SEASON RECORD

			—2-Point—			—3-Point—									
Sea.—Team	G.	Min.	FGM	FGA	Pct.	FGM	FGA	Pct.	FTM	FTA	Pct.	Reb.	Ast.	Pts.	Avg.
68-69—Dallas	78	2682	518	1182	.438	2	15	.133	436	537	.812	394	279	1478	18.9
69-70—Dallas	84	2340	406	925	.439	17	55	.309	300	382	.785	366	272	1163	13.9
70-71—Dallas-Utah	86	2476	.561	1257	.446	49	138	.355	278	357	.779	564	256	1547	18.0
71-72—Utah	84	2040	391	897	.436	13	65	.200	271	341	.795	393	233	1092	13.0
72-73—Utah	84	2585	556	1096	.507	10	40	.250	415	479	.866	423	353	1557	18.5
73-74—Utah	84	3098	581	1162	.500	6	26	.231	300	343	.875	435	417	1480	17.6
74-75—Utah	84	3414	862	1743	.495	10	33	.303	363	422	.860	406	372	2117	25.2
75-76—Utah-St. Louis	78	2961	697	1424	.489	16	43	.372	277	318	.871	319	387	1719	22.0
Totals	662	21586	4572	9686	.472	123	415	.296	2640	3179	.830	3302	2569	12153	18.4

ABA PLAYOFF RECORD

			—2-Point—			—3-Point—									
Sea.—Team	G.	Min.	FGM	FGA	Pct.	FGM	FGA	Pct.	FTM	FTA	Pct.	Reb.	Ast.	Pts.	Avg.
68-69—Dallas	7	196	38	81	.469	0	4	.000	21	25	.840	22	27	97	13.9
69-70—Dallas	6	193	43	89	.483	3	8	.375	15	21	.714	27	27	110	18.3
70-71—Utah	18	569	104	229	.454	9	27	.333	74	86	.860	110	94	309	17.2
71-72—Utah	11	209	49	100	.490	1	5	.200	25	29	.862	24	26	126	11.5
72-73—Utah	10	360	68	132	.515	0	3	.000	33	34	.971	43	47	169	16.9
73-74—Utah	18	747	137	282	.486	0	7	.000	34	37	.919	108	109	308	17.1
74-75—Utah	6	219	54	127	.425	0	0	.000	34	38	.895	24	41	142	23.7
Totals	76	2493	493	1040	.474	13	54	.240	236	270	.874	358	371	1261	16.6

ABA ALL-STAR GAME RECORD

		—2-Point—			—3-Point—								
Sea.—Team	Min.	FGM	FGA	Pct.	FGM	FGA	Pct.	FTM	FTA	Pct.	Reb.	Ast.	Pts.	Avg.
1971—Utah	4	2	4	.500	0	0	.000	2	3	.667	2	0	6	6.0
1974—Utah	24	6	11	.545	1	2	.500	0	0	.000	3	5	15	15.0
1975—Utah	23	4	8	.500	0	0	.000	2	2	1.000	2	2	10	10.0
1976—St. Louis	16	5	11	.455	0	0	.000	0	0	.000	3	2	10	10.0
Totals	67	17	34	.500	1	2	.500	4	5	.800	10	9	41	10.3

NBA REGULAR SEASON RECORD

									—Rebounds—									
Sea.—Team	G.	Min.	FGA	FGM	Pct.	FTA	FTM	Pct.	Off.	Def.	Tot.	Ast.	PF	Dq.	Stl.	Blk.	Pts.	Avg.
76-77—Kan. City	82	3021	1577	747	.474	384	324	.844	128	193	321	338	258	1	119	19	1818	22.2
77-78—Kan. City	82	2653	1271	563	.443	377	322	.854	112	157	269	311	233	3	105	11	1448	17.7
78-79—Los Ang.	82	1583	569	259	.455	104	90	.865	53	92	145	154	171	1	66	11	608	7.4
79-80—L.A.-Utah	81	2392	915	405	.443	196	175	.893	54	173	227	309	232	8	97	3	1004	12.4
80-81—Utah	52	1146	371	160	.431	94	75	.798	17	67	84	161	126	0	33	8	406	7.8
Totals	379	10795	4703	2134	.454	1155	986	.854	364	682	1046	1273	1020	8	420	52	5284	13.9

Three-Point Field Goals: 1979-80, 19-for-50 (.380). 1980-81, 11-for-39 (.282). Totals, 30-for-89 (.337).

NBA PLAYOFF RECORD

									—Rebounds—									
Sea.—Team	G.	Min.	FGA	FGM	Pct.	FTA	FTM	Pct.	Off.	Def.	Tot.	Ast.	PF	Dq.	Stl.	Blk.	Pts.	Avg.
78-79—Los Ang.	8	226	77	37	.481	21	20	.952	7	8	15	14	28	0	9	0	94	11.8

Set professional basketball record by playing in 1,041 consecutive games. . . . Named to ABA All-Star First Team, 1975. . . . ABA All-Star Second Team, 1974. . . . ABA All-Rookie Team, 1969. . . . Member of ABA championship team, 1971.

WILLIAM WARREN BRADLEY
(Bill)

Born July 28, 1943 at Crystal City, Mo.   Height 6:05.   Weight 210.

High School—Crystal City, Mo.

Colleges—Princeton University, Princeton, N. J., and graduate work at Oxford University, Oxford, England.

Drafted by New York on first round (territorial choice), 1965.

Played with Milan Simmenthal of Italian Basketball League, 1965-66.
Played with Oxford University in England, 1966-67.

—COLLEGIATE RECORD—

Year	G.	Min.	FGA	FGM	Pct.	FTA	FTM	Pct.	Reb.	Pts.	Avg.
61-62†	13	....	265	142	.536	125	114	.912	232	398	30.6
62-63	25	....	445	212	.476	289	258	.893	306	682	27.3
63-64	29	....	648	338	.522	306	260	.850	360	936	32.3
64-65	29	....	574	306	.533	308	273	.886	342	885	30.5
Varsity Totals	83	....	1667	856	.513	903	791	.876	1008	2503	30.2

NBA REGULAR SEASON RECORD

Sea.—Team	G.	Min.	FGA	FGM	Pct.	FTA	FTM	Pct.	Reb.	Ast.	PF	Disq.	Pts.	Avg.
67-68—New York	45	874	341	142	.416	104	76	.731	113	137	138	2	360	8.0
68-69—New York	82	2413	948	401	.429	253	206	.814	350	302	295	4	1020	12.4
69-70—New York	67	2098	897	413	.460	176	145	.824	239	268	219	0	971	14.5
70-71—New York	78	2300	912	413	.453	175	144	.823	260	280	245	3	970	12.4
71-72—New York	78	2780	1085	504	.465	199	169	.849	250	315	254	4	1177	15.1
72-73—New York	82	2998	1252	575	.459	194	169	.871	301	367	273	5	1319	16.1

Sea.—Team	G.	Min.	FGA	FGM	Pct.	FTA	FTM	Pct.	Off.	Def.	Tot.	Ast.	PF	Dq.	Stl.	Blk.	Pts.	Avg.
73-74—New York	82	2813	1112	502	.451	167	146	.874	59	194	253	242	278	2	42	21	1150	14.0
74-75—New York	79	2787	1036	452	.436	165	144	.873	65	186	251	247	283	5	74	18	1048	13.3
75-76—New York	82	2709	906	392	.433	148	130	.878	47	187	234	247	256	2	68	18	914	11.1
76-77—New York	67	1027	274	127	.464	42	34	.810	27	76	103	128	122	0	25	8	288	4.3
Totals	742	22799	8763	3927	.448	1623	1363	.840			2354	2533	2363	27			9217	12.4

NBA ALL-STAR GAME RECORD

Season—Team	Min.	FGA	FGM	Pct.	FTA	FTM	Pct.	Reb.	Ast.	PF	Disq.	Pts.
1973—New York	12	5	2	.400	0	0	.000	1	0	2	0	4

NBA PLAYOFF RECORD

Sea.—Team	G.	Min.	FGA	FGM	Pct.	FTA	FTM	Pct.	Reb.	Ast.	PF	Disq.	Pts.	Avg.
67-68—New York	6	64	28	12	.429	13	9	.692	6	2	7	0	33	5.5
68-69—New York	10	419	141	65	.461	39	30	.769	73	40	38	1	160	16.0
69-70—New York	19	616	233	100	.429	43	35	.814	72	60	59	1	235	12.4
70-71—New York	12	368	132	56	.424	19	14	.737	41	43	40	0	126	10.5
71-72—New York	16	594	227	106	.467	56	47	.839	47	54	66	1	259	16.2
72-73—New York	17	587	221	99	.448	50	40	.800	57	45	59	1	238	14.0

Sea.—Team	G.	Min.	FGA	FGM	Pct.	FTA	FTM	Pct.	Off.	Def.	Tot.	Ast.	PF	Dq.	Stl.	Blk.	Pts.	Avg.
73-74—New York	12	425	159	63	.396	29	25	.862	8	20	28	13	39	1	7	3	151	12.6
74-75—New York	3	88	24	9	.375	2	2	1.000	4	5	9	6	5	0	2	0	20	6.7
Totals	95	3161	1165	510	.438	251	202	.805			333	263	313	5			1222	12.9

Elected to Naismith Memorial Basketball Hall of Fame, 1982. . . . Member of NBA championship teams, 1970 and 1973. . . . Named THE SPORTING NEWS College Player of the Year, 1964 and 1965. . . . THE SPORTING NEWS All-America First Team, 1963, 1964, 1965. . . . Outstanding player in NCAA University Division tourney, 1965. . . . Led NCAA University Division in free-throw percentage, 1965. . . . Member of U.S. Olympic Team, 1964. . . . Currently a U.S. Senator (D) from New Jersey.

BILL BRIDGES

Born April 4, 1939 at Hobbs, N. M.   Height 6:06. Weight 235.

High School—Hobbs, N. M.

College—University of Kansas, Lawrence, Kan.

Drafted by Chicago on third round, 1961. (32nd pick).

Draft rights traded by Chicago (Baltimore) with Ralph Davis to St. Louis for Al Ferrari and Shellie McMillion, June 14, 1962.
Traded by Atlanta to Philadelphia for Jim Washington, November 19, 1971.
Traded by Philadelphia with Mel Counts to Los Angeles for Leroy Ellis and John Q. Trapp, November 2, 1972.
Waived by Los Angeles, December 6, 1974; signed by Golden State as a free agent, March 1, 1975.
Played in American Basketball League with Kansas City Steers, 1961-62 and 1962-63.

—COLLEGIATE RECORD—

Year	G.	Min.	FGA	FGM	Pct.	FTA	FTM	Pct.	Reb.	Pts.	Avg.
57-58†			(Freshman team did not play intercollegiate schedule)								
58-59	25	....	307	117	.381	129	74	.574	343	308	12.3
59-60	28	....	293	112	.382	142	94	.662	385	318	11.4
60-61	25	....	334	146	.437	155	110	.710	353	402	16.1
Varsity Totals	78	....	934	375	.401	426	278	.653	1081	1028	13.2

ABL REGULAR SEASON RECORD

Sea.—Team	G.	Min.	2-Point			3-Point			FTM	FTA	Pct.	Reb.	Ast.	Pts.	Avg.
			FGM	FGA	Pct.	FGM	FGA	Pct.							
61-62—Kan. City	79	3259	638	1400	.456	3	12	.250	412	587	.702	1059	181	1697	21.4
62-63—Kan. City	29	1185	312	606	.515	0	2	.000	225	289	.779	437	87	849	29.2

NBA REGULAR SEASON RECORD

Sea.—Team	G.	Min.	FGA	FGM	Pct.	FTA	FTM	Pct.	Reb.	Ast.	PF	Disq.	Pts.	Avg.
62-63—St. Louis	27	374	160	66	.413	51	32	.627	144	23	58	0	164	6.1
63-64—St. Louis	80	1949	675	268	.397	224	146	.652	680	181	269	6	682	8.5
64-65—St. Louis	79	2362	938	362	.386	275	186	.676	853	187	276	3	910	11.5
65-66—St. Louis	78	2677	927	377	.407	364	257	.706	951	208	333	11	1011	13.0
66-67—St. Louis	79	3130	1106	503	.455	523	367	.702	1190	222	325	12	1373	17.4
67-68—St. Louis	82	3197	1009	466	.462	484	347	.717	1102	253	366	12	1279	15.6

Sea.—Team	G.	Min.	FGA	FGM	Pct.	FTA	FTM	Pct.	Reb.	Ast.	PF	Disq.	Pts.	Avg.
68-69—Atlanta	80	2930	775	351	.453	353	239	.677	1132	298	290	3	941	11.8
69-70—Atlanta	82	3269	932	443	.475	451	331	.734	1181	345	292	6	1217	14.8
70-71—Atlanta	82	3140	834	382	.458	330	211	.639	1233	240	317	7	975	11.9
71-72—Atl.-Phil.	78	2756	779	379	.487	316	222	.703	1051	198	269	6	980	12.6
72-73—Phil-LA	82	2867	722	333	.461	255	179	.702	904	219	296	3	845	10.3

Sea.—Team	G.	Min.	FGA	FGM	Pct.	FTA	FTM	Pct.	—Rebounds— Off.	Def.	Tot.	Ast.	PF	Dq.	Stl.	Blk.	Pts.	Avg.
73-74—L.A.	65	1812	513	216	.421	164	116	.707	193	306	499	148	219	3	58	31	548	8.4
74-75—LA-GS	32	415	93	35	.376	34	17	.500	64	70	134	31	65	1	11	5	87	2.7
Totals	926	30878	9463	4181	.442	3824	2650	.693			11054	2553	3375	73	69	36	11012	11.9

NBA PLAYOFF RECORD

Sea.—Team	G.	Min.	FGA	FGM	Pct.	FTA	FTM	Pct.	Reb.	Ast.	PF	Disq.	Pts.	Avg.
62-63—St. Louis	11	204	96	41	.427	27	20	.741	86	9	31	0	102	9.3
63-64—St. Louis	12	240	83	26	.313	19	12	.632	84	24	40	0	64	5.3
64-65—St. Louis	4	145	59	21	.356	15	10	.667	67	9	19	1	52	13.0
65-66—St. Louis	10	421	170	86	.506	43	31	.721	149	28	47	2	203	20.3
66-67—St. Louis	9	369	128	48	.375	67	45	.672	169	22	36	2	141	15.7
67-68—St. Louis	6	216	75	38	.507	25	18	.720	77	14	23	0	94	15.7
68-69—Atlanta	11	442	156	69	.442	48	34	.708	178	37	48	2	172	15.6
69-70—Atlanta	9	381	110	44	.400	27	16	.593	154	29	37	1	104	11.6
70-71—Atlanta	5	229	58	23	.397	9	3	.333	104	5	17	0	49	9.8
72-73—Los Ang.	17	582	136	57	.419	49	38	.776	158	29	68	2	152	8.9

Sea.—Team	G.	Min.	FGA	FGM	Pct.	FTA	FTM	Pct.	—Rebounds— Off.	Def.	Tot.	Ast.	PF	Dq.	Stl.	Blk.	Pts.	Avg.
73-74—L.A.	5	144	41	12	.293	13	6	.462	14	16	30	6	19	0	7	0	30	6.0
74-75—G.S.	14	148	23	10	.435	7	2	.286	13	36	49	7	23	0	9	4	22	1.6
Totals	113	3521	1135	475	.419	349	235	.673			1305	219	408	10	16	4	1185	10.5

NBA ALL-STAR GAME RECORD

Season—Team	Min.	FGA	FGM	Pct.	FTA	FTM	Pct.	Reb.	Ast.	PF	Disq.	Pts.
1967—St. Louis	17	5	4	.800	2	0	.000	3	3	1	0	8
1968—St. Louis	21	9	7	.778	4	1	.250	7	1	4	0	15
1970—Atlanta	15	2	2	1.000	5	1	.200	4	2	1	0	5
Totals	53	16	13	.813	11	2	.182	14	6	6	0	28

Named to NBA All-Defensive Second Team, 1969 and 1970. . . . Member of NBA championship team, 1975. . . . Named to ABL All-Star First Team, 1962. . . . Led ABL in scoring, 1963. . . . Led ABL in rebounding, 1962 and 1963. . . . Set ABL single-game scoring record with 55 points vs. Oakland, December 9, 1962. . . . Member of ABL championship team, 1963.

WILTON NORMAN CHAMBERLAIN
(Wilt)

Born August 21, 1936 at Philadelphia, Pa. Height 7:01. Weight 275.

High School—Philadelphia, Pa., Overbrook.

College—University of Kansas, Lawrence, Kan.

Drafted by Philadelphia on first round (territorial choice), 1959.

Philadelphia franchise moved to San Francisco, 1962.
Traded by San Francisco to Philadelphia for Paul Neumann, Connie Dierking, Lee Shaffer and cash, January 15, 1965.
Traded by Philadelphia to Los Angeles for Jerry Chambers, Archie Clark and Darrall Imhoff, July 9, 1968.
Played with Harlem Globetrotters during 1958-59 season.

—COLLEGIATE RECORD—

Year	G.	Min.	FGA	FGM	Pct.	FTA	FTM	Pct.	Reb.	Pts.	Avg.
55-56†			(Freshmen team did not play an intercollegiate schedule)								
56-57	27	....	588	275	.468	399	250	.627	510	800	29.6
57-58	21	....	482	228	.473	291	177	.608	367	633	30.1
Varsity Totals	48	....	1070	503	.470	690	427	.619	877	1433	29.9

NBA REGULAR SEASON RECORD

Sea.—Team	G.	Min.	FGA	FGM	Pct.	FTA	FTM	Pct.	Reb.	Ast.	PF	Disq.	Pts.	Avg.
59-60—Philadelphia	72	3338	2311	1065	.461	991	577	.582	1941	168	150	0	2707	37.6
60-61—Philadelphia	79	3773	2457	1251	.509	1054	531	.504	2149	148	130	0	3033	38.4
61-62—Philadelphia	80	3882	3159	1597	.505	1363	835	.613	2052	192	123	0	4029	50.4
62-63—San Francisco	80	3806	2770	1463	.528	1113	660	.593	1946	275	136	0	3586	44.8
63-64—San Francisco	80	3689	2298	1204	.524	1016	540	.531	1787	403	182	0	2948	36.9
64-65—S.F.-Phila.	73	3301	2083	1063	.510	880	408	.464	1673	250	146	0	2534	34.7
65-66—Philadelphia	79	3737	1990	1074	.540	976	501	.513	1943	414	171	0	2649	33.5
66-67—Philadelphia	81	3682	1150	785	.683	875	386	.441	1957	630	143	0	1956	24.1
67-68—Philadelphia	82	3836	1377	819	.595	932	354	.380	1952	702	160	0	1992	24.3
68-69—Los Angeles	81	3669	1099	641	.583	857	382	.446	1712	366	142	0	1664	20.5
69-70—Los Angeles	12	505	227	129	.568	157	70	.446	221	49	31	0	328	27.3
70-71—Los Angeles	82	3630	1226	668	.545	669	360	.538	1493	352	174	0	1696	20.7
71-72—Los Angeles	82	3469	764	496	.649	524	221	.422	1572	329	196	0	1213	14.8
72-73—Los Angeles	82	3542	586	426	.727	455	232	.510	1526	365	191	0	1084	13.2
Totals	1045	47859	23497	12681	.540	11862	6057	.511	23924	4643	2075	0	31419	30.1

WILT CHAMBERLAIN

NBA PLAYOFF RECORD

Sea.—Team	G.	Min.	FGA	FGM	Pct.	FTA	FTM	Pct.	Reb.	Ast.	PF	Disq.	Pts.	Avg.
59-60—Philadelphia	9	415	252	125	.496	110	49	.445	232	19	17	0	299	33.2
60-61—Philadelphia	3	144	96	45	.469	38	21	.553	69	6	10	0	111	37.0
61-62—Philadelphia	12	576	347	162	.467	151	96	.636	319	37	27	0	420	35.0
63-64—San Francisco	12	558	322	175	.543	139	66	.475	302	39	27	0	416	34.7
64-65—Philadelphia	11	536	232	123	.530	136	76	.559	299	48	29	0	322	29.3
65-66—Philadelphia	5	240	110	56	.509	68	28	.412	151	15	10	0	140	28.0
66-67—Philadelphia	15	718	228	132	.579	160	62	.388	437	135	37	0	326	21.7
67-68—Philadelphia	13	631	232	124	.534	158	60	.380	321	85	29	0	308	23.7
68-69—Los Angeles	18	832	176	96	.545	148	58	.392	444	46	56	0	250	13.9
69-70—Los Angeles	18	851	288	158	.549	202	82	.406	399	81	42	0	398	22.1
70-71—Los Angeles	12	554	187	85	.455	97	50	.515	242	53	33	0	220	18.3
71-72—Los Angeles	15	703	142	80	.563	122	60	.492	315	49	47	0	220	14.7
72-73—Los Angeles	17	801	116	64	.552	98	49	.500	383	60	48	0	177	10.4
Totals	160	7559	2728	1425	.522	1627	757	.465	3913	673	412	0	3607	22.5

NBA ALL-STAR GAME RECORD

Season—Team	Min.	FGA	FGM	Pct.	FTA	FTM	Pct.	Reb.	Ast.	PF	Disq.	Pts.
1960—Philadelphia	30	20	9	.450	7	5	.714	25	2	1	0	23
1961—Philadelphia	38	8	2	.250	15	8	.533	18	5	1	0	12
1962—Philadelphia	37	23	17	.739	16	8	.500	24	1	4	0	42
1963—San Francisco	35	11	7	.636	7	3	.429	19	0	2	0	17
1964—San Francisco	37	14	4	.286	14	11	.786	20	1	2	0	19
1965—San Francisco	31	15	9	.600	8	2	.250	16	1	4	0	20
1966—Philadelphia	25	11	8	.727	9	5	.556	9	3	2	0	21
1967—Philadelphia	39	7	6	.857	5	2	.400	22	4	1	0	14
1968—Philadelphia	25	4	3	.750	4	1	.250	7	6	2	0	7
1969—Los Angeles	27	3	2	.667	1	0	.000	12	2	2	0	4
1971—Los Angeles	18	1	1	1.000	0	0	.000	8	5	0	0	2
1972—Los Angeles	24	3	3	1.000	8	2	.250	10	3	2	0	8
1973—Los Angeles	22	2	1	.500	0	0	.000	7	3	0	0	2
Totals	.388	122	72	.590	94	47	.500	197	36	23	0	191

ABA COACHING RECORD

Sea. Club	Regular Season				Playoffs	
	W.	L.	Pct.	Pos.	W.	L.
1973-74—San Diego	37	47	.440	T4	2	4

Named to NBA 35th Anniversary All-Time Team, 1980. . . . Elected to Naismith Memorial Basketball Hall of Fame, 1978. . . . NBA Most Valuable Player, 1960, 1966, 1967, 1968. . . . Named to NBA All-Star First Team, 1960, 1961, 1962, 1964, 1966, 1967, 1968. . . . NBA All-Star Second Team, 1963, 1965, 1972. . . . NBA Rookie of the Year, 1960. . . . NBA All-Defensive First Team, 1972 and 1973. . . . NBA Playoff MVP, 1972. . . . Only NBA player ever to score over 3,000 and 4,000 points in a season. . . . Holds NBA single game records for most points, 100, most field-goals attempted, 63, most field-goals made, 36, and shares record for most free-throws made, 28, vs. New York at Hershey, Pa., March 2, 1962. . . . Holds NBA record for most consecutive field goals, 35, February 17-28, 1967. . . . Holds NBA single game record for most consecutive field goals, 18, vs. New York at Boston, November 27, 1963, and vs. Baltimore at Pittsburgh, February 24, 1967. . . . Holds NBA single game record for most free throws attempted, 34, vs. St. Louis, February 22, 1962. . . . Holds NBA single game record for most rebounds, 55, vs. Boston, November 24, 1960. . . . Holds NBA records for most points, 59, most field-goal attempts, 37, and most field-goals made, 22, in one half, vs. New York at Hershey, Pa., March 2, 1962. . . . Holds NBA record for most field-goals attempted in one quarter, 21, vs. New York at Hershey, Pa., March 2, 1962. . . . Holds NBA record for most free-throw attempts, most rebounds and highest scoring average. . . . NBA all-time playoff leader in minutes played and free-throw attempts. . . . Holds NBA playoff game record for most rebounds, 41, vs. Boston, April 5, 1967. . . . Shares NBA playoff game record for most field goals, 24, vs. Syracuse, March 14, 1960. . . . Holds NBA championship series game record for most rebounds in one half, 26, vs. San Francisco, April 16, 1967. . . . Shares NBA championship series record for most free-throw attempts in one quarter, 11, vs. San Francisco, April 16, 1967. . . . NBA All-Star Game MVP, 1960. . . . Holds NBA All-Star Game career records for most minutes played and most rebounds. . . . Holds NBA All-Star Game records for most points in one game, 42, in 1962; most field goals made in one game, 17, in 1962; most free throws attempted in one game, 16, in 1962; most points in one half, 23, in 1962, and most field goals made in one half, 10, in 1962. . . . Shares NBA All-Star Game record for most rebounds in one half, 16, in 1960. . . . Member of NBA championship teams, 1967 and 1972. . . . Led NBA in scoring, 1960, 1961, 1962, 1963, 1964, 1965, 1966. . . . Led NBA in rebounding, 1960, 1961, 1962, 1963, 1966, 1967, 1968, 1969, 1971, 1972, 1973. . . . Led NBA in field-goal percentage, 1961, 1963, 1965, 1966, 1967, 1968, 1969, 1972, 1973. . . . Led NBA in assists, 1968. . . . Named to THE SPORTING NEWS All-America First Team, 1958.

—DID YOU KNOW—

That 1985 Hall of Fame inductee Nate Thurmond posted the only known quadruple-double in NBA history? On the opening night of the 1974-75 season, the 6-11 Thurmond led Chicago to a 120-115 overtime victory over Atlanta by collecting 22 points, 14 rebounds, 13 assists and 12 blocked shots. Steals and blocked shots have only been recorded as official statistical categories in the NBA since 1973-74.

LARRY COSTELLO

Born July 2, 1931 at Minoa, N. Y.   Height 6:01.   Weight 188.
High School—Minoa, N. Y.
College—Niagara University, Niagara Falls, N. Y.
Drafted by Philadelphia on second round, 1954.

Sold by Philadelphia to Syracuse, October 10, 1957.
Syracuse franchise moved to Philadelphia, 1963.
Drafted by Milwaukee from Philadelphia in expansion draft, May 6, 1968.
Played in Eastern Basketball League with Wilkes-Barre Barons, 1965-66.

—COLLEGIATE PLAYING RECORD—

Year	G.	Min.	FGA	FGM	Pct.	FTA	FTM	Pct.	Reb.	Pts.	Avg.
50-51†					Statistics Unavailable						
51-52	28	....	...	131	....	87	58	.667	....	320	11.4
52-53	28	....	...	185	....	191	140	.733	....	510	18.2
53-54	29	....	...	160	....	152	125	.822	....	445	15.3
Totals	85	....	...	476	....	430	323	.751	....	1275	15.0

NBA REGULAR SEASON RECORD

Sea.—Team	G.	Min.	FGA	FGM	Pct.	FTA	FTM	Pct.	Reb.	Ast.	PF	Disq.	Pts.	Avg.
54-55—Philadelphia	19	463	139	46	.331	32	26	.813	49	78	37	0	118	6.2
56-57—Philadelphia	72	2111	497	186	.374	222	175	.788	323	236	182	2	547	7.6
57-58—Syracuse	72	2746	888	378	.426	378	320	.847	378	317	246	3	1076	14.9
58-59—Syracuse	70	2750	948	414	.437	349	280	.802	365	379	263	7	1108	15.8
59-60—Syracuse	71	2469	822	372	.453	289	249	.862	388	449	234	4	993	14.0
60-61—Syracuse	75	2167	844	407	.482	338	270	.799	292	413	286	9	1084	14.5
61-62—Syracuse	63	1854	726	310	.427	295	247	.837	245	359	220	5	867	13.7
62-63—Syracuse	78	2066	660	285	.432	327	288	.881	237	334	263	4	858	11.0
63-64—Philadelphia	45	1137	408	191	.476	170	147	.865	105	167	150	3	529	11.8
64-65—Philadelphia	64	1967	695	309	.445	277	243	.877	169	275	242	10	861	13.5
65-66—						Did Not Play								
66-67—Philadelphia	49	976	293	130	.444	133	120	.902	103	140	141	2	380	7.8
67-68—Philadelphia	28	492	148	67	.453	81	67	.827	51	68	62	0	201	7.2
Totals	706	21198	7068	3095	.438	2891	2432	.841	2705	3215	2326	49	8622	12.2

NBA PLAYOFF RECORD

Sea.—Team	G.	Min.	FGA	FGM	Pct.	FTA	FTM	Pct.	Reb.	Ast.	PF	Disq.	Pts.	Avg.
56-57—Philadelphia	2	16	8	3	.375	1	0	.000	5	2	3	0	6	3.0
57-58—Syracuse	3	134	34	10	.294	14	14	1.000	25	12	6	0	34	11.3
58-59—Syracuse	9	361	121	54	.446	61	51	.836	53	54	40	2	159	17.7
59-60—Syracuse	3	122	47	20	.425	12	10	.833	14	20	15	1	50	16.7
60-61—Syracuse	8	269	103	42	.408	55	47	.854	35	52	39	3	131	16.4
61-62—Syracuse	5	167	51	22	.431	33	29	.879	16	28	21	0	73	14.6
62-63—Syracuse	5	134	37	16	.432	23	19	.826	4	23	27	2	51	10.2
63-64—Philadelphia	5	36	14	3	.214	10	10	1.000	3	4	14	1	16	3.2
64-65—Philadelphia	10	207	53	22	.415	16	11	.688	12	20	43	2	55	5.5
66-67—Philadelphia	2	25	8	6	.750	5	5	1.000	4	3	2	0	17	8.5
Totals	52	1471	476	198	.416	230	196	.852	171	218	210	11	592	11.4

NBA ALL-STAR GAME RECORD

Season—Team	Min.	FGA	FGM	Pct.	FTA	FTM	Pct.	Reb.	Ast.	PF	Disq.	Pts.
1958—Syracuse	17	6	0	.000	1	1	1.000	1	4	2	0	1
1959—Syracuse	18	8	3	.375	1	1	1.000	3	3	1	0	7
1960—Syracuse	20	9	5	.556	0	0	.000	4	2	1	0	10
1961—Syracuse	5	2	1	.500	0	0	.000	0	0	2	0	2
1962—Syracuse				Selected—Injured, Did Not Play								
1965—Philadelphia	11	7	2	.286	0	0	.000	1	2	2	0	4
Totals	71	32	11	.344	2	2	1.000	9	11	8	0	24

MINOR LEAGUE REGULAR SEASON RECORD

			—2-Point—			—3-Point—							
Sea.—Team	G.	Min.	FGM	FGA	Pct.	FGM	FGA	Pct.	FTM	FTA	Pct.	Reb.	Ast.	Pts.	Avg.
65-66—Wilkes-Barre	12	....	54	...	...	2	...	....	53	59	.898	22	83	167	13.9

NBA COACHING RECORD

Sea.	Club	Regular Season			Playoffs			Sea.	Club	Regular Season			Playoffs	
		W.	L.	Pct.	Pos.	W.	L.			W.	L.	Pct.	Pos.	W.	L.
1968-69—Milwaukee		27	55	.329	7†			1974-75—Milwaukee		38	44	.463	4‡	..	..
1969-70—Milwaukee		56	26	.683	2†	5	5	1975-76—Milwaukee		38	44	.463	1‡	1	2
1970-71—Milwaukee		66	16	.805	*1†	12	2	1976-77—Milwaukee		3	15	.167	6‡	..	..
1971-72—Milwaukee		63	19	.768	1‡	6	5	1978-79—Chicago		20	36	.357	3‡	..	..
1972-73—Milwaukee		60	22	.732	1‡	2	4	Totals (10 seasons)		430	300	.589		37	23
1973-74—Milwaukee		59	23	.720	1‡	11	5								

*Won NBA championship.   †Eastern Division.   ‡Midwest Division.

COLLEGIATE COACHING RECORD

Sea. Club	Regular Season W.	L.	Pct.	Pos.	Playoffs W.	L.
1980-81—Utica	13	12	.520	..	..	..
1981-82—Utica	4	22	.154	..	..	..
Totals (2 seasons)	17	34	.333			

NOTE: Costello coached the Milwaukee Does of the Women's Professional Basketball League during 1979-80 season. He also coached at Minoa, N. Y., High School during 1965-66 season.

Named to NBA All-Star Second Team, 1961. . . . Led NBA in free-throw percentage, 1963 and 1965. . . . Member of NBA championship team, 1967. . . . Coach of NBA championship team, 1971.

ROBERT JOSEPH COUSY
(Bob)

Born August 9, 1928 at New York, N. Y.   Height 6:01.   Weight 175.

High School—Queens, N. Y., Andrew Jackson.

College—Holy Cross College, Worcester, Mass.

Drafted by Tri-Cities on first round, 1950.

Traded by Tri-Cities to Chicago for Gene Vance, 1950.
NBA rights drawn out of a hat by Boston for $8,500 in dispersal of Chicago franchise, 1950.
Traded by Boston to Cincinnati for Bill Dinwiddie, November 18, 1969.

—COLLEGIATE PLAYING RECORD—

Year	G.	Min.	FGA	FGM	Pct.	FTA	FTM	Pct.	Reb.	Pts.	Avg.
46-47	30	....	....	91	....	....	45	....	....	227	7.6
47-48	30	....	....	207	....	108	72	.667	....	486	16.2
48-49	27	....	....	195	....	134	90	.672	....	480	17.8
49-50	30	....	659	216	.328	199	150	.754	....	582	19.4
Totals	117	....	....	709	....	....	357	....	....	1775	15.2

NBA REGULAR SEASON RECORD

Sea.—Team	G.	Min.	FGA	FGM	Pct.	FTA	FTM	Pct.	Reb.	Ast.	PF	Disq.	Pts.	Avg.
50-51—Boston	69	....	1138	401	.352	365	276	.756	474	341	185	2	1078	15.6
51-52—Boston	66	2681	1388	512	.369	506	409	.808	421	441	190	5	1433	21.7
52-53—Boston	71	2945	1320	464	.352	587	479	.816	449	547	227	4	1407	19.8
53-54—Boston	72	2857	1262	486	.385	522	411	.787	394	518	201	3	1383	19.2
54-55—Boston	71	2747	1316	522	.397	570	460	.807	424	557	165	1	1504	21.2
55-56—Boston	72	2767	1223	440	.360	564	476	.844	492	642	206	2	1356	18.8
56-57—Boston	64	2364	1264	478	.378	442	363	.821	309	478	134	0	1319	20.6
57-58—Boston	65	2222	1262	445	.353	326	277	.850	322	463	136	1	1167	18.0
58-59—Boston	65	2403	1260	484	.384	385	329	.855	359	557	135	0	1297	20.0
59-60—Boston	75	2588	1481	568	.383	403	319	.791	352	715	146	2	1455	19.4
60-61—Boston	76	2468	1382	513	.371	452	352	.779	331	587	196	0	1378	18.1
61-62—Boston	75	2114	1181	462	.391	333	251	.754	261	584	135	0	1175	15.7
62-63—Boston	76	1975	988	392	.397	298	219	.735	193	515	175	0	1003	13.2
63-64 through 68-69						Voluntarily Retired								
69-70—Cincinnati	7	34	3	1	.333	3	3	1.000	5	10	11	0	5	0.7
Totals	924	....	16468	6168	.375	5756	4624	.803	4786	6955	2242	20	16960	18.4

NBA PLAYOFF RECORD

Sea.—Team	G.	Min.	FGA	FGM	Pct.	FTA	FTM	Pct.	Reb.	Ast.	PF	Disq.	Pts.	Avg.
50-51—Boston	2	....	42	9	.214	12	10	.833	15	12	8	...	28	14.0
51-52—Boston	3	138	65	26	.400	44	41	.932	12	19	13	1	93	31.0
52-53—Boston	6	270	120	46	.383	73	61	.836	25	37	21	0	153	25.5
53-54—Boston	6	260	116	33	.284	75	60	.800	32	38	20	0	126	21.0
54-55—Boston	7	299	139	53	.381	48	46	.958	43	65	26	0	152	21.7
55-56—Boston	3	124	56	28	.500	25	23	.920	24	26	4	0	79	26.3
56-57—Boston	10	440	207	67	.324	91	68	.747	61	93	27	0	202	20.2
57-58—Boston	11	457	196	67	.342	75	64	.853	71	82	20	0	198	18.0
58-59—Boston	11	460	221	72	.326	94	70	.745	76	119	28	0	214	19.5
59-60—Boston	13	468	262	80	.305	51	39	.765	48	116	27	0	199	15.3
60-61—Boston	10	337	147	50	.340	88	67	.761	43	91	33	1	167	16.7
61-62—Boston	14	474	241	86	.357	76	52	.684	64	123	43	0	224	16.0
62-63—Boston	13	413	204	72	.353	47	39	.830	32	116	44	2	183	14.1
Totals	109	....	2016	689	.326	799	640	.801	546	937	314	4	2018	18.5

NBA ALL-STAR GAME RECORD

Season—Team	Min.	FGA	FGM	Pct.	FTA	FTM	Pct.	Reb.	Ast.	PF	Disq.	Pts.
1951—Boston	....	12	2	.167	5	4	.800	9	8	3	0	8
1952—Boston	33	14	4	.286	2	1	.500	4	13	3	0	9
1953—Boston	36	11	4	.364	7	7	1.000	5	3	1	0	15
1954—Boston	34	15	6	.400	8	8	1.000	11	4	1	0	20

BOB COUSY

Season—Team	Min.	FGA	FGM	Pct.	FTA	FTM	Pct.	Reb.	Ast.	PF	Disq.	Pts.
1955—Boston	35	14	7	.500	7	6	.857	9	5	1	0	20
1956—Boston	24	8	2	.250	4	3	.750	7	2	6	1	7
1957—Boston	28	14	4	.286	2	2	1.000	5	7	0	0	10
1958—Boston	31	20	8	.400	6	4	.667	5	10	0	0	20
1959—Boston	32	8	4	.500	6	5	.833	5	4	0	0	13
1960—Boston	26	7	1	.143	0	0	.000	5	8	2	0	2
1961—Boston	33	11	2	.182	0	0	.000	3	8	6	1	4
1962—Boston	31	13	4	.308	4	3	.750	6	8	2	0	11
1963—Boston	25	11	4	.364	0	0	.000	4	6	2	0	8
Totals	....	158	52	.329	51	43	.843	78	86	27	2	147

COLLEGIATE COACHING RECORD

Sea. Club	W.	L.	Pct.	Pos.
1963-64—Boston College	10	11	.455	...
1964-65—Boston College	22	7	.759	...
1965-66—Boston College	21	5	.808	...
1966-67—Boston College	23	3	.885	...
1967-68—Boston College	17	8	.680	...
1968-69—Boston College	24	4	.857	...
Totals (6 seasons)	117	38	.755	

NOTE: Cousy guided Boston College to NIT in 1965, 1966 and 1969 and to NCAA Tournament in 1967 and 1968.

NBA COACHING RECORD

Sea. Club	Regular Season W.	L.	Pct.	Pos.	Playoffs W.	L.	Sea. Club	Regular Season W.	L.	Pct.	Pos.	Playoffs W.	L.
1969-70—Cincinnati	36	46	.439	5†	...	...	1972-73—K.C.-Omaha	36	46	.439	4§	...	...
1970-71—Cincinnati	33	49	.402	3‡	...	...	1973-74—K.C.-Omaha	6	16	.375	...§	...	...
1971-72—Cincinnati	30	52	.366	3‡	...	...	Totals (5 seasons)	141	209	.403		...	...

†Eastern Division. ‡Central Division. §Midwest Division.

Elected to Naismith Memorial Basketball Hall of Fame, 1970. . . . Named to NBA 25th Anniversary All-Time Team, 1970, and 35th Anniversary All-Time Team, 1980. . . . NBA Most Valuable Player, 1957. . . . Named to NBA All-Star First Team, 1952, 1953, 1954, 1955, 1956, 1957, 1958, 1959, 1960, 1961. . . . NBA All-Star Second Team, 1962 and 1963. . . . Holds NBA record for most assists in one half, 19, vs. Minneapolis, February 27, 1959. . . . Holds NBA playoff game records for most free-throw attempts, 32, and most free throws made, 30, vs. Syracuse, March 21, 1953. . . . Holds NBA playoff game record for most points in an overtime period, 12, vs. Syracuse, March 17, 1954. . . . Shares NBA championship series record for most assists in one quarter, 8, vs. St. Louis, April 9, 1957. . . . NBA All-Star Game MVP, 1954 and 1957. . . . Holds NBA All-Star Game record for most career assists, 86. . . . Member of NBA championship teams, 1957, 1959, 1960, 1961, 1962, 1963. . . . Led NBA in assists, 1953, 1954, 1955, 1956, 1957, 1958, 1959, 1960. . . . Named to THE SPORTING NEWS All-America First Team, 1950. . . . Named to THE SPORTING NEWS All-America Second Team, 1949. . . . Member of NCAA championship team, 1947. . . . Commissioner of American Soccer League, 1975 through mid-1980 season.

DAVID WILLIAM COWENS
(Dave)

Born October 25, 1948 at Newport, Ky. Height 6:09. Weight 230.

High School—Newport, Ky., Catholic.

College—Florida State University, Tallahassee, Fla.

Drafted by Boston on first round, 1970 (4th pick).

Traded by Boston to Milwaukee for Quinn Buckner, September 9, 1982.

—COLLEGIATE RECORD—

Year	G.	Min.	FGA	FGM	Pct.	FTA	FTM	Pct.	Reb.	Pts.	Avg.
66-67†	18	....	208	105	.505	90	49	.544	357	259	14.4
67-68	27	....	383	206	.538	131	96	.733	456	508	18.8
68-69	25	....	384	202	.526	164	104	.634	437	508	20.3
69-70	26	....	355	174	.490	169	115	.680	447	463	17.8
Varsity Totals	78	....	1122	582	.519	464	315	.679	1340	1479	19.0

NBA REGULAR SEASON RECORD

Sea.—Team	G.	Min.	FGA	FGM	Pct.	FTA	FTM	Pct.	Reb.	Ast.	PF	Disq.	Pts.	Avg.
70-71—Boston	81	3076	1302	550	.422	373	273	.732	1216	228	350	15	1373	17.0
71-72—Boston	79	3186	1357	657	.484	243	175	.720	1203	245	314	10	1489	18.8
72-73—Boston	82	3425	1637	740	.452	262	204	.779	1329	333	311	6	1684	20.5

Sea.—Team	G.	Min.	FGA	FGM	Pct.	FTA	FTM	Pct.	Rebounds Off.	Def.	Tot.	Ast.	PF	Dq.	Stl.	Blk.	Pts.	Avg.
73-74—Boston	80	3352	1475	645	.437	274	228	.832	264	993	1257	354	294	7	95	101	1518	19.0
74-75—Boston	65	2632	1199	569	.475	244	191	.783	229	729	958	296	243	7	87	73	1329	20.4
75-76—Boston	78	3101	1305	611	.468	340	257	.756	335	911	1246	325	314	10	94	71	1479	19.0

Sea.—Team	G.	Min.	FGA	FGM	Pct.	FTA	FTM	Pct.	Off.	Def.	Tot.	Ast.	PF	Dq.	Stl.	Blk.	Pts.	Avg.
									—Rebounds—									
76-77—Boston	50	1888	756	328	.434	198	162	.818	147	550	697	248	181	7	46	49	818	16.4
77-78—Boston	77	3215	1220	598	.490	284	239	.842	248	830	1078	351	297	5	102	67	1435	18.6
78-79—Boston	68	2517	1010	488	.483	187	151	.807	152	500	652	242	263	16	76	51	1127	16.6
79-80—Boston	66	2159	932	422	.453	122	95	.779	126	408	534	206	216	2	69	61	940	14.2
80-81 and 81-82					Voluntarily Retired													
82-83—Milwaukee	40	1014	306	136	.444	63	52	.825	73	201	274	82	137	4	30	15	324	8.1
Totals	766	29565	12499	5744	.460	2590	2027	.783			10444	2910	2920	90	599	488	13516	17.6

Three-Point Field Goals: 1979-80, 1-for-12 (.083). 1982-83, 0-for-2. Totals, 1-for-14 (.071).

NBA PLAYOFF RECORD

Sea.—Team	G.	Min.	FGA	FGM	Pct.	FTA	FTM	Pct.	Reb.	Ast.	PF	Disq.	Pts.	Avg.
71-72—Boston	11	441	156	71	.455	47	28	.596	152	33	50	2	170	15.5
72-73—Boston	13	598	273	129	.473	41	27	.659	216	48	54	2	285	21.9

Sea.—Team	G.	Min.	FGA	FGM	Pct.	FTA	FTM	Pct.	Off.	Def.	Tot.	Ast.	PF	Dq.	Stl.	Blk.	Pts.	Avg.
									—Rebounds—									
73-74—Boston	18	772	370	161	.435	59	47	.797	60	180	240	66	85	2	21	17	369	20.5
74-75—Boston	11	479	236	101	.428	26	23	.885	49	132	181	46	50	2	18	6	225	20.5
75-76—Boston	18	798	341	156	.457	87	66	.759	87	209	296	83	85	4	22	13	378	21.0
76-77—Boston	9	379	148	66	.446	22	17	.773	29	105	134	36	37	3	8	13	149	16.6
79-80—Boston	9	301	103	49	.476	11	10	.909	18	48	66	21	37	0	9	7	108	12.0
Totals	89	3768	1627	733	.451	293	218	.744			1285	333	398	15	78	56	1684	18.9

Three-Point Field Goals: 1979-80, 0-for-2.

NBA ALL-STAR GAME RECORD

Season—Team	Min.	FGA	FGM	Pct.	FTA	FTM	Pct.	Reb.	Ast.	PF	Disq.	Pts.
1972—Boston.......................	32	12	5	.417	5	4	.800	20	1	4	0	14
1973—Boston.......................	30	15	7	.467	1	1	1.000	13	1	2	0	15

Season—Team	Min.	FGA	FGM	Pct.	FTA	FTM	Pct.	Off.	Def.	Tot.	Ast.	PF	Dq.	Stl.	Blk.	Pts.
								—Rebounds—								
1974—Boston............	26	10	5	.500	3	1	.333	6	6	12	1	3	0	0	1	11
1975—Boston............	15	7	3	.429	0	0	.000	0	6	6	3	4	0	1	0	6
1976—Boston............	23	13	6	.462	5	4	.800	8	8	16	1	3	0	1	0	16
1977—Boston............							Selected—Injured, Did Not Play									
1978—Boston............	28	9	7	.778	0	0	.000	6	8	14	5	5	0	2	0	14
Totals	154	66	33	.500	14	10	.714			81	12	21	0	4	1	76

NBA COACHING RECORD

		Regular Season				Playoffs	
Sea.	Club	W.	L.	Pct.	Pos.	W.	L.
1978-79—Boston		27	41	.397	5†	...	...

†Atlantic Division.

NBA Most Valuable Player, 1973. . . . Named to NBA All-Star Second Team, 1973, 1975, 1976. . . . NBA All-Defensive First Team, 1976. . . . NBA All-Defensive Second Team, 1975 and 1980. . . . NBA Co-Rookie of the Year, 1971. . . . NBA All-Rookie Team, 1971. . . . NBA All-Star Game MVP, 1973. . . . Member of NBA championship teams, 1974 and 1976. . . . Named to THE SPORTING NEWS All-America Second Team, 1970.

ROBERT E. DAVIES
(Bob)

Born January 15, 1920 at Harrisburg, Pa. Height 6:01. Weight 175.

High School—Harrisburg, Pa., John Harris.

College—Seton Hall University, South Orange, N. J.

Signed as free agent by Rochester NBL, 1945.

In military service during 1942-43, 1943-44 and 1944-45 seasons.

—COLLEGIATE RECORD—

Year	G.	Min.	FGA	FGM	Pct.	FTA	FTM	Pct.	Reb.	Pts.	Avg.
38-39†					Statistics Unavailable						
39-40	18	....	....	78		....	56		....	212	11.8
40-41	22	....	....	91		....	42		....	224	10.2
41-42	19	....	....	81		....	63		....	225	11.8
Varsity Totals	59	....	....	250		....	161		....	661	11.2

NBL AND NBA REGULAR SEASON RECORD

Sea.—Team	G.	Min.	FGA	FGM	Pct.	FTA	FTM	Pct.	Reb.	Ast.	PF	Disq.	Pts.	Avg.
45-46—Roch.-NBL	27	....	....	86	....	103	70	.680	....	....	85	..	242	9.0
46-47—Roch.-NBL	32	....	....	166	....	166	130	.783	....	....	90	..	462	14.4
47-48—Roch.-NBL	48	....	....	176	....	161	121	.752	....	....	111	..	473	9.9
48-49—Rochester	60	....	871	317	.364	348	270	.776	....	321	197	..	904	15.1
49-50—Rochester	64	....	887	317	.357	347	261	.752	....	294	187	..	895	14.0
50-51—Rochester	63	....	877	326	.372	381	303	.795	197	287	208	7	955	15.2
51-52—Rochester	65	2394	990	379	.383	379	294	.776	189	390	269	10	1052	16.2

Sea.—Team	G.	Min.	FGA	FGM	Pct.	FTA	FTM	Pct.	Reb.	Ast.	PF	Disq.	Pts.	Avg.
52-53—Rochester	66	2216	880	339	.385	466	351	.753	195	280	261	7	1029	15.6
53-54—Rochester	72	2137	777	288	.371	433	311	.718	194	323	224	4	887	12.3
54-55—Rochester	72	1870	785	326	.415	293	220	.751	205	155	220	2	872	12.1
Totals	569	....	....	2720	....	3077	2331	.758	....	....	1852	..	7771	13.7

NBL AND NBA PLAYOFF RECORD

Sea.—Team	G.	Min.	FGA	FGM	Pct.	FTA	FTM	Pct.	Reb.	Ast.	PF	Disq.	Pts.	Avg.
45-46—Roch.-NBL	7	....	...	28	....	41	30	.732	....	....	13	..	86	12.3
46-47—Roch.-NBL	11	....	...	54	....	63	43	.683	....	....	30	..	151	13.7
47-48—Roch.-NBL	11	....	....	56	....	64	49	.766	....	....	26	..	161	14.6
48-49—Rochester	4	....	51	19	.373	13	10	.769	....	13	12	..	48	12.0
49-50—Rochester	2	....	17	4	.235	8	7	.875	....	9	11	..	15	7.5
50-51—Rochester	14	....	234	79	.338	80	64	.800	43	75	45	1	222	15.9
51-52—Rochester	6	233	92	37	.402	55	45	.818	13	28	18	0	119	19.8
52-53—Rochester	3	91	29	6	.207	20	14	.700	4	14	11	0	26	8.7
53-54—Rochester	6	172	52	17	.327	23	17	.739	12	14	16	0	51	8.5
54-55—Rochester	3	75	33	11	.333	4	3	.750	6	9	11	0	25	8.3
Totals	67	....	....	311	....	371	282	.752	....	....	193	..	904	13.5

NBA ALL-STAR GAME RECORD

Season—Team	Min.	FGA	FGM	Pct.	FTA	FTM	Pct.	Reb.	Ast.	PF	Disq.	Pts.
1951—Rochester	....	6	4	.667	5	5	1.000	5	5	3	0	13
1952—Rochester	27	11	4	.364	0	0	.000	0	5	4	0	8
1953—Rochester	17	7	3	.429	6	3	.500	3	2	2	0	9
1954—Rochester	31	16	8	.500	3	2	.667	5	5	4	0	18
Totals	....	40	19	.475	14	10	.714	13	17	13	0	48

Named to NBA 25th Anniversary All-Time Team, 1970. . . . Elected to Naismith Memorial Basketball Hall of Fame, 1969. . . . NBA All-Star First Team, 1949, 1950, 1951, 1952. . . . NBA All-Star Second Team, 1953. . . . Led NBA in assists, 1949. . . . Member of NBA championship team, 1951. . . . NBL All-Star First Team, 1947 and 1948. . . . NBL Most Valuable Player, 1947. . . . Member of NBL championship team, 1946. . . . BAA All-Star First Team, 1949.

DAVID ALBERT DeBUSSCHERE
(Dave)

Born October 16, 1940 at Detroit, Mich.   Height 6:06.   Weight 235.

High School—Detroit, Mich., Austin Catholic.

College—University of Detroit, Detroit, Mich.

Drafted by Detroit on first round (territorial choice), 1962.

Traded by Detroit to New York for Walt Bellamy and Howard Komives, December 19, 1968.

—COLLEGIATE RECORD—

Year	G.	Min.	FGA	FGM	Pct.	FTA	FTM	Pct.	Reb.	Pts.	Avg.
58-59†	15	....	306	144	.471	101	68	.673	305	356	23.7
59-60	27	....	665	288	.433	196	115	.587	540	691	25.6
60-61	27	....	636	256	.403	155	86	.555	514	598	22.1
61-62	26	....	616	267	.433	242	162	.669	498	696	26.8
Varsity Totals	80	....	1917	811	.423	593	363	.612	1552	1985	24.8

NBA REGULAR SEASON RECORD

Sea.—Team	G.	Min.	FGA	FGM	Pct.	FTA	FTM	Pct.	Reb.	Ast.	PF	Disq.	Pts.	Avg.
62-63—Detroit	80	2352	944	406	.430	287	206	.718	694	207	247	2	1018	12.7
63-64—Detroit	15	304	133	52	.391	43	25	.581	105	23	32	1	129	8.6
64-65—Detroit	79	2769	1196	508	.425	437	306	.700	874	253	242	5	1322	16.7
65-66—Detroit	79	2696	1284	524	.408	378	249	.659	916	209	252	5	1297	16.4
66-67—Detroit	78	2897	1278	531	.415	512	361	.705	924	216	297	7	1423	18.2
67-68—Detroit	80	3125	1295	573	.442	435	289	.664	1081	181	304	3	1435	17.9
68-69—Det.-N. Y.	76	2943	1140	506	.444	328	229	.698	888	191	290	6	1241	16.3
69-70—New York	79	2627	1082	488	.451	256	176	.688	790	194	244	2	1152	14.6
70-71—New York	81	2891	1243	523	.421	312	217	.696	901	220	237	2	1263	15.6
71-72—New York	80	3072	1218	520	.427	265	193	.728	901	291	219	1	1233	15.4
72-73—New York	77	2827	1224	532	.435	260	194	.746	787	259	215	1	1258	16.3

Sea.—Team	G.	Min.	FGA	FGM	Pct.	FTA	FTM	Pct.	—Rebounds— Off.	Def.	Tot.	Ast.	PF	Dq.	Stl.	Blk.	Pts.	Avg.
73-74—New York	71	2699	1212	559	.461	217	164	.756	134	623	757	253	222	2	67	39	1282	18.1
Totals	875	31202	13249	5722	.432	3730	2609	.699			9618	2497	2801	37			14053	16.1

NBA PLAYOFF RECORD

Sea.—Team	G.	Min.	FGA	FGM	Pct.	FTA	FTM	Pct.	Reb.	Ast.	PF	Disq.	Pts.	Avg.
62-63—Detroit	4	159	59	25	.424	44	30	.682	63	6	14	1	80	20.0
67-68—Detroit	6	263	106	45	.425	45	26	.578	97	13	23	0	116	19.3
68-69—New York	10	419	174	61	.351	50	41	.820	148	33	43	0	163	16.3
69-70—New York	19	701	309	130	.421	68	45	.662	220	46	63	1	305	16.1
70-71—New York	12	488	202	84	.416	44	29	.659	156	22	40	1	197	16.4
71-72—New York	16	616	242	109	.450	64	48	.750	193	37	51	2	266	16.6
72-73—New York	17	632	265	117	.442	40	31	.775	179	58	57	0	265	15.6

DAVE DeBUSSCHERE

Sea.—Team	G.	Min.	FGA	FGM	Pct.	FTA	FTM	Pct.	Off.	Def.	Tot.	Ast.	PF	Dq.	Stl.	Blk.	Pts.	Avg.
										—Rebounds—								
73-74—New York	12	404	166	63	380	29	18	.621	25	74	99	38	36	0	7	4	144	12.0
Totals	96	3682	1523	634	416	384	268	.698			1155	253	327	5			1536	16.0

NBA ALL-STAR GAME RECORD

Season—Team	Min.	FGA	FGM	Pct.	FTA	FTM	Pct.	Reb.	Ast.	PF	Disq.	Pts.
1966—Detroit	22	14	1	.071	2	2	1.000	6	1	1	0	4
1967—Detroit	25	17	11	.647	0	0	.000	6	0	1	0	22
1968—Detroit	12	3	0	.000	0	0	.000	4	0	1	0	0
1970—New York	14	10	5	.500	0	0	.000	7	2	1	0	10
1971—New York	19	7	4	.571	0	0	.000	7	3	3	0	8
1972—New York	26	8	4	.500	0	0	.000	11	0	2	0	8
1973—New York	25	8	4	.500	2	1	.500	7	2	1	0	9

Season—Team	Min.	FGA	FGM	Pct.	FTA	FTM	Pct.	Off.	Def.	Tot.	Ast.	PF	Dq.	Stl.	Blk.	Pts.
							—Rebounds—									
1974—New York	24	14	8	.571	0	0	.000	2	1	3	3	2	0	1	0	16
Totals	167	81	37	.457	4	3	.750			51	11	12	0			77

NBA COACHING RECORD

Sea. Club	Regular Season W.	L.	Pct.	Pos.	Playoffs W.	L.	Sea. Club	Regular Season W.	L.	Pct.	Pos.	Playoffs W.	L.
1964-65—Detroit	29	40	.420	4†	..	..	1966-67—Detroit	28	45	.384	5†	..	..
1965-66—Detroit	22	58	.275	5†	..	..	Totals (3 seasons)	79	143	.356		..	..

†Western Division.

Elected to Naismith Memorial Basketball Hall of Fame, 1982. . . . Named to NBA All-Star Second Team, 1969. . . . NBA All-Defensive First Team, 1969, 1970, 1971, 1972, 1973, 1974. . . . Holds NBA All-Star Game record for most field goals made in one quarter, 8, in 1967. . . . Member of NBA championship teams, 1970 and 1973. . . . Youngest coach (24) in NBA history. . . . ABA Commissioner during 1975-76 season. . . . Played major league baseball as a pitcher with the Chicago White Sox, 1962 and 1963 (had 3-4 record in 36 games).

LAWRENCE MICHAEL FOUST
(Larry)

Born June 24, 1928 at Painesville, O.   Height 6:09. Weight 250.

High School—Philadelphia, Pa., South Catholic.

College—LaSalle College, Philadelphia, Pa.

Drafted by Chicago on first round, 1950.

Draft rights selected by Fort Wayne in dispersal of Chicago franchise, 1950.
Fort Wayne franchise transferred to Detroit, April, 1957.
Traded by Detroit with cash to Minneapolis for Walt Dukes, September 12, 1957.
Traded by Minneapolis to St. Louis for Charlie Share, cash and draft rights to Nick Mantis and Willie Merriweather, February 1, 1960.

—COLLEGIATE RECORD—

Year	G.	Min.	FGA	FGM	Pct.	FTA	FTM	Pct.	Reb.	Pts.	Avg.
46-47	26	....	...	103	....	...	49	....	....	255	9.8
47-48	24	....	...	157	....	...	87	....	....	401	16.7
48-49	28	....	...	177	....	164	99	.604	....	453	16.2
49-50	25	....	...	136	....	122	83	.680	....	355	14.2
Totals	103	....	...	573	....	...	318	....	....	1464	14.2

NBA REGULAR SEASON RECORD

Sea.—Team	G.	Min.	FGA	FGM	Pct.	FTA	FTM	Pct.	Reb.	Ast.	PF	Disq.	Pts.	Avg.
50-51—Ft. Wayne	68	....	944	327	.346	396	261	.659	681	90	247	6	915	13.5
51-52—Ft. Wayne	66	2615	989	390	.394	394	267	.678	880	200	245	10	1047	15.9
52-53—Ft. Wayne	67	2303	865	311	.360	465	336	.723	769	151	267	16	958	14.3
53-54—Ft. Wayne	72	2693	919	376	.409	475	338	.712	967	161	258	4	1090	15.1
54-55—Ft. Wayne	70	2264	818	398	.487	513	393	.766	700	118	264	9	1189	17.0
55-56—Ft. Wayne	72	2024	821	367	.447	555	432	.778	648	127	263	7	1166	16.2
56-57—Ft. Wayne	61	1533	617	243	.394	380	273	.718	555	71	221	7	759	12.4
57-58—Minn.	72	2200	982	391	.398	566	428	.756	876	108	299	11	1210	16.8
58-59—Minn.	72	1933	771	301	.390	366	280	.765	627	91	233	5	882	12.3
59-60—Minn.-StL.	72	1964	766	312	.407	320	253	.791	621	96	241	7	877	12.2
60-61—St. Louis	68	1208	489	194	.397	208	164	.788	389	77	165	0	552	8.1
61-62—St. Louis	57	1153	433	204	.471	178	145	.815	328	78	186	2	553	9.7
Totals	817	21880	9414	3814	.405	4816	3570	.741	8041	1368	2889	84	11198	13.7

NBA PLAYOFF RECORD

Sea.—Team	G.	Min.	FGA	FGM	Pct.	FTA	FTM	Pct.	Reb.	Ast.	PF	Disq.	Pts.	Avg.
50-51—Ft. Wayne	3	....	45	14	.311	10	8	.800	37	5	5	....	36	12.0
51-52—Ft. Wayne	2	77	23	12	.522	7	6	.857	30	5	8	1	30	15.0

Sea.—Team	G.	Min.	FGA	FGM	Pct.	FTA	FTM	Pct.	Reb.	Ast.	PF	Disq.	Pts.	Avg.
52-53—Ft. Wayne	8	332	121	48	.397	68	57	.838	111	6	34	2	153	19.1
53-54—Ft. Wayne	4	129	41	11	.268	25	19	.760	38	7	21	2	41	10.3
54-55—Ft. Wayne	11	331	152	60	.395	73	52	.712	107	26	43	0	172	15.6
55-56—Ft. Wayne	10	289	130	49	.377	89	70	.787	127	14	38	2	168	16.8
56-57—Ft. Wayne	2	64	23	13	.565	23	19	.826	25	6	10	0	45	22.5
58-59—Minn.	13	404	134	56	.418	50	41	.820	136	12	47	2	153	11.8
59-60—St. Louis	12	205	74	29	.391	25	20	.800	68	11	36	0	78	6.5
60-61—St. Louis	8	89	20	9	.450	14	8	.571	28	2	13	0	26	3.2
Totals	73	1920	763	301	.394	384	300	.781	707	94	255	9	902	12.4

NBA ALL-STAR GAME RECORD

Season—Team	Min.	FGA	FGM	Pct.	FTA	FTM	Pct.	Reb.	Ast.	PF	Disq.	Pts.
1951—Fort Wayne	..	6	1	.167	0	0	.000	5	2	3	0	2
1952—Fort Wayne					Selected—Injured, Did Not Play							
1953—Fort Wayne	18	7	5	.714	0	0	.000	6	0	4	0	10
1954—Fort Wayne	27	9	1	.111	1	1	1.000	15	0	1	0	3
1955—Fort Wayne	24	10	3	.300	1	1	1.000	7	1	1	0	7
1956—Fort Wayne	20	9	3	.333	4	3	.750	4	0	1	0	9
1958—Minneapolis	13	4	1	.250	8	8	1.000	3	0	3	0	10
1959—Minneapolis	16	9	3	.333	2	2	1.000	9	0	3	0	8
Totals	118	54	17	.315	16	15	.938	49	3	16	0	49

Named to NBA All-Star First Team, 1955. . . . NBA All-Star Second Team, 1952. . . . Led NBA in field-goal percentage, 1955. . . . Shared lead in NBA for rebounding, 1952. . . . Named to THE SPORTING NEWS All-America Fifth Team, 1950.

WALT FRAZIER
(Clyde)

Born March 29, 1945 at Atlanta, Ga. Height 6:04. Weight 205.

High School—Atlanta, Ga., David Howard.

College—Southern Illinois University, Carbondale, Ill.

Drafted by New York on first round, 1967 (5th pick).

Acquired from New York by Cleveland as compensation for anticipated signing of Veteran Free Agent Jim Cleamons, October 7, 1977.

Waived by Cleveland, October 19, 1979.

—COLLEGIATE RECORD—

Year	G.	Min.	FGA	FGM	Pct.	FTA	FTM	Pct.	Reb.	Pts.	Avg.
63-64†	14	....	225	133	.591	85	52	.612	129	318	22.7
64-65	24	....	353	161	.456	111	88	.793	221	410	17.1
65-66					Did Not Play—Ineligible						
66-67	26	....	397	192	.484	126	90	.714	310	474	18.2
Varsity Totals	50	....	750	353	.471	237	178	.751	531	884	17.7

NBA REGULAR SEASON RECORD

Sea.—Team	G.	Min.	FGA	FGM	Pct.	FTA	FTM	Pct.	Reb.	Ast.	PF	Disq.	Pts.	Avg.
67-68—New York	74	1588	568	256	.451	235	154	.655	313	305	199	2	666	9.0
68-69—New York	80	2949	1052	531	.505	457	341	.746	499	635	245	2	1403	17.5
69-70—New York	77	3040	1158	600	.518	547	409	.748	465	629	203	1	1609	20.9
70-71—New York	80	3455	1317	651	.494	557	434	.779	544	536	240	1	1736	21.7
71-72—New York	77	3126	1307	669	.512	557	450	.808	513	446	185	0	1788	23.2
72-73—New York	78	3181	1389	681	.490	350	286	.817	570	461	186	0	1648	21.1

Sea.—Team	G.	Min.	FGA	FGM	Pct.	FTA	FTM	Pct.	Off.	Def.	Tot.	Ast.	PF	Dq.	Stl.	Blk.	Pts.	Avg.
73-74—New York	80	3338	1429	674	.472	352	295	.838	120	416	536	551	212	2	161	15	1643	20.5
74-75—New York	78	3204	1391	672	.483	400	331	.828	90	375	465	474	205	2	190	14	1675	21.5
75-76—New York	59	2427	969	470	.485	226	186	.823	79	321	400	351	163	1	106	9	1126	19.1
76-77—Knicks	76	2687	1089	532	.489	336	259	.771	52	241	293	403	194	0	132	9	1323	17.4
77-78—Cleveland	51	1664	714	336	.471	180	153	.850	54	155	209	209	124	1	77	9	825	16.2
78-79—Cleveland	12	279	122	54	.443	27	21	.778	7	13	20	32	22	0	13	2	129	10.8
79-80—Cleveland	3	27	11	4	.364	2	2	1.000	1	2	3	8	2	0	2	1	10	3.3
Totals	825	30965	12516	6130	.490	4226	3321	.786			4830	5040	2180	12	681	59	15581	18.9

Three-Point Field Goals: 1979-80, 0-for-1.

NBA PLAYOFF RECORD

Sea.—Team	G.	Min.	FGA	FGM	Pct.	FTA	FTM	Pct.	Reb.	Ast.	PF	Disq.	Pts.	Avg.
67-68—New York	4	119	33	12	.364	18	14	.778	22	25	12	0	38	9.5
68-69—New York	10	415	177	89	.503	57	34	.596	74	91	30	0	212	21.2
69-70—New York	19	834	247	118	.478	89	68	.764	149	156	53	0	304	16.0
70-71—New York	12	501	204	108	.529	75	55	.733	70	54	45	0	271	22.6
71-72—New York	16	704	276	148	.536	125	92	.736	112	98	48	0	388	24.3
72-73—New York	17	765	292	150	.514	94	73	.777	124	106	52	1	373	21.9

WALT FRAZIER

Sea.—Team	G.	Min.	FGA	FGM	Pct.	FTA	FTM	Pct.	Off.	Def.	Tot.	Ast.	PF	Dq.	Stl.	Blk.	Pts.	Avg.
									—Rebounds—									
73-74—New York	12	491	225	113	.502	49	44	.898	21	74	95	48	41	1	21	4	270	22.5
74-75—New York	3	124	46	29	.630	16	13	.813	3	17	20	21	4	0	11	0	71	23.7
Totals..............	93	3953	1500	767	.511	523	393	.751			666	599	285	2	32	4	1927	20.7

NBA ALL-STAR GAME RECORD

Season—Team	Min.	FGA	FGM	Pct.	FTA	FTM	Pct.	Reb.	Ast.	PF	Disq.	Pts.
1970—New York	24	7	3	.429	2	1	.500	3	4	2	0	7
1971—New York	26	9	3	.333	0	0	.000	6	5	2	0	6
1972—New York	25	11	7	.636	2	1	.500	3	5	2	0	15
1973—New York	26	15	5	.333	0	0	.000	6	2	1	0	10

Season—Team	Min.	FGA	FGM	Pct.	FTA	FTM	Pct.	Off.	Def.	Tot.	Ast.	PF	Dq.	Stl.	Blk.	Pts.
								—Rebounds—								
1974—New York	28	12	5	.417	2	2	1.000	1	1	2	5	1	0	3	0	12
1975—New York ...	35	17	10	.588	11	10	.909	0	5	5	2	2	0	4	0	30
1976—New York ...	19	7	2	.286	4	4	1.000	0	2	2	3	0	0	2	0	8
Totals..............	183	78	35	.449	21	18	.857			27	26	10	0	9	0	88

Named to NBA All-Star First Team, 1970, 1972, 1974, 1975. . . . NBA All-Star Second Team, 1971 and 1973. . . . NBA All-Defensive First Team, 1969, 1970, 1971, 1972, 1973, 1974, 1975. . . . NBA All-Rookie Team, 1968. . . . NBA All-Star Game MVP, 1975. . . . Member of NBA championship teams, 1970 and 1973. . . . Named to THE SPORTING NEWS All-America Second Team, 1967.

JOSEPH E. FULKS
(Joe)

Born October 26, 1921 at Birmingham, Ky.   Height 6:05.   Weight 190.

High Schools—Birmingham, Ky. (Fr.-Jr.), and Kuttawa, Ky. (Sr.).

College—Murray State College, Murray, Ky.

Signed by Philadelphia BAA, 1946.

—COLLEGIATE RECORD—

Year	G.	Min.	FGA	FGM	Pct.	FTA	FTM	Pct.	Reb.	Pts.	Avg.
41-42	22	....	...	117	....	76	50	.658	....	284	12.9
42-43	25	....	...	135	....	100	67	.670	....	337	13.5
Totals	47	....	...	252	....	176	117	.664	....	621	13.2

NOTE: In military service (Marines) during 1943-44, 1944-45 and 1945-46 seasons.

NBA REGULAR SEASON RECORD

Sea.—Team	G.	Min.	FGA	FGM	Pct.	FTA	FTM	Pct.	Reb.	Ast.	PF	Disq.	Pts.	Avg.
1946-47—Philadelphia	60	....	1557	475	.305	601	439	.730	....	25	199	..	1389	23.2
1947-48—Philadelphia	43	....	1258	326	.259	390	297	.762	....	26	162	..	949	22.1
1948-49—Philadelphia	60	....	1689	529	.313	638	502	.787	....	74	262	..	1560	26.0
1949-50—Philadelphia	68	....	1209	336	.278	421	293	.696	....	56	240	..	965	14.2
1950-51—Philadelphia	66	....	1358	429	.316	442	378	.855	523	117	247	8	1236	18.7
1951-52—Philadelphia	61	1904	1078	336	.312	303	250	.825	368	123	255	13	922	15.1
1952-53—Philadelphia	70	2085	960	332	.346	231	168	.727	387	138	319	20	832	11.9
1953-54—Philadelphia	61	501	229	61	.266	49	28	.571	101	28	90	0	150	2.5
Totals	489	....	9338	2824	.302	3075	2355	.766	....	587	1774	..	8003	16.4

NBA PLAYOFF RECORD

Sea.—Team	G.	Min.	FGA	FGM	Pct.	FTA	FTM	Pct.	Reb.	Ast.	PF	Disq.	Pts.	Avg.
1946-47—Philadelphia	10	....	257	74	.288	94	74	.787	....	3	32	..	222	22.2
1947-48—Philadelphia	13	....	380	92	.242	121	98	.810	....	3	55	..	282	21.7
1948-49—Philadelphia	1	....	0	0	.000	0	0	.000	....	0	1	..	0	0.0
1949-50—Philadelphia	2	....	26	5	.192	10	5	.500	....	2	10	..	15	7.5
1950-51—Philadelphia	2	....	49	16	.327	27	20	.741	16	1	9	0	52	26.0
1951-52—Philadelphia	3	70	33	5	.152	9	7	.778	12	2	13	1	17	5.7
Totals	31	....	745	192	.258	261	204	.782	....	11	120	..	588	19.0

NBA ALL-STAR GAME RECORD

Season—Team	Min.	FGA	FGM	Pct.	FTA	FTM	Pct.	Reb.	Ast.	PF	Disq.	Pts.
1951—Philadelphia	....	15	6	.400	9	7	.778	7	3	5	0	19
1952—Philadelphia	9	7	3	.429	1	0	.000	5	2	2	0	6
Totals	....	22	9	.409	10	7	.700	12	5	7	0	25

Named to NBA 25th Anniversary All-Time Team, 1970. . . . Elected to Naismith Memorial Basketball Hall of Fame, 1977. . . . Named to NBA All-Star First Team, 1947, 1948, 1949. . . . NBA All-Star Second Team, 1951. . . . Holds NBA championship series record for most points in one quarter, 21, vs. Chicago, April 16, 1947. . . . Member of NBA championship team, 1947. . . . Led NBA in scoring, 1947. . . . Led NBA in free-throw percentage, 1951.

HARRY GALLATIN

Born April 26, 1928 at Roxana, Ill.   Height 6:06. Weight 215.

High School—Roxana, Ill.

College—Northeast Missouri State Teachers College, Kirksville, Mo.

Drafted by New York on first round of BAA draft, 1948.

Traded by New York with Dick Atha and Nat Clifton to Detroit for Mel Hutchins and a 1st round draft choice, April 3, 1957.

—COLLEGIATE RECORD—

Year	G.	Min.	FGA	FGM	Pct.	FTA	FTM	Pct.	Reb.	Pts.	Avg.
46-47	31	....	...	149	....	89	53	.596	....	351	11.3
47-48	31	....	465	178	.383	162	109	.673	....	465	15.0
Totals	62	....	...	327	....	251	162	.645	....	816	13.2

NOTE: Played only two years of college basketball.

NBA REGULAR SEASON RECORD

Sea.—Team	G.	Min.	FGA	FGM	Pct.	FTA	FTM	Pct.	Reb.	Ast.	PF	Disq.	Pts.	Avg.
48-49—New York	52	....	479	157	.328	169	120	.710	....	63	127	....	434	8.3
49-50—New York	68	....	664	263	.396	366	277	.757	....	56	215	....	803	11.8
50-51—New York	66	....	705	293	.416	354	259	.732	800	180	244	4	845	12.8
51-52—New York	66	1931	527	233	.442	341	275	.807	661	115	223	5	741	11.2
52-53—New York	70	2333	635	282	.444	430	301	.700	916	126	224	6	865	12.4
53-54—New York	72	2690	639	258	.404	552	433	.784	1098	153	208	2	949	13.2
54-55—New York	72	2548	859	330	.384	483	393	.814	995	176	206	5	1053	14.6
55-56—New York	72	2378	834	322	.386	455	358	.787	740	168	220	6	1002	13.9
56-57—New York	72	1943	817	332	.406	519	415	.802	725	85	202	1	1079	15.0
57-58—Detroit	72	1990	898	340	.379	498	392	.787	749	86	217	5	1072	14.9
Totals	682	....	7057	2810	.398	4167	3223	.773	....	1208	2086	....	8843	13.0

NBA PLAYOFF RECORD

Sea.—Team	G.	Min.	FGA	FGM	Pct.	FTA	FTM	Pct.	Reb.	Ast.	PF	Disq.	Pts.	Avg.
48-49—New York	6	....	56	20	.357	39	32	.821	....	10	31	....	72	12.0
49-50—New York	5	....	52	20	.385	32	25	.781	....	6	23	....	65	13.0
50-51—New York	14	....	140	49	.350	87	67	.770	163	26	57	3	165	11.8
51-52—New York	14	471	122	50	.410	66	51	.773	134	19	45	1	151	10.8
52-53—New York	11	303	86	36	.419	59	44	.746	120	15	29	0	116	10.5
53-54—New York	4	151	35	16	.457	31	22	.710	61	6	12	0	54	13.5
54-55—New York	3	108	42	19	.452	22	17	.773	44	7	11	0	55	18.3
57-58—Detroit	7	182	87	32	.368	37	26	.703	70	11	27	1	90	12.9
Totals	64	....	620	242	.390	373	284	.762	....	100	235	....	768	12.0

NBA ALL-STAR GAME RECORD

Season—Team	Min.	FGA	FGM	Pct.	FTA	FTM	Pct.	Reb.	Ast.	PF	Disq.	Pts.
1951—New York	....	4	2	.500	1	1	1.000	5	2	4	0	5
1952—New York	22	5	3	.600	4	1	.250	9	3	3	0	7
1953—New York	19	4	1	.250	2	1	.500	3	2	1	0	3
1954—New York	28	2	0	.000	6	5	.833	18	3	0	0	5
1955—New York	36	7	4	.571	5	5	1.000	14	3	2	0	13
1956—New York	30	12	5	.417	7	6	.857	5	2	4	0	16
1957—New York	24	7	4	.571	2	0	.000	11	1	3	0	8
Totals (7 games)	....	41	19	.463	27	19	.704	65	16	17	0	57

COLLEGIATE COACHING RECORD

Sea. Club	W.	L.	Pct.	Pos.
1958-59—Southern Ill.	17	10	.630	
1959-60—Southern Ill.	20	9	.690	
1960-61—Southern Ill.	21	6	.778	
1961-62—Southern Ill.	21	10	.677	

NBA COACHING RECORD

Sea. Club	Regular Season				Playoffs	
	W.	L.	Pct.	Pos.	W.	L.
1962-63—St. Louis	48	32	.600	2	6	5
1963-64—St. Louis	46	34	.575	2	6	6
1964-65—St. Louis	17	16	.515	...	..	..
1964-65—New York	19	23	.452	4	..	..
1965-66—New York	6	15	.286	...	..	..
Totals (4 years)	136	120	.531		12	11

Named to NBA All-Star First Team, 1954.... NBA All-Star Second Team, 1955.... Led NBA in rebounding, 1954. ... NBA Coach of the Year, 1963.... Named to NAIA Basketball Hall of Fame, 1957.

THOMAS JOSEPH GOLA
(Tom)

Born January 13, 1933 at Philadelphia, Pa.   Height 6:06.   Weight 205.

High School—Philadelphia, Pa., La Salle.

College—La Salle College, Philadelphia, Pa.

Drafted by Philadelphia on first round (territorial choice), 1955.

Philadelphia franchise transferred to San Francisco, 1962.
Traded by San Francisco to New York for Willie Naulls and Ken Sears, December 5, 1962.

—COLLEGIATE PLAYING RECORD—

Year	G.	Min.	FGA	FGM	Pct.	FTA	FTM	Pct.	Reb.	Pts.	Avg.
51-52	29	....	528	192	.364	170	121	.712	497	505	17.4
52-53	28	....	451	186	.412	186	145	.780	434	517	18.5
53-54	30	....	619	252	.407	254	186	.732	652	690	23.0
54-55	31	....	624	274	.439	267	202	.757	618	750	24.2
Totals	118	....	2222	904	.407	877	654	.746	2201	2462	20.9

NBA REGULAR SEASON RECORD

Sea.—Team	G.	Min.	FGA	FGM	Pct.	FTA	FTM	Pct.	Reb.	Ast.	PF	Disq.	Pts.	Avg.
55-56—Philadelphia	68	2346	592	244	.412	333	244	.733	616	404	272	11	732	10.8
56-57—Philadelphia					In Service									
57-58—Philadelphia	59	2126	711	295	.415	299	223	.746	639	327	225	11	813	13.8
58-59—Philadelphia	64	2333	773	310	.401	357	281	.787	710	269	243	7	901	14.1
59-60—Philadelphia	75	2870	983	426	.433	340	270	.794	779	409	311	9	1122	15.0
60-61—Philadelphia	74	2735	940	420	.447	281	210	.747	692	292	321	13	1050	14.2
61-62—Philadelphia	60	2462	765	322	.421	230	176	.765	585	286	266	16	820	13.7
62-63—S.F.-N.Y.	73	2670	781	363	.465	219	170	.776	507	298	316	7	896	12.3
63-64—New York	74	2156	602	258	.429	212	154	.726	469	257	278	7	670	9.1
64-65—New York	77	1727	455	204	.448	180	133	.739	319	220	269	8	541	7.0
65-66—New York	74	1127	271	122	.450	105	82	.781	289	191	207	3	326	4.4
Totals	698	22552	6873	2964	.431	2556	1943	.760	5605	2953	2708	91	7871	11.3

NBA PLAYOFF RECORD

Sea.—Team	G.	Min.	FGA	FGM	Pct.	FTA	FTM	Pct.	Reb.	Ast.	PF	Disq.	Pts.	Avg.
55-56—Philadelphia	10	360	107	38	.355	60	47	.783	101	58	47	2	123	12.3
57-58—Philadelphia	8	327	109	36	.330	51	38	.745	84	32	24	0	110	13.8
59-60—Philadelphia	9	340	102	42	.412	36	29	.805	95	50	41	3	113	12.5
60-61—Philadelphia	3	127	34	7	.206	20	15	.750	37	15	14	1	29	9.7
61-62—Philadelphia	9	316	70	19	.271	25	19	.760	74	24	38	2	57	6.3
Totals	39	1470	422	142	.336	192	148	.771	391	179	164	8	432	11.1

NBA ALL-STAR GAME RECORD

Season—Team	Min.	FGA	FGM	Pct.	FTA	FTM	Pct.	Reb.	Ast.	PF	Disq.	Pts.
1960—Philadelphia	20	13	5	.385	3	2	.667	4	2	3	0	12
1961—Philadelphia	25	13	6	.462	4	2	.500	5	3	2	0	14
1962—Philadelphia				Injured—Did Not Play								
1963—New York	18	3	1	.333	0	0	.000	2	1	3	0	2
1964—New York	7	0	0	.000	2	1	.500	0	1	2	0	1
Totals	70	29	12	.414	9	5	.556	11	7	10	0	2.9

COLLEGIATE COACHING RECORD

Sea.	Club	W.	L.	Pct.	Pos.
1968-69—LaSalle		23	1	.958	..
1969-70—LaSalle		14	12	.538	..

Elected to Naismith Memorial Basketball Hall of Fame, 1975. . . . Named to NBA All-Star Second Team, 1958. . . . Member of NBA championship team, 1956. . . . NCAA University Division Tournament MVP, 1954. . . . Member of NCAA University Division championship team, 1954. . . . One of only two major-college players ever to score over 2,000 points and grab over 2,000 rebounds in a career. . . . Served as a legislator in Pennsylvania General Assembly.

GAIL CHARLES GOODRICH

Born April 23, 1943 at Los Angeles, Calif.   Height 6:01. Weight 175.

High School—Los Angeles, Calif., Polytechnic.

College—University of California at Los Angeles, Los Angeles, Calif.

Drafted by Los Angeles on first round (territorial choice), 1965.

Selected from Los Angeles by Phoenix in expansion draft, May 6, 1968.
Traded by Phoenix to Los Angeles for Mel Counts, May 20, 1970.
Played out option with Los Angeles; signed by New Orleans as a Veteran Free Agent, July 19, 1976. Los Angeles received two 1st round draft choices (1977 and 1979) and a 1980 2nd round draft choice as compensation. New Orleans received a 1977 2nd round draft choice to complete transaction, October 6, 1976.

Year	G.	Min.	FGA	FGM	Pct.	FTA	FTM	Pct.	Reb.	Pts.	Avg.
61-62†	20	....	385	189	.491	155	110	.710	122	488	24.4
62-63	29	....	280	117	.418	103	66	.641	101	300	10.3
63-64	30	....	530	243	.458	225	160	.711	156	646	21.5
64-65	30	....	528	277	.525	265	190	.717	158	744	24.8
Varsity Totals	89	....	1338	637	.476	593	416	.702	415	1690	19.0

NBA REGULAR SEASON RECORD

Sea.—Team	G.	Min.	FGA	FGM	Pct.	FTA	FTM	Pct.	Reb.	Ast.	PF	Disq.	Pts.	Avg.
65-66—Los Ang.	65	1008	503	203	.404	149	103	.691	130	103	103	1	509	7.8
66-67—Los Ang.	77	1780	776	352	.454	337	253	.751	251	210	194	3	957	12.4
67-68—Los Ang.	79	2057	812	395	.486	392	302	.770	199	205	228	2	1092	13.8
68-69—Phoenix	81	3236	1746	718	.411	663	495	.747	437	518	253	3	1931	23.8
69-70—Phoenix	81	3234	1251	568	.454	604	488	.808	340	605	251	3	1624	20.0
70-71—Los Ang.	79	2808	1174	558	.475	343	264	.770	260	380	258	3	1380	17.5
71-72—Los Ang.	82	3040	1695	826	.487	559	475	.850	295	365	210	0	2127	25.9
72-73—Los Ang.	76	2697	1615	750	.464	374	314	.840	263	332	193	1	1814	23.9

Sea.—Team	G.	Min.	FGA	FGM	Pct.	FTA	FTM	Pct.	Off.	Def.	Tot.	Ast.	PF	Dq.	Stl.	Blk.	Pts.	Avg.
									\multicolumn{3}{}{—Rebounds—}								
73-74—L.A.	82	3061	1773	784	.442	588	508	.864	95	155	250	427	227	3	126	12	2076	25.3
74-75—L.A.	72	2668	1429	656	.459	378	318	.841	96	123	219	420	214	1	102	6	1630	22.6
75-76—L.A.	75	2646	1321	583	.441	346	293	.847	94	120	214	421	238	3	123	17	1459	19.5
76-77—N.O.	27	609	305	136	.446	85	68	.800	25	36	61	74	43	0	22	2	340	12.6
77-78—N.O.	81	2553	1050	520	.495	332	264	.795	75	102	177	388	186	0	82	22	1304	16.1
78-79—N.O.	74	2130	850	382	.449	204	174	.853	68	115	183	357	177	1	90	13	938	12.7
Totals	1031	33527	16300	7431	.456	5354	4319	.807			3279	4805	2775	24	545	72	19181	18.6

NBA PLAYOFF RECORD

Sea.—Team	G.	Min.	FGA	FGM	Pct.	FTA	FTM	Pct.	Reb.	Ast.	PF	Disq.	Pts.	Avg.
65-66—Los Ang.	11	290	92	43	.467	43	29	.674	42	33	35	0	115	10.5
66-67—Los Ang.	3	81	31	11	.355	18	11	.611	9	10	5	0	33	11.0
67-68—Los Ang.	10	100	47	23	.489	18	14	.778	14	14	10	0	60	6.0
69-70—Phoenix	7	265	118	56	.475	35	30	.857	32	38	21	0	142	20.3
70-71—Los Ang.	12	518	247	105	.425	113	95	.841	38	91	38	0	305	25.4
71-72—Los Ang.	15	575	292	130	.445	108	97	.898	38	50	50	0	357	23.8
72-73—Los Ang.	17	604	310	139	.448	79	62	.785	61	67	53	1	340	20.0

Sea.—Team	G.	Min.	FGA	FGM	Pct.	FTA	FTM	Pct.	Off.	Def.	Tot.	Ast.	PF	Dq.	Stl.	Blk.	Pts.	Avg.
									\multicolumn{3}{}{—Rebounds—}								
73-74—L.A.	5	189	90	35	.389	33	28	.848	7	9	16	30	7	0	7	1	98	19.6
Totals	80	2622	1227	542	.442	447	366	.819			250	333	219	1			1450	18.1

NBA ALL-STAR GAME RECORD

Season—Team	Min.	FGA	FGM	Pct.	FTA	FTM	Pct.	Reb.	Ast.	PF	Disq.	Pts.
1969—Phoenix	6	4	2	.500	2	1	.500	1	1	1	0	5
1972—Los Angeles	14	7	2	.286	0	0	.000	1	2	2	0	4
1973—Los Angeles	16	7	1	.143	0	0	.000	2	1	2	0	2

Season—Team	Min.	FGA	FGM	Pct.	FTA	FTM	Pct.	Off.	Def.	Tot.	Ast.	PF	Dq.	Stl.	Blk.	Pts.
								\multicolumn{3}{}{—Rebounds—}							
1974—Los Angeles	26	16	9	.563	0	0	.000	1	3	4	6	2	0	1	0	18
1975—LosAngeles	15	4	2	.500	0	0	.000	0	1	1	4	1	0	0	0	4
Totals	77	38	16	.421	2	1	.500			9	14	8	0	1	0	33

Named to NBA All-Star First Team, 1974. . . . Member of NBA championship team, 1972. . . . Named to THE SPORTING NEWS All-America First Team, 1964. . . . Member of NCAA Division I championship teams, 1964 and 1965.

HAROLD EVERETT GREER
(Hal)

Born June 26, 1936 at Huntington, W. Va. Height 6:02. Weight 175.

High School—Huntington, W. Va., Douglass.

College—Marshall College, Huntington, W. Va.

Drafted by Syracuse on second round, 1958.

Syracuse franchise transferred to Philadelphia, 1963.

—DID YOU KNOW—

That Vince Boryla, the general manager who engineered the deal in the late 1950s to acquire Mel Hutchins for the Knicks, is the man who traded Hutchins' nephew, Kiki Vandeweghe, from Denver to Portland after the 1983-84 season?

Year	G.	Min.	FGA	FGM	Pct.	FTA	FTM	Pct.	Reb.	Pts.	Avg.
54-55†	..	....	....	...	...	....	....	...	...	...	18.0
55-56	23	....	213	128	.601	145	101	.697	153	357	15.5
56-57	24	....	329	167	.508	156	119	.763	332	453	18.9
57-58	24	....	432	236	.546	114	95	.833	280	567	23.6
Varsity Totals	71	....	974	531	.545	415	315	.759	765	1377	19.4

NBA REGULAR SEASON RECORD

Sea.—Team	G.	Min.	FGA	FGM	Pct.	FTA	FTM	Pct.	Reb.	Ast.	PF	Disq.	Pts.	Avg.
58-59—Syracuse	68	1625	679	308	.454	176	137	.778	196	101	189	1	753	11.1
59-60—Syracuse	70	1979	815	388	.476	189	148	.783	303	188	208	4	924	13.2
60-61—Syracuse	79	2763	1381	623	.451	394	305	.774	455	302	242	0	1551	19.6
61-62—Syracuse	71	2705	1442	644	.446	404	331	.819	524	313	252	2	1619	22.8
62-63—Syracuse	80	2631	1293	600	.464	434	362	.834	457	275	286	4	1562	19.5
63-64—Philadelphia	80	3157	1611	715	.444	525	435	.829	484	374	291	6	1865	23.3
64-65—Philadelphia	70	2600	1245	539	.433	413	335	.811	355	313	254	7	1413	20.2
65-66—Philadelphia	80	3326	1580	703	.445	514	413	.804	473	384	315	6	1819	22.7
66-67—Philadelphia	80	3086	1524	699	.459	466	367	.788	422	303	302	5	1765	22.1
67-68—Philadelphia	82	3263	1626	777	.478	549	422	.769	444	372	289	6	1976	24.1
68-69—Philadelphia	82	3311	1595	732	.459	543	432	.796	435	414	294	8	1896	23.1
69-70—Philadelphia	80	3024	1551	705	.455	432	352	.815	376	405	300	8	1762	22.0
70-71—Philadelphia	81	3060	1371	591	.431	405	326	.805	364	369	289	4	1508	18.6
71-72—Philadelphia	81	2410	866	389	.449	234	181	.774	271	316	268	10	959	11.8
72-73—Philadelphia	38	848	232	91	.392	39	32	.821	106	111	76	1	214	5.6
Totals	1122	39788	18811	8504	.452	5717	4578	.801	5665	4540	3855	72	21586	19.2

NBA PLAYOFF RECORD

Sea.—Team	G.	Min.	FGA	FGM	Pct.	FTA	FTM	Pct.	Reb.	Ast.	PF	Disq.	Pts.	Avg.
58-59—Syracuse	9	277	93	39	.419	32	26	.813	47	20	35	2	104	11.6
59-60—Syracuse	3	84	43	22	.512	4	3	.750	14	10	5	0	47	15.7
60-61—Syracuse	8	232	106	41	.387	40	33	.825	33	19	32	1	115	14.4
61-62—Syracuse	1	5	0	0	.000	0	0	.000	0	0	1	0	0	0.0
62-63—Syracuse	5	214	87	44	.506	35	29	.829	27	21	21	1	117	23.4
63-64—Philadelphia	5	211	95	37	.389	39	33	.846	28	30	19	1	107	21.4
64-65—Philadelphia	11	505	222	101	.455	87	69	.793	81	55	45	2	271	24.6
65-66—Philadelphia	5	226	91	32	.352	23	18	.783	36	21	21	0	82	16.4
66-67—Philadelphia	15	688	375	161	.429	118	94	.797	88	79	55	1	416	27.7
67-68—Philadelphia	13	553	278	120	.432	111	95	.858	79	55	49	1	335	25.8
68-69—Philadelphia	5	204	81	26	.321	36	28	.778	30	23	23	0	80	16.0
69-70—Philadelphia	5	178	74	33	.446	13	11	.846	17	27	16	0	77	15.4
70-71—Philadelphia	7	265	112	49	.438	36	27	.750	25	33	35	4	125	17.9
Totals	92	3642	1657	705	.425	574	466	.812	505	393	357	13	1876	20.4

NBA ALL-STAR GAME RECORD

Season—Team	Min.	FGA	FGM	Pct.	FTA	FTM	Pct.	Reb.	Ast.	PF	Disq.	Pts.
1961—Syracuse	18	11	7	.636	0	0	.000	6	2	2	0	14
1962—Syracuse	24	14	3	.214	7	2	.286	10	9	3	0	8
1963—Syracuse	15	7	3	.429	0	0	.000	3	2	4	0	6
1964—Philadelphia	20	10	5	.500	4	3	.750	3	4	1	0	13
1965—Philadelphia	21	11	5	.455	4	3	.750	4	1	2	0	13
1966—Philadelphia ,...........	23	13	4	.308	1	1	1.000	5	1	4	0	9
1967—Philadelphia	31	16	5	.313	8	7	.875	4	1	5	0	17
1968—Philadelphia	17	8	8	1.000	7	5	.714	3	3	2	0	21
1969—Philadelphia	17	1	0	.000	5	4	.800	3	2	2	0	4
1970—Philadelphia	21	11	7	.636	1	1	1.000	4	3	4	0	15
Totals	207	102	47	.461	37	26	.703	45	28	29	0	120

CBA COACHING RECORD

		Regular Season				Playoffs	
Sea.	Club	W.	L.	Pct.	Pos.	W.	L.
1980-81—Phila. Kings		17	23	.425	3†	6	6

†Eastern Division.

Named to NBA All-Star Second Team, 1963, 1964, 1965, 1966, 1967, 1968, 1969. . . . NBA All-Star Game MVP, 1968. . . . Holds NBA All-Star Game record for most points in one quarter, 19, in 1968. . . . Member of NBA championship team, 1967.

RICHIE GUERIN

Born May 29, 1932 at New York, N. Y. Height 6:04. Weight 210.

High School—Bronx, N. Y., Mt. St. Michael.

College—Iona College, New Rochelle, N. Y.

Drafted by New York on second round, 1954.

In military service, 1954-55 and 1955-56 seasons, played with Quantico Marines and Marine All-Star teams. Traded by New York to St. Louis for cash and a 2nd round draft choice, October 18, 1963.

—COLLEGIATE RECORD—

Year	G.	Min.	FGA	FGM	Pct.	FTA	FTM	Pct.	Reb.	Pts.	Avg.
50-51†	..	....	...	...	....	...	...	....	....	....	....
51-52	27	....	...	159	....	...	146	....	....	464	17.2
52-53	21	....	...	139	.491	...	114	.662	....	392	18.7
53-54	21	....	405	171	.422	249	177	.711	....	519	24.7
Varsity Totals	69	....	...	469	....	...	437	....	....	1375	19.9

NBA REGULAR SEASON RECORD

Sea.—Team	G.	Min.	FGA	FGM	Pct.	FTA	FTM	Pct.	Reb.	Ast.	PF	Disq.	Pts.	Avg.
56-57—New York	72	1793	699	257	.368	292	181	.620	334	182	186	3	695	9.7
57-58—New York	63	2368	973	344	.354	511	353	.691	489	317	202	3	1041	16.5
58-59—New York	71	2558	1046	443	.424	505	405	.802	518	364	255	1	1291	18.2
59-60—New York	74	2429	1379	579	.420	591	457	.773	505	468	242	3	1615	21.8
60-61—New York	79	3023	1545	612	.396	626	496	.792	628	503	310	3	1720	21.8
61-62—New York	78	3346	1897	839	.442	762	625	.820	501	539	299	3	2303	29.5
62-63—New York	79	2712	1380	596	.432	600	509	.848	331	348	228	2	1701	21.5
63-64—N.Y.-St.L.	80	2366	846	351	.415	424	347	.818	256	375	276	4	1049	13.1
64-65—St. Louis	57	1678	662	295	.446	301	231	.767	149	271	193	1	821	14.4
65-66—St. Louis	80	2363	998	414	.415	446	362	.812	314	388	256	4	1190	14.9
66-67—St. Louis	79	2275	904	394	.436	416	304	.731	192	345	247	2	1092	13.8
67-68—					Voluntarily Retired									
68-69—Atlanta	27	472	111	47	.423	74	57	.770	59	99	66	0	151	5.6
69-70—Atlanta	8	64	11	3	.273	1	1	1.000	2	12	9	0	7	0.9
Totals	847	27447	12451	5174	.416	5549	4328	.780	4278	4211	2769	29	14676	17.3

NBA PLAYOFF RECORD

Sea.—Team	G.	Min.	FGA	FGM	Pct.	FTA	FTM	Pct.	Reb.	Ast.	PF	Disq.	Pts.	Avg.
58-59—New York	2	77	35	9	.257	14	12	.857	18	15	11	1	30	15.0
63-64—St. Louis	12	428	169	75	.444	85	67	.788	50	49	54	1	217	18.1
64-65—St. Louis	4	125	65	25	.385	25	19	.760	8	21	14	0	69	17.3
65-66—St. Louis	10	399	159	72	.453	76	62	.816	37	79	41	0	206	20.6
66-67—St. Louis	9	228	86	36	.419	30	24	.800	23	39	23	0	96	10.7
68-69—Atlanta	3	32	4	1	.250	2	1	.500	5	7	8	0	3	1.0
69-70—Atlanta	2	56	21	13	.619	7	7	1.000	8	4	6	0	33	16.5
Totals	42	1345	539	231	.429	239	192	.803	149	214	157	2	654	15.6

NBA ALL-STAR GAME RECORD

Season—Team	Min.	FGA	FGM	Pct.	FTA	FTM	Pct.	Reb.	Ast.	PF	Disq.	Pts.
1958—New York	22	10	2	.200	4	3	.750	8	7	3	0	7
1959—New York	22	7	1	.143	5	3	.600	3	3	1	0	5
1960—New York	22	11	5	.455	2	2	1.000	4	4	4	0	12
1961—New York	15	8	3	.375	6	5	.833	0	2	1	0	11
1962—New York	27	17	10	.588	6	3	.500	3	1	6	1	23
1963—New York	14	3	2	.667	3	1	.333	1	1	2	0	5
Totals	122	56	23	.411	26	17	.654	19	18	17	0	63

NBA COACHING RECORD

		Regular Season				Playoffs	
Sea.	Club	W.	L.	Pct.	Pos.	W.	L.
1964-65—St. Louis		28	19	.596	2	1	3
1965-66—St. Louis		36	44	.450	3	6	4
1966-67—St. Louis		39	42	.476	2	5	4
1967-68—St. Louis		56	26	.683	1	2	4
1968-69—Atlanta		48	34	.585	2	5	6
1969-70—Atlanta		48	34	.585	1	4	5
1970-71—Atlanta		36	46	.439	2	1	4
1971-72—Atlanta		36	46	.439	2	2	4
Totals (8 years)		327	291	.529		26	34

Named to NBA All-Star Second Team, 1959, 1960, 1962. . . . NBA Coach of the Year, 1968.

CLIFFORD OLDHAM HAGAN
(Cliff)

Born December 9, 1931 at Owensboro, Ky. Height 6:04. Weight 215.

High School—Owensboro, Ky.

College—University of Kentucky, Lexington, Ky.

Drafted by Boston on third round, 1953.

In military service, 1954-55 and 1955-56, played at Andrews Air Force Base.
Draft rights traded by Boston with Ed Macauley to St. Louis for 1st round draft choice, April 30, 1956.
Signed as player-coach by Dallas ABA, June, 1967.

Year	G.	Min.	FGA	FGM	Pct.	FTA	FTM	Pct.	Reb.	Pts.	Avg.
49-50†	12	....	244	114	.467	58	42	.724	...	270	22.5
50-51	20	....	188	69	.367	61	45	.738	169	183	9.2
51-52	32	....	633	264	.417	235	164	.698	528	692	21.6
52-53			Did Not Play—Kentucky had no team								
53-54	25	....	514	234	.455	191	132	.691	338	600	24.0
Varsity Totals	77	....	1335	567	.425	487	341	.700	1035	1475	19.2

NBA REGULAR SEASON RECORD

Sea.—Team	G.	Min.	FGA	FGM	Pct.	FTA	FTM	Pct.	Reb.	Ast.	PF	Disq.	Pts.	Avg.
56-57—St. Louis	67	971	371	134	.361	145	100	.690	247	86	165	3	368	5.5
57-58—St. Louis	70	2190	1135	503	.443	501	385	.768	707	175	267	9	1391	19.9
58-59—St. Louis	72	2702	1417	646	.456	536	415	.774	783	245	275	10	1707	23.7
59-60—St. Louis	75	2798	1549	719	.464	524	421	.803	803	299	270	4	1859	24.8
60-61—St. Louis	78	2701	1490	661	.441	467	383	.820	718	381	286	9	1705	21.9
61-62—St. Louis	77	2784	1490	701	.470	439	362	.825	533	370	282	8	1764	22.9
62-63—St. Louis	79	1716	1055	491	.465	305	244	.800	341	191	221	2	1226	15.5
63-64—St. Louis	77	2279	1280	572	.447	331	269	.813	377	189	272	4	1413	18.4
64-65—St. Louis	77	1739	901	393	.436	268	214	.799	276	136	182	0	1000	13.0
65-66—St. Louis	74	1851	942	419	.445	206	176	.854	234	164	177	1	1014	13.7
Totals	746	21731	11630	5239	.450	3722	2969	.798	5019	2236	2397	50	13447	18.0

NBA PLAYOFF RECORD

Sea.—Team	G.	Min.	FGA	FGM	Pct.	FTA	FTM	Pct.	Reb.	Ast.	PF	Disq.	Pts.	Avg.
56-57—St. Louis	10	419	143	62	.434	63	46	.730	112	28	47	3	170	17.0
57-58—St. Louis	11	418	221	111	.502	99	83	.838	115	37	48	3	305	27.7
58-59—St. Louis	6	259	123	63	.512	54	45	.833	72	16	21	0	171	28.5
59-60—St. Louis	14	544	296	125	.422	109	89	.816	138	54	54	1	339	24.2
60-61—St. Louis	12	455	235	104	.442	69	56	.811	118	54	45	1	264	22.0
62-63—St. Louis	11	255	179	83	.464	53	37	.698	55	34	42	4	203	18.5
63-64—St. Louis	12	392	175	75	.429	54	45	.833	74	57	34	0	195	16.2
64-65—St. Louis	4	123	75	34	.453	12	6	.500	26	7	14	0	74	18.5
65-66—St. Louis	10	200	97	44	.454	27	25	.926	34	18	15	0	113	11.3
Totals	90	3065	1544	701	.454	540	432	.800	744	305	320	12	1834	20.4

NBA ALL-STAR GAME RECORD

Season—Team	Min.	FGA	FGM	Pct.	FTA	FTM	Pct.	Reb.	Ast.	PF	Disq.	Pts.
1958—St. Louis			Chosen—Injured, Did Not Play									
1959—St. Louis	22	12	6	.500	3	3	1.000	8	3	5	0	15
1960—St. Louis	21	9	1	.111	0	0	.000	3	2	1	0	2
1961—St. Louis	13	2	9	.000	2	2	1.000	2	0	1	0	2
1962—St. Louis	9	3	1	.333	0	0	.000	2	1	1	0	2
Totals	65	26	8	.308	5	5	1.000	15	6	8	0	21

ABA REGULAR SEASON RECORD

Sea.—Team	G.	Min.	2-Point FGM	2-Point FGA	Pct.	3-Point FGM	3-Point FGA	Pct.	FTM	FTA	Pct.	Reb.	Ast.	Pts.	Avg.
67-68—Dallas	56	1737	371	756	.491	0	3	.000	277	351	.789	334	276	1019	18.2
68-69—Dallas	35	579	132	258	.512	0	1	.000	123	144	.854	102	122	387	11.1
69-70—Dallas	3	27	8	12	.667	0	1	.000	1	2	.500	....	....	17	5.7
Totals	94	2343	511	1026	.498	0	5	.000	401	497	.807	436	398	1423	15.1

ABA PLAYOFF RECORD

Sea.—Team	G.	Min.	2-Point FGM	2-Point FGA	Pct.	3-Point FGM	3-Point FGA	Pct.	FTM	FTA	Pct.	Reb.	Ast.	Pts.	Avg.
67-68—Dallas	3	70	14	37	.378	0	0	.000	9	13	.692	13	9	37	12.3
68-69—Dallas	2	45	5	14	.357	0	0	.000	8	10	.800	6	14	18	9.0
Totals	5	115	19	51	.373	0	0	.000	17	23	.739	19	23	55	11.0

ABA ALL-STAR GAME RECORD

Sea.—Team	G.	Min.	2-Point FGM	2-Point FGA	Pct.	3-Point FGM	3-Point FGA	Pct.	FTM	FTA	Pct.	Reb.	Ast.	Pts.	Avg.
1968—Dallas	1	24	4	11	.364	0	0	.000	2	2	1.000	0	5	10	10.0

ABA COACHING RECORD

Sea. Club	Regular Season W.	L.	Pct.	Pos.	Playoffs W.	L.
1967-68—Dallas	46	32	.590	2†	4	4
1968-69—Dallas	41	37	.526	4†	3	4
1969-70—Dallas	22	21	.512	..	..	..
Totals	109	90	.548		7	8

†Western Division.

Elected to Naismith Memorial Basketball Hall of Fame, 1977.... Member of NBA championship team, 1958.... Named to NBA All-Star Second Team, 1958 and 1959.... Member of NCAA championship team, 1951.

JOHN HAVLICEK
(Hondo)

Born April 8, 1940 at Martins Ferry, O.   Height 6:05.   Weight 205.

High School—Bridgeport, O.

College—Ohio State University, Columbus, O.

Drafted by Boston on first round, 1962.

—COLLEGIATE RECORD—

Year	G.	Min.	FGA	FGM	Pct.	FTA	FTM	Pct.	Reb.	Pts.	Avg.
58-59†			Freshman team did not play an intercollegiate schedule.								
59-60	28	....	312	144	.462	74	53	.716	205	341	12.2
60-61	28	....	321	173	.539	87	61	.701	244	407	14.5
61-62	28	....	377	196	.520	109	83	.761	271	475	17.0
Varsity Totals	84	....	1010	513	.508	270	197	.730	720	1223	14.6

NBA REGULAR SEASON RECORD

Sea.—Team	G.	Min.	FGA	FGM	Pct.	FTA	FTM	Pct.	Reb.	Ast.	PF	Disq.	Pts.	Avg.
62-63—Boston	80	2200	1085	483	.445	239	174	.728	534	179	189	2	1140	14.3
63-64—Boston	80	2587	1535	640	.417	422	315	.746	428	238	227	1	1595	19.9
64-65—Boston	75	2169	1420	570	.401	316	235	.744	371	199	200	2	1375	18.3
65-66—Boston	71	2175	1328	530	.399	349	274	.785	423	210	158	1	1334	18.8
66-67—Boston	81	2602	1540	684	.444	441	365	.828	532	278	210	0	1733	21.4
67-68—Boston	82	2921	1551	666	.429	453	368	.812	546	384	237	2	1700	20.7
68-69—Boston	82	3174	1709	692	.405	496	387	.780	570	441	247	0	1771	21.6
69-70—Boston	81	3369	1585	736	.464	578	488	.844	635	550	211	1	1960	24.2
70-71—Boston	81	3678	1982	892	.450	677	554	.818	730	607	200	0	2338	28.9
71-72—Boston	82	3698	1957	897	.458	549	458	.834	672	614	183	1	2252	27.5
72-73—Boston	80	3367	1704	766	.450	431	370	.858	567	529	195	1	1902	23.8

Sea.—Team	G.	Min.	FGA	FGM	Pct.	FTA	FTM	Pct.	Off.	Def.	Tot.	Ast.	PF	Dq.	Stl.	Blk.	Pts.	Avg.
										—Rebounds—								
73-74—Boston	76	3091	1502	685	.456	416	346	.832	138	349	487	447	196	1	95	32	1716	22.6
74-75—Boston	82	3132	1411	642	.455	332	289	.870	154	330	484	432	231	2	110	16	1573	19.2
75-76—Boston	76	2598	1121	504	.450	333	281	.844	116	198	314	278	204	1	97	29	1289	17.0
76-77—Boston	79	2913	1283	580	.452	288	235	.816	109	273	382	400	208	4	84	18	1395	17.7
77-78—Boston	82	2797	1217	546	.449	269	230	.855	93	239	332	328	185	2	90	22	1322	16.1
Totals	1270	46471	23930	10513	.439	6589	5369	.815			8007	6114	3281	21	476	117	26395	20.8

NBA PLAYOFF RECORD

Sea.—Team	G.	Min.	FGA	FGM	Pct.	FTA	FTM	Pct.	Reb.	Ast.	PF	Disq.	Pts.	Avg.
62-63—Boston	11	254	125	56	.448	27	18	.667	53	17	28	1	130	11.8
63-64—Boston	10	289	159	61	.384	44	35	.795	43	32	26	0	157	15.7
64-65—Boston	12	405	250	88	.352	55	46	.836	88	29	44	1	222	18.5
65-66—Boston	17	719	374	153	.409	113	95	.841	154	70	69	2	401	23.6
66-67—Boston	9	330	212	95	.448	71	57	.803	73	28	30	0	247	27.4
67-68—Boston	19	862	407	184	.452	151	125	.828	164	142	67	1	493	25.9
68-69—Boston	18	850	382	170	.445	138	118	.855	179	100	58	2	458	25.4
71-72—Boston	11	517	235	108	.460	99	85	.859	92	70	35	1	301	27.4
72-73—Boston	12	479	235	112	.477	74	61	.824	62	65	24	0	285	23.8

Sea.—Team	G.	Min.	FGA	FGM	Pct.	FTA	FTM	Pct.	Off.	Def.	Tot.	Ast.	PF	Dq.	Stl.	Blk.	Pts.	Avg.
										—Rebounds—								
73-74—Boston	18	811	411	199	.484	101	89	.881	28	88	116	108	43	0	24	6	487	27.1
74-75—Boston	11	464	192	83	.432	76	66	.868	18	39	57	51	38	1	16	1	232	21.1
75-76—Boston	15	505	180	80	.444	47	38	.809	18	38	56	51	22	0	12	5	198	13.2
76-77—Boston	9	375	167	62	.371	50	41	.820	15	34	49	62	33	0	8	4	165	18.3
Totals	172	6860	3329	1451	.436	1046	874	.836			1186	825	517	9	60	16	3776	22.0

NBA ALL-STAR GAME RECORD

Season—Team	Min.	FGA	FGM	Pct.	FTA	FTM	Pct.	Reb.	Ast.	PF	Disq.	Pts.
1966—Boston	25	16	6	.375	6	6	1.000	6	1	2	0	18
1967—Boston	17	14	7	.500	0	0	.000	2	1	1	0	14
1968—Boston	22	15	9	.600	11	8	.727	5	4	0	0	26
1969—Boston	31	14	6	.429	2	2	1.000	7	2	2	0	14
1970—Boston	29	15	7	.467	3	3	1.000	5	7	2	0	17
1971—Boston	24	12	6	.500	2	0	.000	3	2	3	0	12
1972—Boston	24	13	5	.385	5	5	1.000	3	2	2	0	15
1973—Boston	22	10	6	.600	5	2	.400	3	5	1	0	14

Season—Team	Min.	FGA	FGM	Pct.	FTA	FTM	Pct.	Off.	Def.	Tot.	Ast.	PF	Dq.	Stl.	Blk.	Pts.
									—Rebounds—							
1974—Boston	18	10	5	.500	2	0	.000	0	0	0	2	2	0	1	0	10
1975—Boston	31	12	7	.583	2	2	1.000	1	5	6	1	2	0	2	0	16
1976—Boston	21	10	3	.300	3	3	1.000	1	1	2	1	0	0	1	0	9
1977—Boston	17	5	2	.400	0	0	.000	0	1	1	1	1	0	0	0	4
1978—Boston	22	8	5	.625	0	0	.000	0	3	3	1	2	0	0	0	10
Totals	303	154	74	.481	41	31	.756			46	31	20	0	4	0	179

Elected to Naismith Memorial Basketball Hall of Fame, 1983. . . . Named to NBA 35th Anniversary All-Time Team, 1980. . . . NBA All-Star First Team, 1971, 1972, 1973, 1974. . . . NBA All-Star Second Team, 1964, 1966, 1968, 1969, 1970, 1975, 1976. . . . NBA All-Defensive First Team, 1972, 1973, 1974, 1975, 1976. . . . NBA All-Defensive Second Team,

JOHN HAVLICEK

1969, 1970, 1971. . . . NBA Playoff MVP, 1974. . . . Shares NBA record for most seasons played, 16. . . . NBA all-time leader in playoff games. . . . Shares NBA playoff game record for most field goals made, 24, vs. Atlanta, April 1, 1973. . . . Holds NBA championship series record for most points in overtime period, 9, vs. Milwaukee, May 10, 1974. . . . Shares NBA championship series record for most field goals made in one quarter, 8, vs. San Francisco, April 18, 1964. . . . Member of NBA championship teams, 1963, 1964, 1965, 1966, 1968, 1969, 1974, 1976. . . . Selected as wide receiver by Cleveland Browns on seventh round of 1962 National Football League draft. . . . Named to THE SPORTING NEWS All-America Second Team, 1962. . . . Member of NCAA championship team, 1960.

ELVIN ERNEST HAYES

Born November 17, 1945 at Rayville, La.   Height 6:09.   Weight 235.

High School—Rayville, La., Eula D. Britton.

College—University of Houston, Houston, Tex.

Drafted by San Diego on first round, 1968 (1st pick).

Traded by Houston to Baltimore for Jack Marin and future considerations, June 23, 1972.
Traded by Washington to Houston for two 2nd round draft choices (1981 and 1983), June 8, 1981.

—COLLEGIATE RECORD—

Year	G.	Min.	FGA	FGM	Pct.	FTA	FTM	Pct.	Reb.	Pts.	Avg.
64-65†	21	......	478	217	.454	176	93	.528	500	527	25.1
65-66	29	946	570	323	.567	257	143	.556	490	789	27.2
66-67	31	1119	750	373	.497	227	135	.595	488	881	28.4
67-68	33	1270	945	519	.549	285	176	.618	624	1214	36.8
Varsity Totals	93	3335	2265	1215	.536	769	454	.590	1602	2884	31.0

NBA REGULAR SEASON RECORD

Sea.—Team	G.	Min.	FGA	FGM	Pct.	FTA	FTM	Pct.	Reb.	Ast.	PF	Disq.	Pts.	Avg.
68-69—San Diego	82	3695	2082	930	.447	746	467	.626	1406	113	266	2	2327	28.4
69-70—San Diego	82	3665	2020	914	.452	622	428	.688	1386	162	270	5	2256	27.5
70-71—San Diego	82	3633	2215	948	.428	676	454	.672	1362	186	225	1	2350	28.7
71-72—Houston	82	3461	1918	832	.434	615	399	.649	1197	270	233	1	2063	25.2
72-73—Baltimore	81	3347	1607	713	.444	434	291	.671	1177	127	232	3	1717	21.2

									—Rebounds—						
Sea.—Team	G.	Min.	FGA	FGM	Pct.	FTA	FTM	Pct.	Off.	Def.	Tot.	Ast.	PF	Dq.	Stl.	Blk.	Pts.	Avg.
73-74—Capital	81	3602	1627	689	.423	495	357	.721	354	1109	1463	163	252	1	86	240	1735	21.4
74-75—Washington	82	3465	1668	739	.443	534	409	.766	221	783	1004	206	238	0	158	187	1887	23.0
75-76—Washington	80	2975	1381	649	.470	457	287	.628	210	668	878	121	293	5	104	202	1585	19.8
76-77—Washington	82	3364	1516	760	.501	614	422	.687	289	740	1029	158	312	1	87	220	1942	23.7
77-78—Washington	81	3246	1409	636	.451	514	326	.634	335	740	1075	149	313	7	96	159	1598	19.7
78-79—Washington	82	3105	1477	720	.487	534	349	.654	312	682	994	143	308	5	75	190	1789	21.8
79-80—Washington	81	3183	1677	761	.454	478	334	.699	269	627	896	129	309	9	62	189	1859	23.0
80-81—Washington	81	2931	1296	584	.451	439	271	.617	235	554	789	98	300	6	68	171	1439	17.8
81-82—Houston	82	3032	1100	519	.472	422	280	.664	267	480	747	144	287	4	62	104	1318	16.1
82-83—Houston	81	2302	890	424	.476	287	196	.683	199	417	616	158	232	2	50	81	1046	12.9
83-84—Houston	81	994	389	168	.406	132	86	.652	87	173	260	71	123	1	16	28	402	5.0
Totals	1303	50000	24272	10976	.452	7999	5356	.670			16279	2398	4193	53	864	1771	27313	21.0

Three-Point Field Goals: 1979-80, 3-for-13 (.231). 1980-81, 0-for-10. 1981-82, 0-for-5. 1982-83, 2-for-4 (.500). 1983-84, 0-for-2. Totals, 5-for-34 (.147).

NBA PLAYOFF RECORD

Sea.—Team	G.	Min.	FGA	FGM	Pct.	FTA	FTM	Pct.	Reb.	Ast.	PF	Disq.	Pts.	Avg.
68-69—San Diego	6	278	114	60	.526	53	35	.660	83	5	21	0	155	25.8
72-73—Baltimore	5	228	105	53	.505	33	23	.697	57	5	16	0	129	25.8

									—Rebounds—						
Sea.—Team	G.	Min.	FGA	FGM	Pct.	FTA	FTM	Pct.	Off.	Def.	Tot.	Ast.	PF	Dq.	Stl.	Blk.	Pts.	Avg.
73-74—Capital	7	323	143	76	.531	41	29	.707	31	80	111	21	23	0	5	15	181	25.9
74-75—Washington	17	751	372	174	.468	127	86	.677	46	140	186	37	70	3	26	39	434	25.5
75-76—Washington	7	305	122	54	.443	55	32	.582	16	72	88	10	24	0	5	28	140	20.0
76-77—Washington	9	405	173	74	.428	59	41	.695	29	93	122	17	39	0	10	22	189	21.0
77-78—Washington	21	868	385	189	.491	133	79	.594	103	176	279	43	86	2	32	52	457	21.8
78-79—Washington	19	786	396	170	.429	130	87	.669	94	172	266	38	79	3	17	52	427	22.5
79-80—Washington	2	92	41	16	.390	10	8	.800	10	12	22	6	8	0	0	4	40	20.0
81-82—Houston	3	124	50	17	.340	15	8	.533	7	23	30	3	12	0	2	10	42	14.0
Totals	96	4160	1901	883	.464	656	428	.652			1244	185	378	8	97	222	2194	22.9

NBA ALL-STAR GAME RECORD

Season—Team	Min.	FGA	FGM	Pct.	FTA	FTM	Pct.	Reb.	Ast.	PF	Disq.	Pts.
1969—San Diego	21	9	4	.444	3	3	1.000	5	0	4	0	11
1970—San Diego	35	21	9	.429	12	6	.500	15	1	1	0	24
1971—San Diego	19	13	4	.308	3	2	.667	4	2	1	0	10
1972—Houston	11	6	1	.167	2	2	1.000	2	0	2	0	4
1973—Baltimore	16	13	4	.308	2	2	1.000	12	0	0	0	10

								—Rebounds—						
Season—Team	Min.	FGA	FGM	Pct.	FTA	FTM	Pct.	Off.	Def.	Tot.	Ast.	PF	Dq.	Stl.	Blk.	Pts.
1974—Capital	35	13	5	.385	3	2	.667	4	11	15	6	4	0	0	1	12
1975—Washington	17	6	2	.333	0	0	.000	0	5	5	2	1	0	1	0	4
1976—Washington	31	14	6	.429	2	0	.000	3	7	10	1	5	0	1	0	12

Season--Team	Min.	FGA	FGM	Pct.	FTA	FTM	Pct.	—Rebounds— Off.	Def.	Tot.	Ast.	PF	Dq.	Stl.	Blk.	Pts.
1977—Washington	11	6	6	1.000	0	0	.000	0	2	2	1	5	0	0	0	12
ʻ1978—Washington	11	7	1	.143	0	0	.000	3	1	4	0	4	0	1	0	2
1979—Washington..	28	11	5	.455	5	3	.600	4	9	13	0	5	0	1	1	13
1980—Washington..	29	10	5	.500	2	2	1.000	2	3	5	4	5	0	1	4	12
Totals	264	129	52	.403	34	22	.647			92	17	37	0	5	6	126

Named to All-NBA First Team, 1975, 1977, 1979.... All-NBA Second Team, 1973, 1974, 1976.... NBA All-Rookie Team, 1969.... NBA All-Defensive Second Team, 1974 and 1975.... Led NBA in scoring, 1969.... Led NBA in rebounding, 1970 and 1974.... Member of NBA championship team, 1978.... Holds all-time NBA regular season records for games played, minutes played, and personal fouls.... THE SPORTING NEWS College Player of the Year, 1968.... Named to THE SPORTING NEWS All-America First Team, 1967 and 1968.... THE SPORTING NEWS All-America Second Team, 1966.

SPENCER HAYWOOD

Born April 22, 1949 at Silver City, Miss.   Height 6:09.   Weight 225.

High School—Detroit, Mich., Pershing.

Colleges—Trinidad State Junior College, Trinidad, Colo., and University of Detroit, Detroit, Mich.

Drafted by Buffalo on second round, 1971 (30th pick).

Signed as undergraduate free agent by Denver ABA, August 16, 1969.
Terminated contract with Denver ABA and signed by Seattle NBA, 1971.
Traded by Seattle to New York for a 1979 1st round draft choice and cash, October 24, 1975.
Traded by New York to New Orleans for Joe C. Meriweather, January 5, 1979.
Traded by Utah to Los Angeles for Adrian Dantley, September 13, 1979.
Waived by Los Angeles, August 19, 1980; signed by Washington as a free agent, October 24, 1981.
Waived by Washington, March 9, 1983.
Played in Italy during 1980-81 and 1981-82 seasons.

—COLLEGIATE RECORD—
Trinidad State JC

Year	G.	Min.	FGA	FGM	Pct.	FTA	FTM	Pct.	Reb.	Pts.	Avg.
67-68	30	......	675	358	.530	195	129	.662	663	845	28.2

Detroit

Year	G.	Min.	FGA	FGM	Pct.	FTA	FTM	Pct.	Reb.	Pts.	Avg.
68-69	24	......	508	288	.567	254	195	.768	530	771	32.1

ITALIAN LEAGUE RECORD

Year	G.	Min.	FGA	FGM	Pct.	FTA	FTM	Pct.	Reb.	Pts.	Avg.
80-81—Venezia	34	....	601	334	.556	179	132	.737	354	800	23.5
81-82—Carrera	5	175	100	63	.630	32	24	.750	37	150	30.0

ABA REGULAR SEASON RECORD

Sea.—Team	G.	Min.	—2-Point— FGM	FGA	Pct.	—3-Point— FGM	FGA	Pct.	FTM	FTA	Pct.	Reb.	Ast.	Pts.	Avg.
69-70—Denver	84	3808	986	1987	.496	0	11	.000	547	705	.776	1637	190	2519	30.0

NBA REGULAR SEASON RECORD

Sea.—Team	G.	Min.	FGA	FGM	Pct.	FTA	FTM	Pct.	Reb.	Ast.	PF	Disq.	Pts.	Avg.
70-71—Seattle	33	1162	579	260	.449	218	160	.733	396	48	84	1	680	20.6
71-72—Seattle	73	3167	1557	717	.461	586	480	.819	926	148	208	0	1914	26.2
72-73—Seattle	77	3259	1868	889	.476	564	473	.839	995	196	213	2	2251	29.2

Sea.—Team	G.	Min.	FGA	FGM	Pct.	FTA	FTM	Pct.	—Rebounds— Off.	Def.	Tot.	Ast.	PF	Dq.	Stl.	Blk.	Pts.	Avg.
73-74—Seattle	75	3039	1520	694	.457	458	373	.814	318	689	1007	240	198	2	65	106	1761	23.5
74-75—Seattle	68	2529	1325	608	.459	381	309	.811	198	432	630	137	173	1	54	108	1525	22.4
75-76—New York	78	2892	1360	605	.445	448	339	.757	234	644	878	92	255	1	80	80	1549	19.9
76-77—Knicks	31	1021	449	202	.450	131	109	.832	77	203	280	50	72	0	14	29	513	16.5
77-78—New York	67	1765	852	412	.484	135	96	.711	141	301	442	126	188	1	37	72	920	13.7
78-79—N.Y.-N.O.	68	2361	1205	595	.494	292	231	.791	172	361	533	127	236	8	40	82	1421	20.9
79-80—Los Ang.	76	1544	591	288	.487	206	159	.772	132	214	346	93	197	2	35	57	736	9.7
81-82—Washington	76	2086	829	395	.476	260	219	.842	144	278	422	64	249	6	45	68	1009	13.3
82-83—Washington	38	775	312	125	.401	87	63	.724	77	106	183	30	94	2	12	27	313	8.2
Totals	760	25600	12447	5790	.465	3766	3011	.800			7038	1351	2167	26	355	629	14592	19.2

Three-Point Field Goals: 1979-80, 1-for-4 (.250). 1981-82, 0-for-3. 1982-83, 0-for-1. Totals, 1-for-8 (.125).

NBA PLAYOFF RECORD

Sea.—Team	G.	Min.	FGA	FGM	Pct.	FTA	FTM	Pct.	—Rebounds— Off.	Def.	Tot.	Ast.	PF	Dq.	Stl.	Blk.	Pts.	Avg.
74-75—Seattle	9	337	131	47	.359	61	47	.770	20	61	81	18	29	0	7	11	141	15.7
77-78—New York	6	177	85	43	.506	11	11	1.000	19	23	42	12	24	1	2	5	97	16.2
79-80—Los Ang.	11	145	53	25	.472	16	13	.813	14	12	26	4	17	0	0	6	63	5.7
81-82—Washington	7	231	115	57	.496	35	26	.743	16	23	39	7	28	0	4	14	140	20.0
Totals	33	890	384	172	.448	123	97	.789	69	119	188	41	98	1	13	36	441	13.4

Three-Point Field Goals: 1979-80, 0-for-1.

NBA ALL-STAR GAME RECORD

Season—Team	Min.	FGA	FGM	Pct.	FTA	FTM	Pct.	Reb.	Ast.	PF	Disq.	Pts.
1972—Seattle	25	10	4	.400	4	3	.750	7	1	2	0	11
1973—Seattle	22	10	5	.500	2	2	1.000	10	0	5	0	12

Season—Team	Min.	FGA	FGM	Pct.	FTA	FTM	Pct.	Off.	Def.	Tot.	Ast.	PF	Dq.	Stl.	Blk.	Pts.
1974—Seattle	33	17	10	.588	3	3	1.000	2	9	11	5	5	0	0	3	23
1975—Seattle	17	9	1	.111	0	0	.000	1	2	3	0	1	0	0	0	2
Totals	97	46	20	.435	9	8	.889			31	6	13	0	0	3	48

Named to NBA All-Star First Team, 1972 and 1973.... NBA All-Star Second Team, 1974 and 1975.... Member of NBA championship team, 1980.... Named to ABA All-Star First Team, 1970.... ABA Most Valuable Player and Rookie of the Year, 1970.... ABA All-Star Game MVP, 1970.... Led ABA in scoring and rebounding, 1970.... Led NCAA in rebounding, 1969.... Member of U. S. Olympic team, 1968.... THE SPORTING NEWS All-America First Team, 1969.

BAILEY HOWELL

Born January 20, 1937 at Middleton, Tenn.   Height 6:07.   Weight 220.

High School—Middleton, Tenn.

College—Mississippi State University, Mississippi State, Miss.

Drafted by Detroit on first round, 1959.

Traded by Detroit with Bob Ferry, Don Ohl, Wally Jones and Les Hunter to Baltimore for Terry Dischinger, Don Kojis and Rod Thorn, June 18, 1964.

Traded by Baltimore to Boston for Mel Counts, September 1, 1966.

Selected from Boston by Buffalo in expansion draft, May 11, 1970.

Traded by Buffalo to Philadelphia for Bob Kauffman and cash or a draft choice, May 11, 1970.

—COLLEGIATE RECORD—

Year	G.	Min.	FGA	FGM	Pct.	FTA	FTM	Pct.	Reb.	Pts.	Avg.
55-56†					(Statistics unavailable)						
56-57	25	....	382	217	.568	285	213	.747	492	647	25.9
57-58	25	....	439	226	.515	315	243	.771	406	695	27.8
58-59	25	....	464	231	.498	292	226	.774	379	688	27.5
Varsity Totals	75	....	1285	674	.525	892	682	.765	1277	2030	27.1

NBA REGULAR SEASON RECORD

Sea.—Team	G.	Min.	FGA	FGM	Pct.	FTA	FTM	Pct.	Reb.	Ast.	PF	Disq.	Pts.	Avg.
59-60—Detroit	75	2346	1119	510	.456	422	312	.739	790	63	282	13	1332	17.8
60-61—Detroit	77	2752	1293	607	.469	798	601	.753	1111	196	297	10	1815	23.6
61-62—Detroit	79	2857	1193	553	.464	612	470	.768	996	186	317	10	1576	19.9
62-63—Detroit	79	2971	1235	637	.516	650	519	.798	910	232	301	9	1793	22.7
63-64—Detroit	77	2700	1267	598	.472	581	470	.809	776	205	290	9	1666	21.6
64-65—Baltimore	80	2975	1040	515	.495	629	504	.801	869	208	345	10	1534	19.2
65-66—Baltimore	79	2328	986	481	.488	551	402	.730	773	155	306	12	1364	17.3
66-67—Boston	81	2503	1242	636	.512	471	349	.741	677	103	296	4	1621	20.0
67-68—Boston	82	2801	1336	643	.481	461	335	.727	805	133	285	4	1621	19.8
68-69—Boston	78	2527	1257	612	.487	426	313	.735	685	137	285	3	1537	19.7
69-70—Boston	82	2078	931	399	.429	308	235	.763	550	120	261	4	1033	12.6
70-71—Philadelphia	82	1589	686	324	.472	315	230	.730	441	115	234	2	878	10.7
Totals	951	30427	13585	6515	.480	6224	4740	.762	9383	1853	3499	90	17770	18.7

NBA PLAYOFF RECORD

Sea.—Team	G.	Min.	FGA	FGM	Pct.	FTA	FTM	Pct.	Reb.	Ast.	PF	Disq.	Pts.	Avg.
59-60—Detroit	2	72	41	14	.341	8	6	.750	17	3	8	0	34	17.0
60-61—Detroit	5	144	57	20	.351	23	16	.696	46	22	22	1	56	11.2
61-62—Detroit	10	378	163	69	.423	75	62	.827	96	23	48	3	200	20.0
62-63—Detroit	4	163	64	24	.375	27	23	.852	42	11	19	1	71	17.8
64-65—Baltimore	9	350	130	67	.515	70	53	.757	105	19	38	3	187	20.8
65-66—Baltimore	3	94	50	23	.460	11	8	.727	30	2	13	1	54	18.0
66-67—Boston	9	241	122	59	.484	30	20	.667	66	5	35	2	138	15.3
67-68—Boston	19	597	264	135	.511	107	74	.692	146	22	84	6	344	18.1
68-69—Boston	18	551	229	112	.489	64	46	.719	118	19	84	3	270	15.0
70-71—Philadelphia	7	122	45	19	.422	18	9	.500	31	4	25	1	47	6.7
Totals	86	2712	1165	542	.465	433	317	.732	697	130	376	21	1401	16.3

NBA ALL-STAR GAME RECORD

Season—Team	Min.	FGA	FGM	Pct.	FTA	FTM	Pct.	Reb.	Ast.	PF	Disq.	Pts.
1961—Detroit	16	10	5	.500	4	3	.750	3	3	4	0	13
1962—Detroit	8	2	1	.500	0	0	.000	0	1	1	0	2
1963—Detroit	11	3	2	.667	0	0	.000	1	1	2	0	4
1964—Detroit	6	3	1	.333	0	0	.000	2	0	0	0	2
1966—Baltimore	26	11	3	.273	2	1	.500	2	2	4	0	7
1967—Boston	14	4	1	.250	2	2	1.000	2	1	1	0	4
Totals	81	33	13	.394	8	6	.750	10	8	12	0	32

Named to NBA All-Star Second Team, 1963.... Member of NBA championship teams, 1968 and 1969.... Led NCAA major college division in field-goal percentage, 1957.... Named to THE SPORTING NEWS All-America First Team, 1959.

LOUIS HUDSON
(Lou)

Born July 11, 1944 at Greensboro, N. C.   Height 6:05.   Weight 210.

High School—Greensboro, N. C., Dudley.

College—University of Minnesota, Minneapolis, Minn.

Drafted by St. Louis on first round, 1966 (4th pick).

Traded by Atlanta to Los Angeles for Ollie Johnson, September 30, 1977.

—COLLEGIATE RECORD—

Year	G.	Min.	FGA	FGM	Pct.	FTA	FTM	Pct.	Reb.	Pts.	Avg.
62-63				(Freshman team did not play intercollegiate schedule.)							
63-64	24	....	435	191	.439	85	53	.624	191	435	18.1
64-65	24	....	463	231	.499	123	96	.780	247	558	23.3
65-66	17	....	303	143	.472	77	50	.649	138	336	19.8
Totals	65	....	1201	565	.470	285	199	.698	576	1329	20.4

NBA REGULAR SEASON RECORD

Sea.—Team	G.	Min.	FGA	FGM	Pct.	FTA	FTM	Pct.	Reb.	Ast.	PF	Disq.	Pts.	Avg.
66-67—St. Louis	80	2446	1328	620	.467	327	231	.706	435	95	277	3	1471	18.4
67-68—St. Louis	46	966	500	227	.454	164	120	.732	193	65	113	2	574	12.5
68-69—Atlanta	81	2869	1455	716	.492	435	338	.777	533	216	248	0	1770	21.9
69-70—Atlanta	80	3091	1564	830	.531	450	371	.824	373	276	225	1	2031	25.4
70-71—Atlanta	76	3113	1713	829	.484	502	381	.759	386	257	186	0	2039	26.8
71-72—Atlanta	77	3042	1540	775	.503	430	349	.812	385	309	225	0	1899	24.7
72-73—Atlanta	75	3027	1710	816	.477	481	397	.825	467	258	197	1	2029	27.1

Sea.—Team	G.	Min.	FGA	FGM	Pct.	FTA	FTM	Pct.	Off.	Def.	Tot.	Ast.	PF	Dq.	Stl.	Blk.	Pts.	Avg.
73-74—Atl.	65	2588	1356	678	.500	353	295	.836	126	224	350	216	205	3	160	29	1651	25.4
74-75—Atl.	11	380	225	97	.431	57	48	.842	14	33	47	40	33	1	13	2	242	22.0
75-76—Atl.	81	2558	1205	569	.472	291	237	.814	104	196	300	214	241	3	124	17	1375	17.0
76-77—Atl.	58	1745	905	413	.456	169	142	.840	48	81	129	155	160	2	67	19	968	16.7
77-78—L.A.	82	2283	992	493	.497	177	137	.774	80	108	188	193	196	0	94	14	1123	13.7
78-79—L.A.	78	1686	636	329	.517	124	110	.887	64	76	140	141	133	1	58	17	768	9.8
Totals	890	29794	15129	7392	.489	3960	3156	.797			3926	2432	2439	17	516	98	17940	20.2

NBA PLAYOFF RECORD

Sea.—Team	G.	Min.	FGA	FGM	Pct.	FTA	FTM	Pct.	Reb.	Ast.	PF	Disq.	Pts.	Avg.
66-67—St. Louis	9	317	179	77	.430	68	49	.723	48	15	35	1	203	22.6
67-68—St. Louis	6	181	99	44	.444	47	42	.894	43	14	21	0	130	21.7
68-69—Atlanta	11	424	216	101	.468	52	40	.769	59	32	32	1	242	22.0
69-70—Atlanta	9	360	187	78	.417	50	41	.820	40	33	43	1	197	21.9
70-71—Atlanta	5	213	108	49	.454	39	29	.744	35	15	34	2	127	25.4
71-72—Atlanta	6	266	139	63	.453	29	24	.828	33	21	19	0	150	25.0
72-73—Atlanta	6	255	166	76	.458	29	26	.897	47	17	16	0	178	29.7

Sea.—Team	G.	Min.	FGA	FGM	Pct.	FTA	FTM	Pct.	Off.	Def.	Tot.	Ast.	PF	Dq.	Stl.	Blk.	Pts.	Avg.
77-78—L.A.	3	93	38	14	.368	8	7	.875	7	2	9	9	9	0	5	0	35	11.7
78-79—L.A.	6	90	32	17	.531	4	4	1.000	1	3	4	8	6	0	1	0	38	6.3
Totals	61	2199	1164	519	.446	326	262	.804			318	164	196	4	6	0	1300	21.3

NBA ALL-STAR GAME RECORD

Season—Team	Min.	FGA	FGM	Pct.	FTA	FTM	Pct.	Reb.	Ast.	PF	Disq.	Pts.
1969—Atlanta	20	13	6	.462	1	1	1.000	1	1	0	0	13
1970—Atlanta	18	12	5	.417	5	5	1.000	1	0	1	0	15
1971—Atlanta	17	13	6	.462	3	2	.667	3	1	3	0	14
1972—Atlanta	18	7	2	.286	2	2	1.000	3	3	3	0	6
1973—Atlanta	9	8	2	.250	2	2	1.000	2	0	2	0	6

Season—Team	Min.	FGA	FGM	Pct.	FTA	FTM	Pct.	Off.	Def.	Tot.	Ast.	PF	Dq.	Stl.	Blk.	Pts.
1974—Atlanta	17	8	5	.625	2	2	1.000	1	2	3	1	2	0	0	1	12
Totals	99	61	26	.426	15	14	.933			13	6	11	0	0	1	66

Named to NBA All-Star Second Team, 1970. . . . NBA All-Rookie Team, 1967.

GUS JOHNSON

Born December 13, 1938 at Akron, O.   Height 6:06.   Weight 235.

High School—Akron, O., Central.

Colleges—University of Akron, Akron, O.; Boise Junior College, Boise, Idaho, and University of Idaho, Moscow, Ida.

Drafted by Baltimore on second round, 1963 (11th pick).

Traded by Baltimore to Phoenix for a draft choice, April 10, 1972.
Waived by Phoenix NBA, December 1, 1972; signed by Indiana ABA as a free agent, December 15, 1972.

Akron

Year	G.	Min.	FGA	FGM	Pct.	FTA	FTM	Pct.	Reb.	Pts.	Avg.
59-60					(Left school before start of basketball season.)						

Year	G.	Min.	FGA	FGM	Pct.	FTA	FTM	Pct.	Reb.	Pts.	Avg.
62-63	23	....	438	188	.429	105	62	.590	466	438	19.0

NBA REGULAR SEASON RECORD

Sea.—Team	G.	Min.	FGA	FGM	Pct.	FTA	FTM	Pct.	Reb.	Ast.	PF	Disq.	Pts.	Avg.
63-64—Baltimore	78	2847	1329	571	.430	319	210	.658	1064	169	321	11	1352	17.3
64-65—Baltimore	76	2899	1379	577	.418	386	261	.676	988	270	258	4	1415	18.6
65-66—Baltimore	42	1284	661	273	.413	178	131	.736	546	114	136	3	677	16.1
66-67—Baltimore	73	2626	1377	620	.450	383	271	.708	855	194	281	7	1511	20.7
67-68—Baltimore	60	2271	1033	482	.467	270	180	.667	782	159	223	7	1144	19.1
68-69—Baltimore	49	1671	782	359	.459	223	160	.717	568	97	176	1	878	17.9
69-70—Baltimore	78	2919	1282	578	.451	272	197	.724	1086	264	269	6	1353	17.3
70-71—Baltimore	66	2538	1090	494	.453	290	214	.738	1128	192	227	4	1202	18.2
71-72—Baltimore	39	668	269	103	.383	63	43	.683	226	51	91	0	249	6.4
72-73—Phoenix	21	417	181	69	.381	36	25	.694	136	31	55	0	163	7.8
Totals	582	20140	9383	4126	.440	2420	1692	.699	7379	1541	2037	43	9944	17.1

NBA PLAYOFF RECORD

Sea.—Team	G.	Min.	FGA	FGM	Pct.	FTA	FTM	Pct.	Reb.	Ast.	PF	Disq.	Pts.	Avg.
64-65—Baltimore	10	377	173	62	.358	46	34	.739	111	34	38	1	158	15.8
65-66—Baltimore	1	8	4	1	.250	0	0	.000	0	0	1	0	2	2.0
69-70—Baltimore	7	298	111	51	.459	34	27	.794	80	9	20	0	129	18.4
70-71—Baltimore	11	365	128	54	.422	47	35	.745	114	30	34	0	143	13.0
71-72—Baltimore	5	77	30	9	.300	2	2	1.000	25	3	17	0	20	4.0
Totals	34	1125	446	177	.397	129	98	.760	330	76	110	1	452	13.3

NBA ALL-STAR GAME RECORD

Season—Team	Min.	FGA	FGM	Pct.	FTA	FTM	Pct.	Reb.	Ast.	PF	Disq.	Pts.
1965—Baltimore	25	13	7	.538	13	11	.846	8	2	2	0	25
1968—Baltimore	16	9	3	.333	2	1	.500	6	1	2	0	7
1969—Baltimore	18	10	4	.400	8	5	.625	10	0	3	0	13
1970—Baltimore	17	12	5	.417	0	0	.000	7	1	2	0	10
1971—Baltimore	23	12	5	.417	2	2	1.000	4	2	3	0	12
Totals	99	56	24	.429	25	19	.760	35	6	12	0	67

ABA REGULAR SEASON RECORD

Sea.—Team	G.	Min.	2-Point			3-Point			FTM	FTA	Pct.	Reb.	Ast.	Pts.	Avg.
			FGM	FGA	Pct.	FGM	FGA	Pct.							
72-73—Indiana	50	753	128	278	.460	4	21	.190	31	42	.738	245	62	299	6.0

ABA PLAYOFF RECORD

Sea.—Team	G.	Min.	2-Point			3-Point			FTM	FTA	Pct.	Reb.	Ast.	Pts.	Avg.
			FGM	FGA	Pct.	FGM	FGA	Pct.							
72-73—Indiana	17	184	15	56	.268	0	3	.000	3	4	.750	69	15	42	2.5

Named to NBA All-Star Second Team, 1965, 1966, 1970, 1971. . . . NBA All-Rookie Team, 1964. . . . NBA All-Defensive First Team, 1970 and 1971. . . . Member of ABA championship team, 1973.

D. NEIL JOHNSTON
(Known by middle name.)

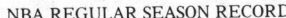

Born February 4, 1929 at Chillicothe, O.   Height 6:08.   Weight 210.

Died September 27, 1978.

High School—Chillicothe, O.

College—Ohio State University, Columbus, O.

Signed by Philadelphia as a free agent, 1951.

Signed as player-coach by Pittsburgh, ABL, 1961.

—COLLEGIATE RECORD—

Year	G.	Min.	FGA	FGM	Pct.	FTA	FTM	Pct.	Reb.	Pts.	Avg.
46-47	7	....		5	....	8	3	.375	....	13	1.9
47-48	20	....	219	67	.306	87	46	.529	....	180	9.0
Totals	27	....	....	72	....	95	49	.516	....	193	7.1

(Signed pro baseball contract in 1948 and became ineligible for his final two years at Ohio State.)

NBA REGULAR SEASON RECORD

Sea.—Team	G.	Min.	FGA	FGM	Pct.	FTA	FTM	Pct.	Reb.	Ast.	PF	Disq.	Pts.	Avg.
51-52—Philadelphia	64	993	299	141	.472	151	100	.662	342	39	154	5	382	6.0
52-53—Philadelphia	70	3166	1114	504	.452	794	556	.700	976	197	248	6	1564	22.3

Sea.—Team	G.	Min.	FGA	FGM	Pct.	FTA	FTM	Pct.	Reb.	Ast.	PF	Disq.	Pts.	Avg.
53-54—Philadelphia	72	3296	1317	591	.449	772	577	.747	797	203	259	7	1759	24.4
54-55—Philadelphia	72	2917	1184	521	.440	769	589	.766	1085	215	255	4	1631	22.7
55-56—Philadelphia	70	2594	1092	499	.457	685	549	.801	872	225	251	8	1547	22.1
56-57—Philadelphia	69	2531	1163	520	.447	648	535	.826	855	203	231	2	1575	22.8
57-58—Philadelphia	71	2408	1102	473	.429	540	442	.819	790	166	233	4	1388	19.5
58-59—Philadelphia	28	393	164	54	.329	88	69	.784	139	21	50	0	177	6.3
Totals	516	18298	7435	3303	.444	4447	3417	.768	5856	1269	1681	36	10023	19.4

NBA PLAYOFF RECORD

Sea.—Team	G.	Min.	FGA	FGM	Pct.	FTA	FTM	Pct.	Reb.	Ast.	PF	Disq.	Pts.	Avg.
51-52—Philadelphia	3	32	10	5	.500	8	6	.750	10	1	8	0	16	5.3
55-56—Philadelphia	10	397	169	69	.408	92	65	.707	143	51	41	0	203	20.3
56-57—Philadelphia	2	84	53	17	.321	6	4	.667	35	9	9	0	38	19.0
57-58—Philadelphia	8	189	78	30	.385	33	27	.818	69	14	18	0	87	10.9
Totals	23	702	310	121	.390	139	102	.734	257	75	76	0	344	15.0

NBA ALL-STAR GAME RECORD

Season—Team	Min.	FGA	FGM	Pct.	FTA	FTM	Pct.	Reb.	Ast.	PF	Disq.	Pts.
1953—Philadelphia	27	13	5	.385	2	1	.500	12	0	2	0	11
1954—Philadelphia	20	9	2	.222	4	2	.500	7	2	1	0	6
1955—Philadelphia	15	7	1	.143	1	1	1.000	6	1	0	0	3
1956—Philadelphia	25	9	5	.556	11	7	.636	10	1	3	0	17
1957—Philadelphia	23	12	8	.667	3	3	1.000	9	1	2	0	19
1958—Philadelpnia	22	13	6	.462	2	2	1.000	8	1	5	0	14
Totals	132	63	27	.429	23	16	.696	52	6	13	0	70

AMERICAN BASKETBALL LEAGUE PLAYING RECORD

			—2-Point—			—3-Point—								
Sea.—Team	G.	Min.	FGM	FGA	Pct.	FGM	FGA	Pct.	FTM	FTA	Pct.	Reb.	Ast.	Pts.	Avg.
61-62—Pittsburgh	5	106	37	15	.405	1	1	1.000	24	16	.667	18	10	49	9.8

ABL COACHING RECORD

		Regular Season				Playoffs	
Sea.	Club	W.	L.	Pct.	Pos.	W.	L.
1961-62—Pittsburgh		41	40	.506	2†	0	1
1962-63—Pittsburgh		12	10	.545	3	..	..

NBA COACHING RECORD

		Regular Season				Playoffs	
Sea.	Club	W.	L.	Pct.	Pos.	W.	L.
1959-60—Philadelphia		49	26	.653	2†	4	5
1960-61—Philadelphia		46	33	.582	2†	0	3
Totals (2 seasons)		95	59	.617		4	8

†Eastern Division.

Named to NBA All-Star First Team, 1953, 1954, 1955, 1956. . . . NBA All-Star Second Team, 1957. . . . Member of NBA championship team, 1956. . . . Led NBA in scoring, 1953, 1954, 1955. . . . Led NBA in rebounding, 1955. . . . Led NBA in field-goal percentage, 1953, 1956, 1957. . . . Played minor league baseball as a pitcher in the Philadelphia Phillies' organization, 1949 through 1951.

SAM JONES

Born June 24, 1933 at Wilmington, N. C.   Height 6:04.   Weight 205.

High School—Laurinburg, N. C., Institute.

College—North Carolina Central College, Durham, N. C.

Drafted by Boston on first round, 1957.

—COLLEGIATE RECORD—

Year	G.	Min.	FGA	FGM	Pct.	FTA	FTM	Pct.	Reb.	Pts.	Avg.
51-52	22	....	263	126	.479	78	48	.615	150	300	13.6
52-53	24	....	370	169	.457	180	115	.639	248	453	18.9
53-54	27	....	432	208	.481	137	98	.715	223	514	19.0
56-57	27	....	398	174	.437	202	155	.767	288	503	18.6
Totals	100	....	1463	677	.463	597	416	.697	909	1770	17.7

NOTE: In military service during 1954-55 and 1955-56 seasons.

NBA REGULAR SEASON RECORD

Sea.—Team	G.	Min.	FGA	FGM	Pct.	FTA	FTM	Pct.	Reb.	Ast.	PF	Disq.	Pts.	Avg.
57-58—Boston	56	594	233	100	.429	84	60	.714	160	37	42	0	260	4.6
58-59—Boston	71	1466	703	305	.434	196	151	.770	428	101	102	0	761	10.7
59-60—Boston	74	1512	782	355	.454	220	168	.764	375	125	101	1	878	11.9
60-61—Boston	78	2028	1069	480	.449	268	211	.787	421	217	148	1	1171	15.0
61-62—Boston	78	2388	1284	596	.464	297	243	.818	458	232	149	0	1435	18.4
62-63—Boston	76	2323	1305	621	.476	324	257	.793	396	241	162	1	1499	19.7
63-64—Boston	76	2381	1359	612	.450	318	249	.783	349	202	192	1	1473	19.4

Sea.—Team	G.	Min.	FGA	FGM	Pct.	FTA	FTM	Pct.	Reb.	Ast.	PF	Disq.	Pts.	Avg.
64-65—Boston	80	2885	1818	821	.452	522	428	.820	411	223	176	0	2070	25.9
65-66—Boston	67	2155	1335	626	.469	407	325	.799	347	216	170	0	1577	23.2
66-67—Boston	72	2325	1406	638	.454	371	318	.857	338	217	191	1	1594	22.1
67-68—Boston	73	2408	1348	621	.461	376	311	.827	357	216	181	0	1553	21.3
68-69—Boston	70	1820	1103	496	.450	189	148	.783	265	182	121	0	1140	16.3
Totals	871	24285	13745	6271	.456	3572	2869	.803	4305	2209	1735	5	15411	17.7

NBA PLAYOFF RECORD

Sea.—Team	G.	Min.	FGA	FGM	Pct.	FTA	FTM	Pct.	Reb.	Ast.	PF	Disq.	Pts.	Avg.
57-58—Boston	8	75	22	10	.455	16	11	.688	24	4	7	0	31	3.9
58-59—Boston	11	192	108	40	.370	39	33	.846	63	17	14	0	113	10.3
59-60—Boston	13	197	117	45	.385	21	17	.809	41	18	15	0	107	8.2
60-61—Boston	10	258	112	50	.446	35	31	.886	54	22	22	0	131	13.1
61-62—Boston	14	504	277	123	.444	60	42	.700	99	44	30	0	288	20.6
62-63—Boston	13	450	248	120	.484	83	69	.831	81	32	42	1	309	23.8
63-64—Boston	10	356	180	91	.506	68	50	.735	47	23	24	0	232	23.2
64-65—Boston	12	495	294	135	.459	84	73	.869	55	30	39	1	343	28.6
65-66—Boston	17	602	343	154	.449	136	114	.838	86	53	65	1	422	24.8
66-67—Boston	9	326	207	95	.459	58	50	.862	46	28	30	0	240	26.7
67-68—Boston	19	685	367	162	.441	84	66	.786	64	50	58	0	390	20.5
68-69—Boston	18	514	296	124	.419	69	55	.797	58	37	45	1	303	16.8
Totals	154	4654	2571	1149	.447	753	611	.811	718	358	391	5	2909	18.9

NBA ALL-STAR GAME RECORD

Season—Team	Min.	FGA	FGM	Pct.	FTA	FTM	Pct.	Reb.	Ast.	PF	Disq.	Pts.
1962—Boston	14	8	1	.125	1	0	.000	1	0	1	0	2
1964—Boston	27	20	8	.400	0	0	.000	4	3	2	0	16
1965—Boston	24	12	2	.167	2	2	1.000	5	3	2	0	6
1966—Boston	22	11	5	.455	2	2	1.000	2	5	0	0	12
1968—Boston	15	5	2	.400	1	1	1.000	2	4	1	0	5
Totals	102	56	18	.321	6	5	.833	14	15	6	0	41

Elected to Naismith Memorial Basketball Hall of Fame, 1983. . . . Named to NBA 25th Anniversary All-Time Team, 1970. . . . NBA All-Star Second Team, 1965, 1966, 1967. . . . Member of NBA championship teams, 1959, 1960, 1961, 1962, 1963, 1964, 1965, 1966, 1968, 1969. . . . Elected to NAIA Basketball Hall of Fame, 1962.

JOHN G. KERR
(Red)

Born August 17, 1932 at Chicago, Ill.   Height 6:09.   Weight 230.

High School—Chicago, Ill., Tilden.

College—University of Illinois, Champaign, Ill.

Drafted by Syracuse on first round, 1954 (6th pick).

Syracuse franchise transferred to Philadelphia, 1963.

Traded by Philadelphia to Baltimore for Wally Jones, September 22, 1965; selected from Baltimore by Chicago Bulls in expansion draft, April 30, 1966.

—COLLEGIATE RECORD—

Year	G.	Min.	FGA	FGM	Pct.	FTA	FTM	Pct.	Reb.	Pts.	Avg.
50-51			(Freshman team did not play intercollegiate schedule.)								
51-52	26	....	365	143	.392	124	71	.573	....	357	13.7
52-53	22	....	397	153	.385	123	80	.650	....	386	17.5
53-54	22	....	520	210	.404	214	136	.636	....	556	25.3
Varsity Totals	70	....	1282	506	.395	461	287	.623	....	1299	18.6

NBA REGULAR SEASON RECORD

Sea.—Team	G.	Min.	FGA	FGM	Pct.	FTA	FTM	Pct.	Reb.	Ast.	PF	Disq.	Pts.	Avg.
54-55—Syracuse	72	1529	718	301	.419	223	152	.682	474	80	165	2	754	10.5
55-56—Syracuse	72	2114	935	377	.403	316	207	.655	607	84	168	3	961	13.3
56-57—Syracuse	72	2191	827	333	.403	313	225	.719	807	90	190	3	891	12.4
57-58—Syracuse	72	2384	1020	407	.399	422	280	.664	963	88	197	4	1094	15.2
58-59—Syracuse	72	2671	1139	502	.441	367	281	.766	1008	142	183	1	1285	17.8
59-60—Syracuse	75	2361	1111	436	.392	310	233	.752	913	168	207	4	1105	14.7
60-61—Syracuse	79	2676	1056	419	.397	299	218	.729	951	199	230	4	1056	13.4
61-62—Syracuse	80	2767	1220	541	.443	302	222	.735	1176	243	282	7	1304	16.3
62-63—Syracuse	80	2561	1069	507	.474	320	241	.753	1049	214	208	3	1255	15.7
63-64—Philadelphia	80	2938	1250	536	.429	357	268	.751	1018	275	187	2	1340	16.8
64-65—Philadelphia	80	1810	714	264	.370	181	126	.696	551	197	132	1	654	8.2
65-66—Baltimore	71	1770	692	286	.413	272	209	.768	586	225	148	0	781	11.0
Totals	905	27772	11751	4909	.418	3682	2662	.723	10103	2005	2297	34	12480	13.8

Sea.—Team	G.	Min.	FGA	FGM	Pct.	FTA	FTM	Pct.	Reb.	Ast.	PF	Disq.	Pts.	Avg.
54-55—Syracuse	11	363	151	59	.391	61	34	.557	118	13	27	0	152	13.8
55-56—Syracuse	8	213	77	37	.481	33	15	.455	68	10	23	0	89	11.1
56-57—Syracuse	5	162	65	28	.431	29	20	.690	69	6	7	0	76	15.2
57-58—Syracuse	3	116	55	18	.327	18	14	.778	61	3	5	0	50	16.7
58-59—Syracuse	9	312	142	50	.352	33	30	.909	108	24	20	0	130	14.4
59-60—Syracuse	3	104	51	15	.294	12	11	.917	25	9	9	0	41	13.7
60-61—Syracuse	8	210	88	30	.341	23	16	.696	99	20	18	0	76	9.5
61-62—Syracuse	5	193	109	41	.376	8	6	.750	80	10	15	0	88	17.6
62-63—Syracuse	5	187	60	26	.433	21	16	.762	75	9	12	0	68	13.6
63-64—Philadelphia	5	185	83	40	.482	20	15	.750	69	16	12	0	95	19.0
64-65—Philadelphia	11	181	67	24	.358	21	15	.714	38	28	20	0	63	5.7
65-66—Baltimore	3	49	11	2	.182	2	1	.500	17	4	5	0	5	1.7
Totals	76	2275	959	370	.386	281	193	.687	827	152	173	0	933	12.3

NBA ALL-STAR GAME RECORD

Season—Team	Min.	FGA	FGM	Pct.	FTA	FTM	Pct.	Reb.	Ast.	PF	Disq.	Pts.
1956—Syracuse	16	4	2	.500	1	0	.000	8	0	2	0	4
1959—Syracuse	21	14	3	.214	2	1	.500	9	2	0	0	7
1963—Syracuse	11	4	0	.000	2	2	1.000	2	1	3	0	2
Totals	48	22	5	.227	5	3	.600	19	3	5	0	13

NBA COACHING RECORD

Sea. Club	Regular Season				Playoffs	
	W.	L.	Pct.	Pos.	W.	L.
1966-67—Chicago	33	48	.407	4†	0	3
1967-68—Chicago	29	53	.354	4†	1	4
1968-69—Phoenix	16	66	.195	7†	..	..
1969-70—Phoenix	15	23	.395	..†	..	..
Totals (4 years)	93	190	.329		1	7

†Western Division.

Named NBA Coach of the Year, 1967.... Member of NBA championship team, 1955.

ROBERT JERRY LANIER JR.
(Bob)

Born September 10, 1948 at Buffalo, N. Y. Height 6:11. Weight 265.
High School—Buffalo, N. Y., Bennett.
College—St. Bonaventure University, St. Bonaventure, N. Y.
Drafted by Detroit on first round, 1970 (1st pick).

Traded by Detroit to Milwaukee for Kent Benson and a 1980 1st round draft choice, February 4, 1980.

—COLLEGIATE RECORD—

Year	G.	Min.	FGA	FGM	Pct.	FTA	FTM	Pct.	Reb.	Pts.	Avg.
66-67†	15	....	....	....	....	....	....	....	....	450	30.0
67-68	25	....	466	272	.584	175	112	.640	390	656	26.2
68-69	24	....	460	270	.587	181	114	.630	374	654	27.3
69-70	26	....	549	308	.561	194	141	.727	416	757	29.1
Varsity Totals	75	....	1475	850	.576	550	367	.667	1180	2067	27.6

NBA REGULAR SEASON RECORD

Sea.—Team	G.	Min.	FGA	FGM	Pct.	FTA	FTM	Pct.	Reb.	Ast.	PF	Disq.	Pts.	Avg.
70-71—Detroit	82	2017	1108	504	.455	376	273	.726	665	146	272	4	1281	15.6
71-72—Detroit	80	3092	1690	834	.493	505	388	.768	1132	248	297	6	2056	25.7
72-73—Detroit	81	3150	1654	810	.490	397	307	.773	1205	260	278	4	1927	23.8

Sea.—Team	G.	Min.	FGA	FGM	Pct.	FTA	FTM	Pct.	—Rebounds—			Ast.	PF	Dq.	Stl.	Blk.	Pts.	Avg.
									Off.	Def.	Tot.							
73-74—Detroit	81	3047	1483	748	.504	409	326	.797	269	805	1074	343	273	7	110	247	1822	22.5
74-75—Detroit	76	2987	1433	731	.510	450	361	.802	225	689	914	350	237	1	75	172	1823	24.0
75-76—Detroit	64	2363	1017	541	.532	370	284	.768	217	529	746	217	203	2	79	86	1366	21.3
76-77—Detroit	64	2446	1269	678	.534	318	260	.818	200	545	745	214	174	0	70	126	1616	25.3
77-78—Detroit	63	2311	1159	622	.537	386	298	.772	197	518	715	216	185	2	82	93	1542	24.5
78-79—Detroit	53	1835	950	489	.515	367	275	.749	164	330	494	140	181	5	50	75	1253	23.6
79-80—Det.-Milw.	63	2131	867	466	.537	354	277	.782	152	400	552	184	200	3	74	89	1210	19.2
80-81—Milwaukee	67	1753	716	376	.525	277	208	.751	128	285	413	179	184	0	73	81	961	14.3
81-82—Milwaukee	74	1986	729	407	.558	242	182	.752	92	296	388	219	211	3	72	56	996	13.5
82-83—Milwaukee	39	978	332	163	.491	133	91	.684	58	142	200	105	125	2	34	24	417	10.7
83-84—Milwaukee	72	2007	685	392	.572	274	194	.708	141	314	455	186	228	8	58	51	978	13.6
Totals	959	32103	15092	7761	.514	4858	3724	.767			9698	3007	3048	47	777	1100	19248	20.1

Three-Point Field Goals: 1979-80, 1-for-6 (.167). 1980-81, 1-for-1. 1981-82, 0-for-2. 1982-83, 0-for-1. 1983-84, 0-for-3. Totals, 2-for-13 (.154).

NBA PLAYOFF RECORD

Sea.—Team	G.	Min.	FGA	FGM	Pct.	FTA	FTM	Pct.	Off.	Def.	Tot.	Ast.	PF	Dq.	Stl.	Blk.	Pts.	Avg.
									___	Rebounds	___							
73-74—Detroit	7	303	152	77	.507	38	30	.789	26	81	107	21	28	1	4	14	184	26.3
74-75—Detroit	3	128	51	26	.510	12	9	.750	5	27	32	19	10	0	4	12	61	20.3
75-76—Detroit	9	359	172	95	.552	50	45	.900	39	75	114	30	34	1	8	21	235	26.1
76-77—Detroit	3	118	54	34	.630	19	16	.842	13	37	50	6	10	0	3	7	84	28.0
79-80—Milwaukee	7	256	101	52	.515	42	31	.738	17	48	65	31	23	0	7	8	135	19.3
80-81—Milwaukee	7	236	85	50	.588	32	23	.719	12	40	52	28	18	0	12	8	123	17.6
81-82—Milwaukee	6	212	80	41	.513	25	14	.560	18	27	45	22	21	2	8	5	96	16.0
82-83—Milwaukee	9	250	89	51	.573	35	21	.600	17	46	63	23	32	2	5	14	123	13.7
83-84—Milwaukee	16	499	171	82	.480	44	39	.886	32	85	117	55	57	1	11	10	203	12.7
Totals	67	2361	955	508	.532	297	228	.768	179	466	645	235	233	7	62	99	1244	18.6

Three-Point Field Goals: 1981-82, 0-for-1.

NBA ALL-STAR GAME RECORD

Season—Team	Min.	FGA	FGM	Pct.	FTA	FTM	Pct.	Reb.	Ast.	PF	Disq.	Pts.
1972—Detroit	5	2	0	.000	3	2	.667	3	0	0	0	2
1973—Detroit	12	9	5	.556	0	0	.000	6	0	1	0	10

Season—Team	Min.	FGA	FGM	Pct.	FTA	FTM	Pct.	Off.	Def.	Tot.	Ast.	PF	Dq.	Stl.	Blk.	Pts.
								___	Rebounds	___						
1974—Detroit	26	15	11	.733	2	2	1.000	2	8	10	2	1	0	0	2	24
1975—Detroit	12	4	1	.250	0	0	.000	2	5	7	2	3	0	2	0	2
1977—Detroit	20	8	7	.875	3	3	1.000	5	5	10	4	3	0	1	1	17
1978—Detroit	4	0	0	.000	2	1	.500	2	0	2	0	0	0	0	0	1
1979—Detroit	31	10	5	.500	0	0	.000	1	3	4	4	4	0	1	1	10
1982—Milwaukee....	11	7	3	.429	2	2	1.000	2	1	3	0	3	0	0	0	8
Totals	121	55	32	.582	12	10	.833			45	12	15	0	4	4	74

Named to NBA All-Rookie Team, 1971. . . . NBA All-Star Game MVP, 1974. . . . Named to THE SPORTING NEWS All-America First Team, 1970.

JERRY RAY LUCAS

Born March 30, 1940 at Middletown, O. Height 6:08. Weight 235.

High School—Middletown, O.

College—Ohio State University, Columbus, O.

Drafted by Cincinnati on first round (territorial choice), 1962.

Signed by Cleveland ABL, 1962; Cleveland dropped out of
ABL prior to 1962-63 season; did not play pro basketball, 1962-63.

Traded by Cincinnati to San Francisco for Jim King and Bill Turner, October 25, 1969.
Traded by San Francisco to New York for Cazzie Russell, May 7, 1971.

—COLLEGIATE RECORD—

Year	G.	Min.	FGA	FGM	Pct.	FTA	FTM	Pct.	Reb.	Pts.	Avg.
58-59†			Freshman team did not play an intercollegiate schedule.								
59-60	27	....	444	283	.637	187	144	.770	442	710	26.3
60-61	27	....	411	256	.623	208	159	.764	470	671	24.9
61-62	28	....	388	237	.611	169	135	.799	499	609	21.8
Varsity Totals	82	....	1243	776	.624	564	438	.777	1411	1990	24.3

NBA REGULAR SEASON RECORD

Sea.—Team	G.	Min.	FGA	FGM	Pct.	FTA	FTM	Pct.	Reb.	Ast.	PF	Disq.	Pts.	Avg.
63-64—Cincinnati	79	3273	1035	545	.527	398	310	.779	1375	204	300	6	1400	17.7
64-65—Cincinnati	66	2864	1121	558	.498	366	298	.814	1321	157	214	1	1414	21.4
65-66—Cincinnati	79	3517	1523	690	.453	403	317	.787	1668	213	274	5	1697	21.5
66-67—Cincinnati	81	3558	1257	577	.459	359	284	.791	1547	268	280	2	1438	17.8
67-68—Cincinnati	82	3619	1361	707	.519	445	346	.778	1560	251	243	3	1760	21.4
68-69—Cincinnati	74	3075	1007	555	.551	327	247	.755	1360	306	206	0	1357	18.3
69-70—Cinn.-S.F.	67	2420	799	405	.507	255	200	.784	951	173	166	2	1010	15.1
70-71—San Fran.	80	3251	1250	623	.498	367	289	.787	1265	293	197	0	1535	19.2
71-72—New York	77	2926	1060	543	.512	249	197	.791	1011	318	218	1	1283	16.7
72-73—New York	71	2001	608	312	.513	100	80	.800	510	317	157	0	704	9.9

Sea.—Team	G.	Min.	FGA	FGM	Pct.	FTA	FTM	Pct.	Off.	Def.	Tot.	Ast.	PF	Dq.	Stl.	Blk.	Pts.	Avg.
									___	Rebounds	___							
73-74—New York	73	1627	420	194	.462	96	67	.698	62	312	374	230	134	0	28	24	455	6.2
Totals	829	32131	11441	5709	.499	3365	2635	.783			12942	2730	2389	20			14053	17.0

—DID YOU KNOW—

That San Antonio Owner Angelo Drossos, Houston Owner Charlie Thomas and former
Denver owner Red McCombs all worked in McCombs' San Antonio car dealership in the
1950s?

JERRY LUCAS

NBA PLAYOFF RECORD

Sea.—Team	G.	Min.	FGA	FGM	Pct.	FTA	FTM	Pct.	Reb.	Ast.	PF	Disq.	Pts.	Avg.
63-64—Cincinnati	10	370	123	48	.390	37	26	.703	125	34	37	1	122	12.2
64-65—Cincinnati	4	195	75	38	.507	22	17	.773	84	9	12	0	93	23.3
65-66—Cincinnati	5	231	85	40	.471	35	27	.771	101	14	14	0	107	21.4
66-67—Cincinnati	4	183	55	24	.436	2	2	1.000	77	8	15	0	50	12.5
70-71—San Fran.	5	171	77	39	.506	16	11	.688	50	16	14	0	89	17.8
71-72—New York	16	737	238	119	.500	71	59	.831	173	85	49	1	297	18.6
72-73—New York	17	368	112	54	.482	23	20	.870	85	39	47	0	128	7.5

Sea.—Team	G.	Min.	FGA	FGM	Pct.	FTA	FTM	Pct.	Off.	Def.	Tot.	Ast.	PF	Dq.	Stl.	Blk.	Pts.	Avg.
									—Rebounds—									
73-74—New York	11	115	21	5	.238	0	0	.000	6	16	22	9	9	0	4	0	10	0.9
Totals	72	2370	786	367	.467	206	162	.786			717	214	197	2			896	12.4

NBA ALL-STAR GAME RECORD

Season—Team	Min.	FGA	FGM	Pct.	FTA	FTM	Pct.	Reb.	Ast.	PF	Disq.	Pts.
1964—Cincinnati..............	36	6	3	.500	6	5	.833	8	0	5	0	11
1965—Cincinnati..............	35	19	12	.632	1	1	1.000	10	1	2	0	25
1966—Cincinnati..............	23	11	4	.364	2	2	1.000	19	0	2	0	10
1967—Cincinnati..............	22	5	3	.600	1	1	1.000	7	2	3	0	7
1968—Cincinnati..............	21	9	6	.667	4	4	1.000	5	4	3	0	16
1969—Cincinnati..............	17	5	2	.400	5	4	.800	6	1	3	0	8
1971—San Francisco	29	9	5	.556	2	2	1.000	9	4	2	0	12
Totals	183	64	35	.547	21	19	.905	64	12	20	0	89

Elected to Naismith Memorial Basketball Hall of Fame, 1979.... Named to NBA All-Star First Team, 1965, 1966, 1968.... NBA All-Star Second Team, 1964 and 1967.... NBA Rookie of the Year, 1964.... NBA All-Rookie Team, 1964. ... Led NBA in field-goal percentage, 1964.... NBA All-Star Game MVP, 1965.... Member of NBA championship team, 1973. ... THE SPORTING NEWS College Player of the Year, 1961 and 1962.... Named to THE SPORTING NEWS All-America First Team, 1960, 1961, 1962.... Member of NCAA championship team, 1960.... Member of U. S. Olympic team, 1960.... Led NCAA in rebounding, 1961 and 1962.... Led NCAA in field-goal percentage, 1960, 1961, 1962.

CHARLES EDWARD MACAULEY
(Easy Ed)

Born March 22, 1928 at St. Louis, Mo. Height 6:08. Weight 190.

High School—St. Louis, Mo., St. Louis University High.

College—St. Louis University, St. Louis, Mo.

Selected by St. Louis as a territorial choice (first round)
in Basketball Association of America draft, 1949.

Drafted by Boston NBA from St. Louis NBA in dispersal draft, April 25, 1950.
Traded with draft rights to Cliff Hagan by Boston NBA to St. Louis NBA for a 1st round draft choice, April 29, 1956.

—COLLEGIATE RECORD—

Year	G.	Min.	FGA	FGM	Pct.	FTA	FTM	Pct.	Reb.	Pts.	Avg.
45-46	23	....	...	94	....	...	71	....	....	259	11.3
46-47	28	....	...	141	....	...	104	....	....	386	13.8
47-48	27	....	324	132	.407	159	104	.654	....	368	13.6
48-49	26	....	275	144	.524	153	116	.758	....	404	15.5
Totals	104	....	...	511	....	....	395	....	....	1417	13.6

NBA REGULAR SEASON RECORD

Sea.—Team	G.	Min.	FGA	FGM	Pct.	FTA	FTM	Pct.	Reb.	Ast.	PF	Disq.	Pts.	Avg.
49-50—St. Louis	67	....	882	351	.398	528	379	.718	....	200	221	....	1081	16.1
50-51—Boston	68	....	985	459	.466	614	466	.759	616	252	205	4	1384	20.4
51-52—Boston	66	2631	888	384	.432	621	496	.799	529	232	174	0	1264	19.2
52-53—Boston	69	2902	997	451	.452	667	500	.750	629	280	188	0	1402	20.3
53-54—Boston	71	2792	950	462	.486	554	420	.758	571	271	168	1	1344	18.9
54-55—Boston	71	2706	951	403	.424	558	442	.792	600	275	171	0	1248	17.6
55-56—Boston	71	2354	995	420	.422	504	400	.794	422	211	158	2	1240	17.5
56-57—St. Louis	72	2582	987	414	.419	479	359	.749	440	202	206	2	1187	16.5
57-58—St. Louis	72	1908	879	376	.428	369	267	.723	478	143	156	2	1019	14.2
58-59—St. Louis	14	196	75	22	.293	35	21	.600	40	13	20	1	65	4.6
Totals	641	....	8589	3742	.436	4929	3750	.761	....	2079	1667	12	11234	17.5

NBA PLAYOFF RECORD

Sea.—Team	G.	Min.	FGA	FGM	Pct.	FTA	FTM	Pct.	Reb.	Ast.	PF	Disq.	Pts.	Avg.
50-51—Boston	2	....	36	17	.472	16	10	.625	18	8	4	0	44	22.0
51-52—Boston	3	129	49	27	.551	19	16	.842	33	11	11	1	70	23.3
52-53—Boston	6	278	71	31	.437	54	39	.722	58	21	23	2	101	16.8
53-54—Boston	5	127	22	8	.364	13	9	.692	21	21	14	0	25	5.0
54-55—Boston	7	283	93	43	.462	54	41	.759	52	32	21	0	127	18.1

ED MACAULEY

Sea.—Team	G.	Min.	FGA	FGM	Pct.	FTA	FTM	Pct.	Reb.	Ast.	PF	Disq.	Pts.	Avg.
55-56—Boston	3	73	30	12	.400	11	7	.636	15	5	6	0	31	10.3
56-57—St. Louis	10	297	109	44	.404	74	54	.730	62	22	39	3	142	14.2
57-58—St. Louis	11	227	89	36	.404	50	36	.720	62	18	23	0	108	9.8
Totals	47	....	499	218	.437	291	212	.729	321	138	141	6	648	13.8

NBA ALL-STAR GAME RECORD

Season—Team	Min.	FGA	FGM	Pct.	FTA	FTM	Pct.	Reb.	Ast.	PF	Disq.	Pts.
1951—Boston	...	12	7	.583	7	6	.857	6	1	3	0	20
1952—Boston	28	7	3	.429	9	9	1.000	7	3	2	0	15
1953—Boston	35	12	5	.417	8	8	1.000	7	3	2	0	18
1954—Boston	25	11	4	.364	6	5	.833	1	3	2	0	13
1955—Boston	27	5	1	.200	5	4	.800	4	2	1	0	6
1956—Boston	20	9	1	.111	4	2	.500	2	3	3	0	4
1957—St. Louis	19	6	3	.500	2	1	.500	5	3	0	0	7
Totals	...	62	24	.387	41	35	.854	32	18	13	0	83

NBA COACHING RECORD

		Regular Season				Playoffs	
Sea.	Club	W.	L.	Pct.	Pos.	W.	L.
1958-59—St. Louis		43	19	.694	1†	2	4
1959-60—St. Louis		46	29	.613	1†	7	7
Totals (2 seasons)		89	48	.650		9	11

†Western Division.

Elected to Naismith Memorial Basketball Hall of Fame, 1960. . . . Named to NBA All-Star First Team, 1951, 1952, 1953. . . . NBA All-Star Second Team, 1954. . . . NBA All-Star Game MVP, 1951. . . . Member of NBA championship team, 1958. . . . Led NBA in field-goal percentage, 1954. . . . Named to THE SPORTING NEWS All-America First Team, 1949. . . . Led NCAA in field-goal percentage, 1949.

PETER PRESS MARAVICH
(Pete)

Born June 22, 1948 at Aliquippa, Pa.   Height 6:05.   Weight 200.

High Schools—Clemson, S. C., Daniels (Fr. and Soph.) and Raleigh, N. C., Needham Broughton (Jr. and Sr.).

Prep School—Salemburg, N. C., Edwards Military Institute.

College—Louisiana State University, Baton Rouge, La.

Drafted by Atlanta on first round, 1970 (3rd pick).

Traded by Atlanta to New Orleans for Dean Meminger, Bob Kauffman and four draft choices (1st round in 1974, 1st and 2nd in 1975, 2nd in 1976), May 3, 1974.
Franchise moved from New Orleans to Utah, 1979.
Waived by Utah, January 17, 1980; signed by Boston as a free agent, January 22, 1980.

—COLLEGIATE RECORD—

Year	G.	Min.	FGA	FGM	Pct.	FTA	FTM	Pct.	Reb.	Pts.	Avg.
66-67†	17	....	604	273	.452	234	195	.833	176	741	43.6
67-68	26	....	1022	432	.423	338	274	.811	195	1138	43.8
68-69	26	....	976	433	.444	378	282	.746	169	1148	44.2
69-70	31	....	1168	522	.447	436	337	.773	164	1381	44.5
Varsity Totals	83	....	3166	1387	.438	1152	893	.775	528	3667	44.2

NBA REGULAR SEASON RECORD

Sea.—Team	G.	Min.	FGA	FGM	Pct.	FTA	FTM	Pct.	Reb.	Ast.	PF	Disq.	Pts.	Avg.
70-71—Atlanta	81	2926	1613	738	.458	505	404	.800	298	355	238	1	1880	23.2
71-72—Atlanta	66	2302	1077	460	.427	438	355	.811	256	393	207	0	1275	19.3
72-73—Atlanta	79	3089	1788	789	.441	606	485	.800	346	546	245	1	2063	26.1

								—Rebounds—									
Sea.—Team	G.	Min.	FGA	FGM	Pct.	FTA	FTM	Pct.	Off.	Def.	Tot.	Ast.	PF	Dq.	Stl.	Blk.	Pts.	Avg.
73-74—Atlanta	76	2903	1791	819	.457	568	469	.826	98	276	374	396	261	4	111	13	2107	27.7
74-75—N. Orleans	79	2853	1562	655	.419	481	390	.811	93	329	422	488	227	4	120	18	1700	21.5
75-76—N. Orleans	62	2373	1316	604	.459	488	396	.811	46	254	300	332	197	3	87	23	1604	25.9
76-77—N. Orleans	73	3041	2047	886	.433	600	501	.835	90	284	374	392	191	1	84	22	2273	31.1
77-78—N. Orleans	50	2041	1253	556	.444	276	240	.870	49	129	178	335	116	1	101	8	1352	27.0
78-79—N. Orleans	49	1824	1035	436	.421	277	233	.841	33	88	121	243	104	2	60	18	1105	22.6
79-80—Utah-Bos.	43	964	543	244	.449	105	91	.867	17	61	78	83	79	1	24	6	589	13.7
Totals	658	24316	14025	6187	.441	4344	3564	.820			2747	3563	1865	18	587	108	15948	24.2

Three-Point Field Goals: 1979-80, 10-for-15 (.667).

NBA PLAYOFF RECORD

Sea.—Team	G.	Min.	FGA	FGM	Pct.	FTA	FTM	Pct.	Reb.	Ast.	PF	Disq.	Pts.	Avg.
70-71—Atlanta	5	199	122	46	.377	26	18	.692	26	24	14	0	110	22.0
71-72—Atlanta	6	219	121	54	.446	71	58	.817	32	28	24	0	166	27.7
72-73—Atlanta	6	234	155	65	.419	34	27	.794	29	40	24	1	157	26.2

Sea.—Team	G.	Min.	FGA	FGM	Pct.	FTA	FTM	Pct.	Off.	Def.	Tot.	Ast.	PF	Dq.	Stl.	Blk.	Pts.	Avg.
79-80—Boston	9	104	51	25	.490	3	2	.667	0	8	8	6	12	0	3	0	54	6.0
Totals	26	756	449	190	.423	134	105	.784			95	98	74	1	3	0	487	18.7

Three-Point Field Goals: 1979-80, 2-for-6 (.333).

NBA ALL-STAR GAME RECORD

Season—Team	Min.	FGA	FGM	Pct.	FTA	FTM	Pct.	Off.	Def.	Tot.	Ast.	PF	Dq.	Stl.	Blk.	Pts.
1973—Atlanta	22	8	4	.500	0	0	.000			3	5	4	0			8
1974—Atlanta	22	15	4	.267	9	7	.778	1	2	3	4	2	0	0	0	15
1977—N. Orleans	21	13	5	.385	0	0	.000	0	0	0	4	1	0	4	0	10
1978—N. Orleans						Selected—Injured, Did Not Play										
1979—N. Orleans	14	8	5	.625	0	0	.000	0	2	2	2	1	0	0	0	10
Totals	79	44	18	.409	9	7	.778			8	15	8	0	4	0	43

Named to NBA All-Star First Team, 1976 and 1977. . . . NBA All-Star Second Team, 1973 and 1978. . . . NBA All-Rookie Team, 1971. . . . Shares NBA record for most free-throw attempts in one quarter, 16, vs. Chicago, January 2, 1973. . . . Led NBA in scoring, 1977. . . . THE SPORTING NEWS College Player of the Year, 1970. . . . Named to THE SPORTING NEWS All-America First Team, 1968, 1969, 1970. . . . Led NCAA in scoring, 1968, 1969, 1970. . . . Holds the following NCAA career records: most points, highest scoring average, most games scoring at least 50 points (28), most field goals made, most field goals attempted, most free throws made (3-year career) and most free throws attempted (3-year career). . . . Holds the following NCAA season records: most points, highest scoring average, most games scoring at least 50 points (10 in 1970), most field goals made and most field goals attempted. . . . Holds NCAA record for most free throws made in one game, 30, vs. Oregon State in 31 attempts, December 22, 1969. . . . Son of former NBL and BAA guard and former college coach Press Maravich.

SLATER MARTIN
(Dugie)

Born October 22, 1925 at Houston, Tex.   Height 5:10.   Weight 170.

High School—Houston, Tex., Thomas Jefferson.

College—University of Texas, Austin, Tex.

Drafted by Minneapolis, 1949.

Drafted by Minneapolis in BAA draft, 1949 (BAA merged with NBL to form NBA later in 1949).
Traded by Minneapolis with Jerry Bird and a player to be named later to New York for Walter Dukes and draft rights to Burdette Haldorson, October 26, 1956.
Traded by New York to St. Louis for Willie Naulls, December 10, 1956.

—COLLEGIATE RECORD—

Year	G.	Min.	FGA	FGM	Pct.	FTA	FTM	Pct.	Reb.	Pts.	Avg.
43-44	14	....	...	75	....	...	34	....	....	184	13.2
44-45 and 45-46					Military Service						
46-47	27	....	...	109	....	...	37	....	....	255	9.4
47-48	25	....	...	126	....	85	65	.765	....	317	12.7
48-49	24	....	...	165	....	...	54	....	....	384	16.0
Totals	90			475			190			1140	12.7

NBA REGULAR SEASON RECORD

Sea.—Team	G.	Min.	FGA	FGM	Pct.	FTA	FTM	Pct.	Reb.	Ast.	PF	Disq.	Pts.	Avg.
49-50—Minneapolis	67	....	302	106	.351	93	59	.634	....	148	162	....	271	4.0
50-51—Minneapolis	68	....	627	227	.362	177	121	.684	246	235	199	3	575	8.5
51-52—Minneapolis	66	2480	632	237	.375	190	142	.747	228	249	226	9	616	9.3
52-53—Minneapolis	70	2556	634	260	.410	287	224	.780	186	250	246	4	744	10.6
53-54—Minneapolis	69	2472	654	254	.388	243	176	.724	166	253	198	3	684	9.9
54-55—Minneapolis	72	2784	919	350	.381	359	276	.769	260	427	221	7	976	13.6
55-56—Minneapolis	72	2838	863	309	.358	395	329	.833	260	445	202	2	947	13.2
56-57—N.Y.-St. L.	66	2401	736	244	.332	291	230	.790	288	269	193	1	718	10.9
57-58—St. Louis	60	2098	768	258	.336	276	206	.746	228	218	187	0	722	12.0
58-59—St. Louis	71	2504	706	245	.347	254	197	.776	253	336	230	8	687	9.4
59-60—St. Louis	64	1756	383	142	.371	155	113	.729	187	330	174	2	397	6.2
Totals	745	....	7224	2632	.364	2720	2073	.762	...	3160	2238	..	7337	9.8

NBA PLAYOFF RECORD

Sea.—Team	G.	Min.	FGA	FGM	Pct.	FTA	FTM	Pct.	Reb.	Ast.	PF	Disq.	Pts.	Avg.
49-50—Minneapolis	12	....	50	21	.420	24	14	.583	....	25	35	....	56	4.7
50-51—Minneapolis	7	....	51	18	.353	27	14	.519	42	25	20	....	50	7.1

—DID YOU KNOW—

That Wilt Chamberlain (28.5) and Nate Thurmond (26.7) combined to average more than 55 rebounds per game in the 1967 NBA championship series? Chamberlain's Philadelphia 76ers defeated Thurmond's San Francisco Warriors, four games to two.

Sea.—Team	G.	Min.	FGA	FGM	Pct.	FTA	FTM	Pct.	Reb.	Ast.	PF	Disq.	Pts.	Avg.
51-52—Minneapolis	13	523	110	38	.345	56	41	.732	37	56	64	4	117	9.0
52-53—Minneapolis	12	453	103	41	.398	51	39	.765	31	43	49	1	121	10.1
53-54—Minneapolis	13	533	112	37	.330	70	52	.743	29	60	52	1	126	9.7
54-55—Minneapolis	7	315	94	28	.298	49	40	.816	28	31	23	0	96	13.7
55-56—Minneapolis	3	121	37	17	.459	24	20	.833	7	15	9	0	54	18.0
56-57—St. Louis	10	439	155	55	.355	74	56	.757	42	49	39	2	166	16.6
57-58—St. Louis	11	416	137	44	.321	63	39	.619	48	40	40	1	127	11.5
58-59—St. Louis	1	18	5	4	.800	0	0	.000	3	2	2	0	8	8.0
59-60—St. Louis	3	58	13	1	.077	4	1	.250	3	8	9	0	3	1.0
Totals	92	2876	867	304	.351	442	316	.715	270	354	342	9	924	10.0

NBA ALL-STAR GAME RECORD

Season—Team	Min.	FGA	FGM	Pct.	FTA	FTM	Pct.	Reb.	Ast.	PF	Disq.	Pts.
1953—Minneapolis	26	10	2	.200	1	1	1.000	2	1	2	0	5
1954—Minneapolis	23	5	1	.200	0	0	.000	0	3	3	0	2
1955—Minneapolis	23	5	2	.400	2	1	.500	2	5	3	0	5
1956—Minneapolis	29	7	3	.429	3	3	1.000	1	7	5	0	9
1957—St. Louis	31	11	4	.364	0	0	.000	2	3	1	0	8
1958—St. Louis	26	9	2	.222	4	2	.500	2	8	3	0	6
1959—St. Louis	22	6	2	.333	2	1	.500	6	1	2	0	5
Totals	180	53	16	.302	12	8	.667	15	28	19	0	40

NBA COACHING RECORD

Sea.	Club	Regular Season				Playoffs	
		W.	L.	Pct.	Pos.	W.	L.
1956-57—St. Louis		5	3	.625	..†	..	..

ABA COACHING RECORD

Sea.	Club	Regular Season				Playoffs	
		W.	L.	Pct.	Pos.	W.	L.
1967-68—Houston		29	49	.372	4†	0	3
1968-69—Houston		3	9	.250	...†	..	..
Totals (2 years)		32	58	.356		..	..

†Western Division.

Named to NBA All-Star Second Team, 1954, 1956, 1957, 1958, 1959. . . . Member of NBA championship teams, 1950, 1952, 1953, 1954, 1958. . . . Named to THE SPORTING NEWS All-America Fifth Team, 1949.

GEORGE McGINNIS

Born August 12, 1950 at Indianapolis, Ind.   Height 6:08.   Weight 235.

High School—Indianapolis, Ind., Washington.

College—Indiana University, Bloomington, Ind.

Drafted by Philadelphia on second round, 1973 (22nd pick).

Signed as an undergraduate free agent by Indiana ABA in lieu of a 1972 1st round draft choice, 1971.

Invoked proviso that for $86,750 he could buy his way out of contract with Indiana ABA; signed by Philadelphia NBA, July 10, 1975 after Commissioner Larry O'Brien revoked a contract McGinnis had signed with New York NBA, May 30, 1975.

Traded by Philadelphia to Denver for Bobby Jones and Ralph Simpson, August 16, 1978.

Traded by Denver to Indiana for Alex English and a 1980 1st round draft choice, February 1, 1980.

Waived by Indiana, October 27, 1982.

—COLLEGIATE RECORD—

Year	G.	Min.	FGA	FGM	Pct.	FTA	FTM	Pct.	Reb.	Pts.	Avg.
69-70†					Did Not Play—Ineligible						
70-71	24	....	615	283	.460	249	153	.614	352	719	30.0

ABA REGULAR SEASON RECORD

Sea.—Team	G.	Min.	2-Point			3-Point			FTM	FTA	Pct.	Reb.	Ast.	Pts.	Avg.
			FGM	FGA	Pct.	FGM	FGA	Pct.							
71-72—Indiana	78	2179	459	961	.478	6	38	.158	298	462	.645	711	137	1234	16.9
72-73—Indiana	82	3347	860	1723	.499	8	32	.250	517	778	.665	1022	205	2261	27.6
73-74—Indiana	80	3266	784	1652	.475	5	34	.147	488	715	.683	1197	267	2071	25.9
74-75—Indiana	79	3193	811	1759	.461	62	175	.354	545	753	.724	1126	495	2353	29.8
Totals	319	11985	2914	6095	.478	81	279	.290	1848	2708	.682	4056	1194	7919	24.8

ABA PLAYOFF RECORD

Sea.—Team	G.	Min.	2-Point			3-Point			FTM	FTA	Pct.	Reb.	Ast.	Pts.	Avg.
			FGM	FGA	Pct.	FGM	FGA	Pct.							
71-72—Indiana	20	633	102	246	.415	4	15	.267	94	150	.627	277	52	310	15.5
72-73—Indiana	18	732	161	352	.457	0	5	.000	109	142	.732	222	39	431	23.9
73-74—Indiana	14	585	117	254	.461	2	7	.286	96	129	.744	166	47	336	24.0
74-75—Indiana	18	731	190	382	.497	23	73	.315	132	192	.688	286	148	581	32.3
Totals	70	2681	570	1234	.462	29	100	.290	431	620	.695	901	286	1658	23.7

ABA ALL-STAR GAME RECORD

Sea.—Team	Min.	2-Point			3-Point			FTM	FTA	Pct.	Reb.	Ast.	Pts.	Avg.
		FGM	FGA	Pct.	FGM	FGA	Pct.							
72-73—Indiana............	34	10	14	.714	0	1	.000	3	6	.500	15	2	23	23.0
73-74—Indiana............	30	7	21	.333	0	0	.000	0	0	.000	11	1	4	14.0
74-75—Indiana............	32	6	13	.462	0	1	.000	6	11	.545	12	5	18	18.0
Totals....................	96	23	48	.479	0	2	.000	9	17	.529	38	8	55	18.3

NBA REGULAR SEASON RECORD

Sea.—Team	G.	Min.	FGA	FGM	Pct.	FTA	FTM	Pct.	Rebounds			Ast.	PF	Dq.	Stl.	Blk.	Pts.	Avg.
									Off.	Def.	Tot.							
75-76—Phila'phia	77	2946	1552	647	.417	642	475	.740	260	707	967	359	334	13	198	41	1769	23.0
76-77—Phila'phia	79	2769	1439	659	.458	546	372	.681	324	587	911	302	299	4	163	37	1690	21.4
77-78—Phila'phia	78	2533	1270	588	.463	574	411	.716	282	528	810	294	287	6	137	27	1587	20.3
78-79—Denver	76	2552	1273	603	.474	765	509	.665	256	608	864	283	321	16	129	52	1715	22.6
79-80—Den.-Ind.	73	2208	886	400	.451	488	270	.553	222	477	699	333	303	12	101	23	1072	14.7
80-81—Indiana	69	1845	768	348	.453	385	207	.538	164	364	528	210	242	3	99	28	903	13.1
81-82—Indiana	76	1341	378	141	.373	159	72	.453	93	305	398	204	98	4	96	28	354	4.7
Totals	528	16194	7566	3386	.448	3559	2316	.651	1601	3576	5177	1985	1984	58	923	236	9090	17.2

Three-Point Field Goals: 1979-80, 2-for-15 (.133). 1980-81, 0-for-7. 1981-82, 0-for-3. Totals, 2-for-25 (.080).

NBA PLAYOFF RECORD

Sea.—Team	G.	Min.	FGA	FGM	Pct.	FTA	FTM	Pct.	Rebounds			Ast.	PF	Dq.	Stl.	Blk.	Pts.	Avg.
									Off.	Def.	Tot.							
75-76—Phila'phia	3	120	61	29	.475	18	11	.611	9	32	41	12	14	1	1	4	69	23.0
76-77—Phila'phia	19	603	273	102	.374	114	65	.570	62	136	198	69	83	2	23	6	269	14.2
77-78—Phila'phia	10	273	125	53	.424	49	41	.837	24	54	78	30	40	1	15	1	147	14.7
80-81—Indiana	2	39	15	3	.200	8	4	.500	2	8	10	7	6	0	2	0	10	5.0
Totals	34	1035	474	187	.395	189	121	.640	97	230	327	118	143	4	41	11	495	14.6

NBA ALL-STAR GAME RECORD

Season—Team	Min.	FGA	FGM	Pct.	FTA	FTM	Pct.	Rebounds			Ast.	PF	Dq.	Stl.	Blk.	Pts.
								Off.	Def.	Tot.						
1976—Phila'phia	19	9	4	.444	4	2	.500	1	6	7	2	2	0	0	0	10
1977—Phila'phia	26	9	2	.222	2	0	.000	5	2	7	2	3	0	4	0	4
1979—Denver	25	12	5	.417	11	6	.545	2	4	6	3	4	0	5	0	16
Totals	70	30	11	.367	17	8	.471	8	12	20	7	9	0	9	0	30

Named to NBA All-Star First Team, 1976. . . . NBA All-Star Second Team, 1977. . . . ABA Co-Most Valuable Player, 1975. . . . ABA All-Star First Team, 1974 and 1975. . . . ABA All-Star Second Team, 1973. . . . ABA All-Rookie Team, 1972. . . . ABA Playoff MVP, 1973. . . . Member of ABA championship teams, 1972 and 1973. . . . Led ABA in scoring, 1975.

RICHARD McGUIRE
(Dick)

Born January 25, 1926 at Huntington, N. Y.   Height 6:00.   Weight 180.

High School—New York, N. Y., LaSalle Academy.

Colleges—St. John's University, Brooklyn, N. Y., and Dartmouth College, Hanover, N. H.

Drafted by New York on first round, 1949.

Drafted by New York on first round of BAA draft, 1949 (BAA merged with NBL later that year to form the NBA). Traded by New York to Detroit for first-round draft choice, September, 1957.

—COLLEGIATE RECORD—
St. John's

Year	G.	Min.	FGA	FGM	Pct.	FTA	FTM	Pct.	Reb.	Pts.	Avg.
43-44	16	....	...	43		...	20		....	106	6.6

Dartmouth

Year	G.	Min.	FGA	FGM	Pct.	FTA	FTM	Pct.	Reb.	Pts.	Avg.
43-44	..	....	...	16		....	9		....	41	....
44-45, 45-46					Military Service						

St. John's

Year	G.	Min.	FGA	FGM	Pct.	FTA	FTM	Pct.	Reb.	Pts.	Avg.
46-47	21	....	...	63		...	37		....	163	7.8
47-48	22	....	...	75		115	72	.626	....	222	10.1
48-49	25	....	...	121		125	72	.576	....	314	12.6

NBA REGULAR SEASON RECORD

Sea.—Team	G.	Min.	FGA	FGM	Pct.	FTA	FTM	Pct.	Reb.	Ast.	PF	Disq.	Pts.	Avg.
49-50—New York	68	....	563	190	.337	313	204	.652	....	386	160	....	584	8.6
50-51—New York	64	....	482	179	.371	276	179	.649	334	400	154	2	537	8.4
51-52—New York	64	2018	474	204	.430	290	183	.631	332	388	181	4	591	9.2
52-53—New York	61	1783	373	142	.381	269	153	.569	280	296	172	3	437	7.2

Sea.—Team	G.	Min.	FGA	FGM	Pct.	FTA	FTM	Pct.	Reb.	Ast.	PF	Disq.	Pts.	Avg.
53-54—New York	68	2343	493	201	.408	345	220	.638	310	354	199	3	622	9.1
54-55—New York	71	2310	581	226	.389	303	195	.643	322	542	143	0	647	9.1
55-56—New York	62	1685	438	152	.347	193	121	.627	220	362	146	0	425	6.9
56-57—New York	72	1191	366	140	.383	163	105	.644	146	222	103	0	385	5.3
57-58—Detroit	69	2311	544	203	.373	225	150	.667	291	454	178	0	556	8.1
58-59—Detroit	71	2063	543	232	.427	258	191	.740	285	443	147	1	655	9.2
59-60—Detroit	68	1466	402	179	.445	201	124	.617	264	358	112	0	482	7.1
Totals	738	17170	5259	2048	.382	2836	1825	.644	2784	4205	1695	13	5921	8.0

NBA PLAYOFF RECORD

Sea.—Team	G.	Min.	FGA	FGM	Pct.	FTA	FTM	Pct.	Reb.	Ast.	PF	Disq.	Pts.	Avg.
49-50—New York	5	....	52	22	.423	26	19	.731	....	27	21	....	63	12.6
50-51—New York	14	....	80	25	.313	53	24	.453	83	78	50	1	74	5.3
51-52—New York	14	546	107	48	.449	86	49	.570	71	90	46	1	145	10.4
52-53—New York	11	360	59	24	.407	55	35	.636	63	70	25	0	83	7.5
53-54—New York	4	68	16	4	.250	5	3	.600	4	5	12	0	11	2.8
54-55—New York	3	75	19	6	.316	12	8	.667	9	12	7	0	20	6.7
57-58—Detroit	7	236	60	25	.417	24	17	.708	33	40	13	0	67	9.6
58-59—Detroit	3	109	32	20	.625	11	7	.636	17	19	10	0	47	15.7
59-60—Detroit	2	42	12	5	.417	3	1	.333	4	9	3	0	11	5.5
Totals	63	1436	437	179	.410	275	163	.593	284	350	187	2	521	8.3

NBA ALL-STAR GAME RECORD

Season—Team	Min.	FGA	FGM	Pct.	FTA	FTM	Pct.	Reb.	Ast.	PF	Disq.	Pts.
1951—New York	..	4	3	.750	0	0	.000	5	10	2	0	6
1952—New York	18	0	0	.000	3	1	.333	1	4	0	0	1
1954—New York	24	5	2	.400	0	0	.000	4	2	1	0	4
1955—New York	25	2	1	.500	2	1	.500	3	6	1	0	3
1956—New York	29	9	2	.222	5	2	.400	0	3	1	0	6
1958—Detroit	31	4	2	.500	0	0	.000	7	10	4	0	4
1959—Detroit	24	7	2	.286	2	1	.500	3	3	2	0	5
Totals	..	31	12	.387	12	5	.417	23	38	11	0	29

NBA COACHING RECORD

		Regular Season				Playoffs	
Sea.	Club	W.	L.	Pct.	Pos.	W.	L.
1959-60—Detroit		17	24	.415	2†	0	2
1960-61—Detroit		34	45	.430	3†	2	3
1961-62—Detroit		37	43	.463	3†	5	5
1962-63—Detroit		34	46	.425	3†	1	3
1965-66—New York		24	35	.407	4‡	..	..
1966-67—New York		36	45	.444	4	‡1	3
1967-68—New York		15	22	.405	..‡	..	..
Totals (7 years)		197	260	.431		9	16

†Western Division. ‡Eastern Division.

Named to NBA All-Star Second Team, 1951. . . . Led NBA in assists, 1950. . . . Named to THE SPORTING NEWS All-America Second Team, 1944.

GEORGE LAWRENCE MIKAN

Born June 18, 1924 at Joliet, Ill. Height 6:10. Weight 245.

High Schools—Joliet, Ill., Catholic (freshman, did not play basketball) and Chicago, Ill., Quigley Prep (sophomore, junior and senior).

College—DePaul University, Chicago, Ill.

Signed by Chicago of National Basketball League, March 16, 1946.

Chicago dropped out of National Basketball League and entered Professional Basketball League of America for 1947-48 season.

PBLA disbanded, November 13, 1947; Chicago was refused a franchise in the NBL and Mikan was awarded to Minneapolis at an NBL meeting, November 17, 1947. (Mikan scored 193 points in the eight PBLA games played by Chicago before the league folded, and led the league in total points and scoring average.)

Signed by Minneapolis NBL, November, 1947.

—COLLEGIATE RECORD—

Year†	G.	Min.	FGA	FGM	Pct.	FTA	FTM	Pct.	Reb.	Pts.	Avg.
41-42†	..	....	...		....	...	...	...	....	....	....
42-43	24	....	...	97	....	111	77	.694	....	271	11.3
43-44	26	....	...	188	....	169	110	.655	....	486	18.7
44-45	24	....	...	218	....	199	122	.613	....	558	23.3
45-46	24	....	...	206	....	186	143	.769	....	555	23.1
Varsity Totals	98	....	...	709	....	665	454	.680	....	1870	19.1

NOTE: Mikan played five years at DePaul.

GEORGE MIKAN

NBL AND NBA REGULAR SEASON PLAYING RECORD

Sea.—Team	G.	Min.	FGA	FGM	Pct.	FTA	FTM	Pct.	Reb.	Ast.	PF	Disq.	Pts.	Avg.
46-47—Chicago-NBL	25	....	....	147	....	164	119	.726	....	....	90	..	413	16.5
47-48—Minn.-NBL	56	....	....	406	....	500	383	.752	....	....	210	..	1195	21.3
48-49—Minneapolis	60	....	1403	583	.416	689	532	.772	....	218	260	..	1698	28.3
49-50—Minneapolis	68	....	1595	649	.407	728	567	.779	....	197	297	..	1865	27.4
50-51—Minneapolis	68	....	1584	678	.428	717	576	.803	958	208	308	14	1932	28.4
51-52—Minneapolis	64	2572	1414	545	.385	555	433	.780	866	194	286	14	1523	23.8
52-53—Minneapolis	70	2651	1252	500	.399	567	442	.780	1007	201	290	12	1442	20.6
53-54—Minneapolis	72	2362	1160	441	.380	546	424	.777	1028	174	268	4	1306	18.1
54-55—					Voluntarily Retired									
55-56—Minneapolis	37	765	375	148	.395	122	94	.770	308	53	153	6	390	10.5
Totals	520	....	....	4097	....	4588	3570	.778	....	....	2162	..	11764	22.6

NBL AND NBA PLAYOFF RECORD

Sea.—Team	G.	Min.	FGA	FGM	Pct.	FTA	FTM	Pct.	Reb.	Ast.	PF	Disq.	Pts.	Avg.
46-47—Chicago-NBL	11	....	....	72	....	104	73	.702	....	....	48	..	217	19.6
47-48—Minn.-NBL	10	....	....	88	....	97	68	.701	....	....	37	..	244	24.4
48-49—Minneapolis	10	....	227	103	.454	121	97	.802	....	21	44	..	303	30.3
49-50—Minneapolis	12	....	316	121	.383	170	134	.788	....	36	47	..	376	31.3
50-51—Minneapolis	7	....	152	62	.408	55	44	.800	74	9	25	1	168	24.0
51-52—Minneapolis	13	553	261	99	.379	138	109	.790	207	36	63	3	307	23.6
52-53—Minneapolis	12	463	213	78	.366	112	82	.732	185	23	56	5	238	19.8
53-54—Minneapolis	13	424	190	87	.458	96	78	.813	171	25	56	1	252	19.4
55-56—Minneapolis	3	60	35	13	.371	13	10	.769	28	5	14	0	36	12.0
Totals	91	....	....	723	....	906	695	.767	....	....	390	..	2141	23.5

NBA ALL-STAR GAME RECORD

Season—Team	Min.	FGA	FGM	Pct.	FTA	FTM	Pct.	Reb.	Ast.	PF	Disq.	Pts.
1951—Minneapolis	....	17	4	.235	6	4	.667	11	3	2	0	12
1952—Minneapolis	29	19	9	.474	9	8	.889	15	1	5	0	26
1953—Minneapolis	40	26	9	.346	4	4	1.000	16	2	2	0	22
1954—Minneapolis	31	18	6	.333	8	6	.750	9	1	5	0	18
Totals	....	80	28	.350	27	22	.815	51	7	14	0	78

NBA COACHING RECORD

		Regular Season				Playoffs	
Sea.	Club	W.	L.	Pct.	Pos.	W.	L.
1957-58—Minneapolis		9	30	.231	4†	..	..

†Western Division.

Elected to Naismith Memorial Basketball Hall of Fame, 1959. . . . Named to NBA 25th and 35th Anniversary All-Time Teams, 1970 and 1980. . . . NBA All-Star First Team, 1949, 1950, 1951, 1952, 1953, 1954. . . . Led NBA in scoring, 1949, 1950, 1952. . . . Led NBA in rebounding, 1953. . . . NBA All-Star Game MVP, 1953. . . . Member of NBA championship teams, 1949, 1950, 1952, 1953, 1954. . . . Member of NBL championship teams, 1947 and 1948. . . . Named to THE SPORTING NEWS All-America First Team, 1944 and 1945. . . . ABA Commissioner during 1968-69 season. . . . Brother of former NBA forward-center Ed Mikan.

ARILD VERNER AGERSKOV MIKKELSEN
(Vern)

Born October 21, 1928 at Fresno, Calif.   Height 6:07.   Weight 230.

High School—Askov, Minn.

College—Hamline University, St. Paul, Minn.

Drafted by Minneapolis on first round, 1949.

—COLLEGIATE RECORD—

Year	G.	Min.	FGA	FGM	Pct.	FTA	FTM	Pct.	Reb.	Pts.	Avg.
45-46					Statistics Unavailable						
46-47	26	....	...	102	....	...	52	....	....	256	9.8
47-48	31	....	...	199	....	...	119	....	....	517	16.7
48-49	30	...	377	203	.538	177	113	.638	....	519	17.3

NBA REGULAR SEASON RECORD

Sea.—Team	G.	Min.	FGA	FGM	Pct.	FTA	FTM	Pct.	Reb.	Ast.	PF	Disq.	Pts.	Avg.
49-50—Minneapolis	68	....	722	288	.399	286	215	.752	....	123	222	...	791	11.6
50-51—Minneapolis	64	....	893	359	.402	275	186	.676	655	181	260	13	904	14.1
51-52—Minneapolis	66	2345	866	363	.419	372	283	.761	681	180	282	16	1009	15.3
52-53—Minneapolis	70	2465	868	378	.435	387	291	.752	654	148	289	14	1047	15.0
53-54—Minneapolis	72	2247	771	288	.374	298	221	.742	615	119	264	7	797	11.1
54-55—Minneapolis	71	2559	1043	440	.422	598	447	.747	722	145	319	14	1327	18.7
55-56—Minneapolis	72	2100	821	317	.386	408	328	.804	608	173	319	17	962	13.4
56-57—Minneapolis	72	2198	854	322	.377	424	342	.807	630	121	312	18	986	13.7
57-58—Minneapolis	72	2390	1070	439	.410	471	370	.786	805	166	299	20	1248	17.3
58-59—Minneapolis	72	2139	904	353	.390	355	286	.806	570	159	246	8	992	13.8
Totals	699	....	8812	3547	.403	3874	2969	.766	....	1515	2812	...	10063	14.4

NBA PLAYOFF RECORD

Sea.—Team	G.	Min.	FGA	FGM	Pct.	FTA	FTM	Pct.	Reb.	Ast.	PF	Disq.	Pts.	Avg.
49-50—Minneapolis	12	....	149	55	.369	60	46	.767	...	18	32	....	156	13.0
50-51—Minneapolis	7	....	96	39	.406	47	31	.660	67	17	35	3	109	15.6
51-52—Minneapolis	13	496	139	60	.432	64	53	.826	110	20	66	4	173	13.3
52-53—Minneapolis	12	400	133	44	.331	66	56	.848	104	24	59	3	144	12.0
53-54—Minneapolis	13	375	111	51	.459	36	31	.861	73	17	52	1	133	10.2
54-55—Minneapolis	7	209	85	30	.353	46	36	.783	78	13	36	4	96	13.7
55-56—Minneapolis	3	90	26	11	.423	20	18	.900	17	2	14	2	40	13.3
56-57—Minneapolis	5	162	83	33	.398	34	22	.647	43	17	29	4	88	17.6
58-59—Minneapolis	13	371	177	73	.412	73	56	.767	93	24	54	3	202	15.5
Totals	85	....	999	396	.396	446	349	.783	....	152	377	...	1141	13.4

NBA ALL-STAR GAME RECORD

Season—Team	Min.	FGA	FGM	Pct.	FTA	FTM	Pct.	Reb.	Ast.	PF	Disq.	Pts.
1951—Minneapolis	..	11	4	.364	4	3	.750	9	1	3	0	11
1952—Minneapolis	23	8	5	.625	2	2	1.000	10	0	2	0	12
1953—Minneapolis	19	13	3	.231	0	0	.000	6	3	3	0	6
1955—Minneapolis	25	15	7	.467	3	2	.667	9	1	5	0	16
1956—Minneapolis	22	13	5	.385	7	6	.857	9	2	4	0	16
1957—Minneapolis	21	10	3	.300	4	0	.000	9	1	3	0	6
Totals (6 games)	..	70	27	.386	20	13	.650	52	8	20	0	67

ABA COACHING RECORD

		Regular Season				Playoffs	
Sea.	Club	W.	L.	Pct.	Pos.	W.	L.
1968-69—Minnesota		6	7	.462	...	..	..

Named to NBA All-Star Second Team, 1951, 1952, 1953, 1955. . . . Holds NBA record for most disqualifications. . . . Member of NBA championship team, 1950, 1952, 1953, 1954. . . . Led NCAA Division II in field-goal percentage, 1949. . . . Named to NAIA Basketball Hall of Fame, 1956. . . . THE SPORTING NEWS All-America Fourth Team, 1949.

EARL MONROE

Born November 21, 1944 at Philadelphia, Pa.   Height 6:03½.   Weight 190.

High School—Philadelphia, Pa., Bartram.

College—Winston-Salem State University, Winston-Salem, N. C.

Drafted by Baltimore on first round, 1967 (2nd pick).

Traded by Baltimore to New York for Dave Stallworth, Mike Riordan and cash, November 10, 1971.

—COLLEGIATE RECORD—

Year	G.	Min.	FGA	FGM	Pct.	FTA	FTM	Pct.	Reb.	Pts.	Avg.
63-64	23	....	...	71	....	...	21	....	....	163	7.1
64-65	30	....	...	286	....	176	125	.710	211	697	23.2
65-66	25	....	519	292	.563	187	162	.866	167	746	29.8
66-67	32	....	839	509	.607	391	311	.795	218	1329	41.5
Totals	110	....		1158			619		....	2935	26.7

NBA REGULAR SEASON RECORD

Sea.—Team	G.	Min.	FGA	FGM	Pct.	FTA	FTM	Pct.	Reb.	Ast.	PF	Disq.	Pts.	Avg.
67-68—Baltimore	82	3012	1637	742	.453	649	507	.781	465	349	282	3	1991	24.3
68-69—Baltimore	80	3075	1837	809	.440	582	447	.768	280	392	261	1	2065	25.8
69-70—Baltimore	82	3051	1557	695	.446	641	532	.830	257	402	258	3	1922	23.4
70-71—Baltimore	81	2843	1501	663	.442	506	406	.802	213	354	220	3	1732	21.4
71-72—Balt.-N.Y.	63	1337	662	287	.434	224	175	.781	100	142	139	1	749	11.9
72-73—New York	75	2370	1016	496	.488	208	171	.822	245	288	195	1	1163	15.5

									—Rebounds—							
Sea.—Team	G.	Min.	FGA	FGM	Pct.	FTA	FTM	Pct.	Off.	Def.	Tot.	Ast.	PF	Dq.	Stl.	Blk.	Pts.	Avg.
73-74—New York	41	1194	513	240	.468	113	93	.823	22	99	121	110	97	0	34	19	573	14.0
74-75—New York	78	2814	1462	668	.457	359	297	.827	56	271	327	270	200	0	108	29	1633	20.9
75-76—New York	76	2889	1354	647	.478	356	280	.787	48	225	273	304	209	1	111	22	1574	20.7
76-77—Knicks	77	2656	1185	613	.517	366	307	.839	45	178	223	366	197	0	91	23	1533	19.9
77-78—New York	76	2369	1123	556	.495	291	242	.832	47	135	182	361	189	0	60	19	1354	17.8
78-79—New York	64	1393	699	329	.471	154	129	.838	26	48	74	189	123	0	48	6	787	12.3
79-80—New York	51	633	352	161	.457	64	56	.875	16	20	36	67	46	0	21	3	378	7.4
Totals	926	29636	14898	6906	.464	4513	3642	.807			2796	3594	2416	13	473	121	17454	18.8

—DID YOU KNOW—

That Billy Paultz tied Hall of Famer Dolph Schayes' all-time professional record of 15 consecutive playoff appearances last year when the Jazz advanced to postseason action?

NBA PLAYOFF RECORD

Sea.—Team	G.	Min.	FGA	FGM	Pct.	FTA	FTM	Pct.	Reb.	Ast.	PF	Disq.	Pts.	Avg.
68-69—Baltimore	4	171	114	44	.386	31	25	.806	21	16	10	0	113	28.3
69-70—Baltimore	7	299	154	74	.481	60	48	.800	23	28	23	0	196	28.0
70-71—Baltimore	18	671	356	145	.407	135	107	.793	64	74	56	0	397	22.1
71-72—New York	16	429	185	76	.411	57	45	.789	45	47	41	0	197	12.3
72-73—New York	16	504	211	111	.526	48	36	.750	51	51	39	0	258	16.1

Sea.—Team	G.	Min.	FGA	FGM	Pct.	FTA	FTM	Pct.	—Rebounds— Off.	Def.	Tot.	Ast.	PF	Dq.	Stl.	Blk.	Pts.	Avg.
73-74—New York	12	407	165	81	.491	55	47	.855	8	40	48	25	26	0	8	9	209	17.4
74-75—New York	3	89	45	12	.267	22	18	.818	1	8	9	6	6	0	4	2	42	14.0
77-78—New York	6	145	62	24	.389	18	11	.611	1	4	5	17	15	0	6	0	59	9.8
Totals	82	2715	1292	567	.439	426	337	.791			266	264	216	0	18	11	1471	17.9

NBA ALL-STAR GAME RECORD

Season—Team	Min.	FGA	FGM	Pct.	FTA	FTM	Pct.	Reb.	Ast.	PF	Disq.	Pts.
1969—Baltimore	27	15	6	.400	12	9	.750	4	4	4	0	21
1971—Baltimore	18	9	3	.333	0	0	.000	5	2	3	0	6

Season—Team	Min.	FGA	FGM	Pct.	FTA	FTM	Pct.	—Rebounds— Off.	Def.	Tot.	Ast.	PF	Dq.	Stl.	Blk.	Pts.
1975—New York	25	8	3	.375	5	3	.600	0	3	3	2	2	0	1	0	9
1977—Knicks..........	15	7	2	.286	0	0	.000	0	0	0	3	1	0	0	0	4
Totals	85	39	14	359	17	12	.706			12	11	10	0	1	0	40

Named to NBA All-Star First Team, 1969.... NBA Rookie of the Year, 1968.... NBA All-Rookie Team, 1968.... Member of NBA championship team, 1973.... Holds NCAA Division II record for most points in a season, 1967.... Outstanding player in 1967 NCAA College Division tournament.... Member of NCAA College Division tournament championship team, 1967.... Named to THE SPORTING NEWS All-America First Team, 1966.... Named to NAIA Basketball Hall of Fame, 1975.

CALVIN JEROME MURPHY

Born May 9, 1948 at Norwalk, Conn.   Height 5:09.   Weight 165.

High School—Norwalk, Conn.

College—Niagara University, Niagara University, N. Y.

Drafted by San Diego on second round, 1970 (18th pick).

—COLLEGIATE RECORD—

Year	G.	Min.	FGA	FGM	Pct.	FTA	FTM	Pct.	Reb.	Pts.	Avg.
66-67†	19	....	719	364	.506	239	201	.841	102	929	48.9
67-68	24	....	772	337	.437	288	242	.840	118	916	38.2
68-69	24	....	700	294	.420	230	190	.826	87	778	32.4
69-70	29	....	692	316	.457	252	222	.881	103	854	29.4
Varsity Totals	77	....	2164	947	.438	770	654	.849	308	2548	33.1

NBA REGULAR SEASON RECORD

Sea.—Team	G.	Min.	FGA	FGM	Pct.	FTA	FTM	Pct.	Reb.	Ast.	PF	Disq.	Pts.	Avg.
70-71—San Diego	82	2020	1029	471	.458	434	356	.820	245	329	263	4	1298	15.8
71-72—Houston	82	2538	1255	571	.455	392	349	.890	258	393	298	6	1491	18.2
72-73—Houston	77	1697	820	381	.465	269	239	.888	149	262	211	3	1001	13.0

Sea.—Team	G.	Min.	FGA	FGM	Pct.	FTA	FTM	Pct.	—Rebounds— Off.	Def.	Tot.	Ast.	PF	Dq.	Stl.	Blk.	Pts.	Avg.
73-74—Houston	81	2922	1285	671	.522	357	310	.868	51	137	188	603	310	8	157	4	1652	20.4
74-75—Houston	78	2513	1152	557	.484	386	341	.883	52	121	173	381	281	8	128	4	1455	18.7
75-76—Houston	82	2995	1369	675	.493	410	372	.907	52	157	209	596	294	3	151	6	1722	21.0
76-77—Houston	82	2764	1216	596	.490	307	272	.886	54	118	172	386	281	6	144	8	1464	17.9
77-78—Houston	76	2900	1737	852	.491	267	245	.918	57	107	164	259	241	4	112	3	1949	25.6
78-79—Houston	82	2941	1424	707	.496	265	246	.928	78	95	173	351	288	5	117	6	1660	20.2
79-80—Houston	76	2676	1267	624	.493	302	271	.897	68	82	150	299	269	3	143	9	1520	20.0
80-81—Houston	76	2014	1074	528	.492	215	206	.958	33	54	87	222	209	0	111	6	1266	16.7
81-82—Houston	64	1204	648	277	.427	110	100	.909	20	41	61	163	142	0	43	1	655	10.2
82-83—Houston	64	1423	754	337	.447	150	138	.920	34	40	74	158	163	3	59	4	816	12.8
Totals	1002	30607	15030	7247	.482	3864	3445	.892			2103	4402	3250	53	1165	51	17949	17.9

Three-Point Field Goals: 1979-80, 1-for-25 (.040). 1980-81, 4-for-17 (.235). 1981-82, 1-for-16 (.063). 1982-83, 4-for-14 (.286). Totals, 10-for-72 (.139).

NBA PLAYOFF RECORD

Sea.—Team	G.	Min.	FGA	FGM	Pct.	FTA	FTM	Pct.	—Rebounds— Off.	Def.	Tot.	Ast.	PF	Dq.	Stl.	Blk.	Pts.	Avg.
74-75—Houston	8	305	156	72	.462	57	51	.895	9	10	19	45	36	2	14	1	195	24.4
76-77—Houston	12	420	213	102	.479	30	28	.933	7	12	19	75	47	1	19	2	232	19.3
78-79—Houston	2	73	31	9	.290	9	8	.889	2	1	3	6	9	0	8	1	26	13.0
79-80—Houston	7	265	108	58	.537	13	13	1.000	4	6	10	26	29	1	11	0	131	18.7
80-81—Houston	19	540	287	142	.495	60	58	.967	7	17	24	57	69	0	26	0	344	18.1
81-82—Houston	3	57	22	5	.227	8	7	.875	2	1	3	4	7	0	1	0	17	5.7
Totals	51	1660	817	388	.475	177	165	.932	31	47	78	213	197	4	79	4	945	18.5

Three-Point Field Goals: 1979-80, 2-for-4 (.500). 1980-81, 2-for-7 (.286). 1981-82, 0-for-3. Totals, 4-for-14 (.286).

—Rebounds—

Season—Team	Min.	FGA	FGM	Pct.	FTA	FTM	Pct.	Off.	Def.	Tot.	Ast.	PF	Dq.	Stl.	Blk.	Pts.
1979—Houston	15	5	3	.600	0	0	.000	0	0	1	5	4	0	2	0	6

Three-Point Field Goals: 1979-80, 2-for-4 (.500). 1980-81, 2-for-7 (.286). Totals, 4-for-11 (.364).

Named to NBA All-Rookie Team, 1971. . . . Holds NBA records for highest free-throw percentage in one season, 1981, and most consecutive free throws made, 78, December 27, 1980 through February 28, 1981. . . . Led NBA in free-throw percentage, 1981 and 1983. . . . Named to THE SPORTING NEWS All-America Second Team, 1969 and 1970.

ROBERT LEE PETTIT
(Bob)

Born December 12, 1932 at Baton Rouge, La.   Height 6:09.   Weight 215.

High School—Baton Rouge, La.

College—Louisiana State University, Baton Rouge, La.

Drafted by Milwaukee on first round, 1954.

Milwaukee franchise transferred to St. Louis, 1955.

—COLLEGIATE RECORD—

Year	G.	Min.	FGA	FGM	Pct.	FTA	FTM	Pct.	Reb.	Pts.	Avg.
50-51†	10	....	...	...	...	...	...	....	...	270	27.0
51-52	23	....	549	237	.432	192	115	.599	315	589	25.6
52-53	21	....	394	193	.490	215	133	.619	263	519	24.7
53-54	25	....	573	281	.490	308	223	.724	432	785	31.4
Varsity Totals	69	....	1516	711	.469	715	471	.659	1010	1893	27.4

NBA REGULAR SEASON RECORD

Sea.—Team	G.	Min.	FGA	FGM	Pct.	FTA	FTM	Pct.	Reb.	Ast.	PF	Disq.	Pts.	Avg.
54-55—Milwaukee	72	2659	1279	520	.407	567	426	.751	994	229	258	5	1466	20.4
55-56—St. Louis	72	2794	1507	646	.429	757	557	.736	1164	189	202	1	1849	25.7
56-57—St. Louis	71	2491	1477	613	.415	684	529	.773	1037	133	181	1	1755	24.7
57-58—St. Louis	70	2528	1418	581	.410	744	557	.745	1216	157	222	6	1719	24.6
58-59—St. Louis	72	2873	1640	719	.438	879	667	.758	1182	221	200	3	2105	29.2
59-60—St. Louis	72	2896	1526	669	.438	722	544	.753	1221	257	204	0	1882	26.1
60-61—St. Louis	76	3027	1720	769	.447	804	582	.724	1540	262	217	1	2120	27.9
61-62—St. Louis	78	3282	1928	867	.450	901	695	.771	1459	289	296	4	2429	31.1
62-63—St. Louis	79	3090	1746	778	.446	885	685	.774	1191	245	282	9	2241	28.4
63-64—St. Louis	80	3296	1708	791	.463	771	608	.789	1224	259	300	3	2190	27.4
64-65—St. Louis	50	1754	923	396	.429	405	332	.820	621	128	167	0	1124	22.5
Totals	792	30690	16872	7349	.436	8119	6182	.761	12849	2369	2529	33	20880	26.4

NBA PLAYOFF RECORD

Sea.—Team	G.	Min.	FGA	FGM	Pct.	FTA	FTM	Pct.	Reb.	Ast.	PF	Disq.	Pts.	Avg.
55-56—St. Louis	8	274	128	47	.367	70	59	.843	84	18	20	0	153	19.1
56-57—St. Louis	10	430	237	98	.414	133	102	.767	168	25	33	0	298	29.8
57-58—St. Louis	11	430	230	90	.391	118	86	.729	181	20	31	0	266	24.2
58-59—St. Louis	6	257	137	58	.423	65	51	.785	75	14	20	0	167	27.8
59-60—St. Louis	14	576	292	129	.442	142	107	.753	221	52	43	1	365	26.1
60-61—St. Louis	12	526	284	117	.412	144	109	.757	211	38	42	0	343	28.6
62-63—St. Louis	11	463	259	119	.459	144	112	.778	166	33	34	0	350	31.8
63-64—St. Louis	12	494	226	93	.412	79	66	.835	174	33	44	0	252	21.0
64-65—St. Louis	4	95	41	15	.366	20	16	.800	24	8	10	0	46	11.5
Totals	88	3545	1834	766	.418	915	708	.774	1304	241	277	1	2240	25.5

NBA ALL-STAR GAME RECORD

Season—Team	Min.	FGA	FGM	Pct.	FTA	FTM	Pct.	Reb.	Ast.	PF	Disq.	Pts.
1955—Milwaukee	27	14	3	.214	4	2	.500	9	2	0	0	8
1956—St. Louis	31	17	7	.412	7	6	.857	24	7	4	0	20
1957—St. Louis	31	18	8	.444	6	5	.833	11	2	2	0	21
1958—St. Louis	38	21	10	.476	10	8	.800	26	1	1	0	28
1959—St. Louis	34	21	8	.381	9	9	1.000	16	5	1	0	25

—DID YOU KNOW—

That three coaches have directed teams in the NCAA Final Four and the NBA championship series? They are Jack Ramsay (St. Joseph's 1961 and Portland 1977); Fred Schaus (West Virginia 1959 and the Los Angeles Lakers 1962, 1963, 1965, 1966) and Bill van Breda Kolff (Princeton 1965 and the Los Angeles Lakers 1968, 1969)?

BOB PETTIT

Season—Team	Min.	FGA	FGM	Pct.	FTA	FTM	Pct.	Reb.	Ast.	PF	Disq.	Pts.
1960—St. Louis	28	15	4	.267	6	3	.500	14	2	2	0	11
1961—St. Louis	32	22	13	.591	7	3	.429	9	0	2	0	29
1962—St. Louis	37	20	10	.500	5	5	1.000	27	2	5	0	25
1963—St. Louis	32	16	7	.438	12	11	.917	13	0	1	0	25
1964—St. Louis	36	15	6	.400	9	7	.778	17	2	3	0	19
1965—St. Louis	34	14	5	.357	5	3	.600	12	0	4	0	13
Totals	360	193	81	.420	80	62	.775	178	23	25	0	224

NBA COACHING RECORD

Sea. Club	Regular Season				Playoffs	
	W.	L.	Pct.	Pos.	W.	L.
1961-62—St. Louis	4	2	.667	...†	...	...

†Western Division.

Elected to Naismith Memorial Basketball Hall of Fame, 1970. . . . Named to NBA 25th and 35th Anniversary All-Time Teams, 1970 and 1980. . . . NBA Most Valuable Player, 1956 and 1959. . . . Named to NBA All-Star First Team, 1955, 1956, 1957, 1958, 1959, 1960, 1961, 1962, 1963, 1964. . . . NBA All-Star Second Team, 1965. . . . NBA Rookie of the Year, 1955. . . . Holds NBA championship series game records for most free-throw attempts, 24, and most free throws made, 19, vs. Boston, April 9, 1958. . . . Holds NBA championship series record for most field goals made in one half, 13, vs. Boston, April 9, 1957. . . . Shares NBA championship series record for most field goals made in one quarter, 8, vs. Boston, April 12, 1958. . . . Shares NBA championship series record for most free-throw attempts in one quarter, 11, vs. Boston, April 9, 1958. . . . NBA All-Star Game MVP, 1956, 1958, 1962. . . . NBA All-Star Game co-MVP, 1959. . . . Holds NBA All-Star Game records for most career field-goal attempts; most rebounds in one game, 27, in 1962, and most rebounds in one quarter, 10, in 1962. . . . Shares NBA All-Star Game record for most rebounds in one half, 16, in 1962. . . . Member of NBA championship team, 1958. . . . Led NBA in scoring, 1956 and 1959. . . . Led NBA in rebounding, 1956.

ANDREW MICHAEL PHILLIP
(Andy)

Born March 7, 1922 at Granite City, Ill. Height 6:02. Weight 195.

High School—Granite City, Ill.

College—University of Illinois, Champaign, Ill.

Drafted by Chicago BAA, 1947.

Drawn by Philadelphia NBA in dispersal of Chicago NBA team, October 6, 1950.

—COLLEGIATE RECORD—

Year	G.	Min.	FGA	FGM	Pct.	FTA	FTM	Pct.	Reb.	Pts.	Avg.
40-41†			(Freshman team did not play intercollegiate schedule)								
41-42	23	....	....	87	....	....	58	....	....	232	10.1
42-43	18	....	....	131	....	57	43	.754	....	305	16.9
			(In military service, 1943-44, 1944-45 and 1945-46 seasons.)								
46-47	20	....	....	81	....	61	30	.492	....	192	9.6
Varsity Totals	61	....	....	299	....	....	131	....	....	729	12.0

BBA AND NBA REGULAR SEASON RECORD

Sea.—Team	G.	Min.	FGA	FGM	Pct.	FTA	FTM	Pct.	Reb.	Ast.	PF	Disq.	Pts.	Avg.
47-48—Chicago	32	....	425	143	.336	103	60	.583	....	74	75	..	346	10.8
48-49—Chicago	60	....	818	285	.348	219	148	.676	....	319	205	..	718	12.0
49-50—Chicago	65	....	814	284	.349	270	190	.704	....	377	210	..	758	11.7
50-51—Philadelphia	66	....	690	275	.399	253	190	.751	446	414	221	8	740	11.2
51-52—Philadelphia	66	2933	762	279	.366	308	232	.753	434	539	218	6	790	12.0
52-53—Ft. Wayne	70	2690	629	250	.397	301	222	.737	364	397	229	9	722	10.3
53-54—Ft. Wayne	71	2705	680	255	.375	330	241	.730	265	449	204	4	751	10.6
54-55—Ft. Wayne	64	2332	545	202	.371	308	213	.692	290	491	166	1	617	9.6
55-56—Ft. Wayne	70	2078	405	148	.365	199	112	.563	257	410	155	2	408	5.8
56-57—Boston	67	1476	277	105	.379	137	88	.642	181	168	121	1	298	4.4
57-58—Boston	70	1164	273	97	.355	71	42	.592	158	121	121	0	236	3.4
Totals	701	15378	6318	2323	.368	2499	1738	.695	2395	3759	1925	31	6384	9.1

BBA AND NBA PLAYOFF RECORD

Sea.—Team	G.	Min.	FGA	FGM	Pct.	FTA	FTM	Pct.	Reb.	Ast.	PF	Disq.	Pts.	Avg.
47-48—Chicago	5	....	46	13	.283	14	10	.714	....	4	11	..	36	7.2
48-49—Chicago	2	....	36	14	.389	11	11	1.000	....	12	9	..	39	19.5
49-50—Chicago	2	....	27	7	.259	13	10	.769	....	12	8	..	24	12.0
50-51—Philadelphia	2	....	15	6	.400	6	3	.500	15	14	9	..	15	7.5
51-52—Philadelphia	3	122	19	8	.421	24	19	.792	14	22	16	1	35	11.7
52-53—Ft. Wayne	8	329	71	24	.338	51	34	.667	32	30	23	1	82	10.3
53-54—Ft. Wayne	4	136	38	13	.342	12	9	.750	12	17	9	0	35	8.8
54-55—Ft. Wayne	11	445	93	30	.323	40	34	.850	60	78	37	0	94	8.5
55-56—Ft. Wayne	10	173	27	9	.333	25	11	.440	26	35	16	0	29	2.9
56-57—Boston	10	128	22	8	.364	15	6	.400	20	17	18	0	22	2.2
57-58—Boston	10	91	21	5	.238	9	7	.778	14	7	20	0	17	1.7
Totals	67	1424	415	137	.330	220	154	.700	193	248	176	2	428	6.4

NBA ALL-STAR GAME RECORD

Season—Team	Min.	FGA	FGM	Pct.	FTA	FTM	Pct.	Reb.	Ast.	PF	Disq.	Pts.
1951—Philadelphia	....	8	3	.375	0	0	.000	10	8	1	0	6
1952—Philadelphia	30	6	4	.667	3	3	1.000	3	6	1	0	11
1953—Ft. Wayne	36	9	4	.444	1	1	1.000	6	8	2	0	9
1954—Ft. Wayne	19	4	1	.250	1	0	.000	3	3	1	0	2
1955—Ft. Wayne	28	4	3	.750	0	0	.000	3	6	3	0	6
Totals		31	15	.484	5	4	.800	25	31	8	0	34

Elected to Naismith Memorial Basketball Hall of Fame, 1961.... Named to NBA All-Star Second Team, 1952 and 1953.... Led NBA in assists, 1951 and 1952.... Member of NBA championship team, 1957.... Named THE SPORTING NEWS College Player of the Year, 1943.... Played minor league baseball in the St. Louis Cardinals' organization.

JAMES C. POLLARD
(Jim)

Born July 9, 1922 at Oakland, Calif.   Height 6:05. Weight 185.

High School—Oakland, Calif., Tech.

College—Stanford University, Stanford, Calif.

Signed by Minneapolis NBL, 1947.

—COLLEGIATE RECORD—

Year	G.	Min.	FGA	FGM	Pct.	FTA	FTM	Pct.	Reb.	Pts.	Avg.
40-41†					Statistics Unavailable						
41-42	23	....	...	103		48	35	.729	....	241	10.5
Varsity Totals	23	....	...	103	....	48	35	.729	....	241	10.5

Note: In military service during 1942-43, 1943-44 and 1944-45 seasons. Played with Alameda, Calif., Coast Guard team.

AMERICAN BASKETBALL LEAGUE RECORD
(Amateur Athletic Union League)

Year—Team	G	FG	FT	Pts.	Avg.
45-46—San Diego Dons	15	84	55	223	14.9
46-47—Oakland Bittners	20	..	..	279	14.0

(Led league in scoring both seasons.)

NBL AND NBA REGULAR SEASON RECORD

Sea.—Team	G.	Min.	FGA	FGM	Pct.	FTA	FTM	Pct.	Reb.	Ast.	PF	Disq.	Pts.	Avg.
47-48—Minn-N L	59	....	....	310	....	207	140	.676	....	....	147	....	760	12.9
48-49—Minneapolis	53	....	792	314	.396	227	156	.687	....	142	144	....	784	14.8
49-50—Minneapolis	66	....	1140	394	.346	242	185	.764	....	252	143	....	973	14.7
50-51—Minneapolis	54	....	728	256	.352	156	117	.750	484	184	157	4	629	11.6
51-52—Minneapolis	65	2545	1155	411	.356	260	183	.704	593	234	199	4	1005	15.5
52-53—Minneapolis	66	2403	933	333	.357	251	193	.769	452	231	194	3	859	13.0
53-54—Minneapolis	71	2483	882	326	.370	230	179	.778	500	214	161	0	831	11.7
54-55—Minneapolis	63	1960	749	265	.354	186	151	.812	458	160	147	3	681	10.8
Totals	497	....	....	2609	....	1759	1304	.741	....	....	1292	....	6522	13.1

NBA PLAYOFF RECORD

Sea.—Team	G.	Min.	FGA	FGM	Pct.	FTA	FTM	Pct.	Reb.	Ast.	PF	Disq.	Pts.	Avg.
48-49—Minneapolis	10	....	147	43	.293	62	44	.710	....	39	31	....	130	13.0
49-50—Minneapolis	12	....	175	50	.286	62	44	.710	....	56	36	....	144	12.0
50-51—Minneapolis	7	....	108	35	.324	30	25	.833	62	27	27	1	95	13.6
51-52—Minneapolis	11	469	173	70	.405	50	37	.740	71	33	34	1	177	16.1
52-53—Minneapolis	12	455	167	62	.371	62	48	.774	86	49	37	2	172	14.3
53-54—Minneapolis	13	543	155	56	.361	60	48	.800	110	41	27	0	160	12.3
54-55—Minneapolis	7	257	104	33	.317	46	33	.717	78	14	13	0	99	14.1
Totals	72	....	1029	349	.339	372	279	.750	....	259	205	....	977	13.6

NBA ALL-STAR GAME RECORD

Season—Team	Min.	FGA	FGM	Pct.	FTA	FTM	Pct.	Reb.	Ast.	PF	Disq.	Pts.
1951—Minneapolis	..	11	2	.182	0	0	.000	4	5	1	0	4
1952—Minneapolis	29	17	2	.118	0	0	.000	11	5	3	0	4
1954—Minneapolis	41	22	10	.455	5	3	.600	3	3	3	0	23
1955—Minneapolis	27	19	7	.368	3	3	1.000	4	0	1	0	17
Totals (4 games)	..	69	21	.304	8	6	.750	22	13	8	0	48

NBA COACHING RECORD

Sea.	Club	W.	L.	Pct.	Pos.	W.	L.
		Regular Season				Playoffs	
1959-60—Minneapolis		14	25	.359	3	5	4
1961-62—Chicago		18	62	.225	5	..	..
Totals (2 years)		32	87	.269		5	4

ABA COACHING RECORD

Sea.	Club	W.	L.	Pct.	Pos.	W.	L.
		Regular Season				Playoffs	
1967-68—Minnesota		50	28	.641	2	4	6
1968-69—Miami		43	35	.551	2	5	7
1969-70—Miami		5	15	.250	...	..	..
Totals (3 years)		98	78	.557		9	13

Elected to Naismith Memorial Basketball Hall of Fame, 1977.... Named NBA All-Star First Team, 1949 and 1950.... NBA All-Star Second Team, 1952 and 1954.... Member of NBA championship teams, 1949, 1950, 1952, 1953, 1954.... Member of NBL championship team, 1948.... Member of NCAA Division I championship team, 1942.

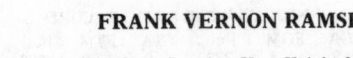

FRANK VERNON RAMSEY

Born July 31, 1931 at Corydon, Ky.   Height 6:03.   Weight 190.

High School—Madisonville, Ky.

College—University of Kentucky, Lexington, Ky.

Drafted by Boston on first round, 1953.

In military service, 1955-56.

—COLLEGIATE RECORD—

Year†	G.	Min.	FGA	FGM	Pct.	FTA	FTM	Pct.	Reb.	Pts.	Avg.
49-50†	16	....	274	109	.398	71	46	.648	..	264	16.5
50-51	34	....	413	135	.327	123	75	.610	434	345	10.1
51-52	32	....	470	185	.394	214	139	.650	383	509	15.9
52-53				Did Not Play—Kentucky had no team							
53-54	25	....	430	179	.416	181	132	.729	221	490	19.6
Varsity Totals	91	....	1313	499	.380	518	346	.668	1038	1344	14.8

NBA REGULAR SEASON RECORD

Sea.—Team	G.	Min.	FGA	FGM	Pct.	FTA	FTM	Pct.	Reb.	Ast.	PF	Disq.	Pts.	Avg.
54-55—Boston	64	1754	592	236	.399	322	243	.755	402	185	250	11	715	11.2
56-57—Boston	35	807	349	137	.393	182	144	.791	178	67	113	3	418	11.9
57-58—Boston	69	2047	900	377	.419	472	383	.811	504	167	245	8	1137	16.5
58-59—Boston	72	2013	1013	383	.378	436	341	.782	491	147	266	11	1107	15.4
59-60—Boston	73	2009	1062	422	.397	347	273	.787	506	137	251	10	1117	15.3
60-61—Boston	79	2019	1100	448	.407	354	295	.833	431	148	284	13	1191	15.1
61-62—Boston	79	1913	979	436	.445	405	334	.825	387	109	245	9	1206	15.3
62-63—Boston	77	1541	743	284	.382	332	271	.816	288	95	259	13	839	10.9
63-64—Boston	75	1227	604	226	.374	233	196	.841	233	81	245	7	648	8.6
Totals	623	15330	7342	2949	.402	3083	2480	.804	3410	1136	2158	85	8378	13.4

NBA PLAYOFF RECORD

Sea.—Team	G.	Min.	FGA	FGM	Pct.	FTA	FTM	Pct.	Reb.	Ast.	PF	Disq.	Pts.	Avg.
54-55—Boston	7	154	54	28	.519	26	19	.731	35	16	27	0	75	10.7
56-57—Boston	10	229	82	38	.463	59	46	.780	43	17	36	1	122	12.2
57-58—Boston	11	352	174	74	.425	59	54	.915	90	16	50	2	202	18.4
58-59—Boston	11	303	192	95	.495	81	65	.802	68	20	52	4	255	23.2
59-60—Boston	13	459	196	81	.413	63	55	.873	100	27	51	1	217	16.7
60-61—Boston	10	300	136	55	.407	75	61	.813	64	23	40	0	171	17.1
61-62—Boston	13	210	104	39	.375	45	41	.911	38	10	38	3	119	9.1
62-63—Boston	13	251	104	37	.356	47	34	.723	35	12	43	1	108	8.3
63-64—Boston	10	138	63	22	.349	21	18	.857	21	10	25	0	62	6.2
Totals	98	2396	1105	469	.424	476	393	.826	494	151	362	13	1331	13.6

ABA COACHING RECORD

Sea. Club	Regular Season				Playoffs	
	W.	L.	Pct.	Pos.	W.	L.
1970-71—Kentucky	32	35	.478	2†	11	8

†Eastern Division.

Elected to Naismith Memorial Basketball Hall of Fame, 1981. . . . Holds NBA championship series game record for most free throws made in one quarter, 9, vs. Minneapolis, April 4, 1959. . . . Member of NBA championship teams, 1957, 1959, 1960, 1961, 1962, 1963, 1964. . . . Named to THE SPORTING NEWS All-America Second Team, 1951. . . . Member of NCAA championship team, 1951.

WILLIS REED JR.

Born June 25, 1942 at Hico, La.   Height 6:10.   Weight 240.

High School—Lillie, La., West Side.

College—Grambling College, Grambling, La.

Drafted by New York on second round, 1964 (10th pick).

—COLLEGIATE PLAYING RECORD—

Year	G.	Min.	FGA	FGM	Pct.	FTA	FTM	Pct.	Reb.	Pts.	Avg.
60-61	35	....	239	146	.611	122	86	.705	312	378	10.8
61-62	26	....	323	189	.585	102	80	.784	380	458	17.6
62-63	33	....	489	282	.565	177	135	.763	563	699	21.2
63-64	28	....	486	301	.619	199	143	.719	596	745	26.6
Totals	122	....	1537	918	.597	600	444	.740	1851	2280	18.7

NBA REGULAR SEASON RECORD

Sea.—Team	G.	Min.	FGA	FGM	Pct.	FTA	FTM	Pct.	Reb.	Ast.	PF	Disq.	Pts.	Avg.
64-65—New York	80	3042	1457	629	.432	407	302	.742	1175	133	339	14	1560	19.5
65-66—New York	76	2537	1009	438	.434	399	302	.757	883	91	323	13	1178	15.5

Sea.—Team	G.	Min.	FGA	FGM	Pct.	FTA	FTM	Pct.	Reb.	Ast.	PF	Disq.	Pts.	Avg.
66-67—New York	78	2824	1298	635	.489	487	358	.735	1136	126	293	9	1628	20.9
67-68—New York	81	2879	1346	659	.490	509	367	.721	1073	159	343	12	1685	20.8
68-69—New York	82	3108	1351	704	.521	435	325	.747	1191	190	314	7	1733	21.1
69-70—New York	81	3089	1385	702	.507	464	351	.756	1126	161	287	2	1755	21.7
70-71—New York	73	2855	1330	614	.462	381	299	.785	1003	148	228	1	1527	20.9
71-72—New York	11	363	137	60	.438	39	27	.692	96	22	30	0	147	13.4
72-73—New York	69	1876	705	334	.474	124	92	.742	590	126	205	0	760	11.0

Sea.—Team	G.	Min.	FGA	FGM	Pct.	FTA	FTM	Pct.	—Rebounds— Off.	Def.	Tot.	Ast.	PF	Dq.	Stl.	Blk.	Pts.	Avg.
73-74—N. Y.	19	500	184	84	.457	53	42	.792	47	94	141	30	49	0	12	21	210	11.1
Totals	650	23073	10202	4859	.476	3298	2465	.747			8414	1186	2411	58			12183	18.7

NBA PLAYOFF RECORD

Sea.—Team	G.	Min.	FGA	FGM	Pct.	FTA	FTM	Pct.	Reb.	Ast.	PF	Disq.	Pts.	Avg.
66-67—New York	4	148	80	43	.538	25	24	.960	55	7	19	1	110	27.5
67-68—New York	6	210	98	53	.541	30	22	.733	62	11	24	1	128	21.3
68-69—New York	10	429	198	101	.510	70	55	.786	141	19	40	1	257	25.7
69-70—New York	18	732	378	178	.471	95	70	.737	248	51	60	0	426	23.7
70-71—New York	12	504	196	81	.413	39	26	.667	144	27	41	0	188	15.7
72-73—New York	17	486	208	97	.466	21	18	.857	129	30	65	1	212	12.5

Sea.—Team	G.	Min.	FGA	FGM	Pct.	FTA	FTM	Pct.	—Rebounds— Off.	Def.	Tot.	Ast.	PF	Dq.	Stl.	Blk.	Pts.	Avg.
73-74—N. Y.	11	132	45	17	.378	5	3	.600	4	18	22	4	26	0	2	0	37	3.4
Totals	78	2641	1203	570	.474	285	218	.765			801	149	275	4			1358	17.4

NBA ALL-STAR GAME RECORD

Season—Team	Min.	FGA	FGM	Pct.	FTA	FTM	Pct.	Reb.	Ast.	PF	Disq.	Pts.
1965—New York	25	11	3	.273	2	1	.500	5	1	2	0	7
1966—New York	23	11	7	.636	2	2	1.000	8	1	3	0	16
1967—New York	17	6	2	.333	0	0	.000	9	1	0	0	4
1968—New York	25	14	7	.500	3	2	.667	8	1	4	0	16
1969—New York	14	8	5	.625	0	0	.000	4	2	2	0	10
1970—New York	30	18	9	.500	3	3	1.000	11	0	6	1	21
1971—New York	27	16	5	.313	6	4	.667	13	1	3	0	14
Totals	161	84	38	.452	16	12	.750	58	7	20	1	88

NBA COACHING RECORD

Sea. Club	Regular Season W.	L.	Pct.	Pos.	Playoffs W.	L.
1977-78—New York	43	39	.524	2†	2	4
1978-79—New York	6	8	.429	..†	..	..
Totals (2 seasons)	49	47	.510		2	4

COLLEGIATE COACHING RECORD

Sea. Club	Regular Season W.	L.	Pct.	Pos.
1981-82—Creighton	7	20	.259	‡8
1982-83—Creighton	8	19	.296	‡10
1983-84—Creighton	17	14	.548	‡4
1984-85—Creighton	20	11	.645	‡4
Totals (4 seasons)	52	64	.448	

†Atlantic Division.
‡Missouri Valley Conference.
Assistant, Atlanta Hawks, 1985-86.

Elected to Naismith Memorial Basketball Hall of Fame, 1981. . . . NBA Most Valuable Player, 1970. . . . Named to NBA All-Star First Team, 1970. . . . NBA All-Star Second Team, 1967, 1968, 1969, 1971. . . . NBA All-Defensive First Team, 1970. . . . NBA Rookie of the Year, 1965. . . . NBA All-Rookie Team, 1965. . . . NBA Playoff MVP, 1970 and 1973. . . . NBA All-Star Game MVP, 1970. . . . Member of NBA championship teams, 1970 and 1973. . . . Member of NAIA championship team, 1961. . . . Elected to NAIA Basketball Hall of Fame, 1970.

OSCAR PALMER ROBERTSON
(Big O)

Born November 24, 1938 at Charlotte, Tenn.   Height 6:05.   Weight 220.

High School—Indianapolis, Ind., Crispus Attucks.

College—University of Cincinnati, Cincinnati, O.

Drafted by Cincinnati on first round (territorial choice), 1960.

Traded by Cincinnati to Milwaukee for Flynn Robinson and Charlie Paulk, April 21, 1970.

—COLLEGIATE RECORD—

Year	G.	Min.	FGA	FGM	Pct.	FTA	FTM	Pct.	Reb.	Pts.	Avg.
56-57†	13	....	...	151	....	178	127	.713	....	429	33.0
57-58	28	1085	617	352	.571	355	280	.789	425	984	35.1
58-59	30	1172	650	331	.509	398	316	.794	489	978	32.6
59-60	30	1155	701	369	.526	361	273	.756	424	1011	33.7
Varsity Totals	88	3412	1968	1052	.535	1114	869	.780	1338	2973	33.8

OSCAR ROBERTSON

NBA REGULAR SEASON RECORD

Sea.—Team	G.	Min.	FGA	FGM	Pct.	FTA	FTM	Pct.	Reb.	Ast.	PF	Disq.	Pts.	Avg.
60-61—Cincinnati	71	3012	1600	756	.473	794	653	.822	716	690	219	3	2165	30.5
61-62—Cincinnati	79	3503	1810	866	.478	872	700	.803	985	899	258	1	2432	30.8
62-63—Cincinnati	80	3521	1593	825	.518	758	614	.810	835	758	293	1	2264	28.3
63-64—Cincinnati	79	3559	1740	840	.483	938	800	.853	783	868	280	3	2480	31.4
64-65—Cincinnati	75	3421	1681	807	.480	793	665	.839	674	861	205	2	2279	30.4
65-66—Cincinnati	76	3493	1723	818	.475	881	742	.842	586	847	227	1	2378	31.3
66-67—Cincinnati	79	3468	1699	838	.493	843	736	.873	486	845	226	2	2412	30.5
67-68—Cincinnati	65	2765	1321	660	.500	660	576	.873	391	633	199	2	1896	29.2
68-69—Cincinnati	79	3461	1351	656	.486	767	643	.838	502	772	231	2	1955	24.7
69-70—Cincinnati	69	2865	1267	647	.511	561	454	.809	422	558	175	1	1748	25.3
70-71—Milwaukee	81	3194	1193	592	.496	453	385	.850	462	668	203	0	1569	19.4
71-72—Milwaukee	64	2390	887	419	.472	330	276	.836	323	491	116	0	1114	17.4
72-73—Milwaukee	73	2737	983	446	.454	281	238	.847	360	551	167	0	1130	15.5

| | | | | | | | | | —Rebounds— | | | | | | |
Sea.—Team	G.	Min.	FGA	FGM	Pct.	FTA	FTM	Pct.	Off.	Def.	Tot.	Ast.	PF	Dq.	Stl.	Blk.	Pts.	Avg.
73-74—Milw.	70	2477	772	338	.438	254	212	.835	71	208	279	446	132	0	77	4	888	12.7
Totals	1040	43866	19620	9508	.485	9185	7694	.838			7804	9887	2931	18			26710	25.7

NBA PLAYOFF RECORD

Sea.—Team	G.	Min.	FGA	FGM	Pct.	FTA	FTM	Pct.	Reb.	Ast.	PF	Disq.	Pts.	Avg.
61-62—Cincinnati	4	185	81	42	.519	39	31	.795	44	44	18	1	115	28.8
62-63—Cincinnati	12	570	264	124	.470	154	133	.864	156	108	41	0	381	31.8
63-64—Cincinnati	10	471	202	92	.455	127	109	.858	89	84	30	0	293	29.3
64-65—Cincinnati	4	195	89	38	.427	39	36	.923	19	48	14	0	112	28.0
65-66—Cincinnati	5	224	120	49	.408	68	61	.897	38	39	20	1	159	31.8
66-67—Cincinnati	4	183	64	33	.516	37	33	.892	16	45	9	0	99	24.8
70-71—Milwaukee	14	520	210	102	.486	69	52	.754	70	124	39	0	256	18.3
71-72—Milwaukee	11	380	140	57	.407	36	30	.833	64	83	29	0	144	13.1
72-73—Milwaukee	6	256	96	48	.500	34	31	.912	28	45	21	1	127	21.2

| | | | | | | | | | —Rebounds— | | | | | | |
Sea.—Team	G.	Min.	FGA	FGM	Pct.	FTA	FTM	Pct.	Off.	Def.	Tot.	Ast.	PF	Dq.	Stl.	Blk.	Pts.	Avg.
73-74—Milw.	16	689	200	90	.450	52	44	.846	15	39	54	149	46	0	15	4	224	14.0
Totals	86	3673	1466	675	.460	655	560	.855			578	769	267	3			1910	22.2

NBA ALL-STAR GAME RECORD

Season—Team	Min.	FGA	FGM	Pct.	FTA	FTM	Pct.	Reb.	Ast.	PF	Disq.	Pts.
1961—Cincinnati	34	13	8	.615	9	7	.778	9	14	5	0	23
1962—Cincinnati	37	20	9	.450	14	8	.571	7	13	3	0	26
1963—Cincinnati	37	15	9	.600	4	3	.750	3	6	5	0	21
1964—Cincinnati	42	23	10	.435	10	6	.600	14	8	4	0	26
1965—Cincinnati	40	18	8	.444	13	12	.923	6	8	5	0	28
1966—Cincinnati	25	12	6	.500	6	5	.833	10	8	0	0	17
1967—Cincinnati	34	20	9	.450	10	8	.800	2	5	4	0	26
1968—Cincinnati	22	9	7	.778	7	4	.571	1	5	2	0	18
1969—Cincinnati	32	16	8	.500	8	8	1.000	6	5	3	0	24
1970—Cincinnati	29	11	9	.818	4	3	.750	6	4	3	0	21
1971—Milwaukee	24	6	2	.333	3	1	.333	2	2	3	0	5
1972—Milwaukee	24	9	3	.333	10	5	.500	3	3	4	0	11
Totals	380	172	88	.512	98	70	.714	69	81	41	0	246

Elected to Naismith Memorial Basketball Hall of Fame, 1979. . . . Named to NBA 35th Anniversary All-Time Team, 1980. . . . NBA Most Valuable Player, 1964. . . . Named to NBA All-Star First Team, 1961, 1962, 1963, 1964, 1965, 1966, 1967, 1968, 1969. . . . NBA All-Star Second Team, 1970 and 1971. . . . NBA Rookie of the Year, 1961. . . . Holds NBA record for most free throws attempted, 22, and most free throws made, 19, in one half, vs. Baltimore, December 27, 1964. . . . Shares NBA record for most free throws attempted in one quarter, 16, vs. Baltimore, December 27, 1964. . . . NBA all-time leader in free throws made, assists and rebounds by guard. . . . NBA All-Star Game MVP, 1961, 1964, 1969. . . . Holds NBA All-Star Game records for most career points; most career field goals made. . . . Shares NBA All-Star Game records for most career free throws attempted; most free throws made in one game, 12, in 1965. . . . Member of NBA championship team, 1971. . . . Led NBA in assists, 1961, 1962, 1964, 1965, 1966, 1969. . . . Led NBA in free-throw percentage, 1964 and 1968. . . . THE SPORTING NEWS College Player of the Year, 1958, 1959, 1960. . . . Named to THE SPORTING NEWS All-America First Team, 1958, 1959, 1960. . . . Led NCAA in scoring, 1958, 1959, 1960. . . . Member of U.S. Olympic team, 1960.

GUY RODGERS JR.

Born September 1, 1935 at Philadelphia, Pa.   Height 6:00.   Weight 185.

High School—Philadelphia, Pa., Northeast.

College—Temple University, Philadelphia, Pa.

Drafted by Philadelphia on first round (territorial choice), 1958.

Philadelphia franchise transferred to San Francisco, 1962.
Traded by San Francisco to Chicago for a draft choice, cash and two players to be designated, September 7, 1966. Jim King and Jeff Mullins sent to San Francisco to complete deal.
Traded by Chicago to Cincinnati for Flynn Robinson, cash and two draft choices, October 20, 1967.
Selected from Cincinnati by Milwaukee in expansion draft, May 6, 1968.

Year	G.	Min.	FGA	FGM	Pct.	FTA	FTM	Pct.	Reb.	Pts.	Avg.
54-55†	15	....	...	...	....	...	...	....	...	278	18.5
55-56	31	....	552	243	.440	155	87	.561	186	573	18.5
56-57	29	....	...	216	....	...	159	....	...	591	20.4
57-58	30	....	564	249	.441	171	105	.614	199	603	20.1
Varsity Totals	90	....		708			351	....	...	1767	19.6

NBA REGULAR SEASON RECORD

Sea.—Team	G.	Min.	FGA	FGM	Pct.	FTA	FTM	Pct.	Reb.	Ast.	PF	Disq.	Pts.	Avg.
58-59—Philadelphia	45	1565	535	211	.394	112	61	.545	281	261	132	1	483	10.7
59-60—Philadelphia	68	2483	870	338	.388	181	111	.613	391	482	196	3	787	11.6
60-61—Philadelphia	78	2905	1029	397	.386	300	206	.687	509	677	262	3	1000	12.3
61-62—Philadelphia	80	2650	749	267	.356	182	121	.599	348	643	312	12	655	8.2
62-63—San Francisco	79	3249	1150	445	.387	286	208	.725	394	825	296	7	1098	14.1
63-64—San Francisco	79	2695	923	337	.365	280	198	.707	328	556	245	4	872	11.0
64-65—San Francisco	79	2699	1225	465	.380	325	223	.686	323	565	256	4	1153	14.6
65-66—San Francisco	79	2902	1571	586	.373	407	296	.727	421	846	241	6	1468	18.6
66-67—Chicago	81	3063	1377	538	.391	475	383	.806	346	908	243	1	1459	18.0
67-68—Chi.-Cinn.	79	1546	426	148	.347	133	107	.805	150	380	167	1	403	5.1
68-69—Milwaukee	81	2157	862	325	.377	232	184	.793	226	561	207	2	834	10.3
69-70—Milwaukee	64	749	191	68	.356	90	67	.744	74	213	73	1	203	3.2
Totals	892	28663	10908	4125	.378	3003	2165	.721	3791	6917	2630	45	10415	11.7

NBA PLAYOFF RECORD

Sea.—Team	G.	Min.	FGA	FGM	Pct.	FTA	FTM	Pct.	Reb.	Ast.	PF	Disq.	Pts.	Avg.
59-60—Philadelphia	9	370	136	49	.360	36	20	.555	77	54	39	3	118	13.1
60-61—Philadelphia	3	121	57	21	.368	20	11	.550	21	15	16	2	53	17.7
61-62—Philadelphia	13	482	145	52	.359	55	35	.636	7	88	57	3	139	11.6
63-64—San Francisco	12	419	173	57	.329	47	33	.702	58	90	46	1	147	12.3
66-67—Chicago	3	97	40	15	.375	5	4	.800	6	18	11	0	34	11.3
69-70—Milwaukee	7	68	14	4	.286	12	9	.750	4	21	7	0	17	2.4
Totals	47	1557	565	198	.350	175	112	.640	173	286	176	9	508	10.8

NBA ALL-STAR GAME RECORD

Season—Team	Min.	FGA	FGM	Pct.	FTA	FTM	Pct.	Reb.	Ast.	PF	Disq.	Pts.
1963—San Francisco	17	6	3	.500	2	1	.500	2	4	2	0	7
1964—San Francisco	22	6	3	.500	0	0	.000	2	2	4	0	6
1966—San Francisco	34	11	4	.364	0	0	.000	7	11	4	0	8
1967—Chicago	28	4	0	.000	1	1	1.000	2	8	3	0	1
Totals	101	27	10	.370	3	2	.667	13	25	13	0	22

Led NBA in assists, 1963 and 1967.... Named to THE SPORTING NEWS All-America First Team, 1958.

WILLIAM FENTON RUSSELL
(Bill)

Born February 12, 1934 at Monroe, La.   Height 6:10.   Weight 220.

High School—Oakland, Calif., McClymonds.

College—University of San Francisco, San Francisco, Calif.

Drafted by Boston on first round, 1956. (3rd pick—Boston traded Ed Macauley and Cliff Hagan to St. Louis for its first-round choice, April 29, 1956.)

—COLLEGIATE RECORD—

Year	G.	Min.	FGA	FGM	Pct.	FTA	FTM	Pct.	Reb.	Pts.	Avg.
52-53†	23	....	...	...	....	...	...	....	...	461	20.0
53-54	21	....	309	150	.485	212	117	.552	403	417	19.9
54-55	29	....	423	229	.541	278	164	.590	594	622	21.4
55-56	29	....	480	246	.513	212	105	.495	609	597	20.6
Varsity Totals	79	....	1212	625	.516	702	386	.550	1606	1636	20.7

NBA REGULAR SEASON RECORD

Sea.—Team	G.	Min.	FGA	FGM	Pct.	FTA	FTM	Pct.	Reb.	Ast.	PF	Disq.	Pts.	Avg.
56-57—Boston	48	1695	649	277	.427	309	152	.492	943	88	143	2	706	14.7
57-58—Boston	69	2640	1032	456	.442	443	230	.519	1564	202	181	2	1142	16.6
58-59—Boston	70	2979	997	456	.457	428	256	.598	1612	222	161	3	1168	16.7
59-60—Boston	74	3146	1189	555	.467	392	240	.612	1778	277	210	0	1350	18.2
60-61—Boston	78	3458	1250	532	.426	469	258	.550	1868	268	155	0	1322	16.9
61-62—Boston	76	3433	1258	575	.457	481	286	.594	1790	341	207	3	1436	18.9
62-63—Boston	78	3500	1182	511	.432	517	287	.555	1843	348	189	1	1309	16.8
63-64—Boston	78	3482	1077	466	.433	429	236	.550	1930	370	190	0	1168	15.0
64-65—Boston	78	3466	980	429	.438	426	244	.573	1878	410	204	1	1102	14.1
65-66—Boston	78	3386	943	391	.415	405	223	.551	1779	371	221	4	1005	12.9
66-67—Boston	81	3297	870	395	.454	467	285	.610	1700	472	258	4	1075	13.4
67-68—Boston	78	2953	858	365	.425	460	247	.537	1451	357	242	2	977	12.5
68-69—Boston	77	3291	645	279	.433	388	204	.526	1484	374	231	2	762	9.9
Totals	963	40726	12930	5687	.440	5614	3148	.561	21620	4100	2592	24	14522	15.1

BILL RUSSELL

NBA PLAYOFF RECORD

Sea.—Team	G.	Min.	FGA	FGM	Pct.	FTA	FTM	Pct.	Reb.	Ast.	PF	Disq.	Pts.	Avg.
56-57—Boston	10	409	148	54	.365	61	31	.508	244	32	41	1	139	13.9
57-58—Boston	9	355	133	48	.361	66	40	.606	221	24	24	0	136	15.1
58-59—Boston	11	496	159	65	.409	67	41	.612	305	40	28	1	171	15.5
59-60—Boston	13	572	206	94	.456	75	53	.707	336	38	38	1	241	18.5
60-61—Boston	10	462	171	73	.427	86	45	.523	299	48	24	0	191	19.1
61-62—Boston	14	672	253	116	.458	113	82	.726	370	70	49	0	314	22.4
62-63—Boston	13	617	212	96	.453	109	72	.661	326	66	36	0	264	20.3
63-64—Boston	10	451	132	47	.356	67	37	.552	272	44	33	0	131	13.1
64-65—Boston	12	561	150	79	.527	76	40	.526	302	76	43	2	198	16.5
65-66—Boston	17	814	261	124	.475	123	76	.618	428	85	60	0	324	19.1
66-67—Boston	9	390	86	31	.360	52	33	.635	198	50	32	1	95	10.6
67-68—Boston	19	869	242	99	.409	130	76	.585	434	99	73	1	274	14.4
68-69—Boston	18	829	182	77	.423	81	41	.506	369	98	65	1	195	10.8
Totals	165	7497	2335	1003	.430	1106	667	.603	4104	770	546	8	2673	16.2

NBA ALL-STAR GAME RECORD

Season—Team	Min.	FGA	FGM	Pct.	FTA	FTM	Pct.	Reb.	Ast.	PF	Disq.	Pts.
1958—Boston	26	12	5	.417	3	1	.333	11	2	5	0	11
1959—Boston	27	10	3	.300	1	1	1.000	9	1	4	0	7
1960—Boston	27	7	3	.429	2	0	.000	8	3	1	0	6
1961—Boston	28	15	9	.600	8	6	.750	11	1	2	0	24
1962—Boston	27	12	5	.417	3	2	.667	12	2	2	0	12
1963—Boston	37	14	8	.571	4	3	.750	24	5	3	0	19
1964—Boston	42	13	6	.462	2	1	.500	21	2	4	0	13
1965—Boston	33	12	7	.583	9	3	.333	13	5	6	1	17
1966—Boston	23	6	1	.167	0	0	.000	10	2	2	0	2
1967—Boston	22	2	1	.500	0	0	.000	5	5	2	0	2
1968—Boston	23	4	2	.500	0	0	.000	9	8	5	0	4
1969—Boston	28	4	1	.250	2	1	.500	6	3	1	0	3
Totals	343	111	51	.459	34	18	.529	139	39	37	1	120

NBA COACHING RECORD

		Regular Season				Playoffs	
Sea.	Club	W.	L.	Pct.	Pos.	W.	L.
1966-67—Boston		60	21	.741	2†	4	5
1967-68—Boston*		54	28	.659	2†	12	7
1968-69—Boston*		48	34	.585	4†	12	6
1973-74—Seattle		36	46	.439	3‡	..	..
1974-75—Seattle		43	39	.524	2‡	4	5
1975-76—Seattle		43	39	.524	2‡	2	4
1976-77—Seattle		40	42	.488	4‡	..	..
Totals (7 seasons)		324	249	.565		34	27

*Won NBA championship. †Eastern Division. ‡Pacific Division.

Selected as "Greatest Player in the History of the NBA" by Professional Basketball Writers' Association of America, 1980. . . . Elected to Naismith Memorial Basketball Hall of Fame, 1974. . . . Named to NBA 25th and 35th Anniversary All-Time Teams, 1970 and 1980. . . . NBA Most Valuable Player, 1958, 1961, 1962, 1963, 1965. . . . Named to NBA All-Star First Team, 1959, 1963, 1965. . . . NBA All-Star Second Team, 1958, 1960, 1961, 1962, 1964, 1966, 1967, 1968. . . . NBA All-Defensive First Team, 1969. . . . Holds NBA record for most rebounds in one half, 32, vs. Philadelphia, November 16, 1957. . . . NBA all-time playoff leader in rebounds and personal fouls. . . . Holds NBA championship series game record for most rebounds, 40, vs. St. Louis, March 29, 1960, and vs. Los Angeles, April 18, 1962. . . . Holds NBA championship series game record for most free throws attempted in one half, 15, vs. St. Louis, April 11, 1961. . . . Holds NBA championship series game record for most rebounds in one quarter, 19, vs. Los Angeles, April 18, 1962. . . . NBA All-Star Game MVP, 1963. . . . Member of NBA championship teams, 1957, 1959, 1960, 1961, 1962, 1963, 1964, 1965, 1966, 1968 (also coach), 1969 (also coach). . . . Led NBA in rebounding, 1957, 1958, 1964, 1965. . . . NCAA Tournament Most Outstanding Player, 1955. . . . Member of NCAA championship teams, 1955 and 1956. . . . Member of U.S. Olympic team, 1956. . . . One of only seven players to average over 20 points and 20 rebounds per game during NCAA career.

ADOLPH SCHAYES
(Dolph)

Born May 19, 1928 at New York, N. Y.   Height 6:08.   Weight 220.

High School—Bronx, N. Y., DeWitt Clinton.

College—New York University, New York, N. Y.

Drafted by Tri-Cities NBL, 1948.

NBL draft rights obtained by Syracuse from Tri-Cities, 1948; Syracuse franchise transferred to Philadelphia, 1963.

—COLLEGIATE RECORD—

Year	G.	Min.	FGA	FGM	Pct.	FTA	FTM	Pct.	Reb.	Pts.	Avg.
44-45	11	....	...	46	....	...	23	....	....	115	10.5
45-46	22	....	...	54	....	...	41	....	....	149	6.8
46-47	21	....	...	66	....	...	63	....	....	195	9.3
47-48	26	....	...	124	....	...	108	....	....	356	13.7
Totals	80	....	...	290	....	...	235	....	....	815	10.2

NBL AND NBA REGULAR SEASON RECORD

Sea.—Team	G.	Min.	FGA	FGM	Pct.	FTA	FTM	Pct.	Reb.	Ast.	PF	Disq.	Pts.	Avg.
48-49—Syr. NBL	63	....	....	272	...	369	267	.724	....	....	232	..	811	12.8
49-50—Syracuse	64	....	903	348	.385	486	376	.774	....	259	225	..	1072	16.8
50-51—Syracuse	66	....	930	332	.357	608	457	.752	1080	251	271	9	1121	17.0
51-52—Syracuse	63	2004	740	263	.355	424	342	.807	773	182	213	5	868	13.8
52-53—Syracuse	71	2668	1002	375	.367	619	512	.827	920	227	271	9	1262	17.8
53-54—Syracuse	72	2655	973	370	.380	590	488	.827	870	214	232	4	1228	17.1
54-55—Syracuse	72	2526	1103	422	.383	587	489	.833	887	213	247	6	1333	18.5
55-56—Syracuse	72	2517	1202	465	.387	632	542	.858	891	200	251	9	1472	20.4
56-57—Syracuse	72	2851	1308	496	.379	691	625	.904	1008	229	219	5	1617	22.5
57-58—Syracuse	72	2918	1458	581	.398	696	629	.904	1022	224	244	6	1791	24.9
58-59—Syracuse	72	2645	1304	504	.387	609	526	.864	962	178	280	9	1534	21.3
59-60—Syracuse	75	2741	1440	578	.401	597	533	.892	959	256	263	10	1689	22.5
60-61—Syracuse	79	3007	1595	594	.372	783	680	.868	960	296	296	9	1868	23.6
61-62—Syracuse	56	1480	751	268	.357	319	286	.896	439	120	167	4	822	14.7
62-63—Syracuse	66	1438	575	223	.388	206	181	.879	375	175	177	2	627	9.5
63-64—Phila.	24	350	143	44	.308	57	46	.807	110	48	76	3	134	5.6
Totals	1059	....	15427	6135	.380	8273	6979	.844	11256	3072	3664	90	19249	18.2

NBA PLAYOFF RECORD

Sea.—Team	G.	Min.	FGA	FGM	Pct.	FTA	FTM	Pct.	Reb.	Ast.	PF	Disq.	Pts.	Avg.
48-49—Syr. NBL	6	....	....	27	...	42	32	.762	....	....	26	..	86	14.3
49-50—Syracuse	11	...	148	57	.385	101	74	.733	....	28	43	..	188	17.1
50-51—Syracuse	7	....	105	47	.448	64	49	.766	102	20	28	2	143	20.4
51-52—Syracuse	7	248	91	41	.451	78	60	.769	90	15	34	2	142	20.3
52-53—Syracuse	2	58	16	4	.250	13	10	.769	17	1	7	0	18	9.0
53-54—Syracuse	13	374	140	64	.457	108	80	.741	136	24	40	1	208	16.0
54-55—Syracuse	11	363	167	60	.359	106	89	.840	141	40	48	3	209	19.0
55-56—Syracuse	8	310	142	52	.366	83	73	.880	111	27	27	0	177	22.1
56-57—Syracuse	5	215	95	29	.305	55	49	.891	90	14	18	0	107	21.4
57-58—Syracuse	3	131	64	25	.391	36	30	.833	45	6	10	0	80	26.7
58-59—Syracuse	9	351	195	78	.400	107	98	.916	117	41	36	0	254	28.2
59-60—Syracuse	3	126	66	30	.454	30	28	.933	48	8	10	0	88	29.3
60-61—Syracuse	8	308	152	51	.335	70	63	.900	91	21	32	2	165	20.6
61-62—Syracuse	5	95	66	24	.364	13	9	.692	35	5	21	0	57	11.5
62-63—Syracuse	5	108	44	20	.455	12	11	.917	28	7	17	0	51	10.2
Totals	103	2687	1491	609	.390	918	755	.822	1051	257	397	10	1973	19.2

NBA ALL-STAR GAME RECORD

Season—Team	Min.	FGA	FGM	Pct.	FTA	FTM	Pct.	Reb.	Ast.	PF	Disq.	Pts.
1951—Syracuse	..	10	7	.700	2	1	.500	14	3	1	0	15
1952—Syracuse				Selected—Injured, Did Not Play								
1953—Syracuse	26	7	2	.286	4	4	1.000	13	3	3	0	8
1954—Syracuse	24	3	1	.333	6	4	.667	12	1	1	0	6
1955—Syracuse	29	12	6	.500	3	3	1.000	13	1	4	0	15
1956—Syracuse	25	8	4	.500	10	6	.600	4	2	2	0	14
1957—Syracuse	25	6	4	.667	1	1	1.000	10	1	1	0	9
1958—Syracuse	39	15	6	.400	6	6	1.000	9	2	4	0	18
1959—Syracuse	22	14	3	.214	8	7	.875	13	1	6	1	13
1960—Syracuse	27	19	8	.421	3	3	1.000	10	0	3	0	19
1961—Syracuse	27	15	7	.467	7	7	1.000	6	3	4	0	21
1962—Syracuse	4	0	0	.000	0	0	.000	1	0	3	0	0
Totals	248	109	48	.440	50	42	.840	105	17	32	1	138

NBA COACHING RECORD

Sea. Club	Regular Season W.	L.	Pct.	Pos.	Playoffs W.	L.	Sea. Club	Regular Season W.	L.	Pct.	Pos.	Playoffs W.	L.
1963-64—Philadelphia	34	46	.425	3†	2	3	1970-71—Buffalo	22	60	.268	4‡	..	..
1964-65—Philadelphia	40	40	.500	3†	6	5	1971-72—Buffalo	0	1	.000	..‡	..	..
1965-66—Philadelphia	55	25	.688	1†	1	4	Totals (5 seasons)	151	172	.467		9	12

†Eastern Division. ‡Atlantic Division.

Elected to Naismith Memorial Basketball Hall of Fame, 1972. . . . Named to NBA 25th Anniversary All-Time Team, 1970. . . . NBA All-Star First Team, 1952, 1953, 1954, 1955, 1957, 1958. . . . NBA All-Star Second Team, 1950, 1951, 1956, 1959, 1960, 1961. . . . Shares NBA record for most seasons played, 16. . . . Shares professional basketball record for most years in playoffs, 15. . . . Member of NBA championship team, 1955. . . . Led NBA in rebounding, 1951. . . . Led NBA in free-throw percentage, 1958, 1960, 1962. . . . NBA Coach of the Year, 1966. . . . Former NBA Supervisor of Referees. . . . Father of Denver Nuggets center Dan Schayes.

—DID YOU KNOW—

That Alex Hannum coached teams from three different cities to the NBA championship series? Hannum went to the finals with the St. Louis Hawks in 1956-57 and 1957-58, the San Francisco Warriors in 1963-64 and the Philadelphia 76ers in 1966-67. He split with the Hawks, won with the 76ers and lost with the Warriors.

WILLIAM WALTON SHARMAN
(Bill)

Born May 25, 1926 at Abilene, Tex.   Height 6:01.   Weight 190.
High Schools—Lomita, Calif., Narbonne (Soph.) and
Porterville, Calif. (Jr. and Sr.)
College—University of Southern California, Los Angeles, Calif.
Drafted by Washington on second round, 1950.

Selected by Fort Wayne in dispersal draft of Washington franchise, January 8, 1951. (Did not report to Fort Wayne).
Traded by Fort Wayne with Bob Brannum to Boston for NBA rights to Charlie Share, 1951.
Signed as player-coach by Los Angeles of American Basketball League, 1961.

—COLLEGIATE PLAYING RECORD—

Year	G.	Min.	FGA	FGM	Pct.	FTA	FTM	Pct.	Reb.	Pts.	Avg.
46-47	10	....	....	....	....	....	....	....	....	41	4.1
47-48	24	....	....	100	....	44	38	.864	....	238	9.9
48-49	24	....	....	142	....	125	98	.784	....	382	15.9
49-50	24	....	421	171	.406	129	104	.806	....	446	18.6
Totals	82	....	....	....	....	....	...	....	....	1107	13.5

NOTE: In military service during 1944-45 and 1945-46 seasons.

NBA REGULAR SEASON RECORD

Sea.—Team	G.	Min.	FGA	FGM	Pct.	FTA	FTM	Pct.	Reb.	Ast.	PF	Disq.	Pts.	Avg.
50-51—Washington	31	....	361	141	.391	108	96	.889	96	39	86	3	378	12.2
51-52—Boston	63	1389	628	244	.389	213	183	.859	221	151	181	3	671	10.7
52-53—Boston	71	2333	925	403	.436	401	341	.850	288	191	240	7	1147	16.2
53-54—Boston	72	2467	915	412	.450	392	331	.844	255	229	211	4	1155	16.0
54-55—Boston	68	2453	1062	453	.427	387	347	.897	302	280	212	2	1253	18.4
55-56—Boston	72	2698	1229	538	.438	413	358	.867	259	339	197	1	1434	19.9
56-57—Boston	67	2403	1241	516	.416	421	381	.905	286	236	188	1	1413	21.1
57-58—Boston	63	2214	1297	550	.424	338	302	.893	295	167	156	3	1402	22.3
58-59—Boston	72	2382	1377	562	.408	367	342	.932	292	179	173	1	1466	20.4
59-60—Boston	71	1916	1225	559	.456	291	252	.866	262	144	154	2	1370	19.3
60-61—Boston	61	1538	908	383	.422	228	210	.921	223	146	127	0	976	16.0
Totals	711	21793	11168	4761	.426	3559	3143	.883	2779	2101	1925	27	12665	17.8

NBA PLAYOFF RECORD

Sea.—Team	G.	Min.	FGA	FGM	Pct.	FTA	FTM	Pct.	Reb.	Ast.	PF	Disq.	Pts.	Avg.
51-52—Boston	1	27	12	7	.583	1	1	1.000	3	7	4	0	15	15.0
52-53—Boston	6	201	60	20	.333	32	30	.938	15	15	26	1	70	11.7
53-54—Boston	6	206	81	35	.432	50	43	.860	25	10	29	2	113	18.3
54-55—Boston	7	290	110	55	.500	38	35	.921	38	38	24	1	145	20.7
55-56—Boston	3	119	46	18	.391	17	16	.941	7	12	7	0	52	17.3
56-57—Boston	10	377	197	75	.381	64	61	.953	35	29	23	1	211	21.1
57-58—Boston	11	406	221	90	.407	56	52	.929	54	25	28	0	232	21.1
58-59—Boston	11	322	193	82	.425	59	57	.966	36	28	35	0	221	20.1
59-60—Boston	13	364	209	88	.421	53	43	.811	45	20	22	1	219	16.8
60-61—Boston	10	261	133	68	.511	36	32	.889	27	17	22	0	168	16.8
Totals	78	2573	1262	538	.426	406	370	.911	285	201	220	6	1446	18.5

NBA ALL-STAR GAME RECORD

Season—Team	Min.	FGA	FGM	Pct.	FTA	FTM	Pct.	Reb.	Ast.	PF	Disq.	Pts.
1953—Boston	26	8	5	.625	1	1	1.000	4	0	2	0	11
1954—Boston	30	9	6	.667	4	2	.500	2	3	3	0	14
1955—Boston	18	10	5	.500	5	5	.500	4	2	4	0	15
1956—Boston	24	8	2	.250	4	3	.750	7	2	6	1	7
1957—Boston	23	17	5	.294	2	2	1.000	3	2	2	0	10
1958—Boston	25	19	6	.316	3	3	1.000	4	3	2	0	15
1959—Boston	24	12	3	.250	6	5	.833	2	0	1	0	11
1960—Boston	26	21	8	.381	1	1	1.000	6	2	1	0	17
Totals	196	104	40	.385	26	22	.846	32	14	21	1	100

COLLEGIATE COACHING RECORD

Sea. Club	W.	L.	Pct.	Pos.
1962-63—Cal St.-Los Ang..	10	12	.454	4§
1963-64—Cal St.-Los Ang..	17	8	.680	2§

§California Collegiate Athletic Association.

NBA COACHING RECORD

Sea.	Club	Regular Season W.	L.	Pct.	Pos.	Playoffs W.	L.
1966-67—San Francisco ...		44	37	.543	1†	9	6
1967-68—San Francisco ...		43	39	.524	3†	4	6
1971-72—Los Angeles*		69	13	.841	1‡	12	3
1972-73—Los Angeles		60	22	.732	1‡	9	8
1973-74—Los Angeles		47	35	.573	1‡	1	4
1974-75—Los Angeles		30	52	.366	5‡	..	..
1975-76—Los Angeles		40	42	.488	4‡	..	..
Totals (7 seasons)		333	240	.581		35	27

*Won NBA Championship.   †Western Division.   ‡Pacific Division.

ABL AND ABA COACHING RECORD

Sea.	Club	Regular Season W.	L.	Pct.	Pos.	Playoffs W.	L.
1961-62—LA-Clev. ABL.....		43	26	.615	..	5	2
1968-69—Los Ang. ABA....		33	45	.423	5†	..	..
1969-70—Los Ang. ABA....		43	41	.512	4†	10	7
1970-71—Utah ABA*		57	27	.679	2†	12	6
Totals (4 seasons)		176	139	.559		27	15

Note: Los Angeles Jets had 24-15 record when they folded after first half of season. Sharman then guided the Cleveland Pipers to ABL championship.

*Won ABA Championship.   †Western Division.

ABL REGULAR SEASON RECORD

Sea.—Team	G.	Min.	—2-Point— FGM	FGA	Pct.	—3-Point— FGM	FGA	Pct.	FTM	FTA	Pct.	Reb.	Ast.	Pts.	Avg.
61-62—Los Angeles	19	346	80	35	.438	8	1	.125	37	34	.919	43	37	107	5.6

Elected to Naismith Memorial Basketball Hall of Fame, 1974. . . . Named to NBA 25th Anniversary All-Time Team, 1970. . . . NBA All-Star First Team, 1956, 1957, 1958, 1959. . . . NBA All-Star Second Team, 1953, 1955, 1960. . . . NBA All-Star Game MVP, 1955. . . . Holds NBA All-Star Game record for most field goals attempted in one quarter, 12, in 1960. . . . Member of NBA championship teams, 1957, 1959, 1960, 1961. . . . Led NBA in free-throw percentage, 1953, 1954, 1955, 1956, 1957, 1959, 1961. . . . NBA Coach of the Year, 1972. . . . Coach of NBA championship team, 1972. . . . ABA Co-Coach of the Year, 1970. . . . Coach of ABA championship team, 1971. . . . Coach of ABL championship team, 1962. . . . Played minor league baseball as an outfielder in Brooklyn Dodgers' organization, 1950 through 1953. . . . Named to THE SPORTING NEWS All-America First Team, 1950. . . . THE SPORTING NEWS All-America Third Team, 1949.

PAUL THERON SILAS

Born July 12, 1943 at Prescott, Ariz.   Height 6:07.   Weight 220.

High School—Oakland, Calif., McClymonds.

College—Creighton University, Omaha, Neb.

Drafted by St. Louis on second round, 1964 (12th pick).

Traded by Atlanta to Phoenix for Gary Gregor, May 8, 1969.
Traded by Phoenix to Boston, September 19, 1972, to complete deal in which Phoenix acquired draft rights to Charlie Scott, March 14, 1972.
Traded by Boston to Denver in three-team deal, in which Curtis Rowe was traded by Detroit to Boston, and Ralph Simpson was traded by Denver to Detroit, October 20, 1976.
Traded by Denver with Willie Wise and Marvin Webster to Seattle for Tom Burleson, Bob Wilkerson and a 1977 2nd round draft choice, May 24, 1977.
Signed by San Diego as Veteran Free Agent, May 21, 1980; Seattle received a 1985 2nd round draft choice as compensation.
Played in Eastern Basketball League with Wilkes Barre, 1965-66.

—COLLEGIATE RECORD—

Year	G.	Min.	FGA	FGM	Pct.	FTA	FTM	Pct.	Reb.	Pts.	Avg.
60-61†	21	....	...	225	....	119	96	.807	568	546	26.0
61-62	25	....	524	213	.406	215	125	.581	563	551	22.0
62-63	27	....	531	220	.414	228	133	.583	557	573	21.2
63-64	29	....	529	210	.397	194	117	.603	631	537	18.5
Varsity Totals	81	....	1584	643	.406	637	375	.589	1751	1661	20.5

NBA REGULAR SEASON RECORD

Sea.—Team	G.	Min.	FGA	FGM	Pct.	FTA	FTM	Pct.	Reb.	Ast.	PF	Disq.	Pts.	Avg.
64-65—St. Louis	79	1243	375	140	.373	164	83	.506	576	48	161	1	363	4.6
65-66—St. Louis	46	586	173	70	.405	61	35	.574	236	22	72	0	175	3.8
66-67—St. Louis	77	1570	482	207	.429	213	113	.531	669	74	208	4	527	6.9
67-68—St. Louis	82	2652	871	399	.458	424	299	.705	958	162	243	4	1097	13.4
68-69—Atlanta	79	1853	575	241	.419	333	204	.613	745	140	166	0	686	8.7
69-70—Phoenix	78	2836	804	373	.464	412	250	.607	916	214	266	5	996	12.8
70-71—Phoenix	81	2944	789	338	.428	416	285	.685	1015	247	227	3	961	11.9
71-72—Phoenix	80	3082	1031	485	.470	560	433	.773	955	343	201	2	1403	17.5
72-73—Boston	80	2618	851	400	.470	380	266	.700	1039	251	197	1	1066	13.3

Sea.—Team	G.	Min.	FGA	FGM	Pct.	FTA	FTM	Pct.	Off.	Def.	Tot.	Ast.	PF	Dq.	Stl.	Blk.	Pts.	Avg.
73-74—Boston	82	2599	772	340	.440	337	264	.783	334	581	915	186	246	3	63	20	944	11.5
74-75—Boston	82	2661	749	312	.417	344	244	.709	348	677	1025	224	229	3	60	22	868	10.6
75-76—Boston	81	2662	740	315	.426	333	236	.709	365	660	1025	203	227	3	56	33	866	10.7
76-77—Denver	81	1959	572	206	.360	255	170	.667	236	370	606	132	183	0	58	23	582	7.2
77-78—Seattle	82	2172	464	184	.397	186	109	.586	289	377	666	145	182	0	65	16	477	5.8
78-79—Seattle	82	1957	402	170	.423	194	116	.598	259	316	575	115	177	3	31	19	456	5.6
79-80—Seattle	82	1595	299	113	.378	136	89	.654	204	232	436	66	120	0	25	5	315	3.8
Totals	1254	34989	9949	4293	.432	4748	3196	.673			12357	2572	3105	32	358	138	11782	9.4

NBA PLAYOFF RECORD

Sea.—Team	G.	Min.	FGA	FGM	Pct.	FTA	FTM	Pct.	Reb.	Ast.	PF	Disq.	Pts.	Avg.
64-65—St. Louis	4	42	10	4	.400	4	3	.750	18	1	6	0	11	2.8
65-66—St. Louis	7	80	18	5	.278	11	8	.727	34	2	11	0	18	2.6
66-67—St. Louis	8	122	36	9	.250	18	11	.611	52	6	17	0	29	3.6
67-68—St. Louis	6	178	51	22	.431	38	27	.711	57	21	17	0	71	11.8
68-69—Atlanta	11	258	58	21	.362	37	19	.514	92	21	32	0	61	5.5
69-70—Phoenix	7	286	109	46	.422	32	21	.656	111	30	29	1	113	16.1
72-73—Boston	13	512	120	47	.392	50	31	.620	196	39	39	0	125	9.6

Sea.—Team	G.	Min.	FGA	FGM	Pct.	FTA	FTM	Pct.	Off.	Def.	Tot.	Ast.	PF	Dq.	Stl.	Blk.	Pts.	Avg.
73-74—Boston	18	574	126	50	.397	53	44	.830	53	138	191	47	51	2	13	9	144	8.0
74-75—Boston	11	405	92	42	.457	25	16	.640	46	84	130	40	45	1	12	2	100	9.1
75-76—Boston	18	741	154	69	.448	69	56	.812	78	168	246	42	67	1	24	6	194	10.8
76-77—Denver	6	141	33	14	.424	24	13	.542	16	24	40	16	23	1	2	4	41	6.8
77-78—Seattle	22	605	94	33	.351	60	41	.683	73	114	187	36	59	0	12	6	107	4.9
78-79—Seattle	17	418	54	21	.389	46	31	.674	40	58	98	19	44	1	9	5	73	4.3
79-80—Seattle	15	257	43	13	.302	13	11	.846	33	42	75	15	29	0	9	2	37	2.5
Totals	163	4619	998	396	.397	480	332	.692			1527	335	469	7	81	34	1124	6.9

NBA ALL-STAR GAME RECORD

Season—Team	Min.	FGA	FGM	Pct.	FTA	FTM	Pct.	Off.	Def.	Tot.	Ast.	PF	Dq.	Stl.	Blk.	Pts.
1972—Phoenix	15	6	0	.000	3	2	.667			9	1	1	0			2
1975—Boston	15	4	2	.500	2	2	1.000	0	2	2	2	2	0	4	0	6
Totals	30	10	2	.200	5	4	.800			11	3	3	0			8

MINOR LEAGUE REGULAR SEASON RECORD

Sea.—Team	G.	Min.	2-Point FGM	FGA	Pct.	3-Point FGM	FGA	Pct.	FTM	FTA	Pct.	Reb.	Ast.	Pts.	Avg.
65-66—Wilkes Barre EBL	5	....	....	25	....	....	0	0	.000	13	21	.619	85	9	63	12.6

NBA COACHING RECORD

Sea.	Club	Regular Season W.	L.	Pct.	Pos.	Playoffs W.	L.
1980-81—San Diego		36	46	.439	5†	..	..
1981-82—San Diego		17	65	.207	6†	..	..
1982-83—San Diego		25	57	.305	6†	..	..
Totals (3 seasons)		78	168	.317		..	..

†Pacific Division.

Named to NBA All-Defensive First Team, 1975 and 1976. . . . NBA All-Defensive Second Team, 1971, 1972, 1973. . . . Member of NBA championship teams, 1974, 1976, 1979. . . . Holds NCAA record for most rebounds in 3-year career. . . . Led NCAA in rebounding, 1963. . . . One of only seven players to average over 20 points and 20 rebounds per game during NCAA career.

NATE THURMOND

Born July 25, 1941 at Akron, O.   Height 6:11.   Weight 235.

High School—Akron, O., Central.

College—Bowling Green State University, Bowling Green, O.

Drafted by San Francisco on first round, 1963.

Franchise name changed to Golden State, 1971.
Traded by Golden State to Chicago for Clifford Ray, cash and a 1975 1st round draft choice, September 3, 1974.
Traded by Chicago with Rowland Garrett to Cleveland for Steve Patterson and Eric Fernsten, November 27, 1975.

—COLLEGIATE RECORD—

Year	G.	Min.	FGA	FGM	Pct.	FTA	FTM	Pct.	Reb.	Pts.	Avg.
59-60†	17	....	....	....	....	....	....	....	208	225	13.2
60-61	24	....	427	170	.398	129	87	.674	449	427	17.8
61-62	25	....	358	163	.455	113	67	.593	394	393	15.7
62-63	27	....	466	206	.442	197	124	.629	452	536	19.9
Varsity Totals	76	....	1251	539	.431	439	278	.633	1295	1356	17.8

Sea.—Team	G.	Min.	FGA	FGM	Pct.	FTA	FTM	Pct.	Reb.	Ast.	PF	Disq.	Pts.	Avg.
63-64—San Fran.	76	1966	554	219	.395	173	95	.549	790	86	184	2	533	7.0
64-65—San Fran.	77	3173	1240	519	.419	357	235	.658	1395	157	232	3	1273	16.5
65-66—San Fran.	73	2891	1119	454	.406	428	280	.654	1312	111	223	7	1188	16.3
66-67—San Fran.	65	2755	1068	467	.437	445	280	.629	1382	166	183	3	1214	18.7
67-68—San Fran.	51	2222	929	382	.411	438	282	.644	1121	215	137	1	1046	20.5
68-59—San Fran.	71	3208	1394	571	.410	621	382	.615	1402	253	171	0	1524	21.5
69-70—San Fran.	43	1919	824	341	.414	346	261	.754	762	150	110	1	943	21.9
70-71—San Fran.	82	3351	1401	623	.445	541	395	.730	1128	257	192	1	1641	20.0
71-72—Golden St.	78	3362	1454	628	.432	561	417	.743	1252	230	214	1	1673	21.4
72-73—Golden St.	79	3419	1159	517	.446	439	315	.718	1349	280	240	2	1349	17.1

Sea.—Team	G.	Min.	FGA	FGM	Pct.	FTA	FTM	Pct.	—Rebounds— Off.	Def.	Tot.	Ast.	PF	Dq.	Stl.	Blk.	Pts.	Avg.
73-74—Gld. St.	62	2463	694	308	.444	287	191	.666	249	629	878	165	179	4	41	179	807	13.0
74-75—Chicago	80	2756	686	250	.364	224	132	.589	259	645	904	328	271	6	46	195	632	7.9
75-76—Chi.-Cleve.	78	1393	337	142	.421	123	62	.504	115	300	415	94	160	1	22	98	346	4.4
76-77—Cleveland	49	997	246	100	.407	106	68	.642	121	253	374	83	128	2	16	81	268	5.5
Totals	964	35875	13105	5521	.421	5089	3395	.667			14464	2575	2624	34	125	553	14437	15.0

NBA PLAYOFF RECORD

Sea.—Team	G.	Min.	FGA	FGM	Pct.	FTA	FTM	Pct.	Reb.	Ast.	PF	Disq.	Pts.	Avg.
63-64—San Fran.	12	410	98	42	.429	53	36	.679	148	12	46	0	120	10.0
66-67—San Fran.	15	690	215	93	.433	91	52	.571	346	47	52	1	238	15.9
68-69—San Fran.	6	263	102	40	.392	34	20	.588	117	28	18	0	100	16.7
71-71—San Fran.	5	192	97	36	.371	20	16	.800	51	15	20	0	88	17.6
71-72—Golden St.	5	230	122	53	.434	28	21	.750	89	26	12	0	127	25.4
72-73—Golden St.	11	460	161	64	.398	40	32	.800	145	40	30	1	160	14.5

Sea.—Team	G.	Min.	FGA	FGM	Pct.	FTA	FTM	Pct.	—Rebounds— Off.	Def.	Tot.	Ast.	PF	Dq.	Stl.	Blk.	Pts.	Avg.
74-75—Chicago	13	254	38	14	.368	37	18	.486	24	63	87	31	36	0	5	21	46	3.5
75-76—Chi.-Cle.	13	375	79	37	.468	32	13	.406	38	79	117	28	52	2	6	29	87	6.7
76-77—Cleveland	1	1	0	0	.000	0	0	.000	0	1	1	0	0	0	0	1	0	0.0
Totals	81	2875	912	379	.416	335	208	.621			1101	227	266	4	11	51	966	11.9

NBA ALL-STAR GAME RECORD

Season—Team	Min.	FGA	FGM	Pct.	FTA	FTM	Pct.	Reb.	Ast.	PF	Disq.	Pts.
1965—San Francisco	10	2	0	.000	0	0	.000	3	0	1	0	0
1966—San Francisco	33	16	3	.188	3	1	.000	16	1	1	0	7
1967—San Francisco	42	16	7	.438	4	2	.500	18	0	1	0	16
1968—San Francisco					Selected—Injured, Did Not Play							
1970—San Francisco					Selected—Injured, Did Not Play							
1973—Golden State	14	5	2	.400	0	0	.000	4	1	2	0	4

Season—Team	Min.	FGA	FGM	Pct.	FTA	FTM	Pct.	—Rebounds— Off.	Def.	Tot.	Ast.	PF	Dq.	Stl.	Blk.	Pts.
1974—Golden St.	5	4	2	.500	1	0	.000	1	2	3	0	0	0	0	0	4
Totals	104	43	14	.326	8	3	.375			44	2	5	0			31

Elected to Naismith Memorial Basketball Hall of Fame, 1984. . . . Named to NBA All-Defensive First Team, 1969 and 1971. . . . NBA All-Defensive Second Team, 1972, 1973, 1974. . . . NBA All-Rookie Team, 1964. . . . Holds NBA record for most rebounds in one quarter, 18, vs. Baltimore, February 28, 1965. . . . Named to THE SPORTING NEWS All-America First Team, 1963. . . . Holds NCAA Tournament record for most rebounds in one game, 31, vs. Mississippi State, 1963.

JACK TWYMAN

Born May 11, 1934 at Pittsburgh, Pa. Height 6:06. Weight 210.

High School—Pittsburgh, Pa., Central Catholic.

College—University of Cincinnati, Cincinnati, O.

Drafted by Rochester on second round, 1955 (10th pick).

Rochester franchise transferred to Cincinnati, 1957.

—COLLEGIATE RECORD—

Year	G.	Min.	FGA	FGM	Pct.	FTA	FTM	Pct.	Reb.	Pts.	Avg.
51-52	16	....	83	27	.325	27	13	.481	55	67	4.2
52-53	24	716	323	136	.421	143	89	.622	362	361	15.0
53-54	21	777	443	174	.393	145	110	.759	347	458	21.8
54-55	29	1097	628	285	.454	192	142	.740	478	712	24.6
Totals	90	....	1477	622	.421	507	354	.698	1242	1598	17.8

NBA REGULAR SEASON RECORD

Sea.—Team	G.	Min.	FGA	FGM	Pct.	FTA	FTM	Pct.	Reb.	Ast.	PF	Disq.	Pts.	Avg.
55-56—Rochester	72	2186	987	417	.422	298	204	.685	466	171	239	4	1038	14.4
56-57—Rochester	72	2338	1023	449	.439	363	276	.760	354	123	251	4	1174	16.3
57-58—Cincinnati	72	2178	1028	465	.452	396	307	.775	464	110	224	3	1237	17.2
58-59—Cincinnati	72	2713	1691	710	.420	558	437	.783	653	209	277	6	1857	25.8
59-60—Cincinnati	75	3023	2063	870	.422	762	598	.785	664	260	275	10	2338	31.2
60-61—Cincinnati	79	2920	1632	796	.488	554	405	.731	669	225	279	5	1997	25.3

Sea.—Team	G.	Min.	FGA	FGM	Pct.	FTA	FTM	Pct.	Reb.	Ast.	PF	Disq.	Pts.	Avg.
61-62—Cincinnati	80	2991	1542	739	.479	435	353	.815	638	323	315	5	1831	22.9
62-63—Cincinnati	80	2523	1335	641	.480	375	304	.811	598	214	286	7	1586	19.8
63-64—Cincinnati	68	2004	993	447	.450	228	189	.829	364	137	267	7	1083	19.9
64-65—Cincinnati	80	2236	1081	479	.443	239	198	.828	383	137	239	4	1156	14.5
65-66—Cincinnati	73	943	498	224	.450	117	95	.812	168	60	122	1	543	7.4
Totals	823	26055	13873	6237	.450	4325	3366	.778	5421	1969	2774	56	15840	19.2

NBA PLAYOFF RECORD

Sea.—Team	G.	Min.	FGA	FGM	Pct.	FTA	FTM	Pct.	Reb.	Ast.	PF	Disq.	Pts.	Avg.
57-58—Cincinnati	2	74	45	15	.333	12	7	.583	22	1	6	0	37	18.5
61-62—Cincinnati	4	149	78	34	.436	8	8	1.000	29	12	18	0	76	19.0
62-63—Cincinnati	12	410	205	92	.449	77	65	.844	98	30	47	1	249	20.8
63-64—Cincinnati	10	354	176	83	.472	49	29	.796	87	16	41	1	205	20.5
64-65—Cincinnati	4	97	48	19	.396	11	11	1.000	17	3	16	1	49	12.3
65-66—Cincinnati	2	11	4	2	.500	2	1	.500	2	0	3	0	5	2.5
Totals	34	1095	556	245	.441	159	131	.824	255	62	131	2	621	18.3

NBA ALL-STAR GAME RECORD

Season—Team	Min.	FGA	FGM	Pct.	FTA	FTM	Pct.	Reb.	Ast.	PF	Disq.	Pts.
1957—Rochester	17	8	1	.125	3	1	.333	0	1	1	0	3
1958—Cincinnati	25	13	8	.615	2	2	1.000	3	0	3	0	18
1959—Cincinnati	23	12	8	.667	4	2	.500	8	3	4	0	18
1960—Cincinnati	28	17	11	.647	8	5	.625	5	1	4	0	27
1962—Cincinnati	8	6	4	.667	3	3	1.000	1	2	0	0	11
1963—Cincinnati	16	12	6	.500	0	0	.000	4	1	2	0	12
Totals	117	68	38	.559	20	13	.650	21	8	14	0	89

Elected to Naismith Memorial Basketball Hall of Fame, 1982.... Named to NBA All-Star Second Team, 1960 and 1962.... Led NBA in field-goal percentage, 1958.

WESTLEY SISSEL UNSELD
(Wes)

Born March 14, 1946 at Louisville, Ky.   Height 6:07½.   Weight 245.

High School—Louisville, Ky., Seneca.

College—University of Louisville, Louisville, Ky.

Drafted by Baltimore on first round, 1968 (2nd pick).

—COLLEGIATE RECORD—

Year	G.	Min.	FGA	FGM	Pct.	FTA	FTM	Pct.	Reb.	Pts.	Avg.
64-65†	14	....	312	214	.686	124	73	.589	331	501	35.8
65-66	26	....	374	195	.521	202	128	.634	505	518	19.9
66-67	28	....	374	201	.537	177	121	.684	533	523	18.7
67-68	28	....	382	234	.613	275	177	.644	513	645	23.0
Varsity Totals	82	....	1130	630	.558	654	426	.651	1551	1686	20.6

NBA REGULAR SEASON RECORD

Sea.—Team	G.	Min.	FGA	FGM	Pct.	FTA	FTM	Pct.	Reb.	Ast.	PF	Disq.	Pts.	Avg.
68-69—Baltimore	82	2970	897	427	.476	458	277	.605	1491	213	276	4	1131	13.8
69-70—Baltimore	82	3234	1015	526	.518	428	273	.638	1370	291	250	2	1325	16.2
70-71—Baltimore	74	2904	846	424	.501	303	199	.657	1253	293	235	2	1047	14.1
71-72—Baltimore	76	3171	822	409	.498	272	171	.629	1336	278	218	1	989	13.0
72-73—Baltimore	79	3085	854	421	.493	212	149	.703	1260	347	168	0	991	12.5

| | | | | | | | | —Rebounds— | | | | | | |

Sea.—Team	G.	Min.	FGA	FGM	Pct.	FTA	FTM	Pct.	Off.	Def.	Tot.	Ast.	PF	Dq.	Stl.	Blk.	Pts.	Avg.
73-74—Capital	56	1727	333	146	.438	55	36	.655	152	365	517	159	121	1	56	16	328	5.9
74-75—Washington	73	2904	544	273	.502	184	126	.685	318	759	1077	297	180	1	115	68	672	9.2
75-76—Washington	78	2922	567	318	.561	195	114	.585	271	765	1036	404	203	3	84	59	750	9.6
76-77—Washington	82	2860	551	270	.490	166	100	.602	243	634	877	363	253	5	87	45	640	7.8
77-78—Washington	80	2644	491	257	.523	173	93	.538	286	669	955	326	234	2	98	45	607	7.6
78-79—Washington	77	2406	600	346	.577	235	151	.643	274	556	830	315	204	2	71	37	843	10.9
79-80—Washington	82	2973	637	327	.513	209	139	.665	334	760	1094	366	249	5	65	61	794	9.7
80-81—Washington	63	2032	429	225	.524	86	55	.640	207	466	673	170	171	1	52	36	507	8.0
Totals	984	35832	8586	4369	.509	2976	1883	.633			13769	3822	2762	29	628	367	10624	10.8

Three-Point Field Goals: 1979-80, 1-for-2 (.500). 1980-81, 2-for-4 (.500). Totals, 3-for-6 (.500).

NBA PLAYOFF RECORD

Sea.—Team	G.	Min.	FGA	FGM	Pct.	FTA	FTM	Pct.	Reb.	Ast.	PF	Disq.	Pts.	Avg.
68-69—Baltimore	4	165	57	30	.526	19	15	.789	74	5	14	0	75	18.8
69-70—Baltimore	7	289	70	29	.414	19	15	.789	165	24	25	1	73	10.4
70-71—Baltimore	18	759	208	96	.462	81	46	.568	339	69	60	0	238	13.2
71-72—Baltimore	6	266	65	32	.492	19	10	.526	75	25	22	0	74	12.3
72-73—Baltimore	5	201	48	20	.417	19	9	.474	76	17	12	0	49	9.8

Sea.—Team	G.	Min.	FGA	FGM	Pct.	FTA	FTM	Pct.	Off.	Def.	Tot.	Ast.	PF	Dq.	Stl.	Blk.	Pts.	Avg.
73-74—Capital	7	297	63	31	.492	15	9	.600	22	63	85	27	15	0	4	1	71	10.1
74-75—Washington	17	734	130	71	.546	61	40	.656	65	211	276	64	39	0	15	20	182	10.7
75-76—Washington	7	310	39	18	.462	24	13	.542	26	59	85	28	19	0	6	4	49	7.0
76-77—Washington	9	368	54	30	.556	12	7	.583	24	81	105	44	32	0	8	6	67	7.4
77-78—Washington	18	677	134	71	.530	46	27	.587	72	144	216	79	62	2	17	7	169	9.4
78-79—Washington	19	736	158	78	.494	64	39	.609	90	163	253	64	66	2	17	14	195	10.3
79-80—Washington	2	87	14	7	.500	6	4	.667	7	21	28	7	5	0	0	3	18	9.0
Totals	119	4889	1040	513	.493	385	234	.608			1777	453	371	5	67	55	1260	10.6

Three-Point Field Goals: 1979-80, 0-for-1.

NBA ALL-STAR GAME RECORD

Season—Team	Min.	FGA	FGM	Pct.	FTA	FTM	Pct.	Reb.	Ast.	PF	Disq.	Pts.
1969—Baltimore	14	7	5	.714	3	1	.333	8	1	3	0	11
1971—Baltimore	21	9	4	.444	0	0	.000	10	2	2	0	8
1972—Baltimore	16	5	1	.200	0	0	.000	7	1	3	0	2
1973—Baltimore	11	4	2	.500	0	0	.000	5	1	0	0	4

Season—Team	Min.	FGA	FGM	Pct.	FTA	FTM	Pct.	Off.	Def.	Tot.	Ast.	PF	Dq.	Stl.	Blk.	Pts.
1975—Washington	15	3	2	.667	2	2	1.000	2	4	6	1	2	0	2	0	6
Totals...............	77	28	14	.500	5	3	.600			36	6	10	0			31

NBA Most Valuable Player and Rookie of the Year, 1969. . . . Named to NBA All-Star First Team and All-Rookie Team, 1969. . . . NBA Playoff MVP, 1978. . . . Member of NBA championship team, 1978. . . . Led NBA in rebounding, 1975. . . . Led NBA in field-goal percentage, 1976. . . . Named to THE SPORTING NEWS All-America Second Team, 1967 and 1968.

CHESTER WALKER
(Chet)

Born February 22, 1940 at Benton Harbor, Mich.   Height 6:07. Weight 220.

High School—Benton Harbor, Mich.

College—Bradley University, Peoria, Ill.

Drafted by Syracuse on second round, 1962 (14th pick).

Franchise transferred from Syracuse to Philadelphia, 1963.
Traded with Shaler Halimon by Philadelphia to Chicago for Jim Washington and a player to be named later, September 2, 1969.

—COLLEGIATE RECORD—

Year	G.	Min.	FGA	FGM	Pct.	FTA	FTM	Pct.	Reb.	Pts.	Avg.
58-59†	15	....	264	146	.553	93	56	.602	246	348	23.2
59-60	29	....	436	244	.560	234	144	.615	388	632	21.8
60-61	26	....	423	238	.563	250	180	.720	327	656	25.2
61-62	26	....	500	268	.536	236	151	.640	321	687	26.4
Varsity Totals	81	....	1359	750	.552	720	475	.660	1036	1975	24.4

NBA REGULAR SEASON RECORD

Sea.—Team	G.	Min.	FGA	FGM	Pct.	FTA	FTM	Pct.	Reb.	Ast.	PF	Disq.	Pts.	Avg.
62-63—Syracuse	78	1992	751	352	.469	362	253	.699	561	83	220	3	957	12.3
63-64—Philadelphia	76	2775	1118	492	.440	464	330	.711	784	124	232	3	1314	17.3
64-65—Philadelphia	79	2187	936	377	.403	388	288	.742	528	132	200	2	1042	13.2
65-66—Philadelphia	80	2603	982	443	.451	468	335	.716	636	201	238	3	1221	15.3
66-67—Philadelphia	81	2691	1150	561	.488	581	445	.766	660	188	232	4	1567	19.3
67-68—Philadelphia	82	2623	1172	539	.460	533	387	.726	607	157	252	3	1465	17.9
68-69—Philadelphia	82	2753	1145	554	.484	459	369	.804	640	144	244	0	1477	18.0
69-70—Chicago	78	2726	1249	596	.477	568	483	.850	604	192	203	1	1675	21.5
70-71—Chicago	81	2927	1398	650	.465	559	480	.859	588	179	187	2	1780	22.0
71-72—Chicago	78	2588	1225	619	.505	568	481	.847	473	178	171	0	1719	22.0
72-73—Chicago	79	2455	1248	597	.478	452	376	.832	395	179	166	1	1570	19.9

Sea.—Team	G.	Min.	FGA	FGM	Pct.	FTA	FTM	Pct.	Off.	Def.	Tot.	Ast.	PF	Dq.	Stl.	Blk.	Pts.	Avg.
73-74—Chi.	82	2661	1178	572	.486	502	439	.875	131	275	406	200	201	1	68	4	1583	19.3
74-75—Chi.	76	2452	1076	524	.487	480	413	.860	114	318	432	169	181	0	49	6	1461	19.2
Totals	1032	33433	14628	6876	.470	6384	5079	.796			7314	2126	2727	23	117	10	18831	18.2

NBA PLAYOFF RECORD

Sea.—Team	G.	Min.	FGA	FGM	Pct.	FTA	FTM	Pct.	Reb.	Ast.	PF	Disq.	Pts.	Avg.
62-63—Syracuse	5	130	53	27	.509	30	22	.733	47	9	8	0	76	15.2
63-64—Philadelphia	5	190	77	30	.390	46	34	.739	52	13	15	0	94	18.8
64-65—Philadelphia	11	469	173	83	.480	75	57	.760	79	18	38	0	223	20.3
65-66—Philadelphia	5	181	64	24	.375	31	25	.806	37	15	18	0	73	14.6
66-67—Philadelphia	15	551	246	115	.467	119	96	.807	114	32	44	0	326	21.7
67-68—Philadelphia	13	485	210	86	.410	112	76	.679	96	24	44	1	248	19.1
68-69—Philadelphia	4	109	43	23	.535	12	8	.667	23	8	5	0	54	13.5
69-70—Chicago	5	178	83	35	.422	33	27	.818	42	11	14	0	97	19.4
70-71—Chicago	7	234	100	44	.440	24	17	.708	50	22	20	0	105	15.0
71-72—Chicago	4	97	38	16	.421	16	13	.813	14	4	7	0	45	11.3
72-73—Chicago	7	229	121	42	.347	37	33	.892	62	14	15	0	117	16.7

Sea.—Team	G.	Min.	FGA	FGM	Pct.	FTA	FTM	Pct.	Off.	Def.	Tot.	Ast.	PF	Dq.	Stl.	Blk.	Pts.	Avg.
									—Rebounds—									
73-74—Chi.	11	403	159	81	.509	79	68	.861	26	35	61	18	26	0	10	1	230	20.9
74-75—Chi.	13	432	164	81	.494	75	66	.880	10	50	60	24	32	2	13	1	228	17.5
Totals	105	3688	1531	687	.449	689	542	.787			737	212	286	3	23	2	1916	18.2

NBA ALL-STAR GAME RECORD

Season—Team	Min.	FGA	FGM	Pct.	FTA	FTM	Pct.	Reb.	Ast.	PF	Disq.	Pts.
1964—Philadelphia	12	5	2	.400	0	0	.000	0	0	1	0	4
1966—Philadelphia	25	10	3	.300	3	2	.667	6	4	2	0	8
1967—Philadelphia	22	9	6	.667	4	3	.750	4	1	2	0	15
1970—Chicago	17	3	1	.333	2	2	1.000	2	1	2	0	4
1971—Chicago	19	9	3	.333	5	4	.800	3	1	1	0	10
1973—Chicago	16	5	1	.200	2	2	1.000	1	0	2	0	4

Season—Team	Min.	FGA	FGM	Pct.	FTA	FTM	Pct.	Off.	Def.	Tot.	Ast.	PF	Dq.	Stl.	Blk.	Pts.
								—Rebounds—								
1974—Chicago	14	5	4	.800	4	4	1.000	0	2	2	1	1	0	0	0	12
Totals	125	46	20	.435	20	17	.850			18	8	11	0			57

Led NBA in free-throw percentage, 1971. . . . Member of NBA championship team, 1967. . . . Named to THE SPORTING NEWS All-America First Team, 1962. . . . THE SPORTING NEWS All-America Second Team, 1961.

JERRY ALAN WEST

Born May 28, 1938 at Cheylan, W. Va.   Height 6:02.   Weight 185.

High School—East Bank, W. Va.

College—West Virginia University, Morgantown, W. Va.

Drafted by Minneapolis on first round (territorial choice), 1960.

Minneapolis franchise transferred to Los Angeles, 1960.

—COLLEGIATE RECORD—

Year	G.	Min.	FGA	FGM	Pct.	FTA	FTM	Pct.	Reb.	Pts.	Avg.
56-57†	17	....		114	....		104	....	....	332	19.5
57-58	28	799	359	178	.496	194	142	.732	311	498	17.8
58-59	34	1210	656	340	.518	320	223	.697	419	903	26.6
59-60	31	1129	645	325	.504	337	258	.766	510	908	29.3
Varsity Totals	93	3138	1660	843	.508	851	623	.732	1240	2309	24.8

NBA REGULAR SEASON RECORD

Sea.—Team	G.	Min.	FGA	FGM	Pct.	FTA	FTM	Pct.	Reb.	Ast.	PF	Disq.	Pts.	Avg.
60-61—Los Angeles	79	2797	1264	529	.419	497	331	.666	611	333	213	1	1389	17.6
61-62—Los Angeles	75	3087	1795	799	.445	926	712	.769	591	402	173	4	2310	30.8
62-63—Los Angeles	55	2163	1213	559	.461	477	371	.778	384	307	150	1	1489	27.1
63-64—Los Angeles	72	2906	1529	740	.484	702	584	.832	443	403	200	2	2064	28.7
64-65—Los Angeles	74	3066	1655	822	.497	789	648	.821	447	364	221	2	2292	31.0
65-66—Los Angeles	79	3218	1731	818	.473	977	840	.860	562	480	243	1	2476	31.3
66-67—Los Angeles	66	2670	1389	645	.464	686	602	.878	392	447	160	1	1892	28.7
67-68—Los Angeles	51	1919	926	476	.514	482	391	.811	294	310	152	1	1343	26.3
68-69—Los Angeles	61	2394	1156	545	.471	597	490	.821	262	423	156	1	1580	25.9
69-70—Los Angeles	74	3106	1673	831	.497	785	647	.824	338	554	160	3	2309	31.2
70-71—Los Angeles	69	2845	1351	667	.494	631	525	.832	320	655	180	0	1859	26.9
71-72—Los Angeles	77	2973	1540	735	.477	633	515	.814	327	747	209	0	1985	25.8
72-73—Los Angeles	69	2460	1291	618	.479	421	339	.805	289	607	138	0	1575	22.8

Sea.—Team	G.	Min.	FGA	FGM	Pct.	FTA	FTM	Pct.	Off.	Def.	Tot.	Ast.	PF	Dq.	Stl.	Blk.	Pts.	Avg.
									—Rebounds—									
73-74—L. A.	31	967	519	232	.447	198	165	.833	30	86	116	206	80	0	81	23	629	20.3
Totals	932	36571	19032	9016	.474	8801	7160	.814			5376	6238	2435	17			25192	27.0

NBA PLAYOFF RECORD

Sea.—Team	G.	Min.	FGA	FGM	Pct.	FTA	FTM	Pct.	Reb.	Ast.	PF	Disq.	Pts.	Avg.
60-61—Los Angeles	12	461	202	99	.490	106	77	.726	104	63	39	0	275	22.9
61-62—Los Angeles	13	557	310	144	.465	150	121	.807	88	57	38	0	409	31.5
62-63—Los Angeles	13	538	286	144	.503	100	74	.740	106	61	34	0	362	27.8
63-64—Los Angeles	5	206	115	57	.496	53	42	.792	36	17	20	0	156	31.2
64-65—Los Angeles	11	470	351	155	.442	155	137	.884	63	58	37	0	447	40.6
65-66—Los Angeles	14	619	357	185	.518	125	109	.872	88	79	40	0	479	34.2
66-67—Los Angeles	1	1	0	0	.000	0	0	.000	1	0	0	0	0	0.0
67-68—Los Angeles	15	622	313	165	.527	169	132	.781	81	82	47	0	462	30.8
68-69—Los Angeles	18	757	423	196	.463	204	164	.804	71	135	52	1	556	30.9
69-70—Los Angeles	18	830	418	196	.469	212	170	.802	66	151	55	1	562	31.2
71-72—Los Angeles	15	608	340	128	.376	106	88	.830	73	134	39	0	344	22.9
72-73—Los Angeles	17	638	336	151	.449	127	99	.780	76	132	49	1	401	23.6

Sea.—Team	G.	Min.	FGA	FGM	Pct.	FTA	FTM	Pct.	Off.	Def.	Tot.	Ast.	PF	Dq.	Stl.	Blk.	Pts.	Avg.
									—Rebounds—									
73-74—L. A.	1	14	9	2	.222	0	0	.000	0	2	2	1	1	0	0	0	4	4.0
Totals	153	6321	3460	1622	.469	1507	1213	.805			855	970	451	3			4457	29.1

JERRY WEST

NBA ALL-STAR GAME RECORD

Season—Team	Min.	FGA	FGM	Pct.	FTA	FTM	Pct.	Reb.	Ast.	PF	Disq.	Pts.
1961—Los Angeles	25	8	2	.250	6	5	.833	2	4	3	0	9
1962—Los Angeles	31	14	7	.500	6	4	.667	3	1	2	0	18
1963—Los Angeles	32	15	5	.333	4	3	.750	7	5	1	0	13
1964—Los Angeles	42	20	8	.400	1	1	1.000	4	5	3	0	17
1965—Los Angeles	40	16	8	.500	6	4	.667	5	6	2	0	20
1966—Los Angeles	11	5	1	.200	2	2	1.000	1	0	2	0	4
1967—Los Angeles	30	11	6	.545	4	4	1.000	3	6	3	0	16
1968—Los Angeles	32	17	7	.412	4	3	.750	6	6	4	0	17
1969—Los Angeles					Selected—Injured, Did Not Play							
1970—Los Angeles	31	12	7	.583	12	8	.667	5	5	3	0	22
1971—Los Angeles	20	4	2	.500	3	1	.333	1	9	1	0	5
1972—Los Angeles	27	9	6	.667	2	1	.500	6	5	2	0	13
1973—Los Angeles	20	6	3	.500	0	0	.000	4	3	2	0	6
1974—Los Angeles					Selected—Injured, Did Not Play							
Totals	341	137	62	.453	50	36	.720	47	55	28	0	160

NBA COACHING RECORD

Sea. Club	Regular Season W.	L.	Pct.	Pos.	Playoffs W.	L.	Sea. Club	Regular Season W.	L.	Pct.	Pos.	Playoffs W.	L.
1976-77—Los Angeles	53	29	.646	1†	4	7	1978-79—Los Angeles	47	35	.573	3†	3	5
1977-78—Los Angeles	45	37	.549	4†	1	2	Totals (3 seasons)	145	101	.589		8	14

Elected to Naismith Memorial Basketball Hall of Fame, 1979. . . . Named to NBA 35th Anniversary All-Time Team, 1980. . . . NBA All-Star First Team, 1962, 1963, 1964, 1965, 1966, 1967, 1970, 1971, 1972, 1973. . . . NBA All-Star Second Team, 1968 and 1969. . . . NBA All-Defensive First Team, 1970, 1971, 1972, 1973. . . . NBA All-Defensive Second Team, 1969. . . . NBA Playoff MVP, 1969. . . . Holds NBA record for most free throws made in one season, 1966. . . . NBA all-time playoff leader in field goals attempted, free throws made and scoring average. . . . Holds NBA playoff game record for most free throws made in one half, 14, vs. Baltimore, April 5, 1965. . . . NBA All-Star Game MVP, 1972. . . . Member of NBA championship team, 1972. . . . Led NBA in assists, 1972. . . . Led NBA in scoring, 1970. . . . Named to THE SPORTING NEWS All-America First Team, 1959 and 1960. . . . NCAA Tournament Most Outstanding Player, 1959. . . . Member of U.S. Olympic team, 1960.

JOSEPH HENRY WHITE
(Jo Jo)

Born November 16, 1946 at St. Louis, Mo.   Height 6:03.   Weight 190.

High Schools—St. Louis, Mo., Vashon (Soph.) and McKinley (Jr.-Sr.)

College—University of Kansas, Lawrence, Kan.

Drafted by Boston on first round, 1969 (9th pick).

Traded by Boston to Golden State for a 1979 1st round draft choice, January 30, 1979.
Sold by Golden State to Kansas City, September 10, 1980.

—COLLEGIATE RECORD—

Year	G.	Min.	FGA	FGM	Pct.	FTA	FTM	Pct.	Reb.	Pts.	Avg.
64-65†	2	....	34	11	.324	15	11	.733	25	33	16.5
65-66†	6	....	88	35	.398	27	18	.667	32	88	14.7
65-66	9	....	112	44	.393	26	14	.538	68	102	11.3
66-67	27	....	416	170	.409	72	59	.819	150	399	14.8
67-68	30	....	462	188	.407	115	83	.722	107	459	15.3
68-69	18	....	286	134	.469	79	58	.734	84	326	18.1
Varsity Totals	84	....	1276	536	.420	292	214	.733	409	1286	15.3

NBA REGULAR SEASON RECORD

Sea.—Team	G.	Min.	FGA	FGM	Pct.	FTA	FTM	Pct.	Reb.	Ast.	PF	Disq.	Pts.	Avg.
69-70—Boston	60	1328	684	309	.452	135	111	.822	169	145	132	1	729	12.2
70-71—Boston	75	2787	1494	693	.464	269	215	.799	376	361	255	5	1601	21.3
71-72—Boston	79	3261	1788	770	.431	343	285	.831	446	416	227	1	1825	23.1
72-73—Boston	82	3250	1665	717	.431	228	178	.781	414	498	185	2	1612	19.7

Sea.—Team	G.	Min.	FGA	FGM	Pct.	FTA	FTM	Pct.	—Rebounds— Off.	Def.	Tot.	Ast.	PF	Dq.	Stl.	Blk.	Pts.	Avg.
73-74—Boston	82	3238	1445	649	.449	227	190	.837	100	251	351	448	185	1	105	25	1488	18.1
74-75—Boston	82	3220	1440	658	.457	223	186	.834	84	227	311	458	207	1	128	17	1502	18.3
75-76—Boston	82	3257	1492	670	.449	253	212	.838	61	252	313	445	183	2	107	20	1552	18.9
76-77—Boston	82	3333	1488	638	.429	383	333	.869	87	296	383	492	193	5	118	22	1609	19.6
77-78—Boston	46	1641	690	289	.419	120	103	.858	53	127	180	209	109	2	49	7	681	14.8
78-79—Bos.-G.S.	76	2338	910	404	.444	158	139	.880	42	158	200	347	173	1	80	7	947	12.5
79-80—Golden State	78	2052	706	336	.476	114	97	.851	42	139	181	239	186	0	88	13	770	9.9
80-81—Kan. City	13	236	82	36	.439	18	11	.611	3	18	21	37	21	0	11	1	83	6.4
Totals	837	29941	13884	6169	.444	2471	2060	.834			3345	4095	2056	21	686	112	14399	17.2

Three-Point Field Goals: 1979-80, 1-for-6 (.167)

NBA PLAYOFF RECORD

Sea.—Team	G.	Min.	FGA	FGM	Pct.	FTA	FTM	Pct.	Reb.	Ast.	PF	Disq.	Pts.	Avg.
71-72—Boston	11	432	220	109	.495	48	40	.833	59	58	31	0	258	23.5
72-73—Boston	13	583	300	135	.450	54	49	.907	54	83	44	2	319	24.5

Sea.—Team	G.	Min.	FGA	FGM	Pct.	FTA	FTM	Pct.	—Rebounds—			Ast.	PF	Dq.	Stl.	Blk.	Pts.	Avg.
									Off.	Def.	Tot.							
73-74—Boston	18	765	310	132	.426	46	34	.739	17	58	75	98	56	1	15	2	298	16.6
74-75—Boston	11	462	227	100	.441	33	27	.818	18	32	50	63	32	0	11	4	227	20.6
75-76—Boston	18	791	371	165	.445	95	78	.821	12	59	71	98	51	0	23	1	408	22.7
76-77—Boston	9	395	201	91	.453	33	28	.848	10	29	39	52	27	0	14	0	210	23.3
Totals	80	3428	1629	732	.449	309	256	.828			348	452	241	3	63	7	1720	21.5

NBA ALL-STAR GAME RECORD

Season—Team	Min.	FGA	FGM	Pct.	FTA	FTM	Pct.	Reb.	Ast.	PF	Disq.	Pts.
1971—Boston	22	10	5	.500	0	0	.000	9	2	2	0	10
1972—Boston	18	15	6	.400	2	0	.000	4	3	1	0	12
1973—Boston	18	7	3	.429	0	0	.000	5	5	0	0	6

Season—Team	Min.	FGA	FGM	Pct.	FTA	FTM	Pct.	—Rebounds—			Ast.	PF	Dq.	Stl.	Blk.	Pts.
								Off.	Def.	Tot.						
1974—Boston	22	12	6	.500	3	1	.333	2	4	6	4	1	0	2	1	13
1975—Boston	13	2	1	.500	6	5	.833	0	1	1	4	1	0	0	0	7
1976—Boston	16	7	3	.429	0	0	.000	0	1	1	1	1	0	2	0	6
1977—Boston	15	7	5	.714	0	0	.000	0	1	1	2	0	0	0	0	10
Totals	124	60	29	.483	11	6	.545			27	21	6	0	4	1	64

Named to NBA All-Star Second Team, 1975 and 1977.... NBA All-Rookie Team, 1970.... NBA Playoff MVP, 1976. ... Member of NBA championship teams, 1974 and 1976.... Named to THE SPORTING NEWS All-America First Team, 1968 and 1969.... Member of U. S. Olympic team, 1968.

GEORGE YARDLEY

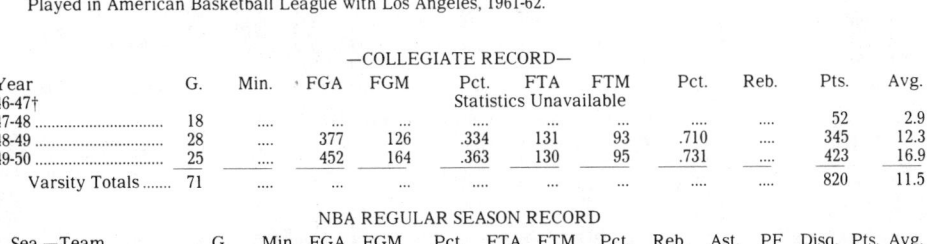

Born November 23, 1928 at Hollywood, Calif.   Height 6:05. Weight 195.

High School—Balboa, Calif.

College—Stanford University, Stanford, Calif.

Drafted by Ft. Wayne on first round, 1950.

Played with the San Francisco Stewart Chevrolets in the National Industrial Basketball League, an Amateur Athletic Union League, during 1950-51 season. (Finished third in the league in scoring with a 13.1-point averge on 104 field goals and 53 field goals for 261 points in 20 games.)

In military service during 1951-52 and 1952-53 seasons. Played with Los Alamitos, Calif., Naval Air Station.

Signed by Ft. Wayne NBA, 1953.

Ft. Wayne franchise transferred to Detroit, 1957.

Traded by Detroit to Syracuse for Ed Conlin, February 13, 1959.

Played in American Basketball League with Los Angeles, 1961-62.

—COLLEGIATE RECORD—

Year	G.	Min.	FGA	FGM	Pct.	FTA	FTM	Pct.	Reb.	Pts.	Avg.
46-47†					Statistics Unavailable						
47-48	18	....	...	...	....	...	...	....	....	52	2.9
48-49	28	....	377	126	.334	131	93	.710	....	345	12.3
49-50	25	....	452	164	.363	130	95	.731	....	423	16.9
Varsity Totals	71	....	...	...	....	...	...	....	....	820	11.5

NBA REGULAR SEASON RECORD

Sea.—Team	G.	Min.	FGA	FGM	Pct.	FTA	FTM	Pct.	Reb.	Ast.	PF	Disq.	Pts.	Avg.
53-54—Ft. Wayne	63	1489	492	209	.425	205	146	.712	407	99	166	3	564	9.0
54-55—Ft. Wayne	60	2150	869	363	.418	416	310	.745	594	126	205	7	1036	17.3
55-56—Ft. Wayne	71	2353	1067	434	.407	492	365	.742	686	159	212	2	1233	17.4
56-57—Ft. Wayne	72	2691	1273	522	.410	639	503	.787	755	147	231	2	1547	21.5
57-58—Detroit	72	2843	1624	673	.414	808	655	.811	768	97	226	3	2001	27.8
58-59—Det.-Syr.	61	1839	1042	446	.428	407	317	.779	431	65	159	2	1209	19.8
59-60—Syracuse	73	2390	1214	549	.452	462	377	.816	570	123	227	3	1475	20.2
Totals	472	15755	7581	3196	.422	3429	2673	.780	4211	816	1426	22	9065	19.2

NBA PLAYOFF RECORD

Sea.—Team	G.	Min.	FGA	FGM	Pct.	FTA	FTM	Pct.	Reb.	Ast.	PF	Disq.	Pts.	Avg.
53-54—Ft. Wayne	4	107	33	16	.485	12	10	.833	24	3	10	0	42	10.5
54-55—Ft. Wayne	11	420	143	57	.399	79	60	.759	99	36	37	2	174	15.8
55-56—Ft. Wayne	10	406	183	77	.421	98	76	.776	139	26	25	0	230	23.0
56-57—Ft. Wayne	2	85	53	24	.453	11	9	.818	19	8	7	0	57	28.5
57-58—Detroit	7	254	127	52	.409	67	60	.896	72	17	26	0	164	23.4
58-59—Syracuse	9	333	189	83	.439	70	60	.857	87	21	29	0	226	25.1
59-60—Syracuse	3	88	39	15	.385	12	10	.833	17	1	9	0	40	13.3
Totals	46	1693	767	324	.422	349	285	.817	457	112	143	2	933	20.3

NBA ALL-STAR GAME RECORD

Season—Team	Min.	FGA	FGM	Pct.	FTA	FTM	Pct.	Reb.	Ast.	PF	Disq.	Pts.
1955—Fort Wayne	22	11	4	.364	4	3	.750	4	2	2	0	11
1956—Fort Wayne	19	7	3	.429	3	2	.667	6	1	1	0	8
1957—Fort Wayne	25	10	4	.400	1	1	1.000	9	0	2	0	9
1958—Detroit	32	15	8	.533	5	3	.600	9	1	1	0	19
1959—Detroit	17	8	2	.250	2	2	1.000	4	0	3	0	6
1960—Syracuse	16	9	5	.556	2	1	.500	3	0	4	0	11
Totals	131	60	26	.433	17	12	.706	35	4	13	0	64

ABL REGULAR SEASON RECORD

Sea.—Team	G.	Min.	FGM	FGA	Pct.	FGM	FGA	Pct.	FTM	FTA	Pct.	Reb.	Ast.	Pts.	Avg.
			—2-Point—			—3-Point—									
1961-62—L.A.	25	948	378	159	.421	37	14	.378	148	122	.824	172	65	482	19.2

Named to NBA All-Star First Team, 1958. . . . NBA All-Star Second Team, 1957. . . . Led league in scoring in 1958 when he became first NBA player ever to score over 2,000 points in a season.

MAX ZASLOFSKY

Born December 7, 1925 at Brooklyn, N. Y.   Height 6:02.   Weight 170.

High School—Brooklyn, N. Y., Thomas Jefferson.

College—St. John's University, Brooklyn, N. Y.

Signed as free agent by Chicago BAA, 1946.

His name drawn out of a hat by New York NBA for $15,000 in dispersal of Chicago franchise, 1950.
Traded by New York to Baltimore for Jim Baechtold, 1953.
Traded by Baltimore to Milwaukee, November, 1953.
Traded by Milwaukee to Fort Wayne, December, 1953.
Coached in ABA with New Jersey Americans and New York Nets, 1967-68 and 1968-69.

—COLLEGIATE PLAYING RECORD—

Year	G.	Min.	FGA	FGM	Pct.	FTA	FTM	Pct.	Reb.	Pts.	Avg.
45-46	18	....	...	59	....	38	22	.579	...	140	7.8

NOTE: Played only one year of college basketball. In Military Service during 1944-45 season.

NBA REGULAR SEASON RECORD

Sea.—Team	G.	Min.	FGA	FGM	Pct.	FTA	FTM	Pct.	Reb.	Ast.	PF	Disq.	Pts.	Avg.
46-47—Chicago	61	....	1020	336	.329	278	205	.737	...	40	121	...	877	14.4
47-48—Chicago	48	....	1156	373	.323	333	261	.784	...	29	125	...	1007	21.0
48-49—Chicago	58	....	1216	425	.350	413	347	.840	...	149	156	...	1197	20.6
49-50—Chicago	68	....	1132	397	.351	381	321	.843	...	155	185	...	1115	16.4
50-51—New York	66	....	853	302	.354	298	231	.775	228	136	150	...	835	12.7
51-52—New York	66	....	958	322	.336	380	287	.755	194	156	183	...	931	14.1
52-53—New York	29	....	320	123	.384	142	98	.690	75	55	81	...	344	11.9
53-54—Balt.-Mil.-F.W.	65	....	756	278	.368	357	255	.714	160	154	142	...	811	12.5
54-55—Fort Wayne	70	....	821	269	.328	352	247	.702	191	203	130	...	785	11.2
55-56—Fort Wayne	9	....	81	29	.358	35	30	.857	16	16	18	....	88	9.8
Totals	540	....	8313	2854	.343	2969	2282	.769	...	1093	1291	...	7990	14.8

NBA PLAYOFF RECORD

Sea.—Team	G.	Min.	FGA	FGM	Pct.	FTA	FTM	Pct.	Reb.	Ast.	PF	Disq.	Pts.	Avg.
46-47—Chicago	11	....	199	60	.302	44	29	.659	...	4	26	..	149	13.5
47-48—Chicago	5	....	88	30	.341	47	37	.787	...	0	17	..	97	19.4
48-49—Chicago	2	....	49	15	.306	18	14	.778	...	6	3	..	44	22.0
49-50—Chicago	2	....	32	15	.469	18	15	.833	...	6	7	..	45	22.5
50-51—New York	14	....	217	88	.406	100	74	.740	58	38	43	..	250	17.9
51-52—New York	14	....	185	69	.373	110	89	.809	44	23	51	..	227	16.2
53-54—Fort Wayne	4	....	36	11	.306	15	13	.867	3	6	7	..	35	8.8
54-55—Fort Wayne	11	....	44	18	.409	20	16	.750	16	18	20	..	52	4.7
Totals	63	....	850	306	.360	372	287	.772	...	101	174	..	899	14.3

NBA ALL-STAR GAME RECORD

Season—Team	Min.	FGA	FGM	Pct.	FTA	FTM	Pct.	Reb.	Ast.	PF	Disq.	Pts.
1952—New York	....	7	3	.429	5	5	1.000	4	2	0	0	11

ABA COACHING RECORD

Sea. Club	Regular Season				Playoffs	
	W.	L.	Pct.	Pos.	W.	L.
1967-68—New Jersey	36	42	.462	4T†	..	..
1968-69—New York	17	61	.218	5†	..	..
Totals (2 seasons)	53	103	.339		..	..

†Eastern Division.

Named to NBA All-Star First Team, 1947, 1948, 1949, 1950. . . . Led NBA in scoring, 1948. . . . Led NBA in free-throw percentage, 1950.

COACHES

ARNOLD J. AUERBACH
(Red)

Born September 20, 1917 at Brooklyn, N. Y.   Height 5:10.

High School—Brooklyn, N. Y., Eastern District.

Colleges—Seth Low Junior College, New York, N. Y., and
George Washington University, Washington, D. C.

—COLLEGIATE PLAYING RECORD—

Seth Low JC

Year	G.	Min.	FGA	FGM	Pct.	FTA	FTM	Pct.	Reb.	Pts.	Avg.
36-37				Statistics Unavailable							

George Washington

Year	G.	Min.	FGA	FGM	Pct.	FTA	FTM	Pct.	Reb.	Pts.	Avg.
37-38	17	....	...	22	....	12	8	.667	....	52	3.1
38-39	20	....	...	54	....	19	12	.632	....	120	6.0
39-40	19	....	...	69	....	39	24	.727	....	162	8.5
Totals	56	....	...	145	....	64	44	.688	....	334	6.0

COLLEGIATE COACHING RECORD
Assistant, Duke University, 1949-50.

NBA COACHING RECORD

		Regular Season			Playoffs				Regular Season			Playoffs	
Sea. Club	W.	L.	Pct.	Pos.	W.	L.	Sea. Club	W.	L.	Pct.	Pos.	W.	L.
1946-47—Washington	49	11	.817	1†	2	4	1957-58—Boston	49	23	.681	1†	6	5
1947-48—Washington	28	20	.583	4†	..	..	1958-59—Boston	52	20	.722	*1†	8	3
1948-49—Washington	38	22	.633	1†	6	5	1959-60—Boston	59	16	.787	*1†	8	5
1949-50—Tri-Cities	28	29	.491	3‡	1	2	1960-61—Boston	57	22	.722	*1†	8	2
1950-51—Boston	39	30	.565	2†	0	2	1961-62—Boston	60	20	.750	*1†	8	6
1951-52—Boston	39	27	.591	2†	1	2	1962-63—Boston	58	22	.725	*1†	8	5
1952-53—Boston	46	25	.568	3†	3	3	1963-64—Boston	59	21	.738	*1†	8	2
1953-54—Boston	42	30	.583	2T†	2	4	1964-65—Boston	62	18	.775	*1†	8	4
1954-55—Boston	36	36	.500	3†	3	4	1965-66—Boston	54	26	.675	*2†	11	6
1955-56—Boston	39	33	.542	2†	1	2	Totals (20 seasons)	938	479	.662		99	69
1956-57—Boston	44	28	.611	*1†	7	3							

*Won NBA Championship.   †Eastern Division.   ‡Western Division.

Selected as the "Greatest Coach in the History of the NBA" by the Professional Basketball Writers' Association of America, 1980. . . . Elected to the Naismith Memorial Basketball Hall of Fame, 1968. . . . Named NBA Coach of the Year, 1965. . . . NBA Executive of the Year, 1980. . . . Winningest coach in history of NBA. . . . Coach of NBA championship teams, 1957, 1959, 1960, 1961, 1962, 1963, 1964, 1965, 1966.

WILLIAM JOHN CUNNINGHAM
(Billy)

Born June 3, 1943 at Brooklyn, N. Y.   Height 6:07.   Weight 210.

High School—Brooklyn, N. Y., Erasmus.

College—University of North Carolina, Chapel Hill, N. C.

Drafted by Philadelphia on first round, 1965.

Signed by Carolina ABA as a free agent, August, 1969.
Returned to Philadelphia, 1974.

—COLLEGIATE PLAYING RECORD—

Year	G.	Min.	FGA	FGM	Pct.	FTA	FTM	Pct.	Reb.	Pts.	Avg.
61-62†	10	....	162	81	.500	78	45	.577	127	207	20.7
62-63	21	....	380	186	.489	170	105	.618	339	477	22.7
63-64	24	....	526	233	.443	249	157	.631	379	623	26.0
64-65	24	....	481	237	.493	213	135	.634	344	609	25.4
Varsity Totals	69	....	1387	656	.473	632	397	.628	1062	1709	24.8

NBA REGULAR SEASON RECORD

									—Rebounds—								
Sea.—Team	G.	Min.	FGA	FGM	Pct.	FTA	FTM	Pct.	Off.	Def.	Tot.	Ast.	PF	Dq.	Stl.	Blk.	Pts.	Avg.
65-66—Philadelphia	80	2134	1011	431	.426	443	281	.634			599	207	301	12			1143	14.3
66-67—Philadelphia	81	2168	1211	556	.459	558	383	.686			589	205	260	2			1495	18.5
67-68—Philadelphia	74	2076	1178	516	.438	509	368	.723			562	187	260	3			1400	18.9
68-69—Philadelphia	82	3345	1736	739	.426	754	556	.737			1050	287	329	10			2034	24.8

Sea.—Team	G.	Min.	FGA	FGM	Pct.	FTA	FTM	Pct.	—Rebounds— Off.	Def.	Tot.	Ast.	PF	Dq.	Stl.	Blk.	Pts.	Avg.
69-70—Philadelphia	81	3194	1710	802	.469	700	510	.729			1101	352	331	15			2114	26.1
70-71—Philadelphia	81	3090	1519	702	.462	620	455	.734			946	395	328	5			1859	23.0
71-72—Philadelphia	75	2900	1428	658	.461	601	428	.712			918	443	295	12			1744	23.3
74-75—Philadelphia	80	2859	1423	609	.428	444	345	.777	130	596	726	442	270	4	91	35	1563	19.5
75-76—Philadelphia	20	640	251	103	.410	88	68	.773	29	118	147	107	57	1	24	10	274	13.7
Totals	654	22406	11467	5116	.446	4717	3394	.720			6638	2625	2431	64	115	45	13626	20.8

NBA PLAYOFF RECORD

Sea.—Team	G.	Min.	FGA	FGM	Pct.	FTA	FTM	Pct.	—Rebounds— Off.	Def.	Tot.	Ast.	PF	Dq.	Stl.	Blk.	Pts.	Avg.
65-66—Philadelphia	4	69	31	5	.161	13	11	.846			18	10	11	0			21	5.3
66-67—Philadelphia	15	339	221	83	.376	90	59	.656			93	33	53	1			225	15.0
67-68—Philadelphia	3	86	43	24	.558	17	14	.824			22	10	16	1			62	20.7
68-69—Philadelphia	5	217	117	49	.419	38	24	.632			63	12	24	1			122	24.4
69-70—Philadelphia	5	205	123	61	.496	36	24	.667			52	20	19	0			146	29.2
70-71—Philadelphia	7	301	142	67	.472	67	47	.701			108	40	28	0			181	25.9
Totals	39	1217	677	289	.427	261	179	.686			356	125	151	3			757	19.4

NBA ALL-STAR GAME RECORD

Season—Team	Min.	FGA	FGM	Pct.	FTA	FTM	Pct.	—Rebounds— Off.	Def.	Tot.	Ast.	PF	Dq.	Stl.	Blk.	Pts.
1969—Philadelphia	22	10	5	.500	0	0	.000			5	1	3	0			10
1970—Philadelphia	28	13	7	.538	5	5	1.000			4	2	3	0			19
1971—Philadelphia	19	8	2	.250	2	1	.500			4	3	1	0			5
1972—Philadelphia	24	13	4	.308	8	6	.750			10	3	4	0			14
Totals	93	44	18	.409	15	12	.800			23	9	11	0			48

ABA REGULAR SEASON RECORD

Sea.—Team	G.	Min.	——2-Point—— FGM	FGA	Pct.	——3-Point—— FGM	FGA	Pct.	FTM	FTA	Pct.	Reb.	Ast.	Pts.	Avg.
72-73—Carolina	84	3248	757	1534	.493	14	49	.286	472	598	.789	1012	530	2028	24.1
73-74—Carolina	32	1190	252	529	.476	1	8	.125	149	187	.797	331	150	656	20.5
Totals	116	4438	1009	2063	.489	15	57	.263	621	785	.791	1343	680	2684	23.1

ABA PLAYOFF RECORD

Sea.—Team	G.	Min.	——2-Point—— FGM	FGA	Pct.	——3-Point—— FGM	FGA	Pct.	FTM	FTA	Pct.	Reb.	Ast.	Pts.	Avg.
72-73—Carolina	12	472	111	219	.507	1	4	.250	57	83	.687	142	61	282	23.5
73-74—Carolina	3	61	9	29	.310	0	2	.000	4	5	.800	16	6	22	7.3
Totals	15	533	120	248	.484	1	6	.167	61	88	.693	158	67	304	20.3

ABA ALL-STAR GAME RECORD

Sea.—Team	Min.	——2-Point—— FGM	FGA	Pct.	——3-Point—— FGM	FGA	Pct.	FTM	FTA	Pct.	Reb.	Ast.	Pts.	Avg.
1973—Carolina.............	20	9	11	.818	0	1	.000	0	0	.000	6	4	18	18.0

NBA COACHING RECORD

Sea.	Club	Regular Season W.	L.	Pct.	Pos.	Playoffs W.	L.		Sea.	Club	Regular Season W.	L.	Pct.	Pos.	Playoffs W.	L.
1977-78—Philadelphia		53	23	.697	1†	6	4		1982-83—Philadelphia*		65	17	.793	1†	12	1
1978-79—Philadelphia		47	35	.573	2†	5	4		1983-84—Philadelphia		52	30	.634	2†	2	3
1979-80—Philadelphia		59	23	.720	2†	12	6		1984-85—Philadelphia		58	24	.707	2†	8	5
1980-81—Philadelphia		62	20	.756	1T†	9	7		Totals (8 seasons)		454	196	.698		66	39
1981-82—Philadelphia		58	24	.707	2†	12	9									

*Won NBA championship. †Atlantic Division.

Named to All-NBA First Team, 1969, 1970, 1971.... All-NBA Second Team, 1972.... NBA All-Rookie Team, 1966. ... Member of NBA championship team, 1967.... Coach of NBA championship team, 1983.... ABA Most Valuable Player, 1973.... ABA All-Star First Team, 1973.... Led ABA in steals, 1973.... Named to THE SPORTING NEWS All-America Second Team, 1965.

ALEXANDER MURRAY HANNUM
(Alex)

Born July 19, 1923 at Los Angeles, Calif.   Height 6:07.   Weight 225.

High School—Los Angeles, Calif., Hamilton.

College—University of Southern California, Los Angeles, Calif.

Signed by Oshkosh NBL, 1948.

Sold by Oshkosh NBA to Syracuse NBA, 1949.
Traded with Fred Scolari by Syracuse to Baltimore for Red Rocha, 1951.
Sold by Baltimore to Rochester during 1951-52 season.
Sold by Rochester to Milwaukee, 1954.
Milwaukee franchise moved to St. Louis, 1955.
Released by St. Louis, signed by Ft. Wayne, 1956.
Released by Ft. Wayne, December 12, 1956; signed by St. Louis, December 17, 1956.

Played for Los Angeles Shamrocks, an Amateur Athletic Union team, during 1945-46 season (averaged 9.8 points per game).

—COLLEGIATE PLAYING RECORD—

Year	G.	Min.	FGA	FGM	Pct.	FTA	FTM	Pct.	Reb.	Pts.	Avg.
41-42†					Statistics Unavailable						
42-43	15	....	....	23	....	20	9	.450	....	55	3.7
43-44-45-46					In Military Service.						
46-47	24	....	....	....	....	....	....	....	....	251	10.5
47-48	23	....	...	108	....	....	....	....	....	263	11.4
Varsity Totals	62	....	...	....	...	...	....	....	....	569	9.2

NBA REGULAR SEASON RECORD

Sea.—Team	G.	Min.	FGA	FGM	Pct.	FTA	FTM	Pct.	Reb.	Ast.	PF	Disq.	Pts.	Avg.
48-49—Oshkosh NBL	62	....	....	126	....	191	113	.592	...	....	188	...	365	5.9
49-50—Syracuse	64	....	488	177	.363	186	128	.688	...	129	264	...	482	7.5
50-51—Syracuse	63	....	494	182	.368	197	107	.543	301	119	271	...	471	7.5
51-52—Balt.-Roch.	66	....	462	170	.368	138	98	.710	336	133	271	...	438	6.6
52-53—Rochester	68	....	360	129	.358	133	88	.662	279	81	258	...	346	5.1
53-54—Rochester	72	....	503	175	.348	164	102	.622	350	105	279	...	452	6.3
54-55—Milwaukee	53	....	358	126	.352	107	61	.570	245	105	206	...	313	5.9
55-56—St. Louis	71	....	453	146	.322	154	93	.604	344	157	271	...	385	5.4
56-57—Ft. W.-St. Louis	59	....	223	77	.345	56	37	.661	158	28	135	...	191	3.2
Totals	578	....	....	1308	....	1326	827	.624	...	....	2143	...	3443	6.0

NBA PLAYOFF RECORD

Sea.—Team	G.	Min.	FGA	FGM	Pct.	FTA	FTM	Pct.	Reb.	Ast.	PF	Disq.	Pts.	Avg.
49-50—Syracuse	11	....	86	38	.442	34	17	.500	....	10	50	....	93	8.5
50-51—Syracuse	7	....	39	17	.436	10	8	.800	47	17	37	3	42	6.0
51-52—Rochester	6	146	42	16	.381	13	8	.615	26	8	30	3	40	6.7
52-53—Rochester	3	52	10	4	.400	8	3	.375	4	2	16	1	11	3.7
53-54—Rochester	6	107	29	12	.414	24	15	.625	22	5	28	3	39	6.5
55-56—St. Louis	8	159	66	21	.318	35	19	.543	29	10	36	3	61	7.6
56-57—St. Louis	2	6	2	0	.000	0	0	.000	0	0	2	0	0	0.0
Totals	43	....	274	108	.394	124	70	.565	....	52	199	....	286	6.7

NBA COACHING RECORD

	Regular Season				Playoffs				Regular Season				Playoffs	
Sea. Club	W.	L.	Pct.	Pos.	W.	L.	Sea. Club	W.	L.	Pct.	Pos.	W.	L.
1956-57—St. Louis	15	16	.484	1T†	6	4	1964-65—San Francisco	17	63	.213	5†	..	..
1957-58—St. Louis	41	31	.569	*1†	8	3	1965-66—San Francisco	35	45	.438	4†	..	..
1960-61—Syracuse	38	41	.481	3‡	4	4	1966-67—Philadelphia	68	13	.840	*1‡	11	4
1961-62—Syracuse	41	39	.513	3‡	2	3	1967-68—Philadelphia	62	20	.756	1‡	7	6
1962-63—Syracuse	48	32	.600	2‡	2	3	1969-70—San Diego	18	38	.321	7†	..	..
1963-64—San Francisco	48	32	.600	1†	5	7	1970-71—San Diego	40	42	.488	3§	..	..
							Totals (12 Seasons)	471	412	.533		45	34

*Won NBA Championship.

ABA COACHING RECORD

	Regular Season				Playoffs	
Sea. Club	W.	L.	Pct.	Pos.	W.	L.
1968-69—Oakland*	60	18	.769	1†	12	4
1971-72—Denver	34	50	.405	4†	3	4
1972-73—Denver	47	37	.560	3†	1	4
1973-74—Denver	37	47	.440	4T†	0	0
Totals (4 seasons)	178	152	.539		16	12

*Won ABA Championship.
†Western Division.   ‡Eastern Division.   §Pacific Division.

NBA Coach of the Year, 1964. . . . Coach of NBA championship teams, 1958 and 1967. . . . ABA Coach of the Year, 1969. . . . Coach of ABA championship team, 1969.

THOMAS W. HEINSOHN
(Tom)

Born August 26, 1934 at Jersey City, N. J.   Height 6:07.   Weight 218.

High School—Union City, N. J., St. Michael's.

College—Holy Cross College, Worcester, Mass.

Drafted by Boston on first round (territorial choice), 1956.

—COLLEGIATE RECORD—

Year	G.	Min.	FGA	FGM	Pct.	FTA	FTM	Pct.	Reb.	Pts.	Avg.
52-53†	15	....	...	97	....	...	70	....	....	264	17.6
53-54	28	....	364	175	.481	142	94	.662	300	444	15.9
54-55	26	....	499	232	.465	215	141	.656	385	605	23.3
55-56	27	....	630	254	.403	304	232	.763	569	740	27.4
Varsity Totals	81	....	1493	661	.443	661	467	.707	1254	1789	22.1

NBA REGULAR SEASON RECORD

Sea.—Team	G.	Min.	FGA	FGM	Pct.	FTA	FTM	Pct.	Reb.	Ast.	PF	Disq.	Pts.	Avg.
56-57—Boston	72	2150	1123	446	.397	343	271	.790	705	117	304	12	1163	16.2
57-58—Boston	69	2206	1226	468	.382	394	294	.746	705	125	274	6	1230	17.8
58-59—Boston	66	2089	1192	465	.390	391	312	.798	638	164	271	11	1242	18.8
59-60—Boston	75	2420	1590	673	.423	386	283	.734	794	171	275	8	1629	21.7
60-61—Boston	74	2256	1566	627	.400	424	325	.767	732	141	260	7	1579	21.3
61-62—Boston	79	2383	1613	692	.429	437	358	.819	747	165	280	2	1742	22.1
62-63—Boston	76	2004	1300	550	.423	407	340	.835	569	95	270	4	1440	18.9
63-64—Boston	76	2040	1223	487	.398	342	283	.827	460	183	268	3	1257	16.5
64-65—Boston	67	1706	954	365	.383	229	182	.795	399	157	252	5	912	13.6
Totals	654	19254	11787	4773	.405	3353	2648	.790	5749	1318	2454	58	12194	18.6

NBA PLAYOFF RECORD

Sea.—Team	G.	Min.	FGA	FGM	Pct.	FTA	FTM	Pct.	Reb.	Ast.	PF	Disq.	Pts.	Avg.
56-57—Boston	10	370	231	90	.390	69	49	.710	117	20	40	1	229	22.9
57-58—Boston	11	349	194	68	.351	72	56	.778	119	18	52	3	192	17.5
58-59—Boston	11	348	220	91	.414	56	37	.661	98	32	41	0	219	19.9
59-60—Boston	13	423	267	112	.419	80	60	.750	126	27	53	2	284	21.8
60-61—Boston	10	291	201	82	.408	43	33	.767	99	20	36	1	197	19.7
61-62—Boston	14	445	291	116	.399	76	58	.763	115	34	58	4	290	20.7
62-63—Boston	13	413	270	123	.456	98	75	.765	116	15	55	2	321	24.7
63-64—Boston	10	308	180	70	.412	42	34	.810	80	26	36	0	174	17.4
64-65—Boston	12	276	181	66	.365	32	20	.625	84	23	46	1	152	12.7
Totals	104	3223	2035	818	.402	568	422	.743	954	215	417	14	2058	19.8

NBA ALL-STAR GAME RECORD

Season—Team	Min.	FGA	FGM	Pct.	FTA	FTM	Pct.	Reb.	Ast.	PF	Disq.	Pts.
1957—Boston	23	17	5	.294	2	2	1.000	7	0	3	0	12
1961—Boston	19	16	2	.125	0	0	.000	6	1	4	0	4
1962—Boston	13	11	4	.364	2	2	1.000	2	1	4	0	10
1963—Boston	21	11	6	.545	4	3	.750	2	1	4	0	15
1964—Boston	21	12	5	.417	0	0	.000	3	0	5	0	10
1965—Boston				Selected—Injured, Did Not Play								
Totals	97	67	22	.328	8	7	.875	20	3	20	0	51

NBA COACHING RECORD

Sea. Club	Regular Season W.	L.	Pct.	Pos.	Playoffs W.	L.	Sea. Club	Regular Season W.	L.	Pct.	Pos.	Playoffs W.	L.
1969-70—Boston	34	48	.415	6†	..	..	1974-75—Boston	60	22	.732	1‡	6	5
1970-71—Boston	44	38	.537	3‡	..	..	1975-76—Boston	54	28	.659	*1‡	12	6
1971-72—Boston	56	26	.683	1‡	5	6	1976-77—Boston	44	38	.537	2‡	5	4
1972-73—Boston	68	14	.829	1‡	7	6	1977-78—Boston	11	23	.324	3‡	..	..
1973-74—Boston	56	26	.683	*1‡	12	6	Totals (9 seasons)	427	263	.619		47	33

*Won NBA Championship. †Eastern Division. ‡Atlantic Division.

Named to NBA All-Star Second Team, 1961, 1962, 1963, 1964. . . . NBA Rookie of the Year, 1957. . . . Member of NBA championship teams, 1957, 1959, 1960, 1961, 1962, 1963, 1964, 1965. . . . NBA Coach of the Year, 1973. . . . Coach of NBA championship teams, 1974 and 1976.

WILLIAM HOLZMAN
(Red)

Born August 10, 1920 at Brooklyn, N. Y. Height 5:10. Weight 175.

High School—Brooklyn, N. Y., Franklin Lane.

Colleges—University of Baltimore, Baltimore, Md.,
and City College of New York, New York, N. Y.

Signed by Rochester NBL, 1945.

Acquired by Milwaukee NBA from Rochester NBA, 1953.

—COLLEGIATE PLAYING RECORD—
Baltimore

Year	G.	Min.	FGA	FGM	Pct.	FTA	FTM	Pct.	Reb.	Pts.	Avg.
38-39					Statistics Unavailable						

CCNY

Year	G.	Min.	FGA	FGM	Pct.	FTA	FTM	Pct.	Reb.	Pts.	Avg.
39-40					Did Not Play—Transfer Student						
40-41	21	....	...	96	....	...	37	....	....	229	10.9
41-42	18	....	...	87	....	...	51	....	....	225	12.5
Varsity Totals	39	....	...	183	...	...	88	...	...	454	11.6

NOTE: In Military Service during 1942-43, 1943-44 and 1944-45 seasons. Played at Norfolk, Va., Naval Training Station and scored 305 points in 1942-43 and 258 points in 1943-44.

NBL AND NBA REGULAR SEASON RECORD

Sea.—Team	G.	Min.	FGA	FGM	Pct.	FTA	FTM	Pct.	Reb.	Ast.	PF	Disq.	Pts.	Avg.
45-46—Roch. NBL	34	....	....	144	....	115	77	.669	....	....	54	....	365	10.7
46-47—Roch. NBL	44	....	....	227	....	139	74	.532	....	....	68	....	528	12.0
47-48—Roch. NBL	60	....	....	246	....	182	117	.643	....	....	58	....	609	10.2
48-49—Rochester	60	....	691	225	.326	157	96	.611	....	149	93	....	546	9.1
49-50—Rochester	68	....	625	206	.330	210	144	.686	....	200	67	....	556	8.2
50-51—Rochester	68	....	561	183	.326	179	130	.726	152	147	94	0	496	7.3
51-52—Rochester	65	1065	372	104	.280	85	61	.718	106	115	95	1	269	4.1
52-53—Rochester	46	392	149	38	.255	38	27	.711	40	35	56	2	103	2.2
53-54—Milwaukee	51	649	224	74	.330	73	48	.658	46	75	73	1	196	3.8
Totals	496	....	....	1447		1178	774	.666			658	....	3668	7.4

NBL AND NBA PLAYOFF RECORD

Sea.—Team	G.	Min.	FGA	FGM	Pct.	FTA	FTM	Pct.	Reb.	Ast.	PF	Disq.	Pts.	Avg.
45-46—Roch. NBL	7	....	....	30	....	31	21	.677	....	....	10	....	81	11.6
46-47—Roch. NBL	11	....	....	42	....	29	22	.759	....	....	22	....	106	9.6
47-48—Roch. NBL	10	....	....	35	....	15	10	.667	....	....	6	....	80	8.0
48-49—Rochester	4	....	40	18	.450	6	5	.833	....	13	3	....	41	10.3
49-50—Rochester	2	....	9	3	.333	2	1	.500	....	0	3	....	7	3.5
50-51—Rochester	14	....	76	31	.408	34	23	.676	19	20	14	....	85	6.1
51-52—Rochester	6	65	15	3	.200	6	1	.167	6	2	3	0	7	1.2
52-53—Rochester	2	14	5	1	.200	4	1	.250	1	1	4	0	3	1.5
Totals	56	....	....	163		127	84	.661			65	....	410	7.3

NBA COACHING RECORD

Sea.	Club	Regular Season W.	L.	Pct.	Pos.	Playoffs W.	L.		Sea.	Club	Regular Season W.	L.	Pct.	Pos.	Playoffs W.	L.
1953-54	Milwaukee	10	16	.385	4†	..	..		1973-74	New York	49	33	.598	2§	5	7
1954-55	Milwaukee	26	46	.361	4†	..	..		1974-75	New York	40	42	.488	3§	1	2
1955-56	St. Louis	33	39	.458	2T†	4	4		1975-76	New York	38	44	.463	4§	..	..
1956-57	St. Louis	14	19	.424	1†	..	..		1976-77	New York	40	42	.488	3§	..	..
1967-68	New York	28	17	.622	3‡	2	4		1978-79	New York	25	43	.368	4§	..	..
1968-69	New York	54	28	.659	3‡	6	4		1979-80	New York	39	43	.476	3T§	..	..
1969-70	New York*	60	22	.732	1‡	12	7		1980-81	New York	50	32	.610	3§	0	2
1970-71	New York	52	30	.634	1§	7	5		1981-82	New York	33	49	.402	5§	..	..
1971-72	New York	48	34	.667	2§	9	7		Totals (18 seasons)		696	604	.535		58	47
1972-73	New York*	57	25	.695	2§	12	5		*Won NBA championship.							

†Western Division.   ‡Eastern Division.   §Atlantic Division.

NBA Coach of the Year, 1970. . . . Coach of NBA championship teams, 1970 and 1973. . . . Member of NBL championship team, 1946. . . . Member of NBA championship team, 1951. . . . Named to NBL All-Star First Team, 1946 and 1948. . . . NBL All-Star Second Team, 1947.

JOHN KUNDLA

Born July 3, 1916 at Star Junction, Pa.

High School—Minneapolis, Minn., Central.

College—University of Minnesota, Minneapolis, Minn.

—COLLEGIATE PLAYING RECORD—

Year	G.	Min.	FGA	FGM	Pct.	FTA	FTM	Pct.	Reb.	Pts.	Avg.
35-36†					Statistics unavailable						
36-37	15	....	...	53	....	53	34	.641	....	140	9.3
37-38	20	....	...	62	....	77	41	.532	....	165	8.3
38-39	17	....	...	71	....	63	40	.635	....	182	10.7
Varsity Totals	52	....	...	186	....	193	115	.596	....	487	9.4

NBA COACHING RECORD

Sea.	Club	Regular Season W.	L.	Pct.	Pos.	Playoffs W.	L.
1948-49	Minneapolis	44	16	.733	*2†	8	2
1949-50	Minneapolis	51	17	.750	*1T†	10	2
1950-51	Minneapolis	44	24	.647	1†	3	4
1951-52	Minneapolis	40	26	.606	*2†	9	4
1952-53	Minneapolis	48	22	.686	*1†	9	3
1953-54	Minneapolis	46	26	.639	*1†	9	4
1954-55	Minneapolis	40	32	.556	2†	3	4
1955-56	Minneapolis	33	39	.458	2T†	1	2
1956-57	Minneapolis	34	38	.472	1T†	2	3
1957-58	Minneapolis	10	23	.303	4†	..	..
1958-59	Minneapolis	33	39	.458	2†	6	7
Totals (11 seasons)		423	302	.583		60	35

*Won NBA Championship.   †Western Division.

Coach of NBA championship teams, 1950, 1952, 1953, 1954.

COLLEGIATE COACHING RECORD

Sea.	Club	W.	L.	Pct.	Pos.
1946-47	St. Thomas	11	11	.500	....
1959-60	Minnesota	12	12	.500	3T
1960-61	Minnesota	10	13	.435	4T
1961-62	Minnesota	10	14	.417	7
1962-63	Minnesota	12	12	.500	4T
1963-64	Minnesota	17	7	.708	3
1964-65	Minnesota	19	5	.792	2
1965-66	Minnesota	14	10	.583	5T
1966-67	Minnesota	9	15	.375	9
1967-68	Minnesota	7	17	.292	9T
Totals (10 seasons)		121	116	.511	

JOSEPH BOHOMIEL LAPCHICK
(Joe)

Born April 12, 1900 at Yonkers, N. Y.   Height 6:05½.   Weight 185.

Died August 10, 1970.

Did not play high school or college basketball.

Played with independent teams, including the Original Celtics, in 1917-18 through 1919-20; 1923-24 through 1925-26 and 1931-32 through 1935-36 seasons.

PRO RECORD

Year Team	League	G	FG	FT	Pts.	Avg.
1920-21—Holyoke	IL	11	14	40	68	6.2
1921-22—Schenectady-Troy	NYSL	32	12	95	119	3.7
1921-22—Brooklyn	MBL	10	6	20	32	3.2
1922-23—Brooklyn	MBL	33	34	109	177	5.4
1922-23—Troy	NYSL	24	13	59	85	3.5
1926-27—New York	NBL	..	..	..	..	7.3
1926-27—New York	ABL	..	..	..	..	...
1927-28—New York	ABL	..	..	..	..	...
1928-29—Cleveland	ABL	39	51	86	188	4.8
1929-30—Cleveland	ABL	52	47	92	186	3.6
1930-31—Cleveland-Toledo	ABL	30	22	49	93	3.1

COLLEGIATE COACHING RECORD

Sea. Club	W.	L.	Pct.	Pos.	Sea. Club	W.	L.	Pct.	Pos.
1936-37—St. John's	12	7	.632	....	1956-57—St. John's	14	9	.609	....
1937-38—St. John's	15	4	.789	....	1957-58—St. John's	18	8	.692	....
1938-39—St. John's	18	4	.818	....	1958-59—St. John's	20	6	.769	....
1939-40—St. John's	15	5	.750	....	1959-60—St. John's	17	8	.680	....
1940-41—St. John's	11	6	.647	....	1960-61—St. John's	20	5	.800	....
1941-42—St. John's	16	5	.762	....	1961-62—St. John's	21	5	.808	....
1942-43—St. John's	21	3	.875	....	1962-63—St. John's	9	15	.375	....
1943-44—St. John's	18	5	.783	....	1963-64—St. John's	14	11	.560	....
1944-45—St. John's	21	3	.875	....	1964-65—St. John's	21	8	.724	....
1945-46—St. John's	17	6	.739	....	Totals (20 seasons)	334	130	.720	
1946-47—St. John's	16	7	.696	....					

NBA COACHING RECORD

Sea. Club	Regular Season				Playoffs	
	W.	L.	Pct.	Pos.	W.	L.
1947-48—New York	26	22	.542	2†	1	2
1948-49—New York	32	28	.533	2†	3	3
1949-50—New York	40	28	.588	2†	3	2
1950-51—New York	36	30	.545	3†	8	6
1951-52—New York	37	29	.561	3†	8	6
1952-53—New York	47	23	.671	1†	6	5
1953-54—New York	44	28	.611	1†	0	4
1954-55—New York	38	34	.528	2†	1	2
1955-56—New York	26	25	.510		....	....
Totals (9 seasons)	326	247	.569		30	30

†Eastern Division

Elected to Naismith Memorial Basketball Hall of Fame, 1966.